# Northwestern University

STUDIES IN *Phenomenology &*

*Existential Philosophy*

Studies in Phenomenology
and Psychology

# Aron Gurwitsch

# Studies in Phenomenology and Psychology

Northwestern University Press

1 9 6 6                    Evanston

Copyright © 1966 by Northwestern University Press
Library of Congress Catalog Card Number: 65–24664
Manufactured in the United States of America

Omnibus eis, viventibus ac mortuis,
qui vitae nostrae testes fuerunt.

# Acknowledgments

ALL THE ARTICLES collected in this volume have already appeared in print. Acknowledgment is made to the following publishing houses, periodicals, and persons for their kind permission to republish the articles which had appeared in the English language and to publish, in English translation, those which were originally published in French or German.

Presses Universitaires de France (Paris) for "Quelques aspects et quelques développements de la psychologie de la forme" ("Some Aspects and Developments of Gestalt Psychology"), *Journal de Psychologie Normale et Pathologique*, XXXIII (1936); and for "La Science biologique d'après K. Goldstein" ("Goldstein's Conception of Biological Science"), *Revue Philosophique de la France et de l'Étranger*, CXXIX (1940).

La Renaissance du Livre (Paris) for "La Place de la psychologie dans l'ensemble des sciences" ("The Place of Psychology in the System of Sciences"), *Revue de Synthèse*, VIII (1934).

*Philosophy and Phenomenological Research* (Buffalo, N. Y.) for "A Non-egological Conception of Consciousness," I (1941); "William James's Theory of the 'Transitive Parts' of the Stream of Consciousness," III (1943); "On the Object of Thought," VII (1947); "Gelb-Goldstein's Concept of 'Concrete' and 'Categorial' Attitude and the Phenomenology of Ideation," X (1949); "The Phenomenological and the Psychological Approach to Consciousness," XV (1955); "The Last Work of Edmund Husserl," XVI (1956) and XVII (1957).

Weidmannsche Buchhandlung (Berlin) for "Rezension von Edmund Husserl, Nachwort zu meinen 'Ideen zu einer reinen Phänomenologie and phänomenologischen Philosophie'" ("Critical Study of Husserl's *Nachwort*"), *Deutsche Literaturzeitung* (February 28, 1932).

*The Journal of Philosophy* (New York) for "The Problem of Existence in Constitutive Phenomenology," LVIII (1961).

Harvard University Press (Cambridge, Mass.) for "On the Intentionality of Consciousness," *Philosophical Essays in Memory of Edmund Husserl,* ed. M. Farber (1940).

Librairie Armand Colin (Paris) for "Présuppositions philosophiques de la logique" ("Philosophical Presuppositions of Logic"), *Revue de Métaphysique et de Morale,* LVI (1951), reprinted in the collection of essays *Phénoménologie–Existence* (Paris, 1953); and for "La Conception de la conscience chez Kant et chez Husserl" ("The Kantian and Husserlian Conceptions of Consciousness"), *Bulletin de la Société Française de Philosophie,* LIV (1960).

Springer-Verlag (Heidelberg) for "Phänomenologie der Thematik und des reinen Ich" ("Phenomenology of Thematics and of the Pure Ego"), *Psychologische Forschung,* XII (1929).

Verlag Anton Hain KG (Meisenheim am Glan) for "Beitrag zur phänomenologischen Theorie der Wahrnehmung" ("Contribution to the Phenomenological Theory of Perception"), *Zeitschrift für philosophische Forschung,* XIII (1959).

Fr. H. L. van Breda (Secretary General at the XIth International Congress of Philosophy, Brussels) for "Sur une racine perceptive de l'abstraction" ("On a Perceptual Root of Abstraction"), *Proceedings of the XIth International Congress of Philosophy,* II (1953).

Martinus Nijhoff (The Hague) and Archives-Husserl à l'Université de Louvain for "Sur la pensée conceptuelle" ("On the Conceptual Consciousness"), *Edmund Husserl 1859–1959 = Phaenomenologica,* IV (1959), already published in English translation in *The Modeling of Mind* (University of Notre Dame Press, 1963).

I wish to thank the translators of the French and German articles, Dr. F. J. Crosson, Mr. D. J. Herman, Miss A. Rosenthal, Dr. R. M. Zaner, and Dr. F. Kersten.

Dr. F. Kersten, with the help of a grant from the Graduate Council of the University of Montana, has carefully attended to the numerous technical details connected with the preparation of the manuscript and the editorial work. I wish to express to him my appreciation and gratitude.

ARON GURWITSCH

Graduate Faculty of Political and Social Science
New School for Social Research
New York
November 27, 1964

# Contents

# Contents

# INTRODUCTION

THE ARTICLES COLLECTED in the present volume were written during a period of more than thirty years, the first having been published in 1929, the last in 1961. They are arranged here in a systematic, not a chronological, order, starting from a few articles mainly concerned with psychological matters and then passing on to phenomenology in the proper sense. Within the latter group, the sequence is from articles dealing with more general questions of principle to those in which rather special questions are discussed. The articles are reprinted or translated unchanged except for "Phenomenology of Thematics and of the Pure Ego," in which a certain number of pages have been omitted because the author has long since come to consider them erroneous.

Almost all of the articles are in the service of Husserlian phenomenology, which they are intended to advance and to develop further rather than merely expound. Only one article, "The Last Work of Edmund Husserl," is purely expository in nature. At first the piece was to be excluded. Several of his students, pointing out the usefulness the article in question might have in the absence of an English translation of *Die Krisis der Europäischen Wissenschaften und die transzendentale Phänomenologie,* finally persuaded the author to have it included as a kind of appendix, in the hope that an English translation of that work of Husserl will appear in the not too distant future and will make a mere report on that work superfluous.

When the author made his first acquaintance with Husserl's philosophy about forty years ago, he was overwhelmed by the spirit of uncompromising integrity and radical philosophical responsibility, by the total devotedness which made the man disappear behind his work. Soon the young beginner came to realize the fruitfulness both of what Husserl had actually accomplished and of what he had initiated, the

promise of further fruitful work. In *Ideen zu einer reinen Phänomenologie und phänomenologischen Philosophie* Husserl had disclosed a
vast field of research and had indicated approaches and methods of
analysis by means of which results of enduring value could be
obtained, to the extent and in the sense in which results of enduring
value may be expected from any human scientific, scholarly, or
philosophical activity. The same holds with respect to *Logische
Untersuchungen,* though this work is more restricted in scope. It was
the style of Husserl's philosophizing, painstaking analytical work on
concrete problems and phenomena rather than the opening up of large
vistas, that made the young student take the decision to devote his life
and work to the continuation and expansion of Husserl's phenomenology—in a word, to become a disciple forever, faithful to Husserl's
spirit and general orientation, but at the same time prepared to depart
from particular theories if compelled to do so by the nature of the
problems and the logic of the theoretical situation. The articles
collected here, as well as his *The Field of Consciousness,* grew out of
that decision which the author now reaffirms with regard to whatever
further systematic work he might do.

As to the general orientation of Husserlian phenomenology, two
leading ideas must be emphasized. The first is that of *constitutive* or
*transcendental phenomenology* or, as it is also called, *phenomenological idealism.* By this is meant the task of accounting for objects of
every description, real as well as ideal, and for objectivity in any sense
whatever in terms of acts and operations of consciousness. To
accomplish radical and ultimate philosophical clarification concerning
objects of any kind—the term *object* understood in the widest possible
sense—the objects must be referred to acts of consciousness, groups
and systematic concatenations of such acts, through which the
objects in question appear and present themselves as those for which
we take them in our life and in our several activities, pre-theoretical,
theoretical, and also non-theoretical, e.g., artistic. In the case of
certain categories of objects—namely, mathematical and logical
entities and, quite in general, those pertaining to a conceptual order—
reference must be made also to the operative procedures by means of
which such objects are constructed, and due allowance must be made
for the basis upon which the operations and constructions rest and
which they presuppose. By means of a descriptive analysis of the
experiences of objects and of objects as experienced, and by that
means alone, it is possible to obtain ultimate clarification of the
respective sense of existence with regard to the several categories of
objects.

Deliberately, the phrase "task" has been chosen. It cannot be repeated often enough or emphatically enough that phenomenological idealism must not be taken for the expression of a thesis or position advanced by means of arguments, defended by refutation and counter-arguments. *Phenomenological idealism must rather be seen as the formulation of a vast and all-encompassing program of research,* highly ramified but concrete throughout. If it is called a philosophical tenet, it is one which cannot be substantiated by the means of argumentative dialectics. Its substantiation is tantamount to the elaboration and development of constitutive phenomenology in its entirety, that is to say, to the gradual realization of the program of research.

Husserl's idea of constitutive phenomenology is in continuity with the classical tradition of modern philosophy, with both the Continental and the British trends. Husserl could rightly claim to bring fulfillment to the "secret longing of modern philosophy." As far as the present historical situation is concerned, the main tendency dominating modern philosophy reaches its culmination in Husserlian phenomenology.

For the formulation and incipient realization of the program of constitutive phenomenology, a new conception of consciousness is required. This brings before us the *theory of intentionality,* the other leading idea here to be mentioned.

If they are defined by intentionality, acts of consciousness prove to be indissolubly connected with sense, signification, and meaning, the latter term taken in a wider sense than the one used to refer specifically to symbolic systems. An act of consciousness is, to be sure, a psychological event which occurs at a certain moment of time. However, it is an event of a particular nature, namely, the actualization of a sense or meaning as an atemporal, irreal, identical ideal entity. Quite in general, consciousness cannot be adequately characterized if it is seen merely as a one-dimensional (temporal) order and sequence of events. Rather, consciousness must be conceived as a correlation between two different realms: that of temporal psychological events, on the one hand, and, on the other hand, that of the ideal entities mentioned. This correlation is of such a nature that, in principle, the same sense or meaning can correspond in strictest identity to an indefinite multiplicity of acts, all different from one another, be it merely by the places which they hold in phenomenal time. Husserl's notion of the noema and his noetico-noematic parallelism seem to us to tend towards this correlation conception of consciousness, in which—we submit—the theory of intentionality receives its definitive shape.

By this token, phenomenology constitutes itself as a *logic* or even (if the meaning of the term is not overstretched) as a *mathematics of consciousness*. Its concern is not with actual occurrences in their actuality but, on the contrary, with possibilities, compatibilities, incompatibilities, and necessities. Whereas the main problem of a primarily noetically oriented study is the temporality of consciousness, in its noematic orientation phenomenology concentrates on the senses and meanings corresponding to the acts. Among the tasks arising here, the first is that of an intentional analysis of a sense or meaning, that is to say, of disengaging the constituents contributing to it in an either manifest or inexplicit and silent way. A further series of questions concerns the forms in which a plurality of senses are combined with one another and synthetized into a systematic group, like the several adumbrational perceptual appearances and presentations uniting into one coherent perceptual experience of an identical thing which presents itself under a multiplicity of aspects. Finally, we mention the fact that a certain phenomenal situation might motivate (in a specifically phenomenological sense of "motivation" having nothing to do with what is treated in the contemporary "psychology of motivation") the transition to a different situation, the simplest example being that of isolated and dispersed elements colligated into one set or collective as a unitary object of a higher order. Inquiries along these lines lead to the disclosure of operations of consciousness and to the establishment of transformation laws. In thus conceiving of phenomenology as a logic of consciousness, one might arrive at a new definition of its difference from psychology. While phenomenology deals with sense as such and with what is contained and implied in it, psychology is concerned with the conditions—multifarious conditions —upon which the actualizing of a certain sense or a different one depends.

The events which have taken place on the philosophical scene during the lifetime of the author—namely, the appearance of the several varieties of *existentialist philosophy*—have only confirmed the conviction he had gained as a young student, not only of the validity of Husserlian phenomenology, but also of the urgent necessity of proceeding in all philosophical endeavors under the guidance of the idea of constitutive phenomenology. The legitimacy of a *philosophical anthropology* is readily granted. It is, however, another question whether philosophical anthropology has reached, can ever reach, the philosophical dimension within which Husserlian phenomenology moves. Existentialist philosophy insists upon the factual existence of man and his involvement in the world. Again the question of access arises, access to the world and to man as existing in the world and being involved in it. Raising the question of access, one is at once referred to acts of consciousness through which one becomes aware of the world, of oneself as man in the world (mundane existent), and of the multiple modes of involvement. Because it omits formulation of the problem of access in terms of consciousness, existential philosophy misses the genuinely radical philosophical dimension.

This criticism also applies to the work of Merleau-Ponty, which one is gratified to see finally receiving in the United States the attention and interest it so fully deserves. Insofar as Merleau-Ponty raises the problem of access to the world and in this connection insists upon the "primacy of perception," he undoubtedly moves along phenomenological lines in Husserl's sense. However, he resolves that problem in terms of the body and the embodied existence, going so far as to speak of the body as "subject" of perception and even of knowledge. Then a second problem of access immediately arises, namely, the problem of access to the very body, and this problem leads back to the acts of consciousness through which we become aware of the body and of our embodied existence. There is no denial that the acts of consciousness here in question are of a particular and specific kind whose nature has to be disclosed and has been disclosed to a large extent by Merleau-Ponty. Notwithstanding their specific particularities, they are acts of consciousness and awareness nonetheless. The necessary reference to consciousness becomes the more apparent as the body with which Merleau-Ponty concerns himself is the "phenomenal body," the body as experienced and lived, not the organism in the sense of an anatomico-physiological system and the subject matter of biochemistry. The body as experienced cannot but prove to be the correlate of acts through which it is experienced and presents itself as the phenomenal body in and with which we live.

In the second of his *Meditations on the First Philosophy*, Descartes has established the privilege of consciousness as the only and universal medium of access to whatever exists. Husserl has renewed and reaffirmed this Cartesian discovery. Constitutive phenomenology can well be characterized as the consistent and radical development of this privilege of consciousness into its last ramifications and consequences. It is this Cartesian and Husserlian principle which we wish to reassert over against existentialism in all its varieties as well as over against all other trends in contemporary philosophy. The privilege of consciousness holds for the world as field of action, involvement, and decision no less than for the world taken as subject matter of uninvolved and disinterested contemplation and study. It holds for the world as a whole as well as for all mundane existents whatever, including the phenomenal body, the Ego as psychosomatic unity, and the human person in its socio-historical concreteness. For this reason, philosophical anthropology, its legitimacy notwithstanding, cannot rightfully lay claim to the rank of the fundamental philosophical discipline.

Many existentialist philosophers refer to *Die Krisis der Europäischen Wissenschaften und die transzendentale Phänomenologie* as a document pertaining to Husserl's "late" period which they contrast with the "earlier" ones. This is not the place to enter into a discussion of the meaning and the validity of this distinction between a "late" and an "early" Husserl. Suffice it to say that the legitimacy of that distinction appears somewhat problematic in the light of the remarkable continuity of Husserl's development, from the first beginnings in *Philosophie der Arithmetik* to the last posthumously published work. *Krisis* has become of interest and importance for existentialist philosophers because in that work Husserl establishes the concept of the life-world (*Lebenswelt*) in contradistinction to the mathematized universe of modern science, especially physics of the Galilean style. The latter is a universe constructed by science, but is constructed on the basis of pre-scientific and pre-theoretical experience of the life-world which thus proves to be the foundation (*Sinnesfundament*) of the scientific universe as well as the soil for all human activities whatever, both theoretical and other. Having laid down the concept of the life-world in the earlier parts of that book, Husserl—it may be recalled—then proceeds in the later parts to opening up an avenue of access and approach from the life-world to transcendental and constitutive consciousness whose intentional correlate the life-world, in turn, proves to be. Read as a whole, even disregarding its connection with Husserl's earlier writings, *Krisis* cannot pass for a document of existentialist philosophy or even be considered as initiating an existentialist orientation.

Expressing the above-formulated reservations with regard to the principles and the general orientation of existentialist philosophy is by no means incompatible with recognizing the important insights and valuable results reached by existentialist writers. Such results and findings must be given their proper place within the developing system of constitutive phenomenology. Precisely because he is convinced of the necessity of pursuing all philosophical work along the delineated general direction of constitutive phenomenology, the present writer does not hesitate to formulate "annexationist" claims with respect to whatever work of value has been and is being done in both contemporary philosophy and other, cognate, disciplines. He does not even confine such claims to existentialist philosophy, but goes as far as extending them to what are commonly considered to be the philosophical antipodes of existentialism, namely, contemporary logic and semantics. It is gratifying to see the first attempts which have been made of late at bringing about a confrontation of recent developments in logic and semantics with the pertinent theories of Husserl. The integration into the context of constitutive phenomenology of results and theories which have been developed within a different context and in a different general orientation will, of course, entail something other than simple acceptance. They will have to be adapted to the new context by means of being reinterpreted in phenomenological terms. On the other hand, one has to be prepared for the possibility of such a confrontation necessitating a revision, a more or less thoroughgoing modification, even a complete abandonment of particular theories established by Husserl or others working along Husserlian lines, without, however, relinquishing the general orientation of constitutive phenomenology.

In the course of his work, the present writer has attempted to confront constitutive phenomenology with some trends in contemporary *psychology*. In a few of the articles here republished, psychology is dealt with from the point of view of a comparative logic or theory of the sciences; that is to say, psychology is treated merely as a subject matter of philosophical analysis, not differently, in principle, from what can be done with regard to any other science, such as mathematics or economics.

Of greater importance and significance in the author's own view are his endeavors to interpret phenomenologically certain psychological theories as well as to use them for the advancement of phenomenological problems. Here, psychology is not looked at from without; rather, the psychological theories are received into the philosophical context and are made instruments, not objects, of analysis. Obviously not all psychological studies lend themselves to such treatment, certainly not those of behavioristic persuasion either in the strict sense or insofar as the interest centers almost exclusively on the occurrence and the statistical average distribution of accomplishments under certain conditions, the accomplishments being taken merely as effects produced without making allowance for the processes themselves in the course of which they result or allowing for their subjective significance (that is, significance for the subject studied by the psychologist, of course, not for the psychologist himself). Only such psychological studies and theories in which the phenomenal data play an essential role and are given proper emphasis can be considered as to their possible integration into the context of phenomenology and as to a possible contribution they might make towards advancing phenomenological understanding. Even though the prevailing interest of psychologists in approaching phenomenal facts and data is primarily explanatory, because—as mentioned before— psychology is concerned in the first place with the conditions under which certain phenomena arise, the very fact that phenomenal facts are taken into consideration and are analyzed on their own grounds and merits leads the psychological theoretician to deal with their sense and meaning in a more or less systematic fashion. With regard to the psychological theories and trends here in question, the distinction must be made between their descriptive and their explanatory phase. It is for the descriptive phase only that phenomenological relevancy and significance as here meant can be claimed.

Because of the specific nature of the problems to which he devoted his endeavors, the present writer has concerned himself primarily, if not exclusively, with the psychology of William James, the Gestalt theory, the work of Gelb and Goldstein, and the functionalistic psychology of Piaget. This is not to imply that the trends and movements mentioned are the only ones in contemporary psychology to have relevancy from the point of view of constitutive phenomenology. The selection is entirely contingent upon the unavoidable limitations which the author, like every worker, has to impose upon the range of his interests.

With regard to *Gestalt theory* the attempt is made to set forth its affinity to Husserlian phenomenology by interpreting the abandonment of the constancy hypothesis as an incipient phenomenological reduction. For this reason, the descriptive analyses of Gestalt theory prove to bear on noemata, and their utilization for phenomenological purposes appears justified. On the other hand, it can be shown that the problem of constitution also arises for the Gestalt theory, provided the latter is sufficiently radicalized, that is, pursued into its philosophical consequences.

By his analysis of the continuity of the stream of consciousness, the experience of time, and, especially, the distinction between "object" and "topic" of thought, *William James* in some sense anticipated Husserlian themes and conceptions. Here again, the logic of the problems and of James's theories points in the direction of constitutive phenomenology, although James's later development proceeded along quite different lines.

The phenomenological significance of the theories established by *Gelb and Goldstein* concerning aphasia, agnosia, apraxia, and the like is too obvious to need explicit comment. In the example of the analysis of a concrete pathological case, the convergence of their theories and some concepts of Husserl's related to the problem of abstraction, or, as one should prefer to say, ideation, could easily be shown. Of still greater significance than this convergence is the import of the theories in question upon the philosophy and phenomenology of logic, especially as far as the class concept is concerned.

In a few of these articles, some of *Piaget's* concepts and theories are referred to; they have been dealt with more extensively in the author's *The Field of Consciousness.* At the present time, no encompassing systematic discussion and interpretation in phenomenological terms of Piaget's work, not only in psychology, but also of his "genetic epistemology," is available. Such a confrontation appears to be an urgent desideratum.

His allowance for, and utilization of results and theoretical notions of, the Gestalt theory has led the present writer to depart from some theories of Husserl.

In the first place, the notion of *hyletic data,* the sense data of traditional philosophy and psychology, has to be abandoned. That leads to a certain modification of the theory of intentionality. In fact, if hyletic data are no longer admitted, intentional acts cannot be characterized either as sense-bestowing or meaning-bestowing, it being understood or implied that the sense or meaning is bestowed upon materials, the hyletic data, which in themselves are devoid of it. Along these lines of reasoning, the present writer has come to develop the aforementioned correlation theory of consciousness, that is to say, to define intentionality as the noetico-noematic correlation. On the noetic side, no distinction is admitted between hyletic data, on the one hand, and, on the other hand, noetic functions which operate on the former in apperceiving, interpreting, animating them and the like. The only distinction is between the noeses as temporal psychological events and the noemata as atemporal ideal entities pertaining to the realm of sense and meaning.

Partly on account of his allowance for the Gestalt theory, partly for immanently phenomenological reasons, the author has established a *non-egological conception of consciousness.* Departing in this respect from Husserl, the author finds himself in agreement with Sartre. By a non-egological conception of consciousness two things are meant. (1) Acts of consciousness are not conceived of as radiating, emanating, issuing, etc., from a center of activity, as manifestations of an agent who lives in the acts. (2) Following from this is the denial of a pure Ego in the Husserlian sense as withstanding or "surviving" the phenomenological reduction, as not reduced to, or better, disclosed as a phenomenon—more exactly, a system of phenomena organized in a

xxiv / PHENOMENOLOGY AND PSYCHOLOGY

specific way. There is only the mundane empirical Ego as a psychosomatic entity or socio-historical person, two aspects of the same reality which for the purposes of analysis, study, and explanation can to some extent abstractively be separated from one another. Because the Ego proves to be a mundane existent, problems of constitution arise with respect to it. Emphatically, the Ego is not the agent of, or a participant in, constitution but rather is its result, correlate, or product. Like all mundane existents, the Ego is constituted, not constituting. It is through acts of consciousness and their interconcatenations that the Ego presents itself as the particular and specific entity for which it is taken in common experience. Precisely because of their concern with the human involvement in the world, the existentialist writers deal with the Ego in its full concreteness, which means in its mundaneity. In this respect, one is indebted to them for insights of great interest and high importance. However, since the Ego as involved in the world is a mundane constitutum or constituendum, all existential analyses require, for the sake of philosophical radicality, supplementation and foundation by a genuinely phenomenological theory of constitution.

As a consequence of his non-egological conception of consciousness, not only does the present writer not speak of a *transcendental Ego* but would also avoid the phrase *transcendental consciousness*. Rather, he would prefer to speak of a *transcendental function* both of consciousness at large and of specific classes of acts of consciousness (such as perception, imagination, abstract thinking, and the like) and even of particular acts. Obviously, there is only one kind of consciousness, but it can be approached from two different points of view. Considered under one perspective, acts of consciousness appear as mundane events among other mundane events to which they stand in relations of various sorts—for instance, in the relation of causal dependency which, incidentally, is not necessarily one-sided. Under this perspective, consciousness is considered in the anthropological sciences, the term taken in the broad sense in which Husserl understands it so as to comprise psychology as well as all other disciplines dealing with man. On the other hand, acts of consciousness can be regarded from the point of view of their presentational function and their contribution towards the constitution of objects of any kind and description whatever. They are considered insofar as through them objects present themselves, or, what amounts to the same, they are considered under the perspective of their intentional correlates, operations and accomplishments. Acts of consciousness are here not conceived simply as events and occurrences taking place under certain conditions. Rather, consciousness is approached as the universal medium of access to, and—

if these terms are properly understood—as the fountain and origin of, whatever exists and is valid. It is this approach which Husserl's constitutive phenomenology takes to consciousness and which we have in view in speaking of considering consciousness under the perspective of its transcendental function. The characterization of phenomenology, whose central notion is that of intentionality, as a logic of consciousness, here receives its full meaning and significance.

Notwithstanding his several departures from some of Husserl's theories, the present writer claims to have remained faithful to the spirit of constitutive phenomenology. Faithfulness to Husserl's intentions is not the same thing as strict adherence to every one of his theories, any more than being the disciple of a master means becoming the partisan of a sect. Nothing could be more alien to Husserl's personality as a scholar and philosopher and no greater disservice could be rendered to his work than "freezing" it into a sectarian doctrine and jealously watching over the purity of the creed. Husserl never intended to found a sect. He initiated a working philosophy, a philosophy living and developing in the actual work of research. It is only in conformity with the nature of the situation and in no way detracts from Husserl's greatness if, building on the foundations which he laid down, phenomenologists who come after him, and whose work he made possible, are led to modifications and revisions of what Husserl himself had never considered as more than initial attempts open to later corrections. Is it too immodest to express the hope that the republication of these articles may have an effect other than merely arousing the "interest" of detached observers who look on phenomenology as some kind of "literary" trend or movement or "cultural product"; that it may to some extent contribute to stimulating actual phenomenological work, actual proceeding into the vast horizons opened up by Husserl?

Studies in Phenomenology
and Psychology

# 1 / Some Aspects and Developments of Gestalt Psychology[1]

## [I] THE DEVELOPMENT AND STATUS OF THE PROBLEM

AT THE BASIS OF THE CONSTITUTION of the physical sciences since Galileo is a basic circumstance which, to the extent that these sciences have progressed, has become increasingly emphasized: the rigorous separation between the reality of the world as it is constructed by these sciences and the qualitative, perceptual, and therefore "subjective" aspect under which the world presents itself to us so far as we are beings endowed with a psychophysical organization.

Considering the representations and constructions of physics as rendering the true and real state of affairs, 19th-century psychology interpreted certain sensory data occurring in consciousness as the effects of physical processes and, at the same time, as signs which refer to the latter without bearing likeness or even similarity to them. Acting as stimuli on the sensory organs or on the nervous system, physical processes produce certain excitations to which the sensory data in question are connected. A particular privilege is assigned to these sensory data; they are considered as the most elementary and simple facts of perception. Accordingly, the principal task of psychology will consist in explaining on the basis of these elements the totality of facts pertaining to sensation and perception—and especially the "abnormal" cases, in which occurs in consciousness a

1. This study represents, in a modified form, some of the lectures I had the honor of giving in 1933–34 at the Institut d'Histoire des Sciences in Paris, under the title "The Historical Development of Gestalt Psychology." I should like to express my appreciation to M. A. Rey for the hospitality with which he received me at his Institute, and MM. Chastaing and Merleau-Ponty, who kindly consented to read the text of this article. (This article was originally published in *Journal de Psychologie Normal et Pathologique*, XXXIII [1936].)

phenomenon different from the one which is expected to occur in the presence of such and such stimuli. Psychology furnishes this explanation by referring either to the psychophysical organization of humans or animals, or to specifically psychological laws, or finally by conceiving certain facts as resulting from the superposition of a multiplicity of elementary data. These facts are therefore considered as complex; in truth, they are different from what they appear to be. The true nature of these facts (understood, of course, as belonging to consciousness) must be distinguished from the immediate impression they leave and which psychological and physiological science analyzes into simpler elements. The separation of reality and appearance is thus brought into the domain of consciousness.

By adopting this orientation (the most eminent defenders of which are Helmholtz and Fechner), psychology admits that it is incapable of determining by its own means what must be conceived as elementary or as complex: for this determination, it needs to be instructed by physics. This appears, for instance, in the discussion concerning the color black—which, some authors believe, must not be taken for a positive sensation but must be interpreted as the absence of all sensation. For the same reason the color white, contrary to all naïve experience, is considered by Young (whose theory is adopted by Helmholtz) not as a simple sensation but as a complex datum containing in equal proportions the three colors passing as fundamental.[2] But it does not follow from this that every sensory datum produced by a simple physical process must, on that account, be considered as also elementary. If it is possible to reduce such a datum to more elementary data and to interpret it as a combination of the latter, one must avail oneself of this possibility. However that may be, it must be kept in mind that, above all, a sensory phenomenon can be considered as elementary only if the physical process corresponding to it is also elementary. Thus, psychology at the outset considers sensory data in terms of their relation to the corresponding physical stimuli. Psychology relies and bases itself upon the results of physics so that it finally appears as an extension of physics.

A fundamental principle implicit in this orientation of psychology —which, we have seen, is not at all arbitrary—is the conformity between stimuli and sensations. When this principle is given a more precise formulation, it becomes the *constancy hypothesis*. Just as every neural element which reacts to a certain kind of stimulus has a well-defined and constant excitability, so too the sensation connected

2. H. von Helmholtz, *Handbuch der physiologischen Optik*, 3d ed. (Hamburg and Leipzig, 1911), II, pp. 119–20.

to the excitation of that element depends exclusively on the stimulus. Hence, *if the same neural element (for example, a circumscribed region of the retina) is repeatedly stimulated in the same manner, the same sensation will arise each time.* Sensations differ from one another as the respective stimulations differ. What determine the nature and intensity of sensory data are the stimuli and nothing else; however—and this point is of primary importance—those stimuli are *local stimuli. Excitation produced in one neural element does not in any way whatever depend upon what happens in other elements, even the most proximate ones.* If, therefore, the same stimulus is applied to such an element one time alone and another time in conjunction with other stimuli (which in turn are applied to proximate elements), the same sensation must in both cases be necessarily connected to the stimulus which is the same in these two constellations. To disengage the actual sensory data contained in a certain perception, one has to discover, given the configuration of stimuli, that which *ought* to take place (according to the constancy hypothesis) in a particular sensory element. Whenever the immediate data seem to conflict with this hypothesis, reference must be made to the effects which are produced by the same stimulus if it comes into play isolatedly. The sensation observed in this case, called normal, must be presupposed as being in reality present also in cases considered as abnormal because they contradict the constancy hypothesis. Such anomalies are explained by reference to the intervention of facts usually conceived of as belonging to a higher level—such as judgment. These anomalies originate, not in the elementary sensory data themselves, but rather in the interpretation which these data are given.

The nervous system as well as psychic life are considered as being composed of a certain number of elements, elementary data or elementary mechanisms functioning independently of one another. Neither psychologically nor physiologically is there genuine cooperation between such separate mechanisms, nor is there any intrinsic coherence among elementary data. The only connection possible is the temporal coincidence of certain elementary data, and this completely fortuitous coexistence cannot give rise to a genuine unity. When some real unity seems to be present, analysis reveals it to be the fortuitous result arising from the accumulation of elementary facts.

This style of thought dominated the entire development of psychology in the 19th century. Aside from the application which Helmholtz made of it in his theory of chromatic vision, one can cite psychophysics as inaugurated by E. H. Weber and T. Fechner and developed by G. E. Müller and others. Therefore, it was almost inevitable that the phenomenon of *Gestalt-qualities* (*Gestaltqualitäten*) would be interpreted by means of these notions and conceptions. We now turn to the Gestalt-qualities.

Following some suggestions of E. Mach, C. von Ehrenfels remarked that when a musical sequence is heard, one receives, in addition to the sensory elements (the notes), a certain impression of a particular nature to which the term "melody" is specifically applied.[3] For a number of reasons—among which are certain effects pertaining to the reproduction and recognition, and above all the transposition, of melodies—Ehrenfels contends that this new impression, to which he gave the name of "Gestalt-quality," cannot be identified either with the ensemble of notes or with the totality of relations existing among these notes. It rather constitutes a special datum, a sensory or quasi-sensory datum not identical with the notes but founded on them. He defined this Gestalt-quality as a "positive content of representation" (*positiver Vorstellungsinhalt*) connected to the presence in consciousness of an ensemble of simple representations which themselves are separable from one another in the sense that they can exist independently of one another. Such a Gestalt-quality arises when the elementary facts on which it is founded are present in consciousness; it comes ready-made from the outside and imposes itself without any mental effort whatever being required to produce it. If perchance the contrary seems to be the case, this is only an appearance. For instance, while listening to a musical piece of some complexity or of excessive length, we may hear the notes without being able to grasp the form and global structure of the entire piece: an inarticulated mass of notes strikes our ears, and we are unable to discern its structure and coherence. In such a case, the effort necessary to resolve the difficulty and to make the Gestalt-quality accessible does not tend to create the latter directly but rather tends to complete the elementary data. According to Ehrenfels, for a Gestalt-quality to arise, it is indispensable for all the simple data which found it to be simultaneously present to consciousness—which can occur either immediately or with the aid of memory.

The melody (to which Ehrenfels refers as only one example among a good many others) makes it possible to establish a general criterion for Gestalt-quality. Let us suppose that there is an ensemble of elementary facts, E, and a datum, F, given with them. If it is possible to vary the elements in E in any fashion while maintaining their relations, and without F being appreciably modified, while, on the other hand, that F loses its characteristics and becomes transformed

3. C. von Ehrenfels, "Über Gestaltqualitäten," *Vierteljahrsschrift für wissenschaftliche Philosophie*, XXIV (1890); cf. I. Meyerson, "Les Images," *Nouveau Traité de Psychologie*, ed. G. Dumas (Paris, 1932), II, pp. 551–53.

genuine simultaneity or of an immediate succession, as in the case of melodies, it is the co-existence in consciousness of separable elementary data, and this co-existence alone, which gives rise to a new sensory element. The latter is a specific datum which, because it is founded on the substratum, can be characterized as being at a higher level than the simple sensations to which it is superadded. On the other hand, so far as the Gestalt-quality is a special impression with its own specific nature, it becomes independent, in some measure, from the substratum. From the descriptive and phenomenal point of view as well as from the functional one this independence can be ascertained by means of the effects which Gestalt-qualities have on psychological processes. In Ehrenfels' conception of Gestalt-quality, there is a genuine *dialectic* which must be remembered. In a different context, Husserl is led to an analogous problem.[5] On entering an assembly-room in which a meeting is going on, one has the impression of being in the presence of a gathering; looking out of the window at night, one perceives a great many stars. Concerning such impressions of collectivities, one may ask: What is their nature? How are they brought about? It is evidently not a question here of a totality of a conceptual, or, as Husserl prefers to say, a categorial, nature, which would be the result of an addition and explicit conjunction of elements.[6] In order to apprehend a categorial totality, it is necessary to go over each of the elements successively and then to combine them all together—a process which takes the more time as the elements to be joined together are the more numerous. Now, the fact that there is a large number of men in the room in no way prevents the observer entering the room from apprehending, at a glance, the entire assemblage as such. On the other hand, the most heterogeneous things can be joined together into a categorial totality—for example, all the things which by chance happen to be found in some room.[7] These remain as diverse and unrelated in this collection as they would otherwise be; the joining does not give to them any character of perceptual unity or any aspect at all.[8] By contrast, a totality which could be designated as "natural" is at first glance presented to perception as endowed with such a character of perceptual unity and as having a certain aspect of oneness. This character of unity is not superimposed from without upon the members of the group and does not derive from a categorial of collecting; rather, it is inherent to what is perceived, is one of

E. Husserl, *Philosophie der Arithmetik* (Halle, 1891), chap. XI.
Cf. E. Husserl, *Logische Untersuchungen* (Halle, 1913), II, iii, § 23.
Cf. C. Stumpf, "Erscheinungen und psychische Funktionen," *Abhandlungen preussischen Akademie der Wissenschaften* (Berlin, 1906), p. 29.
Husserl, *Philosophie der Arithmetik*, pp. 76–81; *Logische Untersuchungen*, § 61.

into F′ when the elements of E are varied *unsystema*
however slightly, then F has to be considered as an au
quality. Ehrenfels discovers by means of this criterio
qualities are found almost everywhere, in every field (
well as in that of every other psychic activity. All r
changes can be cited as examples: slow or rap
movement in a straight line or circular movem(
descending, augmenting, diminishing; growing and sh
ing and contracting; blushing, paling, and so on. In
temporal Gestalt-qualities, there are others whose ele
taneously present to consciousness: such as spatial
kinds and the impressions they make—the tria
elliptical, cubical, and the like. These terms, h(
understood in a qualitative sense and not in a geome
the Gestalt-qualities must also be counted impres
terms such as slender, heavy, and others with aest
Ehrenfels uses the concept which he has introduce(
and confused extension that the most heterogeneo
mentioned side by side. The notion of Gestalt-qual
precision in his article.[4]

Considered by Ehrenfels as a sensory or quasi
Gestalt-quality possesses some rather paradoxical
sensory impression can be assigned a particular s
rise to it. To hear a musical sequence played—a
true for all Gestalt-qualities—there are only t
vibrations of the air, each of which is the cause (
no additional stimulus standing to the melody in
that which obtains between a certain vibratio
corresponding note. The melody appears as a *se*
*impression which does not arise from any stimul*
that one can and must pose the problem conce
although Ehrenfels himself did not do so. Ho
raises amounts to the same thing: do the Gesta
made from the outside and impose themsel
without the intervention of any mental activi
responds in the affirmative, having been
suggestion made by Mach.

Gestalt-qualities are sensory facts which a
they are nevertheless conditioned by the pres
ordinary sensory impressions to which, fo
refers as the "substratum" (*Grundlage*). Wh

4. Cf. A. Gelb, "Theoretisches über Gestaltquali
*logie*, LVIII (1911), chap. II.

the sensory features of it and is part of its constitution. Along with this character of unity there appears, at the same time, an impression of resemblance among the members composing the group, and this impression also constitutes an immediate sensory datum inherent to the perceived as such and does not, therefore, result from explicit comparison. The circumstance that, in one instance, the group is constituted only categorially, that the unity in question is only one of thought, whereas in the other case the group is itself given as such and the character of unity as well as that of group are immediately perceivable data (in the same way as colors, notes, and the like)—this circumstance fundamentally differentiates categorial wholes from wholes of the "natural" type.[9] According to Husserl, immediately perceivable wholes are endowed with *"quasi-qualitative"* or *"figural factors"* (*quasiqualitative Momente, figurale Momente*).

Such factors (*Momente*) are encountered at every turn: we speak of a "heap" of apples, a "line" of trees, a "swarm" of bees, a "flock" of birds, and so on. In all such cases, the elements perceived are separate and do not fuse into one another (as do, for instance, the points of a continuous line). Nonetheless, in their very perceptual appearance, and prior to every activity of categorial thinking, the elements are given as forming a group. To describe what is perceived in a faithful and exact manner, it must be asserted that a group composed of such and such elements is observed in these cases. As is indicated by the various terms we have used, the characters of group and unity (which, in truth, coincide) are not always the same. These characters vary with the objects in question and depend on the properties of these objects; as becomes evident on deeper analysis, the characters also depend on the reciprocal relations among these objects. For example, if some objects are distributed in the visual field, a certain configuration (a quasi-qualitative factor) is perceived. Every variation of spatial relations—bringing nearer, or moving away, equalizing or differentiating distances, parallel or oblique directions—entails a sometimes marked modification of the configuration. If, furthermore, the elements are of different colors, the variation in their relative position entails a modification not only of the spatial configuration but also of the total chromatic impression made by the very configuration —an impression which constitutes a second quasi-qualitative factor. It must be remembered that the sensory variation which is first to be noticed concerns the figural factors and not the relations. A simple and unanalyzed observation discloses that the aspect of the whole has somehow become different; and it is only by virtue of reflection and

9. Husserl, *Logische Untersuchungen*, II, vi, § 51.

analysis that one succeeds in discovering the modifications brought about in the relations. The figural factor as well as the variations which it undergoes are apprehended at a glance, whereas the explicit joining of elements as well as the analysis of relations always require some time.

Quasi-qualitative factors are a πρότερον πρὸς ἡμᾶς, whose conditioned character is disclosed only by subsequent analysis because these factors are a consequence, according to Husserl, of a fusion (*Verschmelzung*) among the elements and the relations of these elements.[10] This analysis, however, is unable either to suppress the immediate character of the figural factor or to transform the unity here in question into a unity of categorial nature. That the elements happen to fuse with one another and form a group whose unity is immediate and perceptual does not mean that they undergo any modification whatever; in their fusion, they do not differ from what they would be if they were taken in isolation. The only effect of fusion is to establish a closer and more intimate relation among the elements than exists among those which have simply been added together—a relation which manifests itself by the presence in perception of a figural factor.

Once again we are confronted with the *dialectic* noted with regard to the concept of Gestalt-quality as established by Ehrenfels. Certain groups of objects, especially homogeneous ones, are given to perception with an immediate character of grouping and unity. This character appears as an autonomous sensory fact. On closer examination, one discovers that this character is conditioned by elementary sensory facts which give rise to it and determine its nature. Apparent in Ehrenfels' notion of Gestalt-quality as well as in Husserl's figural factor, this dialectic confronts us with sensory or quasi-sensory data to which correspond no objective stimuli whatever and, consequently, no excitations in the receptive sense-organs but which nevertheless, all analysis notwithstanding, do not lose the character of sensory immediacy.

## [II] THE DUALISTIC THEORY OF BENUSSI

EHRENFELS AND HUSSERL have merely indicated the existence of the Gestalt-qualities and delimited their descriptive character without, however, explaining them. The first theoreticians to

10. Husserl makes reference to the concept of *Verschmelzung* defined by C. Stumpf, in the latter's *Tonpsychologie* (Leipzig, 1890), II, pp. 64–65, 128–30.

approach Gestalt-qualities from the psychological point of view are the philosophers and psychologists of the *school of Graz,* founded by Alexius Meinong. All the work of this school is based upon certain philosophical ideas which the experimental investigations were designed to substantiate. The limits of this present article do not permit even a brief exposition of the philosophical tendencies of Meinong endorsed by his students; we have to restrict ourselves here to an analysis of the explanation which Vittorio Benussi (the most eminent representative of this school as regards experimental psychology) gives of the phenomenon in question. We shall consider the ideas of Benussi, not as he developed them himself, but in the light of the criticisms to which they have been subjected by the Gestalt theoreticians.[11]

Benussi starts from a fact already noticed by Ehrenfels: the *absence of stimuli* corresponding to Gestalt-qualities.[12] If I hear a melody (or even an interval of two notes), if I perceive geometrical figures, compare the lengths of two lines or brightnesses of two colors —the impression of the melody, musical interval, the figure, the differences of lengths or brightnesses, all constitute an enrichment of perception which has no additional stimulus corresponding to it.[13] Whether or not the difference of brightness between two shades of color is noticed, the stimuli are not thereby altered—hence, neither are the excitations produced by them nor the elementary sensations corresponding to them. According to the constancy hypothesis, such sensations are dependent upon the stimuli in the strictest possible sense. It follows that perceptual phenomena such as these cannot be considered as sensory data of the same kind as the elementary data which depend on, and vary with, the stimuli. And yet one cannot, according to Benussi, doubt the intuitive and even sensory character of form-qualities.[14] He goes so far as to maintain that one is unable to discern these two categories of sensory data by means of descriptive observation alone, so that from the descriptive and immediate point of view one can in no way ascertain any difference between a simple color and a configuration of lines.[15] Only a genetic consideration of

11. K. Koffka, "Zur Grundlegung der Wahrnehmungspsychologie," *Zeitschrift für Psychologie,* LXXIII (1915).

12. V. Benussi, "Über die Motive der Scheinkörperlichkeit bei umkehrbaren Zeichnungen," *Archiv für die gesamte Psychologie,* XX (1911), pp. 391–93.

13. Benussi, "Über die Grundlagen des Gewichtseindrucks," *Archiv für die gesamte Psychologie,* XVII (1910), pp. 92–95.

14. Benussi, "Über die Motive der Scheinkörperlichkeit bei umkehrbaren Zeichnungen," *loc. cit.,* p. 390.

15. Benussi, "Gesetze der inadäquaten Gestaltauffassung," *Archiv für die gesamte Psychologie,* XXXII (1914), pp. 402–3.

these data of a sensory nature—which nevertheless are not caused by specific *stimuli*—leads to a problem.

The remaining alternative seems to be, therefore, to admit that the kind of sensibility which alone had been treated in physiology and psychology is not the only source of perception; that, in addition to this source there exists another, independent of the neural excitations in the sensory organs and therefore independent also of stimuli. To this other source Gestalt-qualities owe their origin.[16] R. Ameseder proposes the term "production" (*Produktion*)—a term which Meinong himself adopts—to designate this other source of perception.[17] In an apparently neutral way Benussi speaks of "representations of extrasensuous provenience" (*Vorstellungen aussersinnlicher Provenienz*).[18]

This "production," designed to account for facts which the known factors of ordinary sensibility leave unexplained, must be interpreted as a psychological factor. Nevertheless, Benussi does not absolutely reject the possibility of specific cerebral processes which would be the physiological substrata of production.[19] J. Lindworsky, who does not belong to the school of Graz but whose ideas are in some respects closely related to those of Benussi, explicitly denies the existence of any physiological substratum whatever corresponding to the understanding of relations—which, without being the same as the perception of Gestalt-qualities, nevertheless leads to analogous problems.[20] At any event, according to Benussi, production must be understood as above all psychological in nature, and therefore it is sufficient to give a purely psychological interpretation of it.

As a mental function, production is obviously not accessible to direct observation. Otherwise a criterion would be available for determining to which category—elementary data or representations of extrasensuous provenience—a given phenomenon belongs. The notion of production is not derived from immediate description; it is required by theoretical principles for filling a gap in the explanation. Concepts of this sort are called by Koffka "functional concepts" (*Funktionsbegriffe*), as distinguished from those which directly render the imme-

16. *Ibid.*, § 1.
17. R. Ameseder, "Über Vorstellungsproduktion," in *Untersuchungen zur Gegenstandstheorie und Psychologie*, ed. A. von Meinong (Leipzig, 1904), p. 488; A. von Meinong, *Über Annahmen*, Erste Aufl., *Zeitschrift für Psychologie und Physiologie der Sinnesorgane*, Erg.-Bd. II (Leipzig, 1902), pp. 8–9.
18. Cf. A. Gurwitsch, *The Field of Consciousness* (Pittsburgh, 1964), p. 65.
19. Benussi, "Zur Psychologie des Gestalterfassens," in *Untersuchungen zur Gegenstandstheorie und Psychologie*, ed. Meinong, pp. 382–83; Benussi, "Experimentelles über Vorstellungsinadäquatheit," II, *Zeitschrift für Psychologie*, XLV (1907), p. 217.
20. J. Lindworsky, "Umrissskizze zu einer theoretischen Psychologie," *Zeitschrift für Psychologie*, LXXXIX (1922), pp. 320–21.

diate observation of psychical realities, to which he gives the name of "descriptive concepts" (*Deskriptionsbegriffe*).[21]

Benussi does not conceal the difficulty involved in defining the exact nature of production. He says that it is a psychical function, a mental operation, an intellectual activity of a certain kind which resembles the act of grouping parts into a whole.[22] It is an activity which is accompanied by a certain effort and requires a certain period of time for its performance.[23]

This separation between facts of a purely sensory provenience and those which are "produced" establishes a definite dualism in the perceptual domain. If I see points which are grouped in some manner, or even only two points (one of which is to the right of the other), it is according to Benussi necessary that production come into play for the constitution of this perception.[24] Sensibility alone can furnish only the impressions of points to which the real points correspond as stimuli. The impression of order among these points—an order perceived, and not thought, but the impression of which has no corresponding stimulus—must proceed from another source than that of pure sensibility. From this perspective, one can evaluate the importance which Benussi ascribes to facts of extrasensuous provenience as far as perception is concerned.

Granting this dualism, the question arises concerning how the two factors constituting perception work together. The answer to this question is determined by the dependence of the Gestalt-qualities on the elementary data. The latter found the phenomena of production which are superadded to these data.[25] Because of this, production cannot be performed unless sensibility has furnished raw materials. The perceptual factor of extrasensuous provenience is applied to these data and organizes them. In other words, the functioning of sensibility is required in order that the activity of production can, in turn, come

21. K. Koffka, *Zur Analyse der Vorstellungen und ihrer Gesetze* (Leipzig, 1912), pp. 2–9.

22. Benussi, "Zur Psychologie des Gestalterfassens," *loc. cit.*, p. 310; Benussi, "Über den Einfluss der Farbe auf die Grösse der Zöllnerschen Täuschung," *Zeitschrift für Psychologie*, XXIX (1902), pp. 386–87; Benussi, "Gesetze der inadäquaten Gestaltauffassung," *loc. cit.*, p. 407.

23. Benussi, "Die Gestaltwahrnehmungen," *Zeitschrift für Psychologie*, LXIX (1914), p. 270. Meinong had already attacked the conception of Ehrenfels (see above, p. 6), according to which Gestalt-qualities emerge spontaneously without the subject having to make any contribution of his own. See A. von Meinong, "Zur Psychologie der Komplexionen und Relationen," *Zeitschrift für Psychologie*, II (1891). Cf. Ameseder, "Über Vorstellungsproduktion," *loc. cit.*, p. 489.

24. Benussi, "Experimentelles über Vorstellungsinadäquatheit," II, *loc. cit.*, pp. 192–93.

25. A. von Meinong, "Über Gegenstände höherer Ordnung und deren Verhältnis zur inneren Wahrnehmung," *Zeitschrift für Psychologie*, XXI (1899), §§ 3, 7.

into play. It is this mechanism which Benussi has in mind when he designates the data of sensuous provenience as *inferiora* and the other data as *superiora*. These terms, introduced by Meinong, indicate two things: the relation of the founding to what is founded (as between *inferiora* and *superiora*), and the circumstance that Gestalt-qualities originate at a higher level than do simple sensations.

A more penetrating understanding of the manner in which, according to Benussi, the two factors of perception work together can be obtained if we consider Figure 1. At one time a vase is perceived, and at other times the silhouettes of two human faces appear to be

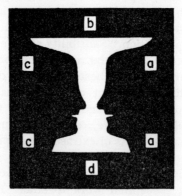

Fig. 1

looking at one another from opposite positions. According to the way in which the figure is viewed, the ensemble of perceptual data is distributed in diverse manners. The line *a-b-c-d* appears in one case as the contour of the vase and in the other as that of the two faces. When one shifts from the one perception to the other, an appreciable transformation occurs. In the perception of the vase, the line is one and continuous, and all of its parts are equivalent; whereas in the perception of the two faces the line is divided into two parts, *a* and *c*— the parts *b* and *d* lose all importance, for nothing would be altered in the phenomenon if these parts were missing.

This figure, taken from E. Rubin, is not univocal, since it can be perceived in different manners.[26] The shift from one way of perceiving it to the other is not accompanied by any change in the objective state of affairs, or in the stimuli; and thus it involves, according to the constancy hypothesis, no modification whatever in the pure sensations. Hence the equivocal character of the figure must be due to production. The ensemble of elementary data depending strictly upon

26. E. Rubin, *Visuell wahrgenommene Figuren* (Copenhagen, 1921), Fig. 3.

the corresponding stimuli, which underlie the act of production itself, does not determine in a univocal way either this act of production or, therefore, what by virtue of that act will be superimposed upon the pure sensations.[27] There is a certain freedom as regards production, a freedom which makes the equivocal character possible.[28] Over and above the absence of specific stimuli, Benussi considers this equivocal character—which is totally absent from simple sensory facts—as a distinctive mark of Gestalten, as opposed to sensations alone. Solely on the basis of this equivocal character, according to him, it is possible to infer the existence of productivity.[29]

This freedom of the so-called superior factor of perception is taken by many psychologists and philosophers as evidence for a special dignity of the human being. Thus, Lindworsky, who denies any physiological, even cerebral, substratum for acts considered as superior to mere sensations, makes this freedom the privilege of man.[30] Restricting the experience of animals to simple sensations, he contends that they are incapable of apprehending a relation, even the most "simple" one. This conception appears completely untenable in the light of Köhler's experiments.[31]

The freedom in question is not, to be sure, absolute. One cannot perceive simply anything one wants in Figure 1. The objective facts, that is to say, the pure sensations corresponding to the stimuli, impose certain limits on the act of production. Within these limits, this act is free to realize one or the other of the two possible perceptions.[32] Production not only gives form to the raw materials furnished by sensibility, but it is, as well, in no way whatever subject to a determinism. The choice it makes between the realizable forms depends only upon our free will. The freedom intrinsic to the productive act by which the elementary data are grouped explains the equivocal character which is found not only in a figure of this kind but quite universally wherever there is a grouping and organizing of pure sensations.

In the case of Figure 1, production has to choose between only two possibilities. There are figures which present more possibilities. Figure 2 can be perceived as flat or three-dimensional. In the first case one

27. Benussi, "Gesetze der inadäquaten Gestaltauffassung," *loc. cit.*, p. 399.

28. Benussi, "Experimentelles über Vorstellungsinadäquatheit," II, *loc. cit.*, pp. 198–99.

29. Benussi, "Zur Psychologie des Gestalterfassens," *loc. cit.*, § 2.

30. Lindworsky, "Umrissskizze zu einer theoretischen Psychologie," *loc. cit.*, pp. 341–50.

31. W. Köhler, "Nachweis einfacher Strukturfunktionen beim Schimpansen und beim Haushuhn," *Abhandlungen der Preussischen Akademie der Wissenschaften* (1918).

32. Benussi, "Zur Psychologie des Gestalterfassens," *loc. cit.*, pp. 386–89.

sees a planimetric figure consisting of all the component lines. In this case, the angle $\alpha = \beta + \gamma$. But, if one sees the figure as three-dimensional, the equation $\alpha = \beta = \gamma = 1R$ holds. Seen as three-dimensional, this figure is still equivocal. One can invert it with more or less difficulty, seeing the same parts of it now in the back, then in front; shifting from one perception to the other, one sees that an apex or an edge which was in front is now placed behind, or inversely. Finally, this figure can be seen as neither flat nor three-dimensional. Without the objective state of affairs undergoing the least modification, one might direct his attention to one or two lines and thus mentally isolate them from the context within which they are found when looking at

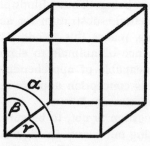

Fig. 2

the figure spontaneously. The lines thus detached from their context are no longer parts either of the planimetric figure or of the apparently stereometric body. They become independent elements, each of which is perceived by itself without being influenced by the data which surround it and without maintaining relations with them. Comparing two lines isolated from the rest of the figure, one will, perhaps, ascertain that one line is longer than the other; whereas when they are seen as two edges of a stereometric body, they seem equal.

Unquestionably, the objective factors suggest one way of perceiving the figure rather than some other.[33] The figure can be so badly drawn that it becomes impossible to see it as three-dimensional; it can be drawn in such a way as to make an inversion of it extremely difficult. Nevertheless, with some practice the observer is able to carry out the instruction given to him, even when that instruction goes contrary to the suggestions arising from the objective factors.[34] Although production is influenced by the objective state of affairs, it never entirely loses its freedom.

33. Cf. Benussi, "Über den Einfluss der Farbe auf die Grösse der Zöllnerschen Täuschung," *loc. cit.*, p. 387.

34. Benussi, "Gesetze der inadäquaten Gestaltauffassung," *loc. cit.*, p. 408.

The same holds for the *geometrico-optical illusions*, a field in which Benussi has done much work and in which he has achieved very remarkable results. The factors on which, for example, Zoellner's illusion depends had long since been studied, and it was established that the size of the angles of intersection, the length of the transversal lines, and the distances between the points of intersection have to be taken into account in explaining the variable magnitude of this illusion.[35] Working with bi-chromatic figures, Benussi has shown that a certain influence stems also from differences in color, and especially of brightness (either between the principal lines and the transversal lines or between these lines and the background).[36] His real accomplishment consists in pointing out that it is in the first instance the manner of perceiving the figure which decides the extent of the geometrico-optical illusions—Zoellner's as well that of Müller-Lyer.[37] *Whenever such a figure is seen as an organized Gestalt, the illusion increases; whenever one succeeds in isolating some of its lines and seeing them as independent elements, the illusion diminishes.*[38] From this, Benussi draws the conclusion that the objective factors which have just been enumerated play a role only so far as they favor one or the other of the two ways of perceiving.[39] These factors have an effect on the extent of the illusion only because of the attitude, synthetic or analytic, which they induce the observer to take.[40] The appearance of the illusion therefore results from the fact that the observer sees an organized Gestalt in the figure, and not a sum of isolated lines.[41] This interpretation constitutes a genuine progress in respect of the prior theories, for which such illusions basically arise from judgment.[42] Furthermore, Benussi shows that, by means of a variation in attitude in respect of a given figure, one can produce the same effects as those which one obtains by objectively modifying the figure.[43] Relying on these results, Benussi opposes the geometrico-optical illusions, which he calls *illusions of extrasensuous* provenience, to the simultaneous

35. V. G. Heymans, "Quantitative Untersuchungen über die Zoellnersche und die Loebsche Taeuschung," *Zeitschrift für Psychologie und Physiologie der Sinnesorgane*, XIV (1897).
36. Benussi, "Über den Einfluss der Farbe auf die Grösse der Zöllnerschen Täuschung," *loc. cit.*
37. Benussi, "Gesetze der inadäquaten Gestaltauffassung," *loc. cit.*, §§ 6–13, 16.
38. Benussi, "Zur Psychologie des Gestalterfassens," *loc. cit.*, p. 403.
39. Benussi, "Gesetze der inadäquaten Gestaltauffassung," *loc. cit.*, pp. 413–14.
40. *Ibid.*, p. 310.
41. *Ibid.*, p. 406.
42. St. Witasek, "Über die Natur der geometrisch-optischen Täuschungen," *Zeitschrift für Psychologie*, XIX (1899).
43. Benussi, "Zur Psychologie des Gestalterfassens," *loc. cit.*, p. 313.

contrast—which is also an illusion but not susceptible to being influenced by factors of a higher level than mere sensibility.[44] In his view, the existence of such illusions constitutes a new proof of the freedom intrinsic to the productive act by which the elementary data of sensibility are organized.

With regard to the freedom of production, the question arises as to what the elementary sensory data become when one shifts from one attitude to another. According to the constancy hypothesis, since the stimuli do not vary, these data remain identically the same.

Let us adopt an analytical attitude as regards Figure 2. This figure then appears neither as plane nor as three-dimensional; instead, one or two lines are isolated. Because it is possible to adopt this attitude in respect of any perceivable object whatever, Benussi's theory can be generalized. The equivocal figures referred to as examples are, instead, exceptional cases; the things with which we are familiar and which surround us (houses, practical objects, animals, men, and the like) are stable and exempt from all equivocalness. Nothing, however, can prevent us from adopting the analytic attitude as regards all these objects, whatever their stability and coherence. The façade of a house, for instance, is given to us as a stable form, coherent and closed; nevertheless, one can with more or less effort succeed in decomposing it into a mass of colored spots and disconnected lines. In a very suggestive way, Mach describes the impression which results when the world is decomposed into a multiplicity of elementary sensory data.[45] Consequently, according to Benussi, every form is equivocal, since it can be perceived either spontaneously or analytically. Benussi's theory is therefore applicable to all Gestalten; those which we have cited are equivocal to a particularly high degree.

Among all the possible attitudes, the *analytic attitude* must be given a particularly *privileged status*. In this attitude, according to Benussi, sensibility alone is at work, and every superior factor is blocked.[46] What is characteristic of this attitude is precisely the absence of all productive activity whatever; accordingly, the pure sensations are neither united nor grouped. In this attitude, the sensations are accessible in their original state, so to speak, just as they are furnished by pure sensibility. There is no inadequacy here, however, if one understands by inadequacy the non-conformity of sensations and stimuli—or, more precisely, the appearance of data

44. Benussi, "Gesetze der inadäquaten Gestaltauffassung," *loc. cit.*, §§ 2 and 3; Benussi, "Zur Psychologie des Gestalterfassens," *loc. cit.*, pp. 384–89.
45. E. Mach, *Die Analyse der Empfindungen*, 9th ed. (Jena, 1922), p. 24.
46. Benussi, "Zur Psychologie des Gestalterfassens," *loc. cit.*, § 19.

other than those which in view of the given stimuli are expected to appear.[47] Nor is there here any equivocalness. What is given in the analytic attitude corresponds (taking into consideration the nature of our receptive organs) to objective reality. In point of fact, this attitude is adopted in the physics laboratory for the practice of measurement.

There is a rather considerable difficulty in the attempt actually to realize this privileged attitude, especially if one attempts to dissociate the familiar things which surround us into sums of sensations. This difficulty is also present in Benussi's experiments on the Müller-Lyer illusion. Although his subjects were very practiced in observations of this kind and had been given instructions to analyze, still under certain objective conditions the illusion did not disappear entirely.[48] Such a result hardly agrees with a theory in which the analytic attitude ought to be the easiest to adopt, since the productive act, involving a mental operation and requiring a certain effort, is totally absent here.[49] This, indeed, is one of the weakest points in the theory.

If one shifts from one to another of the various ways in which a figure can be perceived—including the case in which neither Gestalt nor organization is present—the sensations do not change, since it is the constancy hypothesis which determines the relations between the stimulus and the sensation. The elementary data are the most directly seizable in the analytical attitude. What is in question is not a single perception; it is all those in which the elements composing the figure are isolated and severally apprehended one after the other. Consequently, what is given in perceptions which do not involve production must also be given in the perceptions in which an act superior to pure sensibility organizes the data furnished by the latter. In fact, what distinguishes these two types of perception is just the absence or presence of the higher-level productive act, while the elementary sensory data are the same in both cases. If, for instance, one regards Figure 2 analytically, one cannot avoid ascertaining that angle $a$ is larger than angle $\beta$. If, on the other hand, one sees the same figure as three-dimensional, the two angles are each equal to a right angle. The first way of viewing the figure is privileged; only pure sensations are given, and it seems that whatever is given in this privileged perception must also be contained in the other ones. But this is not the case: for ordinary observation, there are no unequal angles in the figure. The

47. *Ibid.*, p. 403; Benussi, "Gesetze der inadäquaten Gestaltauffassung," *loc. cit.*, p. 406.
48. Benussi, "Experimentelles über Vorstellungsinadäquatheit," *loc. cit.* See esp. the tables listed in §§ 6–8.
49. K. Koffka, "Zur Grundlegung der Wahrnehmungspsychologie," *Zeitschrift für Psychologie*, LXXIII (1915), pp. 52–55.

pure sensations must therefore be present in the form of *unnoticed data*.[50] This consequence is inevitable.

Benussi follows the same direction as Helmholtz and Ehrenfels, although his theory does mark an improvement over that of the latter. According to Ehrenfels, the substratum univocally pre-determines the Gestalt-quality: whenever the same elementary data are given, the same Gestalt-quality is founded on them. If this seems not to be the case, as in the example cited,[51] Ehrenfels maintains that this results from the imagination's modifying the substratum by adding to it or substracting from it and thus indirectly influencing Gestalt-qualities. If it were pointed out that this operation of the imagination is not apparent, Ehrenfels would doubtless be obliged to resort to it as unnoticed, although real. If he seems to succeed in making the Gestalt-quality a univocal function of the substratum, then only on condition of admitting unnoticed psychic facts. This consequence, which cannot be avoided as long as one adheres to the constancy hypothesis, also holds for Benussi's theory. *The constancy hypothesis always leads to the admission of unnoticed data.*

We are now in a position to appreciate the nature of the dualism established by Benussi in the perceptual domain. Perception depends upon two factors, or upon factors pertaining to two classes: the first are external or objective, the second internal or subjective. The concurrence of these two factors in the constitution of what is perceived is conceived in such a way that the object perceived, the perceived *qua* perceived, proves to be composed of two strata; hence it loses its homogeneity and uniformity. These two strata must be distinguished even despite direct observation, with the consequence that the separation between reality and appearance is admitted also in the psychological domain.[52] Each of these strata results respectively from one of the two factors into which the act of perception is divided. One must resort to privileged perceptions in order to establish the nature of each of these two strata and that of each of the two corresponding activities—that is to say, one must resort to those perceptions in which pure sensibility alone is at work and on the basis of which the non-privileged ones are constituted by means of the intervention of the factor of production. What is contained in a privileged perception must also be contained in other perceptions; and, if direct and immediate observation does not reveal the least trace of the content in question, the latter must be assumed to be present in unnoticed form. If we have a perception which is not privileged, it is

50. Gurwitsch, *The Field of Consciousness*, pp. 123–24.
51. See above, p. 6.
52. See above, p. 1f.

always possible to shift to a privileged perception by means of modifications of attitude or disposition and thus to make accessible to direct observation what was at first not accessible. Any perception and the corresponding privileged perception have in common a certain stratum which, in the one, is manifest and, in the other, exists only in unnoticed form. *For the analysis of perception experienced in a certain attitude, one makes use of results obtained under different internal conditions.*[53] From the point of view of method, the constancy hypothesis alone justifies proceeding in this way whenever the external conditions (the objective stimuli and the local circumstances as regards the receptive nerve organs) remain constant in the attitudes considered.

In place of Benussi's theory concerning geometrico-optical illusions, we might refer to *the analysis of musical notes* according to Helmholtz. By means of attention it is possible to discriminate the fundamental note and the overtones from one another.[54] Helmholtz assumes the products of this analysis to be already present in the original and unanalyzed sound, in the form of unnoticed sensations.[55] The same reasoning applies to the problem of constancy (of color, size, form). Perceived objects appear with their familiar and, in a certain sense, "true" properties: they present themselves in, so to speak, their "natural and objective" sizes, forms, and colors and not as they would be given were the retinal phenomena decisive for perception. Once again, it appears necessary to admit the presence of data corresponding to the retinal state of affairs in normal and natural perceptions. Usually these data exist in unnoticed form, but they can be disclosed under the artificial conditions which prevail in the laboratory.

Stumpf was the first to see the need of justifying the constancy hypothesis which is at the root of all these theories.[56] However, while seeking to bring arguments in support of it, he himself abandons it whenever he succeeds in establishing a sufficiently simple law for the explanation of the modifications occurring in a sensation by virtue of its co-existence with other sensations. This is especially striking in his studies concerning audition (to which psychology is indebted for numerous discoveries). Correspondingly, the same holds in other

53. Cf. Koffka, "Zur Grundlegung der Wahrnehmungspsychologie," *loc. cit.,* pp. 26–27.

54. H. von Helmholtz, *Die Lehre von den Tonempfindungen,* 6th ed. (Braunschweig, 1913), chap. IV.

55. W. Köhler, "Akustische Untersuchungen," I, *Zeitschrift für Psychologie,* LIV (1910), pp. 278–83; II, III, IV—*ibid.,* LVIII (1911), LXIV (1913), pp. 96–105; III—*ibid.,* LXXII (1915), pp. 121–39, 148–59.

56. C. Stumpf, *Tonpsychologie* (Hirzel, 1883), I, pp. 11–12, 20–21, 31–34; II, pp. 9–12.

fields—for example, in that of color-vision, where psychologists who prefer Hering's theory to that of Helmholtz no longer need, with respect to simultaneous contrast, to resort to the so-called higher and specifically psychical factors, as this is necessitated by the constancy hypothesis.

In the final analysis, as Köhler remarks, this hypothesis is maintained in practice only in cases in which sufficiently simple means are not yet available for the explanation of phenomena which occur by virtue of, and in, the co-existence of a plurality of psychical facts.[57] The constancy hypothesis leads to the interpretation of every observation in the light of, and with the aid of, the very facts whose existence is at issue. These facts, the unnoticed data, in turn escape all control; they can be neither validated nor invalidated by direct observation. As a consequence, on the one hand, it becomes impossible to pose the problems in such a way as to permit decisions; and, on the other hand, the object of psychology, the immediate data, is renounced in favor of data constructed according to the requirements of a theory. Trying to specify the so-called superior factors in a more exact manner, one ends by conceiving them, in the final analysis, as an ill-defined function X supposed to produce at one time one effect and at another the contrary effect, according to the nature of the case.

## [III] THE FUNDAMENTAL PRINCIPLES OF GESTALT THEORY

To AVOID THE SHADOWY REGIONS of the subconscious, the new doctrines relinquish the constancy hypothesis. Perception is considered as a function of two variables, $x_e$ and $x_i$, such that: $P = F(x_e, x_i)$, where $x_e$ signifies the external conditions and $x_i$ the internal conditions of perception. This formula must be understood in the mathematical sense, which means that of a variation of the function as a whole. The perceived thing is therefore considered as homogeneous, depending, to be sure, upon two variables, but it is no longer taken as composed of two parts or of two strata (the one superimposed upon the other), each of which derives only from a single factor or, if one prefers, from one variable. The latter conception, which is Benussi's, is expressed by the formula $P = F_1(x_e) + F_2(x_i)$. The difference which exists, from the mathematical point of view, between these two formulae indicates the distinction between the theory developed in the school of Graz and *Gestalt theory*.

In the formula $P = F(x_e, x_i)$, one may consider one of the

57. W. Köhler, "Über unbemerkte Empfindungen und Urteilstäuschungen," *Zeitschrift für Psychologie*, LXVI (1913).

variables (for instance, $x_1$) as a parameter and keep it constant while varying $x_e$—which is what one does if one is concerned with pure sensations. The results obtained depend, then, on only a single variable. In the evaluation of these results it must, however, not be overlooked that there exists a parameter; for, *to keep a parameter constant and to disregard it as if it did not exist are not at all the same thing.* This remark summarizes the criticism which, from the perspective of Gestalt theory, is made against the interpretations of traditional psychology. At the same time, it indicates the limits within which studies concerning pure sensations are legitimate.

In a "functionalistic" conception there is no place for privileged perceptions. All perceptions are on the same footing so far as each depends upon two variables. Each must be characterized in terms of the factors which point to the conditions in which it occurs. If two perceptions differ from one another—that is to say, if the perceived objects *qua* perceived are given as different to the simple observation which must precede all theory—this difference must be recognized as a *real one*. In Figure 1, the line *a-b-c-d* (the contour of the vase) must be considered as phenomenally (which is alone relevant) different from the same line forming the contours of the two human faces. If a perception is transformed into another one as a consequence of variations in the internal conditions, this means that the transformation is a thoroughgoing one and not the shift from one perception, of some kind, to a privileged perception supposed as contained in the first one, though in unnoticed form.[58] Gestalt theory gives an absolute primacy to immediate observation, as opposed to every theoretical consideration. The question no longer concerns what *ought* to be given (in terms of a certain theoretical conception, however well-founded it may be) but rather concerns what *is* actually given, what is accessible to direct observation. *In the domain of consciousness no distinction between reality and appearance can be admitted; it is even the essential characteristic of this domain that the distinction mentioned is utterly alien to it.* This is decisive for a theory of consciousness and insures a special philosophical interest in a psychological theory which, like Gestalt theory, follows a strictly descriptive orientation. For this reason it is possible to relate Gestalt theory to Husserlian phenomenology, which is itself devoted to the systematic exploration of consciousness.[59]

Accordingly, the task arises of specifying the conditions in which a

58. Cf. K. Koffka, "Psychologie," in *Lehrbuch der Philosophie*, ed. M. Dessoir, (Berlin, 1925), II, p. 548.
59. See below, "Phenomenology of Thematics and of the Pure Ego," pp. 192–95.

certain perception occurs and of establishing the laws which govern the transformations of one kind of perception into another—especially if these transformations ensue from the variation of internal conditions alone. In these laws Gestalt psychology sees the constants or, if one prefers, the invariants. Traditional psychologists also were looking for constants and believed they had found them in pure sensations. If, however, privileged perceptions are no longer admitted and consequently, as regards any perceived object, there is no room any more for an elementary stratum of psychical data depending only on objective stimuli, these constants cannot be found in *facts* or *data* but reside only in *laws*.

From these few indications one can understand that Gestalt theoreticians (especially Köhler and the group around him) claim to remain even more faithful to the spirit of physics than did earlier psychologists. In fact, the conception expressed by the formula $P = F(x_e, x_i)$, the search for conditions determining the phenomena, the rigorous insistence upon precisely specifying those conditions, the tendency to seek the constants no longer in facts, so to speak in the material, but rather in laws, and, finally, the substitution of the question "how?" for the question "why?"—all these features betray the influence of physics. Even an analogy between Gestalt theory and the Einsteinian theory of relativity has been established.[60] In other respects, this psychological theory could be compared with the theory of quanta.

The essential principle of Gestalt theory—namely, the primacy of immediate observation—entails a certain *methodology*.[61] First of all the descriptive concepts which render just what can be immediately observed and ascertained must be laid down. Functional conclusions of a psychological as well as a physiological nature are derived from these concepts. Thus one comes to establish functional concepts extending beyond the intuitively observed data, concepts which are the necessary tools for theoretical explanation. In pursuit of theoretical construction, consequences of a descriptive nature and predictions capable of verification by direct observation are derived. If the results of this observation agree with the consequences deduced from the functional concepts, not only are the latter confirmed, but one also has the possibility of testing the initial descriptive concepts.

The most fundamental descriptive concept in Gestalt theory which must first be defined is that of *Gestalt* itself. To illustrate it, let us look

60. G. Humphrey, "The Theory of Einstein and the Gestalt-Psychology: A Parallel," *American Journal of Psychology*, XXXV (1924); O. L. Reiser, "Physical Relativity and Psychical Relativity," *Psychological Review*, XXXVII (1930).

61. Koffka, "Psychologie," *loc. cit.*, chap. III, § 5.

at the side *a* of the rectangle (Fig. 3). This side has a certain function within the figure of which it is a part: it limits and closes the figure on the right. It thus contributes to dividing the plane into a part external to the surface of the rectangle and this surface itself.[62] If we isolate it, abstracting from the sides to which it is connected, it is no longer a side of a rectangle but becomes a mere line. As such, it divides the plane into two entirely equivalent parts, a left one and a right one. The line which, objectively speaking, is the same, changes fundamentally (from the phenomenal point of view) by being isolated.

This distinction between the side of a rectangle and a mere line must not be dismissed as a mere subtlety. If the figures are presented in tachistoscopic vision, they expand on appearance and contract on disappearance, a phenomenon designated as $\gamma$ movement.[63] These

Fig. 3

movements are more accentuated if four lines forming a rectangle are presented than if a single line is seen.[64] They also vary according to whether the observer sees a contracted rectangle or a somewhat expanded line in the object. From the functional as well as the phenomenal point of view, a line is totally different from the side of a rectangle, although the stimulus is identical in both cases.

With reference to the example, the following definition of a *Gestalt* can be given.[65] It is an ensemble of items which mutually support and determine one another. Thus they realize a total structure which governs them and assigns to each of them (as a part of the whole) a function or a role to be performed as well as a determinate place in that whole. Each detail exists only at the place at which it plays the role assigned to it by the whole of which it is a part. It can be understood only with regard to the function which characterizes it and to which it owes to be what it is here and now *in concreto*. Its quality, its existence, its *raison d'être*, depend on and are derived from its

62. *Ibid.*, p. 533.

63. F. Kenkel, "Untersuchungen über den Zusammenhang zwischen Erscheinungsgrösse und Erscheinungsbewegung bei einigen sog. optischen Täuschungen," *Zeitschrift für Psychologie*, LXVII (1913), § 11.

64. Cf. Koffka, "Psychologie," *loc. cit.*, p. 553.

65. M. Wertheimer, "Untersuchungen zur Lehre von der Gestalt," I, *Psychologische Forschung*, I (1922), pp. 52–54.

contribution to the whole into which it is integrated, from what the Gestalt in its internal articulation assigns to it. Therefore, when one shifts from one manner of perceiving Figure 1 to the other, one witnesses an actual change of the data—for instance, of the line *a-b-c-d*. The alteration of the functions assigned to the details engenders a profound and radical change of these details themselves which are just what their functions, depending on the total structure, make them be. Hence, from the psychological point of view, the details do not remain the same, although, objectively speaking, they undergo no modification at all. To isolate such a detail and take it in itself is actually to transform it and to effect a change in the object—in the psychological sense of the term—as when the side of a rectangle becomes a mere line.[66] The original object is made to disappear by this procedure, even though it is here a matter merely of a change of mental attitude, and a different object becomes substituted for it whatever the objective state of affairs may be. Furthermore, even if only one of the details which compose a whole of Gestalt structure is modified, this modification is seldom restricted simply to this detail but concerns other details as well, so that the whole Gestalt is affected, loses its original character, and gives way to another Gestalt. This follows immediately from the fact that since the functions depend upon the total structure of the Gestalt, the function of each part depends upon the functions of all the other parts: all these functions mutually demand each other. This circumstance distinguishes the multiplicities which have a total structure from those which are merely sums of their parts. Accordingly, this circumstance might lead to defining the two kinds of multiplicities respectively. In fact, as regards a sum, if one member of it is modified, it is that member alone which is concerned, the other members remaining what they have been, and the sum itself is at the very most decreased or increased by one unit.

The opposite of Gestalt is, on the one hand, a *sum of elements* and, on the other hand, a chaos. A sum is defined as a multiplicity of wholes, each of which consists in only one detail. Such a multiplicity is articulated and fragmented in the extreme, whereas a *chaos* is utterly devoid of all fragmentation, articulation, and differentiation.[67] Both sum and chaos are limit cases. A sum is only approximatively realized, if at all—that is to say, only within a rather restricted part of what is given—and a chaos arises only in very exceptional circumstances.[68] The perfectly clear Gestalt, to the contrary, is in fact

66. See below, "Phenomenology of Thematics," chap. III, § 11.
67. Koffka, "Psychologie," *loc. cit.*, pp. 547–48.
68. Wertheimer, "Untersuchungen zur Lehre von der Gestalt," I, *loc. cit.*, p. 52; Koffka, "Psychologie," *loc. cit.*, p. 547.

often realized, especially in the artificial conditions of the laboratory, where suitable configurations can be used. Thus, what is normally presented is something in between—either in between chaos and Gestalt or in between Gestalt and a sum of disconnected facts.

As regards the direction of mental evolution, one can infer from both ethnological documentation, especially as interpreted by Levy-Bruhl and the observations of W. Stern and J. Piaget concerning the mentality of the child as manifested, for instance, in the acquisition and development of language, that this evolution, in the individual as well as in the human species, goes in the direction of increasing differentiation.[69] It develops from a more or less chaotic state towards increasingly articulated and fragmented Gestalten.

In the light of this conception, the dialectic involved in the concept of Gestalt-quality (Ehrenfels) and in that of figural factors (Husserl) disappears.[70] Gestalt theory admits neither the Gestalt-quality (understood as a special sensory element additional to the substratum) nor the ordinary sensory elements which, for Ehrenfels as well as for Husserl, constitute the substratum. The Gestalt-quality is the Gestalt itself with its intrinsic structure. What used to be called substratum are the parts—more precisely, the constituents of the Gestalt, which exist only within it and only in the role they play in the multiplicity to which they belong. In these terms, the question concerning what happens to the elements if one disregards the role which they have and the function assigned to them simply loses its meaning, because these elements, instead of preserving their phenomenal identity, become totally different from what they were before such abstraction.[71] In this way of conceiving the nature of the parts of an immediate and sensory whole consists the novelty of Gestalt theory as opposed to previous views. The dialectic in such views resulted from observations obtained in certain conditions being utilized for the interpretation of phenomena arising under completely different conditions—a procedure which presupposes the constancy hypothesis.

This strictly descriptive concept of Gestalt entails functional concepts and laws, the most important of which is the *law of pregnance,* or the *law of good Gestalt.* Given the internal and external conditions of perception, the perceived object tends to become the best possible and strongest Gestalt. This strength and this "goodness" of Gestalt mean, phenomenally, a maximum of stability, clarity, and

69. C. and W. Stern, *Die Kindersprache* (Leipzig, 1928); J. Piaget, *Le langage et la pensée chez l'enfant* (Neuchâtel and Paris (1923); *La représentation du monde chez l'enfant* (Paris, 1926).

70. See above, pp. 7–8, 10.

71. M. Wertheimer, "Zu dem Problem der Unterscheidung von Einzelinhalt und Teil," *Zeitschrift für Psychologie,* CXXIX (1933).

good arrangement and, physiologically, a minimum of expense of energy in the corresponding processes of cerebral excitation.[72] Thus, a curve is a better Gestalt than the corresponding polygon.[73] If a disk with two openings is revolved slowly in front of a figure, the latter appears and disappears. Increasing the speed of rotation, one sees uninterruptedly a single figure, but it flickers; increasing the disk's speed still more, the flickering ceases. The minimum speed which, for a given figure, is sufficient to make the flickering cease is called the "critical speed for fusion." Hartmann's experiments show that the critical speed for fusion depends on, among other factors, the geometrical form of the figures; it is higher for a square than for an ellipse, higher for an equilateral triangle than for a square.[74] Of all closed figures of equal area, the circle has the least critical speed for fusion. We shall return to the special privilege of the circle with respect to other forms in connection with the discussion of certain pathological facts.

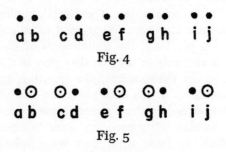

Certain factors governing the constitution of Gestalten can be indicated. If one arranges points along a horizontal line as in Figure 4, one sees the groups *ab/ cd/ ef/ gh/ ij/*.[75] It is very difficult, if not impossible, to see the groups *a/ bc/ de/ fg/ hi/ j/*—a difficulty which increases with the number of points. Here, the *proximity of the points* defines the specific grouping. However, if the points, *b, c, f, g, j* are replaced by small circles (Fig. 5), the groups *a/ bc/ de/ fg/ hi/ j/* will be more easily perceived.[76] The proximity of the points enters into conflict with *resemblance*. Which one will prevail? Will one see pairs

72. Koffka, "Psychologie," *loc. cit.*, p. 546.

73. Cf. E. Lindemann, "Experimentelle Untersuchung über das Entstehen und Vergehen von Gestalten," *Psychologische Forschung*, II (1922), pp. 27–28.

74. L. Hartmann, "Neue Verschmelzungsprobleme," *Psychologische Forschung*, III (1923), § § 6, 8.

75. Wertheimer, "Untersuchungen zur Lehre von der Gestalt," II, *Psychologische Forschung*, IV (1923), pp. 304–8.

76. Wertheimer, "Untersuchungen zur Lehre von der Gestalt," II, *loc. cit.*, pp. 311–15, 320–25.

of circles alternating with pairs of points or see symmetrical forms each of which consists in a point and a circle? This depends upon other factors, in particular the predispositions of the subject resulting from his observations prior to the critical experiment. We shall return to this problem.

If the points are grouped along two lines forming an acute angle (Fig. 6), the point *a* will belong to the point *o* rather than to point *b*, even though it is closer to *b* than to *o*. The factor which becomes relevant here and takes precedence over proximity is that of common direction. The same holds of two curved lines which intersect (Fig. 7): the branches (B, D and A, C respectively), which continue one

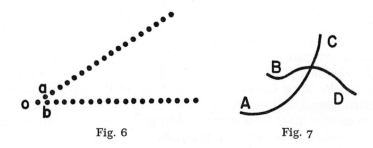

Fig. 6                              Fig. 7

another, appear as belonging together and as forming one single curve. This factor, the most essential one of those we have mentioned, *exemplifies the law of good continuation in conformity with the direction of the curve (Gesetz der kurvengerechten Fortsetzung).*

These factors, however, must not be taken as absolutes. Rather than being efficacious by themselves, they become effective so far as they permit the actualization of the tendency to the best possible Gestalt. They represent specifications of the law of pregnance and come into play to assure its realization.[77] For this reason, there is no absolute hierarchy among these factors. The efficacy of each varies with the particular case; it is relative to the importance which, in each particular case, the factor in question has with respect to the constitution of the Gestalt which is the best possible one under the given conditions. Therefore, if several factors enter into conflict, that factor will prevail which permits the realization of the most pregnant and strongest Gestalt. Just as the parts, which are interpreted by traditional psychology as absolute elements, are considered by Gestalt theory as relative to the function assigned to them within the total structure, so too the value of each factor is relative to the concrete situation in which it is called on to be effective.

77. Cf. Koffka, "Psychologie," *loc. cit.*, pp. 545–46.

It would be a serious mistake to think that these factors merely suggest a certain grouping of points and put a subjective mechanism into play. This interpretation implies that the points as given *at first* are *at first* elements in the traditional sense of the term. To be sure, the grouping of the stimuli favors or even suggests a certain phenomenal grouping, but the points are given *before* the grouping which itself results from a subjective activity and is therefore brought about by factors pertaining to a level higher than simple sensibility. Defended by G. E. Müller, the element conception is at variance with Gestalt theory.[78] Since the latter does not admit any primary raw materials in need of being organized by means of subjective acts, the multiplicities are considered as grouped at the very outset. The factors in question are not clues to the direction of a subjective activity. On the contrary, these factors refer to the objective character of the phenomena. They do not yield an occasion for an act; rather, they denote a structure of the perceived object itself precisely as it presents itself to us in the act of perception. What is in question are formal factors delineating certain general features of the intrinsic structure of given phenomena—such as, for instance, the formal circumstance that a certain structure is dominated by proximity, or by resemblance, or by the common direction of its details.

A consequence indicated by Koffka—which, we submit, is of primary philosophical interest—immediately follows from these theoretical principles.[79] Suppose two lines to be presented to an observer. After he has looked at them for some time, they are concealed from his sight, and he is asked whether these lines were equal in length. He cannot answer this question; he has perceived neither equality nor inequality since he did not regard them from this perspective. They are presented to him again. Looking at them, he notices now that they could form the two vertical sides of a rectangle; thus they leave the immediate impression of equality—an impression which was absent from the preceding observation.

This transition from the first to the second observation involves a real transformation of what is given in perception; each line has become the virtual side of a rectangle—which, as has already been shown, is not at all the same thing as being a mere line.[80] To contend that the lines were of equal length in the first observation, but without this equality being perceived, is tantamount to affirming that the

78. G. E. Müller, *Komplextheorie und Gestalttheorie* (Goettingen, 1923); cf. W. Köhler, "Komplextheorie und Gestalttheorie," *Psychologische Forschung*, VI (1925).

79. Koffka, "Psychologie," *loc. cit.*, pp. 528–34.

80. See above, p. 25.

impression of equality was present in this observation even though it was not noticed—and this, after what we have seen so far, is inadmissible. Since the lines were not of equal length, were they of unequal length? Not at all, because they did not leave an immediate impression of inequality either, which would have been the case had they appeared as the two virtual sides of a trapezoid. It might be maintained that the lines must be one or the other (equal or unequal) and that to infer inequality from the absence of equality is in keeping with the rules of the most elementary logic. This reasoning is perfectly legitimate, provided it concerns *"things,"* and, in this case, the stimuli. It is in the nature of things that, when they are perceived from different aspects, they remain identically the same throughout all the variations which their modes of appearance undergo. This, however, does not hold as regards phenomenal matters. Phenomena are such as they immediately present themselves to consciousness. One must not attribute anything to phenomena which is not actually ascertained in them by means of direct and immediate observation; there is nothing to look for behind them.[81] *Therefore, if certain phenomena appear neither as equal nor as unequal, there is only the conclusion that they have not been considered from the perspective of this relation.* To contend otherwise would be tantamount to asserting that an algebraic equation is large from the circumstance that it is not small. Just as the concepts of largeness and smallness do not apply to algebraic equations, so too certain concepts which are valid for things do not apply to phenomena.

What holds for equality and inequality is also true for identity, resemblance, unity, and the like. All these terms, which are familiar to us as categories, also express certain immediate impressions inherent to phenomena, and it is only in this latter meaning that they apply to phenomena. The area in which the concept of Gestalt is fundamental is at the same time that in which the immediately experienced signification alone of the terms in question has its application. The double signification of these terms, or more exactly the existence for consciousness of categorial relations in the proper sense, leads to a problem which transcends the theoretical means of Gestalt theory and gives rise to a second stage which is connected with the names of Gelb and Goldstein. After having surveyed some experimental investiga-

81. This conception concerning the profound and essential difference between things and phenomena—a further consequence of the abandonment of the constancy hypothesis—is a new point of convergence between Gestalt theory and Husserlian phenomenology. Cf. Husserl, *Ideen zu einer reinen Phänomenologie und phänomenologischen Philosophie,* I (*Husserliana,* Vol. III [The Hague, 1950]), section III, chaps. II–III.

tions bearing out the theoretical views as thus far developed, we shall turn to this new problem.[82]

## [IV] SOME EXPERIMENTAL RESULTS

WE SHALL FOCUS on the double signification of categorial terms, and in particular of identity. Suppose that an observer looks at an object for some time (whether it be at rest, in motion, or even undergoing some sort of change while he regards it). His immediate impression is that he is confronted with an identical object. Suppose, on the other hand, that he perceives a thing again which he has not perceived for some time: he may be convinced that he now sees the same thing which he saw before, whether or not this thing in the meantime underwent some modification.[83] In the first case, there is the experience of an immediate and phenomenal identity; no reasoning, however well-founded, no conviction, e.g., on the part of the observer that he is the victim of an optical illusion, can succeed in suppressing or even weakening the immediate impression. On the contrary, in the second case, where the identity in question is a matter of conviction or assumption and is not immediately felt and lived, the conviction is susceptible of being shaken by contrary reasoning provided it seems plausible.

J. Ternus has studied this *phenomenal identity* working on visual perception of motion.[84] He starts from the following well-known facts. If in tachistoscopic vision one successively presents two bright spots in the same place on a dark background, the observer sees a single spot (if the interval between the presentations is sufficiently brief) which remains at that place as if the presentation had not been interrupted. If, in the second presentation, the bright spot is shown not at the same place as in the first presentation but in another not too distant one, the observer sees a single spot moving from the first to the second place. The phenomenal identity of a single bright spot either at rest or in motion is experienced in these experiments. One has the direct and immediate impression that an identical point is either at rest or jumps

82. For the experimental documentation, see P. Guillaume, "La theorie de la forme," *Journal de Psychologie* (1925); the analyses Guillaume regularly writes in the *Année Psychologique* of the works appearing in *Psychologische Forschung* (the publication of the Gestalt school); and his book *La psychologie de la forme* (Paris, 1937). See also W. Köhler, *Gestalt Psychology* (New York, 1947); K. Koffka, *Principles of Gestalt Psychology* (New York, 1935).

83. Cf. M. Wertheimer, "Experimentelle Studien über das Sehen von Bewegung," *Zeitschrift für Psychologie*, LXI (1912), § 6.

84. J. Ternus, "Experimentelle Untersuchungen über phänomenale Identität," *Psychologische Forschung*, VII (1926).

from the one to the other place. The same holds if, instead of a single spot, several are presented.

Presenting a group of bright spots in such a way that some of them are shown in both presentations at the same places, while the others are shown in different places, one expects to perceive the spots of the first class at rest and those of the second in motion. This would be in conformity with the two elementary laws mentioned, if either would govern, so to speak, in an absolute fashion, the spots to which it refers. The immediate and phenomenal identity, as regards each spot, would follow these elementary laws. The impressions of the bright spots

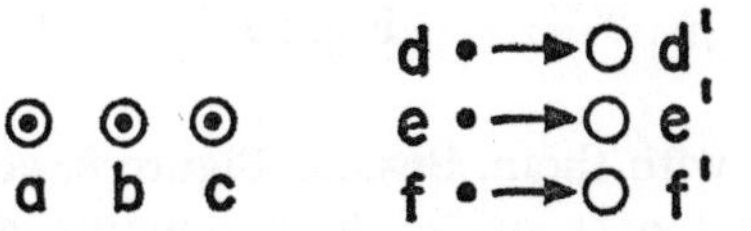

Fig. 8 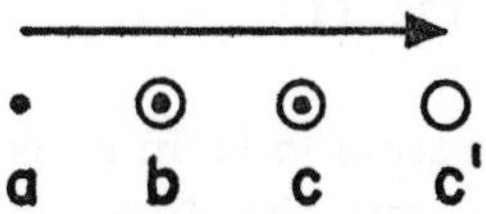        Fig. 9

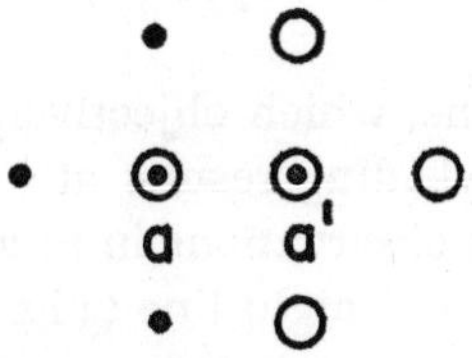

Fig. 10

which, in the two presentations, are presented at the same places would fuse, and one would see, at these places, a single spot at rest. As regards the spots located at different places, the impression left by the first presentation would fuse with that of the second presentation closest to it, and one would see these spots moving from one place to another; one would have the impression of identical spots in motion. In fact, if the spots are arranged as in Figure 8, the spots $a, b, c$ appear as at rest, whereas $d, e, f$ move to the right, respectively identifying themselves with $d', e', f'$.[85]

But, if one presents the arrangement in Figure 9, for example, the three spots $a, b, c$, which lie on a straight line, jump from the left to the right; and the spot $c$ which, according to the elementary law, ought to be seen as at rest identifies itself with $c'$ at the place to which it moves. The same holds for the arrangement in Figure 10. The entire cross which is formed by the points goes to the right, and the phenomenal identity as regards the point $a$, for instance, which

85. As Ternus has done, we symbolize the spots of the first presentation by points and those of the second presentation by small circles.

identifies itself with the point *a′*, is at variance with the elementary law. Figure 11 is another example: the triangle formed by the bright spots moves to the right, and the impression of identity depends upon this motion of the whole and not upon the local conditions.

As opposed to the cases which contradict the elementary laws,

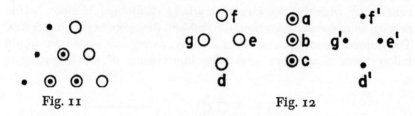

Fig. 11                                   Fig. 12

others seem to be in agreement with them. Besides Figure 8, consider Figure 12: the group composed of spots *a*, *b*, *c* remains at rest, whereas the spots *d*, *e*, *f*, *g*, which form a quadrilateral, move across the stationary group towards the spots *d′*, *e′*, *f′*, *g′* in a manner hard to describe.

Effecting modifications, which objectively speaking are but slight, in those configurations yielding results at variance with the elementary laws, one can obtain observations in accord with these laws. If six spots are arranged along a straight line (Fig. 13), the same results are obtained as with Figure 9: the whole line moves from left to right, and

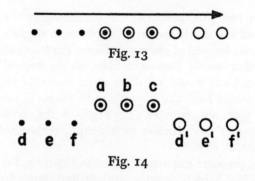

Fig. 13

Fig. 14

the phenomenal identity does not follow the elementary laws. However, if one arranges the six spots as in Figure 14, the spots *a*, *b*, *c* are seen at rest, and the spots *d*, *e*, *f* in motion—precisely what one should expect according to the elementary laws. One obtains the same result when the arrangement of Figure 11 is changed (Fig. 15): the spots *a*, *b*, *c*, forming a triangle, which are given at the same places in both presentations, remain at rest, while the spots *d, e, f,* according to the second elementary law, move to the right.

The arrangement in Figure 16 is very interesting. Instead of spots, there are lines, both of which are seen as moving. The same effect occurs when the lower segments of three lines are hidden from view. But, if the lower segments of only the lines *a* and *c* are hidden, the line *b*, in accord with the elementary laws, is seen at rest, and the line *a* in motion. These results illustrate again and verify the contention according to which there is a difference between a line and the side of a rectangle.[86] The lines *a* and *b*, whether seen in entirety or only in part, appear as the virtual sides of a rectangle. On the other hand, when the length of one differs from that of the other, one has the impression of perceiving simply one line alongside another one.

In the above example, the fluctuation is brought about by means of

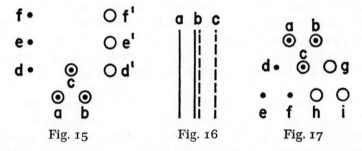

Fig. 15          Fig. 16          Fig. 17

modifications in the objective stimuli. The same result can be obtained by modifying the internal conditions. In Figure 17, one sees the quadrilateral (composed of the spots) oscillate around the axis marked by the spots *a* and *b*, which are at rest. The spot *c*, which, according to the elementary laws, must also appear as at rest, is to the contrary involved in this motion. However, a result conforming to these laws (where the spot *c* is seen at rest) is often obtained. The triangle formed of the spots *a, b, c* is then seen at rest, while the triangle formed by *d, e, f* jumps to the right. This phenomenon occurs especially when one sees in this constellation, even in the first presentation, two triangles whose summits face one another, rather than a quadrilateral. Even in the case of Figure 9 (in which no fluctuation is ordinarily experienced), if the observer attentively fixes his glance midway between the spots *b* and *c*, he can at times experience a phenomenon different from the normal one: the spots *b* and *c* are at rest, while the spot *a* jumps to *c'*. Because of the attitude

86. See above, p. 25.

adopted, the observer resolves the ternary group into a pair plus a point, and these phenomena differ from one another in a fundamental way, from both the phenomenal and the functional point of view.

The above case yields a new illustration and even a new proof of the thesis concerning the double dependence of perception. The variation of conditions, external as well as internal, entails a variation in the perceived objects. Such variation does not affect the perspective or some other subjective characteristic of the perceived object, but the latter *qua* perceived itself and in its entirety. Sometimes as a result of the modification of internal conditions alone, this change in the perceived object has functional consequences. The impressions of motion and of rest, like that of phenomenal identity, vary according to whether the object—which is identical from the point of view of the stimuli—is seen as a ternary group or as a pair plus a point. The functional consequences depend upon the phenomenal aspect of the perceived object and not upon the objective state of affairs.

The results obtained by Ternus fully confirm the views of Gestalt theory. Phenomenal identity is in accordance with the elementary laws, that is to say, the objective state of affairs is decisive when the given spots fall into two groups, either forming a figure. One of these figures is then seen at rest, the other in motion. Such an effect is certain to occur when, as in the case of all the examples mentioned, the spots forming the figure seen at rest are those which are given in identical places in the two presentations, while the other spots form the figure which moves. If, in cases of this kind, only one of the two presentations is given, the observer clearly sees two figures: the one *and* the other, the one besides the other. He has before him a *sum* of two figures. If, on the contrary, all the spots form only one single figure, it is this figure which is displaced in the perceptual field notwithstanding the elementary laws: that is to say, regardless of the local conditions.

These laws must not be misconstrued as valid only for one class of cases, while other cases constitute exceptions. The fact that, in certain conditions, the phenomena follow the elementary laws, is itself a consequence of the law of Gestalt governing all cases. What makes the spots appear as at rest or in motion, what determines phenomenal identity, is the role which they play in the figure they constitute. The spots remain at rest or move according to whether this figure remains at rest or moves, and this is so on account of their existing only as constituents of the figure. On the other hand, all of the factors (internal as well as external) whose supervenient action modifies the normal results have influence only so far as they favor or condition a grouping of spots differing from the normal one. In other words, these factors become efficacious because by virtue of them the total Gestalt which was first given becomes dissolved into two Gestalten, each of which is a whole in its own right.

Which spots, in the experiments of Ternus, are phenomenally and immediately identified with one another? If a ternary group is seen in Figure 9, the spot *c* jumps to the right and becomes identified with the spot *c'*. In the first presentation, this spot is at the extreme right of the group, and it remains, because of its motion, in the same position relative to the group to which it belongs. On the other hand, if the same objective arrangement is perceived as a pair of spots plus a supplementary one, the spot *c*, which in the first presentation is the right-terminal point of the pair, remains at rest and thus occupies the same place in the second presentation and accomplishes the same function with regard to the pair. Finally, the spot *a*, which in the first presentation is additional, by moving to the right and identifying itself with *c'*, remains additional in the second presentation.

Phenomenal identity is established between points which, in the two constellations, have the same function and occupy the same place within the total Gestalt, that is to say, between points which are homologous with regard to the Gestalt. This result throws a new light on the thesis according to which every detail of a Gestalt exists only in the function which this Gestalt assigns to it. It is explained, in turn, by the very general tendency to self-conservation, which is an immediate consequence of the tendency to the best possible Gestalt (under the given conditions). Since the Gestalten which Ternus uses are "good" and "strong," they tend to persevere, and this explains the motions which allow them to appear in the second presentation as they were in the first. The phenomena of rest and motion, as well as that of phenomenal identity, are thus referred to very general principles.

W. Metzger, who has studied shadows in motion, deals with problems similar to those treated by Ternus.[87] In overtaking each other, the shadows trace curves which display themselves gradually in the course of the observation. Metzger asks which curve-segments will, at the points of intersection, be spontaneously joined together and form a total curve, such that one segment appears as the continuation of the other. He shows that factors which are operative in his experiments are the same as those which, according to Wertheimer, govern the constitution and the structure of Gestalten perceived as at rest.[88]

Another example of the application of the law of Gestalt concerns

87. W. Metzger, "Beobachtungen über phänomenale Identität," *Psychologische Forschung*, XIX (1934).
88. Wertheimer, "Untersuchungen zur Lehre von der Gestalt," II, *loc. cit.*

*chromatic thresholds.* If any color is made to appear on an achromatic background, the absolute, and especially the differential, threshold increases with the brightness of the background.[89] Using Figure 18, Gelb and Granit have prepared two series of figures, the colors of which range from white to black, in such a way that each member of the first series, whose figure is of a grey, $g_1$, and the background of another grey, $g_2$ corresponds with a member of the second series, whose figure is the shade $g_2$ and the background $g_1$.[90] These two figures are like the positive and negative proofs of the same photographic plate. With regard to any color, the authors have found its threshold to be higher—to a rather considerable degree—if the color

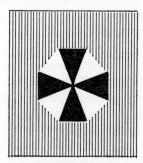

Fig. 18

appears on $g_1$ as figure rather than as ground, the conditions of observation and especially the retinal conditions being equal on both sides. It even happens that, for a grey $g_1$, which is brighter than $g_2$, the threshold is lower when $g_1$ functions as ground and $g_2$ as figure. It follows that the dependence of chromatic thresholds with respect to the brightness of the ground on which a color is presented is not absolute or as rigid as it would have to be if the constancy hypothesis truly expressed the relations between stimulus and sensory datum.

An explanation of these results in terms of Gestalt principles can easily be given. If a colored spot appears on a figure, the latter becomes in some fashion the ground with respect to that spot. But the first figure resists this transformation by virtue of its tendency to self-conservation. By contrast, a ground does not oppose the same resistance to the formation of a figure; it rather favors, to a certain

89. G. Heymans, "Untersuchungen über psychische Hemmung," *Zeitschrift für Psychologie und Physiologie der Sinnesorgane,* XXI (1899), pp. 326–38; G. Revesz, "Ueber die Abhängigkeit der Farbenschwellen von der achromatischen Erregung," *Zeitschrift für Sinnesphysiologie,* XLI (1907).
90. A. Gelb and R. Granit, "Die Bedeutung von Figur und Grund für die Farbenschwelle," *Zeitschrift für Psychologie,* XCIII (1923). Cf. A. Ackermann, "Farbschwelle und Feldstruktur," *Psychologische Forschung,* V (1924).

extent, its appearance. This difference between the properties of the figure and the ground finds an expression in the variable values of the chromatic thresholds on the same grey, according to whether this grey is the shade of the figure or of the ground.

The law of conservation of Gestalt also dissipates the apparent arbitrariness and indeterminateness which, in the opinion of some dualistic psychologists, constitutes the privilege of the so-called "higher" factors, such as disposition.[91] Let us consider a set of points along a horizontal line, as in Figure 4.[92] Let the distances between $a$ and $c$, $c$ and $e$, $e$ and $g$, $g$ and $i$ be denoted by $s$; those between $a$ and $b$, $c$ and $d$, $e$ and $f$, and so on, by $s_1$; and finally, those between $b$ and $c$, $d$ and $e$, and so on, by $s_2$. We have: $s = s_1 + s_2$. If we vary $s_1$ and $s_2$

Fig. 19

Fig. 20

while keeping $s$ constant, we obtain a series of sets of points such that $b$, $d$, $f$, and so on move more and more away from $a$, $c$, $e$, and so on and draw near to $c$, $e$, $g$, and so on. The final set of the series might be Figure 19. Between these extreme sets, there will be some in which $s_1$ and $s_2$ are equal or nearly equal (for example, Fig. 20). It has already been shown that in Figure 4 the factor of proximity brings about the grouping $ab/ cd/ ef/ gh/ ij$, and the same factor imposes the grouping $a/ bc/ de/ fg/ hi/ j$ in Figure 19.[93] What will the natural and spontaneous grouping be in Figure 20 which can be called a critical set? Susceptible of being grouped in one way as easily as in the other, this set is equivocal because neither grouping is imposed nor even suggested in any way. This set belongs to the type of constellations on which Benussi worked to bring out the cooperation of the two factors which, according to him, are indispensable for perception and, at the same time, to bring out the freedom of the activity of production which he considers as superior to pure sensibility. In a case of this kind, the organization of perception seems to depend indeed on the subject and not on formal and objective factors.

91. Koffka, "Psychologie," *loc. cit.*, chap. III, § 4.
92. Wertheimer, "Untersuchungen zur Lehre von der Gestalt," II, *loc. cit.*, pp. 316–17.
93. See above, p. 28.

This apparent indeterminateness disappears in the light of Wertheimer's methodical experiments.[94] When a series of sets of the kind in question is presented to an observer, who has to go through them in order, the observer, if he begins with Figure 4, perceives the critical set grouped according to the rhythm, *ab/ cd/ ef/ gh/ ij.* If, on the contrary, the observer starts from Figure 19, the critical set is articulated with the rhythm, *a/ bc/ de/ fg/ hi/ j.* Those perceptions which precede the critical one decide its organization.

Figures 4 and 19, as well as those which immediately follow them in the series of the sets, are doubtless better and stronger Gestalten as regards the pregnance of their structures than is the critical set. The tendency to good Gestalt makes these strong structures encroach on the sets of lesser pregnance, so that the latter are perceived according to the rhythm of the former. If one goes through the series either in the direction from Figure 4 to Figure 19 or in the opposite direction, a more global Gestalt encompassing, as far as possible, all the sets begins to arise. This global Gestalt has a certain rhythm as its intrinsic structure: either *ab/ cd/* etc. or *a/ bc/* etc. The tendency this global Gestalt has to conserve itself makes it encroach on the critical set and impose on it a rhythm to which, to be sure, it is not averse but which on the other hand it does not suggest by itself.

The influence which past perceptions have on a present one is revealed by such facts. It is this influence which defines what is essential to disposition as well as to *experience.*[95] Traditional psychology defined experience, to which it so often resorted, by *frequency of repetition* whose primary, if not only, effect is to reinforce the associations between the representations involved. By virtue of its very principles, this psychology could not proceed differently.

We shall return at a later point to the difficulty besetting this traditional definition of experience. Gottschaldt has experimentally studied the influence which the frequent perception of certain rather simple figures (*a*-figures) has on the perception of less familiar figures.[96] After the observer has familiarized himself with the *a*-figures, he is presented with *b*-figures, each of which contains one of the *a*-figures as a geometrical part of itself. The influence of experience may consist in an *a*-figure "leaping" into view at the first appearance of a *b*-figure: at first glance the *b*-figure appears as

94. Wertheimer, "Untersuchungen zur Lehre von der Gestalt," II, *loc. cit.,* pp. 319–20.

95. Koffka, "Psychologie," *loc. cit.,* chap. III, § 9.

96. K. Gottschaldt, "Ueber den Einfluss der Erfahrung auf die Wahrnehmung von Figuren," *Psychologische Forschung,* VIII (1926).

composed of an *a*-figure and one or more supplementary figures. It may also happen that at the outset the *b*-figure is perceived without being articulated in terms of the contours of an *a*-figure and that only after a certain time it undergoes a phenomenal and immediately experienced transformation by which it is decomposed into an *a*-figure and the rest. Finally, it is possible that an *a*-figure is at no time seen, though, however, suspected, in the *b*-figure. To these positive cases Gottschaldt opposes those in which the observer suspects that an *a*-figure is contained in a *b*-figure while, in fact, it is not there, and those in which the *b*-figure is seen without any reference to an *a*-figure.

From the results obtained by Gottschaldt, it follows that the mere frequency with which the *a*-figures are exposed, even when the observers were instructed to look very attentively so that they would be able to draw them by memory, has almost no influence whatever on the manner in which the *b*-figures are perceived. The percentage of positive cases is as low for observers who were shown each of the *a*-figures 520 times as it is for those who saw the same figures only 3 times before being shown the *b*-figures. To forestall the eventual objection that with 520 presentations the optimum frequency concerning the efficacy of the *a*-figures is surpassed and that these figures (five of them were used) might mutually inhibit one another as to the effects each of them produces on the later perceptions of the *b*-figures, Gottschaldt made some special experiments involving only a single one of the *a*-figures, varying the frequency of presentation (12, 24, 50, 100, and 200). In these experiments the result was as negative as in the main ones.

However, the results do differ according to whether the observers are instructed to be as passive as possible when confronted with the *b*-figures (to look at them and describe them quite naïvely) or whether, before being shown these figures, they are told that they contain *a*-figures and are asked to look out for them. With respect to the observers in the second class, there is a mean increase of positive solutions amounting to 24%. Still, even with these observers the percentage of positive solutions does not increase with an increase in the frequency of presentation from 5 to 540. Whereas the frequency alone of repeated presentations has only a minimal influence on the way in which the *b*-figures are perceived, the attitude adopted by the observer towards the *b*-figures does play a certain role. It is in keeping with these results that the sporadic positive solutions obtained by some observers who were instructed to remain passive towards the *b*-figures can be explained by the fact that they did not follow the instruction but had a tendency to analyze the figures, a tendency which instructions to the contrary did not entirely counteract. Among the effects resulting from the attitude of the observer or from the internal situation in which he finds himself, one must also count the discouraging influence which a failure with regard to a *b*-figure, extremely difficult to decompose, has upon the perception of another *b*-figure which is a great deal easier to analyze. If the latter is immediately preceded by the very difficult one, the observer does not succeed. The greater frequency of false solutions on the part of observers adopting an analytic attitude than on the part of those who are naïve stems from the same cause. Being pressed by the imposed task, these observers sought to accomplish it by resorting to certain general analogies between the two kinds of figures. Sometimes they were firmly convinced that they had discovered an *a*-figure in a *b*-figure when certain properties of form, either of *b* as a whole or of one or another of the figures into which *b* can be subdivided, recalled some characteristic form of an *a*-figure, even though the latter was not actually contained in the *b*-figure.

However, the attitude of the observer with regard to the *b*-figures is not the only, or even the decisive, factor for the decomposition of these figures; for even the more analytic observers succeeded in decomposing only a very small number of *b*-figures. Beyond the internal factors deriving from the psychological situation of the observer, there is a special and specific factor which in these experiments counteracts the tendency to analyze. This resistance can arise only from global characteristics and properties of the *b*-figures in virtue of which the *a*-figure, while it is a geometrical part of the *b*-figure, does not appear as a phenomenal part of it.

Gottschaldt enumerates some principles concerning the phenomenal absorption of the *a*-figure into the *b*-figure. The lines which make up the contours of the *a*-figure taken in isolation may lose all or part of their function of delimitation if this figure enters into the context of the *b*-figure. Either these lines become internal lines of the *b*-figure, or they delimit subordinate forms into which that figure is articulated but which are totally different from the *a*-figure. This alteration of the contour lines is accompanied by corresponding modifications in the area delimited by these lines. The *a*-figure as a whole of global character possesses one or more principal directions which are no longer preserved in the *b*-figure. Accentuated constituents of the *a*-figure lose this privilege when the *a*-figure becomes integrated with the *b*-figure, or vice versa. Some *a*-figures are characterized by the homology or correspondence of certain lines or points; their relations are modified or even suppressed if to the points and lines belonging to *a* new points and lines are added in *b*. Thus the constituents of the *a*-figure acquire, if they appear in *b*, functions which differ completely from those which the "same" constituents have in the isolated *a*-figure. As a result, the *a*-figure becomes undiscoverable in *b*, thus losing its psychological reality.

Gottschaldt tried to measure the Gestalt consistence of *b*-figures which makes their decomposition difficult (and rather often even impossible) by measuring the average time which a group of 112 observers, to whom the *b*-figures and the corresponding *a*-figures were shown simultaneously, took to discover the *a*-figure in the *b*-figure. This procedure permitted him to classify the *b*-figures in a quantitative manner. The purpose of these measurements was to eliminate the influence of practice. Their results are in perfect accord with the observations made in the main experiments. The few *b*-figures in which the corresponding *a*-figure "leaped" into view are, save for one exception, the same as those which appear as the easiest to analyze in this classification. Quite generally, the number of positive solutions decreases with the increase in the Gestalt consistence of the *b*-figures.

In the course of these experiments, the author found that the more the observers had decomposed or sought to decompose the *b*-figures, the easier became the analysis of succeeding figures and the more the differences resulting from variable consistence among the *b*-figures tended to disappear. Here we have an effect of experience, indeed. Experience, however, cannot be understood as mere repetition, since each figure was presented to each observer only a single time. What is in question here is the formation and development of a function: the more frequently a person performs an action, even if this action applies to variable materials, the better he learns to practice it.

We finally mention an interesting result obtained on very simple *a*-figures and *b*-figures which could easily be decomposed into an *a*-figure plus an additional stroke. If, before exposing the *a*-figure 40 times, the author informed the observer that a figure different from those which were going to be presented to him would appear in the course of the experiment, the *b*-figure was seen at once to contain the *a*-figure as a phenomenal part. If, however, the appearance of the *b*-figure was announced to the observer immediately before its actual presentation, without the other circumstances of the observations being varied, the *b*-figure was not decomposed at its very appearance and was only afterwards sometimes seen to contain an *a*-figure. Gottschaldt imputes this difference to what he calls the internal situation of the observer. The information overthrows the disposition derived from the repeated showing of the *a*-figure, so that the *b*-figure is perceived as if nothing had preceded it. If, in contrast, this information is given at the beginning of the experiment, it has no effect on the disposition (built up in the course of the experiments) by which the manner of perceiving the b-figures is determined.

A conception very different from the traditional one concerning the influence of the past on the present emerges from these observations. When it is a matter of dispositions, the perceptions which have just occurred give rise to a total Gestalt into which the subsequent perceptions are integrated. When, on the other hand, the past influencing the present is a more remote one, its effect is to set up certain internal conditions, to form and progressively perfect functions and aptitudes on which further perceptions depend. Experience modifies the psychophysical organism by setting up conditions which

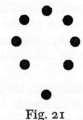

Fig. 21

permit certain typical transformations of Gestalten. All the observations which Köhler has made as to the role of experience in the behavior of the higher apes, as well as those concerning the development of children, in particular the processes of maturation, go to confirm this conception.[97]

Let us study the functional laws in still another domain. Eight small circular disks with a diameter of about 1 centimeter are arranged on the periphery of a circle, and one of the disks is movable along the radius of the circle.[98] If this movable disk is moved out a little from the periphery, we no longer have, geometrically speaking, a circle; from the phenomenal point of view, however, the disks will continue to be arranged along the periphery of a circle, although, it is true, one that is no longer a "genuine" circle but is a "poor" or "bad" one. If the disk is moved out still more from the periphery, one sees something resembling a pear (Fig. 21). If it is moved out still further, it is dissociated from the other disks which now form a genuine circle

97. K. Koffka, *Die Grundlagen der psychischen Entwicklung*, 2d ed. (Osterwieck a/Harz, 1925), chap. V, esp. pp. 186, 222–23; cf. K. Koffka, "Les notions d'héréditaire et d'acquis en psychologie," *Journal de Psychologie Normale et Pathologique* (1932).

98. Koffka, "Psychologie," *loc. cit.*, pp. 550–52.

again, while the mobile disk is an object apart. Analogous observations can be made on a right angle when one of its sides is made movable.[99] If this side is so turned that the right angle becomes an angle of 85°, the latter appears, from the phenomenal point of view, as an imprecise and poor right angle. If the angle decreases still further towards 75°, it no longer appears at all as a right angle. The phenomenal difference between an angle of 85° and one of 75° is, qualitatively, quite different from that between an angle of 75° and one of 65°. However, objectively speaking, there is in both cases the same difference of 10°.

In all these cases, the stimuli are continuously modified. The corresponding phenomena, however, do not vary in a continuous manner. Their transformations take place by sudden jumps from one Gestalt to another, and this implies that there are no intermediate Gestalten between those which are realized. The transformation of Gestalten occurs by levels of pregnance. It is not the case that to every geometrical constellation there corresponds a specific phenomenon; instead, the phenomena develop in a discontinuous way. Such discontinuity, which is at variance with the constancy hypothesis (according to which the differences between sensory data strictly follow those between the corresponding stimuli), recalls some conceptions in quantum theory.

The observations on the circle composed of small disks of which one is slightly displaced and on the right angle slightly diminished in size disclose the law of pregnance from a different point of view. Owing to the tendency to good Gestalt, there exists around every particularly pregnant Gestalt a zone on which that Gestalt encroaches. If one generates a figure by slightly modifying a strong Gestalt, the figure thus generated is placed within that zone. It is perceived, not judged, as signifying this "good" Gestalt from which it appears as derivative. It is taken as an imprecise, "poor" and "bad" realization of this strong Gestalt and not as an independent Gestalt in its own right. Derivative Gestalten appear as perfectible; if it may be so expressed, there is a finality inherent in the strong Gestalt with reference to which the imperfect Gestalten are perceived. It follows that it is not the positions occupied by the points making up a form which determine the structure of this form, but, on the contrary, it is with reference to the form with its intrinsic and characteristic structure that the points are perceived in their respective particular positions as realizing the form in a good or a poor way. Thus, if points are

99. Wertheimer, "Untersuchungen zur Lehre von der Gestalt," II, *loc. cit.*, pp. 318–19.

irregularly arranged around a sine-curve (for instance, in such a way that no point is placed on the curve itself), what is seen is the typical form of the curve and not the geometrical formation which would result from joining the adjacent points by straight lines.[100]

Analogous facts can be ascertained in tachistoscopic observation. Whereas, if a series of letters or words of some length are observed during a certain period of time, one obtains only the impression of a grey stripe from which but a few letters at most emerge, it is possible to discern quite clearly during the same time of observation simple figures such as the circle, the ellipse, and the square.[101] If such simple figures include in their construction some not too significant gaps and are presented in tachistoscopic vision, one perceives apparent movements of the figure, which closes and completes itself.[102] (By "not too significant gaps" are meant "gaps" which do not prevent the remaining part of the figure from realizing the law of the total Gestalt and from exhibiting more or less completely the structure according to which the figure tends to complete itself.) The same apparent movement occurs if one observes in tachistoscopic vision the periphery of a circle marked by twelve points, one of which is slightly displaced towards the interior of the circle.[103] This point appears to move towards the periphery. Below a certain "critical" displacement, a plain circle without any distortion is seen; beyond the "critical" displacement, the point moves towards a privileged place (for example, the center of the circle). If the figures presented in tachistoscopic vision are not as simple as the circle, the ellipse, or the square but are still closed figures, they become simplified and appear as more symmetrical than they are in fact.[104] Above all, pointed ends tend to become curves.

These facts are related to the observations made by W. Fuchs concerning a certain category of hemianoptic patients.[105] If one of the simple figures mentioned before is in tachistoscopic vision presented to a hemianoptic patient in such a way that part of it falls on the blind region of his retina, he sees the entire figure. For the patient to see a complete circle, for example, it suffices to present him with a semi-circle or a little more than that. This phenomenon occurs

100. Koffka, "Psychologie," *loc. cit.*, p. 550.
101. Concerning the notion of simplicity is Gestalt theory, see above, p. 27f.
102. E. Lindemann, "Experimentelle Untersuchung über das Entstehen und Vergehen von Gestalten," *loc. cit.*, pp. 28–29.
103. *Ibid.*, pp. 42–47.
104. *Ibid.*, § 15, and p. 57.
105. W. Fuchs, "Untersuchungen über das Sehen der Hemaniopiker und Hemiamblyopiker: pt. b. Die totalisierende Gestaltauffassung," *Zeitschrift für Psychologie*, LXXXVI (1921).

even when the part of the circle projected onto the weakened region of the retina objectively contains a gap. In general, when a circle, an ellipse, a square, a star, is presented to the patient in this manner, the figure will be completed provided that the part falling on the intact region of the retina already bears within itself the structural law of the Gestalt into which the part is going to be completed. Thus, a hemianoptic patient will not extend an isolated straight line; but, if this line is part of a star, it will be extended so as to complete the figure. With an isolated straight line it does not matter much whether it is a little longer or shorter; its structure is realized by the part falling on the intact side of the retina, and its extension would not make it a better and more pregnant Gestalt. If, however, the line in question is a part of a star, shortening it interferes with the realization of the structure of the star, and the total Gestalt is realized less perfectly. The nature of the Gestalt, in particular the symmetry so essential to it, demands the extension of the line.

What is of greatest importance in the results of Fuchs's investigations is that the phenomena of completion do not occur if, instead of those simple figures, the patient is presented with familiar things, whether irregular or symmetrical, such as a butterfly or the outline of a human face. In such cases as these, he sees only what is projected onto the intact part of his retina. Certainly, these things are also Gestalten, and even stable ones; but Fuchs's investigations show that there are specially privileged Gestalten among which, for instance, are the right angle or the circle. This conclusion is in agreement also with facts previously discussed.

At the same time, these results permit the definitive refutation of the explanation which previous psychology, resorting to experience understood as frequent repetition, had tried to give concerning the psychological origin of privileged Gestalten, as, for example, the right angle. In order for the infant to have repeated experience of the right angle, it is necessary that such an angle be presented to him in a *well-determined position* and that he have it presented to him in this position far more often than in other positions.[106] This is because it is only when the angle is presented in this privileged position that its retinal image is a right angle; all the other positions in which it can be presented yield retinal images other than a right angle. Owing to the motions of both the child himself and the objects, this privileged position, which is only *one* among others, is realized much less frequently than the other possible positions. Accordingly, if the right

106. Wertheimer, "Untersuchungen zur Lehre von der Gestalt," II, *loc. cit.*, pp. 332–33.

angle were not in itself a distinct and privileged Gestalt, the experience of it would never become stabilized for the child. To define experience as a repetition of the same data is to presuppose precisely what must be explained.

Factors analogous to those which enter into Fuchs's observations also come into play in Gelb's experiments on the *separating power of peripheral retinal elements.*[107] Gelb uses two concentric black circles placed on a white background, the observer being instructed to fix his look on their common center. If only a small part of the two peripheries are presented to him, the observer hardly succeeds, under certain conditions of observation, in separating the two black arcs; whereas, if in the same observational conditions he has the two circles presented to him in their entirety, he sees with complete clarity a white circle which separates the two black circles. The contrary effect is obtained if, instead of two circles, one presents two parallel black lines of which the observer fixes one of the extremities. If he is shown only the other extremity of the lines, and that in indirect vision, he separates the two small lines which appear; whereas, if the two lines are seen in their entirety, under the same observational conditions, the separation extends only approximately up to half the length of the lines. The separating power of a peripheral retinal element varies with the total configuration presented, though the conditions of local stimulation are kept constant. This power varies according to whether what appears in indirect vision is or is not indispensable for the subject to obtain a characteristic impression of the configuration. This is the case in the first experiment: in order for two concentric circles to be seen as such, their arcs must be separated throughout. Two parallel lines separated up to approximately half their lengths, on the contrary, already make a rather characteristic impression: they constitute a strong and pregnant Gestalt which would not become any more perfect if the lines were made a little longer.

Gelb sees a connection between his results and the *Aubert-Foerster phenomenon.* Among other facts pertaining to the perceptual domain, they are particularly significant so far as they refute the constancy hypothesis on a most essential point. That hypothesis was at the basis of psychophysics. It seemed to open up the possibility of evaluating the excitability (considered as a constant) of every neural element of a sense organ.[108] According to Gelb's experiments, such a constancy of excitability does not exist: the functioning of a neural element, in

107. A. Gelb, "Grundfragen der Wahrnehmungspsychologie," *Bericht über den 7. Kongress für Experimentelle Psychologie in Marburg* (1921).
108. Cf. above, pp. 4–6.

each concrete case, depends upon global processes which take place in the sense organ as a whole to which the element in question belongs.

## [V] THE LIMIT OF THE CONCEPT OF GESTALT

AMONG THE FACTORS which have contributed most to bringing the problem of Gestalt to the fore, one must count Husserl's discovery of the double meaning of categorial terms such as identity, similarity, unity, and the like. These terms are familiar especially, if not exclusively, as conveying categorial meaning in the proper sense. The question of possibly apprehending at a glance the collective character of any multiplicity—without having the need, or the time, to go systematically through all the members composing such a collection—led Husserl to establish a distinction between two kinds of unity: one which is conceptual, categorial, and in this sense brought about; the other is immediately experienced and given alongside and at once with the sensory data, which, owing to it, appear as forming a unitary group not constituted by any categorial thought.[109] The same distinction has to be made as regards all the categorial terms. If they are taken in their immediate meaning, these terms denote purely phenomenal matters. They designate coherences and contextures directly pertaining to sensory data. Such connections and coherences are features exhibited by the very phenomena; they contribute to the constitution of phenomenal groups of which they are properties. They are, therefore, sensory facts appearing and disappearing in the manner characteristic of all phenomena.

It is the particular merit of Wertheimer to have seen the specific nature of these facts and to have given them their place in psychology. Working on problems similar to those Husserl treated in his *Philosophie der Arithmetik*—namely, psychological problems related to the concept of number—Wertheimer has pointed out that, for example, the number 3 (which to us, especially in arithmetic, denotes a categorial set consisting of any three independent units) is, in the thinking of primitive societies, very much like a Gestalt-quality.[110] For the members of such societies, "3" signifies a phenomenal and immediate characteristic exhibited by certain ternary groups and giving a specific phenomenal appearance to them. In these societies, the word used to count fruit is not used to count men, trees, houses, and so on,

109. Cf. above, pp. 8–9.
110. M. Wertheimer, "Über das Denken der Naturvölker," *Zeitschrift für Psychologie*, LX (1912).

in contradistinction to our concepts of number which are of a purely formal nature and are indifferent to the things to be counted.

The doctrine developed by the Berlin School is obviously sufficient to account for the phenomenal, because the level at which it operates is precisely that one. It is just for this very reason that the categorial, in the strict sense—which by its nature lies beyond the phenomenal level and must, therefore, in principle never be conceived after the model of the phenomenal—constitutes a limit to Gestalt theory. There is a temptation for this theory to confuse the two significations of categorial terms, by making this confusion of the two in favor of their immediate signification, as happened with Koffka.[111]

Distinguishing the immediate and the categorial meaning of the terms in question, one must insist on the specific nature of the latter and do justice to it. Categorial identity is not phenomenal identity; it does not have the nature of an immediately and directly experienced coherence. The number 3 as known in arithmetic must not be mistaken for an intuitive character inherent in a ternary group. Whatever status may be given, in the final analysis, to the categorial, it is certainly not a sensory, nor a quasi-sensory, datum; nor is it exhibited by such data in the manner of a phenomenal feature; nor, finally, is it, in any sense, a phenomenal constituent.[112] Such an interpretation of the categorial is impossible precisely because of its formal and universal nature by virtue of which the categorial is indifferent to the materials to which it may apply—just as, for instance, a number, in the categorial sense, is indifferent to the objects it can be used to count, and these objects, moreover, can be homogeneous as well as heterogeneous.

Facts of this kind cannot be ignored by psychology. For, in order to speak of the categorial and to make use of it, it must be given in one form or another. There must, therefore, be acts of consciousness which are directed towards the categorial and other acts through which it is directly apprehended. Within the limits of this essay, we must abstain from even touching on the question concerning "categorial intuition," an intuition of the categorial which, according to certain Platonic philosophers, must be admitted. However, the expression, "categorial intuition" seems to us to pose the problem rather than solve it. We shall restrict ourselves here to bringing out the problem in question in the light of some findings, thus focusing on one of its aspects.

From the observations on higher apes made by P. Guillaume and I. Meyerson, Köhler, and R. M. Yerkes, it appears that these animals are

111. Koffka, "Psychologie," *loc. cit.*, pp. 548–49, 574–75.
112. Cf. Husserl, *Logische Untersuchungen*, II, vi, §§ 42–46, 51.

capable of intelligent actions.[113] By "intelligent" is meant the aptitude to react to a new situation and to make use of things, without any previous training, in the way most suitable for the concrete situation and at times alone permitting the animal to reach a goal. The distinctive characteristic of such actions—which, to a considerable extent, occur only in certain particularly favorable conditions and in the best moments of the chimpanzee's life—is that the result is not obtained by means of "trial and error" behavior. In trial and error, the final result which the animal obtains is happy only by chance. The conduct leading to the desired effect is *one mode of conduct among others,* all of which are employed and tried by the animal equally; hence, none of them has any intrinsic distinction. The fact that other modes of conduct are not useful, whereas one certain reaction yields a favorable result, is entirely the result of the objective constellation and situation; it is external and even alien to the behavior of the animal. With intelligent actions, on the contrary, the animal may also begin by making random motions; yet at a certain moment he abandons this blind groping and adopts only a single manipulatory conduct that will allow him to solve the problem, just as if he understood the given situation. If at a later time the animal is placed in the same situation, he will immediately, or almost so, make use of the same procedure which resulted in the favorable effect. This procedure will have been learned by him through his experience; whereas, had he followed the method of trial and error and were placed in the same situation, he would have begun again to grope and make random motions.

Let us consider one of Köhler's examples of intelligent action of this kind on the part of a chimpanzee.[114] In the cage there is a tree, and in front of the cage, at a distance greater than the length of the animal's arms from the bars, lies a piece of fruit. The chimpanzee in the cage already knows how to make use of a stick to draw objects near to himself. Perceiving the fruit, he goes to the bars and stretches out his hand, then seeks for a stick. There is no stick in the cage or any object which could be used as a stick.[115] The chimpanzee is perplexed; the situation in which he finds himself consists in the tree

113. P. Guillaume and I. Meyerson, "Recherches sur l'usage de l'instrument chez les Singes," *Journal de Psychologie* (1930, 1931, 1934); W. Köhler, *The Mentality of Apes* (London, 1956); R. M. Yerkes, *The Mental Life of Monkeys and Apes: A Study of Ideational Behavior* (Behavior Monographs, Vol. III, No. 1 [New York, 1916]); Yerkes, *Almost Human* (New York, 1925), chaps. V–VI; Yerkes, *The Mind of a Gorilla* (Genetic Psychology Monographs, Vol. II, Nos. 1–2, 6 [Worcester, Mass., 1926–28]), chaps. IV, VI.

114. Köhler, *The Mentality of Apes*, pp. 103f.

115. Concerning the way in which the most different sorts of objects take on the function of stick for the chimpanzee, see *ibid.,* pp. 31ff.

(a very solid object) on the one hand and on the other hand the field of action oriented towards the fruit. For the animal, this field of action is open and presents a gap which has to be closed. This is indeed the essential structure of what is called a problem of a practical nature. Suddenly, the chimpanzee rushes up to the tree, breaks off a branch and uses it as a stick. What happens and permits the animal to master the situation is the radical transformation which the branch undergoes by becoming a stick. The branch, which was a part of a solid form (the tree), is detached and becomes the intermediary that the chimpanzee needs in the field of action to close the gap. From this action of the chimpanzee, one can derive a definition of intelligence: it consists chiefly in being able to close an open Gestalt by detaching from a closed and solid one a part which now acquires a determinate function in the Gestalt to be completed. Given the solidity of the Gestalt (the tree), this intelligent action of the chimpanzee will be appreciated all the more as he accomplishes it for the first time in his life.

What characterizes the behavior of the kind in question on the part of higher animals is also found, according to the theoreticians of the Berlin School, in the intelligent acts of man.[116] In particular, the radical transformation of Gestalten, the dissociation of one Gestalt and the sudden emergence of another, are of primary importance. Thus the intelligent mentality of man is to a considerable extent approximated by that of the higher apes, so that there seems to be no essential difference between them.

Wertheimer gives some examples of human behavior explainable in terms of this principle.[117] We shall confine ourselves to only two. An attorney has the habit of burning all of his old papers after a certain time; thus, say, he has burned file A. One day he seeks for a receipt belonging to file B. Not finding it in its place, he wonders to what other papers this receipt could be related. Suddenly, the idea strikes him that it is also related to A and that at a certain moment he himself gathered up all the papers relating to A. What happens in this situation is, in principle, the same as what occurred in the action of the chimpanzee. The document which was considered in its relation to the matter B becomes transformed into a document relating to A. Acquiring a place and role in a new context, it becomes different from the phenomenal point of view. Considering what the attorney knows of his own habits, this immediately experienced transformation is sufficient for him to find out what has become of the receipt.

116. Cf. Koffka, "Psychologie," loc. cit., chap. IV, § 4.
117. M. Wertheimer, Über Schlussprozesse im produktiven Denken (Berlin and Leipzig, 1920).

The other example is the following. Given an isosceles triangle, the length of the two equal sides ($s$) and the size of the angle formed by these sides (90°) (Fig. 22), what is its area? Instead of resorting to the formula, $A = \frac{b.a}{2}$, this problem can be easily solved if one imagines the triangle to be turned in such a way that it now appears as indicated in Figure 23. The triangle now proves to be rectangular, both its base and altitude being equal to $s$; the area, therefore, is equal to $\frac{s^2}{2}$. In this case, too, the problem is solved by an actual transformation. The given Gestalt is placed in another position; by the same token the phenomenal values of the two sides change. It will not be denied that, in

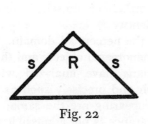

Fig. 22

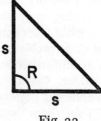

Fig. 23

geometrical problems, one quite often succeeds in discovering a solution in this intuitive manner.

At this point a question arises. Are these examples, taken from human activity, in every respect of the same kind as the performance of the chimpanzee? As for the first example (that of the attorney), one might not hesitate to answer in the affirmative. In general, when it is a matter of practical problems, the behavior of man is of the same psychological structure as that of animals, as far as the shaping principles are concerned. Thus, when in a new and surprising situation, a man uses a tool not designed for that purpose, the notion of Gestalt suffices for a satisfactory explanation. As long as we remain at the level of immediate data, of the phenomenal aspects (even if instantaneous) of objects, and of the immediately experienced transformations which the objects undergo, nothing seems to compel us to go beyond the theoretical principles laid down and elaborated by the Berlin School.

When we consider the geometrical example, however, the case is quite different. The Gestalt which results from the rotation of the triangle yields a solution to the problem posed with regard to the Gestalt first perceived. From the phenomenal and psychological point of view, these two Gestalten are completely different objects, although the one results from the other by means of a transformation which one has followed with one's own eyes. From the geometrical point of view, however, these two Gestalten are not different. The solution to the problem has geometrical significance. This fact must not be overlooked; it points to geometrical thought, or more precisely to the geometrical idea of the triangle. As a geometrical object, it is a matter of indifference how among the diverse manners the triangle can be drawn (in intuition, imagination, or thought). The different phenomenal objects have, therefore, a certain relation to the geometrical object which presents itself by and through the former. Consequently, there exists between them an identity which results from their relation to the geometrical object. This identity is not of the same kind as the immediate and sensory identity treated by Ternus, which he as well as Metzger, following suggestions of Wertheimer himself, have emphatically distinguished from categorial identity.[118]

An analogous problem arises in the perceptual domain. We have insisted on the difference between phenomenal objects and things,[119] a difference which Gestalt theoreticians have analyzed with great clarity. Phenomenal objects are such and precisely such as they are experienced; for them, being and appearing are the same; thus the distinction between reality and appearance is not admissible here. On the other hand, not only do real things permit such a distinction, but beyond that, it is essential to them that they can and must present themselves from different sides and under varying aspects, all the while remaining the same and maintaining their identity throughout modifications usually called subjective (a classification which, incidentally, is correct only in a well-defined sense). It is for this reason that the categories which apply to real things are not applicable, at least in the same sense, to phenomenal objects.

Real things become accessible to us only in and through our experiences and especially our perceptions. But in these experiences phenomenal objects appear to us. Objective things therefore present themselves in phenomenal objects, they are given to consciousness through the phenomenal domain and by means of its mediation; they are, indeed, even constituted in the phenomenal domain. A multiplicity of phenomenal objects, all differing from one another, become mutually related to each other by virtue of their common reference to the same real thing. Owing to these relations, an identity comes to be established between the different phenomenal objects, on account of

118. Ternus, "Experimentelle Untersuchungen über phänomenale Identität," loc. cit., p. 82; Metzger, "Beobachtungen über phänomenale Identität," Psychologische Forschung, loc. cit., p. 9.
119. See above, pp. 23, 30–31.

which an identical real thing appears in each of them. The theory of the Berlin School cannot give an account of this identity, which not only is not phenomenal and immediate but is compatible with a great diversity in phenomenal objects. Indeed, such an identity neither suppresses this diversity, nor is it suppressed by this diversity; instead, it asserts itself through that very diversity.

Problems of this kind inevitably emerge whenever it is not a mere question of practically mastering a situation of vital importance, but when the faculty of Θεωρεῖν (in the Aristotelian sense of the term), which is essential to man, comes into play. Psychology must not fail to take account of such problems; but it cannot do justice to them as long as it relies only on the concept of Gestalt.

Our reservations concerning the Berlin School do not constitute a criticism of a similar kind as that which the Gestalt theoreticians addressed to Benussi's theory or an analogous dualistic system. What is in question is only the delimiting of a certain level with respect to which the conceptions developed in the Berlin School are both legitimate and fruitful. In fact, as far as the level under discussion is concerned, one is indebted to the Gestalt theoreticians for a great number of very important results, and many more can be expected in the future. By delimiting the area under consideration, we indicate, by the same token, another area which is not purely phenomenal, and we point to problems for whose solutions Gestalt theory requires complementation. This need for complementation is the more urgent as Gestalt theory justly claims philosophical interest and significance.

The same idea can be seen from still another point of view. The remarkable performances of the chimpanzees, which are often reminiscent of the manner in which human workers go about doing things, lead to the question about the absence in these animals of even the least indication of *language,* of the verbal function, though they possess almost all the necessary organs of articulation and though their phonetic sounds contain a good number of the elements of human speech. This question is all the more pressing in that the intelligence of these animals comes close to a certain form of human intelligence. In these terms H. Delacroix poses the problem of language as well as of the intellectual functions in general.[120] In the course of their studies of the phenomena of aphasia, Gelb and Goldstein have laid down conceptions by means of which the problems to which we have alluded might be further clarified and which seem to us to have paramount importance for both general psychology and philosophy.

TRANSLATED BY RICHARD M. ZANER

120. H. Dealcroix, "Au seuil du langage," *Journal de Psychologie* (1933).

## 2 / The Place of Psychology
## in the System of Sciences [1]

As we know it today, modern psychology originated contemporaneously with the physical sciences and has been more or less connected with them throughout its development. To be sure, it has not known the continuity distinctive of the physical sciences. Nor has it known that series of progressive successes which constitute the prestige of physics and owing to which physics has been and still is called upon to make the major, if not the exclusive contribution to the formation of a scientific conception of the universe. The course taken by the development of psychology is much more sinuous. Its development was frequently interrupted as a result of the fact that psychological studies often took directions which, sooner or later, revealed themselves to be blind alleys. At any event, the beginnings of psychological studies worthy of being qualified as "scientific," in the modern sense of the term, go back to the 17th and 18th centuries. The thinkers who witnessed the birth of the mathematical and physical sciences, such as Descartes, Hobbes, Locke, Condillac, and Berkeley, were the originators of modern psychology. According to Ernst Cassirer, the first system of scientific psychology, in the sense of the term that has generally been accepted these last centuries, is that which is contained in Malebranche's *Recherche de la Vérité*.[2] In fact, the problems that Malebranche dealt with are largely the same that have preoccupied psychologists during the last century and that still concern us. In the same way certain of his ideas for the solution of these questions are close to some contemporary theories. Thus, with reference to the above mentioned detours, we can observe that con-

1. This article was originally published in *Revue de Synthèse*, vol. VIII (Paris, 1934).
2. E. Cassirer, *Das Erkenntnisproblem in der Philosophie und Wissenschaft der neueren Zeit* (Berlin, 1911), I, pp. 554-55.

temporary psychology is in a certain sense going back toward its beginnings. This remark should be kept in mind; we shall return to it in the course of this study, for the facts and the motives which were at the origin of a science affect the nature of that science and the goals which it aims at attaining.

The simultaneity of the birth of psychology and of physics is more than a simple fact of temporal coincidence. It means, above all, that psychology adopts the methods and the principles of the physical sciences and accepts its procedures. If physics is the more or less realized ideal of what a true science should be—the most perfect form and most adequate realization of scientific tendencies and intentions— then psychology will have to keep itself as close as possible to physics if it is to be raised to the rank of science in the strict sense of the word. And, in fact, modern psychology has, in the course of its history, more than once been conceived as a kind of "physics of the soul," both in its manner of stating its problems as well as in the theories constructed to answer them.

The contributions which could be made by such a psychology to the scientific knowledge of reality would, consequently, be very modest. In this respect, it is not in a position to rival the sciences of physics and chemistry. By studying the most general laws, which apply to the totality of reality, these sciences reveal its fundamental structure. Their field of investigation is unlimited; it is the whole universe. There is no domain of reality, however restricted, or any phenomena or events, however special, which fall outside the competence of these sciences. In comparison to the vast domain of these sciences and their universality, the realm of psychology is very restricted. This is not only because psychology deals with a limited and circumscribed part of that vast region which is the totality of the universe and in comparison to which it is almost nothing. Even if we extend psychology to include comparative psychology and so to cover the fields of primitive, infantile, pathological, and even animal behavior, the case is not altered. The main reason for the restricted nature of psychological studies, even when enlarged to their ultimate limits, is that they depend upon biological and, in particular, physiological research, in such a way that the universal laws of physics and chemistry intervene and support the work of the psychologist from the very outset. This is especially true for the psychology of sensation, for the theory of cerebral localization, for a large part of psychopathology, etc. Psychophysical parallelism, which is almost generally accepted in contemporary psychology, if only as a working hypothesis, teaches the strictest correspondence between psychological phenomena and physiological processes. Even if that doctrine is considered as nothing more than a working hypothesis, the very fact that it stipulates such a correspondence suggests the discovery of physiological constellations to which the experienced states of our consciousness are connected. The very fact that all phenomena and, consequently, any problem of psychology can be approached from a physiological point of view causes psychology to have an added dependence on research that is non-psychological and, in the final analysis, leads back to general physics and chemistry.

In conformity to this state of affairs none of the psychologists who attempted to elevate psychology to the rank of a science in the sense of a "physics of the soul" have claimed for psychology an equal footing with, not to speak of a primacy over, the sciences of physics and chemistry with respect to the formation of a scientific conception of reality. This conception is determined by the sciences which study the universal laws and the general structure of the world to which all special phenomena are reduced. It is their discoveries, such as the principle of the conservation of energy or that of entropy, for example, it is their development, sometimes of a revolutionary character (as in our day the quantum theory)—it is these which mould and modify the ideas we have of the universe. However interesting in themselves, of whatever importance within their special realm, all the discoveries of psychology add but little to the view of reality which we owe to the privileged sciences, nor do they enrich that view to any great extent. All that could be expected of psychology with respect to its contribution to the scientific conception of reality is, as it would seem, that it succeeded in establishing, within its own realm, laws analogous to those of physics or chemistry; or perhaps we could expect it to discover within its own realm some of these laws whose validity would be extended to the domain of consciousness, which, in many respects, is essentially different from nature. Such success would constitute for psychology the proof of its scientific character, for the realm of consciousness would be integrated into the whole of the universe: the same laws that govern nature would be shown to equally govern consciousness which would thereby truly appear as one of its domains. The scientific conquest of the world would be extended to one more region.

A number of studies and even several psychological systems were prompted by this ambition. When the laws of the *association of ideas* were established, the appearance and disappearance of ideas in consciousness was considered as analogous to attraction and repulsion among physical bodies. Hence, a law was sought which would explain this psychological process and which would account for the fact that a given idea evokes this idea rather than another. Such a law, explaining the presence of every idea in consciousness, would dispel as far as possible all apparent fortuitousness in the stream of thoughts. It would be the fundamental law of psychic life, determining and governing all occurrences in it. This law would be in the realm of psychology what the Newtonian law of gravitation is in physics. By comparing the latter with that of the association of ideas by contiguity, one remarks, indeed, a structural resemblance. The role which, in the former, is assigned to the distance separating bodies becomes, in the latter, the frequency with which any two given ideas appear together in the mind. Just as the force of attraction exercised by one body upon another depends only on the geometrical relation between them, the sequence of ideas—according to associationist psychology—is not determined by intrinsic relationships of a qualitative nature, i.e., by relationships founded upon the contents of the ideas; it is determined solely by their temporal proximity, by the mere fact of their frequent co-existence. Associationism is not only inspired by Newtonian physics; it applies and extends it to the realm of psychology.

The difference between the associationism of the 17th and 18th centuries and the theory of gravitation consists in the fact that, on the one hand, the existence of the given bodies which act upon one another does not depend upon these very effects, while, on the other hand, the presence of an idea gives birth to another which previously did not exist. This difference will vanish with the psychology of Herbart. He conceives of the unconscious as a kind of basement of the soul, the place of ideas which are not actually given but which were, and will be, so again; whereas consciousness is the place of actual ideas, i.e., of ideas which have managed to become actual. A threshold of consciousness separates as well as connects the two areas of the soul. This threshold must be passed in order for unconscious ideas to appear in the full light of consciousness. Those which cease to be conscious recede beneath this threshold without, however, ceasing to exist.[3] Ideas, or, as Herbart calls them, representations, are endowed with a certain force, intensity, or energy enabling them to pass the threshold against the resistance of opposing representations of lesser force or energy, the latter being, in turn, pushed back from consciousness into the unconscious. This energy is susceptible of gradations and, according to its degree of intensity, lifts ideas to a higher or lower point above the threshold, the zero point of consciousness.

These conceptions made it possible for Herbart to construct a real mechanics of the soul. If physics is the ideal that every science must imitate, and, to vary a remark of Kant's, if a science deserves that name only to the extent that physics can be found in it, then

3. The meaning given to the term "threshold of consciousness" by Herbart is utterly different from that of contemporary psychology, and especially of psychophysics since Fechner.

psychology was never again destined to reach that degree of perfection to which Herbart had raised it. This is not because his psychological studies made abundant use of mathematical formulae but because all the fundamental concepts of the physics of his time have a place in his psychological system. Here ideas attract and repel one another reciprocally. The association of ideas means for Herbart no longer the mere fact that one idea is followed by another. The first idea actually pulls the next idea from the unconscious in which it pre-existed and attracts it. Psychic life is explained mechanically by the laws of attraction and repulsion. The whole of this life consists in such elementary events. The reciprocal actions among ideas combine with one another in several ways and mutually support or cancel out each other. The whole of conscious life results from such combinations, interferences, and mutual interactions of elementary processes. This notion is reminiscent of the kinetic theory of gases.

Herbartian psychology, dominant for several decades in Germany and, still more, in Austria, was sharply criticized and attacked toward the end of the last century. Yet it has survived these criticisms under various forms. The problem of the so-called span of consciousness, for example, owes its origin to that psychological system, and so does the concept of "apperception" which is so important and fundamental in Wundt's psychology. Through Wundt Herbartian psychology found its way into psychoanalysis. The theory of the repression of desires and of other emotional tendencies whose gratification is forbidden by collective morality and which the "psychic censor"—the representative and executor of that morality—does not tolerate, even when they merely present themselves to consciousness, recalls Herbart's "mechanics of the soul." For these tendencies, when pushed outside of the realm of consciousness, fall into the unconscious where they continue to exist and from which they sometimes emerge manifesting themselves in dreams, in slips and similar kinds of faulty acts, and, after diverse transformations, in neurotic symptoms.

The distinction between what is manifest and what is only latent in the soul presupposes that the soul be conceived on the model of adjoining areas in which the various psychical elements—conceived on the model of atoms—are distributed so that they are able to move from one area to the other. For his theory of the transformation of latent tendencies Freud made use of another great principle borrowed from physics, namely, that of the conservation of energy. In psychoanalysis the libido is what energy is in physics. The forbidden desires reappear, not as such, but in disguise; they mask or change their objects and take on symbolic forms. The libido that animates them, or which they are, is capable of manifesting itself in various ways, but the same libido, or, more precisely, the same libidinal energy, lies behind and is even contained in all those forms. Besides this dissimulation, brought about by the censor acting in us, there are real transformations of the libido: the sublimations. Freudianism discovers the transformed libido at the basis and heart even of the highest human activities such as art, science, religion, etc. These activities are sustained by psychical energies which fundamentally are vital energies. They spring from the fact that, to a certain extent, man has the power to divert his libidinal energy from its original aims and to choose new goals for it. So far as he succeeds in this, he becomes capable of devoting himself to these activities considered as "higher" for the sole reason that they are approved by society. He then enjoys a special social recognition because he puts the gratification of his personal emotional tendencies at the service of society. A man suffering from neurosis is, on the other hand, constantly struggling with emotional tendencies which he has repressed and whose true nature he fails to recognize. In seeking to gratify them he collides with the demands of reality, and especially with those of social life. He dissipates all his forces in conflicts and struggles of this kind.

If Freud was able to interpret both normal and pathological psychical phenomena in his own special way and to understand them from a unifying point of view, it is not because of the very general and, hence, imprecise manner in which he deliberately defined the notion of libido but, instead, because of his conception of libido as a form of energy. For Freud, man resembles a closed physical system endowed with a certain quantity of energy. This energy can be distributed in diverse ways, it can take on various forms, it can change the modes of its manifestation, but it can neither be diminished nor augmented. Because of this conception Freud attempts to discover the same driving force in all human attitudes and activities, however diverse they may appear at first sight, and to reduce them to the most elementary and original forms of the libido: those that it assumes at the beginning and in the early phases of life.

Some concepts of physics, especially of contemporary physics, can be found in *Gestalt psychology*. From the very beginning, W. Köhler has made use of analogies from physics in order to show that his central thesis was rather akin to certain conceptions current in physics.[4] He attempted to introduce these conceptions into psychology,

---

4. W. Köhler, *Die physischen Gestalten in Ruhe und in stationärem Zustand* (Berlin, 1920).

with the result that Gestalt theory appears as truly applying physical conceptions to psychology. The main conception which Köhler and other theoreticians of Gestalt psychology have introduced from physics is that of the *field* and of dynamic processes of a global structure. According to Gestalt theory, the psychical life as well as human and animal behavior cannot be accounted for in terms of isolated processes taking place independently of each other in such a manner that the "wholes" resulting from fortuitous combinations would be merely sums of elementary facts. In contradistinction to the Herbartian conception, what we experience are always states whose structure and articulation are intrinsically global, and such states—both static and dynamic—constitute our whole life. These global states or "Gestalten" which we experience contain, to be sure, components and constituents. The latter, however, are not, according to Gestalt theory, primary elements which by their combination would yield the whole. Nor would it be exact to say that Gestalt theory maintains the priority of the whole with regard to the parts or constituents. This thesis, so often wrongly attributed to Gestalt theory, belongs, in truth, to other schools of psychology dealing with wholes, such as that of Driesch. Gestalt theory does not recognize "parts" at all in the traditional sense of elements which, whether they are combined with one another or are taken in isolation, retain their identity. One should rather speak of *moments* of the whole. Such moments are entirely determined by the total structure of the whole of which they are moments; they are what they are only at the place they occupy within this structure, a place assigned to them by its specific nature. At this place they perform the function necessary for the articulation of the whole; they have their existence only in their function with regard to the whole. Such moments cannot be considered posterior to the whole to which they belong.

The state of affairs just described is akin to the case of an electrically charged body: the global distribution of electricity depending upon the stereometric form of the body determines all local distributions, the latter being comprehensible only with regard to the former. An entire electrostatic field is formed whose details cannot be accounted for unless it be by reference to the global structure of the field to which they belong. We are never, according to Gestalt theory, in the presence of multiplicities of isolated sensations, volitions, impulses to act; we are always placed in a field of perception, of action, etc. These fields have their proper articulation: they have a center with regard to which they are organized, they have privileged or "vectorial" directions tending towards the center, and they even have slopes.[5] If an animal is placed in front of food, the animal is placed in a field of action whose center is the food and whose vectorial directions are constituted by the most direct accesses to the food. The animal follows these directions when rushing to the food.

If one approaches an electrically charged body with a metal stick, not only will the local repartition of electricity be influenced, but the entire field will be disturbed and another field of a new structure and a new electrical distribution will be established. Something similar is observed in the case of apparently only partial modifications of psychological fields, modifications "objective" as well as "subjective"— the latter being caused, for instance, by a new direction given to attention. The effect of such modifications does not consist in something being added to, or subtracted from, a circumscribed portion of the field. On the contrary, the field is disturbed in its entirety, and more often than not it will be superseded by another field of a different articulation. This can be observed in the behavior of animals whose direct access to the food is blocked. There comes a moment when they "understand" the situation: they discover a round-about way that will lead them to their goal.[6] This discovery which, according to Köhler, is a sign of intelligence, marks the transition from one field of action— where the animal failed—to another which has the same nucleus but whose "vectorial" directions are altogether different. Things are still more complex when the situation requires the interposition of intermediary goals in such a way that the resulting field becomes more articulated and more differentiated than the preceding one. These transitions, incidentally, are discontinuous. One may, to be sure, contrive intermediary fields which would gradually lead from the initial to the final field, as though any and every constellation of "elements" could become a psychological field. As a matter of fact, certain constellations distinguished by their particular structure are privileged in alone being realized. What lies between the initial and the final fields are states which are transitory, turbulent, confused, and chaotic, in contradistinction to the special clarity, firmness, and stability of the final field. We see the extent to which these conceptions of Gestalt theory were inspired by ideas concerning the emission of energy familiar in quantum physics.

Thus far we have followed a series of ideas which on account of our intellectual and scientific tradition appear to be particularly

5. The fact that Köhler adopts such notions in psychology is very significant. It shows how serious he was in introducing into psychology ways of thinking current in physics.

6. See the examples mentioned by W. Köhler, *The Mentality of Apes.*

suggestive. Yet the results are rather meager: psychology does not seem to deepen or to enrich our scientific knowledge of reality to a considerable extent. At the most, we can observe how some of the great ideas of physics are reflected in contemporary psychological systems, how attempts have been made at introducing these ideas into the domain of psychology. Fortunately for psychology, this direction, which has thus far been followed exclusively, is not the only possible or even the most important one.

To evaluate the role of psychology among the other sciences and to determine its place within their system, one must, in our opinion, adopt the historical point of view. The ultimate meaning of a science (especially of a science like psychology where nearly everything— principles, methods, primordial data, and, in a way, even the subject matter—is subjected to debate) can be disengaged only by taking into account the motives and ideas that were at its source, the problems and theoretical needs that gave rise to its birth. The historical, or genetic, orientation must be followed consistently. As a consequence, it is not sufficient to note the simultaneity of the origin of modern psychology with that of the physical sciences. The meaning of this simultaneity must be clarified by asking how and why the existence of the physical sciences entailed the creation of modern psychology. The limitations of this article only permit us to hint at this historical relation. We shall limit ourselves to the indication of those problems that emerge rather than proposing solutions for them, since it is a matter of *direction* of work and thought which contemporary psychology has only begun to follow.

It has often been pointed out that the decisive difference between psychology and the sciences of physics and chemistry consists in that it is precisely the very "subjective" data and qualities discarded by these sciences which constitute the subject matter of psychology. Among these data are to be included not merely the so-called secondary qualities and the "subjective" impressions *par excellence* such as pleasure and pain, or emotional states such as joy, suffering, and other passions; of equal, if not still greater, importance is the very fact that the ambient world in which we live carries the imprint of humanity: it is a human world. We are surrounded with familiar objects which offer themselves as serving these or those purposes and as having to be manipulated in this or that way. Furthermore, there are objects of value, of various types of value: aesthetic value, religious value, etc. Our surrounding world is characterized by the presence of objects which are not the neutral objects from which objective science takes its departure but which have significance and relevancy. Psychology cannot overlook these purely "subjective" data, cannot ignore the fact that the objects which surround us exhibit qualities of this kind. Even if an objective psychology were possible, those facts would not disappear, and with them all the problems concerning them would recur.[7] The difference between psychology and the physical sciences manifested itself also in our previous discussions concerning the transfer of conceptions of physics into the domain of psychology. To be sure, there is a striking analogy between the psychological field and the field in the sense of physics. But this analogy is more of a formal nature than it is concerned with respective contents. Such things as a desired goal that one tends to reach is nowhere to be found in the domain of physics. Generally speaking, all entities and all features that figure in psychological fields are absolutely alien to those dealt with in physics. The fact that the same way of looking at things is practiced in different domains is very significant from a certain point of view. Nevertheless, the psychological field is not reduced to the field of physics, nor are both reduced to something more general, as, for example, in the theory of electric waves the phenomena of light and those of electricity appear as facts of the same order.

This dualism is a consequence of the peculiar nature of modern physics. As opposed to Aristotelian and medieval physics, modern physics starts by breaking with the ambient world as it is known to the common man, and each of us is, in his daily life, such a common man. Reality is not as it presents itself but as it is constructed by science, that is to say, by the scientific endeavors of the human mind. This construction is obtained only by mathematical analysis as opposed to ordinary perception.[8] The "elementary realities," writes Brunschvicg, "are not given to us immediately; nor are they susceptible of being so, for they are not at the human scale." [9] But our ambient world as we know it in our everyday experience is not modified by the scientific interpretation of reality; it never ceases to surround us with all the sensible appearances and with all the "subjective" qualities that it exhibits. It is this fact that, historically as well as systematically speaking, gives rise to psychology.

In this world of everyday experience we can see a sort of natural illusion, an error into which our human constitution forces us and from which science emancipates us without, however, making the illusion disappear altogether. This is the position taken by Malebranche. The truly psychological parts of his *Recherche de la Vérité*

7. Rather than discuss behaviorism here, we refer the reader to the critique in W. Köhler, *Gestalt Psychology* (London, 1930).

8. L. Brunschvicg, *De la connaissance de soi* (Paris, 1931), p. 144.

9. *Ibid.*, p. 64.

have no other aim than to show the errors to which we are exposed and to explain their origin in a manner which one may already consider as naturalistic. The first psychological system, in the modern sense of the term, thus presents itself under the form of a science of errors, and its final goal is to enable us to avoid them. Hence, psychology serves the scientific conquest of the universe only in an indirect way. This fact is not without importance for psychology's later development and often manifested itself in the course of its history, as when, for example, studies concerning acuity of vision were undertaken by psychologists for the sake of the need of astronomers to make their observations as exact as possible.

The frame of reference with respect to which Malebranche raised his problems is still relevant to us. However, the problems themselves must be stated in a different and even inverse way.

The true structure of reality may be as science reveals it. However, not only must scientific theories be verified in terms of "subjective" phenomena and our experiences of them, but, what is more, it is only by starting from the ambient world in which we never cease to exist that the scientific conquest of reality can be undertaken. This conquest, realized by constructions of the mind, is a creation of the mind. It is not a creation made once and forever at a certain moment in time. Instead, it is accomplished in the course of a continuous progress throughout history. Psychology, as a science of the mind, finds itself confronted with the problem of how the human mind, whose most familiar and elementary data are those related to the ambient world, can arrive at a scientific representation of reality by starting from such a basis. The question does not concern particular conceptions at a certain stage of historical development; instead, it concerns the general way of looking at things which is at the basis of physical science. There are methods and procedures which are alien to the natural naïveté of man but indispensable to scientific constructions. To mention only one problem: abstracting from the qualities of instrumentality, of value, and also from the secondary qualities, seeing in every object only a special case of a physical body in general to which the laws of physics apply, requires a mental operation in whose nature, conditions, presuppositions, and origin psychology cannot help being interested. The same holds for the notions used in the physical and chemical sciences, which differ greatly in their logical structure and nature from the notions current in everyday experience with which traditional logic had alone concerned itself. Owing to the fact that man is capable of creating a science, there accrues to psychology the task of description and analysis of the psychological processes resulting in this creation.

Nor is this all. Comparative psychology teaches us that the ambient world, as we adults know it, is in turn itself the product of an evolution, and even of a revolution. Without mentioning primitive and animal mentalities, the study of the child's mentality also puts us in the presence of a world whose nature is altogether different from ours. The works of Stern, Piaget, and others reveal that the objects belonging to the infantile world are characterized either by their functions and uses or by some particularly striking features and that, consequently, there exist for the child differences and identities totally different from those we admit.[10] On the other hand, the things pertaining to the world of the child are devoid of the substantial identity which for us adults is one of the most essential characteristics of an object and, incidentally, is an indispensable condition of scientific knowledge.[11] The transition from the infantile world to the world of the adult does not take place gradually but marks one of the great intellectual revolutions in human life. Today, one attributes to language, more precisely, to "representative language," a major role in the revolutionary process.[12] However, the fact that at a certain phase infantile language becomes "representative language," while it was not so before, is itself a symptom of the transition from the infantile to the "objective" representation of the world. Of course, as this language is gradually acquired, it facilitates the formation of the "objective" representation and contributes toward its consolidation. With the problem of the origin of the "objective" representation of the world, all the old questions, so often debated, as to the origin of the concepts of space, time, etc., recur. These questions will have to be reformulated in terms of comparative and evolutionary psychology. Thus, with respect to the ambient world of the adult, psychology finds itself confronted with a task analogous to that which it faced with regard to the universe constructed by science. Neither one nor the other is given ready made; both derive from mental operations, active or passive; and to psychology falls the task of explaining the products of the mind by describing and analyzing the processes that result in them.

We are witnessing a reversal of problems. Man no longer is, as he was in Antiquity and in the Middle Ages, at the zenith or, at least, at a privileged level of reality. Nor does he insert himself in the totality of

10. W. Stern, *Psychologie der frühen Kindheit* (Leipzig, 1923); J. Piaget, *Le langage et la pensée chez l'enfant* (Neuchâtel and Paris, 1923); *La représentation du monde chez l'enfant* (Paris, 1926).
11. See K. Bühler, *Die geistige Entwicklung des Kindes* (Jena, 1931).
12. See K. Goldstein, "L'analyse de l'aphasie et l'étude de l'essence du langage," *Journal de Psychologie Normale et Pathologique* (1933); E. Cassirer, "Le langage et la construction du monde," *Journal de Psychologie Normale et Pathologique* (1933), pp. 25–26.

the objective universe. It is no accidental fact at all that the rise of the modern science of nature was accompanied by the discovery of the *cogito*, that is to say, of consciousness. As a conscious being, man belongs to a special realm: the realm of "subjectivity," altogether separated from the objective world, the universe of "extension," the totality of physical things. This "subjective" realm of consciousness, inaccessible, as Malebranche had already seen,[13] to explanatory methods of physics and of almost no significance in comparison with the universe of "extension," is nevertheless privileged in a most important respect. Consciousness is the general medium of constitution. Every objective universe, the ambient world of our everyday life as well as the scientific representation of the world, arises through acts of consciousness. Nothing can exist nor have validity for us unless we experience it (experience being understood in the widest possible sense of the term). The claim to objectivity and validity contains a reference to the realm of consciousness, to certain processes of constitution. By virtue of that conception of consciousness, which is faithful to Descartes' intentions,[14] its place can be assigned to psychology within the system of the sciences. It is not one science among the others; instead, it is their foundation. Its main task is not to enrich our knowledge of reality as the physical and chemical sciences do but to account for the very knowledge of reality. In this manner psychology approaches philosophy, which is to say that by a sufficient radicalization of the problems of psychology we reach the philosophical dimension.

TRANSLATED BY DANIEL J. HERMAN

13. N. Malebranche, *Recherche de la Vérité*, Book III, chap. VII, sec. 4.
14. See especially *Méditations* II.

# 3 / Goldstein's Conception
## of Biological Science [1]

To the memory of Adhémar Gelb

THE LIVING ORGANISM has very often been conceived as composed of a certain number of elementary mechanisms that are more or less independent of one another. Each of the mechanisms has its mode of operation or its specific function. The organism's life is explained by the cooperation among these elementary mechanisms; its actions and reactions result from the partial effects which mutually reinforce, inhibit, and modify one another. A knowledge of these is therefore necessary for the study of the organism. But only if it is exposed to an isolated stimulation can the operation of one of these mechanisms be established. It is therefore necessary to examine it under conditions which, as far as possible, permit one to exclude every influence deriving from another elementary mechanism. The elementary or primitive vital phenomenon is in these terms, then, seen to be the response to a localized stimulation affecting one receptive organ—that is to say, the reflex. The goal of the biological sciences is supposedly to construct the organism's life starting from reflexes; it is to compose that life by means of the latter.

Goldstein brings out the difficulties of such a conception. Because of the increasing complexity of the phenomena in question, it becomes necessary to resort to higher-level regulatory centers whose task would be to coordinate the multiple reflexes and to guarantee the cooperation of the isolated elementary mechanisms. One is thus led to superimpose hypotheses which are at times mutually incompatible (because one or another of them have been constructed *ad hoc*) in order to explain phenomena which cannot, it would seem, be accounted for in any other fashion. As biological theory thus becomes increasingly compli-

1. This article—originally published in *Revue Philosophique de la France et de l'Etranger*, CXXIX (Paris, 1940)—is chiefly concerned with K. Goldstein, *Der Aufbau des Organismus* (The Hague, 1934).

cated, by the same token it loses its unity. Finally, because of the necessity to resort to factors that arise at progressively higher levels and centers, biology so conceived becomes involved in an infinite regress. In any event, it is not by following such a course that one can succeed in explaining organismic facts by means of a single principle.

The author abandons the traditional direction of biological research: proceeding from the "lower" to "higher," the biologist begins with so-called simple facts and moves from these to facts which are considered complex. The notions of "simplicity" and "complexity," indeed, are among the most problematic notions in biology. The "simplicity" of some particular datum must not be defined in terms of the relationship it has to the observer but should be framed in terms of the relationship it has to the organism in question; because of this circumstance a knowledge of this organism is necessary. The point of departure for biological research, therefore, cannot be the disconcerting multiplicity of observed particular data concerning an organism; rather, it ought to be the organism itself.

The latter, according to Goldstein, is a centralized whole. Although the total organism is articulated in members, in organs and systems of organs, it is nevertheless not composed of their juxtaposition. The total organism is neither a "sum" formed from parts, nor does it stand opposed to those parts in the sense of being at a higher level than they. There can be no question, furthermore, of an antagonism or polarity between the tendency to unity and the multiple tendencies which would belong specifically to the parts of the organism. Any theory which, with the notion of "entelechy" or that of an analogously higher-level entity, would establish a distinction, even a sort of tension, between the organism itself and its organs, is rejected by Goldstein. In reality, the organism is nothing other than the articulated and centralized total system of its parts. It follows from this that it is not at all possible to conceive the life of the organism as the result of the actions of its parts, nor is it possible to admit an interdependence and an interaction among the particular organs. This problem concerning the reciprocity of actions arises when we consider an isolated datum and when we study it in itself as an absolute, rather than viewing it in its relationship with the total organism. *Every vital manifestation must be related to the organism in its totality; it must be viewed as an expression of this organism, of its concretely actual state, of general tendencies which govern it.* The entire organism is engaged in every action and reaction even when these are effectuated only by means of some organs or by a single one. In the latter case, to speak only of the nervous system, the innervation of the organ in question plays a special role and occupies the foreground. Now, this *foreground process* is accompanied by other nervous excitations which constitute the background relative to it. Foreground and background demand and reciprocally support each other: a certain formation of the background is necessary to the foreground. In consequence of this, no datum, however localized it may appear, is alien or neutral with respect to what goes on at any other place in the organism. If a new stimulation is applied to an organism while it is performing some action, that action is stopped or modified. This occurs, not because of a reciprocal interaction of parts, but because of the alteration of the conditions in which the organism performs the action. To understand a reaction as regards its relation to the organism, to determine the bearing and signification of this reaction for the organism, it is indispensable to take into account these conditions and especially the initial conditions in which the organism is found when a task is imposed on it.

Of these conditions, one of the most essential is the *degree of centralization*. In fact, a number of phenomena (pathological, experimental, as well as those concerning infants) can be explained by means of the relaxation of centralization—whether the latter be weakened by sickness, by an operation which the animal has undergone, by any kind of experimental arrangement; or whether, as in the case of infants, the normal degree of centralization of the organism has not yet been obtained because of incomplete maturation. For this reason there is a resemblance between certain modes of behavior found specifically in infants and certain phenomena observed in adult patients. This resemblance in no way permits us to infer, as is done in psychoanalysis, a survival of infant attitudes in the unconscious. It is explained instead by the fact that similar effects are produced by the same cause: namely, the relaxation of centralization.

Goldstein's conception throws a new light on the phenomenon of the reflex. Rather than a primitive and fundamental fact which would be the constitutive element of life, the reflex appears as a fact which is produced and can exist only in special laboratory conditions, the experimental arrangement permitting one to bring about a certain isolation in the organism. The author goes so far as to maintain that these experimental arrangements create the reflex. So far as it is produced in the artificial conditions present in the laboratory, the reflex must not be considered as a "natural" action of the organism and cannot, accordingly, serve as the point of departure for a general biological conception. Discussions concerning the reflex have too often failed to take into account the rather profound modification which the experimental arrangement introduces into the organism.[2] The organism responds to a task with which it is confronted in manners and in ways which may, and do, vary from one organism to another; however, for a given organism, the response has a remarkable constancy. For every organism, there are attitudes, postures, and so on, which are privileged and which the organism seeks to adopt. The distinction of this *privileged behavior* is subjectively expressed by the feeling of convenience and ease which the subject experiences when he adopts it, and it is expressed objectively by the precision and accuracy of the actions, the lower level of the thresholds, and so on. When the organism has been agitated or excited by a stimulation, what permits it to re-establish its equilibrium is this tendency to adopt privileged behavior. This tendency secures the order inherent in the processes of the organism and determines their direction. Finally, this tendency guarantees the constancy of the reactions of the organism to the same external situations and, by means of this, the constancy of the very milieu in which the organism lives, the milieu which it itself creates by means of its activities.

We must here restrict ourselves as regards Goldstein's biological conception to some rather summary indications and neither trace its theoretical development nor give a résumé of its documentation.[3] We propose instead to explicate some of the philosophical and methodological principles of his work. Notwithstanding the abundance of documentation and theoretical explanation, we must consider his work according to his own intention: as a methodology and philosophy of biological science.

To consider particular facts in their relation to the organism as a whole and to view them from the perspective of the latter, it is necessary to gain some idea of what the organism as a whole is. This can be done only on the basis of the observation of particular facts pertaining to the organism, and these can be established only by adopting the analytical and experimental method. For a positive biological theory there is no other means of access. Now, the biological importance of these particular facts can be appreciated only relative to the organism. But that one must begin in biological theory with a consideration of the organism seems to lead immediately into a vicious circle. In point of fact, however, this vicious circle only points to the impossibility of moving directly from particular facts to the organism. To be sure, the conception of the organism requires that one begin from particular facts, and it is necessary as well to remain in close

2. As regards the reflex, see below, pp. 79–80.
3. We have given a more detailed exposition of this in "Le fonctionnement de l'organisme d'après K. Goldstein," *Journal de Psychologie Normale et Pathologique,* XXXVI (1939), pp. 107–38.

contact with these facts. Nevertheless, the elaboration of the notion of organism cannot be accomplished by means of a simple pulling together of simple facts; this elaboration requires a cognitive function which differs from those cognitive activities bearing only on observed facts. In other words, the idea of the organism (which, in order to understand all particular facts relative to that organism, is conceived on the basis of them) pertains to a level different from that of the particular facts themselves.

This passage from the level of facts to a different one, a movement which is truly a μετάβασις εἰς ἄλλο γένος, is not found exclusively in biology. The physical sciences are also well acquainted with the difference between a pure empiricism and theoretical construction. In these sciences, also, theoretical construction is not at all obtained by means of a simple accumulation, comparison, and classification of facts. Here as well, there is a leap from the observation of facts (which is at the basis of all theory) to the conception of ideal symbolic entities. In this connection Goldstein refers to the methodological reflections of Heinrich Hertz concerning the nature of those entities which figure in the theoretical constructions of physics and especially concerning the symbolic character of these entities. Such symbolic entities have neither a resemblance nor a conformity with the given things they symbolize, with the exception of the following relation: the conclusion which we draw by means of certain operations from the initial symbols must, in turn, symbolize the facts resulting from those with which we started. It is true that biological symbols differ from those of the physical sciences insofar as they are less abstract or, more exactly, less formalized than the latter. The symbols employed in biology remain closer to the observed phenomena, and this circumstance differentiates them from the symbolic entities conceived by physicists. The symbols utilized by the latter, in the extreme case, can be signs defined solely by the formal characteristics of the operations performed on them.

The reason for this difference is that the physicist substitutes mathematical symbols for all perceptual facts, whereas the biologist leaves intact the observed facts which underlie his theory. He considers these facts as real manifestations of the organism, although their relation to that organism and the evidence which they provide as regards it constitute a problem to be solved for each particular case; and, beyond that, such a relationship constitutes a general methodological problem to which we shall return at a later point.

It is therefore necessary that biological symbols have a qualitative and concrete content. The individuality of the organism must be taken into account in any notion developed of it. This notion is therefore an idea or a Gestalt in the sense in which Goethe uses this term, and the act of "creative imagination" by means of which it is conceived can be characterized as an intuition (also in the sense in which Goethe uses it) based on positive facts. Notions thus oriented toward the individuality of the organism do not involve anything that can rightly be suspected as mystical or metaphysical.

To be sure, the ideas which the biologist creates, however conformed and adapted they may be to the observed facts on the basis of which they are conceived, remain ideal symbols. That the idea belongs to a different level than the facts is constantly emphasized by Goldstein. The totality which is the organism must not be passed off as a reality of the same nature as those realities which are the members of the organism, the organs and systems of organs—the totality is not a reality which would be added to, or superimposed upon, the latter. In such an interpretation, the organism would be conceived as a higher-level entelechy opposed to lower-level entelechies, and one would be forced to admit a polarity between the whole and its parts—a conception which the author rejects, as we have already said.[4] We are *not seeking a metaphysical entity designed to found being*, but we are *looking for an idea, an intelligible principle which would make the observed phenomena comprehensible*, an idea which permits us to explain these phenomena in detail, if one takes account of the conditions in which they originate.

Among such conditions it is necessary to include those which the experimenter imposes by means of the arrangement of his experiment. In these terms, the observed facts are considered as the modes in which the idea appears and manifests itself under certain conditions. These facts follow by necessity from the idea, because they appear as its variations under the conditions in question. The idea of the organism is determined and defined in the course of the investigation. Beginning from, and based upon, particular facts obtained by means of the analytical and experimental method, an idea of the total organism capable of making these data understandable emerges. This idea stimulates further investigations, because certain consequences which result from it can in turn be confronted with new facts. The discovery of such data is thus often suggested by the theoretical idea which one is examining. If these data do not confirm the idea, one corrects or relinquishes it and seeks to conceive, on a broader basis, another idea of the organism—an idea which in its turn will be tested in new observations, and so on. In this manner, by means of a

4. See above, p. 70.

*dialectical progress of experience,* one reaches an increasingly adequate knowledge of the organism.

This knowledge, however, is never definitive or complete; on the contrary, it remains approximative. But this does not signify that the validity and certainty of a biological theory depend only upon the number of facts which it explains. To be sure, the amount of data which a theory makes intelligible is not without importance as regards its verification; but the number alone is not in itself decisive, since the particular facts which one observes have qualitatively different values. And the task of biological science is not only to explain the observed facts but also to do justice to their qualitative value. Each datum must be related to the organism as a whole, and its place and role in this whole must be ascertained; that is to say, the importance and significance of each datum as regards the nature and life of the organism in question must be made explicit. Therefore, however numerous may be the facts which support a biological theory, a single new fact is capable of making that theory collapse. Given the conditions in which it occurs, if this new fact is disclosed as sufficiently important for the nature of a living being, it requires a different idea of the organism, such that the facts established prior to this discovery now appear in a new light.

In these terms, it is experience and not the theoretical conception which determines the progress of biological investigation. In fact, if each particular datum is considered in the light of the idea of the organism, every new discovery obliges us to revise this idea and at times to reconceive our theory from top to bottom, since one cannot stop until this new datum has been given its place in the structure of the organism as a whole. If, to the contrary, one began from particular and isolated facts established by means of the analytical method— such as reflexes, so-called inhibitions, and the like—biological research would be guided by certain theoretical notions which could not but be preconceived: precisely those notions which govern the selection, and especially the interpretation, of the facts which one is studying. Confronted with a new datum, one seeks above all to conserve these theoretical notions: they are modified, additional elements are introduced, new hypotheses superimposed upon those notions, a plurality of explanatory principles are admitted, and so on. Considering these theoretical notions as fundamental and as definitively established, one may even go so far as to bypass or to ignore data which do not conform to these notions, instead of challenging and, eventually, abandoning them.

Goldstein's conception is very far from philosophical *empiricism*.

Yet it is much closer to *empireia* than views of empiricistic inspiration. For at the basis of empiricist principles are certain theoretical ideas concerning the manner in which things must take place. Because they are not subjected to discussion, these ideas acquire a more or less dogmatic character; thus they prevent an impartial study of facts, and their predominance stands in the way of progress in research. The investigator who approaches the facts with these theoretical notions and who seeks to conceive the life of the organism in their terms risks being unknowingly misled into a metaphysics hidden under apparently scientific formulae.

Goldstein's *empirical,* but *not empiricist,* orientation requires the application of some methodological principles to the studies of the human beings as well as of animals, to studies of normal as well as abnormal persons. If one observes a plurality of symptoms in a patient, one must never assign a predominant importance to one symptom at the expense of the others. Because one of the symptoms, for accidental reasons, strikes the observer or because he approaches them with preconceived theoretical ideas, he is led to consider one symptom as *the* central and fundamental one of which the others are derivatives. The correct method consists, instead, in describing as completely as possible the totality of observed symptoms and treating them all on the same level. All the symptoms must be referred to the organism (which has been changed in a certain way because of the sickness) and must be considered as expressions of this alteration in activities of the most diverse kinds. It is only when one has arrived at an idea of the modifications suffered by the organism (that is to say, at the end of analysis) that it is possible to decide whether one of the symptoms has a particular importance—and this not from the point of view of the observer but from the point of view of the organism itself. The principal aim of the analysis of a patient is to disclose the manner in which he performs an action, to discover the way by which he reaches a resolution to a problem which has been posed to him.

It is, accordingly, not sufficient to abide only by the objectively final result, that is to say, to limit oneself to ascertaining whether the patient has been successful or has failed as regards a requested task. Although patients often reach a positive solution to the problem, they approach it in a way which differs from that of normal subjects—a way which the observer, without deeper analysis, would at first be tempted to believe the only possible one. However, when the patient is forced to adopt the procedure of the normal subject, he ends in failure. The analysis of the path followed by the patient, of the detours and expedients to which he has recourse, of the situations in which he is successful and in which he fails, of the reasons which prevent him from acting in the same way as the normal subject, and finally of the incorrect solution which he sometimes produces instead of the required solution—all such considerations, that is to say, are indispensable for a full understanding of the disorders which the patient suffers and of the modifications he has undergone as a consequence of his injury or illness.

It is sufficient to cite the works of Goldstein and his collaborator, A. Gelb, concerning the disturbances of language, works which made the fruitfulness of these methodological principles for concrete investigations quite evident.[5]

Goldstein does not admit *negative explanations:* that is to say, explanations in terms of which one fact is reduced to the weakening, inhibition, suppression, and the like of another fact. For example, Babinski's phenomenon is considered as an important reflex as regards animals. Since it has no importance for man, it is assumed to be inhibited. In certain lesions this inhibition is weakened or suppressed, and, accordingly, the reflex reappears. Goldstein rejects this explanation. Instead, he refers Babinski's phenomenon to the very general relation between the cortical region and movements of flexing —movements which, according to Goldstein, are at a higher level than the movements of extension. This superiority appears in a number of very different facts. In the case of lesions, entailing a general dedifferentiation, the movements of extension (because they are more primitive) acquire a certain preponderance. Accordingly, Babinski's phenomenon appears, of which Goldstein, by the same token, explains several variations which thus far had not been understood. In this explanation the phenomenon in question loses its singularity: it is revealed as a particular case of a very general law, as the special form under which, in certain internal conditions of the organism and within a given concrete situation, a very general relation finds its expression and manifestation.

Obviously Goldstein's explanation offers the advantage of higher rationalization. This advantage consists in making it unnecessary to have recourse to specific reflexes of any kind, of having to consider the importance of these reflexes, and having to construct hypotheses concerning inhibition and lack of inhibition as to these reflexes. If one begins his explanation on the basis of the latter notions, every phenomenon, as for example Babinski's, appears, properly speaking, as a unique fact which as such calls for a special explanation. Once

5. Cf. the presentations which Gelb and Goldstein have given of their conception of aphasic disorders, in the *Journal de Psychologie Normale et Pathologique* (1933).

specific reflexes and interactions among them are admitted, one is obliged to resort to regulatory and coordinating centers, the definition of which necessarily remains empty. In fact, all that one can say concerning these superimposed mechanisms is that they fulfill the functions for which they were designed. Furthermore, suppose two opposed processes to take place simultaneously in the organism; it is impossible to decide which of them must be considered as inhibited and which as inhibiting, which as normal and which as modifying the former, unless one allows oneself to be guided by a preconceived theoretical idea.

For these reasons Goldstein proposes to eliminate altogether the notions of inhibition and non-inhibition and to explain observed phenomena by referring them to the concrete situation in which a certain organism finds itself. When two stimuli which, if applied separately, would set in motion two opposed processes, are simultaneously applied to a patient afflicted with certain cerebral disorders, one never observes an effect in the sense of a resultant of forces. Either one of the two stimuli dominates, or else two opposed phases alternate with one another and the phase which is most conspicuous and which has the longest duration corresponds to the stronger stimulus. In a biological explanation, one must therefore never refer to processes which would have to take place so as thereby to conclude that they are inhibited from the fact that in reality they do not take place. On the contrary, one must strictly abide by the facts actually observed. If one cannot explain a particular phenomenon in this manner, it is better to provisionally renounce the interpretation than to construct one in a more or less *ad hoc* manner.

Especially as regards man, perfect centralization is not the normal case, if one means by this the most frequent one. It is to the contrary an exceptional occurrence, the gift, if one may so express it, of particularly happy moments. One ordinarily witnesses a certain alternation of opposing phases in almost all acts—even in those involving arbitrary innervation, which are the most centralized of motor facts. Quite often this alternation is not directly observed but must be disclosed by special methods. In infants, in patients, and in animals having undergone an operation, the phenomenon of alternation is pronounced: one can also bring it about in the normal adult by means of certain experimental arrangements. In all these cases, the alternation expresses a relaxation of centralization, and it is an immediate consequence of this relaxation. This relationship becomes evident from the general ideas which Goldstein advocates as to the functioning of the nervous system, especially the functioning of an isolated part of this system. One can thus conclude that if the alternation occurs in all acts, even in those performed with the greatest concentration, this is the result of the circumstance that centralization is always more or less imperfect in man. Thus, the fact that alternation to some extent characterizes all normal acts in human life testifies to the imperfection of this being—who, because he is the most complicated of living beings, attains a perfect degree of centralization only very rarely and then only with great difficulty.

Goldstein starts not from the most frequent but from the ideal case (that of perfect centralization), precisely because, according to him, the "less" perfect can be understood only in terms of the "more" perfect but never inversely. The same is true as regards the relation between parts and whole. It is only when one considers the organism as a whole that it is possible to understand the facts which occur in its particular organs, even those which take place under conditions of isolation. But there is no way at all to reconstruct the life of the organism beginning from those facts—beginning from reflexes, for instance. Defined by the constancy of the relation between stimulation and reaction, the *reflex* occurs when an organ is stimulated isolatedly in such a way that the rest of the organism is not permitted to partake in the reaction: that is to say, when placed in constant conditions. If these conditions were not constant or if the organ to which a stimulus is applied were not isolated as far as possible from the rest of the organism, the response given to the stimulation of the particular organ would be altered as a result of the relation of each organ to the whole of the organism.

Phenomena analogous to reflexes are also observed outside of artificial experimental circumstances, when, for example, an organ is abruptly and suddenly stimulated or when the intensity of the stimulation surpasses the capacities of the organism. There is an isolation in these cases as well, because the stimulation is released in the organism before it has time to adapt itself to the new and unforeseen situation. The reflex is therefore not, as Sherrington maintains, an abstraction; it exists in reality and occurs in the organism. But it is a "non-natural" fact in the sense that it appears only in well-determined conditions which differ considerably from those in which the "natural" reactions of the organism take place. The latter reactions, therefore, are not composed of reflexes and are not understandable on the basis of results obtained under artificial conditions.

Inversely, it is indeed possible to explain the reflex on the basis of the normal functions and to interpret it as a special case of "natural" reactions of the organism. According to Goldstein, what is called a reflex is nothing other than the most primitive biological reaction, consisting in turning towards a stimulus. Incidentally, some facts which had been qualified as instinctual are reduced to this primitive reaction and thus lose their specific character. The isolation in the case of reflexes entails a dedifferentiation of the nervous substratum in question, so that there remains only the most primitive manner of reacting to a stimulation and of compensating for it. The reflex therefore proves to be the special form which the life of the organism assumes in certain well-determined conditions, so that one can dispense with reflexes as specific facts.

It thus becomes evident that such a particular phenomenon, which takes place only in highly special conditions, cannot serve as the point of departure for the explanation of reactions occurring in the varied conditions of natural life, reactions in which the organism as a whole is engaged—which is their most important and distinctive characteristic. Indeed, the inflexibility of reactions which take place under the special conditions created by isolation sharply contrasts with the flexibility and the prompt adaptation to the vicissitudes of the situation which characterize the "natural" reactions of the living being. If, then, one starts from the organism as a whole and takes into account centralization and its relaxation, one can explain reflexes, the antagonism and alternation of opposed phases, the predominance which certain needs and tendencies acquire (the sexual need, for example), a predominance which in psychoanalytic theory plays a major role and is considered as the principal vital fact. If, to the contrary, one starts from facts considered as absolute without allowing for their place in the organism's life—that is to say, the conditions under which they occur—one cannot arrive at an understanding of that life. It is necessary in this sense to admit the notion of totality as the category which constitutes the object of biology.

Goldstein derives this methodological orientation not on the basis of abstract reasoning but from empirical and experimental work bearing directly on concrete phenomena. It is of the greatest interest therefore to note the affinity, underlined by the author himself, between his conception of biological science and the speculative ideas of Parmenides regarding ὄν and ὄντα. Goldstein believes that he has established this parallel in detail. Thus, for instance, Parmenides' contention that the μὴ ἐον cannot be an object of knowledge is taken up again by Goldstein in his methodological precept not to admit negative explanations. Again following Parmenides, knowledge must bear on the one and unique ὄν, with unity in differentiation, and not on the ὄντα, that is to say, the multiple objects separated from, and opposed to, one another. Goldstein sees a connection between this idea and the

views he advocates concerning biological data resulting from isolation
—for example, reflexes, starting from which, if we take them for
something other than the product of isolation and attribute to them an
absolute character, does not permit us to arrive at the truth concerning
the organism's life.

Goldstein refers to the interpretation of Parmenides given by
Riezler.[6] According to Riezler, the One does not denote the totality of
ὄντα—men, animals, plants, stones, and the like. The intrinsic structure of the ὄν must not be confused with the order of the cosmos.
There is a problem concerning the passage from the structure of the ὄν
to the order among the ὄντα, a problem which Parmenides himself did
not pose but which continuously occupied subsequent thinkers.

Goldstein believes that he is confronted with an analogous problem. The organism as a totality, according to him, is an idea which
pertains to a level different from that of the particular organismic
facts. As we have seen, it is a principle which founds knowledge.[7] The
idea is designed to explain the appearance of observed data, to permit
us to understand why the organism, in virtue of its intrinsic structure,
behaves (in a particular case) in such and such a way rather than in
another. On the one hand, particular facts express the organism; on
the other, the idea which is developed concerning the organism
permits us to establish an order among these facts—that is to say,
makes it possible to conceive them as the manifestations of the
organism when placed in certain conditions. The relation between
particular facts pertaining to the organism and the organism as a
whole thus becomes problematic: in what way are these facts
contained in the organism? Is, perhaps, the relation in question
different from that of the contained to the containing? In other words:
from the point of view of the organism and from that of biological
science, *what is an observed fact?*

According to Goldstein, the notion of "fact" itself becomes quite
problematic. This is so, we recall, because it is a question not only of
ascertaining the appearance of a certain fact but also and mainly of
determining its reality for the organism.[8] That is to say, the problem is
to establish the place a fact has in the life of a determinate organism.
Every fact which is observed or brought about by means of an
experimental arrangement (a patient's symptom, for example) is a
response of the organism to a certain situation. This response depends

6. K. Riezler, *Parmenides* (Frankfurter Studien zur Religion und Kultur der
Antike, ed. W. Otto [Frankfurt, 1933]).
7. See above, p. 74.
8. See above, 79f.

on more than the question posed—that is to say, on the situation in which it occurs—for it is impossible to appreciate that response except through reference to the nature of the organism which gives it. An observed fact therefore acquires its reality for an organism only by means of the idea in terms of which the organism is conceived. Such a fact never exists merely alongside other facts, nor is it added to them; it has reality for the organism only by virtue of its accord with other facts which have been previously ascertained, facts upon which we relied when we conceived the idea of the organism in the first place. Reality can therefore be attributed to a fact only when it is related to the organism in question—that is to say, to the idea which this fact itself helps to elaborate.

For this reason Goldstein can define the reality of a fact in terms of its contribution to knowledge, and this definition expresses the dialectic of biological knowledge. With respect to any new fact, therefore, there arises a problem concerning its reality for the organism, of its contribution to knowledge, of the role it plays in a certain organism's life, of its significance for that life. In particular, there arises the question as to whether this fact is a "natural" reaction or a "non-natural" phenomenon which, as in the case of reflexes, takes place only in very special conditions or in limit-situations. In this sense the author recommends a certain skepticism with respect to a great many facts which, although established by means of the most exact methods, have not contributed very much to the progress of science.

One has to start from the particular facts because there is no other point of departure. Among the facts established by means of analytical methods it is necessary to seek those which are essential for the organism studied—that is to say, to determine which of them manifest the tendency of this organism to adopt a privileged mode of behavior and which accordingly express its constancies.[9] Thus, in order to establish the materials which are indispensable for the conception of the idea of an organism, it is necessary to consider the particular facts only as materials: *they indicate the organism and refer to it, rather than provide a direct access to it.* The elaboration of this idea cannot be accomplished by means of a mere synthesis of facts or by means of an induction, though one must make use of the facts, so to speak, as a springboard. As in all symbolic knowledge, an act of "creative imagination" comes into play in this elaboration. One can evaluate the significance of a fact for a given organism only in the light of the idea as established in this manner.

9. See above, p. 72.

Goldstein in no way doubts the existence of facts established by means of the experimental and analytical method. But he does not simply accept them as such; they can be considered as facts having the sense of biological reality only when they are integrated into science, when they have found their place in the idea of the organism. Therefore, a fact must be seen as a problem rather than simply being taken for a datum.

In terms of that perspective Goldstein considers *physical and chemical facts* which can be ascertained in the organism. Many authors admit neither psychological analysis nor an analysis of behavior, seeking to substitute physiological research for them—namely, an examination of the organism by means of the method of physics and chemistry. They give preference to these methods because of the precision and the exactness of the results obtained by means of them. With such a procedure, they believe, one can more adequately approach the organism and develop a more direct idea of the functioning of the living substance. According to Goldstein, however, facts established by means of physical methods (those of chronaxia, for instance) do not open up a direct access to the activity of the nervous system; all that one can ascertain in this manner are reactions of the system under the special condition here in question, namely, the action of electrical current. From these reactions one derives conclusions concerning the functioning of the nervous system, its excitability, the development of excitation, and so on. The situation is therefore the same as the one in which one finds oneself, if one relies on facts disclosed by means of psychological analysis: here as well, one ascertains reactions—one cannot ascertain anything else by any method—and one develops, on the basis of these reactions, an idea of the activity of the nervous system, an activity to which one can have access in no other way.

The electro-physiological methods and phenomenological analysis of psychical behavior as well as somatic behavior can reciprocally confirm one another. To give this confirmation its full force, one must make the two methods as independent of one another as possible. But one has to insist on the reciprocity of the confirmations. If it is possible to conclude from increased chronaxia that there will be disturbance in tachistoscopic vision, one can by the same token inversely infer an increased chronaxia from disturbances ascertained in tachistoscopic vision. With one as well as with the other method, certain altered reactions are disclosed which permit us to conceive an idea of the modified functioning of the nervous system in such a way that, on the basis of this conception, one can predict disorders in other reactions, which can be verified by the other method. Neither method, however, permits a more direct access to the organism than the other. They both furnish only the facts—that is to say, the material necessary for the conception of an idea of the organism's functioning. And it is only when this idea becomes more complete and encompassing that it is possible to appreciate the biological value of facts discovered by means of the physical and chemical methods—for example, the importance of minute quantities of certain endocrine substances in the formation of sexual characteristics, or chemical processes involved in transplantation of tissues, and so on.

The examination of the organism by means of electro-physiological methods, therefore, yields only these reactions; it does not provide direct and immediate apprehension of the physical processes which go on in the living substance. Nor must one overlook the modification which is brought about in the functioning of the organism by the very use of these methods. If a certain experimental arrangement is applied to it, the organism is placed in very special conditions which differ considerably from those of its normal life. Here again, the most important difference consists in the more or less complete artificial isolation of certain regions or of certain organs. The facts established by means of the methods of physics and chemistry are, to a great extent, conditioned by the use of these methods. Accordingly, one must not take it for granted that these self-same reactions also take place when the organism performs under the normal conditions of its life.

Goldstein's conception concerning the *relations between the psychical and the somatic* is in conformity with his interpretation of facts as pure materials. It is from the perspective of medical practice and not from a philosophical or speculative one that he approaches this problem. Certain authors view somatic phenomena as primary and consider psychical facts as dependent on them; certain contemporary psychiatrists, on the other hand, tend to see in psychical facts if not the unique, at least the principal, expression of life, and thus they consider somatic facts as conditioned by the psychical. For the one as well as for the other group, the relation between the two spheres is defined by influence: either the somatic acts on the psychical or vice versa, or there is an interaction between the two. Whether such an action be unilateral or reciprocal, its admission presupposes that the psychical and the somatic are considered as two realms which are not only different but also separated from one another. This is indeed the common presupposition of both groups, and, according to Goldstein, that is precisely their fundamental error. If one breaks the unity of the organism's life, dividing it into a somatic and a psychical realm, one can no longer reconstruct that original unity. From this unity one must start, and to this unity one must refer the facts designated as psychical or as somatic respectively. Facts such as these must be considered only as vital manifestations of the organism, hence as materials whose organismic reality is in question.

As a result the whole question concerning primacy—whether it be of the somatic or of the psychical—appears badly formulated. Accordingly, the author does not admit the idea of an interaction between the two; on the other hand, he does not doubt the particular nature of the somatic nor of the psychical. However, in the biological order, it is only by means of the analysis of a given organism placed in a particular situation that it is possible to appreciate the role played, in certain concrete conditions, either by the somatic or the psychical. Accordingly, what is ascertained is not an interaction of the one on the other but the reaction of the organism as a whole—under the predominance sometimes of what is called somatic and sometimes of what is called psychical. Before emphasizing the difference between the somatic and the psychical, the relationship of both to the organism as a whole must be insisted upon. It is only on the basis of the essential structure of the organism that it is possible to bring out the importance and significance of both the somatic and, especially, the psychical for that organism's life.

In philosophical anthropology *nature* has too often been opposed to *spirit*, or *mind*. According to Scheler, the human being is constituted by an antagonism between life (impulses and blind drives) and spirit (which by itself is powerless). Through the latter, man becomes an ascetic of life; he acquires the faculty of taking a negative position with respect to life—a faculty upon which is founded the superiority of man over all other living beings. This negation of the vital sphere permits the spirit to borrow from it the energy it needs in order to manifest itself. It thus manages to direct life, which by itself knows neither ideas nor values; the spirit directs life by making use of the energy which it takes from it.

This conception of man, according to Goldstein, or of life and spirit, as two opposed, if not hostile, principles, considers the phenomena by isolating them or considers facts that are the result of actual isolation. The definition of the vital sphere by impulses and blind drives does not suffice even to explain the behavior of the animal. The facts which one could cite to support such an explanation are, in general, observed in special situations which condition a certain behavior, and these conditions differ considerably from those in which the animal finds itself in its normal life. The needs of the animal are integrated into an individual organization; they are forms which manifest this organization in determinate conditions. Consequently, they indicate that organization and point to it, rather than either define or compose it. It is possible to explain those needs and also the special forms they take under conditions of isolation, provided one refers them to the organism and takes account of the particular situations in which they arise. If, however, one starts from the needs and attempts to construct in their terms the life of the animal, one is led to add them together, to superimpose one on the other, and finally one is again confronted with the same difficulties which present themselves when one seeks to explain normal actions and reactions by means of reflexes.

As regards man, the relaxation of centralization as a consequence of sickness, poisoning, or an abnormal efficacy of external stimuli entails a behavior characterized by an increased predominance of the affective life, of impulses and drives. But the behavior of the human patient must not be compared to that of the animal. Morbid behavior is disordered or automatized; what it lacks, in any case, is this relation to the organism as a whole which characterizes behavior of animals. The description of the vital sphere given by Scheler does not render life in itself but applies to certain forms of life under conditions of isolation.

At the same time, spirit must not be conceived merely as a negative and purely inhibiting factor with respect to life. Owing to spirit or mind, the human being is able to put a distance between himself and the world, so to speak, to stop the course of things and to consider possibilities, eventualities, and the like. Man therefore acquires a certain independence as regards external things and assumes the attitude of a spectator with respect to them. The image which man himself thus creates of the world and which permits him to foresee things enables him to intervene in the course of things and to modify it. This ability is not, however, simply superimposed upon the vital sphere. Its presence in man makes all his vital functions undergo a conversion—not a negation—such that none of these functions is for man what it is for the animal. Goldstein even goes so far as to maintain that for man all action, whatever it may be, is set in motion by consciousness (defined as the function of objectification). If this faculty is weakened, a predominance of the affective life can result, as we have already pointed out. But this weakening can equally entail such a narrowing contraction of the milieu in which the patient lives that there is no longer room even for the vital. Goldstein cites the case of a patient who had lost all spontaneity in his relationships with the world; he had also lost it in his sexual life. In the case of this patient, the reduction of spirituality was not accompanied by a reinforcing of affectivity. One must not conceive man as a being who possesses something over and above what he possesses in common with the animals.

The antagonism between vitality and spirituality is a well-known fact. This antagonism results from the general imperfection of the human being and from the fact that just because of his spirituality this being is exposed to the danger of falling into catastrophic situations. Such a situation materializes when the equilibrium in which man lives with his milieu is broken and a new adaption is not yet established. In such situations the centralization is obviously weakened to a very high degree. The antagonism in question expresses this state of transition between an order which has been shaken and a higher-level order; it is precisely at this point that spirit appears as the negation of life. Accordingly, one must refer this antagonism to the situation in which it arises and consider it as generated by that special situation.

One is inevitably forced, however, to resort to a regulatory principle if one takes this antagonism as an absolute and interprets it in terms of two principles which are inherently opposed to one another. One can by no means achieve a reconstruction of the unity of the human being in this manner. Once again, one must take one's departure from this unity—that is to say, from the "more" perfect, although it is less frequently realized. Only then is it possible to comprehend the phenomena which occur under conditions of isolation. These phenomena appear as symptoms of the modifications which these special conditions make the human being undergo in his unity. The problem is not, therefore, how to compose the human being in terms of two principles which are independent of one another, principles which Scheler has hypostatized; it is rather one of assigning to both vitality and spirituality the place which they respectively occupy in the organization of the human being in general and to determine the concrete role which each of them plays, for man, in determinate circumstances. For Goldstein, vital facts as well as those pertaining to spirituality are but materials for the conception of the idea of the human organism. Refusing to rely on a preconceived idea concerning an original opposition between vitality and spirituality, he considers them from the perspective of their relationship to the organism as a whole.

Assuredly, as regards man, there is a tension between vitality and spirituality. But this tension is not evidence for two opposed principles which would make up the human being. It must be viewed from within the unity of this being: it expresses a profound duality at the very heart of that unity. Vitality and spirituality not only co-exist in the human organism and are indissolubly connected to one another, but within that very connection there is a relation of tension between them. This duality characterizes man and distinguishes him from animals. It is at the basis of all the creations and all the works of civilization.

To consider facts as materials whose organismic significance is established in the light of the idea which they themselves help to conceive and thus to define biological science as a dialectic between the level of facts and that of ideas is to draw on *Platonism* in the interpretation of biological science. More exactly expressed, it is to rediscover Platonism as the motive force or the mainspring of this science. Goldstein does not cite Plato; but there are in his work sufficient passages which are of distinctly Platonic inspiration. To draw a line of demarcation between "empirical investigation" and "philosophical reflection" seems artificial to him because nothing empirical can be understood except in the light of ideas and because the finite does not become intelligible except by its relationship to the infinite. Scientific knowledge consists in establishing order among facts. Now, such an order can be established only on the basis of ideas, which are at a level different from that of the facts. One may summarize the conception of facts which Goldstein advocates by the words of Goethe, which are also of Platonic inspiration: "Das Höchste wäre: zu begreifen, dass alles Factische schon Theorie ist." (The highest insight would be: to understand that every fact is already a theory.)

To avoid all misunderstanding, it should be emphasized that Goldstein is not putting observed facts in doubt, any more than he is doubting the value of analytic methods which permit the ascertainment of those facts, and that he emphasizes the importance of facts obtained by these methods for the elaboration of the idea of the organism. The conception of this idea has no other basis nor any other point of departure than observed facts. What is in question is not these facts as such but, rather, the evidence which they provide for the reality of the organism; it is their significance for the organism. And, we should remember, in this Platonic conception one does more justice to the facts than in an empiricism in which, while appealing to these facts, one approaches them with theoretical ideas which in the last analysis cannot but be preconceived.

TRANSLATED BY RICHARD M. ZANER

# 4 / The Phenomenological
and the Psychological Approach
to Consciousness [1]

BOTH PHENOMENOLOGY AND PSYCHOLOGY are concerned with consciousness in general as well as with specific acts of consciousness such as perception, memory, comprehension of meaning, reasoning, etc. Yet, the theoretical orientation and perspective in which consciousness is studied in psychology is highly different from that of phenomenology.

Psychology has developed into a positive science not different, in principle, from other positive sciences, especially physics. Considered from the psychological point of view, acts of consciousness appear as *mundane events,* i.e., events which occur in the same real world and in the same objective time as any other events. Of particular interest among such other events are certain organismic or physiological processes and physical processes to which acts of consciousness stand in the relationship of causal or functional dependence. In this sense, psychology is in logical continuity with, and relies partly upon, the physical and biological sciences.

Phenomenology, on the contrary, has been established and developed by Husserl as a philosophical, not a positive, discipline and as a philosophical discipline in the most radical sense conceivable. Phenomenology concerns itself with the fundamental problems of knowledge and experience, both scientific and the pre-theoretical experience which we have of the surrounding perceptual world and by which we are guided in our everyday life. Whereas positive sciences take for granted the objects with which they deal and concern themselves with their exploration and theoretical explanation, phenomenology poses

1. Part of this article was read, in modified form, before the General Seminar of the Graduate Faculty, New School for Social Research, on October 14, 1953; it was originally published in *Philosophy and Phenomenological Research,* XV, no. 3 (1955).

[89]

the question of the existence of objects and of the meaning of their existence. The term "object" is here used in the most inclusive sense so as to comprise real objects, natural things (animate as well as inanimate) and cultural objects (e.g., instruments, books, works of art, and the like), and ideal unities of the kind which play a role in mathematics and logic and, further, historical and social entities such as political institutions, economic systems, legal orders, etc.

Aiming at ultimate clarification and justification of all knowledge and experience, phenomenology considers acts of consciousness primarily, if not exclusively, with regard to their cognitive or presentational function. It is through acts of consciousness and systematically grouped and concatenated acts that objects, processes, events, and occurrences of any description whatever appear and display themselves as to what they are and as to what they count for in our conscious life—in our practical, theoretical, artistic, etc., life. Among such events and occurrences there must be included those physiological and physical processes upon which, in the psychological perspective, acts of consciousness prove to depend functionally. Hence in the phenomenological orientation, consciousness obviously cannot be considered as one mundane domain beside others. On the contrary, consciousness proves to be a privileged realm, in a certain sense prior to every mundane domain, insofar as for its very existence every mundane domain necessarily refers to consciousness, viz., to those acts and systems of acts through which items pertaining to the domain in question present themselves. This specific phenomenological approach to consciousness, i.e., the consideration of acts of consciousness with regard to their presentational function and not as mundane events occurring in the real world, has been opened up and rendered possible by a special methodological device which Husserl calls the *"phenomenological reduction."*

Considering the profound difference in theoretical orientation and approach, every attempt at comparing or even contrasting with each other psychological and phenomenological theories proves to be in need of a preparatory legitimation and justification. It is the purpose of the present essay not only to contrast the psychological with the phenomenological approach to consciousness but also to prepare the ground for a legitimate utilization of concepts and results deriving from *Gestalt theory* for the advancement of phenomenological theories of consciousness. We shall embark upon showing that one of the fundamental principles of Gestalt theory, viz., *the dismissal of the constancy hypothesis*, lends itself to a phenomenological interpretation by means of which it may be disclosed as an *incipient phenomenological reduction*. Owing to this interpretation, some of the concepts of Gestalt theory—to be more specific, its descriptive concepts—may acquire phenomenological relevancy and validity. Here we shall not go beyond legitimating the use of concepts of Gestalt theory within the context of phenomenology. Their actual utilization is to be left to concrete analytical work on specific phenomena.

To substantiate our thesis, we shall first present the phenomenological reduction. Next we shall consider the growth of the idea of psychology as a positive science out of the conceptions of modern physics. This discussion will permit us to assign to the constancy hypothesis its logico-historical place with respect to the system of modern sciences. Finally we shall embark upon developing the philosophical consequences which derive from the dismissal of the constancy hypothesis in Gestalt theory.

## [I] THE PHENOMENOLOGICAL REDUCTION

AT EVERY MOMENT of conscious life, we find ourselves within the perceptual world, amidst things and objects of the greatest diversity: natural objects as well as objects of value or cultural objects, inanimate things as well as animals. Within this world, there live with us our fellow-men to whom we are standing in relationships of the most various kinds. All those objects and things, living beings, fellow-men, etc., appear and are taken as real existents. They pertain to the real world which encompasses all existents including ourselves.

Living in the *"natural attitude"* (*natürliche Einstellung*), which is the attitude not only of everyday experience but also of any activity whatever (with the sole exception of radical philosophical reflection as carried out in specific phenomenological considerations), we simply accept the existential character with which the perceptual world and whatever it contains present themselves.[2] In all dealings with real mundane existents, in all perceiving, reasoning, exploring, planning, acting, etc., there is implied or involved the existential belief, i.e., belief in the existence of what concerns us. To be sure, the existential belief is not permanently stated and formulated; the existential character of the things and beings encountered is not on every occasion disengaged, rendered explicit, and posited. Such rendering explicit

2. As to "natural attitude," see E. Husserl, *Ideen zu einer reinen Phänomenologie und phänomenologischen Philosophie* (referred to hereafter as *Ideen*), §§ 27f. (All our references to *Ideen* are to the 2d edition, 1922, which is a reprint of the 1st edition, 1913. The Louvain edition, ed. W. Biemel [*Husserliana*, Vol. III (The Hague, 1950)], gives on the margin the pagination of the previous editions.) Cf. also M. Farber, *The Foundation of Phenomenology* (Cambridge, Mass., 1943), pp. 522ff.

and formulation through a judgment about existence is, of course, always possible. As a rule, however, the existential belief involved in all our activities assumes a rather implicit and inarticulate form. This belief is not so much a premise entailing consequences but rather a general thesis which, unformulated and unthematized, underlies and supports all mental activities and upon which we proceed in all our dealings with mundane existents.[3] The eventual thematization of the existential belief is but a subsequent formulation of that general thesis. In its very thematization, the thesis in question appears as having been implied, previously to its disclosure, in the mental activity of the past moment and, thus, as not having been brought into being by its being rendered explicit.

Instead of abiding by the natural attitude, we are free to subject the general existential belief to the *phenomenological reduction*. The existential belief is "put out of action," no "use is made of it," it is "bracketed," "suspended."[4] It is not as though the existence of the world and of mundane existents were denied or doubted or, instead of being admitted as certain, were held as merely probable, etc. That would be modalization rather than suspension of the existential belief. Strictly speaking, the phenomenological reduction does not concern the existential belief itself or the existential character exhibited by the things perceived and the perceptual world at large. Instead, it concerns the role which the existential belief is permitted to play within the context of phenomenology. In this sense, the phenomenological reduction may be considered as a methodological device resorted to for the sake of arriving at radical and radically justified philosophical knowledge.[5] Every perceived thing which in the natural attitude counts as a real existent continues so to count under the phenomenological reduction. The same holds for the perceptual world as a whole, which continues to present itself as existing and as the real world. However, whereas, in the natural attitude, the existential belief is simply accepted, implicitly and unreflectingly as a rule, acceptance of the belief is withheld under the phenomenological reduction, which for this reason proves to be an ἐποχή, i.e., suspension or withholding of assent. Though reduced, because no longer accepted as a basis upon which to proceed, the existential belief continues to be experienced.[6]

3. Husserl, *Ideen*, pp. 52ff.
4. *Ibid.*, §§ 31f. and Abschnitt II, chap. IV; Farber, *The Foundation of Phenomenology*, pp. 526f. A very clear, though brief, presentation is given by A. Schutz, "Some leading concepts of phenomenology," *Collected Papers* (The Hague, 1962), I, pp. 99–117.
5. It is thus interpreted by Farber, *ibid.*, pp. 561f.
6. E. Husserl, *Cartesian Meditations*, trans. D. Cairns (The Hague, 1960), pp. 19f.: "Meanwhile the world experienced in this reflectively grasped life goes on

Therefore, it is misleading to speak of the existential belief as being disregarded, set aside, suppressed, eliminated, and the like.[7] In truth, the existential belief and, correspondingly, the existential character of real things are so far from being disregarded that, on the contrary, that character is explicitly disengaged and, along with other characters exhibited by those things, subjected to radical reflection and analysis. It is one of the most important tasks of phenomenology to provide an ultimate clarification of the very existence of perceptual things and the perceptual world at large.

Before we proceed to developing the consequences of the phenomenological reduction, let us first point out that its performance appears imperative for the sake of radical philosophical clarification. If we are confronted with a real world to which we belong ourselves, it is because this world and whatever it comprises presents itself through certain acts and concatenated systems of acts of consciousness, especially perceptual consciousness, as that which it is for us, as existing and with a specific sense of existence. Correspondingly the same holds for the universe as conceived and constructed by science and for non-perceptual domains as, for example, logic and mathematics, with respect to those acts and act-systems through which the domains in question are constructed and elaborated. To formulate and to advance radical philosophical problems concerning the domains mentioned as well as the perceptual world, concerning the specific sense of existence and validity characteristic of each of those domains, to achieve final clarification and justification of the fundamental concepts and categories related to the several domains, etc., we have to consider acts of consciousness. Especially those acts have to be taken into consideration through which the entities pertaining to any domain appear in the mode of original and authentic self-presentation. Thus the pre-eminent task of philosophy may be defined as *accounting for objects of every type and kind and for objectivity in every conceivable sense in subjective terms*, i.e., in terms of acts of consciousness which with respect to the objects in question have experiential and presentational function.

The essential reference of objects to acts of consciousness moti-

---

being for me (in a certain manner) 'experienced' as before, and with just the content it has at any particular time. It goes on appearing, as it appeared before; the only difference is that I, as reflecting philosophically, no longer keep in effect (no longer accept) the natural belief in existence involved in experiencing the world—though that believing too is still there and grasped by my noticing regard."

7. Such misunderstandings are not infrequent; cf., e.g., V. J. McGill, "A Materialistic Approach to Husserl's Philosophy," in *Philosophical Essays in Memory of Edmund Husserl*, ed. M. Farber (Cambridge, Mass., 1940), pp. 239f.

vates the phenomenological reduction. First of all this reference has to be rendered explicit. As a consequence, consciousness comes to be disclosed as a unique and uniquely privileged realm, prior to every domain, including the perceptual world.[8] On the basis of this disclosure, the methodological procedure of bracketing or suspending the existential belief which pertains to the natural attitude proves necessary in order to avoid a *circulus vitiosus*. This *circulus vitiosus* becomes most conspicuous in the case of perception. As long as the phenomenological reduction is not performed, consciousness is considered as integrated into, and part of, the real world. In other words, consciousness is considered as a well-circumscribed particular mundane domain. Hence acts of perception are interpreted as causally dependent upon real things and physical events both inside and outside the organism of the perceiving subject. Real things as well as physical processes appear as to what they are through acts of perception and through acts of scientific elaboration and interpretation, based upon, and starting from, perceptions. In the final analysis, they have to be accounted for in terms of acts of perception. Perception is thus explained with reference to real things and physical processes which, in turn, have to be accounted for in terms of perceptual consciousness.

By the phenomenological reduction, the integration of consciousness into the real world is severed. Consciousness is no longer regarded as a particular mundane domain among other domains, nor are acts of consciousness considered as mundane events which occur in the real world and, therefore, depend causally or functionally upon other mundane events. Under the phenomenological reduction, acts of consciousness are considered solely as experiences of objects, as experiences (this term understood in the broadest possible sense) in and through which objects appear, present themselves, and are apprehended as those which they are and as which they count. By the

8. The privilege and priority of consciousness in the sense under discussion was formulated for the first time by Descartes in his *Meditations*. Summarizing his analysis of perception, Descartes writes (*Philosophical Writings*, selected and translated by N. K. Smith [New York, 1958, 1911], pp. 190ff.): "What now shall I say of the mind itself, i.e., of myself? . . . What am I to say in regard to this I which seems to apprehend this piece of wax so distinctly? Do I not know myself much more truly and much more certainly, and also much more distinctly and evidently, than I do the wax? For if I judge that the wax is or exists because I see it, evidently it follows, with yet greater evidence that I myself am or exist, inasmuch as I am thus seeing it. . . . If the apprehension of the wax has seemed to me more determinate and distinct when sight and touch, and many causes besides, have rendered it manifest to me, how much more evidently and distinctly must I now know myself, since all the reasons which can aid in the apprehension of the wax, or of any body whatsoever, afford yet better evidence of the nature of my mind."

phenomenological reduction, *consciousness* is fully disclosed as a *unique realm of absolute priority,* because it reveals itself as the medium of access to whatever exists and is valid.[9] The phenomenological reduction permits us not only to make but also to exploit this disclosure, i.e., to render it fruitful for concrete analyses and investigations.

Conversely, in consequence of the suspension of the existential belief, the real world as a whole as well as particular real existents can no longer be simply accepted as existing but must be taken merely as presenting themselves and appearing as existing. We have emphasized that the existential belief is by no means eliminated or nullified, even though its acceptance and assent to it are withheld. If the existential belief is preserved under the phenomenological reduction, it can be preserved only as a matter of experience, i.e., as an experienced belief. Correspondingly, the existential character of any real thing or event continues to be taken into account after, so to speak, receiving an *index,* viz., the index of being meant and intended.[10] With that index affixed to it, the existential character as meant and intended through acts of experience is subjected to phenomenological investigation. Since the existential character concerns all attributes, properties, qualities, etc., of any real existent, the index of being meant is affixed to the existent as a whole. In other words, within the context of phenomenology the real existent will henceforth be taken merely as a meant existent, meant as—exactly and only as—it actually appears through a given act of experience. The attachment of the index in question serves the purpose of rendering explicit the *essential condition of every object to be an object for consciousness,* to present itself through, and to be intended by, acts of experience. In this sense alone are the *perceptual world* and *all mundane existents,* transformed into, or, more correctly, *disclosed as, phenomena.*[11] Phenomenology is concerned throughout with phenomena in the sense mentioned—that is, not with things and objects *simpliciter,* but with "things" and

9. Cf. Husserl, *Ideen,* §§ 47ff., 142; E. Husserl, *Formale und transzendentale Logik* (Halle, 1929), §§ 61, 94f., 104; Husserl, *Cartesian Meditations,* §§ 7f. and pp. 47f.

10. Cf. *Ideen,* p. 142.

11. Husserl, *Cartesian Meditations,* pp. 20f., 32 ". . . the whole world, when one is in the phenomenological attitude, is not accepted as actuality, but only as an actuality-phenomenon." A very clear presentation of the phenomenological reduction from the point of view of its function to disclose the world as a phenomenon has been given by G. Berger, *Le cogito dans la philosophie de Husserl* (Paris, 1941), chap. III. Berger writes (p. 54) "Ce qui s'opère, dans la réduction phénoménologique, c'est moins le passage de l'objet au sujet, que *la prise de conscience du monde en tant que phénomène—qua cogitatum—. . . . il y a une catégorie plus profonde que celle d'être ou de non-être, c'est celle d'objet pensé"* (italics added).

"objects" as they appear through acts of consciousness. Obviously, phenomenological investigations must be carried out in a *strictly descriptive orientation,* since after the performance of the phenomenological reduction we are left only with "things" and "objects" meant and intended and which, accordingly, have to be *taken as they are meant and intended*—i.e., *as they present themselves in* actual or potential *experience.*[12] No reference to any reality not actually appearing and given through the act of experience under consideration must be permitted to intervene in phenomenological analyses. Through a given perception a thing presents itself under a certain aspect, from one of its sides, as far away or as nearby, etc. Phenomenology of perception has to start with the "thing" perceived, taken exactly as it stands before the experiencing subject's mind and in that very mode of presentation in which it actually appears through the perception under discussion. The "thing" thus characterized is the *perceptum qua perceptum,* as we may be permitted to say, varying Husserl's expression *cogitatum qua cogitatum;* another technical term used by Husserl is *perceptual noema.*[13] However, phenomenology does not confine itself to descriptive analyses of single perceptions. The ultimate goal of the phenomenology of perception is to account for the objective real thing in subjective terms, that is, in terms of perceptions and perceptual noemata. Hence problems arise concerning the relation between perceptual noemata and the real thing which, through different perceptions, appears in varying modes of presentation and is still experienced as one and identically the same. These problems are the *transcendental problems of the constitution* of real things.[14]

## [II] PSYCHOLOGY AS A POSITIVE SCIENCE

To THE PHENOMENOLOGICAL APPROACH to consciousness there is opposed the psychological approach. By that we mean the interpretation of acts of consciousness as real mundane events. Let us trace the root of this "naturalistic" conception of consciousness, at least as far as modern psychology is concerned.

The perceptual world in which we live and act in our everyday experience is for us the paramount reality. Throughout all our conscious life, the perceptual world is given to us as really existent. In

12. Cf. Husserl, *Cartesian Meditations,* p. 36.
13. Cf. Husserl, *Ideen,* § 41, 88ff., 97; Husserl, *Cartesian Meditations* II. See also our article "On the Intentionality of Consciousness," below, pp. 124–40.
14. For the formulation and development of these problems, cf. Husserl, *Ideen,* § 86 and Abschnitt IV.

the natural attitude its existence is simply taken for granted. All science and knowledge, all cognitive endeavor essentially refers to and is oriented with respect to the perceptual world, since it is the goal and aim of scientific knowledge to establish the truth concerning reality.

Since Galileo the pursuit of scientific knowledge has assumed the form of the elaboration, by way of construction and inference, of the scientifically true and valid universe of physics. This universe is entirely and exclusively characterized and determined by its mathematical structure. It is throughout conceived in mathematical terms. Between the perceptual world in which we live, such as it is familiar to us in everyday experience, and the true and scientifically valid universe, as it is conceived and constructed in physical science, a gulf has come to be opened up and, in the course of the development of physical science, has been widened progressively. Yet it must be kept in mind that the elaboration of the true physical universe is undertaken for the sole sake of explaining the perceptual world. All constructs and constructions of physics are subject to the decisive test of correspondence to, and in this sense agreement with, perceptual experience. Their only *raison d'être* is to provide an explanation and account of events and processes which occur in the perceptual world —our paramount reality and, if the term reality is understood in its strict sense, our only reality. Therefore no departure from the natural attitude is involved in the transition from perceptual knowledge and common experience to scientific explanation or in the corresponding substitution of the universe as constructed and elaborated in physical science for the perpetual world. The existential belief which pervades perceptual experience is carried over into the scientific interpretation of the world and underlies the elaboration of the universe of physics in the form of an implicit and unreflecting acceptance of the existence of the perceptual world. A complication arises insofar as a secondary existential belief—viz., belief in the validity of the scientific elaboration and the constructed universe of physics—is added to, or, rather, founded upon, the primary existential belief in the perceptual world. Here we cannot go beyond mentioning this complication, any more than we can enter into discussing or even presenting the philosophical problems which, as Husserl has set them forth, are involved in the very constitution and existence of modern physics, i.e., physics since the time of Galileo.[15]

In the natural attitude, we conceive of ourselves as mundane existents among other mundane existents. The perceptual world

15. E. Husserl, *Die Krisis der Europäischen Wissenschaften und die transzendentale Phänomenologie*, ed. W. Biemel (*Husserliana*, Vol. VI [The Hague, 1954]), § 9.

which comprises whatever exists comprises our body. In this world our body acts upon other bodies, both animate and inanimate, and is acted upon by them. If, in the course of the elaboration of the scientifically true and valid universe, physical systems (i.e., systems which are characterized entirely and exclusively in mathematical terms) come to be substituted for perceptual things as known and accepted in common experience, this also holds for the human body. Accordingly, a special physical system, the *organism* as conceived in anatomy and physiology is substituted for the *body* as given and familiar in the immediate experience of everyday life. The exposure of the human body to influences or actions of its environment has then to be reformulated in terms of physical processes which are propagated in the surroundings of a given organism and thus reach that organism. When some of these physical processes, which for this very reason are called stimuli, impinge upon specific parts of the organism, the sense organs, they provoke certain processes within the organism. Such organismic processes, which must be conceived in conformity with the ideas and conceptions prevailing in physical science, are, in turn, correlated and concomitant with the appearance of sense data. From the very conception of the organism as a physical system among other physical systems, it follows that internal organismic processes, e.g., those to which data of sense experience are correlated, must be construed as, in principle, of the same kind and nature as the external processes by which the former are aroused.

The distinction between "body" and "organism," a distinction that plays a role of increasing importance in contemporary philosophical and psychological literature, is of comparatively recent date. It seems that Scheler was the first to have made it.[16] We borrow the terms "body" and "organism" with the specific sense with which they are here used from Köhler, who emphatically insists upon the distinction in question.[17] "If the chair is seen 'before me,'" Köhler writes, "the 'me' of this phrase means my body as an experience, of course, not my organism as an object of the physical world."[18] Traditionally the identification between "body" and "organism" had been taken for granted as a matter of course. Revealing in this respect is Descartes' description of the naïve opinion and belief which, previous to the universal doubt, we have of our body: "I thought that I possessed a face, hands, arms, and that whole structure to which I was giving the

16. M. Scheler, *Die Wissensformen und die Gesellschaft* (Leipzig, 1926), pp. 361ff.

17. W. Köhler, *Gestalt Psychology* (New York, 1947), pp. 5ff.

18. *Ibid.*, p. 22n.

title 'body,' composed as it is of the limbs *discernible in a corpse.*" [19] Descartes' description bears out the thesis of Sartre, according to whom the substitution of the "organism" for the "body" depends upon the body's being considered, not as it is experienced by the living, embodied, and involved subject, but as it appears to an onlooking, disinterested, and detached observer.[20] Following a similar line of thought, Merleau-Ponty has set forth the difficulties which beset the idea of an explanatory biology—explanatory in the style of physics— and, in general, the very conception of the body as a physical system.[21] Over and against that conception, Merleau-Ponty insists upon the *corps phenomenal* as the subject matter of biological science.[22]

Through the preceding discussion we have tried to disclose the intimate connection between modern physics and modern psychology. It seems more than a mere historical coincidence that with Male- branche, as Cassirer has pointed out, the first genuine psychologist makes his appearance in modern philosophy.[23] According to Husserl, the very idea of Galilean physics, if consistently and radically pursued in its consequences, motivates the idea of a naturalistic psychology.[24] Modern psychology has developed not only in historical continuity but also in *logical continuity* with modern physics. What must be stressed is not so much the definition of psychological concepts in analogy to concepts of physics.[25] More important is the reference to physics in the very formulation of psychological problems, especially problems con- cerning perception. To account for perception, the psychologist ac- cepts, and starts from, the universe as conceived in physical science and considers the human organism as a physical system acted upon by physical events.[26] Independently of any theories to be advanced, the very problems which the theories of psychology are meant to solve are determined by allowance for the science of physics.[27] In this sense,

19. Descartes, *Philosophical Writings*, p. 184 (italics added).

20. J. P. Sartre, *L'être et le néant* (Paris, 1943), pp. 365ff.

21. M. Merleau-Ponty, *La structure du comportement* (Paris, 1942), pp. 195ff., 256ff.

22. M. Merleau-Ponty, *Phénoménologie de la perception* (Paris, 1945), pp. 110ff., 122ff., 403f.

23. E. Cassirer, *Das Erkenntnisproblem in der Philosophie und Wissenschaft der neueren Zeit* (Berlin, 1911), I, pp. 554f.

24. Husserl, *Die Krisis der Europäischen Wissenschaften und die transzenden- tale Phänomenologie*, §§ 10f.

25. A few examples by which that analogy is illustrated have been discussed above, "The Place of Psychology in the System of Sciences," pp. 57ff.

26. Cf. the classical formulation by H. von Helmholtz, *Handbuch der physiologischen Optik*, 2d ed. (Hamburg and Leipzig, 1896), pp. 584ff.

27. Cf. G. Marcel, *Journal métaphysique* (Paris, 1935), p. 124: ". . . le mode de représentation des rapports de l'âme et du corps, dépendant de la façon

modern psychology, both empiricistic and intellectualistic, has been dominated by what Merleau-Ponty calls *le préjugé du monde.*[28] Gestalt theory does not depart from this orientation of psychology with respect to physics. In the first chapter of his *Gestalt Psychology* Köhler points to the perceptual world as the basis from which every science, physics as well as psychology, starts and has to start, since there is no other point of departure. He then defines it as the task of psychology to conceive of organismic processes in such a way that the appearance of the perceptual world, including the phenomenal body, will be explained as resulting from these processes.[29] Köhler's formulation may well serve as an illustration of the orientation of psychological problems with regard to physical science.

Our historico-logical reflections have brought us before the very roots of the idea of psychology conceived as a positive science. At once it appears that the psychological, in contradistinction to the phenomenological, approach to consciousness involves an explanatory orientation—explanation understood in that specific sense which the term has acquired in modern science.[30] If acts of consciousness are considered as mundane events beside other mundane events, questions are bound to arise concerning the conditions, both internal and external, with respect to a given organism, under which a certain conscious event rather than a different one occurs. The systematic study of such conditions and of the multiple functional relationships which come into play here constitutes the subject matter of the positive science of psychology. The very fact that consciousness lends itself to both a psychological-explanatory and a phenomenological approach betrays its ambiguous nature: on the one hand, acts of consciousness depend causally or functionally upon extra-conscious facts and events and in this sense prove their effects; on the other

---

dont le corps même est pensé, dépend indirectement de ce mouvement même par lequel l'esprit se réalise dans la science . . . la notion que l'esprit peut se faire des rapports de l'âme et du corps doit être fonction du mouvement par lequel la notion du corps se construit. Or cette construction du corps se révèle solidaire dans une mesure extraordinairement étroite de la construction même du monde extérieur."

28. Merleau-Ponty, *Phénoménologie de la perception,* Introduction.

29. Köhler, *Gestalt Psychology,* p. 7: "To the influence of other physical objects my organism responds with processes which establish the sensory world around me. Further processes in the organism give rise to the sensory thing which I call my body."; p. 22n., "My body is the outcome of certain processes in my physical organism, processes which start in the eyes, muscles, skin, and so forth, exactly as the chair before me is the final product of other processes in the same physical organism."

30. The legitimacy of the "explanatory" style in question in psychology has been challenged by Merleau-Ponty, *La structure du comportement,* pp. 177ff. and 256ff.; *Phénoménologie de la perception,* pp. 58ff., 112f.

hand, they have cognitive and presentational functions with regard to *all* mundane things and events, including those very facts upon which they depend causally.

## [III] THE CONSTANCY HYPOTHESIS AND ITS DISMISSAL

IF CERTAIN SPECIFIC external physical processes (stimuli) strike sense organs, they arouse, as we have mentioned, internal organismic (physiological) processes with which the experience of sensory data is correlated. Hence the question arises concerning *the relationship between the stimuli,* on the one hand, *and both the provoked physiological processes and the concomitant sense experiences,* on the other. This question is bound to arise from the conception of the organism as a physical system acted upon by external physical events.

Historically speaking, the *constancy hypothesis* represents the first attempt at establishing the mentioned relationship.[31] According to the constancy hypothesis, genuine sense data are completely determined by, and depend only and exclusively upon, local stimulation. Whenever the same well-circumscribed area of a sense organ (e.g., the retina) is stimulated by the same external physical process, the same sense data cannot fail to appear. They appear regardless of the general conditions which prevail in the organism, regardless also of other processes which take place at the same time, even when these processes occur not only in the same sense organ but also in parts adjacent to the circumscribed area in question. In other words, genuine sense data produced by a certain local stimulation do not even depend upon simultaneous stimulations in their immediate environment. Continuous change in the local stimulation is accompanied by continuous change in the corresponding sensations.[32] Quite in general, differences between sensations are strictly proportional to differences between arousing stimuli.

If it happens—as it does more often than not—that actual perceptual experience does not display those sensations which on the basis of the given local stimulation must be expected to occur, the "deviation" is ascribed to factors other than mere sensibility. Such factors, in whatever fashion their nature may be specified, "distort" in

31. For the following brief presentation of the constancy hypothesis and its consequences, see Köhler, *Gestalt Psychology*, chaps. III–IV; K. Koffka, *Principles of Gestalt Psychology* (New York, 1935), chap. III. Of necessity we must here confine ourselves to a few theoretical statements.

32. Cf. Helmholtz, *Handbuch der Physiologischen Optik*, p. 569.

a certain sense the genuine sensations. Owing to the intervention of non-sensuous factors, we are confronted, in common perceptual experience, not with genuine and authentic data of sense but with the products of operations of the factors mentioned upon the original sensations as exclusively determined by local stimulation. Further, whatever features perceptual experience exhibits in excess of mere sensations must also be the result of operations of extra-sensuous factors. Among the yieldings of such factors must be reckoned the *Gestaltqualitäten* of C. v. Ehrenfels, Husserl's *figurale Momente*,[33] all kinds of forms of organization, articulation, structure, grouping, inner coherence, and the like. None of these features can, properly speaking, pass for a genuine datum of sense experience. All of them must be considered as contributed by factors other than sensibility and as imposed upon the genuine data of sense.[34] *The constancy hypothesis entails a thoroughgoing dualism* which finds its expression in the current distinction between *sensation* and *perception*. Genuine sense data as depending only upon local stimulation serve, so to speak, as raw materials for factors of a non-sensuous nature by means of which the former are interpreted, organized, grouped, articulated, structured, etc. Because of the operation of the factors in question, common experience hardly ever confronts us with sensations in their original and authentic state. By means of appropriate techniques, however, it is possible to inhibit the operation of organizing factors and actually to experience genuine sensations. For that end, the adoption of a specific "analytical" attitude is sometimes sufficient. It must be stressed that the sense data in their genuine state which are disclosed by such techniques had already been experienced previously to their disclosure, though in a *non-noticed form*. The constancy hypothesis makes unavoidable the admission of sensations experienced but not noticed.

In 1913 Köhler explicitly discussed the constancy hypothesis and its consequences, some of which, as he brought out, are not even compatible with one another.[35] His main contention concerns the unverifiability of the constancy hypothesis, which, of course, may by no means pass for self-evident. No direct or indirect experimental confirmation of either the constancy hypothesis itself or of the

33. C. von Ehrenfels, "Über Gestaltqualitäten," *Vierteljahrsschrift für wissenschaftliche Philosophie*, XIV (1890); E. Husserl, *Philosophie der Arithmetik* (Halle, 1891), pp. 217ff.

34. Cf. the critical discussion of V. Benussi's explanation of the features in question on the basis of the constancy hypothesis by K. Koffka, "Zur Grundlegung der Wahrnehmungspsychologie," *Zeitschrift für Psychologie*, LXXIII (1915); see also above, "Some Aspects and Some Developments of Gestalt Psychology," II.

35. W. Köhler, "Über unbemerkte Empfindungen und Urteilstäuschungen," *Zeitschrift für Psychologie*, LXVI (1913).

consequences which it entails appears conclusive, because the interpretation of the experimental findings proves to depend upon the admission of the constancy hypothesis.[36] As result of his critical discussion and examination, Köhler suggests dismissing the constancy hypothesis altogether.

It must be kept in mind that the constancy hypothesis is only one special or, rather, specifying assumption concerning the nature of the relationship between stimulating physical processes and aroused data of sense experience. Dismissing *one* possible hypothesis as to the relationship in question hence by no means purports challenging the existence of that relationship or putting it in question in any conceivable sense. The dismissal of the constancy hypothesis does not *ipso facto* and of necessity entail discarding the very idea of psychology as a positive science, i.e., departing from the orientation of psychology with respect to physics. In the actual development of Gestalt theory, the constancy hypothesis has come to be replaced by a different conception of the relationship in question. In this new conception, the assumption of autochthonous organizational forms and processes within the nervous system plays a predominant role.

Here, however, we are not concerned with the development of Gestalt theory along the lines of a positive science of psychology. Rather, we wish to show that *the dismissal of the constancy hypothesis can be interpreted as a potential or incipient phenomenological reduction or as a phenomenological reduction in germinal form.*[37] Thus interpreted, and that of necessity means *radicalized,* the dismissal of the constancy hypothesis opens up a possible avenue of approach to the phenomenological conception of consciousness, a conception which, as we have seen, is radically opposed to the psychological conception.

Along with the constancy hypothesis, the traditional dualism in the account of perceptual experience, i.e., the distinction between sensation and perception, is discarded as well. Sensations as exclusively determined by, and depending upon, local stimulation may no longer be singled out as genuine sensory facts to be contrasted with the contributions and yieldings of sources other than sensibility in the proper sense. No allowance for stimulations or, in general, any extra-conscious or extra-perceptual reality may be made in the description and analysis of what appears through a certain perception. To be sure,

36. For technical discussions of this question and related ones, which pertain to experimental psychology, we refer to Köhler's article, *ibid.,* as well as his book *Gestalt Psychology,* and to Koffka, *Principles of Gestalt Psychology.*

37. For the first time, we have ventured a phenomenological interpretation of Gestalt theory along similar lines in "Phenomenology of Thematics and of the Pure Ego," below, pp. 192–95.

within the "content" of a given perception, elements or, better, components and constituents may be distinguished and discriminated from one another. (By the "content" of a perception or, as we may likewise say, the percept, we mean that which is perceived and presents itself through the perception in question.) It is, however, no longer permissible to classify such components and constituents according to their provenience. *All these components and constituents —in general, all features displayed by perception—must be treated on the same footing; they must all be recognized as data and facts of genuine sense experience.* One must include, among such constituents, properties of the kind mentioned before,[38] which are characteristic of organized, structured, and articulated groups and wholes. In their totality, these components, constituents, and features build up the given percept. Following the dismissal of the constancy hypothesis, the percept has to be considered as a homogeneous unit, though internally articulated and structured. It has to be taken at face value; as that which it presents itself to be through the given act of perception and through that act alone; as it appears to the perceiving subject's consciousness; as it is meant and intended (the term "meaning" understood in a properly broadened and enlarged sense) in that privileged mode of meaning and intending which is perceptual presentation. In other words, the percept as it is conceived after the constancy hypothesis has been dismissed proves to be what we called the *perceptum qua perceptum,* the *perceptual noema* or the *perceptual phenomenon.*[39] Those concepts which were established and elaborated under the phenomenological reduction now reappear in consequence of the dismissal of the constancy hypothesis. For this reason, we submit, the dismissal of the constancy hypothesis may justifiably be considered an incipient phenomenological reduction.

Because Gestalt theory is led to the concept of noema, those of its notions and results which refer to the phenomenal data of immediate experience acquire phenomenological significance and validity. Analyses pursued along the lines of Gestalt theory prove to be noematic analyses. To submit a percept to an analysis of that kind does not mean decomposing it into elements in the traditional sense. Rather, such analysis aims at disengaging the components and constituents as essentially determined and defined by the role which they play for the total structure of the percept. It means the disclosure of their specific significance for, and contribution towards, that which, through the given act of perception, presents itself, taken exactly as it actually

38. Cf. above, p. 102.
39. Cf. above, pp. 95ff.

appears. Briefly it amounts to the disclosure of the components as *noematic* constituents.

Analyses of this style may well be characterized as descriptive. This characterization certainly purports faithful rendering of the experienced phenomena. However it purports still more. The *perceptum qua perceptum*—and, quite in general, the *cogitatum qua cogitatum*—must be analyzed and described solely on its own grounds and merits, without any reference to an extra-phenomenal reality. To express the point more precisely, no extra-phenomenal reality may be admitted as basis or presupposition of the descriptive analysis, nor may it be permitted to intervene "from without" in such an analysis. The only form in which an extra-phenomenal reality may come to play a role is that of a reference to such a reality being actually displayed as a phenomenal feature. In other words, if a *cogitatum qua cogitatum* actually points and refers beyond itself, this pointing reference may, and must, be disclosed and disengaged exactly as, and in precisely the sense in which, it is exhibited by, and contained in, the phenomenon under consideration. This condition is fulfilled in the perceptual experience of material things. Through every single perception, the perceived thing appears in a one-sided manner of presentation: it presents itself from a certain side, under a certain aspect, in a certain orientation—e.g., as near or remote, as lying straight ahead or as located more or less sideways, etc.[40] Every such one-sided perceptual presentation, however, contains references beyond itself to further perceptual appearances of the self-same thing under different aspects, from other sides, in different orientations, and so on. In a descriptive analysis along the lines of Gestalt theory, the perceived thing must be taken exactly as it is given and appears through the single perception under examination. By virtue of the descriptive orientation of the analysis, this implies that allowance must be made for the mentioned references beyond itself which the single perceptual appearance in question displays as phenomenal features of its own. Thus we find ourselves confronted with the problem of the relationship between the *thing as it appears,* viz., through a single perception, and the *thing as it really is,* i.e., the thing under the systematically organized and intrinsically coherent totality of its possible aspects. On the very grounds of Gestalt theory, there arises the task of accounting for things as they really are in terms of things as they are experienced, meant, intended, given in actual or

40. This is Husserl's theory of perceptual adumbration. Cf. his *Ideen* §§ 41ff., 97f., 135, 149f.; his *Cartesian Meditations*, §§ 17ff.; and his *Erfahrung und Urteil* (Hamburg, 1954), § 8.

potential perceptual presentation: i.e., in terms of perceptual noemata. In other words, we are brought before the transcendental problems of constitution, the very problems with which phenomenology is concerned. In this context, the role of the dismissal of the constancy hypothesis functioning as a phenomenological reduction in germinal form becomes most manifest. At the same time, it appears that, in order to be made philosophically fruitful, the dismissal of the constancy hypothesis has to be developed beyond the incipient stage into the phenomenological reduction in the full sense of the term.

# 5 / Critical Study
## of Husserl's *Nachwort*[1]

HUSSERL'S *Ideen zu einer reinen Phänomenologie und phänomenologischen Philosophie* appeared in the year 1913. In the recent "Postscript" (*Nachwort*) (identical with the Foreword to the English edition of 1931), Husserl explicates the *Ideen*, it is true, but only in reference to a few major points. This self-explication is naturally limited in its range. Husserl stresses there what he saw as essentially new and, understood in a radical sense, as philosophical in the enterprise initiated as a first beginning, according to his own words, but with full awareness of the goal.

Indeed, the *Ideen* signifies a decisive turning point as well in the history of Husserl's phenomenology. In essential parts of the *Logische Untersuchungen*, which appeared in 1900–1901 (in the Prolegomena as well as in the first four Investigations), the concern was still "pure logic": the self-sufficiency belonging to the logical sphere as a sphere of ideal Being, the rejection of naturalizing and psychologizing the logical itself, recognition of its own peculiar nature, its independence over against the reduction of logical, ideal unities and entities to dispersed multiplicities of real psychic contents. The elaboration of the logical itself as to its proper nature—carried out in explicit debate against contemporary logic as well as against classical British philosophy—culminates in the plan of a *mathesis universalis*, a completed part of which Husserl offered in the third Logical Investigation ("On the Doctrine of Wholes and Parts"). In the last two Logical Investigations, however, Husserl is no longer oriented, in a direct and

1. This article, originally published in *Deutsche Literaturzeitung* (1932), criticially discusses E. Husserl, "Nachwort zu meinen 'Ideen zu einer reinen Phänomenologie und phänomenologischen Philosophie,' " in *Jahrbuch für Philosophie und phänomenologische Forschung* (Halle, 1930), XI, pp. 549–70.

straightforward manner, towards ideal unities, ideal states of affairs, and the like in order to formulate pure and simple predicative propositions about them. Instead, especially in the Sixth Investigation, dedicated to "phenomenological clarification of knowledge," the thematic view is reflectively directed to consciousness of idealities, to the different ways in which species and the logical in general are intended, when they are "emptily" or only symbolically meant, and in particular to the ways in which they offer themselves in bodily presence in "categorial intuition." Here, too, Husserl takes up the problems of the coincidence of intending and meaning acts and the intuitions "fulfilling" them—phenomena of "fulfillment" standing under the headings of "truth" and "evidence."

These expositions reach their climax with the introduction of the concept of "categorial intuition" along with its differentiation from "sensuous intuition." With these positive demonstrations, Husserl finally and definitively refutes the traditional and classical theories of abstraction. The motive for this turning from the things themselves to consciousness-of-the-things was formulated by Husserl as follows in the introductory remarks in the second volume of the *Logische Untersuchungen:* one cannot be satisfied with "developing pure logic merely in the same way as our mathematical disciplines, viz., as a system of propositions established with naïve-material [*naivsachlich*] validity; instead, along with this one must strive for philosophical clarity concerning those propositions—i.e., for insight into the essence of the ways of knowledge coming into play together with the effectuation and ideally possible applications of such propositions, for insight also into the sense-bestowings and objective validities essentially constituting themselves through the ways of knowledge." With these words the setting of the problem for the *Ideen* is already prepared.

In the *Ideen* there is also a concern, this time exclusively, for consciousness. Consciousness is understood eidetically as the "eidos consciousness-at-large," so that each *de facto* consciousness, each *de facto* mental state, is considered only as a case of, as an example of, consciousness-at-large as well as of its genera or species (e.g., perception, memory, phantasy [*Phantasie*], and, again, color perception, sound perception, etc.). From its being *factual,* no act of consciousness derives any privilege or priority over what is merely conceived or phantasied, i.e., possible consciousness. The eidetic inquiry into consciousness and all its most universal structures is effected now, however, in an attitude which is radically changed over against attitudes pertaining to "natural life" as well as to the positive sciences. As Husserl emphasizes in the *Nachwort,* everything rests on the comprehension of this change in attitude which was already now and then practiced in the *Logische Untersuchungen*—but which was not explicitly characterized as such prior to the *Ideen*—and on whose meaning as well as import the greatest stress is laid.

The existential thesis, in which the world, in "natural life" as well as in the positive sciences, is simply there for me and accepted by me loses its unquestionable validity through the *"transcendental-phenomenological reduction."* I do not draw into doubt the universal existential thesis, nor do I modalize it in the sense that I concede to the world existence of lesser certainty than that thesis claims. I only set out of action the universal existential thesis; I practice an *epoché* over against it, without modifying it as it is continuously present to me. Setting out of action the otherwise continuously operative and naïvely accepted natural existential thesis opens up the possibility for the disclosure and thematic treatment of a wholly new, infinitely extended realm of Being which, for the most part, remains concealed in the attitude of the positive sciences no less than in "natural life": the realm of pure consciousness, the "world of consciousness purely as such," comes into the field of view of the phenomenologist. Instead of abiding by existing and unquestionably accepted things *per se,* as phenomenologists we turn to phenomena and concatenations of phenomena in which those things appear in transcendentally purified consciousness and present themselves as just the things which they are also in the natural attitude—i.e., as *actually existing things.* Under the phenomenological *epoché* we deal with thing-phenomena, with "things" just as they appear, and within the limits in which they appear, but also *only within these limits and in the manners of their appearing.* In other words, the world yields its place to the "world-phenomenon," the latter to be taken *precisely in the way, but also only in the way, in which it is a world-phenomenon.* That is to say, it is taken as a world-phenomenon carrying in itself the claim to existential validity in the sense of the natural existential thesis.

Performance of the transcendental-phenomenological reduction opens up the possibility for a radical formulation and treatment of philosophical problems beyond merely tracing them back to their roots and pursuing them to their very origins. Nothing is unquestionably accepted as matter of course; whatever lays claim to existence and validity is put under the obligation of legitimating itself in transcendental consciousness. The latter is the only Being absolute, a "first-in-itself" and irreducible, as already appears from its resisting Descartes' attempt at universal doubt—an attempt guided by different motives and directed toward other goals. Whatever claims existence and validity must legitimate this claim by showing itself as that which it claims to be. Thus the sense of the claim to existence in general and, more particularly, all possible claims—i.e., claims to existence in every conceivably possible sense (existence of physical things, of real psychological events as well as all modes of existence comprised under the heading of ideal existence and admitting further distinctions and differentiations)—are clarified and legitimated by constitutional phenomenological inquiries (under the heading of "Phenomenology of Reason") in the field of pure consciousness. The sense of existence at large is disclosed. The sense in which objects pertaining to the several regions can legitimately be said to exist (in the final analysis, the sense of existence of the very regions themselves) is also disclosed. This occurs by means of investigating intentional consciousness *of:* its teleology, the teleological productions issuing from its intentionality. Such investigations are oriented towards, and guided by, the objective entities which in the natural and all quasi-natural (e.g., mathematical) attitudes (i.e., objectively directed attitudes) are unquestionably accepted. That is to say, those objective entities function as "ontological clues" for constitutional phenomenological inquiries.

With this philosophizing, starting from an "absolute beginning," grounded in an "ultimate foundation," and inspired by "ultimate self-responsibility," which does not rely upon any pre-given and matter-of-course point of departure, Husserl renewed and radicalized the λόγον δ/δόναι of Plato in the sense of a truly absolute "autonomy of knowledge."

*"Transcendental-phenomenological idealism"* arises in the manifold and manifoldly directed inquiries made possible on the basis of "transcendental subjectivity" uncovered by the "reduction." This "idealism" is radically different from the historical forms of idealism, especially from "psychological idealism," in that it does not formulate a philosophical standpoint. It does not take issue with the natural existential thesis, nor does it modify it in such a way that in a new thesis the existence meant in the natural one is degraded to mere appearance in some respect or other. In no way does it maintain that what the natural existential thesis refers to is not true Being, which must be sought for elsewhere. No *thesis about existence* is formulated at all and, hence, no counter-thesis is formulated over against the "realistic" one. The reason for this is that the transcendental-phenomenological reduction only puts the natural existential thesis out of operation; but in no way and in no sense does it affect it. Scheler misunderstands just this reduction when he maintains that the specific reality-character of the real world is canceled by it and that something like a realm of pure essences results, freed from the weight

of reality.[2] This misunderstanding rests on the confusion of the eidetic with the transcendental reduction. Both have so little to do with each other that even in the natural attitude or in the positive-scientific attitude we make continuous use of the one (the eidetic reduction) when we speak in the mode of the "at large" (*Überhaupt*), e.g., when we speak about melody at large, a melody of a certain type, a mathematical function in general, the state at large, the species red, etc., without ever having to resort to transcendentally purified consciousness. On the other hand, performance of the transcendental without the eidetic reduction discloses the flow of "my" transcendentally purified mental states in phenomenal time, without stating anything in the mode of essential universality about these mental states and their interconnections.

It is not a matter of advocating an "idealistic" thesis over against a "realistic" one, but a question of clarifying the sense of existence of which we continuously make use in the non-phenomenological attitude. As truly existing, the world remains existing and in no respect is it interpreted as a mere sham world; but the sense in which it is accepted as existing and the right with which it is thus accepted come to radical and evident explication. Thus we reach a level above the traditional conflict between realism and idealism which moves in the opposition of thesis and counter-thesis; positive constitutional analyses and discoveries take the place of "arguments." When we speak of idealism here, that is because transcendental consciousness proves to be the only and unique realm of absolute Being. All other entities are constituted in sense-bestowings of phenomenological consciousness, are intentional correlates of sense-unities and sense-concatenations, and prove to be, seen in this way, relative to "transcendental subjectivity." The latter can be called the primal basis for all legitimacy and validity; this "transcendental subjectivity" itself is—as Husserl now says—" 'irrelative,' " i.e., relative only to itself.

The transcendental phenomenological reduction, moreover, underlies the difference between phenomenology and every kind of psychology, even descriptive and "phenomenological psychology." Husserl stresses this distinction again, while at the same time he emphasizes the reform of psychology implied in transcendental phenomenology. This reform depends on further developing (in the correct direction) the concept of *intentionality* introduced by Brentano as the basic concept of descriptive psychology and on the actual and concrete

2. Cf. M. Scheler, "Realismus-Idealismus," *Philosophischer Anzeiger*, II (Bonn, 1927), pp. 281f.; Scheler, *Die Wissensformen und die Gesellschaft* (Leipzig, 1926), pp. 352f.

utilization of the new conception of consciousness which Brentano made possible with his doctrine. Intentionality is not a property which belongs to mental states as coloredness pertains to natural things: intentionality is not a natural property of consciousness at all, since consciousness is radically distinct from nature. Consciousness can be conceived as essentially intentional only when intentionality is understood as *productive intentionality (leistende Intentionalität)*, i.e., seen in its *teleological function*. "The genuine psychology of intentionality," resulting in its reformed shape from transcendental phenomenology, ". . . proves to be nothing other than constitutive phenomenology in the natural attitude." Psychology of intentionality is oriented towards an object, meant as identically the same, which appears as such in a multiplicity of subjective processes directed to it. The one and self-same object comes to present itself in, and endures throughout, this very multiplicity, appearing from various sides, in different orientations, manners of givenness, with varying existential characters, in different modes of "position-taking of the ego," etc. Just this appearing and presenting itself, enduring, etc., fashion the theme of the psychology of intentionality. Its radical opposition to nature is grounded in the fact that consciousness is essentially intentionally productive. On that account consciousness cannot be described and investigated in the same way as nature; it is not even sufficient to introduce intentionality as an additional descriptive fundamental concept. On this basis Husserl directs the reproach of "psychological naturalism" against the traditional descriptive psychology of "sense data" which goes back to Locke. He has in view the whole of contemporary psychology. Even Gestalt psychology is referred to the Lockean school, since "stated in terms of principle, it makes no difference whether one allows psychic data to "'atomistically' drift together like sanddunes. . . , or whether one takes them as parts of wholes which, be it in empirical or *a priori* necessity, can only be given as such parts." If one further considers the fact that the psychology of sense data conceives sense data in (as one must say today) a thoroughly constructive manner, orienting them to the generating stimuli, so that a strict correspondence and parallelism obtains between stimuli and sensations, then one understands that psychology as such persists in the natural attitude, positing the "human ego" as "real object" in the pre-given world and allowing it to undergo manifold influences from that world. Such a procedure might be entirely legitimate in psychology as a "science in the dogmatic attitude." Yet on this very account, psychology proves to be totally different from transcendental phenomenology, and it becomes fully clear that (and why) psychology cannot function as the basis of philosophy if the philosophical motive is that of radical presuppositionlessness.

By referring Gestalt psychology to the Lockean tradition, Husserl overlooks its essential novelty. It is not a question of a new theory or description of sense data when Wertheimer opposes the "Gestalt thesis" to the "bundle thesis." [3] It seems that Husserl, in the statement cited above,[4] has that opposition alone in view. This opposition acquires its full and concrete sense only in connection with the relinquishment of the constancy hypothesis.[5] As a consequence of this relinquishment, the description and investigation of what is given to consciousness is emancipated from considerations concerning constellations of stimuli. What is given must be taken and described at face value. No knowledge of objective things and events, no considerations as to what "must" occur, given certain stimuli, and the relations between them, must influence pure description. The latter must not be modified nor obscured by what we learn about the world from the natural sciences. So little is it a matter of a new thesis concerning "sense data," or even of the assertion that sense data only exist as "parts of wholes," that the concept of sense data itself, as well as that of parts in general, becomes a problem for Gestalt psychology. In the final analysis, when the consequences of the relinquishment of the constancy hypothesis are pursued to their ultimate conclusion, even the very concept of stimulus becomes a problem. Just that in which Husserl sees the significance of the *epoché*—exclusion of all knowledge resting on everyday experience of the world and of all knowledge derived from the positive sciences, an exclusion combined with the disclosure of the "world of consciousness purely as such"—is attained by the relinquishment of the constancy hypothesis. This relinquishment has a function and significance for Gestalt theory which is similar to the transcendental phenomenological reduction within Husserl's phenomenology. To be sure, Husserl has developed his theory of the reduction with the utmost methical consciousness of the goals to be reached and under explicit emphasis of the principles involved.

The differences between Gestalt theory and phenomenology are indisputable and have their basis in the fact that Gestalt theory is psychology, while Husserl's phenomenology aims at, and prepares the

3. M. Wertheimer, "Untersuchungen zur Lehre von der Gestalt, I," *Psychologische Forschung,* I (1922).

4. Husserl, "Nachwort," *loc. cit.,* p. 565.

5. Cf. W. Köhler, "Über unbemerkte Empfindungen und Urteilstäuschungen," *Zeitschrift für Psychologie,* LXVI (1913).

ground for, a universal philosophical science. Notwithstanding these differences resulting from divergencies of general theoretical orientation, there is a common ground for these two lines of inquiry upon which they meet one another and upon which they can be further developed, the one with the help of the other. Precisely the problems dealt with in the first and, up to now, only volume of the *Ideen* lie upon this common ground.[6] Furthermore, Gestalt-theoretical investigations which are not limited to "normal adult civilized men" but extend to animals (Köhler), children (Koffka, K. Lewin), and brain-injured patients (Gelb and Goldstein) and which allow for Lévy-Bruhl's work on primitive mentality lead to problems which are also of significance for Husserl's phenomenology, although he has not pursued them. This extension of the investigations can and even must be carried out in an attitude which does not presuppose any pregiven "objectivity."

Although the natural world falls to the *epoché*, it plays the role of an "ontological clue" for constitutive phenomenology, since the contents of the world, such as natural objects, objects of value, animals, men, social institutions, etc., are the correlates of the corresponding teleologically productive intentionalities. But what is the natural world —just as *natural* and not already interpreted in theoretical terms? What is the mode of existence of its contents, and how are these to be suitably characterized? Further, what is the sense of that natural existential thesis which is put out of operation in the *epoché* and of which we make continuous use in natural life? And, finally, what is this natural life itself, and by what is it essentially characterized? In the present *Nachwort* Husserl does not enter into these problems related to a "systematical, all-embracing description, exhaustive in breadth and depth, of whatever is encountered in the natural attitude," which he had designated in the *Ideen* itself as a "highly important, scientific task scarcely seen up to now," problems which have become acute in present-day philosophic discussions in Germany. This omission is probably explained by the fact that this *Nachwort* was used as the Foreword to the English edition of the *Ideen,* and that the situation of English philosophy is very different from the German. Hence, we confine ourselves here to mere mention of those problems. As to Husserl's defense against the reproach of "intellectualism," his defense seems to us superfluous because the reproach itself is pointless. Philosophy as clarification of the world and, more particu-

6. See below, "Phenomenology of Thematics and of the Pure Ego," pp. 175–286, in which the attempt has been made, on the basis of an awareness of this common ground, to develop certain problems in Husserl's phenomenology by means of views drawn from Gestalt theory.

larly, as clarification in a radical sense—in which alone the clarification deserves to be called philosophical—can by its very nature be nothing else than "intellectualistic" because clarity and clarification are precisely matters of intellect.

TRANSLATED BY FREDERICK KERSTEN

# 6 / The Problem of Existence
## in Constitutive Phenomenology [1]

IN THIS DISCUSSION the term "phenomenology" will be used to refer to Husserl's constitutive phenomenology and not to later philosophical trends, which, whatever their kinship with Husserl's phenomenology, have developed in somewhat different directions. First, a brief sketch of the fundamental principles of phenomenology with special regard to the problem of existence will be presented. Next, the terms will be set forth in which ontological problems can be treated in phenomenology. Last, two ontological theses will be submitted.

## [I]

PROBLEMS REGARDING BEING and existence have concerned phenomenology since its beginnings. As early as in *Logische Untersuchungen,* Husserl's interest in these problems is manifest. There he raises the question of the ontological status of "general objects" (universals), meanings, concatenations of meanings, numbers, and other ideal entities. Ascribing to them an ontological status of their own, Husserl refuses to conceive of existence at large after the model of two special types of existence and modes of being: the one particular to material things, the other to psychological acts and events as interpreted in the empiricist tradition. Ontological interests prevail still more in *Ideen,* the key work of constitutive phenomenology. This prevalence appears not only in Husserl's conception of formal and material ontologies and his notion of regional ontologies

1. Presented in a symposium on "Phenomenology" at the 58th annual meeting of the American Philosophical Association, Eastern Division, December 29, 1961, and published in the *Journal of Philosophy,* LVIII (1961).

[116]

but also, and mainly, in the very goal that he set for constitutive phenomenology and to which he devoted all his subsequent philosophical endeavors.

One may formulate this goal as that of giving an account of objects of every description (perceptual material things; cultural objects or objects of value like tools, books, and the like; constructs of science; ideal entities of any sort; and so on) and of treating objectivity in every conceivable sense in subjective terms, that is to say, in terms of acts of consciousness. Objects (this term is to be understood in the broadest and most comprehensive sense) appear to us through acts of consciousness and especially through systematically organized concatenations and groupings of such acts. Through systematically concatenated acts, objects present themselves to us as those which they are for us, as what we take and accept them for in our several mental activities—practical, theoretical, artistic, and the like. Through acts of consciousness, objects not only exhibit their qualities and properties but also reveal themselves as real or existent; they present themselves as existing in a certain specific mode, viz., that mode which is characteristic of, and peculiar to, a certain order of existence and in which objects must exist if they are to pertain to that order under consideration.

It must be noted that the converse is also true. We have no way of access to objects, beings, objectivity, or existence other than through acts of consciousness and experience—the term "experience" like the term "object" being understood in the broadest sense and by no means confined, as traditional empiricism has it, to the presence of sense data. Whatever object we consider is for us what it is experienced as. It refers to an organized and systematized multiplicity of acts and processes. Some of these acts play a privileged role—those, namely, which function as primordial apprehensions and genuine presentations of their objects. In the case of real things pertaining to the external world, this privileged role is played by acts of perception in contradistinction to acts of memory, expectation, mere representation, and the like. As far as their cognitive or presentational function is concerned, the latter acts may be characterized as "derivative" in comparison with perception.

Raising ontological problems, therefore, means, on phenomenological grounds, embarking upon investigations of acts of consciousness, especially the privileged acts of genuine apprehension, through which the object in question presents itself as existing and from which it derives the specific meaning of its existence. There obtains a thoroughgoing strict correlation between objects and intertextures of acts of consciousness, so that Husserl speaks of an "equivalent of consciousness" with respect to every object.

Sketchy and superficial though the preceding outline of constitutive phenomenology certainly is, it suffices, perhaps, to show that, if Husserl and those who follow him engage in detailed, painstaking, and sometimes even minute descriptions and analyses of both consciousness in general and special classes of acts—perception, imagination, abstraction, etc.—they do so for the very sake of an ultimate clarification and account of objectivity. Consciousness is the subject matter of phenomenology and even its exclusive subject matter. However, consciousness commands a paramount interest exactly as the universal and only medium of access to objects. In phenomenology, consciousness is throughout considered in this light, that is, under the aspect of its presentational function. This appears most clearly in the theory of the intentionality of consciousness, a theory of such fundamental importance that its complete elaboration in all its ramifications may be said to be tantamount to the full development of phenomenological philosophy.

By the same token, an apparent paradox seems to find an explanation. Notwithstanding his prevalent interest in objectivity—a concept which assumes with him a great many differentiations—Husserl never wrote a treatise on ontology. What is more, in none of his writings do we find an ontological theory developed in a systematic and sustained fashion and presented under the heading of ontology. The explanation of this fact seems to me to lie in the very orientation of constitutive phenomenology. Given the nature of such a phenomenology, no ontological inquiry is to be pursued directly; the inquiry must proceed, so to speak, in an oblique manner. Whatever ontological results are attained, they are obtained as by-products, though much desired and searched for, of investigations bearing upon and concerned with subjective conscious life. In fact, if consciousness is recognized as the universal and only medium of access to whatever exists, there is no longer the possibility of approaching being and existence directly and immediately. There remains but the approach by way of the experience and consciousness of being and existence.

## [II]

WHICH, THEN, are the terms in which ontological problems are to be stated on phenomenological grounds?

1. Phenomenology does not aim at discovering a realm of being behind, beneath, or beyond (in any conceivable sense) the perceptual

world of everyday experience or apart from some other order of existence already familiar to pre-philosophical mental activity. It does not claim a special philosophical "intuition" enabling one to penetrate into a "new world" accessible only to such "intuition" but otherwise not open to sight. Nor does phenomenology set out to construct such a "new world." Its procedure is neither speculative nor constructive. What phenomenology endeavors to do is to *clarify* the concept of existence and the different though, perhaps, somewhat related meanings which that concept assumes with respect to the several orders of existence with which we concern ourselves: the existence of real things belonging to the perceptual world, mathematical existence, existence of propositions, and so on. With the notions of being and existence, we are in a situation repeatedly described by Plato, which is neither that of complete and full knowledge nor that of total ignorance. Undoubtedly, the words in question have meaning for us, but their meaning is inexplicit, penumbral, obfuscated.

2. On phenomenological grounds, clarification is not to be expected from "formal" procedures—that is, by setting up a tentative definition which is then progressively amended, corrected, and refined so as to meet certain demands and requirements, however plausible and well founded. Neither can the desired clarification be expected from an analysis of the use of the mentioned terms in ordinary discourse, since it is just as they are used in ordinary discourse that those terms are in obvious need of clarification. Here, as everywhere, phenomenological clarification demands that concepts be confronted with the entities to which they refer, as these entities present themselves in genuine, primordial, and aboriginal apprehension. The yieldings of such apprehensions, and those yieldings alone, determine the justified and legitimate meaning of the concept to be clarified. In other words, the more or less symbolic and empty concept, whose meaning is inexplicit and somehow obscure, is measured and gauged by the concept fulfilled. Such fulfillment is brought about by the appearance of the entity meant in itself—that is, its appearance in the form of bodily presence. With respect to the notions of existence and being, this demands, as mentioned before, inquiry into the intertexture of acts of consciousness through which an object presents itself as existing in a certain mode.

3. The phenomenologist must abstain from operating with any preconceived notions of what "true being" and—most closely related hereto—"true knowledge" are; when one does so operate, then, in the name of such preconceived notions, other modes of being are denied ontological status altogether. This applies to the style of metaphysics developed in the 17th century in intimate connection with the rise of

modern physical science. As Husserl has shown in his posthumously published book *Die Krisis der Europäischen Wissenschaften und die transzendentale Phänomenologie,* perhaps the most fundamental presupposition of that metaphysics was the view, taken for granted, that mathematical knowledge represented the ideal and the norm of "true knowledge." Referred to this standard, the perceptual world as it is familiar in everyday experience came to be considered a mere subjective appearance concealing or, at the most, pointing to an underlying "true" reality to be conceived as a mathematical manifold. In a phenomenological orientation, every form of knowledge and every mode of being must be treated on its own grounds and merits. Different orders of existence have already been mentioned. There are also different levels of objectivity and even different worlds in another sense. These may be illustrated by the following enumeration: the world of the child (much information of an ontological nature may also be derived from the writings of Jean Piaget); the world of our historico-cultural group as distinguished from the worlds of other such groups, both contemporary and belonging to the historical past; the world in the sense of the life-world common to the whole human race and invariant with respect to the conceptions that change from one cultural-historical group to another—here, I submit, would be a possible starting point for a new interpretation of Aristotelian science. Treating those different worlds and different levels of objectivity on their own grounds and merits in no way implies treating them on a par. There can be no question of "relativism," and the distinction between objectivity of a higher level and that of a lower level must not be blurred. Yet the question arises: what is the basis for the superiority of the former and the ground of this superiority? This question concerns the very meaning of that superiority. It appears that objectivity of a higher level is founded upon and in this sense presupposes objectivity of a lower level. In any event, no mode of existence related to objectivity in a higher sense may be permitted to pass for the "only mode of true existence" so as to eclipse totally what in respect to it may be considered an "inferior mode of existence."

4. As mentioned before, the distinction between different orders of existence was introduced rather early by Husserl and was never relinquished. Still, in the last period of his life—the first literary document of that period being the *Formale und transzendentale Logik* of 1929—Husserl insisted upon what he called the life-world (*Lebenswelt*) as *the* fundamental order of existence. By life-world is meant the world as we encounter it in everyday experience, the world in which we pursue our goals and objectives, the world as the scene of all our human activities. Not only must the life-world be distinguished

from the universe of science in the specific modern sense—the universe of science being constructed and not immediately experienced—but the experience of the life-world, which is perceptual experience, must be taken in its original immediacy, i.e., as we have it independently of, and prior to, conceptualization of any kind. For this reason Husserl speaks of pre-predicative experience. As the fundamental order of existence, the life-world underlies all other orders, including the conceptual orders like those of logic and mathematics; also the several artistic domains belong here. On phenomenological grounds, all orders of existence have to be accounted for in terms of specific acts and functions of consciousness. But—and herein the privileged status of the life-world becomes manifest—the mental functions in question operate upon and in this sense presuppose findings encountered in the life-world. Though orders of existence other than the life-world preserve their specific nature and also their autonomy with respect to the life-world, they can be understood only on the basis of the latter. In accounting for them, one has to start from the life-world. Because of the privileged status of the life-world, the theory of perception plays a prominent role in the writings of Husserl as well as other phenomenological authors.

## [III]

LET US NOW TURN for a moment to the phenomenological theory of perception. Through every single perception, the thing perceived presents itself by way of what Husserl calls "one-sided adumbration." The thing is perceived from a certain standpoint; it appears under a certain aspect, in a certain orientation, from a certain side, etc. On the other hand, every single perception is a perceptual apprehension and experience of the thing itself. The theme of even a single perception is not the aspect under which the thing appears, as though there were no difference between a one-sided perception of a thing and the appearance of a visual phantom. On the contrary, the theme of an act of perception is the very thing itself, although, through a single perceptual act, it is given in a one-sided manner of presentation. Every single perception thus points and refers beyond itself to further perceptions through which the thing will present itself under aspects different from its present manner of appearance. To express the point differently, every perception is interwoven with anticipations of what further perceptions will yield. Such anticipations may be more or less indeterminate and vague, but they are never totally devoid of all specification. The "equivalent of consciousness" related to a perceivable thing is not a single perception but is a systematically organized group, i.e., a perceptual process whose intrinsic coherence consists in the harmony and agreement among all its phases. Later phases confirm anticipations that had been more or less vague and empty. Throughout the perceptual process, the thing in question appears under a multiplicity of varying aspects which are not only compatible with, but also fit into, one another. The identity and existence of the thing, its being in reality what it appears to be at a certain phase of the perceptual process, depend upon or, if one prefers, correspond to, the perceptual process developing harmoniously, all its phases mutually continuing and confirming one another. However, from the fact that a certain perceptual process has thus far developed harmoniously, no guarantee, no certainty can be derived of its continuing thus to develop in the future. Not only is it sometimes necessary to correct details, but in principle there is also the possibility of a disintegration of a perceptual process—any process—so that the yieldings of its several phases would no longer fit together. In such a case, the process itself would lose its coherence and unity. Rather than experiencing *one* sustained process, the subject would be confronted with a succession of unrelated and disconnected perceptual appearances. This possibility defines in an important respect the ontological condition of real things insofar as it shows their existence to be affected by an essential contingency. Real things have but presumptive existence. They can be posited as existent only with the proviso that later phases of the perceptual process will be in harmony and agreement with one another and with earlier phases. This consequence of the phenomenological theory of perception substantiates and confirms Leibniz's contention of the essentially contingent nature of the *vérités de faits* related to real things and events, truths whose opposite never implies a contradiction or absurdity.

To conclude this discussion, a few remarks about the notion "order of existence." It is here taken to denote a systematic context of objects —this term understood in the broadest possible sense—which, on account of their qualitative determinations and very natures, have something to do with, are related to, one another or, to express it more generally, have relevancy for one another. Orders of existence are constituted by, and have unity on the strength of, specific *principles of relevancy*. Accordingly, orders of existence differ from one another by their underlying constitutive relevancy principles. In my book *The Field of Consciousness* I have endeavored to substantiate the thesis that the notion of existence contains a necessary and essential reference to that of order of existence. For an object—of any description whatever—to exist means that it is inserted into a context based upon and, therefore, dominated by, a specific relevancy principle. *Existence means existence within a system* at a certain place in the latter and, hence, in well-defined relationships with other objects pertaining to the same systematic context. To illustrate, one may refer to mathematical existence and, more specifically, to the system of natural numbers. Every number holds a definite place within the system; one might even go so far as to say that a number is nothing but a certain place within that systematic context. In any event, the number has its existence among, with reference to, and *only* with reference to, other members of the system in question. As to reality, i.e., the perceptual world of everyday experience, the most general underlying relevancy principle is spatio-temporality. For an object or event to be real, it must occur at a certain place in time and space and, hence, in definite spatio-temporal relations to other real objects and events. The object in question thus appears with reference to the world, as pertaining to it, as mundane. Its mundaneity belongs to the very meaning of its existence. On the other hand, there is no possible experience of the world except from the vantage point of a concrete mundane object or situation. Correspondingly the same can be asserted with regard to all other orders of existence generally.

It is the phenomenological analysis of the horizonal structure of consciousness that leads to this ontological thesis. When we deal with an object and choose it as the theme of our mental activity—of whatever kind our mental activity may be—our conscious life is never confined to the exclusive experience of our theme. At the time of our dealing with the theme, we are aware, in varying degrees of clarity and explicitness, of other objects and events. Our theme presents itself in a total field of consciousness. Within that field, a line of demarcation must be drawn between those items which merely happen to be co-present with our theme and those which, in addition to being co-present with the theme, are experienced as intrinsically related or relevant to it. The totality of the co-present items of the second class may be said to form the *thematic field* with respect to the given theme which occupies the center of that field. Thus we perceive a thing amidst other things, i.e., in a certain perceptual surrounding. A proposition that engrosses our mind refers and points to other propositions from which it follows as their consequence. An order of existence turns out to be an indefinite extension of a thematic field. Conversely, a concrete thematic field may be regarded as a circumscribed segment of an order of existence. It is the emergence of every theme from a thematic field and its experienced appearance within such a field that determine the meaning of the existence of every object as existence within a systematic context or order of existence.

# 7 / On the Intentionality of Consciousness[1]

THE INTENTIONALITY of consciousness may be defined as a relation which all, or at least certain, acts bear to an object. In this manner, Brentano introduced the notion into contemporary philosophy. Seeking to account for the difference between what he calls "physical phenomena" and what he calls "psychical phenomena," Brentano found, among other characteristics, that the latter are distinguished by a relation to, or a direction towards, an object.[2] This directedness of psychical phenomena is interpreted by Brentano as their containing within themselves an "immanent" object-like entity. Although Husserl takes over Brentano's notion of intentionality, he raises some objections against this interpretation.[3] His examination of Brentano's conception of intentionality finally leads him to abandon it completely; but he agrees with Brentano in acknowledging the existence of a highly important class of mental facts—for which Husserl reserves the title of acts—which have the peculiarity of presenting an object to the subject.[4] Experiencing an act, the subject is aware of an object, so that the act may be characterized, as Husserl shows, as a *consciousness of* an object whether real or ideal, whether existent or imaginary.

1. This article was originally published in *Philosophical Essays in Memory of Edmund Husserl*, ed. M. Farber (Cambridge, Mass.: Harvard University Press, 1940). Copyright © 1940 by the President and Fellows of Harvard College. Reprinted by permission of the publishers.
2. F. Brentano, *Psychologie vom empirischen Standpunkt*, ed. O. Kraus (Leipzig, 1924), Book II, chap. I, para. 5.
3. E. Husserl, *Logische Untersuchungen* (Halle, 1913), II, v, §§ 9–11; Husserl, *Ideen zu einer reinen Phänomenologie und phänomenologischen Philosophie* (Halle, 1929), § 90. Lack of space forbids us to summarize Husserl's criticism of Brentano's doctrine; some essential differences between Brentano's and Husserl's conceptions are emphasized by L. Landgrebe, "Husserl's Phänomenologie und die Motive zu ihrer Umbildung," in *Revue Internationale de Philosophie*, I.
4. Husserl, *Logische Untersuchungen*, II, p. 378.

This peculiarity, however, ought not to be considered as a real quality or as a real property of acts, such, for example, as intensity, which is held by many psychologists to be a real property common to all sense data. In fact, one would be bestowing on an act a magic or at least mysterious power were one to ascribe to the act, under the heading of intentionality, a real quality which makes it transcend itself to seize an object belonging, as is the case in the perception of a real thing, to a universe external to the sphere of consciousness, to which the act, though endowed with the transcending quality, nevertheless remains tied. Conscious acts confront us with objects; experiencing such an act, the subject is aware of an object, and he is so aware owing to the reference the act bears in itself to the object. The objectivating function of consciousness is, however, a problem rather than a simple datum which one could content himself to take notice of. In fact, the objectivating function involves a whole complex set of problems. Out of these we choose the most elementary one. *To be aware of an object means that, in the present experience, one is aware of the object as being the same as that which one was aware of in the past experience, as the same as that which, generally speaking, one may be aware of in an indefinite number of presentative acts.* Identity in this sense is, no doubt, constitutive of objectivity (*Gegenständlichkeit*). But, even if considered on the most elementary level, the identity of objects, inasmuch as it is a conscious fact—and it is only for this reason that we have any knowledge of it and may talk of it—turns out to be an insoluble problem for the traditional conception of consciousness. We shall go on to show, if possible, that the treatment of this problem leads to a new conception of consciousness that is radically opposed to the traditional one.

## [I]   THE PROBLEM OF IDENTITY AS STATED BY HUME

LET US CONSIDER the problem of identity in its most accentuated form, as stated by Hume concerning perceptible things.

Following Locke and Berkeley, Hume asserts "that our ideas of bodies are nothing but collections formed by the mind of the ideas of the several distinct sensible qualities, of which objects are composed, and which we find to have a constant union with each other." [5] Now

---

5. D. Hume, *A Treatise of Human Nature*, ed. T. H. Green and T. H. Grose (London, 1890), I, pp. 505–6. Cf. J. Locke, *An Essay Concerning Human Understanding*, Book II, chap. XXIII, especially §§ 6, 14; G. Berkeley, *A Treatise Concerning the Principles of Human Knowledge*, in *Works*, ed. A. C. Fraser, Vol. I (Oxford, 1901), p. 258.

the "sensible qualities" in question are identified, by Hume as well as
by his predecessors, with the sensations which are produced in the
mind when a perceptual act is experienced; these "sensible qualities"
are taken for real elements, of which the perceptual experience is
composed; consequently they pass for real elements of consciousness
itself, i.e., for elements existing within consciousness. Hence the
object, being composed of the same data which figure in the perceptual experience, turns out to be a real element of this experience and
to coincide with it; at any rate, the object itself is also conceived to
exist within consciousness and to be a content of it. This thesis is
indeed defended by Hume. "Those very sensations, which enter by the
eye or ear, are . . . the true objects . . . there is only a single
existence, which I shall call indifferently *object* or *percep-*
*tion* . . . understanding by both of them what any common man
means by a hat, or shoe, or stone, or any other impression conveyed to
him by his senses." [6] This thesis is presented by Hume not as a result
of philosophical inquiry but as the opinion of the "vulgar," i.e., the
opinion of all of us, when, without philosophizing, we live in the
natural attitude and are concerned with any things we find in our
surroundings.

Nevertheless, a problem inevitably arises in this connection.
Taking up again the observation of a thing we have already observed
some time ago, as, for example, shutting and opening our eyes
alternately, we obtain a set of sense data. The latter may resemble
one another to a very high degree, yet they remain distinct from one
another and do not fuse, in any manner whatever, into a single one.
We can enumerate these multiple sense data by means of the
perceptual acts which we experience successively and to which
the data belong respectively. Nevertheless we believe—we do so as the
"vulgar"—that we are in the presence not of a set of objects, however
much they resemble one another, but of one single object appearing as
identically the same in every one of the successive experiences. In the
very face of the multiplicity of sense data, the identity of the object
and our belief in it must be accounted for, without forgetting that the
object is conceived as a complex composed of sense data. In these
terms Hume stated the problem, and the solution he adduced for it is
well known.[7] Because of the resemblance among the sense data, the
mind passes so smoothly and so easily from one to another that it is
scarcely aware of the transition. This resemblance puts the mind in a

6. Hume, *A Treatise of Human Nature*, I, p. 491.
7. *Ibid.*, p. 493: "The very image, which is present to the senses, is with us
the real body; and 'tis to these interrupted images we ascribe a perfect identity";
cf. pp. 491–94.

state similar to that in which it is when it surveys, without interruption, an unchangeable object for some time; this latter state gives rise to the idea of identity.[8] Thus, on account of the double resemblance, the mind mistakes similarity for identity. Whereas there is in fact only a succession of sense data, of which none, when it has disappeared, can be brought into existence again, the imagination misleads us to believe that such data, having ceased to appear, i.e., to exist, can return as the same when the interrupted observation is taken up again. The belief in the singleness of the perceived object rests on confounding resembling, yet distinct, sense data with identical ones.[9]

The mere presence to the mind of sensuous data composing an object is not sufficient for giving rise to the idea of its identity. Hume is perfectly right in emphasizing that the notion of identity needs that of time.[10] This means, in the case under discussion, that the object perceived now, after opening the eyes again, is held to be the same as that which appeared before shutting the eyes. Perceiving the object, the mind must recall previous perceptions; the impressions which are now present to the mind must be attended with ideas, which, although resembling the former at all points, differ from them, according to Hume's doctrine, with respect to force and vividness. In order to conceive identity, the mind must confront itself with a plurality of items. But as soon as it has done so, it must overlook not only the differences as to intensity but also, and chiefly, the fact that it has presented to itself a plurality of items. Since identity consists in the illusion of holding the resembling but distinct items to be a single one, the function of the imagination in producing this illusion is such as to abolish the condition that is indispensable to put the imagination into function.[11]

This illusion therefore can subsist only as long as the subject is inattentive to what really happens in his mind. The contradiction, however, between the experienced succession of sense data and the

8. We shall come back later to the identity of an object observed uninterruptedly for some time.

9. Cf. Hume, *A Treatise of Human Nature*, I, p. 535.

10. *Ibid.*, pp. 489–90.

11. In the excellent analysis which J. Laporte ("Le scepticisme de Hume," in the *Revue Philosophique de la France et de l'Étranger*, CXV [1933], pp. 92–101) gives of the passages of the *Treatise* referred to here, he emphasizes the stress Hume laid on the "operation" of the mind in producing the illusion of identity. Laporte's analysis, however, renders the more obvious the contradiction upon which we insist. The operation of the mind does not consist in making something out of the materials for which this operation is employed, as is the case when objects are united into an ensemble, when they are numbered, when a perceived matter of fact enters into a judgment and undergoes categorial formation, and so on. Here, on the contrary, the operation, as it were, has to make disappear, before the mind, the materials necessary to set it going.

irresistible propensity created by imagination to mistake them for a single and identical one is too striking to be overlooked. To disentangle itself from this contradiction, the imagination devises the further fiction of a "continued existence" ascribed to the "broken and interrupted appearances." [12] But this new fiction cannot help Hume, since only in case the identity of the object, perceived after the interruption with that perceived before it, has been established may the question be raised as to the existence of the object during the interruption.

The case is the same with the identity of an object observed for some time without interruption.[13] Under these circumstances, identity means "*invariableness* and *uninterruptedness* of any object, through a supposed variation of time." Variation of time implies succession and change, if not in the object in question, which is supposed to be permanent and unaltered, then in the co-existent objects. Nevertheless, the unchangeable object is imagined to participate in these changes, without suffering, in itself, any modification whatever.[14] Again, on the one hand, succession and variation of time must not only happen in fact but must also be experienced by consciousness, for otherwise there would be only a single permanent object, and the mind would be given the idea, not of identity, but of unity. On the other hand, the transition from one moment to another, which constitutes duration and variation of time, must scarcely be felt, no other perception or idea must be brought into play, in order that the disposition of the mind might be such as to continue surveying one permanent, unchangeable, identical object.[15] Variation of time must be felt, but not enough to produce any alteration in the mind's activity. Once more the operation of imagination is in contradiction to the very condition of this operation.

If Hume's explanation of identity is untenable, it is not because identity is held to be a "fiction," i.e., a creation of imagination. Had Hume contented himself with asserting that identity is no matter of sensibility but results from another mental faculty—namely, imagination—he would have advanced a two-factor theory of perception. Such a theory is, no doubt, open to criticism, but it cannot be rejected as inconsistent, the main objection which, it seems, is to be made against Hume's theory. His task is to account for the fact that the perceiving

12. Hume, *A Treatise of Human Nature*, I, pp. 494–97. We must disregard here Hume's account of continuous existence.

13. *Ibid.*, pp. 489–90.

14. It will be shown later that the "participation" of an object which stands before consciousness for some time, and which during this time is given as permanent and identical, in those changes which constitute its presence-time and its duration, is not a "fiction" but an immediately experienced fact.

15. Hume, *A Treatise of Human Nature*, I, p. 492.

subject, experiencing these impressions and by means of them, is aware of something identical, despite impressions being "internal and perishing existences," subject to variation of time, so that none of them when once passed can ever return.[16] But there is no room in Hume's doctrine both for *identity* and for *temporality*. It is highly significant that Hume talks of our tending to "disguise, as much as possible, the interruption," to "remove the seeming interruption by feigning a continued being." [17] If we could sacrifice either identity or temporality, we would get rid of the irreconcilable contradiction in which these principles stand to each other; but we cannot, because of the irresistible tendency created by the imagination to ascribe identity to resembling perceptions, on the one hand, and because, on the other hand, the interruptions of these perceptions are too striking to be overlooked.[18] *Identity and temporality turn out then, for Hume, not only to oppose but even to exclude each other.* These principles stand in a perpetual struggle with each other. As long as we are inattentive enough, we may believe in identity, although in reality there is merely a succession of resembling items. Philosophical reflection comes to show the falsehood of this belief, without, however, being able to shake it seriously.[19] According to whether we adopt the attitude of practical life or the philosophical one, we waver from instinctive and natural opinion to "studied reflections," without ever gaining a conclusive solution of the problem.[20] Thus Hume fails to account for a very simple fact, familiar to the "vulgar" in their everyday lives, the fact formulated by saying: The thing I see now, I saw some time ago, and tomorrow I shall take up its observation. In a case like this, identity as well as temporality stand before the subject's mind, whether his attention bears upon the one or upon the other.

The ultimate reason for Hume's failure is to be sought, I submit, in his general conception of consciousness. ". . . the true idea of the human mind," he says, "is to consider it as a system of different perceptions or different existences, which . . . mutually produce, destroy, influence, and modify each other. . . . One thought chases another, and draws after it a third, by which it is expelled in its turn." [21] *Consciousness is then conceived as a unidimensional sphere of being, whose fundamental structure consists only and exclusively in temporality.* What constitutes the mind "are the successive perceptions only," the mind being "nothing but a bundle or collection of

16. *Ibid.*, p. 483.
17. *Ibid.*, pp. 488, 496.
18. *Ibid.*, p. 494.
19. Cf. *ibid.*, pp. 497–98, 501–5.
20. *Ibid.*, pp. 535–36.
21. *Ibid.*, pp. 541–42.

different perceptions which succeed each other with an inconceivable rapidity, and are in a perpetual flux and movement." [22] Hume expressly likens consciousness to a theatre; but it is, so to speak, a theatre without a stage. In modern terminology, one could compare consciousness with a perpetual succession of cinematographic pictures.

Whatever differences may exist among the different kinds of perceptions, "primary qualities," "secondary qualities," passions, affections, and so on, insofar as they are perceptions, i.e., contents of consciousness, they must be taken to be on the same footing and to have the same manner of existence.[23] That is to say, all of them are real events happening in the stream of consciousness; they appear and disappear, and every one of them has its place in this stream with relation to other events belonging to the same stream. Nothing can ever be found in consciousness but such an event, one picture among others which precede or succeed it and which in their succession constitute the conscious life.[24] Being aware of an object is reduced to the mere presence in consciousness of a real content.[25] Hence the identification mentioned above of sensible qualities with sensations, through which the former appear, both designated, as a rule, by the same terms, as color, smoothness, raggedness, and so on.[26] After all, the object as composed of real contents of consciousness must itself become a real element in the conscious stream. For consciousness conceived in this way there can indeed exist nothing identical.[27]

Though formulated by Hume in the most explicit manner, this conception of consciousness as a unidimensional sphere constituted by the mere succession of real events was already effective with Locke and with Berkeley and—as far as I can see—it has been embraced more or less explicitly by all philosophers up to the present day. With regard to the problem under discussion, it makes no great difference whether the perceptions are considered, with Hume, as distinguishable

22. *Ibid.*, pp. 534–35.
23. Cf., *ibid.*, pp. 480, 482–83.
24. Cf., *ibid.*, p. 487: " . . . nothing is ever really present to the mind, besides its own perceptions."
25. Cf., *ibid.*, p. 483: ". . . every thing which appears to the mind is nothing but a perception, and is interrupted, and dependent on the mind."
26. See Husserl's criticism of this confusion in *Logische Untersuchungen*, II, v, § 2, and *Ideen*, § 41.
27. It is worth noting that even the identity of objects undergoing a real change, by the addition or diminution of parts, is explained by Hume in some cases by inattention. The essential condition of ascribing identity in such cases is that the changes be insignificant enough not to strike the mind. (*A Treatise of Human Nature*, I, pp. 537–38.)

and separable from one another [28] or whether, like James [29] and Bergson, one lays stress upon the continuity of the stream of consciousness and upon the interpenetration of the mental states, so that demarcations may no longer be drawn to separate them from one another.[30] This conception constitutes the ultimate sense of what Husserl calls *psychologism.*[31] What is true for perceptible objects belonging to the real world holds good also for mathematical entities, for significations, propositions, and for all kinds of products of logical thinking. Reduced to the real elements and contents which constitute the acts of awareness of them, none of these objects can ever be apprehended as the same, in an indefinite number of acts. Since objectivity is to be defined by this sameness of the object as opposed to the multiple acts, whether they be experienced by one person or by different persons, on the basis of the conception of consciousness under discussion there can be no objects at all, of any kind whatever.

## [II] HUSSERL'S NOESIS–NOEMA DOCTRINE

THE PRECEDING DISCUSSION leaves us with the problem of how identical and identifiable objects may exist for, and stand before, a consciousness whose acts perpetually succeed one another; every one of these acts, in addition to their succeeding one another, incessantly undergoing temporal variations. For what is meant by James's "stream of thought" and by Bergson's *durée* does express an experienced reality, of which we may become conscious at any moment, if we are attentive to what happens in our conscious lives.

A solution has been given to this problem by Husserl by means of his theory of intentionality; and as far as I know, it is the only one that exists. Lack of space prevents me from studying the growth of this theory throughout Husserl's writings. When in the *Logische Untersuchungen* he tackled intentionality for the first time, Husserl was not yet dealing with the problem we have emphasized. His theory of intentionality gradually got a reference to this problem, and though this reference did not become manifest until the *Formale und transzendentale Logik*, it seems to us that the form in which intentionality is advanced in the *Ideen*, chiefly in the *noesis-noema*

28. *Ibid.*, p. 495.
29. W. James, *The Principles of Psychology* (London, 1908), I, pp. 237–43.
30. H. Bergson, *Essai sur les données immediates de la conscience*, chap. II.
31. Cf. *Formale und transzendentale Logik* (Halle, 1929), §§ 56–58, 62, 65.

doctrine, already constitutes an answer to our problem. Taking the noesis-noema doctrine into consideration from this point of view, we shall proceed beyond what was explicitly formulated by Husserl himself.

When an object is perceived, there is, on the one hand, the act with its elements, whatever they may be: the act as a real event in psychical life, happening at a certain moment of phenomenal time, appearing, lasting, disappearing, and, when it has disappeared, never returning. On the other hand, there is what, in this concrete act, stands before the perceiving subject's mind.[32] Let the thing perceived be a tree. This tree, at any rate, presents itself in a well-determined manner: it shows itself from this side rather than from that; it stands straight before the observer or occupies a rather lateral position; it is near the perceiving subject or removed from him at a considerable distance, and so on.[33] Finally, it offers itself with a certain prospect, e.g., as giving shade, or, when the subject perceiving the tree recalls to his mind his past life, the tree perceived appears in the light of this or that scene of his youth. What has been described by these allusions is the *noema of perception*—namely, the object just (exactly so and only so) as the perceiving subject is aware of it, as he intends it in this concrete experienced mental state. It is with respect to the noema that the given perception is not only a perception of this determined object but is also that awareness of the object rather than another; that is to say, the subject experiencing the act in question, the *noesis,* finds himself confronted with a certain object appearing from such a side, in the orientation it has, in a certain aspect, and so on. Hence the noema may also be designated as the perceptual sense.

The noema is to be distinguished from the real object.[34] The latter, the tree for instance, as a real thing appears now in this determined manner; but it may offer itself from a different side, at another distance, in a different orientation and aspect; and it does so in fact when the subject goes around it. It shows itself in a multiplicity of perceptions, through all of which the same real tree presents itself; but the "perceived tree as such" varies according to the standpoint, the orientation, the attitude, etc., of the perceiving subject, as when for instance he looks at the tree from above or at another time perceives it while in the garden. Indeed, a real thing may not present itself as such except by means of a series of perceptions succeeding one another.[35]

32. Husserl, *Ideen,* § 88.
33. E. Husserl, *Cartesian Meditations,* trans. D. Cairns (The Hague, 1960), pp. 39f.
34. Husserl, *Ideen,* §§ 89–90.
35. *Ibid.,* §§ 42, 44, 143.

These perceptions enter into a synthesis of identification with one another, and it is by, and in, this synthesis and the parallel synthesis among the corresponding noemata that what appears successively constitutes itself, for consciousness, into this real thing which it is, one and identical as opposed to the multiple perceptions and also to the multiple noemata.[36] Hence problems arise as to the relation of the act and its noema to the real thing perceived through the act and, further, as to what relations the noemata uniting themselves by the synthesis of identification bear to one another.[37] At any rate, it is obvious that the real object ought not to be confounded with a single noema.

On the other hand, the noema is distinct from the act in the sense that it does not constitute a part, an element, a factor of the act and does not really exist within consciousness, as the act does.[38] When, looking at a thing, we alternately shut and open our eyes again, without any change in the position of our body or in the direction of the glance, we experience a number of perceptual acts, all different from one another. Through every one of these acts, however, not only does the same object offer itself, but it appears also in the same aspect and orientation, from the same side, at the same distance, and so on. The tree presents itself now in exactly the same manner as it did a moment ago, as it did yesterday, as it is expected to do tomorrow. The "perceived tree as such" is identically the same, notwithstanding the variety of the acts to which it corresponds. *In the noema,* then, *we have something identical* which, for this very reason, ought not to be mistaken for an element of the corresponding act. Were it such an element, it would appear and disappear with the act, and it would be tied up, as the act is, to the place the latter occupies in phenomenal time.

The noema, as distinct from the real object as well as from the act, turns out to be an irreal or ideal entity which belongs to the same sphere as meanings or significations. This is the sphere of sense (*Sinn*).[39] The irreality of entities belonging to this sphere lies, first of all, in their atemporality, i.e., in a certain independence of the concrete act by which they are actualized, in the sense that every one of them may correspond, as identically the same, to another act, and even to an indefinite number of acts. Noemata are not to be found in perceptual life alone. There is a noema corresponding to every act of memory, expectation, representation, imagination, thinking, judging,

36. *Ibid.*, §§ 41, 86, 135, 145, 150; Husserl, *Cartesian Meditations*, §§ 17–18.
37. Husserl, *Ideen*, §§ 98, 128–31.
38. *Ibid.*, § 97.
39. *Ibid.*, § 133.

volition, and so on.[40] In all these cases, the object, matter of fact, etc., in itself, towards which the subject directs himself through the act, is to be distinguished from the object just, exactly just, as the subject has it in view, as, through the act, the object stands before the subject's mind. With regard to judging, the difference is between *objects about which* and *that which is judged as such.*[41] It is worth noting that somehow James anticipated Husserl's notion of the noema of thinking and judging.[42]

Husserl's noesis-noema doctrine, which we must content ourselves with summarizing briefly, far from being a constructive or explanatory theory, is simply a descriptive statement of an objectivating mental state, i.e., of a mental state through which the experiencing subject is confronted with an object. Every mental state of this kind must then be accounted for in terms of identity as well as of temporality. The traditional conception of consciousness, in which emphasis is placed upon temporality, the succession of acts and the variations each act undergoes by its duration, is certainly not false, since the fact emphasized is a real fact of consciousness. But this conception is incomplete and unilateral. No mental state is to be conceived only and exclusively as a real and temporal event in the stream of consciousness, without any reference to a sense. This reference is overlooked in the traditional conception. *Identity is to be acknowledged as a fact irreducible to any other; it turns out to be a fact of consciousness, no less authentic and no less fundamental than temporality is.* Thus we are led to a duality. And it must be stressed that this duality holds good even for the most elementary level of consciousness, where the question concerns the repeated appearance of an object in the same manner of presentation, without there being a need for going on to consider the appearance of an object one time in perception, another time in memory, representation, etc., and, still more, to take into consideration the successive presentations of an object, appearing as identically the same, from various sides and in the most different aspects.

## [III]  TEMPORALITY AND IDENTITY

BEFORE SETTING OUT the general conception of consciousness implied in, and following from, the noesis-noema doctrine,

40. *Ibid.*, §§ 91, 93–95.
41. Husserl, *Formale und transzendentale Logik*, §§ 42, 44–45, 48.
42. James, *The Principles of Psychology*, I, pp. 275–76.

let us look at the nature of this duality and at the relation between the terms composing it.

That identity is a fundamental fact in conscious life does not signify a permanent explicit awareness of it. In all perceiving, thinking, judging, and so on, in all theoretical and practical life, we make use of the identity of the objects we deal with. When perceiving a thing, for instance, we take it for the same as that perceived some time ago, or when thinking of a proposition, we hold it to be the same as the one which we demonstrated yesterday, and then go on to verify this demonstration (the same as that performed yesterday) or to reason further upon the basis of this proposition. So we may behave and so we do behave, without necessarily grasping identity in an explicit way, although all of our behavior is constantly guided by it. The object with which we are concerned is our theme, and our only one; as a rule, the identity of this object does not constitute a secondary theme accompanying the former. But, of course, identity may be rendered explicit to the subject's mind and may be taken as a theme. How then does it become so? In what way do we get an originary awareness of identity?

A perceived object offers itself in a certain manner of presentation. Experiencing such a perception, we are free to remember past perceptions and to look forward to future perceptions, so that to all these mental states, past as well as future ones, there corresponds the same noema as that corresponding to the present experienced perception. Thus we become aware in an originary way of the noema and of its identity, as distinct from, and opposed to, the multiple acts to which it corresponds. It is of no importance if the past experiences are recalled with a more or less exact temporal determination or if the moment at which the future acts are expected to happen may be foreseen with some exactness. It is not even necessary that the acts taken into consideration be recalled perceptions—i.e., appear as having been present at a past moment—or that the experiences considered as future be expected really to happen. For our present purposes, it will be quite sufficient to conceive acts as possible or potential, as differing from one another and also from the present perception, and yet as actualizing the same noema. Acts through which the same object appears and offers itself in the same manner of presentation can differ from one another only as to the moments in conscious time at which each of them takes place. At any rate, *we may not render identity of the noema explicit and ascertain it by an originary experience unless we also become aware of the temporality of consciousness.*

Noematic identity may be brought up to explicitness, even without taking into consideration acts different from the present experienced one, on the condition that there be reflection upon the duration of the latter. Duration consists in, and manifests itself for consciousness by, an incessant transformation of every "actual now" into a "having just been an actual now." When time is elapsing, the present moment does not sink into the past, so that it could not be recalled again to the mind, except by reproduction; on the contrary, the present moment, ceasing to be present, is yet retained in "primary memory" and takes the form of "having just been present." [43] At once what has just been present, relative to the actual now, when transformed in the manner mentioned, undergoes a transformation in its turn, passing into a "retention of a retention"; it is then removed still more from the occasional actual now, until it disappears from immediate memory, no longer being retained.[44] Thus reflecting on what really happens in consciousness, at every moment we find a continuous variation and transformation: a continuous passing of the present phase into a retained one and then of a phase given in a retention of any degree into a retention of a higher degree, a continuous iteration of this transformation.[45] Upon these incessant variations is based the stream-character of consciousness, which, owing to their continuity, is experienced as a unidimensional order.[46] What is involved in these transformations is, however, not the object perceived or its manner of presentation but only its temporal orientation, its temporal modes of appearance.[47] In other words: what is concerned is the act rather than its noema, the fact that a perceived object as such stands before consciousness rather than the perceived object as such itself. Looking at the stream elapsing, we become explicitly aware of the fact that the perceived object as such has already appeared for a long time, or that it has just begun to appear, and—if we also allow for protentions—that we expect it to continue appearing, or that we foresee interruption of its appearance, and so on. Once more, *explicit awareness of identity requires that of temporality* and, in the case just analyzed, even of *intrinsic temporality*. Hume was then perfectly right in referring to temporality when he sought to account for identity.

On the other hand, were there nothing identical standing before

43. As to the difference between "primary memory" (retention) and "secondary memory" (reproduction), see E. Husserl, *Vorlesungen zur Phänomenologie des inneren Zeitbewusstseins* (Halle, 1928), § 19.

44. *Ibid.*, §§ 8, 10.

45. *Ibid.*, § 39 and Supplement I.

46. *Ibid.*, § 36 and pp. 466–67.

47. *Ibid.*, §§ 30–31 and Supplement IV.

consciousness, awareness of temporality would no longer be possible. With this hypothesis, retentional modifications could no longer be variations in the temporal orientations of something which may successively assume different temporal orientations. The very reality of conscious life, when an act is an enduring one, is a phase of present actuality most intimately connected with a whole continuity of phases retained (in retentions of various degrees), all these phases being related to one another and the phase of present actuality constituting a limit of this continuity.[48] With identity hypothetically omitted, however, instead of this continuity of phases there could be only a set of punctiform act-impulses among which one would bear the character of actual presence, whereas the others would be given characters different from one another as well as from that of the former. All these act-impulses, though simultaneously given, would still remain in isolation from one another; at any rate, they would lack the intrinsic relationship to connect them into a unitary act—for the unity of an enduring act is possible only with regard to something identical whose appearance may assume different temporal phases.[49] Conscious life being in incessant variation, at every moment one set of such act-impulses would be displaced by another one, without any intrinsic reference between them; for such a reference supposes the same to pass from one temporal phase into another. At every moment, then, the unity and the continuity of conscious life would be broken off. Experienced time consists just in the progressive removal either of a certain phase of an act or of the act in its entirety from the actual now, in such a way that what is being removed appears as having been, a moment ago, nearer to the actual now than it is at present. Therefore a consciousness for which nothing was identical, as in the hypothesis under discussion, could not become aware of time. Consequently for such a consciousness time would not exist at all.[50]

It is then by way of the very same reflection that the subject, in an originary way, ascertains the identity of the object offering itself in a certain manner of presentation, of the noema, as well as the temporality of the noema's appearance, the duration of its appearance, and all changes the duration carries with itself. Temporality and identity are, no doubt, poles opposed to each other. As against Hume, however, *they are poles which do not exclude but require each other. Temporality and identity are related to each other like the terms of a*

48. *Ibid.*, § 16. For the sake of brevity we confine the discussion to the intrinsic temporality of an enduring act.

49. *Ibid.*, Supplement XI.

50. *Ibid.*, pp. 376–77.

*correlation.* This is indeed the nature of the duality to which Husserl's noesis-noema doctrine leads.

## [IV] THE CORRELATION CONCEPTION OF CONSCIOUSNESS

To EACH ACT there corresponds a noema—namely, an object just, exactly and only just, as the subject is aware of it and has it in view, when he is experiencing the act in question. *Consciousness* is not to be mistaken for a mere unidimensional sphere composed of acts, as real psychical events, which co-exist with and succeed one another. Rather, it ought to be considered as a *correlation, or correspondence, or parallelism between the plane of acts, psychical events, noeses, and a second plane which is that of sense (noemata).* This correlation is such that corresponding to each act is its noema, but the same noema may correspond to an indefinite number of acts. It is then not a one-to-one correspondence.

The noetico-noematic correlation is what the term intentionality must signify. In this light the formula consciousness *of* something is to be understood: a conscious act is an act of awareness, presenting to the subject who experiences it a sense, an ideal atemporal unity, identical, i.e., identifiable.[51] It is not by virtue of favorable circumstances calling for an explanation and for a reduction to more elementary facts but by virtue of what constitutes the nature of consciousness itself that an experienced act bears a reference to a sense. Consciousness is to be defined by its bearing reference to a sphere of sense, so that *to experience an act is the same thing as to actualize a sense.* Hence every fact of consciousness must be treated in terms of the relation *cogito-cogitatum qua cogitatum,* and no mental state may be accounted for except with regard to the objective sense (*gegenständlicher Sinn*), of which the experiencing subject becomes aware through this act.[52]

Intentionality means the objectivating function of consciousness. In its most elementary form, this function consists in confronting the subject with senses, ideal unities, to which, as identical ones, he is free to revert an indefinite number of times. No sooner than this elementary structure of the objectivating function has been established,

51. Husserl, *Cartesian Meditations,* p. 33.
52. *Ibid.,* p. 36; Husserl, *Formale und transzendentale Logik,* p. 120; Husserl, "Nachwort zu meinen 'Ideen zu einer reinen Phänomenologie und phänomenologischen Philosophie,'" in *Jahrbuch für Philosophie und phänomenologische Forschung* (Halle, 1930), XI, 6.

problems may be tackled as to higher structures of intentionality, concerning, for instance, syntheses by means of which particular perceptual senses are united into systems which are the real perceptual things, concerning categorial forms bestowed upon the perceptual data in thinking, concerning syntactical operations by which, in apophantics, more and more complicated meanings and significations are constructed from simpler ones, and so on.[53] All structures of intentionality rest upon the noetico-noematic correlation, which, for this reason, is the most elementary structure. But it is, at the same time, also the most fundamental and the most universal one, since every sense entity, of whatever kind and of whatever degree of complication, is an identical and identifiable unity, to which the subject may come back again and again. Thus the noetico-noematic parallelism enters into all forms of mental activity; and it is to it that one is led by the basic problems of logic.[54]

The objectivating function belongs to an act, but not as taken in itself and as isolated from other mental states. On the contrary, this function is possessed by an act even when the latter has the distinctive character of evidence or self-presentation, on account of its being inserted into the whole of the experiencing life and only with regard to this whole.[55] Objectivity is identifiableness, i.e., the possibility of reverting again and again to what, through the present experienced act, is offered to consciousness and the possibility of so doing whether in the same or in any other mode of awareness.[56] This holds good for real as well as ideal objects.[57] It holds good also for "inner perception." When a present experienced mental state is grasped by an act of reflection and is thus made the object of this act of inner perception, the latter possesses the character of evidence, since the apprehended act is offered directly, immediately, and bodily, not by memory or in any symbolic manner. Nevertheless, it is not on this account that the act of inner perception is objectivating; it is so only because what appears through it, although its self-presentation never can be actualized again, may yet be recalled later and may be so an indefinite number of times.[58] Objectivity and identity, then, have sense with regard to a multiplicity of acts—that is to say, with reference to the temporality of conscious life. These analyses of Husserl concerning

53. Husserl, *Logische Untersuchungen,* II, vi, chap. VI; II, iv, § 3; Husserl, *Formale und transzendentale Logik,* § 13.
54. Husserl, *Formale und transzendentale Logik,* § 73.
55. *Ibid.,* pp. 142–43.
56. *Ibid.,* p. 139.
57. *Ibid.,* §§ 61–62.
58. *Ibid.,* pp. 140–41 and § 107b.

objectivity, by which he has cleared up the ultimate meaning of his struggle against psychologism,[59] throw a new light upon the correlation conception of consciousness advanced here.

Though never formulated by Husserl in quite explicit terms, this conception seems to be at the root of a large part of his theories, and, when his work is considered in its growth, this conception reveals itself, I submit, to be one of the teleological goals towards which phenomenology is tending.

59. *Ibid.*, §§ 56–57, 65, 67.

# 8 / On the Object of Thought [1]

IN CONTRAST to the objectivistic trend which, to a large extent, prevails in contemporary philosophy and psychology, phenomenology has insisted upon the orientation toward subjectivity, i.e., consciousness. It is to the defense and, if possible, the elaboration of this orientation that the present discussion is devoted. We propose to discuss a concept which is of central importance in this respect—namely, the concept of what may be called the "subjective object." Provisionally and roughly defined, it is the concept of the object not as it really is but as it appears to the experiencing subject's mind through a given act of consciousness. What is meant by this is called noema in Husserl's terminology.

Since, as far as I can see, William James was the first to lay down the concept of the subjective object, it seems appropriate to begin by expounding some of James's pertinent ideas. His term for the concept in question is "object of thought" as distinguished from "topic"; it is this term with the sense James gives to it that I borrow as title of the present paper. It must be remarked that in dealing with theories of James, we are concerned only with James the psychologist—that is, with ideas which James advanced in his *Principles of Psychology;* we shall have to disregard his later philosophical development. In the second part of my argument, I shall attempt to radicalize James's methodological reflections so as to open an avenue of approach towards constitutive phenomenology.

According to James, a most essential character of mental states or thoughts consists in their cognitive function or knowing reference to

1. Paper read at the meeting of the Phenomenological Society, April 27, 1946, at Hunter College, New York City. It was not possible to include here all the discussion. The original version was published in *Philosophy and Phenomenological Research*, VII (1947).

extramental facts. Such a fact is known to the mental state through which it presents itself and it is also known to the psychologist who studies the mental state in question, no matter whether the latter is his own experience or that of another person. The psychologist's knowledge of the extramental fact is assumed to be "true"; to be, at least, as true and as complete but, usually, more true and more complete than that of the mental state under examination. We shall see presently that the knowledge of the psychologist extends in any case further than that of the mental state studied, since the former includes elements altogether absent from the thought in question, even when the latter happens to be one of the psychologist's own experiences. In this case, the knowledge which the psychologist has as a psychologist is obviously not conveyed to him by his mental state which he is just studying but is derived from other sources, as, for instance, previous experiences concerning the extramental fact in question. In the case of introspective analysis, the psychologist has a double knowledge of the extramental fact concerned: (1) the knowledge he owes to his mental state which he is actually experiencing and goes on to analyze in introspection; (2) the knowledge which he has insofar as he is a psychologist and which James terms the "psychologist's reality."

The "psychologist's reality" comprises first of all the extramental fact which, in the case of perception, stimulates a certain section of the nervous system and provokes nerve and brain processes to which there corresponds the mental state to be studied. We must keep in mind that this mental state is not only aroused by, but also bears knowing reference to, that extramental fact. As far as this fact is concerned, the psychologist accepts the common-sense belief. This belief is supplemented by what the psychologist learns from the physical sciences. Thus, when he has to discuss the perception of a black body, the psychologist will take account of the fact that no light is reflected from the surface of that body. The "psychologist's reality," furthermore, includes the organic conditions of the stimulation and finally comprises a knowledge properly to be called psychological: the knowledge, namely, of what mental state other than the actual one would be given rise to if the same extramental fact would stimulate the nervous system under conditions different, in this or that respect, from the present ones.

The "thought's object" is the specific knowledge which the thought studied has of the extramental fact or, as James likewise calls it, of the "topic" to which it bears cognitive reference. Accordingly, James defines the object of thought as the thought's "entire content or deliverance neither more nor less." Surveying the various examples James cites to illustrate his concept and the manifold applications he makes of it, one may summarize as follows. Whenever a mental state occurs, something appears to the experiencing subject's mind. This something may be a sense datum as well as the meaning of a comparatively complicated sentence. It might be given directly, as in sense perception, or in a rather symbolic manner. The something in question appears in a certain light, under a certain aspect, surrounded by a halo, escorted by fringes, swimming in a network of relations, and so on. What thus stands to the mind or to the thought studied, such—but exactly and only such—as it actually does, is the "thoughts' object." This object *is* what it is experienced and known *as* through the particular mental state considered.

The preceding description may well be taken as a provisional characterization of Husserl's concept of noema. As James distinguishes between "topic" and "object" of thought, so does Husserl between the "object which is intended" and the "object as it is intended." The latter is to be taken just as it is intended, just as it is determined in the way in which it presents itself, in just the manner in which it is meant through the act of consciousness under consideration. To give one example, the distinction is between the meaning or sense of a proposition, that which is formulated and stated by the proposition, on the one hand, and, on the other hand, that about which the statement is made, the "objectivity" (*Gegenständlichkeit*)—in Husserl's terminology—about which something is asserted and to which the proposition refers by means of its meaning. I refer to this example because some ideas which James developed on this subject come rather close to certain aspects of Husserl's elaborate theory of meaning. Lack of space forbidding, I must refrain from pursuing the line along which there is agreement between James and Husserl as to the mentioned problem, and I must also forsake surveying the elaboration of concepts analogous to that of the "object of thought" in contemporary psychological sciences. I have in view the abandonment of the constancy hypothesis in Gestalt theory, the studies of the late Gelb and Prof. Goldstein on the psychical effects of brain injuries, the late Lévy-Bruhl's account of mental functions in primitive societies, the views of the phonological school in linguistics, Max Weber's *verstehende Soziologie* and especially his distinction between *objektiver* and *subjektiver Sinn*.

Turning to the second part of my argument, the radicalization of James's methodological reflections and the transition to constitutive phenomenology, I must, to begin with, characterize James's general position in which he established the concept of object of thought.

This position is that of the psychologist, psychology being considered as a natural science, all philosophical questions being deliberately put aside. Within the real world there are two domains: the domain of things known or to be known and the domain of mental states knowing, neither domain being reducible to the other. The cognitive function of mental states is simply posited, and every inquiry as to its possibility or general nature is explicitly excluded. Thus a dualism and even a kind of pre-established harmony between things and thoughts is assumed. It is this dualism which gives rise to the specific philosophical questions. The line along which we are going to formulate these problems is, however, entirely different from that which James followed in his philosophical development subsequent to the *Principles of Psychology*.

The radicalization of the methodological reflections consists in enlarging the scope of the psychological point of view so as to apply it to that which falls within the "psychologist's reality." In a universal reflection, the psychologist makes himself aware of the fact that whatever he knows as a psychologist about the "topic" and about other items which pertain to the "psychologist's reality" is the result of certain experiences. Just because he adopts the point of view of natural science, the psychologist does not consider the topic and other elements of the "psychologist's reality" as metaphysical entities, but he takes them as a matter of experience. From the point of view of empirical science, a thing is what it is known as, to refer to Hodgson's fortunate formulation of the sound principles of British empiricism. There is then a relation between any element of the "psychologist's reality" and experiences, both actual and possible, through which that element is known as that which it is, displays its qualities, properties, and determinations, appears in its real existence, and exhibits the meaning of its existence. For the sake of simplicity, let us suppose that the psychologist is studying a mental state of his own. He is then confronted with a "thought's object," i.e., with the topic just—exactly and only just—as it stands to his mind through the mental state he is studying. But the psychologist does not lose sight of the topic as it really is. In the radicalization in question, the topic is considered in its relations to experiences, not only to the mental state which the psychologist is studying, at least not to this mental state alone, but also to experiences he has had in the past and which, in certain circumstances, the psychologist is free to repeat. Between these experiences, there is accordance, convergence, and conformance, by virtue of which all of them present themselves as experiences of the topic in question. The same holds, correspondingly, for the other elements of the "psychologist's reality," e.g., for the organic conditions of the stimulation. Here too, there is reference to experiences, though not to mere perceptions but to the latter as embodied in scientific interpretation and elaboration. The experiences which are here in question exhibit some complexity and a rather complex stratification.

Proceeding in this way, the psychologist becomes a psychologist throughout with regard to whatever exists and is valid for him; or, for that matter, he becomes a philosopher. By the same token, an *incipient* phenomenological reduction is performed, incipient because it is not yet the phenomenological reduction in the developed and elaborated form in which Husserl has formulated it in the *Ideen* and, later, in the *Cartesian Meditations*. But the essential principle, the consideration of every object with reference to experience and to groups of experiences, is already laid down.

To exemplify the reference of a real existent to the experiences through which the existent appears and is known as that which it is, let us glance at perception. When we perceive a thing, we do so from a certain standpoint and a certain distance. The thing is near to, or remote from, us; it offers itself from this side or from that; it is seen under a certain aspect; situated in a perceptual field, the thing appears under the perspective of these or those other things belonging to that field. As we change our standpoint, come nearer to, go farther away, or go around the thing, the latter presents itself from different sides and appears under varying aspects and perspectives. We are here confronted with the phenomena which Husserl has brought out in his theory of perceptual adumbration (*Wahrnehmungsabschattung*). Allowance must furthermore be made for the experiences of the causal properties of the thing. If we go beyond the perceptual level, account must be taken also of the idealizing processes through which the causal properties receive mathematical formulation and find expression in the concepts of physics like mass, conductivity of heat, index of refraction, electrical conductance. Thus we are in the presence of a plurality of mental states, all different from each other and yet all referring to the same real existent. James has laid down the "principle of constancy in the mind's meanings" to the effect that "the same matters can be thought of in successive portions of the mental stream, and some of these portions can know that they mean the same matters which the other portions meant." Adopting the point of view of psychology as a natural science, James could content himself with simply asserting this principle and with ascertaining its dominance in consciousness. If through the radicalization of the psychological point of view, we pass to the phenomenological level, the principle mentioned proves to be a title for far and deep reaching investigations. In fact, the identity of the object in the face of the multiple experiences referring to the former is the fundamental problem of constitutive phenomenology whose aim is to account for the object or existent in terms of the pertinent experiences.

Let us finally consider the form in which the dualism between the "thought's object" and the topic appears on the phenomenological level. Considered in its reference to the multiple relevant experiences, the topic proves itself an "object of thought," related, to be sure, not to this or that particular experience but to the totality of experiences through which it becomes or may become known as that real existent which it is. In this sense, the topic turns out to be an "object of thought" of a higher order. To put it in Husserl's terminology, through each of the experiences in question, the topic presents itself in a certain mode of appearance; to each of these experiences there corresponds a noema, viz., the topic as appearing under a certain aspect and perspective. To the totality of experiences there corresponds, ideally, the topic under the totality of its possible aspects and perspectives. In other words, the "topic" is a noematic entity itself; more precisely it proves the systematic concatenation of noemata. Now, the particular experience under consideration belongs to the group of experiences through which the topic discloses and unfolds itself in its properties, qualities, and determinations. Accordingly, the noema which corresponds to this experience belongs itself to the noematic system in question. Hence the relation between the "object of thought" and the "topic" is that between a member of a system and the system itself; there is the corresponding relation between a particular experience and the coherent group of experiences to which the former belongs. The problems which arise in this connection concern (1) the phenomenal features through which the reference and pertinence of this particular noema to the noematic system is given and (2) the nature of the coherence of the noematic system and of the group of corresponding experiences. The latter question refers, so to speak, to the dynamics of conscious life. Earlier we mentioned the accordance, conformance, and convergence between experiences which are experiences of one and the same object. These terms refer to the internal structure of the system and group in question. Problems of this type arise with regard to all domains, perceptual and other, with which constitutive phenomenology deals.

I am well aware of how little sympathy James, especially the older James, would have had for the arguments presented here as a continuation and development, let alone interpretation, of his intentions. If, notwithstanding the intentions of the historical James, I started from his methodological reflections, it is because James brought out the foundation problems of psychology with such clarity and rigor that motives become apparent which lead towards the phenomenological position. In the present phase of phenomenology, it seems to me important to insist upon the possibility of disengaging such motives from the foundation problems of the sciences. Phenomenology is not detached from the sciences, not separated from them by an unbridged gulf, but is accessible from the sciences. Accessibility means continuity by motivation. This holds not only for psychology but applies also to the foundation problems of the other sciences, the mathematical and physical sciences as well as the historical and social sciences. As to the latter, I refer to the work done by Alfred Schutz. If phenomenology keeps in contact with the sciences and if, on the other hand, the foundation problems of the sciences are set forth in a radical way as to their philosophical implications, much clarification and advancement may be expected with regard to the foundation problems along these convergent lines of research.

# 9 / The Kantian and Husserlian
Conceptions of Consciousness [1]

A COMPARATIVE STUDY of Kant's theoretical philosophy with Husserlian phenomenology could have been attempted, indeed, should have been attempted, as early as 1913, following the publication of the first volume of Husserl's *Ideen zu einer reinen Phänomenologie und phänomenologischen Philosophie*—the only volume of the *Ideen* to appear during Husserl's lifetime. This work, in which Husserl outlines the program of constitutive phenomenology and indicates the general lines along which this program is to be realized, has a clearly Kantian inspiration. Indeed, the first generation of Husserl's students had already perceived this orientation.

If one seeks a motto for the whole of Husserl's work, one could not do better than to refer to the few phrases which Kant places at the head of his *Analytic of Concepts*, when he speaks of his intention to descend into the depths of the mind to discover the notions of the understanding, which are found therein prepared in at least a germinal form. Indeed, in the history of modern thought between Kant and Husserl one does not find a theoretician of subjectivity who is of comparable depth. Neither for Kant nor for Husserl, furthermore, is this concern for subjectivity an end in itself. They both seek to give an account of objectivity by means of the analysis of the life of consciousness, or of subjective life. Objects of every kind are viewed from the perspective of their origination and formation within the life of consciousness. To give an account of objectivity, it is necessary to bring out and make explicit the contribution of subjectivity to the constitution of objects. Husserl's intentions can be characterized, somewhat *grosso modo* certainly, in such terms as these, but they are

1. Originally, this was a lecture delivered before the Société Française de Philosophie, April 25, 1959. The lecture was published in the *Bulletin de la Société Française de Philosophie* (1960).

descriptive as well, at least to a considerable extent, of the intentions of Kant. There are, in fact, some Husserlian doctines which are highly reminiscent of parallel theories advanced by Kant.

We shall choose two examples more or less at random and begin by considering the phenomenological theory of perception as established by Husserl. When we perceive an object, we perceive it from a certain point of view, and we can move from one point to another. From each of these points of view the perceived thing presents itself from a certain aspect and in a certain orientation. As we move around the thing, looking at it from different points of observation, the aspects change, the perceptual presentations of the same thing undergo variations. However, among the varying aspects there is not only a compatibility but even more a harmony and accordance. The aspects glide into one another, and, owing to this continuation and harmony, as a result of this accordance, the perspectives, the perceptual adumbrations become fitted together and form a coherent and system-atized group. It is in virtue of this grouping that perceptions, perceptual acts which can be dispersed in time, are in turn organized into one process, the unity of which depends upon the relation of accord and harmony between the perceptual perspectives under which the object appears. As is known, Husserl insists emphatically on this relation of harmony and concordance. According to him, the identity and the very existence of the perceived thing depend on that relation.

These analyses remind us of Kant's formula found in the first edition of the *Transcendental Deduction of the Categories.* Posing the question concerning the relation of representations, or ideas, phenom-ena, sensory data, to the object, Kant gives his well-known answer: in order for the representations to be related to an object, there must exist between them this relation of concordance and conformity which is required by the very notion of objectivity.

To consider another example, let us look briefly at the theory regarding the consciousness of phenomenal time. Husserl presented this theory in his *Vorlesungen zur Phänomenologie des inneren Zeitbewusstseins* and returned to it in his posthumous work *Erfahrung und Urteil,* where he studies the phenomena in a more detailed and differentiating manner.[2] The notions of protention and particularly of retention are at the center of the Husserlian theory concerning the experience of time. At each moment of time, a certain immediately past phase of the temporal stream is still retained. This immediately

2. The first of Husserl's works mentioned above was edited by Martin Heidegger and published in *Jahrbuch für Philosophie und phänomenologische Forschung* (Halle, 1928), Vol. IX. The second was edited by Ludwig Landgrebe (Hamburg, 1954).

past phase is not purely and simply past but is rather a "past which has just been present." This immediate past is a phase of the flowing time which was present a moment ago, which is no longer present but is still retained as having just been present.

This theory reminds us of some remarks which Kant makes concerning the synthesis of the imagination, or more exactly, the synthesis of reproduction by the imagination. Speaking of a line which is traced in thought, of a number, of a temporal interval, Kant maintains that if, for example, the segments of the line which one has just been drawing were effaced and forgotten, a whole line could never result. Therefore, the present phase of the action of drawing the line must still contain the phases which have preceded it—that is to say, those which have just been present. Here again we find another convergence of a Husserlian theory with views formulated by Kant.

However, even though encouraged by such more or less haphazardly chosen convergences, if one goes on to compare the two philosophies more systematically, a most embarrassing situation arises.

We remarked at the beginning that Kant's as well as Husserl's concern with the life of consciousness, or subjectivity, is in the service of their respective interests in objectivity. However, what is it that Kant understands by "objectivity"? And, what is its meaning for Husserl? When Kant speaks of objectivity, of an objective world, he has in mind mathematical science, the mathematical physics of his time, that is, Newtonian physics—the physics which describes the objective world. For Husserl, on the contrary, the notion of objectivity has a great many shades of meaning. When Husserl speaks of objectivity, he is not thinking exclusively or even primarily of the mathematical science of his time; he is not thinking of Einstein's physics or of quantum physics.

First and foremost there is the objectivity of a world for me, of a world with respect to which I disregard every contribution deriving from Others. It is possible—indeed, it is necessary—to effect such a reduction of the world to what pertains to me alone; thereby the first notion of objectivity is made explicit. Subsequently, there is the objectivity of our world as it is for us, the objectivity of our surrounding environment in the sense of the milieu wherein I live with my fellow-men who belong to the same social and historical group as I. This world is the world of a certain society at a certain phase of its history. A good example of such a world is perhaps that of a primitive tribe or a historical world such as that of the ancient Egyptians. On this basis a second notion of objectivity arises: that of the world as pertaining to a certain historico-social group. A third notion of objectivity relates to the Husserlian conception of the human life-world (*Lebenswelt*) in general. The life-world understood in this sense is conceived by Husserl as an invariant with respect to the multiple socio-historical environments, between which there are often considerable differences. This life-world is the same for all human beings and for all societies. The objectivity belonging to the scientific universe as it is elaborated by the physical sciences appears only at an even higher, and perhaps the final, level.

Whereas Kant had a single notion of objectivity, Husserl develops a whole series of notions, between which there can be no other unity— we submit—than that which Aristotle called "unity by analogy."

Let us consider another example. In *Erfahrung und Urteil* and especially in his other posthumously published work, *Die Krisis der Europäischen Wissenschaften und die transzendentale Phänomenologie*,[3] Husserl advanced a theory of "pure sensibility." This phrase makes us think of Kant's "transcendental aesthetics," the goal of which is to provide the grounds for geometry. Perhaps it does not contain the whole of Kant's theory of mathematics, but it is surely a central and fundamental part of it, and especially of his theory of geometry.

When Husserl speaks of "pure sensibility," by contrast, his concern is with the role of our organism, of our own body, in perception. He describes the kinaesthesias which we experience when we move about in our perceptual field, and he studies the correlations between these kinaesthetic experiences and the unfolding of the perspectives pertaining to perceived things, which we mentioned at the beginning. This "pure sensibility" belongs to what Husserl calls "pre-predicative experience," which precedes all sorts of idealizations. What characterizes the world as it presents itself to us in pre-predicative experience is that not even the most elementary logical operations, not to speak of geometrical idealizations, have yet made any contribution to it.

For Kant, perceived space is geometrical space. In his view, the axioms of geometry can, so to speak, be read off the intuition of space, which is the condition for all perception and experience. According to Husserl, to the contrary, because pre-predicative experience is at the root of every idealization and of every elaboration pertaining to a higher level, the axioms of geometry and all geometrical idealizations in general arise on the basis of perceptual space, in virtue, of course, of processes of a very specific kind whose details call for special examination.

Here is another instance in which Kant and Husserl make use of

3. Ed. W. Biemel (*Husserliana,* Vol. VI [The Hague, 1954]).

the same terminology but do not speak of precisely the same things.

Faced with such a situation, it seems advisable to forego altogether every comparison which would proceed theory by theory and doctrine by doctrine. Rather, we should attempt to go straight to the heart of things.

Let us inquire into the conception of consciousness, or understanding, which Kant has established as distinguished from that which Husserl advocates.

As regards Kant's conception, let us glance briefly—perhaps too briefly—at a certain phase of the "transcendental deduction of the categories," namely the notion of the "pure transcendental apperception," a notion which—it seems to us—is at the center not only of the deduction but also of the entire *Kritik der reinen Vernunft*.

As is known, all representations, ideas, phenomena, sensory data, and so on are for Kant subject to the condition of being mine or, as Kant more prudently expresses it, to the condition of being able to be apprehended as mine, as belonging to an identical Ego. The sensory data which form a multiplicity and which change, vary, and succeed one another stand opposed to the identical Ego, to the Ego conceived as strictly one. In order for the sensory data to be apprehended as mine, it is not enough that as regards each sensory datum I reflectively apperceive that it is given to, and experienced by, me, that it belongs to the same experiential flux as my other sensory data. Such a reflection would still not permit me to account for the strict identity of my Ego. The latter itself would in some way partake of the vicissitudes of sensory data; it would become involved in the change and variation which these data undergo; it would be dispersed along with its sensory data. In order for me to have consciousness of the identity of my Ego as opposed to the multiplicity of my sensory data, I must perform on these one single function, an identical action (*identische Handlung*), always the same. *The Ego*, asserts Kant, *cannot apperceive itself in its own identity except by apperceiving by the same token the identity of the function by means of which the multiplicity of sensory data is reunited into a context governed by certain laws.* In order for the Ego to be able to apprehend itself as an identical Ego, it must unify the sensory data.

Two kinds of unity can be distinguished from one another: on the one hand, that unity which exists between all the sensory data in virtue of their common relation to an identical Ego; on the other hand, the unification which the function or action of the identical Ego brings about between the sensory data. The originality of the Kantian thesis consists in identifying these two unities or, more exactly, in regarding each of them as a necessary and indispensable condition for the other.

It is almost trivial to state that if the sensory data did not belong to an identical Ego, this Ego could not perform any function on them. What is not trivial is to affirm that the converse is also true. In fact, Kant maintains that in order for the sensory data to belong to an identical Ego, this identical Ego must effect a unification between the sensory data. This unification is, according to Kant, an indispensable condition for the strict identity of the Ego of the pure transcendental apperception.

This pure transcendental apperception, or the transcendental Ego, is exhausted in an action or in an actual function admitting of an inner articulation, of which the categories as Kant conceives them are the conceptual fixations. Pure transcendental apperception is defined by this articulated action and by this action alone.

In order to determine the nature of the synthetic action of unification, one has to remember that the sensory data are received under the conditions of time and space. For our purposes here, however, time is more important than space. Sensory data occur either simultaneously or in succession. The operation of synthetically unifying the sensory data occurring under the condition of time consists in ratifying (or not ratifying) their temporal relations—for example, conferring a legal title upon their factual succession. If the succession of temporal data is ratified, the mere fact of this succession is legitimated and conceived as a special case of a general law. The objectification of sensory data always has the meaning, for Kant, of a ratification and legitimation of their temporal relations.

The Kantian conception of consciousness, which we have sketched rather superficially, is activistic and functionalistic. The life of the understanding consists in an action, in a single action which is always the same. The pure transcendental apperception is one with its action; it is but its articulated action.

It seems to us, though this assertion cannot be substantiated here, that Kant's notion of consciousness derives from the monadology of Leibniz. To be sure, there can be no question of a reinstatement or of a simple renewal of the Leibnizian conception of the monad. This conception has, in the hands of Kant, undergone a transformation which is fundamental, but the transformation is continuous. As a substance, the Leibnizian monad is essentially characterized by its activity. Precisely the same holds for the understanding as Kant conceives it. Although the activity of the monad is specified differently from that of the pure transcendental apperception, the latter stands to the former in a relation of filiation. The direction in which Kant has transformed the Leibnizian concept of the monad is determined by his adopting the analyses and even some of the theses of Hume, at least to a certain extent and within certain limits. It was thus unavoidable that the Leibnizian idea of the active monad should undergo a transformation.

Let us now turn to the Husserlian conception of consciousness.

It has to be emphasized at the outset that the notion of synthesis is not at all alien to Husserlian thought. Husserl's notion of synthesis exhibits a higher differentiation than that of Kant, who only knew one single synthesizing function. Husserl, however, makes a distinction between active and passive syntheses. All perceptual syntheses are passive, whereas the active syntheses come into play in the constitution of logical, mathematical, and similar entities. To simplify our exposition we are going to restrict ourselves to the passive synthesis of perceptual life.

The first question which arises concerns the materials which enter into the synthesis, the materials between which synthetic unity is established. With respect to Kant, the question is easily answered: the materials on which the pure transcendental apperception imposes unity are sensory data (conceived in more or less the same manner as by Hume). It is from this side that Hume's views have penetrated Kant's thinking. In the Husserlian theory of perception, however, the question concerning the materials which become unified by means of the passive synthesis is much more complicated.

Let us return again to the perceptual process. I perceive a house from a certain point of view, and this house (it does not matter whether it is familiar to me or not) presents itself under a certain aspect, in a certain perceptual adumbration, in a certain orientation (from far or near, in front of me or at the side, and so on). Perceived from another point of view, the same house presents itself under a different aspect, and it is between these aspects (which vary according to the points of view) that the perceptual synthesis is passively established. What, then, is this house perceived, as presenting itself under a certain aspect rather than under another? The question concerns the house *qua* perceived, precisely and strictly as it appears through a determinate perceptual act or, more briefly, the house perceived as such. Obviously, the house *qua* perceived in the above sense cannot be considered as a mere sum of sensory data in the sense in which Hume uses the term. No more can the house *qua* perceived be taken as the real house *qua* physical thing, a thing which can be perceived from diverse points of view and present itself under different aspects. For here we have to do with the house appearing under one well-determined aspect and not under another one.

Finally, one must distinguish the thing perceived as such from the perceptual act. A rather simple reflection will serve to make this clear.

Suppose that we place ourselves at a certain point of observation from which we look at the house without moving, and suppose that we alternately close and open our eyes. Each time that we open our eyes, we experience an act of perception, which, once it is past, can never recur, as this generally holds for all acts of consciousness. Thus we have to distinguish the perception which we experienced before closing our eyes from the one which we are experiencing now that we have opened them again. We find, therefore, a multiplicity of perceptual acts which differ from one another (be it only because of their places in phenomenal time) and which can be enumerated. Meanwhile we perceive not only the same house *qua* physical thing but are also confronted with the same thing as presenting itself to us under the same aspect; briefly, we are faced with the same house perceived as such. The latter being neither the physical house nor an act of consciousness, we have to recognize the perceived *qua* perceived as a special and specific entity—"perceptual noema" is the technical term which Husserl uses. For this entity there was no place in traditional thought, because the only distinction admitted was that between things or physical events, on the one hand, and, on the other, acts of consciousness.

The passive synthesis which we are here considering is effected between the perceptual noemata. In the course of the perceptual process developing while we walk around the house so as to see it from all sides, the diverse aspects under which the house appears not only succeed one another in time but beyond this continuously glide and blend into one another. To borrow a phrase of Merleau-Ponty which quite adequately expresses the passivity of the perceptual synthesis, a "synthesis of transition" becomes established between the perceptual noemata. But here we must forsake embarking even upon a superficial study of the perceptual process.

These reflections have led us to the notion which is at the center of the Husserlian conception of consciousness: namely, that of *intentionality*. It has all too often been remarked that, according to this conception, every act of consciousness is a consciousness *of* something, that every act of love is a love *of* something, and so on. It is necessary, however, to analyze the phenomena more precisely instead of contenting ourselves with a formula which is almost merely verbal.

The analysis of the example taken from our perceptual experience has made us aware of both an opposition and a correlation between an identical and identifiable unity—the perceptual noema—and an indefinite multiplicity of acts of consciousness, all different from one another, if only by their respective places in phenomenal time. Acts of perception are intentional acts because, through each of them, a perceived thing appears under a certain aspect and in a certain mode of perceptual presentation—because, in one word, to each of them there corresponds a perceptual noema, and—we remember—the same noema can correspond to a multiplicity of acts. What is fundamental here is the notion of noema. According to a very telling remark made by Berger some years ago, Husserl has discovered a category which is more fundamental than that of being or of non-being: namely, the category of the object intended as such, of the object as intended through a concrete act of consciousness.[4]

What is true for perceptual life is valid quite generally, as can be shown on any example. Let us take an example from the sphere of linguistic symbols and their understanding. I can state the Pythagorean Theorem as often as I wish; or, let us suppose that I formulated it yesterday after having deduced it from other theorems, say from the very axioms of Euclidean geometry, and this morning I return to the result of my geometrical reflections in order to deduce further consequences from it. My act of yesterday evening is not this morning's act, and yet it is the same Pythagorean Theorem which I deduced yesterday and which I take as the point of departure for my thought today. Here again, it is necessary to insist on the identity of the thing intended, precisely *as* it is intended, in opposition to an indefinite multiplicity of acts through which it is intended. Incidentally, it matters but little that the Pythagorean Theorem is true. Even if I say that "three and four are nine," in order to be able to recognize this proposition as false, I must intend and apprehend it as an identifiable and identical proposition. This proposition must be intelligible, and it must have the mode of existence proper to propositions. Whenever I formulate this false proposition, it is the same falsity which I state, doing this on different occasions, i.e., through different acts.

It follows from these considerations that consciousness must not be conceived as a unidimensional series of events in the manner of traditional thought, which saw in consciousness only a series of events succeeding one another in time. To be sure, such a conception is not false, because temporality is in fact a basic law of consciousness. It is not, however, the only one. What we must say is that the traditional conception is simply incomplete, because the events in question here are events of a very particular kind. They are the events through which noemata are presented, apprehended, and actualized. As indicated by the parallel we have established between perceptual con-

4. G. Berger, *Le cogito dans le philosophie de Husserl* (Paris, 1941), p. 54.

sciousness and the comprehension of linguistic expressions, noemata pertain to the same domain as meanings. One can even call them meanings, provided one understands this term in a much wider sense than is usual. *We are thus led to define consciousness by the correlation between two levels: on the one hand, the level of multiple acts, psychological events, which take place in time; on the other, the level of meanings, of significations, of noemata.* We may perhaps be permitted to refer to an article in which we sought to advance this conception of consciousness as a correlation and to show that Husserl's analyses not only agree with this interpretation of intentionality but even tend toward it as their *telos*.[5]

It is possible (by means of the example of the perception of a stable thing) to demonstrate the superiority of the Husserlian conception of consciousness as against that advocated by Kant. The problem which we have in view here is concealed in Kant because of the preeminence he gives to the relation of causality in both the *Kritik der Reinen Vernunft* and *Prolegomena*. To bring this problem out, we shall take a glance at the Kantian analysis of the relation of causality.

Suppose we have the same experience or do the same laboratory experiment on several occasions. For instance, we heat a metal rod and observe a certain elongation. It is common to speak of a repetition of the same observation, of the same experience or the same process. Let us consider this more carefully. Each time that we do the experiment in question, we measure the length of the rod; we heat it and measure its length again. Each experience furnishes us with a series of sensory data: the first one with the data $a_1, a_2 \ldots, a_n$; the second one with the data $b_1, b_2 \ldots, b_n$, and so on. Comparing these two series, we find that the sensory data respectively resemble one another: $a_1$ is similar to $b_1$, $a_2$ is similar to $b_2$, $a_n$ is similar to $b_n$. One can go even further to say that these sensory data are totally like each other respectively, but they can never be taken as identical because the first series occurred, let us say, twenty minutes before the second. Though there may be similarity between the sensory data— even, if one wishes, perfect likeness—there can never be identity. What is identical is the law which governs the relation between the rise of the temperature and the extent of the elongation. According to Kant, the identity of the law is guaranteed by the identity of the function pertaining to the pure transcendental apperception which, on each occasion, operates in the same manner. Properly speaking, there is no repetition of the same process; there is only an identical law

5. See above, "On the Intentionality of Consciousness."

which governs an entire series of processes. Furthermore, there is a similarity or likeness between the sensory data which appear each time the experience is had.

This brief analysis will help us to understand the difficulty which the Kantian theory faces when it deals with the perception of a stable thing. Let us consider the example of which Kant himself made use (without, however, sufficiently analyzing it): the perception of a house. Kant remarks that I can look at this house from top to bottom or else from the bottom to the top. Sensory data successively follow one another in each observation, but their succession is not ratified by the pure transcendental apperception, in contradistinction to the case of the causal relation where the sensory data succeed one another not only in fact but also by rights. To simplify the matter, let us suppose that we always look at the house in the same direction, say, from top to bottom, and that we do this several times. Each time we experience a sequence of sensory data: the first time, the sequence $a_1, a_2 \ldots$ , $a_n$; the second time, the sequence $b_1, b_2 \ldots , b_n$, and so on. Here again, $a_1$ and $b_1$, $a_2$ and $b_2$, up to $a_n$ and $b_n$, are similar to one another or are respectively alike, but they are in no way identical. Contrary to the causal relation, there is here nothing identical, not even a law. How, therefore, can we speak of the "same thing" and maintain that it is perceived on several occasions? Under these conditions, it is hard to see how the consciousness of identity could ever emerge or by what right we can say, as in fact we do at every moment and without the least hesitation, that the diverse perceptions are all, in spite of the differences between them, perceptions of the same house.

Kant's theory fails in the face of a problem which, we repeat, is concealed in the case of the causal relation. Before, we were confronted not only with different sequences of sensory data but also with different physical processes (the actual elongation of the rod each time it is heated). In the case we are now considering, however, the perceived thing stands, in its very identity, over against a multiplicity of perceptions or sensory data.

We have taken these sensory data as psychical facts, refusing to adopt the interpretation of Paton, who has suggested that Kant deliberately identified "sensory data" with "sensible qualities" as states of things.[6] If this interpretation is in keeping with Kant's intentions, the criticism which Husserl has expressed as regards Locke and the entire empiricist school also applies to Kant. This criticism consists in pointing out the confusion of sensory data (*Empfindungen*) considered as psychical facts with the sensible qualities of things which,

6. H. J. Paton, *Kant's Metaphysic of Experience* (London, 1936), Vol. II, pp. 266ff., 306f.

while presenting themselves by means of sensory data, in no way coincide with these.[7] Husserl considers this confusion as an hereditary vice of modern thought, both philosophical and psychological; it is facilitated and even suggested by the fact that the sensory data and sensible qualities are expressed by the same words—such as "red," "hot," "hard."

In conclusion, we now ask where our reflection has led us. The result is certainly not a rapprochement between Husserlian and Kantian thought. Fundamentally, only the divergences have appeared.

Nevertheless the result of our considerations is not wholly negative, for this reflection does permit us to place the theory of intentionality into a historical perspective and thereby to make it appear in all its significance and importance.

In the history of modern thought three principal conceptions of consciousness have been advanced. The first is that of empiricism, the classical British school inaugurated by Locke and brought to its completion by Hume. According to this conception, consciousness is a mosaic of sensory data and images derived from these data. There is no internal connection whatever between all these facts; they merely co-exist or succeed one another. Hume has compared the mind to a kind of theatre where "perceptions" (including both what he calls "impressions" and what he calls "ideas") appear, disappear, and combine in numerous ways.[8] Hume adds that this comparison must not be pushed too far, because the stage of a theatre on which events take place has a certain stability, whereas the mind is reduced by him entirely to a heap of "perceptions" which are and remain isolated from one another.

It was against this conception of consciousness that Leibniz and Kant reacted; Leibniz to Locke, and Kant to Hume. Leibniz and Kant established the second principal conception of consciousness by insisting on the activity and spontaneity of the mind. In the Kantian theory, we recall, the understanding is conceived as function, operation, action.

The third principal conception of consciousness is established by Husserl. Although the term "intentionality" was borrowed from Brentano, who in turn took it from scholasticism, it is Husserl who gave to it a completely new and original meaning. For Husserl, the theory of

7. Husserl, *Logische Untersuchungen* (Halle, 1913), II, i, pp. 128ff.; Husserl, *Die Krisis der Europäischen Wissenschaften und die transzendentale Phänomenologie*, p. 27n. As to the confusion in question in Kant, cf. H. A. Prichard, *Kant's Theory of Knowledge* (Oxford, 1909), pp. 134ff., 209n.3, 231ff., 280ff.

8. D. Hume, *A Treatise of Human Nature*, ed. L. A. Selby-Bigge (Oxford, 1951), p. 253.

intentionality is not merely one phenomenological theory among others. The idea of a fully completed phenomenology is nothing other than the idea of a theory of intentionality developed in all directions, followed out to its final ramifications.

## DISCUSSION [9]

M. BERGER

—I welcome the opportunity to express the thanks of our society to M. Gurwitsch. We have enjoyed a great deal the considerable ease and at the same time rigorous precision with which he has treated his subject, harmoniously developing the task he has set himself.

I am certain that, in the audience, there are a great many questions ready to be asked. I do not want to delay them; I want only to say to M. Gurwitsch how much I was struck by the truth of one of his remarks, one to which he returned in several places: it is neither fair nor fruitful to compare two philosophies point by point. Though they may perchance employ the same vocabulary, they nevertheless give wholly different and even opposed meanings to the same terms because their fundamental intentions, or their general climate, can hardly be called similar.

You have shown quite well how the philosophy of Kant is focused on the activity of consciousness, whereas that of Husserl has an aversion to everything which evokes the idea of a "constructive" synthesis. This circumstance seems to me all the more important because contemporary philosophy has often been tempted to emphasize again this "activity of the mind" and to give it still more reality and significance than it had even for Kant.

You know, as do I, my dear friend, how much the word "construction" could irritate Husserl. Everything connoting operation, manipulation, or synthesis in the active sense in which it is often understood by our contemporaries seemed to him in radical opposition to his own thought. I am, indeed, certain that he would not have permitted the substitution of the notion of *receptive passivity* for that of *constructive activity,* because, for him, consciousness was neither active nor passive. Such notions as these are meaningful only in the mundane sense. The relation which connects consciousness to its objects has a radical originality above and beyond all "mundane" actions. You have shown very well that, for Husserl, consciousness does not operate or

9. Discussion following the lecture as presented before the Société Française de Philosophie, April 25, 1959.

fabricate anything. The distinction between the "ego" and the "world" thus permits one to avoid the difficulties and ambiguities which one finds in Descartes. When the latter, for instance, says "I exist," "the world exists," "God exists," one may ask whether the same word, even analogically, can be used for that which cannot simply be taken for three modes of being.

However, I want to allow your listeners to pose their questions to you. First, one of our colleagues, M. André Leroy, who is well acquainted with Hume's thought.

M. A. LEROY

—I admit that it is not the relation to Hume which has particularly attracted me in this exposition, and, if I were not afraid of abusing Professor Gurwitsch's time, I would only point out that a good many of the things which he has said have prompted me to think of Whitehead. When you spoke, quite justly, of that first contact indicated by Husserl in his last work, of the crisis of consciousness, I just wondered if there were not in this connection some relation to what Whitehead called the world of "physical feelings." For Whitehead, however, the relating is established by the opposition, by the objectivation, by the subject himself, at least to a certain degree.

Furthermore, there is another extremely interesting idea which, however, seems to be expressed very differently by Whitehead. When at the level of knowledge a projection onto the object or the recovery of the object by means of the needs and desires of the subject takes place, this recovery can be accomplished in two ways, according to Whitehead. However, at the level of the involvement of consciousness [*au stade de la prise de conscience*] the subject recovers his desires and sees an extremely different world. This position is at once close to, and yet very different from, Husserl's, as you have indicated it. It is quite similar because there is that kind of combination which I would venture to call "synthetic." At the same time, there is something which I do not see in Husserl (I do not know him too well, but you will tell me if I am wrong)—there is at the same time a considerable difference because, for Whitehead, there are needs or desires which intervene and are not simply a kind of strictly intellectual knowledge.

Is it true that I can attribute to Husserl, in this instance, a more intellectual knowledge than the kind of knowledge which I believe Whitehead maintains?

M. GURWITSCH

—Husserl would probably have replied that Whitehead starts from man considered as a mundane being and that, in order to thus start, he has to presuppose the world in which man finds himself situated, just as a mundane being. For this reason Whitehead's philosophy would be for him one more mundane philosophy among others—that is to say, a philosophy which at the very outset accepts the world without raising the question concerning the sense or meaning of the existence of the world. In this regard, Husserlian phenomenology is of a radicalism unheard of before. As it seems to me, such would be the reply which Husserl would have given had he known the work of Whitehead, of which, however, I am not sure.

To return to your first question, it is indeed very interesting to see parallels between certain ideas which Whitehead has expressed in his *Science and the Modern World* and some views which Husserl formulated in his *Krisis*—parallels which the late Alfred Schutz had already pointed out in several of his writings. It appears from such parallels that for contemporary thought the very existence of science has become a problem in a sense completely unknown in philosophical tradition and that this problem has emerged in completely different currents of thought which even ignore one another. One can take it as a confirmation by convergence that we are faced with a truly genuine problem. To express the matter in a way somewhat similar to that of Husserl, in a certain sense we understand scientific theories, but we do not understand science. The point is that the very existence of a science with the style of modern science has become problematic for us. It seems to me that in his writings on science Whitehead has seen a great many of the things which are related to this problem.

M. LEROY

—I appreciate your comments very much. What seems to me very interesting is, as you have pointed out, that these two thinkers have begun with very different styles, the one from the outset being mundane and, as it were, without subjectivity, whereas Husserl, who cannot dispense with objectivity, relies on a primitive subjectivity which only gradually objectifies. That shows, I believe, that we have another view of human knowledge and of human science especially.

M. GURWITSCH

—Permit me to add one more remark. You say that for Husserl knowledge is more subjective than it is for Whitehead. This is so precisely because Husserl poses the radical question concerning the very sense of the existence of the world and of real things. Therefore, he must endow perception with a privilege which it never had known in the history of philosophy. The reason for this is that by means of perceptual consciousness we establish contact (I am seeking to express myself in the most neutral way possible) with the real world, the *Lebenswelt,* the surrounding world. To be sure, perception enjoys a privilege in many respects for Husserl, but the one which I have mentioned seems to me most important.

M. E. WOLFF

—M. Gurwitsch has stated that Kant was above all concerned with a theory of science and not so much with a theory of perception. I think that by and large this is correct; still, there is all the same a theory of perception in Kant, and I have in particular studied it in my book, *Du rôle de l'imagination dans la connaissance chez Kant.* This theory of perception is found not only in the first edition of the "transcendental deduction of the categories," to which you have referred but also in the *Vorlesungen über die Metaphysik,* in which Kant gives the example of a spectator who arrives in a cathedral (I believe it is Saint Peter's in Rome) where there are a great many objects. It is necessary by means of a synthetic activity of perception to accomplish the unity of these objects.

Kant has on the other hand spoken of the *Vorhersehungsvermögen* which seems to me very closely related to Husserl's notion of "protention."

With respect to the passive and active syntheses, this distinction can be found in Kant's *Prolegomena:* the level of the "rhapsody" of perceptions and the level of the apperception of ordered themes. This is precisely a point which I have developed in my complementary thesis. However, I believe that already in this apparently passive synthesis there appears a connective power, because for Kant the mind is never completely passive, and it is the subconscious activity of the imagination which precedes the appearance of that of the apperception. And, if we recall the distinctions between the three syntheses— first, the synthesis of apprehension in perception, then that of reproduction in the imagination, finally that of recognition in concept —in the main all the work is accomplished, the apperception only becoming consciously aware of the subterraneous work of the imagination. And I think that there is in Kant a theory of perception, of an active perception, for there is never complete passivity of perception. I prefer the expressions of Kant, who opposes the ordered synthesis to the spontaneous synthesis. Still, already in the spontaneous synthesis, already in the appearance of this spontaneous activity of the imagination, there is an active synthesis which, however, does not arrive at an order as stable as the synthesis effected by scientific reflection.

I want, moreover, to stress the fact that this manner of coordinating the data belonging to the senses, the "sensoria," in order to bring about the unity of the object, is very close indeed to the "bestowing of sense"—to employ what I believe is a Husserlian expression, in any case a phenomenological one. When diverse sensory elements are thus coordinated and unified, their unity has at the same time been given sense or meaning. I am aware that the recognition in the concept belongs to the sphere of the transcendental apperception in the proper sense, whereas everything else belongs to the domain of the imagination. But after all, the main work was done by the imagination which preceded the apperception, and the synthesis is by itself signifying, I believe. It gives rise to sense or meaning (signification), and I think that one can thus defend oneself against the possible objection of phenomenologists—namely, by pointing out that the synthesis makes a signification arise.

M. GURWITSCH

—It is indeed correct that the imagination plays a primary role for Kant, and I am very far from contesting that. You are also correct to recall the importance which he has attributed to it in the *Anthropologie in pragmatischer Hinsicht*, as well as in the *Kritik der reinen Vernunft*. However, the synthesis of apprehension and that of the imagination only have a preparatory task. Objectivation is the work of the pure transcendental apperception alone. If one can speak of the syntheses of imagination and of apprehension as passive, this is only because, according to Kant, they contribute nothing to objectivation. Husserl's contention, on the contrary, is that the constitution of the perceptual world, whose objectivity (primordial objectivity) founds every higher-level objectivity, is effected by means of passive syntheses. And I cannot conceal a certain uneasiness at seeing parallels drawn between Husserlian notions and those of Kant (who, incidentally, speaks of "receptivity" rather than "passivity").

You maintain that the Kantian synthesis can be considered as a bestowal of sense. Here I cannot agree with you, because the synthesis of pure transcendental apperception as Kant conceived it only ratifies temporal relations between sensory data. For this reason he needs the schematism. The sensory data received under the conditions of time are dispersed and scattered. On the other hand, there is the pure transcendental apperception in its articulated functioning. The two must meet, they must come into contact, as Rotenstreich has shown in a study on the Kantian theory of the schematism.[10] Let us grant that the contact is established: what, then, can the functioning of

---

10. N. Rotenstreich, "Kant's Schematism in Its Context," *Dialectica*, X (1956).

apperception accomplish? It can ratify or not ratify the temporal relations. Objectivation consists entirely in legalizing the temporal relations and conferring upon them a title of right. Then, and only then, does the succession of data become objective. At the beginning of the "second analogy" Kant expressly affirms that the apprehension of the manifold is always successive and that the question arises whether it is also successive in the object itself. "Bestowal of sense or meaning," as Husserl understands it, is something completely different. It must be emphasized, as M. Berger has just done, that consciousness does not manufacture meaning; it is rather the actualization of meaning. Consciousness and meaning go and belong together; there is no act of consciousness which is not the actualization of a meaning.

At the higher level of active synthesis new problems arise, with which, however, we are not concerned here. Thus, I do not see how the Kantian syntheses can fulfill the function which falls to the theory of intentionality.

M. HYPPOLITE
—I should like to ask M. Gurwitsch, whose exposition I greatly admired, if there is not another difference between Kant and Husserl. Syntheses, and in particular those which concern the world, are for Husserl capable of being disconfirmed. There can be non-ratification for Husserl, and in his *Ideen* the world itself as a synthesis achievement is problematic. The existence of the world is problematic insofar as it is a synthetic unity, whereas for Kant there is necessarily a synthetic unity of experience.

I think that this only extends what you have said. The theory of evidence, in the end, and the possibility of invalidation, seem to me in consequence fundamental for Husserl; whereas for Kant there can never be an invalidation of the unity of experience conceived *a priori*.

M. GURWITSCH
—Certainly. Only to simplify my exposition, I have supposed all along that the perceptual process develops without corrections or modifications.

It seems to me, indeed, that Kant has raised the problem of error—which must arise in every philosophy of whatever persuasion.

Finally, you are quite right if you say that it is in the *Ideen* that the problem concerning the existence of the world is considered. However, according to Husserl, the world is not dubitable; it is only contingent, and contingency is something other than dubitability.

M. HYPPOLITE

—The sense of the synthesis by which the world is continually confirmed. . . .

M. GURWITSCH

—This synthesis is never completed or definitive. It is valid only with proviso; that is to say, provided that the perceptual process continues developing in the future as it has up to the present. But there is never any guarantee that this process will in fact continue developing without discordances, that it will not necessitate corrections. This defines the contingency of the world. One can say that Husserl has assumed the task of clarifying the nature of contingent truths, to use Leibniz' language. Every truth related to mundane facts is contingent; it is not necessary. The world can be different from what it is in fact; the world exists, but it could be the case that it not exist. We have no reason whatever to doubt the existence of the world; such a doubt would not be well founded—even, not founded at all. There remains, however, the problem concerning the meaning of the contingency of the world as a whole, as well as of every mundane fact; of the meaning of the contingency, of facticity itself.

If for Kant this problem hardly plays any role, this is, I think, because of his notion of the thing-in-itself. Although he does not permit himself any speculation on the thing-in-itself, it is not only admitted in his system but also supports the system in a certain sense. For the very same reason, Kant never posed the problem of Others in his theoretical philosophy, nor that of intersubjective communication, as Husserl has done. The identity of the phenomenal world for all subjects is guaranteed by the identity of the thing-in-itself. This notion has been rejected by Husserl, just as it had been discarded in German neo-kantianism and also in German post-kantianism already at the end of the 18th century. This is another divergence between Kant and Husserl.

I tried to bring out some of these divergencies in examples almost arbitrarily chosen. One could make a longer list of these, and the results to which one would come would be quite surprising. Yet, while emphasizing the divergencies and differences of climate, one must remember the express claim maintained by Husserl that he seeks to realize the deepest intentions of Kant. On the very first page of his *Cartesian Meditations*, Husserl characterizes phenomenology as a neo-cartesianism, although he finds himself obliged to abandon almost the whole doctrinal content of Descartes' philosophy. *Mutatis mutandis*, Husserl could have used the very same words as regards Kant's theoretical philosophy.

One must distinguish Kantianism from the philosophy of Kant himself, who was the first to express in a certain form a philosophical tendency which has become a living force in history. It is a distinction of the same kind as the one which must be made as regards Plato: Platonism is something different from the set of doctrines which the historical Plato advanced.

#### M. HYPPOLITE

—I did not exactly want to speak of this contingency of the world in its totality. I want to say that there is a level of perception at which we can encounter a kind of causality which breaks down, in which the approximation of causality is not of the same type as the one necessary to a synthesis elaborated by science. For Kant, the demonstration must absolutely rely on the absolute unitary character of synthesis. We must refer to concepts *a priori* which make a succession and a simultaneity of the facts necessary, and necessary in one sense alone. On the other hand, for Husserl there are degrees, and that appears to us, to us moderns, as a beginning of a prodigious intentional analysis, in relation to that of Kant.

#### M. GURWITSCH

—Agreed. What you have brought up here is pertinent to the different attitudes which Kant and Husserl have taken towards science. For Kant, Newtonian science expresses the constitution of the real world, whatever it may be that we perceive. Newtonian science exists, and philosophy has to account for it. It is one of the principal aims which governs the system of the *Kritik der reinen Vernunft*—a system which must be conceived in such a way that the Newtonian universe can result from it. Consequently, the syntheses can never fail, because otherwise, given the existence of Newton's science, philosophy would miss its task. Husserl, by contrast, moves in an entirely different direction. He even considers the possibility that the world could be such that there would not be science of the style of modern science. If we possess such a science, it is in no way by necessity; it is, as one can say with a little exaggeration, almost owing to a happy chance.

#### M. HYPPOLITE

—We could therefore say that for Husserl the function of intentionality is, in its different degrees, to unveil our contingent relation to the world in all its forms . . .

#### M. GURWITSCH

—Yes, and the Husserlian analysis is not oriented toward the justification of any science . . .

M. HYPPOLITE

—But the manifestation of this fundamental relation . . .

M. BERGER

—With reference to the very interesting point touched upon by M. Hyppolite, I want to give you the occasion to furnish some explanation of a problem which, as you know, preoccupied Husserl: that of the "origin of the world."

Most philosophers treat that question by giving a causal explanation. For them, to explain the origin of anything whatever is to relate it to the agent which produced it—whether it be constructed out of preexistent elements or created *ex nihilo*. Already with Kant such an explanation is not possible, since time is a form of sensibility, and causality is a category of the understanding. Between reality in itself and the world of phenomena there is a relation *sui generis* with which the commentators are, generally, less concerned than they are with the transcendental aesthetic or analytic.

Considering the origin of the world, the *Ursprung der Welt*, Husserl, like Kant, could utilize neither the concept of causality nor that of production. But, since he refuses to relate the world to "an absurd thing-in-itself," he puts himself under the obligation to elaborate on original theory (which does not appear very clearly). The notion of "unveiling," of which M. Hyppolite has spoken, could put us on the way to a solution. But does this correspond to Husserl's intentions? Or do you think that, for him, the origin of the world poses an insoluble problem? I would like to know your feelings on this point.

M. GURWITSCH

—A number of Husserlian manuscripts in fact bear, unless I am mistaken, the title "The Origin of the World."

As you have correctly stated the phrase *Ursprung der Welt* has no causal-mundane meaning. It is not at all a question of a cosmogony in the traditional sense. Besides, it is a peculiarity of the German language that certain words have a plurality of sometimes highly different meanings. The word *Ursprung*, for example, can also have the meaning of ἀρχή, "root." Although he modifies the term, Husserl takes it in such a sense.

The world has its origin in constitutive consciousness; it is in this consciousness that the world arises such as we know it. Let us understand this. The consciousness in question here evidently cannot be that of an individual human being or a divine consciousness of which we are totally ignorant. What, then, is in question?

In the *Krisis*, Husserl has devoted two sections to what he calls the "correlational *a priori*" (*Korrelationsapriori*).[11] The meaning of this notion is roughly the following: each object can be taken as a clue which leads us back to the acts of consciousness, to the groupings and concatentations of acts, through which the object in question presents itself such as it figures in our conscious life, be it theoretical or practical. Certain of these acts play a privileged role: namely, those which are originary apprehensions of the object. This is the case, for instance, of perception in contradistinction to memory and representation. To raise the problem concerning the origin of any object whatever is, therefore, to conceive a program for analytical work. The task consists in making explicit the "equivalent of consciousness"—to use a term Husserl once employed in his *Ideen* [12]—with respect to this object. The "equivalent of consciousness," to repeat, is nothing other than the group of systematically organized acts through which the object in question appears such as we take it to be.

Generalizing this idea, and pushing its generalization to the end, we come to formulate the problem of the origin of the world: what are the acts of consciousness through which the world as it is familiar to us presents itself to us? Now, the world is not one mundane object among others. To raise the problem of the phenomenological origin of this sheet of paper, for example, is to engage oneself in the analysis of a perceptual process, the development of which is subject to the condition of concordance between its successive phases. Since the world, however, is not an additional mundane object, the study of its phenomenological origin must be pursued in a different direction.

Let us start from the fundamental distinction between figure and ground, as advanced in Gestalt theory. The generalization of this distinction yields the notion of "horizon." Being interested in this sheet of paper, I deal with it, I choose it as my perceptual theme. However, I perceive the sheet of paper as situated on the table; I thus perceive it on a background. Furthermore, the table is located in this room, this room in the Sorbonne, the Sorbonne in Paris, Paris in France. References to other things which can be perceived spread out in all directions originating in the theme of our present perception. The system of such references (which can be more or less vague, imprecise, and indeterminate) constitutes the consciousness which we have of

11. Husserl, *Die Krisis der Europäischen Wissenschaften und die transzendentale Phänomenologie*, §§ 46, 48.

12. Husserl, *Ideen zu einer reinen Phänomenologie und phänomenologischen Philosophie*, ed. W. Biemel (*Husserliana*, Vol. III [The Hague, 1950]), p. 319.

the world. Every perceived object appears in an horizon which extends or can be extended to infinity. This confers on the object the sense of its mundaneity.

On the other hand, we never have access to the world except from a particular mundane object—that is to say, from a certain point of view. A certain consciousness of the world accompanies the consciousness we have of every object we perceive. The inverse as well is true: every perceived object is necessarily a mundane object, by reason of the aforementioned references to the horizon which continues indefinitely. In brief, at every moment of our perceptual life we are conscious of the world which appears, in a certain sense, centered on a particular object—namely, the one which is our present perceptual theme.

I hope that these few remarks remain faithful to Husserl's intentions.

I will be permitted perhaps to add a few words on the subject of the phenomenological reduction. It is often said that by means of it the world becomes a phenomenon. However, the phenomenological reduction in no way effects any change or transformation. The world continues to be what it has always been, prior to the reduction; the objects which it encompasses remain as they were all along. The phenomenological reduction creates nothing; however, it does reveal something. In an attitude which can be called "pre-philosophical," we naïvely take the things as real beings, as mundane existents. We do this and we can do it, because, in virtue of certain acts of consciousness and groups of such acts, the objects present themselves *as* real, mundane existents. Precisely this circumstance is disclosed and made explicit by means of a reflection in which one can see the initial step of the phenomenological reduction. One may therefore say that the world reveals itself as a phenomenon; this signifies that it does not *become* a phenomenon but rather that it has always been one— although, if one can so express it, without our being aware of it. We can adopt one or the other of two attitudes. In the attitude which can be called naïve—the natural attitude according to Husserl—we accept things simply as we encounter them in our experience, and we proceed on this basis. This is what we do in both the pre-scientific and the scientific attitude—briefly, in every attitude whatever, with the sole exception of the phenomenological attitude. To adopt the latter is to become interested not so much in things themselves as in their manner of appearance and presentation, and thus we become interested in their "equivalent of consciousness." The problem of the phenomenological origin, be it of the world as a whole or of a mundane being, always concerns an "equivalent of consciousness."

**M. DUSSORT**

—I would like, if I may, to venture two remarks.

The first goes in the direction of what M. Gurwitsch said—namely, that Husserl considered phenomenology as a neo-cartesianism. As for his "intention," one could also consider it as a neo-kantianism. This is precisely what Husserl himself said in Freiburg in 1924, when he presented himself as the successor to Kant who, like Descartes, had been a *Bahnbrecher*, someone who opens the way, a trailblazer. Therefore, on this point I am in complete accord with M. Gurwitsch.

The second remark would perhaps be a little critical, if indeed I have correctly understood and comprehended what M. Gurwitsch has said. I would make it *a propos* your allusion to the Husserlian distinction between passive and active synthesis. I think you said that perception is the privileged example of passive synthesis and, as regards active synthesis, you said that it was reserved for logical thought . . .

**M. GURWITSCH**

—Among others . . .

**M. DUSSORT**

—But, for example, "recollection" (the act of memory) is an active synthesis which is not of the order of logical thought, whereas retention is a passive synthesis. Whether I would like it or not, I cannot help experiencing retentions; but I can, *voluntarily*, remember or not remember a remote past. The latter belongs to the sphere of the "I can," as Husserl said in his *Vorlesungen.*

It would therefore perhaps be necessary to develop a trichotomy: passive synthesis, pre-logical active synthesis, and the active synthesis which is *properly* logical.

**M. GURWITSCH**

—Permit me, if you will, to begin by addressing myself to your second point. I am afraid that there is a misunderstanding of which I am guilty: I have cited logical thought and mathematical thought as examples of active synthesis. One could give other examples of this synthesis; for example, all artistic activity. But I cannot follow you as regards your remarks concerning memory proper as opposed to retention.

What essentially characterizes the active synthesis is that an object of a higher order or level is constituted on the basis of data of a lower order. Let us consider the collecting of elements of any kind (for example, of all the persons now in this room) into a set. This is one of the most elementary active syntheses. Doubtless the activity in question here is not a physical but a mental activity. Correlatively, what results is not a real totality but a categorial set; it is, if you will, already a set in the mathematical sense. For the elements to be collected, they must be given. If these elements are real objects, they are given by means of the passive syntheses of perceptual life.

Let us consider another example: one begins with simple propositions, $p_1$, $p_2$, and so on, and then combines them as it is done in modern logic. This combination gives rise to a new proposition, $P$, which is more complex and includes the other propositions, $p_1$, $p_2$, and so on, as constituents. A new meaning is constituted on the basis of pre-given meanings. The latter themselves are already a result of active syntheses, but these pertain to a level of activity lower than the one to which the active synthesis related to the proposition $P$ belongs.

These examples furnish a criterion for the activity of synthesis. This activity denotes two things: new objective entities are constituted, and their constitution is based upon pre-given elements which in the final analysis are perceptual objects such as they are presented in the passive synthesis of pre-predicative experience.

We are faced with a completely different situation, however, in the case of explicit recollection—as when I go back into my past (for instance, to a certain period of my youth which I now seek to reconstruct). This requires an effort on my part, and it is no doubt because of this effort that you have spoken of activity here. From the psychological point of view you are certainly correct. By the same right, you could as well speak of activity as regards perception: when I walk around a house in order to perceive it from various sides, this motion certainly implies an activity on my part, even a physical activity—that of walking. However, it is not this purely psychological aspect which interests Husserl. According to him, the question must always be asked as to whether an object of a new order or of a new level results from the synthesis which is under examination. Considered from another perspective, the difference between the active synthesis and the passive synthesis can be reduced to this: the real world, the life-world (*Lebenswelt*), the world in which we find ourselves, is not only contingent but, beyond this, is not created by man. On the other hand, logic is certainly a human creation, as is mathematics, or works of art, and the like.

Finally, let us return to the remarks which Husserl made on Kant in the Freiburg lecture, as well as on other occasions. He has repeatedly expressed a preference, even a marked one, for Hume rather than for Kant. According to Husserl, Kant did not fully see the problems which Hume had already posed in all radicality. In other texts, he says that Kant did have a presentiment for phenomenology but that unhappily it was hardly more than a foreshadowing, and that Kant permitted himself to be misled into constructions. At times, Husserl speaks of Kant with a certain *malaise,* even irritation. What we have to remember and to emphasize here is the express claim which Husserl has so often repeated: namely, that of realizing the intentions of Kant, intentions which Kant himself understood but imperfectly.

M. DUSSORT

—He has said that Kant was a de facto phenomenologist, naïvely. In other words, that Kant sometimes did phenomenology without being aware of it . . .

M. GURWITSCH

—No! I do not think that he said that.

M.DUSSORT

—But yes! In the Preface to the Freiburg lecture.

M. GURWITSCH

—Perhaps we can come to agreement if we refer ourselves to the passage in his *Ideen,* where Husserl speaks of phenomenology as the "secret nostalgia" of all modern thought.[13] Descartes had already come very close to it, but unfortunately he allowed his own greatest discovery to escape him. Hume was already on phenomenological grounds, but his eyes were blinded. Kant had a prescience of phenomenology. By definition, a "nostalgia" is not fulfilled. Therefore, Husserl was very far from attempting to transform all the great thinkers of modern philosophy into phenomenologists. In his historical presentations (which are, incidentally, not among the most fortunate of his writings), Husserl is interested only in a certain aspect of the thought of his predecessors. He was sometimes led to results which the historian feels obliged to rectify. But, after all, phenomenology did not fall full-bodied from the sky; it has its genealogy, it has historical roots, and Husserl was correct in pointing to very strong motifs which, through the course of the history of modern thought, moved toward phenomenology.

13. Husserl, *Ideen zu einer reinen Phänomenologie und phänomenologischen Philosophie,* pp. 118f.

**M. BERGER**

—We want to express our sincere thanks to M. Gurwitsch for his excellent exposition and the replies which he has given to his diverse interlocutors.[14]

TRANSLATED BY RICHARD M. ZANER

14. At the time this exposition and discussion was to be put into print, M. Gaston Berger met his accidental death—on November 13, 1960. Respect to his memory was paid in the issue of this *Bulletin* pertaining to the meeting of November 26, 1960.

# 10 / Phenomenology of Thematics and of the Pure Ego: Studies of the Relation between Gestalt Theory and Phenomenology [1]

WITH REGARD to its problems, the present work is concerned with Husserl's *Ideen zu einer reinen Phänomenologie und phänemenologischen Philosophie*, Volume I.[2] According to the *Ideen*, phenomenology is an eidetic science of consciousness and its most general structures. This fundamental conception serves as the basis on which the present analyses are developed and defines the historical standpoint of this essay. It will be phenomenology in the sense established by the *Ideen*.

Stated generally, as far as the orientation and problems of this essay are concerned, we shall not go beyond the *Ideen*. As far as the former is concerned, the phenomenological reduction is, so to speak, the avenue of access to phenomenology and its object, pure consciousness; as far as the problems are concerned, the point of view pertaining to intentionality is of basic significance. This is expressed by the distinction between noesis and noema, real and intentional phenomenological analysis, the doctrine of the hyletic, and so forth. In Husserl's own words, intentionality is the general theme of phenomenology and psychology; it is that which grants to consciousness its specific sense, denoting the fundamental component of the essence, "consciousness-at-large."

Finally, the investigations of the *Ideen* culminate in the functional problems related to the "phenomenology of reason" where phenomenology, by extending the Kantian inquiry, becomes transcendental phenomenology as far as it concerns itself with the constitution of

1. The original version of this article appeared in *Psychologische Forschung*, XII (1929).
2. Cited hereafter as *Ideen*. Page numbers refer to the original edition (Halle, 1913) and are printed in the margin of the Louvain edition, ed. W. Biemel (*Husserliana*, Vol. III [The Hague, 1950]).

objects pertaining to all possible regions. Inasmuch as this sketch indicates in general outline the setting of problems of the *Ideen,* it delineates the framework of the present essay as well.

The phenomenological reductions supply the undiscussed foundation, the tacit presuppositions. From the very beginning we move in the sphere and attitude acquired by exercising the *epoché,* the bracketing of the "natural world" and all real as well as ideal objects, i.e., whatever is transcendent to consciousness. That with which we have to deal is always tacitly presupposed as transcendentally purified, as the residuum of the *epoché.* On that account the reductions will not be explicitly discussed, because they are already presupposed as performed throughout the whole inquiry.

The problems of constitution, phenomenology as transcendental, remain in the background into which these investigations always, to be sure, protrude but never explicitly intrude. Constitutional problems are referred to whenever they appear as relevant; we shall explicitly designate the points at which constitutional problems arise, but we shall not pursue them or make them an object for inquiry. The problems of constitutive phenomenology form the ever-present horizon of our analyses, yet solely the horizon and never the field. Accordingly, this essay has epistemological goals but is not itself epistemological— just as it is oriented towards a transcendental philosophy without being itself transcendental philosophy.

Instead, the theme of the present inquiry revolves around what lies between the undiscussed foundation of the phenomenological reduction and the problems pertaining to transcendental phenomenology: the sphere of pure consciousness. Just as in Husserl, so here the concept of intentionality is considered as the central concept pertaining to this realm. However, in the more detailed development of the doctrine of intentionality a deviation from Husserl's teaching has become necessary on account of, and in connection with, his doctrine of hyletics and its problems. So far, however, as intentionality signifies that it is of the essence of states and processes of consciousness to have a presentifying or presentational function, this essay finds itself in agreement with Husserl's *Ideen.* As does the *Ideen,* so the present essay begins with pure consciousness in the form of the cogito: something is given to me; I am presented with, or confronted by, something objective. The inquiry is dedicated to the cogito and its noematic correlates. What does it mean that something objective is given? What is, in every case, the given? And what do changes in the cogito signify? These are questions whose answers we seek here.

Our essay thus fits into the framework which Husserl's *Ideen* allots to phenomenology; and it does that as much with respect to the point of departure as with respect to the formulation of problems. The attempt will be made to further develop and advance Husserl's analyses but also to modify them in some respects. Apart from phenomenological motives, still other lines of thought will prevail, especially those which have their origin in Gestalt theory. The goal of our study is to further certain phenomenological problems with the help of Gestalt-theoretical theses, to supplement Husserl's analyses by insights arrived at in Gestalt theory, as well as to correct some of his tenets, and in general to advance phenomenology along these lines beyond the stage reached by Husserl's *Ideen*. All this is accomplished, however, essentially in the spirit of the *Ideen*. Conversely, we shall point out the philosophical and, in particular, the epistemological problems arising out of Gestalt theory, at least intimating the way in which they originate.

Let us now present those Husserlian doctrines with which we shall deal in what follows.

In the pregnant sense, consciousness is characterized by intentionality, the "peculiarity of subjective processes 'to be consciousness of something.'" In particular, we encounter this peculiarity in the explicit cogito, in mental states in which we are actually busied with something, where we are presented with, or directed to, something, concerned with some object or other.[3] Calling the something with which we concern ourselves the theme of our busiedness, we accordingly designate by "cogito" those acts in which we actually busy ourselves with a theme, and for "cogito" the expression "thematic consciousness," "consciousness of a theme," can be substituted, so that the terms "theme" and "thematic" always connote actual busiedness.

For Husserl, these *cogitationes* are "specific acts of the ego" which emerge from the "changing stream" of subjective processes (*Erlebnisse*).[4] The pure ego engages himself in them; "in every actual cogito a 'regard' issuing from the pure ego is directed to the 'object' of the corresponding correlate of consciousness, to the thing, the state of affairs, etc., and effects the highly multiform consciousness *of* it." The pure ego's "'regard' passes 'through' each actual cogito to the object. This ray of vision varies with each cogito, with the new ⟨cogito⟩ newly darting forth and disappearing with it."[5] "Each 'cogito'. . . 'emanates from the ego,' it 'lives' 'actually' in it. The pure ego is the 'pure' subject of the act." As "'pure' subject of the act," the ego necessarily belongs to the cogito and cannot be erased from it by means of any reduction. "The 'being-directed-to,' 'being-busied-with,' 'taking a position towards,'

3. Cf. *Ideen*, I, § 84.
4. *Ibid.*, p. 58.
5. *Ibid.*, § 57.

178 / PHENOMENOLOGY AND PSYCHOLOGY

experiencing, suffering from,' *necessarily* contain in their essence the fact that they are 'away from the ego' or, in a converse direction, 'towards the ego.'" [6] "*Each* act, of whatever kind, can start in this *mode of spontaneity belonging, so to speak, to the creative beginning* in which the pure ego makes its appearance as subject of spontaneity." "Thesis and synthesis come into being while the pure ego actually takes the step and each new step; the ego itself lives in the step and 'makes an appearance' with it. The positing, positing-thereupon, precedent-positing and consequent-positing, etc., are its *free spontaneity and activity;* it lives in the theses, not in the mode of a passive dwelling-therein, but they are rays which radiate from it as a primal source of originations. Each thesis begins with an initiating, with a point of *originary positing.* . . . This 'initiating' belongs . . . to the thesis as such as a distinctive mode of originary actuality." [7]

The pure ego is active in *cogitationes* and lives in them; it lives in every actual cogito in a special sense corresponding to the specific nature of the cogito in question: in perception it is a pure perceiving ego, in phantasy it is a pure phantasying ego, in wishing it is a pure wishing ego, in valuing it is a pure valuing ego, etc. It is, however, always one and the same identical pure ego which lives in respectively varying modes. Mental states come and go, and along with them the modes of activity of the pure ego, but the pure ego itself, active in these modes, is identical over against all possible and actual change in mental states.

Mental states not having the form of the cogito and which are still intentional processes—for the cogito is a *special* form of intentionality—likewise have their share in the pure ego even when they do not possess the special ego-relatedness peculiar to *cogitationes.* They allow of being transformed into actual *cogitationes* and are a "*potential perceptual field* in the sense that whatever does not thus appear (sc. not in the form of a *cogitatio*) can be attended to by a special perceiving (an attentive perceptual [*gewahrendes*] cogito)." [8] Similarly, an explicit cogito, an operative act, can "be transformed into an 'inoperative' one by way of attentional modification," can become an "act impulse" (*Aktregung*) and thereby lose the character of an "act proper." [9] A similar but still different pattern occurs "when the pure ego effects a new step, and when it . . . 'still maintains in grasp' what it just was holding in grasp: apprehending the new thematic object, or rather apprehending a new member of the total theme as a primary

6. *Ibid.,* § 80.
7. *Ibid.,* § 122.
8. *Ibid.,* pp. 169, 232.
9. *Ibid.,* p. 236.

theme, while still holding onto the previously grasped member as belonging to the same total theme."

From the standpoint of these essential possibilities, the inactualities, understood in the broadest and most general sense, are interpreted as the "background of consciousness" pertaining to the pure ego; they are considered as "its field of freedom." It lives in actual *cogitationes*, it can grasp inactualities, they are at its disposal, it has power and freedom over them. The ego turns to what is given in an inactual mode of consciousness and, accordingly, makes it thematic; the ego brings an inactuality into its field of vision; or, conversely, the ego "releases" the theme "from its grasp," withdraws, and turns away from it.

In these last statements we have already entered into Husserl's doctrine of "attentional modifications." [10] This is what he calls those modifications of consciousness in which something is given to consciousness in the form of the cogito, while what was previously given in this form loses its attentional actuality. Husserl had already referred to the connection between attention and intentionality in the *Logische Untersuchungen.* [11] In fact, in comparing with one another the several modes of actuality such as "grasping," "holding in grasp," "still maintaining in grasp," "releasing from grasp," we find the mode "holding in grasp" to be identical with the mode of being-busied-with-something-in-the-form-of-the-cogito, the mode "still maintaining in grasp" to designate a certain form of inactuality, while the other modes refer to modifications of the cogito, i.e., of thematic consciousness.

It is in conformity with these connections and affinities that Husserl attributes to the "attentional formations in the modes of actuality the *character of subjectivity* in a distinctive way." "The attentional ray is given as issuing from the pure ego and terminating in something objective, directed to, or turning away from it. The ray does not separate itself from the ego but is itself and remains a ray of the ego. The 'object' is confronted; it is a goal only in relation to the ego (and thus posited by it), ⟨it is⟩ not itself 'subjective.' A position-taking, which carries the ray of the ego itself, is by this means an act of the ego itself; the ego acts or undergoes something, is free or conditioned. The ego . . . 'lives' in such acts. This living denotes . . . a multiplicity of describable ways in which the pure ego lives within certain intentional subjective processes having the general mode of cogito, as the 'free agent' that it is." Such modes of living

10. *Ibid.,* § 92.
11. Husserl, *Logische Untersuchungen,* 2d ed. (Halle, 1928), II, i, p. 409; "Aufmerksamkeit ist eine auszeichnende Funktion, die zu Akten in dem . . . Sinne von *intentionalen* Erlebnissen gehört." Similarly, p. 164.

belonging to a free agent, its "freely going out from itself, going-back-into-itself, its spontaneous doing, experiencing, undergoing something from the objects," define the sense of subjectivity at large and of the attentional in particular.

The interpretation of attention and attentional formations as subjective in the sense mentioned entails a certain conception of what results from attention and its modifications as regards noematic content. To be sure, there can be no question of merely external additions "supervening to something remaining identical; . . . rather, the concrete noemata change through and through." Still, attentional formations are various "modes of the manners of given-ness of the identical." The noematic content remains identically the same over against "mere alterations in the distribution of attention and its modes." Throughout the attentional modifications the same object with the same patent features and the same set of undeter-mined components given in a non-intuitive mode continues to present itself in the same manners of appearance and orientation, exhibiting the same doxic characters. Only at times is the one, then the other of its features and moments attended to in a privileged way; and one and the same feature is now " 'primarily paid attention to,' " now only secondarily, the one time " 'still just noticed' " ('*noch eben mitbe-merktes*'), the other time " 'fully noticed'—although always still appear-ing." The usual comparison of attention with an illuminating spotlight is endorsed by Husserl. "That which, in a specific sense, is paid attention to is found in the more or less bright beam, but it can also retreat into the half shadow and into full darkness. . . . This change in illumination does not change what appears as to its own sense-content, but brightness and darkness do modify its manner of appearance. . . ."

As a consequence of this doctrine, the attentional modifications denote, "on the noematic side, their own genus of characterizations—the identical noematic nucleus notwithstanding." "It is a question of necessary modes pertaining to manners of givenness of what is identical." The same holds for the modes of actuality, "holding in grasp," "still maintaining in grasp," etc.

The present essay is concerned with the doctrines just presented; above all with the egological interpretation of the cogito and the attentional, as well as with the conception which sees a "primal source of generations" in the pure ego, emphasizing its spontaneity. In the further course of our study we shall also consider the Husserlian doctrines founded on, or connected with, the egological interpretation of the cogito—thus, e.g., Husserl's doctrine of *hyle* and *morphé*. Above all, however, we shall examine the theory of attention which sees in this function some sort of light-source illuminating what the light is projected upon without materially changing anything in it, so that attentional modes are interpreted as kinds of characters.

In Section I of this essay we investigate the structure of that which presents itself to consciousness in the mode of cogito or, as we may also say, the structure of the theme. What does it mean to say of something given that it forms our theme? In this way we formulate the chief problem of this section.[12] In this connection we shall also attempt to incorporate into phenomenology the basic theses of Gestalt theory, and in an appendix to this section we shall outline the epistemological problems involved in Gestalt theory.

Section II begins with a distinction within that which is co-given with the theme. A certain domain of that which is co-given with the theme proves to be privileged. We shall embark upon an analysis of the internal structure of this domain, its belongingness to the theme, and, conversely, the theme's relatedness to that privileged domain. These analyses will lead us to the distinction of two types of Gestalt connections. Parallel to the noematic distinction within what is co-given, there is a noetic one concerning the concept of inactuality. Finally, we shall attempt to define the concept of actual consciousness, the concept of consciousness in the mode of cogito, and—noematically —the concept of what is given in this mode.

Section III deals with the attentional modifications and attempts to make the results of the two previous sections fruitful with regard to the problems in question. According to their essential accomplish-ments, three series of attentional modifications are distinguished. The concept of attention as a unitary function always performing the same service in the same way will have to be relinquished. From the analyses of the thematic modifications consequences are drawn which bear on the problem of parts and, especially, on Husserl's distinction of *hyle* from animating functions. This leads to an interpretation of the concepts of noesis and intentionality different from the sense in which Husserl understands these notions.

Section IV attempts to provide an outline of a phenomenology of the pure ego. Referring to the distinction within the co-given made in Section II, we shall seek access to the pure ego. However, we offer only an outline. In the foregoing sections it will have been shown that none of the motives pertaining to the area of problems concerning the pure ego may be allowed to intrude into a study of thematizing con-sciousness.

Finally, we note that all of Husserl's concepts which are not made

12. For essential suggestions concerning the problems treated in this section, the author is indebted to the lectures and seminars of Professor Gelb.

explicit objects for investigation are to be understood precisely in the sense given by Husserl in his writings, especially in the *Ideen*. Above all, this is true of the concept of noema.

## [I]  PHENOMENOLOGY OF THE THEME

### 1 / *Terminological Note*

As UNDERSTOOD in our normal manner of speaking, "theme" is synonymous with "object." We are accustomed to call the theme of the respective act the object of a perception, of a doubt, of an act of thinking, of ascertaining, wishing, and the like.

When, with Husserl and Twardowski, we distinguish the "content" from the "object" of acts, or, relatedly although not equivalently, the "noematic" from the "objective," the term "theme" directly refers to what is designated in the preceding contrast with "object." [13] The theme of a thing-perception, for instance, is the perceived thing itself, e.g., the tree standing in the garden, the "transcendent" tree which is subject to physical laws and can become an object of physical inquiries into its properties as a thing. But we do not designate as theme of this perception the "sense" of the tree-perception, "the perceived tree" (*das Baumwahrgenommene*), the noema corresponding to the act of perception.[14] We would not do that as long as we maintain the "natural attitude" towards the world; and all objective sciences related to "objects," to "transcendent" entities of any description whatever, including numbers, arise in this attitude and remain in it.[15] The identification of "theme" and "object" is in line with the "natural attitude" throughout.

But phenomenological investigations are radically and essentially different from inquiries into things in this sense. They take place by virtue of the "transcendental reduction" which makes phenomenological investigation possible in the first place. In our inquiry we are no longer concerned with objects, but instead we are concerned with what remains of them as residuum of the *epoché*. Transcendent entities as such fall to the *epoché*, and only united multiplicities of "senses" remain. Phenomenological investigation is directed to those "senses" and is so directed in the attitude of reflection.[16] If we take

13. K. Twardowski, *Zur Lehre von Inhalt und Gegenstand der Vorstellungen* (Vienna, 1894). Husserl, *Logische Untersuchungen*, II, i, 12ff.; *Ideen*, I, § 129.

14. Husserl, *Ideen*, I, p. 184.

15. Cf. *ibid.*, Pt. II, chap. I.

16. Cf. *ibid.*, § 77.

"theme" in the usual sense as synonymous with "object," then a phenomenology of the theme is never concerned with the theme itself but always only with conscious acts of the theme and, correlatively, with "theme" in the sense indicated when the word is enclosed in quotation marks: i.e., phenomenology deals with the theme exactly, precisely, only as, and only *so far as* it is presented to consciousness.[17] Content as the sense of consciousness directed towards the theme and being busied with it, the noema of the theme belonging to "thematic consciousness"—in a word, the theme-noema—forms the subject matter of investigation of a noematically oriented phenomenology of the theme.

This situation justifies our diverging from the normal linguistic use which identifies theme with object. Without exception, in what follows we shall designate with "theme" that which is given to consciousness, precisely just as and only to the extent to which it is given and as it is disclosed by a strictly descriptive analysis. When we speak of the theme of an act of consciousness, we mean, accordingly, the "object" as it stands before our mind, as it is meant and intended through the act in question. In the present essay, the term "theme" has a noematic meaning, and a phenomenology of the theme is a noematic analysis.

## 2 / *Theme as "Sense" or the Noematic What*

HOWEVER, we do not consider the full and concrete noema. Instead, we are concerned with a stratum of the noema disengaged by abstraction, this being the most fundamental stratum of the structure of the full noema.

Following Husserl's discussions in the *Ideen* of the structure of the full noema, we discern it in three distinctive strata. To every noema there belongs a precisely circumscribable content, a set of predicates pertaining to it "which is unfolded by a description confining itself within a certain delimitation, namely, by a ⟨description⟩ which *avoids all 'subjective' expressions as a description of the 'object meant, just as it is meant.'* "[18] The noematic stratum in question comprises all the content, all the material components of the noema, as well as all of its "formal ontological" and "material ontological" determinations. Even certain indeterminacies belong to this stratum, which, in fact, is the fundamental noematic stratum. It determines the "what" of the

17. This way of designating the noematic with quotation marks is employed in the *Ideen*.

18. Husserl, *Ideen*, I, § 130.

consciousness in question so far as, by descriptions of the kind indicated, the noematic object is explicated with respect to its determinacies and indeterminacies, with respect to that which it "is" and what it is meant as being. Which object is meant in a given case, which determinations—in both formal and material respects—pertain to the meant object as what and how it is meant, is defined by the stratum in question designated as matter of the act (the designation made in the *Logische Untersuchungen* [19]). The stratum's function of indicating the determinations and the content of what is given to consciousness is sometimes rendered in the *Ideen* by the term "What" (*Was des Bewussten*), which is equivalent to the expression "sense," while the concept of "nucleus" has a somewhat different meaning.[20] In what follows we shall adopt the designation of the stratum established as "sense" or as noematic What, and we shall take both expressions as synonomous.

The noematic stratum just delimited, abstractively isolated, defines a concept of noematic "objectivity"—namely, the concept of the "object in the How of its determinations." Let us contrast this concept with another concept of the "object in the How": the "object in the How of its manners of being and givenness." A second noematic stratum different from the first comes to the fore: the stratum of characters. It comprises the characters of being as well as those of manners of presentation. In the noetically oriented *Logische Untersuchungen* this stratum, in contradistinction to that of the "matter," is denoted as "quality" of the act.

As third stratum, in the *Ideen* we have the "central point of unity," "the pure X in abstraction from all predicates." From this "innermost moment" of the noema, which can be identically the same for noemata with various determinations of content, thus for noemata which differ from one another as to the noematic What, syntheses of identification take their departure—syntheses in which the same object is constituted in the sense of a transcendent entity. For the problems pertaining to the "phenomenology of reason," extended to objects of every description, the concept of this central point of unity is fundamental. The concept explains how the same thing presents itself as identical through multiplicities of adumbrations and, at the same time, how unity is bestowed on the multiplicity of adumbrations.

The problems holding our interest are far removed from those pertaining to "phenomenology of reason." It is not relevant for the phenomenological analysis of the given "theme" as such that the latter is susceptible of being combined with other themes into encompassing

19. Husserl, *Logische Untersuchungen*, II, v, § 20.
20. Husserl, *Ideen*, I, § 131.

sense unities correlated to transcendent entities. Nor, on the other hand, does it matter how that which is present to consciousness is characterized, whether as present or past, whether as simply existing or as doubtful, and so forth. Our concern is with the analysis of what is present to consciousness, and this analysis must be carried out in the greatest possible generality. Differences between "qualities" of acts and peculiarities of certain "qualities" are of little relevancy. On the other hand, the noematic What must not be subjected to any limitation with regard to singular and regional content. We deal with the stratum of the noematic What in broadest generality, i.e., extended to any What of any content whatever. Accordingly, "theme" in our sense is not the noema *simpliciter*, the full, concrete noema; instead, it is the content of the What in the noema, the noematic sense.

## 3  /  *The Problem of Structure in Thing-Perception*

To BEGIN WITH, let us formulate a problem with regard to perceptual noemata. A "box" stands there, with its "front" facing me. I see the "thing" there, and, apprehending it as a "thing," I "know" that it has a "back." The "form," "shape," and "color" of the "front" are intuitively given to me; of that which belongs to the "back" I have a more or less obscure, inexplicit "knowledge." Obviously the "back" belongs to the noematic What, but, of course, only to the extent to which, and in just the way in which, I am conscious of the "back." That of which I am conscious is a "box seen from the front," the "back" of which is not "seen," although I am somehow conscious of it. Materially determinate [21] components of the "back" belong to the noematic sense and must be allowed for in a noematic description. In asking *what* is given through this perceptual act, we must include the components of the "back" so far, but also only so far, as there is consciousness of them. Even when we know nothing in detail about the "back," suppose nothing and expect nothing, the situation is essentially the same. Let us suppose that the "back" of the "box" appears as totally undetermined when we see it from the "front"; in a noematic description of the What we express this state of affairs like this: the "thing" whose "front" is completely determined with respect to "color," "shape," "form," etc., also has a "back" which is *somehow* "colored," *somehow* "formed," *somehow* "shaped."

---

21. "Materially determinate" understood in contrast to that which belongs to the characters, and not, as is usual, in contrast to ontological, both formal and regional. In this sense, not only are terms such as "colored," "rough," etc., meant under the heading of the materially determinate, but also "property," "figure," "relation," and so forth.

This state of affairs is grounded in the nature of thing-perception. What is seen, what is "actually presented," is inserted into a domain of what is not seen and is more or less indeterminate along certain dimensions. And this domain necessarily belongs to what is presented in the mode of originarity. Owing to the very nature of adumbration, what "genuinely appears" is surrounded by what is "not actually presented," and even empty and undetermined components belong to it. What is "actually seen" requires, according to the nature of perceptual experience, just a surrounding of this sort. Husserl has quite correctly observed that what " 'genuinely appears' forms, in the full thing-sense, a *dependent* part which can only possess sense unity and sense independence in a whole *necessarily* containing empty and indeterminate components." [22]

What is the relation of components of the "back" to those of the "front"? How are we to conceive their connectedness?

To begin with, let us disregard forms of connection which result from peculiarities proper to certain qualities, as, for example, color and figure between which there obtains a connection of a definite and specific nature. Setting aside what Stumpf [23] called "partial contents" (*Teilinhalte*), we limit our problem to "independent contents" (*selbständige Inhalte*). Our problem is then to understand how parts and qualities, which by their nature are not dependent upon one another, become related to each other when they enter into the unity of *one* thing-noema.

A possible answer to this question would be to say that it is an aggregate. This would signify that the noematic What is composed of elements which happen to be given together. Element is added to element, their relatedness consists exclusively in their co-existence, their connection is purely an "existential connection" in Wertheimer's sense.[24] Since the elements are simply juxtaposed to one another, their totality simply presents a sum; an adequate noematic description would have to be no more than an enumeration: this and this and that, etc. In the enumeration, the elements stand side by side as *equipollent items,* connected to one another solely by an "and." On the basis of this conception, one can account for the difference between elements which function as components of the "front" and those which function as of the "back" in no other way than by resorting to

22. Cf. *Ideen,* I, pp. 80, 286.
23. C. Stumpf, *Über den psychologischen Ursprung der Raumvorstellung* (Leipzig, 1873), § 5.
24. M. Wertheimer, "Untersuchungen zur Lehre von der Gestalt," I, *Psychologische Forschung* (1922), I, pp. 48ff.

the manner in which the one and the other elements present themselves to consciousness, i.e., to the characters of the one or the other dimension. First of all, one might resort to differences in clarity. To be sure, it is quite possible that the components of the "back," in contradistinction to those of the "front," appear only as blurred, as indistinct and obscure. But *that* is not decisive, and it is not by this mode of obscurity *alone* that they are set off from the components of the "front."

We can convince ourselves of this with the following example: in the darkness of the forest we see something obscurely with uncertain outlines which "looks like a man." [25] What is given to us is confused, appearing as though veiled in a mist. Our "apprehension" wavers, now and then changing (it seems more like a tree). Although *everything* is veiled in darkness and obscurity, we still distinguish what we "see" of the supposed "man," say, his face, and what is turned away from us, his back which, nevertheless, belongs to what is perceived. For we indeed believe that we see a man, and his non-"seen" back does belong to him. Thus, resorting to differences in clarity is of no avail. Even when everything given to us is obscure and confused, i.e., unstable, there still remains for perceptual consciousness the difference between what is seen and what is not seen, between the "front" and the "back" of a "thing." And the problem remains as to the nature of the relation in which these components stand to one another, as to how their connectedness is to be conceived.

Nor does it help to resort to the difference between what is given perceptually and what is represented.[26] We can, indeed, represent the "box." We then have nothing given perceptually; and while we represent the "box-thing as seen from the front," the represented components of the back enter into the noema of remembering (*Erinnerungsnoema*) as noema of a remembered *"thing."* Hence, in the noema of remembering, in which *everything* is represented and where nothing at all is perceptually given, we encounter the same phenomenological difference as in the perceptual noema. Accordingly, we have the same problem again.

The situation recurs no matter what characters we might consider. When we say that the "back" is only distinguished from the "front" by modificatory manners of givenness, the possibility continually remains that the entire noema takes on the modification in question. In such a

25. Taken from Husserl, *Ideen*, I, p. 215.

26. Paralleling this distinction is the one introduced by H. Cornelius between the "mediately" and "immediately" given. Cf. *Transzendentale Systematik* (Munich, 1916), p. 89.

case, there is no longer a difference in manners of givenness as to the several components, but the phenomenological difference of "front" and "back," and accordingly the problem of their interrelation, remain as they were before. It follows that the interpretation of the noematic What as an aggregate, with respect to which we can only resort to characterizations for the difference mentioned, is not sufficient and that the structure of the noematic What, the relation of the component parts, entering into and forming the sense, ought not to be understood in terms of mere addition.

The problem posed here has not been dealt with by Husserl. "We obtain by explication and conceptual formulation a closed set of formal or material predicates, of predicates determined as to content ⟨sachhaltig bestimmten⟩ or else undetermined (emptily meant)." [27] Our problem concerns the inner structure of just this set.

## 4 / Generalization of the Problem

ABANDONING THE LIMITATION to the perceptual experience of things and posing the question in full generality, we are confronted with the problem of the *inner* structure of the noematic sense at large. When the noematic What contains a plurality of constituents, of what kind is that plurality? How is the noematic sense formed out of constituents? In what kind of relation do these constituents stand to one another? Formulated in this all-inconclusive generality, the question concerns noemata of any content whatever.

A figure, such as $\mathcal{S}$, which can be "apprehended" as a large Latin S or a small Greek $\varphi$, contains a curved line and a loop. How does the curved line fit together with the loop? What is their relation when the figure is "apprehended" as a large Latin S; what is it when "apprehended" as a small Greek $\varphi$? Or: a theoretical line of thought which I survey "at a glance," e.g., a mathematical proof, is composed of single steps, of single thoughts. How are they related to one another? How do they fit into each other? Correspondingly, the same question can be raised with regard to the melody which, as it were, at one glance I memorially hold in grasp without passing from note to note in remembering the melody. In this case, I also have parts; in what way are they connected? Finally, the problem also concerns "partial contents" and their discrimination and discernment. Husserl has distinguished several meanings of the term "abstraction." Taken in *one* of these meanings (the one we have in mind here), abstraction denotes the act

27. Husserl, *Ideen*, I, p. 270.

"through which an abstract content (= partial content) is discerned, i.e., without being separated, becomes the object of an intuitive representation especially directed to it."[28] Our question concerns the structure of the noematic sense correlative to this act of abstraction. The abstract content "appears in and with the concretum in question from which it is abstracted, but specifically it is intended and, being thus intended, . . . also intuitively given, as that which it is intended as." The problem concerns precisely *how* the abstract content appears "in" the concretum in question and *how,* on the other hand, it is distinguished and "accentuated."

## 5 / The Concept of Gestalt

LET US RETURN to the figure described above. The function of the curved line is different depending on whether the figure is seen as a small Greek $\varphi$ or as a large Latin S. In the first case, it is a dangling appendix; in the other case, "the figure rests upon it." This difference is of a genuinely phenomenal nature. It is so decisive for the What of the given that in the two "apprehensions" a totally different "object" presents itself, and not a certain identical sense datum which, while undergoing different apprehensions, continues being given as the same sense datum.[29]

The curved line is not a content with properties of its own. Instead, it is defined and determined by the configuration to which it belongs and by the role which it plays in the configuration. No juxtaposed contents are given at all which stand in a mere "and-connection" as the "bundle thesis" (*Bündelthese*) would have it. On the contrary, what is given are contents and totalities structured throughout in a specific way.[30] These Gestalten have their "distribution of emphasis" peculiar to them; they have, so to speak, their "centers of gravity," and they have them where they are required by their proper nature and their inner structure.[31]

What a "part"—better stated, constituent—of a certain Gestalt is, how it stands in it, is determined by the structure of this Gestalt.[32] The

28. Husserl, *Logische Untersuchungen*, II, ii, § 41.
29. Cf., in contrast, V. Benussi, "Gesetze der inadäquaten Gestaltauffassung," *Archiv für die gesamte Psychologie*, XXXII (1914), pp. 399f.
30. Cf. Wertheimer, "Untersuchungen zur Lehre von der Gestalt," I, *loc. cit.*, p. 52.
31. Cf. K. Koffka, "Psychologie," in *Lehrbuch der Philosophie*, ed. M. Dessoir (Berlin, 1925), II, p. 558.
32. M. Wertheimer, "Über Gestalttheorie," *Symposion* (1925), I, i, p. 43.

part is not something in and for itself, regardless of whatever else is given together with it. Rather, a "part . . . is something . . . *different* as the part of a certain constellation than when it is the part of another constellation; for what it is, the constellation to which the given belongs as part is essential." [33] For Gestalt theory, the converse problem arises—namely, the problem of the constitution for consciousness of a sense datum indifferent to its insertion into the context within which it is given. This leads to the further problem regarding the very concept of the identical stimulus which persists as identically the same throughout all "apprehensional change." Just that which was taken for granted as self-evident by traditional description and analysis becomes a problem here.

What kind of relation obtains between the constituents of a given Gestalt? In the noematic What there are privileged constituents: they "stand out," they carry the "accent," they have an incomparably heavier emphasis than the other constituents. They determine the character, the sense of the noematic What, and that means that they derive their emphasis and their central importance from the structure and the properties pertaining to the Gestalt as a whole. We often say: for a certain appearance, this or that feature is "characteristic," it is "the chief matter" in it, referring thus to certain privileged constituents in the appearance.[34] Around the "privileged" constituents are grouped the others, leaning on the former which, so to speak, form the stem about which the latter thrive.

This state of affairs suggests that the privileged constituents be called formative and that those which surround them be called formed constituents. Everywhere and always the formative and formed constituents are to be distinguished from one another, though, of course, only abstractively. They are always interwoven in the way in which what is emphatic is interwoven with what is subordinate, what is "outstanding" with what leans on it. This occurs in the way in which

33. Wertheimer, "Untersuchungen zur Lehre von der Gestalt," II, *loc. cit.*, iv, p. 329. Correspondingly, Koffka, "Psychologie," *loc. cit.*, pp. 533, 551, and *passim*.

34. "Appearance" is used here in Husserl's sense, *Ideen*, I, p. 275.

What is "characteristic" in an appearance is to be distinguished from the "characteristic appearance" which Cornelius introduced (*Transzendentale Systematik*, p. 205) and to which Husserl's concept of "normal" appearance (*Ideen*, I, p. 82) also refers.

Both authors speak of a distinctive appearance among the multiple adumbrations of an identical thing. We, however, have in view here privileged constituents of every particular appearance. Every appearance, even if it is itself not a characteristic one, has constituents which are characteristic of it. Both concepts are not without relation to one another so far as the characteristic components of an appearance, if the latter is itself a "characteristic appearance" (in Cornelius' sense), can have a special significance for the identical thing whose appearance it is.

a sense determinant is interwoven with that whose function in the structural framework in which it stands is derived from the sense determinant and which, as it were, only exists for the sake of what is formative.

Accordingly, we have indicated several possibilities for the concrete particularization of the interrelation between constituents, which is essential to such a structural framework. The specification of the particularization depends, in every case, upon the properties belonging to the Gestalt in question as a whole. Thus, there arise types of interrelations of the formative and formed constituents which are precisely determined by the typical properties of the Gestalt. For the moment, we shall put aside the distinction between "independent" and "partial contents." As yet we cannot answer the question of whether or not this distinction rests on a fundamentally typical difference in structure, so that structural types fall into two classes. A solution would presuppose the complete development of a structural typology.[35]

Let us survey a few concrete examples of typical interrelations. Lying before me is a rectangular piece of cardboard, the color of which "interests" me. In the noematic What the color is "prominent" and gives its stamp to what is experienced; correspondingly, the noetic act is determined as an "experience of color." But I do indeed see a rectangle colored in a certain way; I also see the surface as to its shape. The "being-rectangular" belongs to the noematic What; however, the rectangular shape is covered by the color; it "carries" the color. The color dominates; it is the quality of a surface on which it lies, and in that alone the "function" of the rectangular surface is exhausted. Or, in the case of S we come to say that the loop is added to the curved line as a kind of ornament. The sense of what is experienced is determined by the curved line to which the loop is subordinate. The function of the loop consists exclusively in sustaining and, perhaps, supplementing the sense of what is experienced, as determined by the curved line, in accordance with this determination.[36] The loop also belongs to the sense of what is experienced, yet does not determine it. It partakes of a sense whose characteristic

35. As is known, C. von Ehrenfels limited Gestalt-qualities to contents separable from one another and thus, in our sense, to independent contents. Cf. "Über Gestaltqualitäten," *Vierteljahrsschrift für wissenschaftliche Philosophie*, XIV (1890), pp. 262f.

36. The term "sense" does not refer to the meaning of the "sign." "Sense" is to be understood here as when Husserl (*Ideen*, I, p. 274) speaks of the sense of an intuition (*Anschauungssinn*). Quite apart from its meaning, the figure in question exhibits the described structure in its very appearance. The question is here of nothing else than of how the figure "looks." The state of affairs discussed in the text is also encountered in ornaments, although they do not have meaning, nor are they "signs."

stamp is determined by something else. The structure comprises both the formative and the formed constituents, but both in different ways. The structure is anchored in the "center of gravity" of the Gestalt and, so to speak, "radiates" out from that center, while the other constituents are placed within the framework of this structure, but only as *inserted* in it, *not as determining it.*

Again, I "see" the "front" of a "thing," and in "apprehending" it as the "front of a thing" I have some consciousness of the "back." Even when the noematic description of the "back" yields only indefinite predicates, this indeterminacy is, to that extent, neither total nor "absolute," i.e., equally indifferent to all possible determinations *whatever,* as the "back" with its constituents is inserted into the sense of that which is given to consciousness and is part of that sense. Because the noema under discussion is a perceptual one, the noematic What is determined by the "visible front." This fact entails a certain delimitation for the indeterminacy of the "back" and certain lines of possible determination. When what I see is, e.g., the "façade" of a "house," the "back of the thing" contained in the noematic What is a "back of the house." No matter how indefinite the "back" may be with regard to "shape," "coloration," etc., it is pre-delineated to the extent that it must conform to the sense of the perceptual noema which is determined by the "seen façade." Obviously, this is not to assert that quite in general in every thing-noema the perceptually given is formative in contradistinction to what is given as represented. In the example chosen for the sake of simplicity, this is indeed the case. But it need not always be so: The "sensuously" given can be irrelevant for what I "perceive" in comparison with what is "memorially given to consciousness" and, in general, with what, in Cornelius' sense, is not "immediately given" (e.g., "illusions," unstable perceptions, and the like).

## SOME EPISTEMOLOGICAL PROBLEMS CONCERNING GESTALT THEORY

WITH REFERENCE to perceptual experience, we repudiated the conception of the noematic What as an aggregate because it does not do justice to the descriptive findings of consciousness. This refutation is susceptible of being generalized beyond perceptual consciousness. To that conception we opposed the Gestalt thesis according to which the phenomenal findings have to be taken at face value and must not be "explained away." Gestalt psychologists arrived at that thesis on the basis of empirical work on concrete psychological problems, and it has to be further verified by experimental results. This thesis is connected with the fundamental problem of Gestalt psychology, as of psychology at large. It is especially because of this connection that Gestalt psychology acquires philosophical relevance. The problem concerns the constancy hypothesis.[37]

Traditional psychology conceived the psychological subject as placed in the world of objective stimuli. Sense data were conceived of as coordinated, element for element, in a strictly univocal way, to the corresponding objective stimuli. What is sensuously experienced depends only and exclusively on the stimuli in question: to like stimuli correspond like sensations; to stimuli differing slightly from one another correspond sensations also differing slightly from one another, etc. The "objective" world of stimuli was accepted as a "self-evident" basis, a "natural" presupposition for psychological work, requiring no justification nor any discussion. Likewise, the supposition that sensations are unambiguous and continuous functions of the corresponding stimuli seemed self-evident.

If we relinquish the constancy hypothesis and take whatever is given to consciousness just as it presents itself in its phenomenal nature, apart—at least to begin with—from all theoretical interpretation, we dispense with orienting the data of consciousness *beforehand* to objective stimuli, and we allow their descriptive nature to come into its rights independently of all theoretical constructions. Such a methodological procedure entails some very important consequences. We must be clear about the fact that the objects, of which we speak as experienced, must in fact be considered *exclusively as they are experienced.* In other words, we are not dealing with things, states of affairs, events *simpliciter,* or with objects in the sense of transcendent entities; instead, we are concerned with all that just as it is given and appears through the act of consciousness under discussion. The inquiry moves in the noematic rather than the objective realm. Whatever we speak of is bracketed in quotation marks and is to be understood in this modified sense. We do not speak of objects as they are; on the contrary, we concern ourselves with *what is given and how it is given.*

Precisely by abandonment of the constancy hypothesis the realm of the noematic is opened up to psychology, and psychology deals only with this noematic realm. In approaching the noematic sphere from the side of psychology, the greatest stress must be laid on the peculiar nature of this realm. We must always keep in mind the profound difference between the noema and the thing (the real physical thing),

---

37. Cf. W. Köhler, "Über unbemerkte Empfindungen und Urteilstäuchungen," *Zeitschrift für Psychologie,* LXVI (1913), pp. 51ff.

as well as the fact that all insights into affairs acquired under the guidance of the principles of Gestalt psychology are precisely insights into "affairs" (in the accordingly modified noematic sense).[38] This is of primary interest and importance in dealing with logical problems from the points of view of Gestalt theory.[39] It would be interesting to see what becomes of the paradoxes which arise in this connection when the distinction between the noema and the actually existing thing is consistently carried through.

When the theses of Gestalt theory are pursued into epistemological dimensions (theses resulting from relinquishment of the constancy hypothesis), not only is the world of stimuli, the world of things, suspended but also—we submit—the whole transcendent sphere, the entire stock of objects with which we deal in the "natural attitude." Understood in this way, the procedure of Gestalt theory, in taking the psychic purely descriptively and disregarding all constructions, has the same significance and methodical function for psychology as the transcendental reduction has for phenomenology. Objects in the normal sense of the word fall away, and noemata alone are left over; the world *as it really is* is bracketed, the world *as it looks* remains. All statements move within this circle. At this juncture, the problem of the constitution of objects becomes acute for Gestalt theory in its epistemological extension. Just as phenomenology is led to the problems pertaining to the "phenomenology of reason," so problems of the very same kind also arise for epistemologically oriented Gestalt theory. They concern the concatenations of consciousness through which a transcendent object manifests itself in a multiplicity of mental acts and processes directed to it as *one identical object* over against this multiplicity which comprises mental acts of highly different contents. The question also concerns the directedness of mental acts to this transcendent object; the question concerns how different mental acts are interwoven with each other so as to make one and the same object appear, how the object so constituted legitimates itself as "truly existing," and on what grounds, quite generally, the distinction between *"true being"* and mere illusory appearance is justified with regard to the transcendent realm.[40]

The Kantian problems of constitution as to the "unity in a multiplicity," the possibility of transcendent objects and, correlatively, the possibility of objective knowledge concerning actually existing objects—generalized to apply to objects of every region—also arise for

38. Cf. Husserl, *Ideen*, I, § 89.
39. As, for example, in M. Wertheimer, *Über Schlussprozesse im produktiven Denken* (Berlin, 1920).
40. See the development of the problems in Husserl, *Ideen*, I, § § 135ff.

a theory of knowledge which, in the sense of Wertheimer's Gestalt thesis, takes its departure from the original orderedness, structured-ness, and organization of the immediately given, the primal phenom-enological material. Arising within Gestalt theory, these epistemolog-ical problems are certainly not the same as for Kant, who develops his transcendental questions on the basis of the Humean doctrine of the "chaotic sensuous material" which is in need of being ordered and organized because it exhibits nothing of that in itself. The problems of the "synthetic unity of multiplicities" are modified in accordance with, and as a consequence of, the new and improved—*essentially* improved—conception of the primal phenomenological material. Obviously, the sense of the problems in question depends upon the way in which the nature of the multiplicity is interpreted. It must be stressed that the transcendental problems are only *modified,* by no means eliminated, for Gestalt theory.

## [II]  THEME AND THEMATIC FIELD

### 1  /  *A Phenomenological Difference within the Co-given*

FOLLOWING HUSSERL, *cogito* designates a distinctive mode of intentionality. The theme as the noema of the act in which we are busied with something, in which we "live," is given in this distinctive mode. As yet we cannot account for the sense of this distinctiveness of what is peculiar and specific to cogitative intentionality. Before we enter into a noetic analysis, we must, instead, carry the noematic analyses further, since a noetically directed inquiry requires contin-uous recourse to the noematic aspects.[41] However, the privilege accruing to the cogito as a special mode of intentionality functions as an index for the special and distinctive way in which the theme is given to consciousness along with what is "also there." [42] In saying "also there" for consciousness, the way is shown upon which our inquiry must strike out: just this which is "also there" must now be considered.

41. We can point out the peculiar parallelism between phenomenology and psychology. Just as in the former the noetic investigation is oriented towards the noematic, so in the latter "functional concepts" are oriented towards, and founded upon, the descriptive ones. For this, cf. Husserl, *Ideen*, I, p. 204, and K. Koffka, *Zur Analyse der Vorstellungen und ihrer Gesetze* (Leipzig, 1912), pp. 9ff.; Koffka, "Psychologie," *loc. cit.*, pp. 539ff.

42. In the further course of this inquiry, we shall show that bringing out the cogito *alone* is not sufficient and that still further modes of intentionality are to be distinguished.

Let us begin with a few indications furnished by Husserl's analyses of thing-perception in order to generalize our conclusions beyond the perceptual experience from which we take our departure. Every mental state has its environment in the sense that what is experienced through it, its noema, has surroundings, a noematic environment, also given in experience. When I apprehend a thing in the mode of the cogito, I grasp it as emerging from a background. Turning to the thing so grasped, and busying myself with it, I am conscious of the components of this background which, in spite of being set off from my theme, are conjoined with it in a peculiar way. The thing, of which I am conscious in the mode of cogito, is given as part of my "natural surrounding world," as a thing among things; other things are "contiguous," juxtaposed, forming together with it a "perceptual field" —precisely that part of the "natural surrounding world" which falls directly into my perception. I observe, e.g., the inkwell on my desk. Round about it lie pencils, paper, books, etc.; they are co-given while I am directed to the inkwell in the mode of cogito: they form the "objective background" of the inkwell. In this "objective background" there appear diverse things, among them those just named; but even more: there appears to me through the window part of the front of my neighbor's house. This front also is experienced as a component part of the "objective background"; I am not cogitatively turned to it, but what I experience as co-given is the perceptual appearance of things, and those acts through which the front appears to me are as legitimately called intentional acts as those through which the papers, books, etc., present themselves to me.

All these components pertaining to the background, such as pencils, papers lying about the inkwell, the front of the neighboring house which I see through the window, parts of the wall of the room which I happen to see, and whatever other objective components I am conscious of while being cogitatively turned to the inkwell: do all these belong *undifferentiatedly* and *in the same way* to the background of my present consciousness; do they all carry the *same* phenomenological character of co-givenness? And do the acts in which all this is presented have, likewise, *undifferentiatedly* the same mode of intentionality—namely, that of non-cogitative background intentionality? It is not alone a question of what *perceptually* appears to me in my cogitative apprehending of the inkwell as a component of the "objective background" belonging to it; it is not alone a question of co-appearing things. Indeed, arising memories, emerging wishes—in greater or lesser nearness or farness of background—also belong to the domain of the co-given, which, taken in its full completeness, coincides with the "horizon of originarity (*Originaritätshorizont*) of the pure ego," understood in an appropriately modified sense. The domain of the co-given comprises an enormous variety and heterogeneity. Our immediate task is to establish essential distinctions within this huge domain, to delimit, so to speak, its natural provinces.

In preparation for that, however, a side comment on the concepts employed is in order. The modification suggested for the concept of "horizon of originarity" is motivated by the coordination of the "horizon of the Now" with the "horizons of Before and After" in the *Ideen* (I, § 82). Husserl understands by "horizon of originarity of the pure ego" the sum total of all mental states which, with respect to any "experienced Now" (*Erlebnis-Jetzt*), have the temporal index of "given simultaneously in originarity." In this manner, the dimension of simultaneity is coordinated with the dimensions of Before and After, and these three dimensions together form the "whole phenomenological time-field of the pure ego." Now, consciousness of the just-past is, however, itself again a Now; the "horizons of Before and After" with reference to a certain "experienced Now" are, along with their temporal indices, actually co-given with the "experienced Now" in question. We thus arrive at the modified concept of the "horizon of originarity" which—as mentioned above—coincides with the concept of the domain of the co-given. We prefer this concept to the Husserlian one of the "phenomenological time-field," first of all, because it more pregnantly expresses the matter on hand and, furthermore, because the problems concerning phenomenological time, which indeed arise here, should not yet be spelled out. (This will be done in Section IV, although only in a preliminary way.)

From a temporal point of view, three dimensions are to be distinguished within the domain of the co-given. One of them consists of the sum total of all mental states co-given with the "experienced Now" in question—consciousness of which always assumes the mode of cogito—equally in the "form of originarity of the 'Now' "; these are the impressionally simultaneous states—that is, the "horizon of originarity of the 'Now' " in Husserl's sense. A second dimension comprises all the mental states actually co-given with the "experienced Now" through which something carrying the index of "pastness" presents itself: the "horizon of Before." A third dimension comprises the actually co-given mental states through which something carrying the index "futurity" appears: "the horizon of After."

We obtain the most important concept of the co-given when we consider that it is through a *present* mental state that we become conscious of both the past and the future; that is to say, the noematic correlate of the present state is characterized temporally as having been or as yet to come.

## 2  /  The "Natural" Surroundings of a Thing

WE HAVE SAID that the inkwell has its surroundings. In ordinary linguistic usage, we ascribe to it what is found "nearby"— e.g., the pen and papers lying on the desk. We do not, however, ascribe to the surroundings of the inkwell the walls of the room and the front of the neighboring house. Yet it is not a matter of spatial distances as such, of distances in the sense of analytic geometry where differences of distance are considered as different quantities of the same entity, *viz*, "distantiality." Instead, it is a matter of a quality in a pre-eminent sense. The "surroundings" themselves do not signify, as in the theory of functions, the totality of things whose distance from the given one, of which they form the "surroundings," is smaller than a certain magnitude. It denotes, on the contrary, a certain phenomenal quality, a quale which is *immediately* given and which, by its very nature, does not lend itself to measurement. Similarly, the terms "neighborhood," "relative proximity," "moderate proximity," "immediate surroundings," "wider surroundings," "close by," "next to," and others designate phenomenological *qualities* and not distances in a merely quantitative sense.

Having the inkwell as our theme and observing that an object in its surroundings moves away from the inkwell without leaving our visual field, we may pay attention to the places at which the moving object stops and to the changes in relations which the moving object has to our inkwell at those several places. What we observe does not consist in mere distantiality undergoing different quantitative determinations. Instead, the changes reach much deeper. Qualities previously present are replaced by totally different ones as expressed by the following descriptions: the object is no longer within the "surroundings" of the inkwell, it is now "far away from it"; or, the object no longer lies within its "immediate proximity," it has "moved out," etc.[43]

43. E. Rubin, *Visuell wahrgenommene Figuren* (Copenhagen, 1921), p. 50, has referred to these relations in his attempt to clarify what it means to speak of "ground as background," without, however, explicitly formulating the principle involved. "Es ist . . . ein willkürlicher und unnatürlicher Sprachgebrauch, zu sagen, dass der Schornstein, der weit draussen rechts eben sichtbar ist, für die Figur, die ich gerade vor mir halte und betrachte, Hintergrund sei. Der unwillkürliche Sprachgebrauch rechnet jedenfalls nur mit dem als Hintergrund, was . . . leidlich nahe bei der Figur liegt . . . Wenn der Grund ein einfarbiges oder gleichmässig gemustertes Feld ist, ist es hauptsächlich der Teil des Feldes, der direkt bei der Figur liegt, woran man denkt, wenn man vom Grunde spricht." Without it being explicitly stated, these words contain a reference to the specific qualitative characters of "directly next to" and "moderately close." Precisely such qualitative characters determine the linguistic use.

The presence of genuinely qualitative characters also appears from the fact that the old eristic questions, which are senseless because they approach qualitative phenomena from quantitative points of view (e.g., at least how many elements are required to make a heap?), can also be asked here: at what distance, for example, does an object cease to be "close to another one"? In general, within the phenomenal realm, one never deals, at least in the beginning, with qualitatively neutral distances in the sense of analytic geometry. Phenomenal "distances" always exhibit qualitative features; they are thus not distances in the genuine sense of the term.[44]

As a consequence, there arises here again the problem of how, in the sense of analytic geometry, distances are constituted for consciousness and from which *specific* features this constitution takes its departure.

The phenomenological characteristic of these surroundings of the thing and its situatedness in them may be explicated as follows. The inkwell, which is my theme, appears within a certain field in which pen and paper are found. "Material relations" (*sachliche Bezüge*) obtain between pen and paper and the inkwell.[45] The inkwell belongs to the surrounding field; it is bound up with this field as with its "natural" environment. Even though it is singled out and made the theme of a "special attention," the singling out requires and presupposes the surroundings from which the theme cannot be totally severed. It always remains attached to a surrounding "fringe," just to its environment. This attachment is not accidental so far as a fringe belongs to cogitative consciousness with essential necessity, and the components of the fringe contribute their part to the structure of the perceptual field in which the theme is encountered. These components cannot be varied at will, or, rather, it is not as though such a variation would consist merely in the substitution of other components for those which happen to be given now, as in the case of an aggregate where changes concerning certain items remain strictly confined to those very items. The components belonging to the fringe have some significance for that whose fringe they form.

My theme is the inkwell, but that inkwell in just this environment in which it is situated here and now. When the environment changes, the inkwell can still be my theme. But I must not forget to add: the

44. Cf. also the derivation of the "factor of nearness" as a Gestalt factor in Wertheimer, "Untersuchungen zur Lehre von der Gestalt," II, *loc. cit.*, p. 308. However, Wertheimer has in mind a Gestalt-moment different from the one meant here and by Rubin. For this difference, see 6 of the present section.

45. W. Köhler, "Intelligenzprüfungen an Anthropoiden," *Abhandlungen der Preussischen Akademie der Wissenschaften* (1917), I, p. 173. Cf., however, 6 of the present section.

same inkwell in a new environment. Always a theme is located within some environment or other. It is impossible to perceive a thing without environment, a thing *simpliciter*, severed from *any* environment.

Obviously what holds for thing-perception also holds beyond perceptual consciousness for remembering, expecting, phantasying, etc. What was said about the location of a thing in its environment and about the qualitative character of this environment itself does not involve any specific peculiarity of consciousness in the form of "originarity." Modifications of manners of presentation do not affect the relation between the theme and its environment or surroundings. The latter likewise undergoes the modification in question. As the remembered has its background, its co-remembered environment, so also in the case of phantasy a phantasied environment is co-given.

## 3 / *The Thematic Field*

THE PHENOMENOLOGICAL STATE of affairs discussed in the preceding analyses is not restricted to consciousness of things alone. For every theme, for every mental state of the form of *cogitatio*, there is a domain of the co-given. If I am dealing with an *eidos* and live in the performance of the act in question, I am, at the same time, conscious of many other things: other eidetic objects related to the *eidos* on which my attention is fixed; individual, concrete substrata possibly founding my ideational acts; that part of the "natural environment" which I happen to have directly before me, such as the desk, walls of the room, etc. Further, I also have some awareness of what lies behind my back, is in my house, in the garden, in the street, in the city in which I am, of the time of day, and the like. Memories, expectations, wishes arise. With reference to all this the same holds as was previously stated in the analysis of cogitative consciousness of things. As a consequence, we are confronted with the same problem as before, a problem concerning *thematic consciousness as such*. For every cogito there is a domain of the co-given, with regard to which we now ask: is this domain a unitary one in the sense of admitting no inner differentiations of an essential nature? Do all components belonging to it stand undifferentiatedly side by side as co-given in a unitary sense equal for all of them? With regard to the way in which they are given to consciousness, are all these components to be characterized as appearing together, one with another? Or is co-givenness a general heading which requires further differentiation, and, accordingly, does the term "background of consciousness" possibly conceal equivocations?

Suppose I think about a theory of Descartes, say the union of body and mind. Many things may come to mind: the connection in which this problem arises in Descartes' philosophy, the great historical consequences which this theory has had, etc. I always have such additional and subsidiary thoughts which indicate the direction in which my thinking moves, my "attitude" (*Einstellung*).[46]

Thinking about something is never a stupid staring at it. These subsidiary thoughts belong to the background of consciousness; they are co-given while I am thinking about the theory in question, just as is, e.g., the just-occurring expectation of a visit which I am to receive this evening. However, such subsidiary thoughts are attached to my theme in an entirely different way. While I have them "I do not digress from the matter at hand." When I deal with the theory in question, while interested in (*eingestellt auf*) the context of Descartes' philosophy as a whole, it is certainly appropriate that inner motivational connections between that theory and other doctrines of Descartes present themselves to mind.

We must note a distinction here. Dealing with the union of mind and body as theme under the perspective of the connectedness of the several Cartesian theories and with the motivatedness of each by the others is one consideration. Making this connectedness itself a theme in some attitude or other is a different consideration.[47]

However, the case is different when, while I am dealing with the theory in question under the perspective of its systematic place within the whole of the Cartesian philosophy, some thoughts concerning the historical consequences of that theory occur to me. This is a "disturbing subsidiary thought," an "intrusion" into the movement of my thinking—just as when expectation of this evening's visit had occurred to me. And the same holds, though we do not speak of "disturbances," for the part of the "natural surrounding world" which I happen to have in front of me while thinking about that theory of Descartes. Within the domain of the co-given the fundamental distinction must be drawn between that which "belongs to my theme" and determines my attitude and that which does not belong to it—and this distinction is of greatest importance for all investigations into this domain.

"Forms" in Stumpf's sense are not *special* but are, at most, distinguished and privileged cases of "sets" (*Inbegriffe*) if we

46. "Attitude" is a very important concept in this connection. What has traditionally been meant by attitude as well as change of attitude (*Einstellungsänderung*) and the like is most closely related to findings of the kind described here and in what follows.

47. With regard to both this difference and the connection which obtains here, see section III, 13.

designate the domain of the co-given as a "set," which conforms to Stumpf's term.[48] However, both "sets" and "forms" are considered by Stumpf as "correlates of functions of colligation"—a view which we cannot accept. Descriptively speaking, a function of colligation is not at work in whatever would be designated as "set" in Stumpf's sense, and certainly not in those cases which are being discussed here—not to speak of "forms" such as a melody, a spatial figure, etc., which are thematic unities, unitary themes.

The attempt at phenomenological clarification of what is meant by "attitude" leads to the eidetic insight that thematic consciousness is not a staring at something and that the theme is not, as it were, an isolated point. Consciousness is, in general, not the presence of a content surrounded by a chaotic manifold of any other contents whatever; and thematic consciousness does not consist, as one usually asserts of attention, in a beam of light being cast upon a certain content while a chaotic confusion of other contents fills the regions of shadow and darkness. We must beware of taking literally the metaphor of the "illuminating light" of attention. Beyond that, the correctness of this analogy remains very much in question. In general, the distinction between "noticed" = "illuminated," and "unnoticed" = "unilluminated" parts of consciousness misses essential phenomenological structures. Indeed, this whole problem must be approached from an entirely different side. Neither that upon which "attention is fixed" nor "what is left aside by it" ought to be described as in some way illuminated, as though the different degree of illumination were the single or even the essential descriptive difference.

To the contrary, the phenomenological structure, to which all studies concerning attention and the like must refer, is the following: within the sum total of what is co-given with the theme, there is a partial domain of what has a special connection with the theme, materially belongs to it, or however we wish to express it. We shall call this partial domain, which determines the attitude in which we are dealing with the theme, the thematic field. Our next analyses are devoted to the structure of this field.

In our first attempt at delimiting a certain sub-domain, the thematic field, within the domain of the co-given, we concerned ourselves with the sense in which we speak of the surroundings of a thing. However, the type of thing-perception discussed on pp. 198–200 was a special one. When I merely look at a thing, taking it as one thing

48. C. Stumpf, *Erscheinungen und psychische Funktionen* (Berlin, 1907), p. 29.

among others in front of me, surroundings and thematic field coincide indeed. But I can also deal thematically with a thing in other ways. I can, e.g., think of its usefulness in certain situations, or of the role which it once played in my life, etc. In that case, the surroundings, in which I happen to perceive the thing in question, do not coincide with the thematic field belonging to it as my theme; it may then be that nothing of what lies near to it or in its neighborhood belongs to the thematic field. Instead, the thematic field comprises situations in which the thing can be of use, or those in which it had once figured, etc., always according to the attitude in which I am actually dealing with a thing as theme. On pp. 198–200 a special case was singled out for methodological reasons. This case is now subsumed under a universal eidetic law.

## 4 / *The Structure of the Thematic Field*

WE NEVER DEAL with a theme *simpliciter;* instead, we confront a theme standing in a field. Our attitude is determined by the thematic field, and we deal with the theme as pertaining to this field. The thematic field itself is a context of "objects" intrinsically related as materially belonging together. The form in which all items belonging to the thematic field are connected with both each other and the theme is not the form of the "and-connection" in which anything whatever can be connected with anything else whatever, however disparate and for which material relationships or relations of relevancy are of no account. Since the items in question belong together on the basis of their properties and their *material* contents, there obtains between them a "Gestalt connection" (*Gestaltverbindung*) which in every given case is specified in accordance with the specification of those material relations. The thematic field is not a conglomeration of any contents whatever, not like a box in which sundry things can be put and from which they can be taken out, a conception which is at the basis of problems of the "range of consciousness" and the "narrowness of consciousness" and which necessarily leads to these pseudoproblems.

The thematic field is a set of *materially* related objects. The theme, with which we are dealing, is inserted into this framework of sense. *Qua* theme, it has a special and privileged place; it is what we are concerned with, and the components of the thematic field are co-given with the theme. This distinction of the theme is decisive for the structure of the thematic field. The thematic field has a center and is oriented with reference to this center.[49] Whether or not a co-given item belongs to the thematic field, how it is inserted in this field, which place it has there, etc.—all this depends upon its relation to the theme. The ground (thematic field) is organized around the figure (theme). There is always given a thematic field organized and oriented with respect to this theme. Whatever is experienced as pertaining to the thematic field has "directedness to the center."

Turning to thoughts which we were already having but which merely "crossed our mind" without our explicitly grasping them and being directed to them has frequently been accounted for in terms of an altered direction of attention. The third section of this essay is dedicated to problems of attention in particular. However, without prejudging the issue, phenomenologically we can describe here the turning to a theme as well as the being turned to it. This is connected with the problems of attention so far as we not only speak of functions and accomplishments of attention with respect to "attention turning to something new," hence with respect to modifications, but also as the "static" "having in view," "being directed to something as theme" is considered a matter of attention. How are we now to formulate the descriptive nature of "taking into grasp" and "holding in grasp"? I sit here and allow thoughts to "cross my mind"; mathematical theorems, for instance, present themselves to me without my thematically dealing with any one of them. I am aware of a variety of propositions, of obscure, confused, and unarticulated thoughts in a more or less nascent state. Suddenly an orientation comes into unordered train of mathematical "phantasies" and musings; what was still simply floating by acquires relatedness to a thought of which I am aware clearly and articulately as my theme and which dominates my field of consciousness, centralizing and directing it.

That earlier, wandering train of thought is now no longer experienced. In accordance with its material connectedness with the theme, that which pertains to the background of consciousness acquires a definite place within the thematic field. We say that an orientation has been brought about, and this involves two things: the field of consciousness has acquired a center, and the thematic field is

49. Rubin's investigations are relevant here so far as the figure-ground relationship studied by him is a special case of the general relation of theme to thematic field—namely, that which we mention on pp. 202–3. In fact, the "attitude" of the observer in the psychological experiment is as described there: one looks at what there is to see, as "impartially, naïvely, and untheoretically" as possible. Accordingly, some of Rubin's results are susceptible of an appropriate generalization, since they are grounded not in the specific nature of the visual realm but in the relation of theme to thematic field. We can generalize the terms "figure" and "ground" beyond the visual realm in which they arose and identify them with the concepts of theme and thematic field.

organized with respect to it. The components of the thematic field are ordered in accordance with their relations to the theme. The duality involved in such orientation is precisely what characterizes the figure-ground relationship in the sense of Rubin, who has studied it in the visual realm.

As stated, the problems of attention will not be discussed until the third section because they become more accessible to analysis when the so-called attentional alterations are taken into consideration. However, this much has already been established: turning to, and being turned to, a theme cannot be accounted for in terms of distribution of illumination, but rather in terms of organization of the field of consciousness—that is to say, in terms of *that which is given*. We cannot follow Ribot, who speaks of a dominating idea which darkens and dislodges the rest of what is still there for consciousness.[50] It is not a matter of obscuring or brightening but is one of organization.

For a theme "to be taken into grasp" and for "thoughts to come into order" is one and the same thing. Correlative with becoming-figure and being-figure of the theme is becoming-oriented and being-oriented of the thematic field; both are brought about by one and the same process. Consequently, a theme is always a "theme in a thematic field." It is erroneous to speak of the "theme *simpliciter*" without mentioning its relation to, and its insertion into, the thematic field, just as it is also inappropriate to speak of the thematic field without taking into consideration its organization and orientation with reference to the theme.

A further feature is still to be mentioned. Not all items pertaining to the ground have the same relationship to the figure. Material relations may differ from one another: they may, for example, be more or less close. Along with them there is variation in the position which the components of the thematic field occupy with respect to the theme. Some items belonging to the ground have only remote or mediated material relations to the theme or are related to less essential moments (e.g., only formed ones); others immediately hang together with the theme or with what is essential (e.g., with the formative moments). They stand nearer to the theme, belong more to it. In such ways nearer and farther zones are delimited within the thematic field, according to the closer and looser material relations between its items and the theme.[51]

50. T. Ribot, *Psychologie de l'attention* (1885), p. 6.
51. The same example which serves Rubin, *Visuell wahrgenommene Figuren*, p. 50, for demonstrating the phenomenological characteristic of the "background" (in our terms, the surroundings) can also serve as an example of zones: a grease

From the nearer to the farther zones transitions are continuous. We can almost speak of one and the same quality as admitting of degrees, if we allow material connectedness with the theme to be considered a quality. All these zones lie within the thematic field; what belongs to any of them, even the farthest, is essentially differentiated from whatever lies outside the thematic field because these latter items have no material relatedness to the theme and are only and solely given simultaneously with it, co-given with the theme, and nothing more.[52] For this reason, there is no continuous transition from the thematic field to that which does not belong to it. At this juncture a leap occurs, and the *merely co-given* is *not* integrated into the thematic field as its farthest zone: its difference from that field is essential and radical.

## 5 / *The Place of the Theme in the Thematic Field*

THE THEME, as the "organizing center," is inserted into the thematic field. The relation of theme to thematic field is reciprocal; it is a correlation. Besides, as we have repeatedly pointed out, between the theme and the thematic field there obtains a "Gestalt connection." For such a connection, in contradistinction to a mere sum, it is characteristic that any "part" entering into it is not totally independent of other "parts" with which it is thus connected. In the case of a "Gestalt connection," in contrast to an aggregate of single "elements" merely added to one another, a context is given with laws of its own, such that each "part" has its place by virtue of these laws and is not indifferent to what occurs in other "parts."

Thus the inkwell looks differently on the desk than when I put it on the piano. It is displaced, "does not belong there," is not found in its authentic milieu.[53] In an analogous way I can deal with Descartes' theory of the union of mind and body at one time with regard to its historical significance and at another time as to its connections with Descartes' philosophy as a whole. The changed horizon, the new

spot on a white sheet of paper belongs to a figure if it is "very close by" it; but if it appears at the edge of the sheet of paper, it does not belong to the ground of the figure. When the spot (supposed as moveable) is gradually displaced from a position near the figure over to the edge, phenomena of transition and even jump are experienced, the grease spot moving from a near zone into more and more remote ones and, finally, leaving the thematic field altogether.

52. For the sense of mere co-givenness without material connectedness, see section IV, 1.

53. Let us remark in passing that the concept of the "authentic milieu" of a thing is to be distinguished from that of its "natural surroundings" as established in pp. 198–200.

perspectives under which the theme appears do not leave it un-affected: "the theme looks different either time." If it is true that to understand a scientific proposition and really to penetrate its sense requires seeing it in its connection with other propositions relevant for it—that is to say, with reference to, and in its significance for, the whole discipline to which it pertains—in other words, under its horizon,[54] then the proposition in question is not indifferent to changes in its horizon, and the changed attitude in which I now think about my theme means something for my theme itself. It "somehow" looks differently, and its "function"—of which it makes sense to speak only in relation to the thematic field in question—changes with the thematic field.

Nevertheless, the theme—understood as always in the noematic sense—remains *the same in strict identity*. It is the same "inkwell" which I see on the desk and on the piano; and it is the *same* theory of Descartes which I can think about in this or that attitude. The theme as the noematic What, established in section I, 2, preserves itself as the *same* in different thematic fields and over against change in attitude.[55] The theme is independent to a high degree over against its thematic field. It is not absorbed into its thematic field or exhausted by its function and significance for that field. Rather, it has its own subsistence over and above its function in its thematic field. That is to say, the distinctiveness it has within its thematic field—namely, of organizing that field—is not even its primary distinction but, rather, derives from the latter.

The primary distinction of the theme consists in its peculiar independence with regard to whatever else belongs to the thematic field. Self-sufficient, unitary, and delimited, resting entirely on itself, it stands in the thematic field which fades into the indefinite in several directions. The thematic field has no boundaries and cannot have them—it comprises indeterminacies of many kinds; the theme, on the contrary, is confined within well-defined boundaries. Owing to them, the theme stands forth from the field in sharp outlines, as a completed and self-contained unity, delimited with regard to whatever is extrinsic to it.

The theme rests wholly on itself and is self-sufficient so far as it requires no supplementation from without in order to be what it is. According to Rubin, the "fundamental difference" between figure and ground consists in the figure having "thing-character" and the ground

---

54. Cf. Wertheimer's remark in "Über Gestalttheorie," *loc. cit.*, p. 44.
55. For the invariance of the theme over against changes in attitude, see section III, 5.

"stuff-character." [56] This, in specific visual terms, is what we mean quite generally by delimitedness and self-containedness of the theme in contrast to the thematic field open on all sides. The same holds not only for Rubin's description of the contour, which is always experienced as delimitation of the figure and only has a subordinate, if any, significance for the ground, but also for what he says about the unformedness of the ground and the formedness of the figure, etc.[57] Finally, what Rubin says about the greater "impressiveness" (*Eindringlichkeit*) of the figure over against the ground also belongs here, the concept of "impressiveness," as Rubin himself observes, requiring still further clarification.[58]

Because of its delimitedness and self-containedness, the theme is given as separable from the thematic field. We have the impression of being able to remove the theme from the field in which it happens to stand in a given concrete case and of being able to place it in another thematic field just as it is without modifying it in any way whatever. Thus, I have the impression that I could, e.g., put the inkwell on my desk into another environment, for instance, on the piano, without changing it in any respect whatever. We have the same impression when we see a grey figure, e.g., a grey circle on a white background; we believe that the circle could also be placed on a black background without undergoing any change. It must be stressed that what is here in question is nothing else than the impression which we have in regard to an actual theme in its field. It must not be objected that the grey circle does not, *as a matter of fact,* behave in the way mentioned and that its color changes according to the laws of color contrast when the circle is transported from the white to the black background field. We are not speaking here of what *factually* happens in the *factual occurrence* of change in environment; we are speaking solely of the impression we have with regard to the theme, of its phenomenological *habitus.* There is no doubt that the theme itself can undergo modifications, and even deep-reaching ones along several dimensions, as a result of a change of the attitude in which it is *hic et nunc* actually given as theme. In the present context, it is only a question of how the theme looks when we direct our regard to it while dealing with it.

This peculiar nature of the theme, which we shall designate as its consistency, will play its role in the discussion of the so-called attentional modifications.

56. Rubin, *Visuell wahrgenommene Figuren,* pp. 46ff.
57. *Ibid.,* chap. I, § 5. Cf. especially p. 36, where Rubin describes how a field, experienced as ground, becomes a figure by undergoing "ein formendes Wirken": "Der Grund wird gestaltet."
58. *Ibid.,* pp. 67ff.

6 / *Two Types of Gestalt Connection*

THE GESTALT CONNECTION, as contrasted with the mere "sum," is characterized by the items concerned having an "inner bearing" in relation to one another and materially belonging together, while in the case of the "sum" disparate items, which as to their contents may be totally unrelated to one another, are merely given together: anything whatever is existentially connected with anything else whatever, anything whatever is added onto, and joined with, anything else whatever. From this point of view, both the theme as the total system of its constituents and the union comprising the theme and the thematic field are Gestalt connections. However, they are Gestalt connections of rather different kinds.

Let us consider how the constituents of the theme are connected with one another within the unity of the theme. These constituents are in no sense independent, nor can they be extracted from the structural framework. As to the "formed" constituents, this obviously follows from their subordinate role. They are exhausted in being substrata, supports, continuations, and the like for other constituents. They are what they are only with respect to something else; or, as we can say, they exist only for the sake of something else. What they are is determined by their function within and for the structural whole into which they are integrated. Such a function changes from structural framework to structural framework along with the frameworks themselves. What they are as constituents of one Gestalt they are not as constituents of a different one. The way they look, their "physiognomy," their entire *habitus,* changes, and this holds regardless of whether they are subordinate or dominant in the new structure.

The same is to be said of the formative constituents. They, too, are enmeshed in their structural framework and cannot be separated from it. Their dominant role is assigned to them in virtue of the structural framework as a whole, and it is only *within* that structural framework that they can play that role. They also are subject to the laws of the whole, and what holds in general for all constituents of a Gestalt also holds for the formative ones: each has its function and stands at the place required by the sense of the whole. Whatever a formative constituent might be outside a certain Gestalt, it is, in any case, not the same as within that Gestalt. Furthermore, the formative constituent is in need of the formed ones for its support, continuation, supplementation. Formed constituents are by no means superfluous and like mere trimmings in the sense that they could be lacking without their absence impairing the structuration of the theme. In their subordinate and merely supporting function they contribute indispensably to the thematic sense, and the formative constituent requires them for its being formative. Were they lacking, the theme would be incomplete, fragmentary; in any event, it would not be what it is. They must be given for the formative constituent to fulfill the function assigned to it by the structural whole. The examples discussed in section I, 5 can serve as illustration. Consider how in the apprehension of the $\varphi$ the loop is in need of the curved line without which the $\varphi$ would not be complete, would, properly speaking, not be a $\varphi$ at all. Quite in general, no constituent of a Gestalt is independent of the other constituents.[59] Each one requires the others, all carry one another, each is in need of the others.

Let us now contrast this with the consistency of the theme: its independence and separableness with regard to the thematic field. This consistency obtains, we must still add, only for the theme with respect to the field, not conversely. The components belonging to the field form the background on which the theme appears. If among all the co-given items the components of the thematic field have a certain distinction, they have it on account, and only on account, of their material relatedness to the theme. The thematic field is the horizon opened up with respect to the theme. Obviously, there can be no question of the independence and separability of the horizon, which by its very nature is related and, in this sense, relative to the theme.

We must not allow ourselves to be misled by the habit of speaking, e.g., of the "mathematical attitude," as though there were a thematic field which could be co-given to *every* mathematical theorem and, hence, would be independent and separable with regard to any special one. Considering the *concrete* thematic field which belongs to a *concrete* theorem as theme, we see how intimately it is connected with it and how it stands and falls with it. *In concreto* there is no general *"mathematical attitude" simpliciter* at all; the horizon pertaining to one theorem is as different from the horizon of another theorem as both theorems are from one another. Only what is concretely given is decisive, and to this we must always return. What we mean by "mathematical attitude" in a concrete case changes from case to case, according to the case.

The independence of the theme from the field is not absolute. Otherwise, the field would just be superadded to the theme; accordingly, the figure-ground structure and the Gestalt connection between theme and thematic field would become unintelligible. The independ-

---

59. See section III, 18 for the sense in which we can speak of "independent parts" of a Gestalt.

ence of the theme is not only limited by the *essential law* according to which a field belongs to any theme, so that a theme cannot be without a thematic field, but of still greater importance, perhaps, is the following: we have the impression that the theme can be transferred from the present thematic field to a different one, without its material content and its status as a theme undergoing any alteration. However, the different thematic field cannot be just *any* other thematic field whatever; it can be only such a one as exhibits certain specifications.

This condition of specification derives from the material bonds between field and theme, the thematic field being a *material* (*sachlich*) horizon and not a "horizon of originarity." A given theme does not fit into just any thematic field; the thematic field belonging to an artistic object appropriately contains artistic objects; to a mathematical proposition belongs a mathematical horizon, and not just any set of mathematical objects can suitably function as horizon of a certain theorem. Rather, with regard to every theorem there is a more or less wide range of possible thematic fields into which it fits, and among them some *may* but *need not* be distinguished. Again, we are only speaking here of what pertains to the appearance of the theme.

Confronting the unity of the theme with that comprising both theme and thematic field, two distinct kinds of Gestalt connection emerge, and the one must not be interpreted in terms of the other. Above all, the theme must not be misconstrued as a formative constituent of the thematic field, nor must the structure consisting of formative and formed constituents be confused with the entirely different field structure. Both Rubin and Wertheimer as well as other authors close to the latter discuss Gestalt connections and Gestalt moments. But while Rubin has studied figure-ground relations, which are a special case of the relation of theme to thematic field, Wertheimer deals almost exclusively with constituents *within the Gestalt,* endeavoring to show that the Gestalt is not composed of parts added together and that, correspondingly, its constituents themselves are to be taken not as parts in the sense of independent "elements" but as dependent members whose being and function are determined by the structural whole of the Gestalt. The two authors, therefore, do not consider the same structure.[60] Accordingly, terms which arise in the analysis of the one type of Gestalt connection can be valid only in a modified sense for the other type. Such is the case with Wertheimer's "factor of nearness" posited as a *Gestaltfaktor* in the sense that

60. It remains an open question whether the two types distinguished here are the only ones or whether there is a system of possible types of Gestalt connection.

"comprehensive togetherness (*Zusammengefasstheit*)—*ceteris pari-bus*—results *in the sense of the smallest distance.*" [61] For Wertheimer, comprehensive togetherness means "resulting *in uno*"; what results *in uno* belongs together, forms a unitary contexture in which (dependent) constituents are contained. The "factor of nearness" also plays a role in our analyses of the surroundings of a thing; but in this case there is no question of "resulting *in uno.*" The thing emerges and stands out from its surroundings. It is not a constituent within a contexture but is a contexture itself and in its own right, appearing on the background of its surroundings. Over against the latter, the thing presents itself as self-contained and self-sufficient. The thing does not belong to the surroundings; on the contrary, the surroundings belong to the thing.[62] Hence, the "factor of nearness as a *Gestaltfaktor*" has a different sense according to the kind of Gestalt connection which is in question.

In the literature on this and related problems, the difference we have emphasized has still not been given its proper due. Köhler [63] defines—though only in passing—the material relation between two things [64] as a "*context owing to the properties* of those things themselves . . . , not their frequent occurring together, successively or simulataneously." By this, however, he designates what is characteristic of and essential to the Gestalt connection as such in opposition to the mere "sum." In fact, Köhler's definition holds for both established types of Gestalt connection, but for each in a different and peculiar way. Koffka,[65] who reports Rubin's analyses, concerns himself with the connection between the figure-ground relation and the problems of attention, a connection brought out by Rubin himself. Attention is devoted to the figure and, conversely, the part of the perceptual field to which attention turns becomes the figure (Koffka limits himself here, as does Rubin, to the visual realm). "What does attention mean here? Certainly not clarity, but instead: *emphasis* (*Gewicht*), *center of gravity.* The chief emphasis in a field lies on the figure, and when I put the chief emphasis at a place in the field, the figure appears there." Koffka then interprets weightiness and distribution of emphasis in terms of the structure of the Gestalt, i.e., the figure itself which has "its own center" and within which the distribution of

61. Wertheimer, "Untersuchungen zur Lehre von der Gestalt," II, *loc. cit.*, p. 308.

62. This holds in full generality for the relations between theme and thematic field at large.

63. Köhler, "Intelligenzprüfungen an Anthropoiden," *loc. cit.*, I, p. 173.

64. The reference is not to thing in the proper sense but in the frequent usage where it signifies object, moment in the object, property of the object, and the like.

65. Koffka, "Psychologie," *loc. cit.*, p. 588.

emphasis is "determined by the total properties of the Gestalt." Exemplifying his interpretation by the experience of ambiguous figures in "varying apprehension," where the center of gravity is displaced along with the variation of "apprehension," he parallels these phenomena with the structure of the thematic field whose center of gravity is the theme. Consider, however, how different are the phenomenological characteristics of both structures and how in both cases a totally different phenomenon is meant by "center of gravity and emphasis."

7 / *Actual and Inactual Consciousness, and the Cogito*

AS A DISTINGUISHING FEATURE of intentional experiences, the cogito is considered by Husserl as a "mode of performance" of acts, obviously as a distinctive mode of performance. Objects are given to us through acts—this belongs to intentionality as such. When we "live in acts," "are absorbed in their performance," are directed in a pre-eminent way to the objects which present themselves through these acts, and busy ourselves with them, we experience consciousness in the form of cogito. The objects given to consciousness in this form are noticed, attention is devoted to them, we are "thematically dealing" with these objects.[66] "*Attention is a distinctive function which belongs to acts . . . in the sense of intentional subjective processes.*" For its part, attention presupposes acts through which the objects, to which we are to pay attention, present themselves to consciousness. Attention is thus related to the cogito in such a way that acts in the form of cogito are acts in which our attention is turned to the theme of the cogito. Intentionality *simpliciter,* we have noted, is an essential feature of *all* acts so far as through them objects are made to present themselves. Now we see that cogitative intentionality has to be distinguished as a special and privileged mode.[67] The acts, namely, in which we are thematically dealing with objects are acts of cogitative intentionality.

In the *Ideen*, the "distinctive attentional function," as well as the nature of cogitative consciousness and, in general, the cogito as such, are more precisely determined by ego-relatedness (*Ichhaftigkeit*).[68] Here a distinction refers us to the analyses by means of which we endeavored to delimit a distinctive partial domain within the total domain of the co-given: the distinction, namely, between that with

66. Husserl, *Logische Untersuchungen*, II, pp. 409ff.
67. That this distinction is still not sufficient will be immediately seen.
68. See the presentation of the relevant Husserlian doctrines in the Introduction, pp. 177ff.

which we are dealing, "primarily" or "incidentally," and that of which we are also aware, but in addition to, and besides, our theme, which is only co-given with the theme without being materially related to it (as, e.g., a wish which arises "from the background" while we are following a theoretical line of thought). What pertains to the thematic field was singled out from the totality of items co-given with the theme in question.

Recalling our previous analyses, we must say: when, over against the inactualities which by essential necessity belong to the actualities like a surrounding fringe, the actualities (understood in the most general sense) determine "the pregnant sense of the expression 'cogito,' 'I have consciousness of something,' 'I perform an act of consciousness,'" [69] and when, on the other hand, intentionality is the general law of *all* consciousness, we cannot simply oppose actuality to inactuality, cogitative intentionality to mere intentionality. We must distinguish which kind of inactuality is involved, whether an object presented through inactual consciousness does or does not belong to the thematic field. This distinction must be made with regard to all inactualities, including, e.g., "act-impulses" in the broadest sense, i.e., both acts which are about to arise and those which are no longer performed (*ausser Vollzug geraten*).[70] The importance which this distinction has, especially for "acts 'no longer performed,'" will become apparent when, in the next section, we consider attentional modifications where just this distinction will provide a classificatory principle for these modifications. There we shall show the different senses in which it can be said of an act that it is "no longer performed."

The difference between what is "primarily" and what is "incidentally" noticed is especially suitable for defining the sense of actuality in contradistinction to inactualities of all kinds and for clarifying the phenomenological nature of the cogito. Understood in noematic terms, this distinction leads to what we have described under the heading of theme and thematic field. I am "primarily" concerned with my theme, "incidentally" dealing with items pertaining to the thematic field. I am "absorbed" in my theme while "living" in those acts which make the theme present. But I am not "absorbed" in the thematic field, nor do I "live" in those acts through which it is given to me. That is to say: acts in which something is primarily noticed, acts of attention in the pregnant sense, in which attention is directed to something, grasps something, or in whatever other psychological terms it might be

69. Husserl, *Ideen*, I, p. 63.
70. *Ibid.*, p. 236.

expressed (quite in general, consciousness in the form cogito) is consciousness whose objective correlate presents itself as theme.

The concept of cogitatively dealing with something thus purports that this something is a theme over against both its thematic field and whatever else is co-given. In contradistinction to other modes of intentionality, cogitative intentionality is the form of intentionality pertaining to acts of consciousness whose object is given as theme. Problems of attention concern the peculiar nature of acts through which something is experienced as theme; they concern the nature of thematic consciousness *qua* thematic consciousness. In this manner, the connection is established between the phenomenology of attention and the problems discussed in our analyses. As a peculiar feature of certain acts, attention designates a noetic phenomenon whose noematic correlate is here in question. On that account the phenomenological clarification of attention requires the translation into noetic terms of the noematically directed analyses of theme, thematic field, and the domain of the co-given; in other words, the noetic analyses are parallel to the noematic ones.

Now, the question still remains concerning the specific ego-relatedness of the cogito. Nowhere in our analyses did we encounter the pure ego intervening in acts in the form of cogito, nor, for that matter, a "pure subject of the act" at all as a phenomenological finding. In full measure we appropriate the arguments with which Husserl, in the first edition of the *Logische Untersuchungen,* repudiated the assertion "that the relationship to the ego belongs to the essential structure of the intentional subjective process [*Erlebnis*] itself." [71]

In this respect, we revert to Husserl's initial position in contrast to his later one, especially as his thought later developed in the *Ideen.* His polemics, in the first edition of the *Logische Untersuchungen,* against Natorp and the Kantian Ego of the "pure apperception" appear convincing to us because they correspond more adequately to the phenomenological findings than do the descriptions in the *Ideen* where each act is presented as an act of the ego and each act-peculiarity as the peculiar way in which the ego is active in his living performances. For Natorp, who was not without influence as to Husserl's position in the *Ideen,* the ego belongs to consciousness "as the other point of reference besides that of which there is consciousness, in just the relation which consciousness means for both." [72] To be sure, in spite of all agreement between Natorp and

71. Husserl, *Logische Untersuchungen,* 1st ed. (Halle, 1901), II, pp. 342ff., 355ff.

72. P. Natorp, *Allgemeine Psychologie nach kritischer Methode,* pp. 27f.

Husserl, an essential difference separates these thinkers. Although he views it as "the common, ultimate center of reference with regard to the content of which it has consciousness," Natorp does not consider the ego to be a "phenomenological datum"; according to him, the ego does not manifest itself in phenomenological findings, nor is it under the obligation of such a legitimation.[73] Natorp accepts the ego as a "supposition": necessarily posited, not as fact and appearance, but as the ground "of all fact and all appearing," "as the ultimate ground of being with regard to unification and, accordingly, as the possibility of unity—in a word, as the *ground* of unity at large."

This "original," "pure ego, the ego of consciousness-at-large," is not accessible to "static" observation, i.e., of such a kind which "always accepts as given only a definitely delimited collection of contents." Rather, we must take into consideration the dynamics of conscious life, its continuous flowing, where "collecting of contents" continuously passes into a "collection of contents" and where there are no discrete connective unities (*Verknüpfungseinheiten*) rigorously separated from one another. Here, where all singularization is suspended, in the "all-encompassing ideal unity of conceptual thinking" over against both the "absolutely singularized experiential *moment*" (*Erlebnismoment*) and the "concrete, definitely delimited experiential *context*" (*Erlebniszusammenhang*), we reach the "all-encompassing ideal *unity* of consciousness" (*Bewusstseinseinheit*), the Kantian "appreception" or the "pure ego." [74] "It is solely in thinking that we are conscious of the ego *as such* and that, accordingly, it becomes in fact actual as subject of consciousness," while in the "experiential moment" as well as in the "delimited experiential context" it appears merely as potency in comparison with the actualization which it undergoes in "conceptual thinking." On this basis, we understand that supposition of the pure ego as idea which, in its highest actualization, has a tendency towards universal consciousness and "which is not merged into the delimited and, in this delimitation, continuously changing complexes of contents, but, on the contrary, in itself limitless and enduring (in the sense in which an idea endures), surpasses all these complexes, hence, again, does not appear in them but, as ground of appearing (in the way in which the idea is ground), 'makes all of them possible.' " [75]

Natorp's thesis concerning the actualization of the pure ego in the flux of life encompassing all singularizations, where "the ego relation" becomes "all-embracing in its concreteness and actuality" will occupy

73. *Ibid.*, p. 85, and especially II, §§ 6f.
74. *Ibid.*, X, § 7.
75. *Ibid.*, II, § 7.

us later on.[76] This thesis bears the stamp of Marburg neo-Kantianism; its connection with Kantian theories is obvious and has been pointed out by Natorp himself.[77] Here we cannot enter into a discussion of the principles which underlie the position of the Marburg school. But we must note that suppositions concerning the ego of the kind made by Natorp are not admissible in the phenomenal realm.

Indeed, if the question as to the possibility and validity of objective unities is to be answered in terms of phenomenal data, connections between such data, and "rational" motivations pertaining to those connections, then the problem cannot be raised again concerning the possibility of those very phenomenal data and findings. Quite in general, within the phenomenological realm the question is not *how* something is possible but *what* is possible. With respect to phenomenally given unities, it makes no sense to ask about a ground of unity by virtue of which they "are made possible." As a matter of principle, phenomenological concepts must be descriptively legitimated; they must find their validation in findings pertaining to the sphere of consciousness. Their justification extends so far, but also *only so far,* as they can be legitimated in phenomenal data—this is the fundamental principle of all phenomenological analysis. While Natorp, in his discussion with Husserl, does not assert a descriptively ascertainable ego moment in the mental state or process and does not consider the pure ego as a "phenomenological finding," it is just *this* thesis that is essential to Husserl's changed position in the *Ideen*.

For the very reason that Husserl, according to the tendency of his work, emphasizes the descriptive phenomenological character of the ego in the cogito and explicitly recognizes "the pure ego as a phenomenological datum" only so far as its "immediate, evidently ascertainable essential nature and co-givenness with pure consciousness reaches," [78] we cannot accept his standpoint in the *Ideen*, which is at variance with "phenomenological findings." In the analyses of thematic consciousness we did not encounter a descriptively ascertainable ego moment as involved in every act of the form cogito, not to speak of the ego as a "primal source of generations" out of which acts radiate. As we have already said, we must revert to

76. Cf. below, section IV, 4, pp. 281ff.
77. The "levels of subject relations" and the threefold division of sensation (experiential *moment*), "precisely delimited representation" (experiential *context*), the "ideal unity of conceptual thinking" (ideal *unity* of consciousness [X, § 7]), which correspond to the "levels of objectivation," can be compared with the Kantian "synthesis of apprehension in intuition," "synthesis of reproduction in imagination," "synthesis of recognition in concept." I. Kant, *Kritik der reinen Vernunft*, 1st ed. pp. 77ff.
78. Husserl, *Ideen*, I, p. 110. In context, these statements are directed against Natorp's supposition.

Husserl's original position in the first edition of the *Logische Untersuchungen* over against his changed standpoint in the *Ideen*.

What is essential in this matter appears in the following statement: ". . . When we live, so to speak, in the acts in question, when we are absorbed, e.g., in a perceptual experience of an appearing event, or in a play of phantasy, in the reading of a fairy tale, in the performance of a mathematical proof, and the like, there is nothing to be noted of the ego as point of reference with regard to the acts performed. The representation of the ego may . . . with special facility . . . be especially evoked . . . , but only when it is actually evoked and unites itself with the act in question, do 'we' relate 'ourselves' to the object in such a way that something descriptively ascertainable corresponds to this relating of the ego. What is then present descriptively in actual experience [*Erleben*] is a composite act which contains the representation of the ego as one part and the representing, judging, wishing, etc., of the state of affairs in question as the other part. The ⟨straightforward⟩ experience itself does not consist in a complex which contains the representation of the ego as a partial experience." [79]

This holds precisely for the mode cogito, considering that it is in this mode that the objects of the acts in which we are living are given to consciousness. Cogito and attention, which prove to be closely connected with one another, are not to be understood as a kind of special light cast by the ego onto its objects. The "searchlight theory" of attention has to be abandoned altogether. Variations in attention or in attentional directions must not be interpreted as modifications of illumination or of directions of illumination; even the subjective character of attention, maintained by Husserl, becomes a problem for us. We thus approach the problems pertaining to the phenomenology of attentional modifications, which, as will be shown in the following section, are akin to the thematic modifications and will be treated together with them.

## [III] THEMATIC MODIFICATIONS AND ATTENTION

### 1 / *The Traditional Theory of Attention*

HUSSERL'S THEORY of attention, as presented in the Introduction, scarcely differs in essential points from the conception advocated by the majority of psychologists. His view has much in common with theirs even if we disregard the notion of intentionality

79. Husserl, *Logische Untersuchungen*, 1st ed., II, pp. 355f.

wherein attention becomes the name for modes of performing acts which, because through them objects are made to present themselves to consciousness, are required by and underlie that "discriminating and emphasizing factor." In this respect Husserl himself refers to the writings of Lipps and Pfänder.[80] According to Fröbes,[81] Pfänder indeed advocates the prevalent and universally accepted standpoint of today. Let us elaborate a few aspects of this standpoint which are of importance for our problems.

In the first place, we have to mention the "subjectivity of attention" in a double sense. On the one hand, it is taken as a function emanating from the "psychological subject" or from the ego, as an act of the ego in the sense that the ego lives or is active in an act when he is attentively directed to some object.[82] Not only is the ego co-experienced, but it belongs essentially to the act; it is experienced as the center out of which the attentional rays radiate.

Pfänder, who follows Husserl rather closely and sees the *problems* in question clearly and sharply, speaks of a nearness of the "psychic subject" to the objects with regard to attention.[83] To be sure, terms such as "nearness and farness" and likewise background and foreground of consciousness are metaphorical and should not be used without caution. Still, Pfänder believes that, if the care required is exercised, just these figurative expressions are appropriate to account for the essential features of attention. Figuratively speaking, "the object side of object consciousness" does not offer a "flat surface" but, just in view of the facts pertaining to attention, is more adequately represented by a relief, the *Beachtungsrelief*. The highest point of this relief is the point nearest the "attentive subject," and its base is farthest away from him. To speak of the highest point of a relief, and likewise of foreground and background, requires a point of reference "with respect to which the one is in the fore, the other is behind." In the case of object consciousness, this point of reference is, obviously, the psychic subject. One cannot but combine the thought of the psychic subject with that of objects which stand in the foreground or background of consciousness and thus take for granted that what stands in the foreground of consciousness is nearer the subject and is noticed by him, while what stands in the background is farther away from the subject and not particularly noticed.[84]

Besides subjectivity in the sense of ego relatedness, there is still

80. Husserl, *Ideen*, I, p. 192n.
81. I. Fröbes, *Lehrbuch der experimentellen Psychologie* (Freiburg, 1917), II, p. 72.
82. Thus, e.g., T. Lipps, *Leitfaden der Psychologie* (Leipzig, 1907), p. 59.
83. A. Pfänder, *Einführung in die Psychologie* (Leipzig, 1904), II, 3, § 5.
84. *Ibid.*, p. 358. See pp. 352, 357, 367.

another sense in which the attentional function is considered as subjective by Husserl as well as by the majority of writers. I can turn to an "unnoticed" object without the fact that my attention is directed to it making it undergo any alteration as to content. It is taken for self-evident that the noematic nucleus, with respect to its material content, maintains itself in strictest identity over against change in attention and that modifications of this kind merely entail a change of characters, *all* of which attach to the *same identical* noematic nucleus.

The majority of thinkers go along with Husserl in this respect. Stumpf, who expresses himself with utmost caution, presenting his assertions merely as "theses or hypotheses" and refusing to make the recognition of psychic functions as facts of consciousness conditional upon the acceptance of his assertions which we are about to report, writes: "Nothing whatever need be varied in an individual appearance by functional variation. . . . Evidently, such independent variability is not maintained for all cases. I only hold that it *can* take place, not that it always and necessarily does take place." [85] However, in the concrete examples which Stumpf then discusses, his theorem of the "mutually independent variability" of appearances and functions seems to us to be applied beyond the admissible limits.[86] Such is the case when, for instance, he states that along "with transformation of the unnoticed into something noticed a variation in the appearance itself need not necessarily occur." [87] Singling out an element from an unarticulated total mass does not change the total mass. "The sound which I apprehend at first as unanalyzed, then as analyzed; or, likewise, the initial unitary impression of food in which I soon discern both a sweet and a sour component . . . remain what they were." "In this vein, suppose that, coming out of a theatre in a pensive mood, we have seen the lamps of a lighted street or heard the strokes of the church clock, and now turn our attention to the row of lights or to the further strokes of the clock. What we at this moment perceive as lights and chimings must already have been in existence before we noticed them. Lights and chimings existed, of the same kind and at the same spatial and temporal distances, occasionally even of the same intensity as are now perceived, and not an unnamable unitary something." [88]

Within certain limitations and reservations (which follow from

85. Stumpf, *Erscheinungen und psychische Functionen*, p. 15.
86. We immediately note that the determination of just these limits forms one of the tasks of the present inquiry.
87. Stumpf, *Erscheinungen und psychische Functionen*, pp. 17f.
88. Stumpf, *Tonpsychologie* (Leipzig, 1883–90), II, pp. 9ff. ". . . Überall verändert Aufmerksamkeit, Übung und sonstige psychische Einflüsse im individuellen Leben wesentlich nur die *Auffassung* der Empfindungen, die Empfindun-

the constancy hypothesis), Stumpf, in agreement with Lipps, allows the possibility of intensification of sensations by attention; however, this increase in intensity has to be considered as "indirect." [89] Pfänder follows Stumpf and Husserl here. He recognizes the difference between "object of object consciousness" and objective thing (although not as consistently and explicitly as Husserl later made this distinction in the *Ideen* where it led to the concept of noema) and emphasizes that only what "is actually an object of object consciousness for the psychic subject" may be taken into consideration.[90] "One must take no account of the actual existing external world, its actual multiplicity and extension." "If different men simultaneously direct their attention to one and the same actual painting as a whole, these different men do not, for this reason, have the same objects before them." Correspondingly, the same holds for a single psychic subject at different times of his life. The differences which Pfänder has in mind here concern only the "inner variety" of what is noticed. The objects in question only differ from one another so far as at one time *more* of what is actually present is attentively grasped than at another time. The differences merely concern the "range" of what is noticed, which can vary from case to case. But if the "inner variety" is given and if the "range" of the noticed neither decreases nor increases, the object remains the same over against all the attentional modifications which are still possible under these conditions.[91] Shifting the "emphasis of attention," for example, affects in no way the identity of the object which on diverse occasions presents itself in a different *Beachtungsrelief.* When "a painting in its signification . . . is the object of attention, there can be in the chief focus of ⟨the psychic subject's⟩ attention the colors and their decorative effect, or the distribution of light and brightness-composition, or the forms, the sweep and composition of lines, or the entire mood, or the kind of feeling and striving of certain represented objects, etc. In each case, the total whole has a different *Beachtungsrelief.*" Yet, it is identically the same object whose *Beachtungsrelief* varies. A similar case is that of a "simple object," as when, for example, a uniformly colored surface is attentively observed. "At one time the color, so to speak, is the basis, the form, the summit of the relief; at another time the color

___

gen selbst nur ganz ausnahmsweise und in sehr geringem Masse." For Stumpf, the exceptional cases are incidental. "Sensuous material" is "identical and invariable . . ., given the objective impressions" (p. 12).

89. *Ibid.,* I, pp. 71ff., 373ff.; Lipps, *Leitfaden der Psychologie,* pp. 6off. Cf. William James, *Principles of Psychology* (New York, 1890), I, pp. 425ff.

90. See the exposition in Pfänder's *Einführung in die Psychologie,* II, 2, § 1, and pp. 361ff.

91. *Ibid.,* pp. 369ff.

is prominent over the retreating form." But it is the identical "simple object" which can "have a different *Beachtungsrelief* with respect to the attention directed to it." When a picture, for instance, is appraised differently by different people, or when different people react differently to the same situation, it is, among other reasons, because emotional effects and reactions depend on the "form of the *Beachtungsrelief*" (that is, on which part or moment of the object is located at the summit of the relief); and they also depend on what the relief presents at its various altitudes. But the reason is not that different objects underlie the different appraisals and reactions.

Finally, it is taken for granted that attention is a *unitary* function and that its accomplishment is always the same regardless of where it is directed in a concrete case. This conception is common to all theories of attention. According to Husserl and Pfänder, the nature of this function consists in making prominent, pointedly bringing out, bringing closer, and illuminating; all these circumlocutions are found in both writers. Stumpf [92] sees its "primary effect" as a "noticing," a notion closely related to Husserl's and Pfänder's. Lipps considers the notion that the mental state to which attention is directed displaces other mental states and asserts itself against them.[93] Ribot speaks of a *"monoïdëisme"* or a tendency to *"monoïdëisme."* [94] However the function of attention may be specified in the several theories, all of them agree in considering the accomplishment of attention not to depend in any way on the objects to which attention is directed or on the sense in which it is turned to them. The same is held concerning attentional modifications, the variation in attention or change of its direction. All these theories speak of *attention simpliciter* and see as a unitary phenomenon what, upon closer analysis, is resolved into a series of rather different and, partly, even unconnected phenomena.

2 / *The Direction of the Further Investigations*

THESE THESES of the traditional theory of attention have to be discussed. Their examination requires an analysis of the phenomenological findings which those very theses pretend to express —in other words, a testing of the legitimacy of such a pretense. We shall pursue these analyses along the lines of our previous investigations. To establish the connection with the latter, we recall what we found above concerning the relationship of attention (as this term is

92. Stumpf, *Tonpsychologie*, II, p. 278.
93. Lipps, *Leitfaden der Psychologie*, p. 60.
94. Ribot, *Psychologie de l'attention*, pp. 6ff., 63, and *passim*.

commonly understood, apart from any theory) to thematic consciousness. There we identified acts of attention—i.e., acts in which we are attentively directed to something—with consciousness in the form of the cogito. We found the noematic correlate of consciousness of this form in the theme, while the thematic field, and whatever else still belongs to the domain of the co-given, proved to be the noematic correlates of inactual consciousness.

By virtue of their results, these analyses of theme and thematic field suggest a certain further line of exploration: definite essential possibilities for thematic modifications are pre-traced by the peculiar nature of the theme and the structural organization of its constituents, by the place which the theme has in its field, by the specific structure of the field, and its distinctiveness within the domain of the co-given. The possibility of thematic modifications is grounded in the essential situation that the theme has constituents and lies within a field. A theme can cease to be a theme, and something else can become the theme that somehow, in some mode or other, except the mode of cogito, was experienced (or perchance was not even experienced at all). We shall pursue these possible thematic modifications which are of strictly prescribed types. Thus, the attentional modifications will appear by themselves and find their places in the series of the thematic modifications. It is in this framework that we propose to study the attentional modifications and confront the aforementioned theses with the phenomenological findings. The point of view according to which the thematic modifications are arranged will become apparent in the course of our discussion.

With the study of the thematic modifications the connection with Husserl's analyses in the *Ideen* will be re-established. As stated in the Introduction, inactualities are conceived by Husserl as susceptible of possible actualization. With respect to every object not experienced through an act in the form of cogito, there obtains the possibility that the consciousness of it assumes this form. In which different senses this possibility of actualization is to be understood, what, according to the several typical cases, the actualization accomplishes, and whether —as Husserl teaches—it is to be interpreted as a specific ego-act will on this occasion also be made a topic of discussion.

## 1. First Series of Thematic Modifications

### 3 / *Enlargement and Elucidation of the Thematic Field*

A THEME is given in a thematic field. A variety of events can take place within the field. For instance, it is broadened: the range of what is co-given as materially belonging to the theme becomes larger so far as new items, previously not experienced, now appear. Throughout this enlargement we abide by our theme, continuing to deal with what we have been dealing before. But our theme has now acquired a wider horizon. Its "import," its "significance" may have changed, as, for example, when I think about a scientific theory and there is broadening of the range of facts or other items for which it has relevancy. The theory itself about which I am thinking remains the same—also noematically—and I continue to have *it* as theme, not the total range for which it has relevance.[95] But the variety and quality of its material relations, the possibilities of connection, the aspects which it opens up, have become different. Such modifications are possible in all areas of conscious life and everywhere are of the same type, thus also in perceptual consciousness. In conjunction with the broadening of the perceptual field in which the thing is situated, the relations and relational possibilities multiply. Or the horizon of memories belonging to a certain thing broadens: again the same thing continues being given, but it has acquired a new "meaning," a new significance for the whole of my life, it appears in a new light; I see it —the noematically same thing—in a different attitude. Only its perspective has changed; it itself remains identically the same. The modifications concern only its history, say; or, perhaps, the thing appears now for the first time under the perspective of my life-history. This can go so far that the thematic field becomes totally changed, as will be shown presently. Again, this possibility is to be strictly distinguished from that other one which is much more likely to be actualized in everyday life, the possibility, namely, that the situation itself in which the thing in question played its role will become the theme and that the thing will become only a member of that situation, being nothing for itself and existing only under the perspective of the situation. Obviously the nature of the noematic objects involved determines the particular sense in which the enlargement is to be understood in a concrete case with regard to aspects and perspective.

Correspondingly, the same holds for variations in the opposite direction, although these are comparatively seldom actualized. Narrowing of the thematic field purports a narrowing of the horizon, the theme loses connecting links, the variety of its material relations is reduced.

Along with these modifications must also be considered those in which the thematic field is not enriched by *increase* of components not

95. We are dealing here with the same difference already considered above, pp. 201f. Cf. also p. 243f.

previously given but in which components which had appeared in a certain obscurity, nebulosity, and confusedness become elucidated, clarified, and determined to a higher degree than before. The thematic field is never fully determined; it never displays itself in full clarity and transparency. It always contains obscurities and fades into indefiniteness. Some of what belongs to the field is given in full clarity and determination, while much else is veiled and undetermined; and this indeterminateness has degrees: from a confusion in which broad outlines are still visible although finer contours merge with one another, to that degree of unclarity where there is but misty obscurity. However, this obscurity is not obscurity *simpliciter;* rather, it is obscurity affecting a thematic field. That is to say, the attitude as determined by the thematic field bestows a specific tinge upon the obscurity affecting the field. Dealing with a certain mathematical proposition, I can say in general terms that I am adopting a mathematical attitude; and this generality, which from case to case is differently specified, refers to the meant obscurity.[96] The experienced relatedness of the obscurity to the field purports that, however veiled, confused, and undetermined the items of the thematic field may be, they still pertain to the theme and are "somehow" materially related to it—the term "somehow" indicating that, apart from this pertinence to the theme at large, any more precise and proper specification of the kind of the material pertinence is more or less lacking. Whatever possibilities of connection there are might be entirely undetermined: perspectives are opened up only insofar as we know that there are perspectives in this or that direction, which is, again, only roughly delineated.

Now, let us say, the obscurity is dispelled, and the horizon is clarified. Components of the field acquire determinations, their possible connections with the theme, previously indicated only in the rough, appear with increased precision. Here, too, one can speak of enlargement: an obscure horizon has been clarified, and that purports further and freer perspectives. Undetermined presumptions are more or less intuitively filled; the theme now stands in a determined horizon, and its material relations to the components of the clarified thematic field are given with some preciseness. Such clarification can be of different sorts. It may happen that the field continues being shrouded in almost absolute darkness, and only directions in which connections are possible appear in comparative clarity. It is no longer a pure "somehow," for the field has acquired some determination, even

96. Cf. the discussions on p. 210. Phenomenally speaking, mathematical attitude means something different from case to case; that implies that the obscurity is also different from case to case.

though only as to the mentioned directions. It may also happen that the obscurity is dispelled and the thematic field presents itself in clarity. However, this clarity is never total. There is always obscurity somewhere in the field; in the case under consideration, the clarification may have occurred in the center of the field around the theme, while the obscurity has withdrawn into the outer zones of the field. That the thematic field is always affected by obscurity and contains components only roughly outlined is the result of its not being precisely delimited but fading into the indefinite. Yet, this "indefinite" is always related to the field; for the obscurity in question is not just *any* obscurity but one which affects a particular thematic field. Between the extremes we have considered are other possibilities at the intermediate levels.[97]

The preceding analyses have significance for the method of clarification—more precisely, for the "non-genuine levels of clarity," the "extensive broadenings of the extent of clarity." [98] A fully exhaustive phenomenological description of these processes would have to take into account all essential conditions such as the structures of both the theme and the thematic field and would have to show the essentially different intermediate phases through which these processes can lead. As a matter of fact, "non-genuine clarification" is nothing else than the thematic modification considered in the present section.

Properly speaking, these thematic modifications are not very significant, though, to be sure, not as trivial as they might appear at first. The expression "increase (or decrease) of field-components" is to be construed with a certain caution: it must not be taken to mean that further components are simply superadded and the previously given possible connections remain what they have been all along, while new ones appear in addition to them. Even in comparatively insignificant modifications we find a reorientation of the theme. While new components emerge in the thematic field, or while the latter is elucidated, or while what was farther away comes closer, the emphasis

97. In the *Ideen*, I, p. 49, Husserl has described the possible results of such clarification with respect to the "natural surrounding world." This limitation is not essential; *mutatis mutandis*, what is said there can be transferred to consciousness of every kind. However, in view of the obscurity deriving a tinge from the thematic field, we hesitate to speak of "an empty obscurity of dark undeterminateness," an expression which does not do justice to the phenomenon in question. Husserl ascribed this clarification to the "elucidating regard of attention" (*aufhellenden Blick der Aufmerksamkeit*). Thus we are confronted with a first accomplishment of the attentional function, an accomplishment which we try to understand in its specific nature.

98. Cf. Husserl, *Ideen*, I, p. 127ff. The "genuine levels of clarity" belong in a different context.

within the field is differently distributed so that the field varies in its "looks." New motives, we may say, become efficacious, and this is not without influence upon the old ones. The thematic field in which the theme is situated undergoes a certain change; the theme is now differently oriented to that field and differently inserted in it.

## 4 / Radical Modification of the Thematic Field

WHAT WE HAVE just said holds in full measure for an entire change in attitude. As we have already pointed out, an identical theme "looks" different in varying attitudes. The theme is not so independent of the field as to be totally unconcerned by modifications of the latter; it is not as though even in the case of an "unlimited variation" of the field the theme remained identically the same and maintained its "physiognomy" in every respect. Let us recall that a "thing" which—also noematically speaking—remains the same presents itself in another light when set into another environment: the "inkwell" on the "desk" has different relations to its environment and appears under a different perspective than when the same "inkwell" is set on the "piano." Let us consider a still more pregnant example. Take the following proposition, understood, of course, within the frame of the transcendental reduction: a grey, which, physically speaking, remains the same, appears brighter in a darker environment than in a less dark environment. Let this proposition be our theme, and let us refer it to Helmholtz's system of physiological optics. We see the proposition in question inserted into a certain theoretical context as an horizon. We now vary our attitude. As before, we abide by our theme; but the horizon changes: Helmholtz's system is replaced by Hering's theory.[99] Again our proposition is inserted into a theoretical context. But observe how completely different it appears in the thematic field: Hering's theory of colors as compared to Helmholtz's. While we continue dealing with the same proposition, our attitude has varied, and our theme, which has remained the same, fits into the new thematic field as determined by the changed attitude in a way different than before. Because the thematic modifications of the dimension under discussion here are of an almost extreme kind, we can observe in this example in a fully pregnant manner the changes and variations in the relatedness of the theme to its field. Though in a less striking, less radical way, we also experience

99. We explicitly emphasize that our theme is the aforementioned proposition in the one or the other attitude. But our theme is not one of those theories themselves, the proposition in question being merely emphasized and accentuated among other theorems with which it is interwoven. We have already referred to this difference.

variations in the thematic field, as when components of the thematic field, which were only loosely connected to the theme, now "draw nearer" to it, so that the theme is primarily oriented to them, or when new components appear in the field with which the theme is connected—always the new orientations and connections penetrating and modifying the old ones. This defines the sense of the reorientation of the field and the import of this reorientation for the theme itself. In virtue of modifications of the kind just mentioned, the theme, being inserted into a *different* thematic field, is inserted into that field in a *different* way. Therefore, these modifications must not be interpreted as a mere increase of components and possible connections, with everything else remaining just as it was. Such an interpretation is already precluded by the structure of the thematic field, i.e., the unity of the theme and the thematic field as a Gestalt connection.

## 5 / *The Essential Accomplishment of This Series of Thematic Modifications*

THE MODIFICATIONS DESCRIBED can be interpreted as accomplishments of the attentional function, and, indeed, they were thus interpreted. Now we must ask: what is essential to the noematic accomplishment of these modifications? Obviously it consists in the theme remaining unchanged as identically the same throughout the thematic modifications grouped in this series. We can go so far as to say that the invariance of the theme throughout the variations described founds their inner kinship and yields the point of view from which they belong together. This type of thematic modification is the only one admitting of such invariance.

However, this invariance is not absolute; it concerns the noematic What of the theme merely with respect to its content—merely as to what it is in itself, apart from its relation to other items and its possible insertion into any contexts. In the latter regard, there are modifications, and even appreciable ones. But the theme itself as self-enclosed and delimited is not thereby affected; it remains as it was. The invariance thus involves, if one will, a stratum which can be isolated only by abstraction; yet it is an independent stratum of fundamental importance. The aforementioned proposition from the psychology of colors remains in itself the same, whatever the attitude in which I might deal with it; it is the *one* definite meaning-entity with which I am concerned in each and every attitude. I can bring the thing which I perceive into different surroundings without changing anything in it; in all surroundings it remains one and the same thing which is given to me as my identical theme—just as the Pythagorean theorem is *one* identical theorem in whichever attitude it may become my theme.

The connection between the invariance of the theme with regard to changes in attitude and the consistency of the theme within the thematic field (which has been brought out above[100]) is apparent. On the one hand, that consistency is the essential phenomenological ground of this invariance; on the other hand, the special position which the theme holds in the thematic field manifests itself in that very invariance.

Let us mention that all those cases are here excluded in which along with changes in attitude the theme itself also undergoes modifications of any kind. If a colored figure is placed upon a different background, its color changes according to the laws of color-contrast. In such cases in which a modification of the theme itself occurs, the possibility under discussion is not actualized, and other laws come into play. Obviously such cases are here not taken into consideration, and they do not fall under the purview of phenomenology which is concerned merely with *possibilities*.[101]

## 2. Second Series of Thematic Modifications

### 6  /  *Variation in Theme as Alteration of Its Status*

WE NOW TURN to modifications belonging to a new dimension whose possibility likewise is grounded in the phenomenologically essential situation that a theme is given in a thematic field. The modifications of the second series differ from those of the first by their noematic accomplishments. More than before we shall now deal with modifications and their accomplishments commonly comprised under the heading of attention.

Following Husserl, the domain of the co-given in its totality is to be characterized as a "potential perceptual field in the sense that a peculiar perceiving (an attentive cogito) can turn to anything so appearing," i.e., belonging to this domain, just as, conversely, whatever is actually, i.e., cogitatively, given can lose its actuality when the "attentive cogito" turns away from it.[102] Carrying out in the domain of the co-given the differentiation, not made by Husserl himself, by means of which the thematic field is delimited as a partial domain of a special kind, we can refer the aforementioned possibility of actualiza-

100. Section II, 5.
101. Cf. the remarks on p. 208.
102. Husserl, *Ideen*, I, p. 169; cf. also § 35.

tion to this partial domain alone. In view of our present purpose, such a restriction is admissible; it permits us to formulate in full pregnancy the problems of attention in which we are interested. On the one hand, we thus confine the expression of "the fringe of consciousness which belongs to the essence of a (cogitative) perception experienced in the mode of 'advertence to the object' " to the thematic field as defined by us. On the other hand, we can still say, adopting Husserl's generalization with regard to all "cogitationes whatever in the sense of the examples as enumerated by Descartes," that it is of the essence of thematic consciousness, i.e., of the unity of theme and thematic field, that "free turnings" are possible in such a manner that a component part of the fringe becomes the new theme while the old theme "fades away," yet still continues to appear, but now as a component part of the fringe belonging to the new theme.

The following possibilities obtain when we turn away from our theme. (1) The theme completely disappears from consciousness. (2) It continues being given, i.e., is co-given, but belongs only to the partial domain other than the thematic field—cf. Husserl's example of the whistle (*Ideen*, I, p. 254); here the theme is "released from grasp." (3) The theme ceases to be theme and now belongs to the thematic field of the new theme. It is "still in grasp" and still partakes of thematic consciousness so far as the latter concerns both the theme and the thematic field. The manner in which the thematic field is given can quite generally be characterized by the expressions "also in grasp" or "still in grasp"—the latter serving especially the modification under discussion. In what follows we shall only deal with the third of these possibilities. It is not difficult to see what is accomplished by this modification.

We experience how that which was the theme loses this distinction. Having been the center of a field oriented and organized with respect to it, it now fits into another organization differently determined. It is essential that this new organization, the newly organized field, have a new center of reference and orientation. In contradistinction to the modifications of the first series, the old theme is now dislodged from its central place and loses its privileged status, the latter passing on to what had been a component of the thematic field.

*Mutatis mutandi*, the same holds for the acquisition as for the loss of that privileged status. We experience how that which had been inserted in an organization in a more or less subordinate position now acquires a dominant one, becomes the center of organization of the thematic field, so that what is co-given with it fits into the new organization and is oriented with respect to its center. We have to stress that we experience the actual occurrence of these modifications themselves, not only their accomplishments as results. Both loss and acquisition of that peculiar independence which essentially characterizes the figure over against its ground are experienced as occurring before our very eyes—that is to say, as a variation of the noemata.[103]

## 7 / Constancy of the Theme

LET US NOW INQUIRE into the specific sense of this series of modifications. It is determined by its noematic accomplishment just as, quite generally, the sense of any modification of consciousness whatever is determined by its noematic accomplishment. Here we progress from one theme to another; however, to a theme which was materially related to the one "held in grasp" before, both belonging to one and the same sphere of objects. Thus a certain area, such as that designated by the "mathematical attitude," or the "geometrical attitude," etc., can remain unaffected by the variation and be common to the thematic fields belonging to the old and new themes, the reason being that the movement from theme to theme takes place within one and the same objective sphere.

In the *first series* of thematic modifications, an identical theme was preserved over against sometimes radical variations in its thematic environment; it remained the same in strict identity. Change in its orientation in the thematic field does not impair its identity in any way whatever. Now we are dealing with a modification which, in a certain sense, does not affect the theme either. To be sure, it discontinues being theme and loses this privileged status; becoming a component of the ground, it assumes a corresponding status. Nevertheless, as to its material content, it remains what it was. Let us consider an example. I review, let us say, the several steps of a mathematical demonstration with which I am acquainted. In each step of the demonstration the theme is the proposition arrived at in the step in question; the propositions preceding it and leading to it, as well as those which are to follow, are co-given with my theme and form its thematic field. Now I take a further step: the proposition to which I was just directed does not vanish from consciousness, but it is no longer my theme, since I have turned to a different proposition. The old theme, which now belongs to the thematic field of the new theme, as well as the new

103. Rubin, *Visuell wahrgenommene Figuren*, p. 69, gives a highly illustrative example from the visual realm. According to him, one can "almost intuitively experience" the loss of figure-quality.

theme which previously belonged to the thematic field of the old theme, remain in themselves what they were. They are such and such determined propositions of which I am conscious as the same in strict identity. As we have already noted before, we here exclude the case where the propositions enter into new relations and connections with one another such that a different theme, new with respect to its What, results—a case which we shall consider later.

What is characteristic of this situation actualized in reviewing the several steps of a demonstration, as well as in counting, consists just in that I go step by step without the demonstration as such becoming my theme or without the objects to be counted being given to me as a unitary group—a case in which counting in the genuine sense is precluded. Here the several items through which I pass step by step can be called elements, because they remain distinct from one another, and no synthesized total theme results.[104] As they are gone through, these elements remain what they were; all items remain unchanged with respect to their What and their sense content. We can speak of a constancy of elements.

## 8 / The Shaping of the Field of Consciousness by the Modifications of This Series

THE MODIFICATION under discussion leaves the theme unchanged with regard to its What, apart from alterations entailed by the loss of theme status. The theme remains constant with respect to its inner structure. By this formulation of constancy, however, only one side of the present situation is described. The other side concerns the shaping of the field of consciousness, i.e., of the unity of theme and thematic field. In this regard, there is a change which we, again, experience as a process and not only as to its result. The field of consciousness, whose components have possibly all remained the same, appears different when organized with respect to this theme *qua* theme than when organized with respect to a different theme. The heap of elements to be counted "looks" different when I consider it from the standpoint of the second element as my theme as compared to when I consider it from the standpoint of the first. This difference in "looks" is not the result of the memory of having already taken a counting step, although such memory is itself necessarily required for the process of counting, which would be impossible without it. Counting as such is not the issue here, however. Rather, we are analyzing the kind of experience which underlies the process of counting and establishes it: the experience of going through the

104. We shall clarify this expression on pp. 244–48.

elements, one after the other; and it is with reference to that experience that the memories in question supervene.[105]

Correspondingly, the same holds for our other example: the mathematical demonstration surveyed from the point of view of one step presents itself differently from the way it presents itself when it is surveyed from the standpoint of another step, even though all particular theorems pertaining to the demonstration remain distinct and discriminate and do not "merge" or interweave with one another (which would yield new noematic objects). What is essential to, and characteristic of, the modification under discussion consists in the components and items of the field of consciousness—the field in which I move while passing from item to item—remaining, each one in itself, what it is and not being affected with regard to material content. Nevertheless, the field in which I move undergoes at every step from theme to theme an alteration, so far as its center of reference and organization and, accordingly, its "physiognomy" changes. Finally, the several components acquire new relations and orientations, or the old ones disappear: the acquisition and loss of the theme status may be mentioned first in this respect. These alterations notwithstanding, all the items to be taken into consideration remain the same with respect to their material What. Here we are confronted with an identity which involves no constitutional problems but is the identity of the immediately given over against modifications of a specific kind.

Husserl and those in agreement with him had in mind this identity of elements—here, indeed, one can speak of "elements"—over against the alteration of the field of consciousness when advocating the thesis that attention consists *merely* in giving preference to certain contents or objects, the function of attention being to throw brighter light on the items concerned without thereby changing in any way their material content. As far as *this* accomplishment of attention is concerned, Pfänder's theory of *Beachtungsrelief* can be advanced with a certain justification. Here we have the case of an "additive sum" (*Und-Summe*) admitted by Wertheimer as an exception, possible only "under definite characteristic conditions, only within very narrow limits and perhaps only in approximation." [106] To be sure, there can be no question here of an "additive sum" in the pure and pregnant sense of what Wertheimer called the "bundle thesis." Perhaps Koffka's formulation of the "and-connection of isolated . . . fully articulated

---

105. By this, obviously, we do not pretend to present a complete phenomenology of counting, into whose problems we cannot enter here.

106. Wertheimer, "Untersuchungen zur Lehre von der Gestalt," I, *loc. cit.*, p. 52.

partial wholes" (*Teilganze*) appears more adequate.[107] However, the "partial wholes" are not so much isolated from, but rather delimited with regard to, one another, and, furthermore, the expression "and-connection" must be taken *cum grano salis*. The "elements" are not totally alien, indifferent, and without any bearing on one another, even though they are, to a rather high degree, independent of one another. Perhaps one does justice to this state of affairs only by considering the Gestalt connection binding up the thematic field to the theme as somehow relaxed. However, there is an appreciable difference between a Gestalt connection, however relaxed, and a pure "additive sum," and just this difference prevents us from speaking here of an "and-connection."

It is *this* kind of experience which has especially been treated in the literature on the psychology of attention and on kindred topics and with respect to which the traditional theories are justified. A case in point is G. E. Müller's theory, although that theory is correct only for the experience under discussion. In his dictations on the doctrine of the *distinctio rationis* he states: "We can . . . apprehend the objects in two ways. Either we allow an object to partake of our attention singularly, notwithstanding its connection with other objects (singular apprehension), or we apprehend a complex of several objects given in a certain spatio-temporal connection and as distinct from one another also in their totality (collective apprehension)." [108] Müller takes it for granted that the objects in question are given as the same in both apprehensions, so that any objects whatever are susceptible of being apprehended in either way. Furthermore, it seems objectionable to consider, as Müller does, the "complexes of appearances" as sums of their "elements" and correspondingly to symbolize them. Husserl's refutation of scepticism with respect to parts in the sense of portions (*Stücke*) is to be accepted only with similar restrictions. To be sure, the connections between the contents in the experiences under discussion must not be construed, with Husserl, as successions and coexistences; were they existential connections, Husserl's analysis would be correct *a fortiori*. Still, with this proviso, Husserl's assertions hold under the restriction mentioned. Presupposing an experience of the type under consideration, we can, in fact, say with regard to Husserl's example of the homogeneous white surface: "The boundaries drawn in imagination do not produce the portions but only delimit them. Obviously these portions were actually present in the unitary content, 'white surface.' The content without boundaries fixed in identical

107. Koffka, "Psychologie," *loc. cit.*, p. 548.
108. Published by F. Schumann, in *Zeitschrift für Psychologie*, XVII, pp. 107f.

intention *coincides* with the same content changed by that imagination; it *coincides* with the former in respect of the delineated parts. The parts were and are still in the whole, only not as discriminate unities in themselves." [109]

As we said with regard to the material content of the items concerned, the traditional theory of the accomplishment of attention is correct for the aforementioned sphere of thematic or, if one prefers, attentional modifications. But it is correct *only* for this sphere. It was the main mistake to have disregarded this limitation. The noematic accomplishment pertaining to the specific experience of going through a series of "elements" and making "element" after "element" the theme was taken as *standard accomplishment* of attention, attention being considered as a unitary function always of the same accomplishment, all other attentional accomplishments being interpreted or, more correctly, reinterpreted in terms of the standard case. One tried to discover the standard accomplishment in all attentional functions.

It is worth noting that the modes of actuality or (noematically) modes of givenness, as described by Husserl, are in correspondence with the results of our analyses of theme and thematic field as well as of the thematic modifications under discussion. Thus, the mode "holding in grasp" is identical with "*being* a theme"; "grasping" designates the process of turning to a theme, the "becoming a theme"; the "still maintaining in grasp" refers to the case, dealt with above, in which what was the theme is now given as a component of the thematic field belonging to a new theme now "held in grasp." It is not without hesitation that we speak here of *modes,* because this expression might convey the idea that we were dealing here with modes in the sense of characters. Although the term "character" does not occur, Husserl's analyses do not preclude the interpretation that he did in fact consider "modes of attention" as well as "modes of actuality" or "modes of givenness" as characters in the genuine sense of the term. [110] That is to say, modes could be understood in the sense in which one and the same noematic nucleus can be differently characterized, as when, e.g., the *same* is originarily present or represented, appears as simply existing or else as questionable, doubtful, presumable, etc. Modes of actuality cannot be considered as modes in the same sense as the "characters" in the sphere of presentations and representations or as the "characters of belief" and the corresponding "existential characters." [111] These modes are not characters at all in the pregnant

---

109. Husserl, *Logische Untersuchungen,* II, ii, § 39.

110. Cf., e.g., *Ideen,* I, p. 254: ". . . die Gegebenheitsweise des . . . 'Vermeinten als solchen' ändert sich. . . ."

111. Cf. *ibid.,* §§ 99, 103, 104.

sense of the term; they do not form a special group among the totality of characters. Their function does not consist in determining the manner in which something is present to consciousness. When what "had been held in grasp" is now only "maintained in grasp," it undergoes the alterations indicated above which are connected up with the loss of the theme status. In the variations of genuine characters there are no such alterations of the material nucleus of the noema, even though they merely concern its orientation and hardly its material content proper. For example, they do not occur when something which was given as simply existing becomes questionable, etc., whereby we abstractively exclude the possibility of new rational motives becoming operative.

Modes of actuality also do not have the peculiarity essential to genuine characters which permits us, with reference to characters, to speak of modifications in a very special sense. Among the characters of a certain group there is always one which is distinctive in that all the other characters of the group in question refer back to it and have the sense of "modifications of" it—i.e., of the primal character which is not modified, so that the modified ones appear as its derivatives. But "still maintaining in grasp" is not a modification in that sense of "holding in grasp." This is in keeping with the mentioned alteration. We must not be led astray by the little word "still." It serves to distinguish this relinquishment of the theme from a different one which Husserl calls "releasing from grasp," whereby "what is released from grasp" no longer belongs to the thematic field but at most is "merely co-given." Besides this, the "still" can imply that while I "still maintain something in grasp" I happen to remember that I "had held it in grasp" before. This, however, does not make the "still maintaining in grasp" a modification in the genuine sense of the "holding in grasp," quite apart from the fact that phenomenologically speaking "that which is still maintained in grasp" and "that which was in grasp," taken purely in themselves, are two different things and that their coincidence is possible only by means of an additional thought.[112]

Cogitative consciousness does not function as the primal form of a series of characters which refer back to it in "noematic intentionality" as modifications of it, just as thematic modifications are not genuine modifications when—as appears natural—we define this concept with regard to structures of characters. When we speak here of modifications, we use the term not in the pregnant sense but in a rather vague one where modification signifies variation or alteration in some respect or other.

112. Cf. in this connection section IV, 1 and 2.

Actual consciousness and inactual consciousness do not stand to each other as primal form and derivative.[113] There obtains between them a relation of a kind of which there is no analogue as far as characters are concerned. By virtue of a law, inactualities, and even inactualities of different dimensions, belong to every actual consciousness of any object. This law is also expressed in the fact that what is given is always a theme in a field. This again hangs together with the fact that modes of actuality do not have the same importance for problems pertaining to the "phenomenology of reason," as developed by Husserl, which genuine modifications and characters have.

## 3. Third Series of Thematic Modifications

So FAR AS their noematic accomplishments are concerned, the thematic modifications now to be considered are totally different from those studied thus far. It is only from the point of view of this radical difference that modifications are grouped together here which still differ from one another in regard to their noematic accomplishment. From the point of view by which we are guided in the present investigations, what unifies the modifications of the third series in contradistinction to those considered thus far is the fact that in and through them the theme is affected in a deep-reaching way (although differing from case to case) with regard to its very material content.

### 9 / *Restructuration of the Theme*

To BRING OUT the first modification we recall the structure of the theme which is not a "psychic element" in the sense of a "simple idea." We refer to the analyses offered in Section 1 (especially pp. 189–92) where, within the noematic What, we encountered the structure comprising both the formative and the formed constituents; and we mentioned there several possibilities for the specification of that structure. The problem now to be posed is this: what happens when, in that structure, a change occurs, e.g., when one of its constituents changes its function?

For the sake of concreteness let us return to our earlier examples. We spoke there of a rectangular piece of cardboard the color of which "interested" us, and we described the noema pertaining to this perceptual experiencing by saying that, as the dominant constituent the color lies on the rectangular surface which supports the color and serves as its foundation; it is a color of such and such a hue, of such

113. Derivative not in the Humean sense but in the sense of Husserl's presentations in *Ideen*, I, §§ 99, 104.

and such a brightness, saturation, etc.; it covers its support. Let our "interest" now "change"; "we are interested" in the form of the piece of cardboard. Now it is the rectangular shape which carries the emphasis and determines the physiognomy of what is given. The color becomes a mere quality *of* the rectangle; it is spread over the surface as a kind of filling. Or, take a new "change": "we are interested" in the contour. By virtue of its delimiting function the contour seems to comprise and to compress whatever lies within. It becomes "active" and forming with regard to what is contained within it. The latter is concerned by, and undergoes something from, the contour, so as to become "its content" in a special and especially pregnant sense.[114] Then—again a change—just this "content" comes into its own. The contour loses its distinctive position, becomes a mere boundary and no longer has a delimiting function. It no longer compresses; it has lost its activity.

We experience something similar as to the figure discussed on p. 188. If, as one usually says, the S-"apprehension" is superseded by the $\varphi$-"apprehension," neither curve nor loop remain what they were. The curve loses its function of being the stem which it was in the case of the S. Its static function changes to the extent that, as the curve of $\varphi$, it no longer has any static function at all but is, instead, merely an appendix. The loop, in turn, decorative and arabesque as S-loop, now becomes central and determinative for the sense of what is seen. The appendix goes off from it, is suspended by it. As the S-loop, it is the upper closure in which the curve terminates; when it is seen as $\varphi$-loop, the curve emerges from it. Examples of this sort are abundant, but the figure published by Rubin holds special interest.[115] We observe how the boundary between white and black changes its "looks" and is totally transformed when we see it one time as the contour of the white vase and another time as that of the two black faces looking at each other.

Always—and we must not forget this—we are speaking only of what is phenomenally given and its physiognomy, never of constellations of physical stimuli or of things.

10 / *The Result of Restructuration*

IN OUR FIRST ANALYSES we encountered the theme as Gestalt, all of its constituents being related to one another by virtue of Gestalt-connection. The modifications introduced in the previous

114. Cf., in this connection, Rubin, *Visuell wahrgenommene Figuren*, pp. 36ff. What Rubin says about a field, which had been a ground, becoming a figure can easily be applied to the experiences now under discussion.

115. *Ibid.*, Fig. 3. See above, p. 14.

section, which occur within the theme itself, are to be understood on the basis of the Gestalt thesis, which provides us with the decisive point of view.

According to Koffka's definition, "in the Gestalt every part has its place and its property as part of the whole, i.e., stated differently: in the Gestalt all parts support each other reciprocally; the change of *one* member cannot remain without influence on the whole Gestalt." [116] That definition not only confirms our assertion that the theme is a Gestalt but also allows us to understand the modifications under discussion. In these modifications a new theme emerges, a different datum results. One theme is superseded by another, one material What replaced by a different one. None of the constituents remain what they were. When the Gestalt in which a certain constituent had a definite function no longer exists and the constituent is integrated into a new contexture, it takes on a function in accordance with this new contexture and its properties as a whole. This new function can be *toto coelo* different from the old one.

Whether and to what extent it is different depends on the particular nature of the Gestalten in question. Certain special cases are possible in which the two Gestalten exhibit high similarity, sometimes even, in a certain sense, likeness. There are, however, other possibilities—by far more frequently actualized—in which the situation is entirely different. In the latter cases, which alone were taken into consideration in the selection of examples in the preceding section, a totally different theme emerges in restructuration, and, accordingly, no constituent and no detail is unaffected. Nothing remains what it was. A stroke in one configuration of lines (e.g., the contour of Rubin's goblet) and the "same" stroke—the "same" objectively speaking, i.e., as far as the physical stimulus is concerned—in *another* configuration (the contour of the two faces) appears phenomenally as totally different; it *is* by no means the same stroke.

Objective identity becomes a problem. Now we can state in concrete terms what was said in general ones in the appendix to Section 1, concerning the epistemological problems arising from the point of view of Gestalt theory. The problem is this: how does the constitution of the identical stimulus come about? How does the experience arise, and how is it phenomenologically constituted, on the basis of which we can speak of one and the same stimulus differentially "apprehended," "construed," and organized, but presupposed as always identical, only from case to case "looking" different in its very identity? By the same token the question is simultaneously posed

116. Koffka, "Psychologie," *loc. cit.*, p. 551.

concerning the phenomenological constitution of the basis on which theories, such as Benussi's theory of production, can be established and which these theories presuppose.

A different theme emerges in restructuration, this modification yielding another What with regard to its material content. The precise sense in which this new theme is different, the direction which the material alteration takes cannot be decided generally and *a priori,* certainly not for this whole dimension. The specific accomplishment of such a modification depends in every concrete case on the nature of the Gestalt in question and on the kind and the direction of the modifications of which this Gestalt admits by its very nature. This is very important because the specific structure of a given Gestalt is only revealed by the disclosure of the modifications of which it admits.

It must be stressed that the result of restructuration, as far as the constituents of the theme in question are concerned, is *in principle* the same whether the constituents are "independent" or "dependent" parts.[117] In both cases a materially different noematic What emerges. To be sure, "independent" parts allow of still another modification besides that of restructuration—namely, that of singling out. This, however, does not impair the possibility of restructuration whose accomplishment is in no way influenced by the possibility of still other modifications which, in the present context, have to be left out of consideration. We have to disclose the essential accomplishment of re-structuration, distinguishing it from those of other possible modifications. For that reason, in the preceding section, we have chosen two illustrative examples, of which the one involves only "dependent" and the other only "independent" constituents. We have—and we are entitled to do so—disregarded this distinction in the analysis of the examples as well as in the development of the general theoretical considerations. As a matter of fact, it makes no difference whether the constituents concerned by restructuration do or do not admit of still other modifications.

11 / *Singling Out*

UNDER THIS HEADING we shall deal with a thematic modification which has a certain kinship to restructuration. However, singling out must not be interpreted as a limiting case of restructuration. We must not be misled by the fact that singling out is not possible with regard to all Gestalten and their constituents, there

117. Independent and dependent in Stumpf's sense, *Über den psychologischen Ursprung der Raumvorstellung,* p. 109.

hardly being any Gestalt which admits of this modification with respect to *each* of its constituents. While restructuration is essentially universal and can involve any constituent, the constituents are distinguished from one another as to whether they are or are not susceptible of being singled out, and this differentiation has great and important consequences with respect to the problem of parts in general.

To take a concrete example, consider a configuration of lines— e.g., a row of parallel vertical lines. This row is our theme, and each line belonging to the configuration is a constituent of the theme. Such a constituent of a configuration has a function ascribed to it by the sense of the configuration,[118] e.g., the function of being the left terminal line. Now we single out this line—that is to say, we make it our theme. This differs from centering the configuration around it as one of its constituents. It now no longer functions as the left terminal of the row; it does not have any function at all derived from the configuration, since it is no longer experienced as one of its constituents. Whatever accrued to it as a constituent in a certain structural framework disappears as soon as it no longer pertains to that framework. The line is no longer the same as before; a different object has superseded it.

A line as theme by itself (an isolated line) and a line as constituent of a configuration of lines are different objects having scarcely anything in common. Koffka has thoroughly discussed the phenomenal difference between two parallel vertical lines and two sides of a rectangle, the objective-physical data being the same.[119] He writes: ". . . A line alone is phenomenally . . . different from the side of a rectangle. To mention only one point, the latter has an inside and an outside, the former, in contrast, two completely equivalent sides." Especially impressive is one of Wertheimer's examples.[120] If we see the formation $\varphi$ as unitary, it appears as a large ornamented Latin V. If we single out the ornamentation at the upper left, it becomes a $\sigma$, and the rest apart from this ornamentation appears as a $\gamma$.

We can see with particular clarity the result of singling out in this extreme and hence very pregnant example. Singled out, the item becomes a different object in the phenomenal sense; properties which it now has it did not have before, and those which it had before it now no longer has. It is not the same item differently apprehended, but it

118. On sense, cf. above, p. 191n. 36.
119. Koffka, "Psychologie," *loc. cit.*, pp. 531ff.
120. Wertheimer, "Untersuchungen zur Lehre von der Gestalt," II, *loc. cit.*, p. 331, Fig. 46.

has become another throughout. The view that there is an identical datum and that only its "apprehension" changes derives from the "constancy hypothesis," the phenomenological parallel of which—the theory of *hyle* and *morphé*—we shall discuss later.

Concerning the rest of the configuration or, more generally, of the structural framework from which the constituents in question are severed, there are two possibilities. This structural framework can remain the same as what it was notwithstanding the separation of the constituent singled out—e.g., in the row of parallel vertical lines, which remains such a row even though one of its lines has been isolated and separated from it. In such a case, singling out affects only what it directly concerns, leaving the rest of the previously given Gestalt unchanged as to its nature. This depends upon properties pertaining to the Gestalt in question as a whole. Namely, if the "rest" already exhibits the structure of the whole so that the constituent in question fits into this structure without essentially contributing towards it, the Gestalt, though it is no longer given as theme, may continue exhibiting its characteristic structure, the severance of that constituent notwithstanding.[121]

The second possibility is that the "rest" of the configuration also changes completely, as, for example, in Wertheimer's figure. In that case, the "rest" does not yet realize the law of the whole; the constituent singled out contributed essentially towards the previously given Gestalt which can no longer appear after the constituent in question has been separated from it. In one with the singling out, the whole experience, including the attitude, can undergo a profound change, which is the case in Wertheimer's example where we were first directed to the Latin alphabet and then directed to the Greek one.

According to the two possibilities, the changes occurring in the "rest" of the Gestalt can, following Wertheimer, be characterized as "in conformity" or "not in conformity" to structure.[122] Independent of these possibilities and valid for both is the changed relation which the constituent singled out has to the "rest" of the structure. Since it is

121. Cf. Koffka, "Psychologie," *loc. cit.*, pp. 552ff., concerning movements of closure in Gestalten. "Good continuations and completions" also belong here (cf. Wertheimer, "Untersuchungen zur Lehre von der Gestalt," II, *loc. cit.*, pp. 324ff.), and certain psychopathological findings in brain-injured patients (cf. W. Fuchs, "Untersuchungen über das Sehen der Hemianopiker und Hemiamblyopiker," in *Psychologische Analysen hirnpathologischer Fälle*, ed. A. Gelb and K. Goldstein [1921]). See also A. Gelb and K. Goldstein, "Zur Frage nach der gegenseitigen funktionellen Beziehung der geschädigten und der ungeschädigten Sehsphäre bei Hemianopsie," *Psychologische Forschung*, VI (1925), pp. 191ff.

122. Wertheimer, "Untersuchungen zur Lehre von der Gestalt," II, *loc. cit.*, p. 315.

now our theme and the rest is co-given with it, it stands to the "rest" in the same relation as the figure to the ground. That is to say: the type of Gestalt connection where the line appears as a constituent of a structural framework which was our theme as a whole is replaced by the other type where the line as an independent theme lies in the thematic field to which the "rest of the configuration" also belongs. The figure-ground correlation supersedes the connection obtaining between the constituents of a Gestalt.

In contradistinction to restructuration, a constituent singled out and isolated is no longer given as a constituent. However such a constituent might change its function and, accordingly, its phenomenal look in restructuration, it always has *some* function in a structural context and maintains the status of a constituent. It is precisely that status which it loses by being singled out. Therefore, singling out must be considered as a more radical modification than restructuration. This greater radicality is not due to increase but rather stems from the two modifications belonging to different dimensions. Common to both modifications is the fact that by their virtue a different theme is given, but the sense in which it is different is not the same in either case. The loss of the status as a constituent is the characteristic result of singling out, and precisely that does not occur in restructuration.

On the occasion of the problem of parts we shall return later to singling out and develop the consequences of our present analysis for this problem.

## 12 / *Synthesizing*

THERE IS AN INVERSE modification for singling out. Separating out a constituent from a structural context is the opposite of a modification whose result consists in what was previously given as an independent theme now becoming a constituent and, as such, fitting into a Gestalt. For illustration we use an example especially appropriate for bringing out the particular nature of this modification which we propose to call synthesizing. We shall describe the experience in question, differentiate it from experiences of other kinds, but also point out the connections which obtain and the transitions which are possible by virtue of certain laws.

We are dealing with Descartes' theory of the union of mind and body under the perspective of Descartes' philosophy as a whole. What is meant by this we know from our analyses of theme and thematic field. Now a change occurs with regard to our theme. It grows into its ground and merges with it; or, expressed from the other point of view, the ground absorbs the theme and pervades it. A new theme results on a new ground. No longer is the theory of the union of mind and body given for itself on the background of other Cartesian theories, but it has become a moment in a system of thought, arising out of it, integrated into it, and having its definite place within it. Our new theme is Descartes' philosophy, perhaps centered on the theory of the union of mind and body; but this doctrine is for our thematic consciousness only a constituent of the total theme. Even as a dominant constituent it is supported and required by the total theme and, therefore, refers to the other constituents. Previously a certain theory was given under the perspective of Descartes' philosophy; now we have Descartes' philosophy as theme, that philosophy itself and, as such, perhaps centered on that special theory. The latter is now no longer separable from its thematic context, figuring only as a constituent of context.

## 13 / Synthetic and Synthesized Consciousness

IN THE LITERATURE outside of Gestalt theory, the phenomena in question, e.g., the appearance of a total theme, are discussed in terms of colligating consciousness. Underlying that discussion is the implicit presupposition, formulated by G. E. Müller, that there are essentially two possible apprehensions, the "singular" and the "collective," and that in the case of either apprehension the objects concerned remain identically the same as to the properties peculiar to them.[123] The same presupposition is also made by Husserl in his analysis—mentioned along with Müller's statements—concerning the parts being contained in the whole. As we can see from the noematic accomplishment of singling out, the skeptical objections that what is originally given might be changed by phantasied division cannot be so simply dismissed as it is by Husserl.[124]

We previously indicated the experience of a certain kind to which Husserl's analysis applies. The situation is different, however, in the case of a unitary total theme. A homogeneous white surface has, as unitary total theme, no parts; to draw them in imagination means to articulate the surface, and a surface articulated in a certain way is something different from the homogeneous one. If such a part of the surface is especially paid attention to and becomes prominent, it is isolated, singled out, and all consequences of this modification follow. Correspondingly the same holds when a given articulation is abol-

123. See above, pp. 234f.
124. See Husserl, *Logische Untersuchungen*, II, ii, §§ 38, 39.

ished. We cannot say that "the parts are manifestly there, but . . . they lack discriminating qualitative discontinuity and the character of segregation with respect to the parts with which they merge." If the parts merge into an inarticulated unity, the result is not only a "homogeneous unity from which inner differentiations have vanished" but also and first of all a *thematic unity* which might have constituents but does not have parts susceptible of being apprehended either singularly or collectively and still in themselves remaining identically the same. No phenomenological state of affairs must be interpreted in terms of possibilities considered as already actualized, when in fact this actualization takes place in phenomenologically different experiences, even though it might depend upon allegedly mere subjective modifications (attention, etc.). One must not, as does Husserl, assume that in a thematic unity all parts already actually exist in strict identity *qua parts* which result from *one* and therefore from all possible divisions and articulations.

We arrive here at a phenomenological distinction which Husserl touched upon without pursuing it consistently, so that its full significance escaped him. We can best bring out this difference by considering Husserl's analysis of "plural loving" which he carried out to show that certain syntaxes appearing at first as doxic are not *merely* doxic.[125]

It makes a difference whether one says, "The mother who lovingly looks upon her little flock embraces in *one* act of love each child singly and all together"; or whether one calls the loving many-rayed: "The group of children loved as the object of loving is a collective object." "Just as noetically a ray of love radiating out from the ego is split up into a bundle of rays, each of which is directed to a single object, so too as many *noematic characters of love* as there are objects colligated at the time are apportioned to the collective object of love . . ." The ambiguity already lies in the words "each child singly" in the first sentence quoted.

The difference in question is the following: in one case (that of synthesized consciousness) the noema of loving (as well as of the perceptual representation which underlies the loving) is the flock of children as a unitary object. The love is directed to the flock, and each child partakes of the love so far as he is one of the flock, a constituent of the theme. No colligating occurs in the underlying representation either; what is perceptually represented is the flock comprising the children as a unitary object, and the love is directed to this unitary object. In contradistinction to Husserl's formulation, this act of love is

125. Husserl, *Ideen*, I, § 121. See also § § 118–19.

*one,* and so is the underlying representation. There is no colligating consciousness in any sense whatever; hence, noematically speaking, there is no collective object. The love being directed to the flock as one unitary act, the corresponding noema is a *loved flock of children.*

In the other case (that of synthetic consciousness) the flock is constituted in "an articulated polythetic synthesis"—that is to say, in a colligating one. The representation is "many-rayed"; "this and this are taken together." The flock arises through colligation; it is not a unitary object, and the consciousness of it is not—as for Husserl—a "synthetic unitary" consciousness, at least not in the sense of the previous case. The noematic structure corresponds to the noetic one. Both the representation and the love founded on it are "plural." To every child colligated in the representation belongs his noematic character of loved. The children are colligated not merely doxically but also as objects of love; between child and child stands an "and" of love in which the doxic "and" is included in the familiar way.

As an expression of *this* consciousness the proposition, "The mother . . . embraces in *one* act of love each child singly and all together," is inadequate so far as there is not *one* act here—neither of representation nor of love. The noematic correlate pertaining to *this* consciousness is a *flock of loved children (Schar geliebter Kinder),* and that is distinct from a *loved flock of children (geliebte Kinderschar).*[126]

To this distinction corresponds precisely the one mentioned before, between the totality of steps in a demonstration and the demonstration itself as a unitary whole, or the one between the row of elements to be counted and the group, etc. All these examples illustrate the difference between synthetic and synthesizing consciousness, a difference which, in the final analysis, amounts to that between additive sum and Gestalt.

Koffka has shown the difference between "one plus one" and "pair" in a very instructive example.[127] Objectively the same lines can be seen either as two, one at the left and the other at the right, or else as the parallel sides of a rectangle. "That is to say: I now no longer see one line and still another line but instead see a unitary figure to which the two lines belong as essential constituents." ". . . The phrase 'two lines' is already ambiguous as a description of the phenomenal state of

126. Obviously, this is not a doxic colligation but a love-colligation, just as the corresponding colligating is a love-colligating—a "valuing"—and not a doxic one, so long as the mother simply lives in this consciousness without actualizing the doxic thesis included therein. Our critique in no way affects Husserl's assertion to be illustrated by this example: "Besides the doxic (logical) 'and' there is also an axiological and practical 'and.' "

127. Koffka, "Psychologie," III, 3, *loc. cit.*

affairs. It can mean $1 + 1$, and it can mean a pair of members pertaining to a Gestalt." The process in which "one plus one" becomes "pair" or, quite in general, the and-connection becomes a unitary Gestalt, is precisely the modification of synthesizing.

We cannot follow Husserl when he maintains that "the simply objectivated [*Vergegenständlichte*] and the synthetically unified are actually the same and that the subsequent thesis or extraction foists nothing into synthetic consciousness but apprehends what the latter yields." The states of affairs in question must not be considered simply from the point of view of synthesis, in our special case of colligating or relating. In speaking of a total object or of a total theme, it makes a difference whether it is constituted in polythetic syntheses or appears through a unitary act. In the latter case, there is no colligating nor a going from item to item.

Neglected in the *Ideen*, this distinction is pointed out by Husserl himself in the *Logische Untersuchungen*. There he emphasized that it is not the same when a group of particular items is meant as a group, i.e., as a unitary object, as when it is meant as a colligated plurality.[128] With regard to universality he writes: "It is . . . presented in the manner of a unitary thought, and only thus or in a corresponding 'genuine' [*eigentlichen*] form can it come to consciousness as a universality. . . . No matter how many particular items we may go over and how eagerly we may colligate them, at best, all *A* would be presented, if the extension of the concept were really exhausted, and, yet *all A* would not be presented: the logical presentation would not be effectuated." Similarly, he writes in his critique of Berkeley's theory of representation: "In a unitary pulse, in a homogeneous act *sui generis* the consciousness of all *A* is effectuated, in an act which has no components referring to all of the single *A*'s, and which could be neither produced nor replaced by a sum or interweaving of single acts. . . ."[129] What holds for universality also holds for rather limited sets. Yet, neither here nor in the *Philosophie der Arithmetik*, where Husserl likewise emphasized the unitary nature and the simplicity of "figural factors."[130] has the problem been formulated in full radicality. Husserl adopts a point of view which we shall discuss later.

Pfänder has also seen that in experiences of the kind under discussion *one* object comes to consciousness; but the unity is for him that of the act of attention.[131] We can "gradually telescope and condense an extended manifold in such a way that it can be

128. Husserl, *Logische Untersuchungen*, II, ii, § 26.
129. *Ibid.*, II, ii, § 29.
130. Husserl, *Philosophie der Arithmetik* (Halle, 1891), pp. 227ff.
131. Pfänder, *Einführung in die Psychologie*, pp. 362ff.

apprehended by means of one grasp of attention." In such a process, it is, according to Pfänder, not the object itself, i.e., the objective manifold, that becomes unitary in undergoing a certain transformation. Rather, we apprehend this manifold in a certain way; we "compress" and unify it so that it can be grasped by a single act of attention. The unity pertains to the psychic function and not to the noematic "object." Because Pfänder conceives of attention as a function of the psychic subject, and because a sufficiently radical formulation of the concept "object of object-consciousness" (*Gegenstand des Gegenstandsbewusstseins*) in the sense of Husserl's noema is lacking in his theory, he is led to this "subjectivistic" interpretation of the situation. For this reason he fails to see in their full depth the problems pertaining to these phenomenological states of affairs as well as to realize the far-reaching consequences entailed by the latter.

James's position in respect of the problems under discussion is very extreme and radical. He denies that a "plurality of *ideas*" in the proper sense can be given at all, and maintains that "however complex the object may be, the thought of it is one undivided state of consciousness." [132] Taken strictly, there is, according to James, never a plurality of simultaneously given ideas. Later we shall discuss the consequences which James draws from this position, untenable in this exaggerated and extreme form. Instead, the following problems must be raised. What is it that is given "in a single pulse of consciousness"? Which articulation is exhibited by what is thus given? In which sense is it unitary, with its constituents belonging together, and in which sense not? In how many and in which different senses must we speak of belonging together and being given together?

It must still be noted that the possibility of the thematic modification of synthesizing hangs together with the "law of Gestalt supplementation" [133] which thus finds its place within the context of phenomenology.

## 14 / The General Transformation Law

THE RESULTS of the preceding analyses allow the formulation of an important general phenomenological law. To every phenomenal datum there correspond others into which the former can be "transformed." This is not to be understood with respect to modes of presentation which change while the noematic nuclear stratum which is given in those various modes remains identically the same. On the

132. James, *The Principles of Psychology*, I, p. 405, and see also pp. 276ff.
133. Cf. Koffka, "Psychologie," *loc. cit.*, p. 576.

contrary, a certain noema is replaced by another differing from it as to the nuclear stratum, the transformation yielding a new material What. Such possibilities of transformation stand under definite laws. Whenever a theme is given in a thematic field, this situation by its very nature implies the possibility that through a new act the entire field of consciousness is made a unitary theme to which, in turn, a new thematic field belongs. The same possibility of synthesizing obtains with regard to this new field of consciousness, etc. Furthermore, there are the possibilities of transformation in the opposite sense which we discussed under the heading of "singling out." Here, too, to certain noemata there correspond others by which the former may be superseded; here again the modification is, as to its possibility, grounded in the very nature of the experienced situation in question. Finally, we mention the thematic modifications arising in restructuration to confine ourselves to mentioning those modifications in which the theme undergoes a radical alteration involving its material What.

Possibility of transformation purports that phenomenal data of a certain kind correspond to others, highly different from them, in such a way that the nature of the former predetermines which other data of a definite and well-defined type may be substituted for them. The actualization of such a possibility is not a mere factual occurrence, i.e., not a psychological process affected with the contingency characteristic of whatever is a matter of fact. On the contrary, the factual event is here the actualization of an eidetic possibility, though it remains a merely factual, i.e., contingent, circumstance that one rather than another among the possibilities in question is actualized in a given case.

Not only noemata of the same content of sense, differing from one another only with respect to manner of presentation and character, refer to, and are connected with, one another, according to laws. This holds also for noemata which differ precisely in regard to their content of sense. However, inter-noematic connections of the latter kind must not be misconstrued, and differences as to material content must not be interpreted as those of manners of presentation. The fact that such relations obtain between noemata of different material content, that a given noema by virtue of its nature and structure refers to certain others which might arise out of it—or, more properly expressed, into which it may be transformed—is certainly not without importance for the problems of constitutive phenomenology.

Understanding the concept of transformation in this sense, we shall have to interpret differently from Husserl the law of the "transformation of polythetic acts into monothetic ones." [134] We consider it as a special case of the general law of transformation. The transformation of polythetic acts into monothetic ones is synthesizing and has to be understood accordingly. We cannot follow Husserl, who writes: ". . . The synthetically constituted collection"—i.e., the actual one arising in syntheses by colligating one and one and one, etc.— becomes "objective in a special sense; it becomes the object of a simple or plain doxic thesis through the reference of a simple thesis to the just originarily constituted collection, thus through a peculiar noetic linking of a thesis to the synthesis." There is here the same confusion of synthetic and synthesizing consciousness which has already appeared in Husserl's analysis of collective love and leads to the view that the synthetically colligated is given only in a different mode, i.e., in another manner of presentation, but remains unmodified otherwise, especially as far as material content is concerned. A plurality is colligated by a synthetic act; a "one-rayed" thesis is directed to this collection and "gathers" from the synthetic act the plurality which "'originarily' can come to consciousness but by means of a synthesis." This plurality presents itself to consciousness as identically the same object as when it is originarily colligated, but it is now given in a different mode. Because the monothetic acts, into which polythetic ones can be transformed, gather their objects from the latter, they are founded acts presupposing by their nature and sense the originary syntheses which underlie them and make them possible.

In opposition to Husserl's view, we must insist upon the peculiar nature of synthesized consciousness in contradistinction to synthetic consciousness. Precisely the noematic What differs from one to the other. The law of transformation is reciprocal: monothetic acts can also be transformed into polythetic acts. Both kinds of consciousness are independent of one another; to neither can primacy or originarity be attributed. Their difference is not one of obscurity and distinctness, as though what is given as synthesized were unarticulated and obscure and, when unfolded step by step, would become distinct and articulated without its material content undergoing any change.[135]

## 4. The Problem of Parts

THE INTERPRETATION of the structure of the noema in terms of the Gestalt theory leads to important consequences for the

134. Husserl, *Ideen*, I, § 119.
135. Cf., in contrast, Husserl, *Ideen*, I, § 123.

theory of parts and wholes. Here, we shall pursue this problem in only two directions: in relation to the theory of "Gestalt-qualities" and, furthermore, in regard to the distinction between "independent and dependent" parts.

## 15 / *"Gestalt-Qualities"*

CONCERNING THE PROBLEM of Gestalt-qualities, we are especially interested in one point regularly discussed in the older literature on this subject. To bring out that point, let us look at the theories of several writers.[136]

Ehrenfels maintained that the "Gestalt-quality" requires a presentational complex, a sum of presentations, and is founded upon it: e.g., a melody requires "a sum of single auditory presentations with different temporal determinations linked to one another." [137] In his essay, he poses the problem of whether a Gestalt, i.e., a presentational complex to which a Gestalt-quality belongs, is *more* than the sum of the parts contained in the complex. As is known, he answers in the affirmative. "The proof for the existence of 'Gestalt-qualities' in our sense . . . is provided by . . . the . . . similarity of melodies and figures notwithstanding the thoroughgoing diversity as to their auditory or spatial substrata." [138] Such a "substratum," consisting in a presentational complex, i.e., in a sum of elements, is indispensable for the presence of a Gestalt-quality. The latter, which Ehrenfels describes as a new "positive presentational content" [139] and, more particularly, as a presentational content *sui generis,* supervenes to the substratum. According to him, a Gestalt-quality is, "so to speak, a new element beyond and above that complex." [140]

With this distinction between the substratum as a sum of elements and the Gestalt-quality as a new psychic element, Ehrenfels has pointed out the direction for the further discussion of the problem. Meinong has expressed this distinction, upon which he himself emphatically insists, in a very pregnant way contrasting the *inferiora* to the *superius.*[141] The same distinction underlies Benussi's theory of

136. A detailed, critical review of the older literature can be found in A. Gelb, "Theoretisches über 'Gestaltqualitäten,'" *Zeitschrift für Psychologie,* LVIII (1911).

137. C. von Ehrenfels, "Über 'Gestaltqualitäten,'" *Vierteljahrsschrift für wissenschaftliche Philosophie,* XIV (1890), pp. 252ff.

138. *Ibid.,* p. 258.

139. Cf. *ibid.,* pp. 261f.

140. *Ibid.,* p. 256.

141. A. Meinong, "Über Gegenstände höherer Ordnung und deren Verhältnis zur inneren Wahrnehmung," *Zeitschrift für Psychologie,* XXI (1889), § 3.

production, for which the constancy hypothesis provides a further foundation.[142]

Husserl has been led to results similar to Ehrenfels, but along different lines.[143] Husserl focuses on the problem of how we come to the instantaneous apprehension of a sensuous multiplicity as a multiplicity (e.g., a troop of soldiers, a pile of stones), without first going from element to element and then colligating all the elements at once. This problem leads him to the hypothesis of the "quasi-qualitative figural factors," a hypothesis which he finds borne out by psychological experience. These "figural factors," by which Husserl means hardly anything different from Ehrenfels' "Gestalt-qualities," are *signs* which *can immediately be apprehended* in the perception of a sensuous multiplicity . . . and by which the character of multiplicity can be recognized." [144] Fusion (*Verschmelzung*) occurs—either between the members of the multiplicity, or between the relations (involving all or only some of them) which obtain within the multiplicity, or, finally, between the former as well as between the latter or even between both. By virtue of this fusion, a new quality arises "which confers upon the appearance of the whole multiplicity an *immediately sensible special character,* so to speak, a sensuous quality of the second order." This quality of the second order is the "figural factor."

Husserl insists upon *Verschmelzung* (fusion), which he conceives entirely in Stumpf's sense, and in accordance with this he emphasizes that the elements between which fusion occurs can also appear as identically the same apart from fusion, i.e., be given isolatedly.[145] The "quasi-qualitative characters" are "the πρότερον πρὸς ἡμᾶς with respect to the elementary relations conditioning them." On the one hand, they are founded upon the elements of the multiplicity and upon the relations between those elements; and, on the other hand: "We apprehend the quasi-qualitative character of the whole perceptual experience as simple, and not as a collection of contents and relations. But what is simple for our first apprehension proves, in subsequent analysis, to be multiple." Here "multiplicity is not a mere plurality but is a plurality of parts unified into a whole in the strictest sense of the word." Hence, it is something different from, and *more* than, a mere sum.

142. V. Benussi, "Zur Psychologie des Gestalterfassens," § 3, in *Untersuchungen zur Gegenstandstheorie und Psychologie,* ed. A. Meinong (Leipzig, 1904); Benussi, "Gesetze der inadäquaten Gestaltauffassung," *Archiv für die Gesamte Psychologie* XXXII (1914), § 1.

143. Husserl, *Philosophie der Arithmetik,* chap. XI.

144. *Ibid.,* p. 225.

145. *Ibid.,* p. 231.

These ideas are perfectly in line with Husserl's previously mentioned refutation of skepticism concerning parts in general.

Just as with Ehrenfels and Meinong and Benussi, so with Husserl
we also have the stratification of *inferiora* and *superius*. Upon an
underlying matter a "higher" datum, a "quality of the second order" is
founded. It makes no difference how this relation of foundation is
conceived as to particular details: whether, following Ehrenfels, the
*superius* is automatically connected with the *inferiora* or, according to
Benussi, a certain freedom is left to "productions." What is essential
and common to all these writers is the dualism as such: on the one
hand, sensuous elements which are simply given and which, even
without it being explicitly stated, are conceived of according to the
constancy hypothesis; on the other hand, a higher stratum, above
those elements but founded on them.

## 16 / *Husserl's Concept of* Hyle

WE ENCOUNTER a similar dualism in still another theory,
which we consider at this point because of its direct relevancy to
problems of Gestalt-qualities, but also because it appears to us
symptomatic of a frequent approach to phenomenological and psychological problems. The importance of that theory goes far beyond the
problems concerning wholes and parts.

Benussi's distinction between presentations and presentational
processes of sensuous and extrasensuous provenience has its phenomenological counterpart in Husserl's concepts of "sensuous ὕλη" and
"intentional μορφή." [146] Under the heading of hyletic data Husserl
groups whatever is given in the way of "sensation," the latter term
understood so broadly as to include not only sensations in the ordinary
psychological sense but also "feeling sensations," etc., in general
whatever belongs to "phenomenology" in Stumpf's sense. [147] Above and
beyond the hyletic data, there is an "'animating' sense-bestowing

146. Cf. Benussi, "Gesetze der inadäquaten Gestaltauffassung," *loc. cit.*, p.
400, and "Zur Psychologie des Gestalterfassens," *loc. cit.*, pp. 382f; Husserl,
*Ideen*, I, § 85.

147. Cf. C. Stumpf, *Zur Einteilung der Wissenschaften* (Berlin, 1907), pp.
28ff. Considering in his article, "Über Gefühlsempfindungen" (*Zeitschrift für
Psychologie*, XLIV [1907], § 1, esp. pp. 4ff.), "sensuous feelings" as a class of
sensations and distinguishing them from emotions (*Gemütsbewegungen*) (cf. pp.
7ff. and, further, his article, "Über den Begriff der Gemütsbewegung,"
*Zeitschrift für Psychologie*, XXI [1899], p. 52), Stumpf prepares the way for the
radical and thoroughgoing distinction between appearances and functions, as
formulated in his later writings, "Erscheinungen und psychische Funktionen" and
"Zur Einteilung der Wissenschaften." What Husserl calls ὕλη coincides with
Stumpf's concept of appearance, likewise μορφή with function. On terminological
differences, see *Ideen*, I, note to § 86.

stratum," the stratum of the noetic, from which consciousness derives its specific sense as *intentional* consciousness. This sense-bestowing stratum denotes what is genuinely psychic in a concrete experience.

*Nous* transforms hyletic data into intentional experiences; it is owing to it that something is meant in subjective processes, that the latter have intentional reference or a presentational or presentifying function. The "sensuous which in itself has nothing of intentionality" is alien to sense, a mere datum. *Hyle* itself means nothing but is merely given, a multitude of contents which acquires sense and order only through noetic functions. The hyletic itself is "formless stuff," merely present and nothing more.[148]

In the First Investigation ("Expression and Meaning") in *Logische Untersuchungen*, Husserl elaborates this distinction between hyletic data and animating noesis in a more concrete way. "As to the descriptive difference between the appearance of the physical sign and the significational intention which makes it an expression, it appears most clearly if we turn our interest to the sign itself, e.g., to the printed word as such. Doing this, we have an external perception (or an external intuitive presentation) like any other, and its object loses the character of being a word. If it then functions again as a word, the character of its presentation is totally changed."[149] "We know very well from our own experience what differentiates the mere word as a sensuous complex from the word as significant. . . . The sensuous appearance of an object does not change when it becomes a symbol for us; nor, conversely, when we disregard the significancy of what normally functions as a symbol. Nor is it the case that a new psychic content has been added to the old one, as though a sum or connection of congenerous contents were given. Rather, the same content changes its psychic appearance, we feel differently about it, it does not appear to us as merely a sensuous mark on paper; instead, what physically appears has become a sign which we understand."[150] Later on, the difference between the "physical and mental aspects" of the *unitary total act,* which is considered as the meaningful expression, is described in terms of difference of activity.[151] "The expression is perceived, but 'our interest does not live' in this perceiving; unless we are distracted, our attention is directed, not to the signs, but to what is

148. The inner kinship of this doctrine of *hyle* and *morphe* with Benussi's views appears most clearly in Husserl's formulation: "Sensibility in a narrower sense denotes the phenomenological residuum of what is mediated through the 'senses' in normal outer perception" (*Ideen,* I, p. 173).
149. Husserl, *Logische Untersuchungen,* II, p. 40.
150. *Ibid.,* p. 66.
151. *Ibid.,* Fifth Investigation, § 19.

signified." The predominant activity belongs to the sense-bestowing acts. This prevalence of the sense-bestowing acts, the noetic functions founded upon hyletic data, is explicitly referred to as a case of the general fact of attention.

The justification for considering these analyses as a paradigmatic special case of his general theory of *hyle* and *morphe* appears from the kinship which Husserl finds between "understanding apprehension" and "objectivating apprehensions." In the case of the latter, "on the basis of an experienced complex of sensations, the intuitive presentation (perception, phantasy, imagination, etc.) of an object (e.g., of an external thing) arises." [152] Both cases, whatever differences recognized by Husserl himself might exist between them, are akin so far as sensuous data are interpreted and hyletic elements undergo animating apprehensions. This alone is important in our present context; the differences hardly matter.

Our concern here is not with the understanding of meaningful expressions as such. However, the understanding requires the signs which are to be understood to have a certain physiognomy, to be articulated in a specific way even as "physical objects." If Chinese letters are presented to me, the difference between me and one who knows Chinese is not only that he understands them and I do not, but the letters also look different to him than they do to me. What is immediately given to either of us, what either perceives, is not the same object. Holding that hyletic data are organized and articulated by meaning-bestowing and understanding acts, one cannot say that the appearance of the word on paper as a physical event is, with respect to its sensuous aspect, left unchanged by the animating acts. In this case, the mental aspect of the expression forms and articulates its physical aspect. However, Husserl correctly considers the signifying act to be a founded one which presupposes the appearance of a physical substratum and which, in its very being founded upon that appearance, fuses with it into a unitary total act. So considered, this meaning-bestowing act requires an underlying substratum which is articulated in a specific way. The problem concerning the articulation of the formless *hyle* is pushed back. Accordingly, between the meaning-bestowing acts, on the one hand, and the sensuous hyletic data, on the other hand, a third noetic intermediary stratum would have to be assumed in order for that articulation to be brought about. A merely descriptive analysis fails to ascertain such an intermediary stratum. Even when the latter is posited as an assumption, there is

152. *Ibid.*, First Investigation, § 23.

still the problem as to whether hyletic data, with respect to their "sensuous appearance," remain really unchanged with regard to different noeses operating upon them.

Just this problem is the crux of Husserl's basic conception of his hyletics, as it is of Stumpf's "phenomenology." From our analyses it results that there can be no question of the alleged independence of a hyletic stratum. A "sensuous item," as we have shown, can be altered in many ways and in different directions along with a shift of attention, attitude, "manner of apprehension." Such an item is not a constant datum with determined properties of its own; it changes from case to case. No hyletic datum is in any way independent with regard to a "higher stratum." It is only at its place within an organized structure that a sensuous item becomes what it is in a given case.

The two-strata theory is untenable, as far as both Gestalt-qualities and the theory of the *hyle* in general are concerned. It is not the case that a new element, the melody, is superadded to the complex of notes; nor is each of the latter within the melodic contexture the same which it would be apart from that contexture when it appeared alone. What this note is depends upon the melodic contexture, and only within such a contexture does it exist as that which it is. The (objectively) same note as constituent of one melody is not what it is as constituent of another one, and extracted from every melodic contexture, taken in isolation, it is something different again.[153] None of these phenomena must be considered as in any respect privileged or primary with regard to another. Each one of them has to be taken on its own grounds and merits.

Quite in general, sensuous material is not articulated by means of higher functions. What is immediately given, the phenomenological primal material, is given only as articulated and structured. Data devoid of all articulation, hyletic data in the strict sense, do not exist at all. What is given depends on the structural connections within which it appears.[154] There are no data remaining unaffected by changes in organization, articulation, etc. Nor does the "same material complex admit of multiple apprehensions discretely shifting into one another." [155] In such a case there is no "same material complex"; under certain conditions, each component may undergo a profound change.

This refutation of the *hyle* in general has important consequences. Acts of consciousness as psychological events do not consist of two

153. Cf. Wertheimer, "Untersuchungen zur Lehre von der Gestalt," II, *loc. cit.*, p. 350.
154. See above, pp. 189f.
155. Cf. Husserl, *Ideen*, I, § 93.

strata—a hyletic one and a noetic one. A separation between *hyle* and *morphe* is not even abstractively possible, for disregarding *morphe* and concentrating upon *hyle* alone entails a change in what is given. It purports the appearance of something new and different which neither by virtue of fusion, however intimate, nor in any other form of which one might think, was contained in what had previously been given. Hyletic reflection as reflection on the *hyle alone* is thus not reflection in the proper sense. It is a thematic modification—namely, singling out: a constituent is extracted from its thematic context and made into a theme for itself. This, however, is a farther reaching and more radical transformation of the phenomena than Husserl admits.

That which the analysis and description of acts of consciousness as real psychological events must recognize as ultimate, beyond which it cannot proceed, is *consciousness of* sense or meaning, while for intentional analysis the ultimate fact and datum is the sense or meaning itself as a structured whole.

This necessitates a redefinition of the concepts of noesis and intentionality. By the term "noesis" we can no longer denote an organizing and apprehending function turning hyletic data into a vehicle of sense or meaning, a special and specific function to which consciousness owes its character of intentionality. After the distinction between *hyle* and *morphe* has been abandoned, the term "noesis" extends to the *experienced act of consciousness in its entirety*. Every act of consciousness as a real psychological event is a noesis to which corresponds a noema as its intentional correlate. The concept of intentionality refers to this relation between noesis and noema. It designates the peculiar nature of the noesis, which is to be in correspondence with a noema, in such a way that one and the same noema can belong to a plurality of noeses. Indeed, the noema is ideal, atemporal and reiterable, while the mental states as events of consciousness are temporal and, on that account, can never recur, once they have passed.

Before we conclude this section, something remains to be said about W. James's controversy with Stumpf concerning the concept of *Verschmelzung*. In the center of that controversy is just the tenet of Stumpf which is fundamental to Husserl's theory of "figural factors": the assertion that contents which are "fused" with one another exist within that relation of *Verschmelzung* as precisely the same contents they would be if they appeared separately from one another, each one taken in itself.[156] James objects that this view rests on the "psycholo-

156. Stumpf, *Tonpsychologie*, I, pp. 106f.; II, pp. 64f., and *passim*.

gist's fallacy par excellence," because for what is present to consciousness, for the "content of thought," an object, an actual thing in its objective reality is substituted.[157] In a polemic against Helmholtz, which he would also extend to Stumpf, James argues that "what perception fails to discriminate (when it is 'synthetic') is not *sensations* already existent but not singled out, but new objective *facts*, judged truer than the facts already synthetically perceived. . . . These new facts, when first discovered, are known in states of consciousness never till that moment exactly realized before, states of consciousness which at the same time judge them to be determinations of the same *matter of fact* which was previously realized."[158] Similarly, later, "When simultaneous red and green light make us see yellow, when three notes of the scale make us hear a chord, it is not because the sensations of red and green and of each of the three notes enter the mind as such, and there 'combine' or 'are combined by its relating activity' into the yellow and chord, it is because the larger sum of light-waves and of air-waves arouses new cortical processes, to which the yellow and the chord directly correspond."[159]

James develops this position with utmost consistency and opposes it especially to the associationist psychology of thinking.[160] He denies that the thought of an object is composed of as many presentational elements as the object has parts, a particular presentation corresponding to every part of the object. The thought of a complex object is not itself, according to James, complex. On the contrary, it is a unitary totality.

17 / *Stumpf's and Husserl's Theory of "Independent and Dependent Parts"*

STUMPF, followed by Husserl, starts from the fact that presentational contents appear together.[161] Analyzing combinations of contents, one finds that contents belong together in different ways. From the point of view of their belonging together, all contents appearing together fall into one of two classes: "independent contents and content-parts" (*Teilinhalte*).

Stumpf writes: "One is confronted with independent contents when the elements of a presentational complex can by their nature

157. James, *The Principles of Psychology*, I, pp. 196f.
158. *Ibid.*, I, p. 521n.
159. *Ibid.*, II, p. 30.
160. Cf. *ibid.*, I, pp. 276ff.
161. Stumpf, *Über den psychologischen Ursprung der Raumvorstellung;* Husserl, "Psychologische Studien zur elementaren Logik," I, *Philosophische Monatshefte*, XXX (1894); Husserl, *Logische Untersuchungen*, II, III.

also be presented separately; with content-parts when this is not the case." [162] The connections into which independent contents enter are rather loose, in that they can be dissolved and their elements presented separately. Whether combined with one another or not, the elements as such are the same. The dissolution of a complex yields the very same elements separately which previously had been given in conjunction. In accordance with this is Stumpf's distinction between simple and complex presentations: "When several notes are simultaneously presented . . . , we call this a complex presentation, but the presentation of the single note . . . a simple one." [163] Husserl's example of a non-reciprocal dependence of two contents likewise belongs here. "A line which together with any others founds a configuration is an independent content; the configuration itself, however, is dependent with respect to the line." [164] The line as such is what it is both within the configuration, to which it contributes, and apart from the configuration, extracted from it, taken by itself, and separated from the other lines.[165]

As to content-parts, the situation is totally different. Content-parts cannot exist or even be imagined without one another. By its very nature such a part is in need of others for its existence and appearance. Such contents "penetrate each other; they are within, not outside of, one another." Accordingly, they change along with each other; they hang together functionally in such a way that the change of one content also involves the other. With regard to the connection of color and extension, Stumpf says that "the quality partakes, in some way, of the change in extension." [166] Husserl further develops Stumpf's reasoning: "The extension can remain the same while the color changes; the color can remain the same while the extension and the figure change in any way whatever. . . . But there still remains a place for functional dependencies in the change of the factors, which . . . are not exhausted by what the species ideally comprise. The color factor, as an immediate content-part of the intuited concrete object, is not already the same in two concrete intuitions if the quality,

162. Stumpf, *Über den psychologischen Ursprung der Raumvorstellung*, p. 109. Husserl follows him literally in *Logische Untersuchungen*, II, p. 230.

163. Stumpf, *Über den psychologischen Ursprung der Raumvorstellung*, pp. 3f.

164. Husserl, "Psychologische Studien zur elementaren Logik," *loc. cit.*, pp. 163f.

165. Accordingly, in the *Logische Untersuchungen*, II, p. 227, conjunctions of independent contents are called "in sich zerstückte bzw. zerstückbare Ganze." "Die Teile . . . haben den Charakter miteinander verknüpfter 'Stücke' "; and on p. 238: "ein Ding oder ein Stück von einem Dinge kann für sich vorgestellt werden, d.h. es ist, was es ist, ob auch alles ausser ihm zu nichte würde."

166. Stumpf, *Über den psychologischen Ursprung der Raumvorstellung*, pp. 112ff.

the lowest difference of the genus Color, is the same." [167] "With regard to *certain* contents we have the evidence that the change or the elimination of at least one of the contents given together with them (but not included in them) must change or eliminate those contents themselves." Stumpf sets forth *how* content-parts exist together: " 'being presented' together indeed means here more than mere temporal co-existence in presentation. Quality appears *in* extension, extension *in* quality; they penetrate each other. It is not like having simultaneously present a note and a tactile or olfactory datum."

With this, as well as with the rejection of the interpretation of the situation in a summative sense, the Gestalt thesis is already anticipated. Indeed, all that Stumpf and Husserl say about the way in which content-parts are given together applies to the constituents of a Gestalt as to their existence with, and within, one another. In all the examples considered, we have encountered Gestalt connections and Gestalten. In this sense, constituents of a Gestalt are dependent parts. But the assertion that Gestalten and their constituents are in question extends beyond the cases discussed by Stumpf and Husserl as examples of dependent parts. The thing with its parts is also a Gestalt, and the parts are its constituents; similarly the configuration with respect to its lines, the melody with respect to its notes, etc.

In the older literature on Gestalt-qualities, the problem was posed exclusively with regard to the latter cases, i.e., with regard to complexes "consisting of elements separable from one another (i.e., presentable without each other)," [168] and the case of dependent parts was explicitly excluded. Asserting that *all* those cases are on a par, so far as all of them involved the structural connection of constituents within a total Gestalt, we seem to relinquish Stumpf's differentiation of parts, in the sense that *all parts prove to be dependent* and that the existence of independent parts in Stumpf's and Husserl's sense must be denied altogether.

Fundamental to the differentiation in this form is the separability of dependent parts. "Separability means nothing else than that we can keep this content identical in the presentation despite unlimited variation (arbitrary, not restricted by any law grounded in the *essence* of the content) of the contents connected and somehow co-given; and this means that the content remains unaffected by the removal of any set of co-given contents." [169]

What happens in actual separation? With reference to the results

167. Husserl, *Logische Untersuchungen*, II, iii, §§ 3, 4.
168. Ehrenfels, "Über 'Gestaltqualitäten,' " *loc. cit.*, p. 262.
169. Husserl, *Logische Untersuchungen*, II, iii, § 5.

of our discussion concerning the operation of singling out, we deny that a part extracted from a complex is and continues being experienced as the same as what it was within the complex. Complexes are not composed of elements which can be extracted from one complex, taken in isolation, then combined again into a different complex, and throughout these operations remain given as identically the same. Extracting a constituent from its framework and taking it in itself results in the appearance of a new and different theme in the place of the old one. No constituent of a structural framework is self-sufficient or self-contained, none has properties and qualities pertaining to it once and for all, hence in all combinations. Every constituent must be considered with reference to the structural framework into which it is integrated *hic et nunc* and within which it has a certain function and plays a definite role.

Whatever a constituent might be outside the given framework, e.g., within a different framework or taken in isolation—we note that these words conceal a constitutional problem—it is, in any event, different from what it is *hic et nunc* as a constituent of the framework in question. Thus, e.g., the curve in the figure on page 188 can be experienced only as curve of the S or of the $\varphi$. To be experienced as a curve *simpliciter*, it has to be singled out. Then, however, neither a $\varphi$ nor an S is given; rather, there is a curve to which a loop is joined from above. This loop no longer belongs to the theme which is the curve alone. Though curve and loop are not separated by any spatial interval, the loop, like any other line in the proximity of the curve, pertains to the surroundings of the latter, to its thematic field. Only through an experience of this sort is the "curve" given as such, as a curve *simpliciter*, which, phenomenally speaking, is highly different from the curve of an S or of a $\varphi$. Only in the case of *this experience* through which the curve presents itself as a theme in its own right can what we previously found concerning the consistency of the theme be applied to the relation of the curve to the loop; this is distinguished from the other cases in which no "curve" *per se*, but rather the curve of an S or a $\varphi$, is given. Here the difference between the two types of Gestalt connections, as previously set forth, must be taken into consideration.

In the sentences quoted above, Husserl defines separatedness rather than separability. Both those sentences and the immediately following ones present a phenomenology of the content as already singled out and made into a theme "in itself," not, however, a phenomenological description of a constituent susceptible of being singled out, though not singled out actually. Failing to differentiate between the two means to overlook the fact that by being actually singled out, the content in question undergoes a qualitative change and is, phenomenally speaking, no longer "the same."

When Husserl qualifies the line within a configuration as an independent content, he has in view our capacity to freely vary in imagination the entire surroundings of the line, all that appears together with it, while the line itself is maintained in its identity. As to its descriptive content, to be sure, the line does not remain absolutely identical. However, "nothing in the content of this 'appearance' evidently requires a functional dependency of its changes with respect to those of the co-existing 'appearances' as necessary." [170] Precisely such a "functional dependency" is asserted by Koffka because of the difference between a line and the side of a rectangle. If the side is transformed into a line, it undergoes a far-reaching modification, its physiognomy changes, and it becomes phenomenally different. Husserl and Koffka diverge, because they do not describe the same experience. What Husserl has in mind is the line as theme; even if this line is given together with other lines, it alone is aimed at by the thematic consciousness, while the other lines belong to its surroundings. The line is a figure on a ground and therefore exhibits consistency and independence which pertain to the figure. For Koffka, however, the theme is not the line in question on a background of other lines, but the configuration itself as perceptually given, and the line belongs to this configuration as a constituent of the theme. Hence we deal with another experience, correctly analyzed by Koffka. Both Husserl and Koffka are correct in their descriptions, which refer to different phenomenological situations.

The basic error in Stumpf's and Husserl's definition of independent and dependent parts seems to consist in foisting into a phenomenological datum as already contained in it that which results from it by virtue of a modification, but not otherwise. The possibility or impossibility of singling out a constituent from a contexture is permitted to play a decisive role for the description of the experience of the constituent within the contexture—that is to say, when it is not yet singled out. In other words, a given concrete phenomenon is not taken for what it is in itself but is interpreted under the perspective of another phenomenon into which it can be transformed. In opposition to Stumpf's and Husserl's theory, we distinguish two questions, although these two are not unrelated. The first question is whether a certain item is integrated into a contexture so that it comes to

170. *Ibid.*, II, p. 231.

thematic consciousness only so far as the contexture comprising it is our theme, or whether it is our theme in its own right. The second question is whether or not a certain constituent of a Gestalt allows of a certain modification, here that of singling out. The problems must be treated separately. An item which *can* be singled out must be sharply distinguished from one which *is* singled out actually.

18  /  *A New Distinction between Independent and Dependent Parts*

BY THE PRECEDING REMARKS a direction is indicated in which a new distinction between independent and dependent parts may be attempted. Undoubtedly, the distinction in question is somehow justified, though the specific justification and explanation given by Stumpf and Husserl lays itself open to the objections mentioned. The distinction we are going to propose can, however, not be applied so widely as Husserl claimed for his theory. It is limited to the phenomenological sphere and does not allow of being extended to the ontological realm. We arrive at this distinction by means of the following consideration:

Two kinds of Gestalt-constituents are to be distinguished. Those of the first kind admit of restructuration but of no more. According to the case in question, they assume a corresponding function; hence their function can change from case to case. In all cases, however, they remain constituents *of*. Starting from a certain Gestalt, we progressively arrive at different ones in which the constituent of the first kind plays its role as determined by the Gestalt in question and undergoes the corresponding phenomenal alterations. If we speak of "the constituent" to which this happens, we do so for the sake of simplicity, eschewing a constitutional problem which is involved here. Whatever noemata might result by virtue of restructuration, it never happens that a constituent of the kind under consideration appears as figure on the ground of other constituents. Just this possibility, however, obtains with regard to Gestalt-constituents of the second kind.

The crucial question is whether an item is and remains a constituent throughout all thematic modifications or, by contrast, can lose the status of a constituent. Differently expressed, the question is whether its Gestalt connections with other items are of necessity always of only one type or whether it can enter into Gestalt connections of the other type as well. The two types of Gestalt connections are sharply distinguished from one another; neither is in any sense a kind of limiting case which the other might continuously approach. There is no transition at all from the one to the other.

However pithily a constituent appears as formative, whether it can be severed, in imagination, from all other constituents or by its own nature is always in need of being complemented by certain other constituents, whether it can become a theme itself and in its own right or can be given to thematic consciousness only as a constituent within a structural context—this does not depend on its pithiness as a formative constituent: that is to say, on the degree to which it contributes to the sense of the noematic What. From the experience of Gestalt-constituents as mutually demanding and supporting each other, there is, in the direction of increasing pithiness of a certain constituent as formative, no way leading to the experience of that constituent as standing in the figure-ground relation with regard to the other constituents. Because of the discontinuity between the two types of Gestalt connections, the difference between constituents which can enter into connections of both types and those confined to a connection of one type only may serve as a principle of classification.

Items which can be experienced only as constituents of a Gestalt into which they are integrated and which resist all attempts at severing them from any thematic Gestalt contexture and making them into themes "in themselves," because they prove to be in need of something else by which they are supported or at least complemented, may be called *items not lending themselves to being singled out or made independent*. Those which can become themes "in themselves" and are not in need of structural contexts within which alone they can be given to thematic consciousness will be called *items susceptible of being made independent*. By way of abbreviation we may continue speaking of independent and dependent items, but these terms, obviously, have another sense here than in the writings of Husserl and Stumpf.

The examples by which Stumpf and Husserl illustrate the difference between independent and dependent parts in their sense can also be referred to for the definition proposed here. However, we can do this only insofar as what Stumpf and Husserl call independent or dependent parts are, in the sense of our analyses, items respectively susceptible or not susceptible of being made independent. The reason for this is that we do not contest the difference itself, but only its interpretation. For us it is not the same whether a content *can be made* independent or *is made* independent. Referring to our previous discussion of the modification of singling out and its noematic accomplishment, we deny that an item which is susceptible of being singled out remains phenomenally the same when it is singled out. This is the central point in our divergence from Stumpf and Husserl, who maintain that an item can merely be isolated and otherwise remain what it is, whereas according to our analyses a *materially* different What, a new theme, results from such isolation.

Whether or not a certain item can be singled out depends upon its nature. An eidetic possibility is here in play.[171] The possibility of certain modifications, among them that of singling out or making independent, is grounded in the very nature of the items and contents. This state of affairs appears to be of great importance for problems of constitution.

## 19 / *Résumé of the Analyses of Attentional Modifications*

THE CONCEPTION of attention as subjective in the sense of ego relatedness rests on the assumption that variations in the direction of attention do not affect the material content of what is given. Only on this assumption does the comparison with a beam of light make any sense. Since it must be admitted that modifications occur to that which appears, although it remains unchanged with respect to its material content, these modfications come to be interpreted as changes in illumination.[172] Quite in line with the theory of the cogito as ego-related, of the pure ego as living in its *cogitationes* and directing its glance at the objects through its *cogitationes,* one is led to the view that subjectivity pertains to "attentional formations in a pre-eminent way." Attentional modifications are interpreted as modifications of the glance of the ego moving from one objective component to another or illuminating one such component in varying ways. It follows that in the attentional modifications the pure ego must be descriptively accessible in a special and pre-eminent way.

The results of our analyses contradict precisely the thesis that attentional modifications are without import for the noematic material What. We have shown that the noema is affected just as to its material content and that, furthermore, the sense and the direction of its alteration varies from case to case. Attentional modifications must, therefore, not be considered as changes in illumination; nor is the comparison with the moving beam of light appropriate at all. On the contrary, attentional modifications affect the material content of the noema to such an extent that a radically different noema results. In no respect can such alterations and modifications be compared with

171. Cf. *ibid.,* II, iii, §§ 5ff.

172. Husserl emphasizes that attentional modifications—"without detriment to the identical noematic nucleus"—concern the very noemata themselves and "form a special genus of ⟨noematic⟩ characterizations." Cf. *Ideen,* I, p. 191.

variations concerning manners of presentation and existential modes, variations in the course of which one and the same noematic nucleus comes to be characterized in varying ways. In contradistinction to the traditional theory of attention, our analyses lead to the result formulated by Koffka: "What had been considered as a mere variation of attention, a variation of clarity concerning parts, the total situation remaining otherwise unchanged, proves to be an actual division entailing far-reaching consequences." [173]

Furthermore, we have seen that in contradistinction to what is usually ascribed to it, attention is not a unitary function whose accomplishment is always the same. From the point of view of their noematic accomplishment, the attentional modifications must be classified into three series, each one of them being characterized by accomplishments of a specific nature. Not only is it by virtue of attentional modifications that the noema can be changed at all in regard to its material content, but also the sense and essential direction of that change varies from modification to modification. On that account the task is not to replace *one* theory of attention *simpliciter* by a different one. Rather our argument is that attention at large and in general does not exist at all in the sense of a unitary function. As the term is customarily used, attention is an equivocal collective name for several heterogeneous phenomena which must be distinguished from one another, each of them exhibiting a structure of its own and presenting special problems.[174] One should not speak at all of attention in general but should indicate in every concrete case which *specific* attentional modification is meant, with its *specific* noematic accomplishment belonging only to the modification in question.

We cannot endorse Husserl's view of an "identical noematic nucleus" which is varyingly illuminated by a unitary attentional function and among whose components and constituents sometimes one, sometimes another, is rendered conspicuous and brought into prominence. Opposing Husserl's view, we point to the following state of affairs finding expression in the general transformation law. To every datum correspond other data, to every theme in its thematic field other themes in their fields, in such a way that any given experience motivates certain transitions as possible. Which transitions they are depends upon the very nature and structure of the given experience in accordance with definite phenomenological laws. If the actually given theme is superseded by one of those which are related to it in the mentioned way, the transition from theme to theme is the actualiza-

173. Koffka, "Psychologie," *loc. cit.*, p. 548.
174. In this connection, cf. *ibid.*, III, 8.

tion of a possibility obtaining by virtue of a certain law. Thus, we are confronted with a system of different noemata interconnected in such a way that each one of them contains motivations for possible transitions to any one of the others.

By our analyses an essential foundation of the theory concerning the ego-relatedness of attention is undermined. The examination of the phenomena themselves leads to the same result as in the case of the static cogito. We find no "pure subject of the act" engaged in attentional modifications; the latter are not experienced as changes of ego-directedness or as shifts of the glance of the ego. The phenomenologically faithful description discloses no pure ego living in *cogitationes* and no "attentional ray emanating from the ego and terminating in the object." Here as before, with the reference to the phenomenological findings we must revert from Husserl's standpoint in the *Ideen* to his position in the first edition of *Logische Untersuchungen*.

## [IV] OUTLINE OF A PHENOMENOLOGY OF THE PURE EGO

### I / *Marginal Consciousness*

IN OUR PREVIOUS ANALYSES we delimited within the domain of the co-given a partial domain and distinguished it under the heading of thematic field. We now consider the other partial domain of the co-given, which comprises what we shall call marginal data or objects. Noetically, we shall speak of marginal consciousness. Examples of marginal data were already referred to in the first sections of Section II. When the inkwell on the desk is my theme, the seen walls of the room, the part of the front of the neighboring house which appears through the window, etc. are marginal data; similarly, arising memories, emergent wishes, feelings of pleasure, displeasure, etc. Furthermore, it is through marginal consciousness that I am aware of the "natural world" which is continually "there" for me, whatever I might be dealing with, and which "continuously surrounds the actual perceptual field." Speaking of "perceptual field," we do not take the term in the narrow and technical sense in which it is used with regard to thing-perception. Rather, we construe it in a broader sense as synonymous with "field of consciousness," the field with which I am thematically concerned.

The term "marginal consciousness" is meant to indicate that the total field of consciousness can be symbolized by a circle. The theme with which we are dealing occupies the center of this circle; it stands in the thematic field, which—to abide by the metaphor—forms the area of the circle; and around the thematic field, at the periphery as it were, the objects of marginal consciousness are arranged. As to the latter, there is still the distinction to be made between those which have and those which have not some relation to the theme without being relevant to it—that is to say, a purely external relation. To exemplify this difference, for which we use the terms "halo" and "horizon," respectively, consider the case that, while dealing with a mathematical proposition, we recall our having already thought about this proposition before, having demonstrated it, etc., and simultaneously experience a wish arising (e.g., to go outdoors). This distinction might have importance for some problems of phenomenology, especially for functional problems.

Among the components of the halo must be mentioned all the data the awareness of which is expressed in the "transformation laws" established in phenomenology—that is to say, in propositions of the form: to every mental state of such and such a kind corresponds a different mental state of such and such a determinate kind. Also belonging here is the possibility of reflection which obtains with regard to every mental state as such. This is so because all the possibilities here in question are experienced possibilities. Awareness of such possibilities of transformation and transition is attached to, and linked with, thematic consciousness; the experienced possibilities have some relation, but no material relevancy, to the theme. Obviously, there is no permanent awareness of all the possible transitions. The halo is not a set of constant data surrounding and accompanying every mental state. Rather, these data incessantly emerge and fade away. What alone is constant and permanent is the experienced pertinence to the halo which characterizes all its components.

It is through data pertaining to the halo that we become aware of the duration of mental states. Awareness of duration, as is known, consists in experiencing phenomenal time as elapsing while dealing with the theme or, differently expressed, in experiencing the theme as extending throughout a segment of phenomenal time. That is to say, by virtue of data pertaining to the halo we have a marginal awareness of our having been dealing with the same theme and a marginal anticipation of our continuing to deal with it. As we are retentionally aware of our having been dealing with our theme, so we also have awareness of retentions belonging to the phase just past, etc. Correspondingly the same holds with respect to the dimension of protentions. In dealing with the theme, we experience it as gliding through time. In perpetual flux, each Now changes into a just-Now, every retention of any degree into a retention of a higher degree.[175] It is always the same theme with which we are confronted, and while it remains identically the same, its margin perpetually changes. Through the multiple retentions and protentions referring to, and intertwined with, one another, the duration of mental states manifests itself. Phenomenologically speaking, duration is nothing other than the experience of the theme as surrounded by an ever-changing marginal halo in such a way that in every actual, i.e., originary, marginal awareness, the past marginal awareness is still retained.

A further question concerns the form in which what is given through marginal consciousness is organized with what is given through thematic consciousness—that is to say, the nature of the connection between the area of the circle and its periphery. Marginal consciousness, we recall, comprises more than just the awareness of duration. I am absorbed in thought; a wish arises and fades away, the noise of steps is heard, etc. While I deal with my theme, heterogeneous items are co-given. But my theme remains the same over against the variations which may and do occur in marginal consciousness. It preserves its identity in the strictest sense of the word. In no way is it concerned by what takes place in the margin.

The thematic field is also basically unaffected by marginal data and their change. This is because what is given through marginal consciousness, even when related to the theme, has no bearing upon its material content. Such relations concern the experiencing, having experienced, expecting to experience, etc. of the theme but not its material What. As to the latter, the data of marginal consciousness are merely superadded to the theme in a merely additive sense. Here we are precisely at the point of additive connection and where, in fact, something + something is given. Using again the metaphor of the circle, we may say that the periphery denotes the locus of the + signs, or, more correctly stated, the + signs form the periphery. The margin is in an and-connection with both the theme and the thematic field. It is one of the characteristic properties of the and-connection that when $A_1 + A_2$ is given, $A_2$ can undergo modifications which do not concern

175. Cf. Husserl, *Ideen*, I, § 81. It is inconsequential for our purposes whether, following Husserl, one conceives the "actual Now" as punctual, as "an enduring form for always new matter" so that the impressional phase appears as a limiting phase, or with Cornelius (*Transzendentale Systematik*, pp. 166ff., and *Psychologie als Erfahrungswissenschaft*, pp. 128ff.), one speaks of a "duration of the present." If it is admitted, as does Cornelius, who only denies continuity, that while dealing with one and the same theme one can distinguish phases, no exception can be taken to our presentation in which we leave it open whether such distinguishing takes place continuously or not continuously.

$A_1$. However, we do not agree with Wertheimer that the and-connection is actualized only in rare, exceptional cases. Rather, it is *always* actualized: to every thematic consciousness belongs a margin. We now see the full significance of the division of the domain of the co-given into the thematic field and the margin. One should not, however, denote the thematic field as co-given. It is better to reserve this designation for the margin which supervenes to that to which it has no material relevancy.

In the margin itself there are structured and unified wholes which can become themes, as, for example, the part of the "natural world" with which we happen to be confronted. These co-given data compose a field of potentiality; they lend themselves to thematic perception in the sense that any moment we are free to relinquish the theme and to turn to this part of the surrounding world. As long as we do not do that, but abide by our thoughts, marginal data are only "potential themes" supervening to the actual one. The connection with one another of the data which in their totality form the margin has also the character of a sum. A wish which happens to emerge may have no intrinsic relation to the given part of the surrounding world; they are only experienced simultaneously. As the wish and the perception are superadded to one another, so both of them are superadded to the theme to which they are, both of them, irrelevant. Marginal consciousness must not be misconstrued as an amorphous, chaotic accumulation of contents utterly lacking form, structure, and articulation. Such an accumulation of totally shapeless contents is never experienced, not even marginally. If marginal consciousness has an additive structure, the reason is that the potential themes, each one of them a well articulated whole, having no relevancy to another, are not interlinked into a unity encompassing all of them by virtue of their respective contents. For this reason, the previously discussed possibilities of thematic modification do not obtain with regard to marginal consciousness as a whole. The particular items of the sum are, each one of them, structured and articulated, but their organization with one another is symbolized by the + signs. Disappearance or variation of one item does not affect the others, which remain what they are. Thus, the additive character does not refer to the proper nature of the potential themes but refers only to their organization with both one another and the actual theme.

The identical theme is preserved, while the co-given margin changes in manifold ways and in many respects. The theme remains the same not only throughout its duration and over against modifications of the horizon, but its identity manifests itself in still other ways. In dealing with a theme, we may remember having already dealt with it, the identical theme, at a certain time. It is identically the same in every "experiential context" (*Erlebnisumgebung*).[176] One and the same identical theme can, on principle, be given at any time—i.e., on principle, it can be surrounded by any marginal consciousness whatever; it fits into any marginal consciousness. No marginal consciousness contributes to it, which means that none affects it. Here there is not the same situation as obtains in the case of the relationship between figure and ground; the self-sufficiency and independence of the figure mean that it may be transposed on different grounds—within certain limits arbitrarily chosen—without thereby being affected. Here there is no such restriction as expressed by the phrase, "within certain limits," because there is no material relation whatever between theme and margin. Any marginal consciousness may function as a "natural" experiential context of any theme; no marginal consciousness has any privilege with respect to any theme whatever. Every marginal consciousness can accompany every theme in the like manner—that is to say, with like indifference.

In this connection, we might note before proceeding, a question is answered which is bound to arise from the definition of the essential nature of consciousness by intentionality. Considering that to every theme as noematic unity there corresponds a multiplicity, in principle indefinite, of mental states, all of them being experiences of the same, how, then, do their diversity and plurality manifest themselves? One cannot resort to accidental particulars which may or may not be present, as, for example, phantasy images which may happen to accompany acts of thinking. Rather, the question must be raised with respect to the experienced intending itself, which is the essential component of the act of thinking as a psychological event really occurring. To see the significance of the problem, consider that intentional acts, noeses, can be described only with reference to the noema, the one over against their multiplicity: namely, as multiple and diverse experiencings of the same. How, then, can we be aware of them as multiple and diverse, seeing that their noematic correlate is one? We answer: by virtue of the marginal consciousness which belongs to each mental state and individuates it. By necessity, the marginal consciousness concomitant with any mental state must be different from that pertaining to another mental state. The marginal consciousness belonging to a later mental state cannot be the same as that belonging to an earlier one, even if the same noema corresponds to both mental states. This is so because in principle there obtains the possibility that the marginal consciousness belonging to the later

176. Experiential context means as much as marginal consciousness.

mental state comprises the memory of the earlier one, including its marginal consciousness. It is in this way that quite in general a mental state phenomenologically manifests itself as later than another one.[177] The possibility in question precludes in principle the identity of two margins. On this account the *principium identitatis indiscernibilium* does not hold for mental states which are not *indiscernibilia* in that they differ precisely with regard to the marginal consciousness necessarily belonging to them.[178]

## 2 / *The General Reflection*

MARGINAL CONSCIOUSNESS founds a further and essentially new possibility of relinquishing the actual theme and turning to a new one. However, it does not seem appropriate to speak here of thematic modifications since these changes are not confined to the theme and the thematic field. Having been dealing with, e.g., a mathematical theorem, we now pay attention to some happening in our surroundings which already had appeared to us, of which we had been marginally aware. It is not material that the new theme had already appeared; we may just as well turn to a new theme which suddenly emerges. At any event, the mathematical theorem is no longer our theme, nor does it belong to the background out of which the presently actual theme arises. Yet, it has not vanished from consciousness; at least this is not necessary. In principle, a memory of what has just been our theme can be marginally co-experienced with the theme now actual, a possibility not confined to what has just been. While actually dealing with a theme, anything whatever can be (marginally) co-given as carrying the phenomenological index of "having once been a theme."

Among the great many items of which marginal awareness is possible, we are here interested exclusively in marginal memories of the kind mentioned. At any moment of our conscious life anything whatever can be marginally co-given as already experienced. There is, furthermore, the possibility of remembering the noesis rather than the noema: we remember our having experienced the theme in question. Our remembering does not move straightforwardly; it takes place reflectively. What we have marginal co-awareness of is our previous mental state, our having experienced. The potential theme is a noesis;

---

177. Cf. H. Bergson, "Introduction à la métaphysique," *Revue de Métaphysique et Morale*, XI (1903), p. 5.

178. In this connection, cf. Husserl, *Ideen*, I, p. 167. As to the concept of "experiential context" (*Erlebnisumgebung*), Husserl has, however, not made the distinction between the thematic field and the margin.

we remember the past act of experiencing the theme in question.[179] It makes no difference whether the theme, whose corresponding noesis is marginally co-given, is or is not different from the present one.

A simple example would be the following: I go to a city in which I have already been before; standing in front of a building, I remember having already seen it, and the remembrance of my previous seeing is the co-given potential theme. A mental state thus remembered can be remembered with greater or lesser determinateness. It may be that large portions of the marginal consciousness belonging to it are co-remembered. For instance, I know under which circumstances of my life I had that experience, part of what was contemporaneous with it being also remembered. "Contemporaneous" means that it pertained to the margin of that past experience, to the horizon of simultaneity with respect to the Now of that experience. What is meant by greater or lesser temporal determinateness of the remembrance of a mental state refers to the greater or lesser extent of both richness as to details and distinctness of the co-remembered marginal consciousness. Every remembrance of a noesis is also one of the margin pertaining to that noesis. This remembered margin, which, as just said, presents itself in greater or lesser articulateness and distinctness, passes into an undetermined horizon, fades into the vague, even in several dimensions. However, the remembered margin always points to the actual Now. Two determined regions, the Now and the Then, are separated by a mist; but they are not just separated, for in separating them the mist also mediates between them. In one dimension the mist points forward to the actual Now.

What is co-given in this manner can become the theme at any moment. We relinquish what we have been dealing with as a theme and turn to the mentioned components of its margin. We then live in the memory of the past mental state, and what this remembering yields now becomes our theme. In this sense we reflect. The co-remembered marginal consciousness with its mist enters into our thematic consciousness. All the results of our previous discussions concerning the theme, the thematic field, and the possibilities of transition grounded in the theme-thematic field relation correspondingly apply to what in the reflective attitude is given as theme. Becoming a theme, the past experience appears within a thematic field

179. In this connection, cf. Husserl, *Ideen*, I, §§ 77–78. It is in the sense of these sections, and in no other sense, that reflection is meant here as the attitude in which the experiencing of that which is experienced is made the object and even the theme of our additional act, unreflective in turn. We pass over in silence some problems concerning the phenomenology of memory, which require clarification. Considering the goal of our discussion, we may safely do so within the present context.

which comprises still further experiences remembered as past. Among the components of this thematic field, the presently actual experience is privileged so far as it is free from the mist in which certain regions of the field are shrouded.

The mist can clear away. Here and there experiences emerge with increasing determinateness and distinctness as clearly discriminated from one another, until finally—in the ideal case, possible in principle —the mist entirely dissolves. A chain of remembered distinct experiences leads from the Then to the Now, the Now being the experience of "reflecting on the chain," an experience which by means of a reflection of the second degree can be rendered explicit and, in this sense, objectivated. For every past experience, i.e., remembered as past, the possibility obtains of being made the initial member of a chain leading from it to the Now.[180] This chain presents itself as one of remembered experiences which immediately follow one another and which are thus not connected by intermediary members. However, it is not necessary that the ideal case be actualized and the mist be fully dissipated. Nothing essential changes when the mist still prevails in some regions of the chain, thus mediating between those which are cleared up.

The Now alone is privileged in the chain which terminates in it and somehow partakes of its originarity. All other members are, in principle, on a footing with each other. Thus the following theorem can be formulated: Because of the possibility of reflecting on past experiences, in this very reflecting an order-relation is established which mediates between any one experience and any other, so that both are comprised as members of a chain terminating in the present experience. This law holds for all mental states so far as, in principle, every one can become an object of reflection in memory.

To every past experience, however remote, belongs a chain of mental states terminating in the Now and comprising the former as a member. A peculiar circumstance must still be mentioned in regard to the chains which belong to two mental states. Among any two or more of such chains, there is always one which contains all the others or into which the others are inserted as partial chains. If to every pair of mental states there belongs a chain mediating between them, it is still not necessary that the one be inserted into the other as a partial chain. It may happen that one of the chains is not expanded up to the present Now but extends only so far as to mediate between the two mental states in question. In this case, there is a third chain leading from one

180. Following Husserl, *Ideen*, I, § 141.

mental state of one pair to one of the other pair, and in this third chain the two other chains may, in turn, be inserted.

Proceeding in the opposite direction, i.e., starting from the Now and going "backward" in recollective reflection, we may, in principle, encounter and incorporate every mental state along this way. Assuming an "ideal memory," one single reflection of this kind would yield an uninterrupted order of our past mental states, an order nowhere clouded by misty indeterminednesses. Every mental state with its full margin, i.e., with all that which had been simultaneous with it, would find its place within that order. No mental state can elude that order which is nothing other than our whole past conscious life. All the other chains mentioned in the preceding passage would be inserted into this *one* chain as its parts. The totality of our past mental states allows of being organized along this one chain, extending in one dimension. For an "ideal memory" all possibilities of recollection are actualized, and it admits of no determinable indeterminacies. We, who have no "ideal memory," are not able to reconstruct an *uninterrupted* order of our past life when we reflect in the manner described; we do encounter misty indeterminacies whose clarification, possible in principle, never succeeds completely. Nevertheless, the order of our past life, terminating in the present and pointing to the future, is unitary and self-contained, and nothing can escape from it. It is one single chain, here and there clouded in misty indeterminacy, clarifiable but not clarified.

Every mental state which we remember, even though it might suddenly emerge isolatedly, lays claim to being incorporated into this one and single chain. The experiential context of the mental state in question may be shrouded in almost total mistiness, and more or less large stretches of the chain leading to it may be highly or even totally undetermined; still, whatever is undetermined, in principle, lends itself to determination, as the mist may be cleared up. Whatever mental state is not incorporated into the chain is susceptible to such incorporation. Every remembered experience presents that claim to incorporation, a claim which can never be relinquished, though it may sometimes happen to be difficult or even impossible to redeem it, depending upon the factualities of mental life. But the claim as such obtains and essentially belongs to the remembered mental state, remembered as to be incorporated. As far as the present experience, the Now, is concerned, the claim is *ipso facto* redeemed because of its privileged position as point of reference in which the chain terminates and from which it descends into the past. Here there are no possibilities, actualizable in principle but not happening to be actualized. As for the Now, the acme of our life, the possibilities are always by necessity actualized.

Bergson posited a distinction between, on the one hand, "time" in the sense of a "homogeneous medium in which our conscious states are ranged alongside one another as in space, so as to form a discrete multiplicity," and, on the other hand, "pure duration." [181] This coincides with the difference between going in the chain from one mental state to the other and—by means of synthesizing—making our conscious life as a unitary whole our theme.[182] Bergson himself uses the metaphor of the chain: "We set our states of consciousness side by side in such a way as to perceive them simultaneously, no longer in one another, but alongside one another; in a word, we project time into space, we express duration in terms of extensity, and succession thus takes the form of a continuous line or a chain, the parts of which touch without penetrating one another." [183] On the other hand, "We can . . . conceive of succession without distinction and think of it as a mutual penetration, an interconnection and organization of elements, each one of which represents the whole and cannot be distinguished or isolated from it except by abstract thought." [184] We cannot enter here into a discussion of the problems to which Bergson refers; but it must be noted that Bergson means by *durée* more than duration of mental states, as the term is employed here. *Durée* denotes the ongoing conscious life in its totality, in the sense of the continuously flowing stream of consciousness.

## 3 / Problems of Phenomenological Time: The Stream of Consciousness

As ENCOUNTERED in what we call the general reflection, mental states present themselves in an order of succession. The order in which they are arranged does not depend upon whether they are experiences of the same theme or of themes materially akin to one another or, finally, of themes between which there obtains any relationship of relevancy. By its nature this order is not determined by the sense of the mental states. They appear in this order as they succeed upon one another, each mental state taken exactly as it presents itself in memory and with all that which belongs to it:

181. H. Bergson, *Essai sur les données immédiates de la conscience*, chap. II. Trans. F. L. Pogson, *Time and Free Will* (New York, 1910), p. 90.
182. Cf., in this connection, Bergson, "Introduction à la métaphysique," *loc. cit.*, pp. 4ff.
183. Bergson, *Essai sur les données immédiates de la conscience*, p. 101.
184. *Ibid.*

namely, as a consciousness of a theme in a thematic field, surrounded by a margin. The order disclosed by the general reflection is a mere existential order, no allowance being made, in principle, for the sense of mental states nor for concatenations of sense. Therefore, that order, the chain, can be called indifferent to sense. What counts in it is only succession and simultaneity. The law of its structure requires that every mental state be incorporated into it at a definite place; it is an unambiguous but otherwise indifferent order.

This existential order of mental states is a temporal order. Thus we are led to an aspect of phenomenological time which, however, is different from that of the temporal duration of mental states. Still, here too, we are dealing with phenomenological, and not with physical, i.e., measurable, time.[185] Hence, temporality can be understood in a double sense; in the sense of duration as it pertains to every particular mental state, on the one hand, and, on the other hand, in the sense of the temporal order between mental states as dovetailed into the chain. From this distinction it does, of course, not follow that there is no relation between time as duration and time as order. The fundamental determinations of the phenomenal order-time have their phenomenological "origin" in the essential properties of the chain. For instance: one-dimensionality, the concepts of earlier and later, that of the temporal between, etc., and whatever might be involved herein. In the present context, we cannot go beyond those few remarks concerning the problems of phenomenological time.

In speaking of the stream of consciousness one appropriately means the actually ongoing life itself, with regard to which Bergson's concept of *durée* is as fundamental as the concept of duration in our sense. We experience the stream of consciousness also when, in dealing with a theme, we become aware of its duration. We hold fast to the theme while its margin is in flux; as an enduring unity, the theme "glides" through a continuously varying and changing margin, changing, however, in accordance with certain laws. The case is similar when in passing to a new theme we are still aware of the old one as just having been our theme—that is to say, when the retention of it accompanies our present thematic consciousness; especially at the moment of experiencing the transition when the one theme fades away and the other begins to emerge.

It is different in experiencing the chain or parts of it. Then we remember past mental states as fitting into a definite, strictly unambiguous one-dimensional order. Between these mental states there might

185. Bergson tends to interpret "time" in the sense of a "homogeneous medium" as objective, physical time. Cf. "Introduction à la métaphysique," *loc. cit.*, pp. 18ff.

be gaps to be filled by further remembered mental states. The chain, descending from the Now into the past, has no terminal point at its "lower" end: there is no first mental state. At the present Now, its only terminal point, the chain is involved in a continuous transformation; continuously accretions take place, the present Now in which the chain terminates continuously gliding forward. Along with experiencing the chain, i.e., order-time, we at once experience this transformation of the chain and the gliding forward of the Now while dealing with the chain. That is to say, we also experience duration. The connection between order-time and duration-time rests on this state of affairs. However, there is no reciprocity: in experiencing duration, it is not necessary that the chain be given as well.

## 4 / The Pure Ego

THE PHENOMENOLOGICALLY REDUCED pure ego is nothing but the chain along which all experiences are ordered and which terminates in the present Now continuously gliding forward. By the pure ego is meant, first of all, a thoroughgoing unity of all mental states: all of them belong to the ego, as the ego belongs to them. In terms of the unity as phenomenally exhibited by the chain, it is indeed possible to account for whatever had been ascribed to the hypostatized "subject of the act," the ego-relatedness as a specific feature of mental states or a specific component contained in their structure, the "pure apperception" in the sense of Natorp, and the like. It is a unity of mental states so far as there is only *one* chain which comprises *all* mental states and from which none can be severed. Because all mental states without exception partake in the unity in question, *the manner of this participation is, in principle, the same for all.* We cannot, therefore, follow Husserl in maintaining that the phenomenological ego lives in every actual cogito in a specific sense, that it is a perceiving pure phenomenological ego in perception, a phantasying one in phantasy, a joyous one in joy, etc. This implies that though the pure ego is identically the same with regard to all *cogitationes* and even in general with regard to all mental states whatever, the ego manifests itself in every mental state of a certain kind in a special way corresponding to the specific nature of the kind in question. Being the same for all mental states, its manifestations vary according to specific differences between mental states. Husserl's later formulations undoubtedly point in this direction.[186] In the course of our analyses we did not discover

186. In *Logische Untersuchungen*, II, v, § 8, referring to phenomenological differences between acts such as perception, remembering, phantasy, etc., Husserl argued against Natorp's assertion that the relation to the ego is "one and the

the relatedness to the ego in the form of a descriptive feature inherent in the mental states. The latter are not experienced, as the theory we criticize would have it, as emanating from the ego, as activities of the ego and the like. Hence, the foundation on which that theory rests seems to be undermined.

The participation of the mental states in the pure ego, which is in principle the same for all, regardless of generic differences between them, i.e., regardless of whether they are perceptions, phantasies, experiences of joy, etc., consists in the following: all these diverse mental states are members of the chain given in the general reflection. Considering the structure of the chain, along which the remembered mental states are arranged merely from the temporal point of view, the sense of "being a member" must obviously be, on principle, the same for *all* mental states of any description whatever. This chain is the concatenation of all mental states belonging to one consciousness; it is nothing other than a thoroughgoing context in which every mental state is related to every other one.[187] Unity is here not to be understood in the proper sense, for the concatenation of all experiences does not exhibit unity as do, for example, the acts which are unified by means of syntheses of identification and whose unity is a genuine one. The concatenation in question is thoroughgoing and unique: thoroughgoing because no mental state is excluded, unique because there is only *one* concatenation of this kind. Because of that uniqueness we cannot endorse Husserl's distinction between the "phenomenological ego of the moment" and the "phenomenological ego in extended time." [188] Since by its very nature and sense the phenomenologically reduced ego is a context which, beyond the present moment, i.e., the

same . . . for all content however varying in many respects." Husserl's polemic is the more justified as Natorp identifies the intentional relation and the presentational function of mental states with their relatedness to the ego. (Cf. Natorp, *Allgemeine Psychologie nach kritischer Methode*, chap. II, § 2.) The conception of the pure ego as here advocated, which, to a large measure, coincides with Husserl's position in the first edition of the *Logische Untersuchungen*, does not lay itself open to the objections raised to Natorp's thesis of the homogeneousness of the relatedness to the ego with regard to *all* mental states. In fact, with reference to his concept of the ego in the *Logische Untersuchungen*, Husserl himself implicitly maintained the homogeneousness of the relatedness in question for all mental states (*Logische Untersuchungen*, 1st ed., II, pp. 356ff.). For this homogeneousness to be asserted, however, the pure ego must be conceived as a "concrete complex of experiences."

187. This is the place for Cornelius' fundamental idea that the "unity of personal consciousness" is an ultimate, irreducible basic fact. (Cf. Cornelius, *Transzendentale Systematik*, p. 53.) Cornelius' concept of personal consciousness is free from all reification and, therefore, has a different meaning than the same expression as used by Husserl.

188. Husserl, *Logische Untersuchungen*, 1st ed., II, p. 332. In the 2d edition, Husserl has suppressed this passage.

Now, comprises conscious life in its entirety, there can be no question of a "phenomenological ego of the moment." It is true that what is experienced at the present moment has special significance for the ego; the chain with which we identify the ego terminates in the Now. However, this distinctive function of the present moment does not mean that there is an ego of the moment. That would imply that the ego of one moment would be different from that of another moment. The ego is not exhausted in the Now, which is merely the ever-changing climax of its life.

The context of the entire conscious life is *necessary* in the sense that every mental state must be inserted into it. Every mental state can, in principle, become the occasion on which the context is experienced, and the mental state itself then appears as belonging to that context. The experience of the pure ego is always possible—that is to say, this possibility can be actualized at any moment. Only in this sense does the "I think" accompany all my presentations. The phenomenological ego is not a special datum presenting itself along-side whatever else is given; it is not an additional or secondary theme which never disappears, always persists throughout all thematic change. As long as we live in straightforward experience, we are not aware of the ego, but we can, in principle, become aware of it at any moment. This possibility is grounded in that of noetic reflection to which all mental states lend themselves in principle. The acts through which we are actually conscious of the phenomenological ego are acts of reflection and, more particularly, of a special kind of noetic reflection which we designate as the general reflection. The possibility of the general reflection obtains *eo ipso* in one with the possibility of noetic reflection at large. In this sense, but *only in this sense,* can this unity of conscious be considered as "demanded by the intrinsic nature of the *cogitationes.*" [189]

By the fact that all mental states are by necessity inserted into the context of consciousness, they are characterized as *my* mental states. Their belonging to the context of consciousness makes them my experiences in contradistinction to those of other conscious beings. This means nothing else than that if a mental state does not pertain to one context of consciousness, it must necessarily belong to a different one. Because the insertion of all mental states into the context of consciousness is necessary—more correctly expressed, is by necessity always possible—the index "mine" also necessarily pertains to all mental states. Of course, that index does not denote a descriptive tinge or feature so attached to the mental states that they could not be

189. Cf. Husserl, *Ideen,* I, p. 61.

experienced except as thus tinged. In accordance with what we maintained concerning the pure ego as always necessarily *actualizable*, though not always *actualized*, we characterize the index "mine" as follows: mental states can be so apprehended in a certain reflection, always by necessity possible, that they appear as *mine* "even though I am not conscious of them as such," [190] namely, when I do not perform this reflection. The necessity by which the index "mine" pertains to all mental states proves to be an essential possibility: mental states *can* be apprehended in a certain attitude and, if so apprehended, *must* be experienced as "mine." This possibility is, again, founded upon that of noetic reflection.

The context of our consciousness is given in the general reflection. The acts through which that occurs are, like all acts of reflection, "immanently directed" acts.[191] That is, their noematic and objective correlates are mental states, and "one and the same unbroken stream of experience . . . mediates continuously" between those mental states and the apprehending acts of reflection. Orienting the concept of objectivity with respect to that of transcendence, the genuine and only phenomenologically legitimate concept of subjectivity comes to be defined by way of contrast to transcendence. Because no transcendent object is constituted by the unity and order between mental states as arranged along the chain, the order in question is a subjective order. Correspondingly, the subjectivity of mental states consists in, and only in, their being members of the chain in the aforementioned way, in their forming an order of experiences as a merely temporal order yielding nothing "objective" whatever, i.e., nothing transcending the sphere of mental states as psychological events and occurrences.

So far as phenomenology studies mental states under this aspect, their "subjective" aspect, it is itself subjectively oriented, and its central concept is, therefore, that of the pure ego. The subjectivity understood in this sense, the only legitimate one, is to be distinguished from that subjectivity which we have in view when we say of a state of consciousness such as repentance that it is eminently subjective, meaning that it arises from the depth of the subject and involves the subject in his innermost core. In such cases, by "subject" is meant the person, in our example, the moral person, who is concerned by repentance in his depth and center. Referring to and, therefore, presupposing the person, this concept of subjectivity does not belong to pure phenomenology.

In reply to Husserl's criticism in the first edition of the *Logische*

190. Cf. Kant, *Kritik der reinen Vernunft*, B, 132.
191. Cf. Husserl, *Ideen*, I, pp. 68f.

*Untersuchungen,* Natorp points out that "phenomenological findings" are by no means required for the pure ego.[192] Such a point or unity of reference "need not, even cannot, manifest itself in any given limited context." It is erroneous to search for a "given, definitely delimited content." Instead, one has to take into consideration the actual flux of conscious life in which "such definitely delimited totalities of contents never exist except by arbitrary reflection." The authentic ego is not to be found "in complexes of contents always delimited and, because of this delimitation, continuously changing"; on the contrary, "in itself unlimited and persisting" it surpasses all such special complexes of contents.

Our theory does justice to Natorp's correct idea expressed in these statements—namely, that no static consideration of the phenomena of consciousness opens up an access to the pure ego and that, instead, the dynamics of conscious life, its flux and change, has to be taken into account. We established a relationship between the all-encompassing totality of "complexes of contents" and the pure ego, going so far as to identify the ego with that totality. Just those arguments of Natorp which we mentioned seem to impose this conclusion. This, however, does not mean endorsement of Natorp's supposition of the center of reference, any more than his interpretation of the intentional relation as ego-relatedness. One has to abandon the conception of the pure ego as an enduring center within the flux of appearances, as being opposed to the flux in such a way as not to be concerned by it, as somehow standing above the flux. It is the sum total of whatever acts of experience emerge; it is involved in the flux without thereby losing its identity. Indeed, the ego is the flux itself, that one well determined identical totality which, however, is never accomplished or finished, but rather involved in perpetual growth.

In the first edition of the *Logische Untersuchungen,* Husserl presents a theory of the pure ego which almost entirely coincides with the one we defend here. Not only does he reject the necessary point of reference and unity in Natorp's sense, and even any center of reference altogether, but Husserl also maintains that in the case of a "straightforward experience" the ego is not at all given as part or component of the act. It is only on the basis of objectivating reflection that a mental state can come to be characterized as a state of the ego.[193] (Keeping to the meaning which the terms in question always have for Husserl, we call the reflection objectivating because in being

192. Husserl, *Logische Untersuchungen,* 1st ed., II, v, § 8; Natorp, *Allgemeine Psychologie nach kritischer Methode,* chap. II, § 7.
193. Husserl, *Logische Untersuchungen,* 1st ed., II, p. 357.

apprehended by an act of reflection, the mental state thus apprehended becomes the object of the act of reflection.) This is to say that the ego is given through reflection and cannot be given except through reflection. A closer examination of this reflection was the task we set ourselves in the previous analyses. Husserl, furthermore, identifies the phenomenological ego with the stream of consciousness as the unity of consciousness resulting from "psychic states interweaving with one another." [194] "Obviously the ego is no special entity floating above the multiplicity of experiences; rather, it is just the unity resulting from their connection with one another." [195] The phenomenological ego is nothing else than the unity of consciousness, a real complex of mental states. "Contents have . . . their ways of cohering, according to certain laws, with one another, of fusing into more comprehensive unities, and, by virtue of their thus becoming and being unified, the ego or the unity of consciousness is already constituted without there being any need of a special ego-principle supporting all contents and unifying them once more." [196]

This view, according to which the phenomenological ego is but a "unified totality of contents"—a view with which we fully agree—is abandoned in the *Ideen*. Whereas according to the *Logische Untersuchungen* the pure ego is immanence itself, Husserl speaks in the *Ideen* of "a quite peculiar—non-constituted—transcendence, a transcendence in immanence." [197] In the *Logische Untersuchungen* the pure ego was identified with the stream of consciousness, but now their relation becomes a problem. The ego somehow faces its mental states; over against the unceasing flux of experiences it is, as in Natorp's treatise, an invariable identical unity. The ego and the stream of mental states are two; they are correlates, necessarily related to one another, but they are not identical. The stream of consciousness, the filled concrete phenomenological time is the "time-field of the pure ego which it can traverse from any one of 'its' experiences along the three dimensions of before, after, and simultaneous." [198] The sphere of experiences thus becomes a field of free activity for the pure ego. Herein is rooted the necessary correlation between ego and stream of consciousness.

The ego is no longer considered as a totality of mental states interwoven with one another. This is expressed in frequent formula-

194. *Ibid.*, p. 325. Stream of consciousness is used here in a rather vague sense, without taking into account the distinction made above.
195. *Ibid.*, p. 331.
196. *Ibid.*, p. 376.
197. Husserl, *Ideen*, I, p. 110.
198. Husserl, *Ideen*, I, p. 165.

284 / PHENOMENOLOGY AND PSYCHOLOGY

tions to the effect that "through its mental states the ego directs itself to what is other than itself." In contradistinction to what Husserl had taught in the *Logische Untersuchungen,* intentionality is now conceived as a relation between *ego* and object and no longer as the fundamental essential feature of mental states *qua* acts of consciousness. If it is the latter, then only because the mental states are interpreted as ego-states, the ego, the subject of experiencing essentially belonging to the mental states themselves as their necessary "center of reference." According to Husserl's theory in the *Ideen,* since the ego directs itself to objects through mental states, the intentional relation proceeds from the subject of the act, and the subject becomes relevant for this relation.

Equally remarkable is the role ascribed to reflection in the *Ideen.* The field of experiences being considered as a field of free activity for the ego, acts of reflection are interpreted as actualizations *par excellence* of his freedom. The very possibility of reflection indicates the nature of the relation between the ego and the stream of consciousness, the ego confronting the stream. Through acts of reflection, the ego apprehends "its" mental states and, so to speak, appropriates them. Its freedom with regard to its experiences consists and manifests itself in such appropriation and even in the capacity of such appropriation. Mental states belong to the ego also when it experiences in the mode of "straightforward direction." Through its mental states the ego then directs itself in several different ways to the objects in question. Through acts of "reflective experience" the ego becomes aware of the mental states pertaining to the stream of consciousness as its own; by virtue of reflecting on them, the ego asserts its freedom and its "domination" over its mental states. The possibility of reflection grounded in the nature of mental states is equivalent to the possibility for the ego to apprehend its mental states and, thus, to become aware of them as its own.

As to the relation between the ego and the stream of mental states, it follows that the stream is now conceived as a field of free performances of *cogitationes* pertaining to one and the same ego. *Cogitationes* are ways in which the pure ego lives as a "free agent": going out of itself, returning to itself, spontaneously doing, etc.[199] The ego's freedom, "its free spontaneity and activity" are essential to the ego; they are its characteristic, if not its only assignable properties. Freedom is here meant in two distinct though intrinsically related senses: the freedom *to* perform, namely, with respect to the stream of experiences, and the freedom *in* every performing so far as the latter is considered as a mode of life of a free agent active in it.

199. *Ibid.,* p. 192.

After the preceding analyses, there seems to be no need of any further explicit criticism of the theory developed in the *Ideen* concerning the relation between the ego and the stream of consciousness. Phenomenological analyses lead to the identification of the pure ego with the stream or context of consciousness. Hence, the pure ego can no longer be said to confront the stream, to stand in any sense outside or beyond it, any more than the stream of consciousness can be considered as a field for free activities of the pure ego.

A final word. We maintained that our theory of the pure ego does justice to the phenomenological situation and makes intelligible what other writers tried to account for in their theories of the pure ego. However, as to Kant's theory of pure apperception a few remarks might not be out of place.

As is known, Kant takes pure apperception as the point of departure for the transcendental deduction of the pure concepts of the understanding. Accordingly, the spontaneity of action essentially belongs, following Kant, to the pure apperceptions. It is only in being conscious of the identity of the function by which I synthetically unify the dispersed manifold of sensuous data into the unity of an object that I am conscious of the identity of myself. Transcendental pure apperception is not possible without the synthetic function of unification of the manifold, and it manifests itself in this very function.[200]

There is no doubt that the pure ego as conceived above cannot serve as the basis for a transcendental deduction. At this point, Kant's attempt seems to lay itself open to a certain criticism. It may be asked whether Kant succeeded in accomplishing what he had set out to do, i.e., whether the unity of self-consciousness provides an appropriate basis for his transcendental deduction. The question is to what extent and whether the consciousness of an identical function effectuating synthesis, i.e., a function unifying a dispersed manifold, is essentially connected at all with a "pure, original" consciousness of the identity of the self. Even granted that, the further question remains whether this function and what it accomplishes does account for the constitution of the objective world. Unifying representations into *one* consciousness [201] is by no means the same as establishing a context, an inner contexture between that which is represented. Unity of consciousness is not

200. Kant, *Kritik der reinen Vernunft*, A, 108: "Das Gemüt könnte sich unmöglich die Identität seiner selbst in der Mannigfaltigkeit seiner Vorstellungen, und zwar a priori denken, wenn es nicht die Identität seiner Handlung vor Augen hätte, welche alle Synthesis der Apprehension (die empirisch ist) einer transzendentalen Einheit unterwirft und ihren Zusammenhang nach Regeln a priori zuerst möglich macht."

201. See the important formulation, "Denken aber ist Vorstellungen in einem Bewusstsein vereinigen" (Kant, *Prolegomena*, § 22).

consciousness of unity. A dispersed manifold unified, i.e., joined together according to fundamental principles *a priori* which have their roots in pure apperception, does not yield that intrinsic unity of content as between the different appearances or sides of the same thing which refer to, and are concatenated with, one another. It is just in their interconcatenation, their mutual references to, and their supporting and supplementing of, one another, that the diverse appearances determine the sense of the thing, as, conversely, the thing requires that kind of intrinsic contexture among its appearances and is even nothing other than their contexture. The necessary and universally valid "synthetic unity of perceptions" in Kant, however, is but a manifold of elements joined together according to rules.

So much for the problems pertaining to transcendental philosophy. Here we cannot go beyond stating that the pure ego, as the context of acts of consciousness, does not and cannot serve as the basis for a transcendental philosophy or as the basis for a valid approach to problems of constitution.

TRANSLATED BY FREDERICK KERSTEN

# 11 / A Non-egological Conception
## of Consciousness [1]

IN THE FIRST EDITION of the *Logische Untersuchungen*,
Husserl did not admit an ego different from the empirical one, and
consequently he rejected all theories in which the acts of consciousness are held to spring from a center of conscious life. A highly
important class of conscious facts—the intentional acts—have the
peculiarity of confronting the experiencing mind with an object, but
relatedness to the ego is no essential feature of these acts. [2] Certainly
an idea or a representation of the ego may appear; it may even easily
appear, or, expressed otherwise, there may possibly exist a special
disposition or readiness for its appearing. But only if it does actually
appear may the act in question be experienced as connected with, or
related to, the ego. This is, however, not a general rule. On the
contrary, when the subject pays more attention to the object presented
to him by the act which he experiences, he becomes more absorbed in
dealing with this object, and the more the subject "forgets" himself,
i.e., the less the chance that a representation of his ego intervenes in
his conscious activity and operations. While the subject is certainly
aware in such a case of his actual dealing with the object, he does not,
however, experience it as a manifestation of his personal life, much
less as emerging from a presumed center of his life. To ascertain that
the act he experiences is his, the subject must first adopt the attitude
of reflection, and then he may bring the act thus grasped into relation
with his ego. The latter, however, is nothing other than a complex or
unity of mental facts. Whether we consider the "phenomenal ego"—
i.e., the complex of those mental facts of which the subject is
conscious at an actual moment of time in any mode of awareness

1. This article was originally published in *Philosophy and Phenomenological
Research*, I (September, 1940–June, 1941).
2. Husserl, *Logische Untersuchungen* (Halle, 1900–1901), II, v, §§ 4, 8, 12b.

whatever—or the "psychical ego"—which contains the "phenomenal ego" as a part and exceeds it, just as the material thing contains and exceeds that which falls under direct observation in a concrete experience—in either case we are concerned only with acts, real conscious events, mental facts, and with the complex they form. If they are united into complexes, this is because of their co-existence and succession and because of the relation the facts of consciousness bear to one another, but not by virtue of a special entity distinct from the conscious facts, which would have to support these facts and institute unity among them. What is meant by the ego is nothing apart from this united complex. It derives its unity and its coherence from the very acts that enter into it and constitute it; and it is nothing other than the organized totality of these acts. Hence when the subject, reflecting upon the act he experiences, ascertains that this act is his, this only means that the act in question is a part of that complex and has its place within this united and organized whole. In this theory there is obviously no place for a center or a pole of conscious life from which the acts might issue or emerge.

Later Husserl changed his mind and endorsed Natorp's theory which he had subjected to an explicit critical discussion in the first edition of the *Logische Untersuchungen*. In the *Ideen*, indeed, we find a manifestly egological conception of consciousness. Husserl here advocates the "pure ego" as different from the empirical ego, viz., not only from the psychophysical but also from the mere psychical ego.[3] Unlike the latter, the "pure ego" is not affected by the phenomenological reduction; it does not undergo the transformation into a phenomenon presenting itself to consciousness and constituted into what it is for us by means of certain experiences. The phenomenological reduction leaves us with the field of transcendentally purified experiences. Every such experience—inasmuch as it is an intentional act—must be characterized at once as "being directed toward" and as "coming out from." To the strictly phenomenological observation the intentional act appears thus as a ray directed towards the object and issuing from a center or a source of radiancy. It may happen that the direction of the ray is reversed, so that it is experienced as going to the ego instead of coming out of it, when, for instance, the ego undergoes something due to the object. At any rate, the phenomenological analysis reveals the acts as emanating from a source called the "pure ego."

3. Husserl, *Ideen zu einer reinen Phänomenologie und phänomenologischen Philosophie* (Halle, 1913), Vol. I, §§ 54, 57, 80. (Hereafter cited as *Ideen*. Page numbers are those of the first edition, corresponding to page numbers in the margins of the Louvain edition, ed. W. Biemel [*Husserliana*, Vol. III, The Hague, 1950].)

The latter lives "in" its acts which are "its modes of life as the going freely out of oneself, or going back upon oneself, spontaneous doing, experiencing something from objects, suffering, and so forth." [4] "In every wakeful *cogito* a 'glancing' ray from the pure ego is directed upon the 'object' of the correlate of consciousness . . . , the thing, the fact, and so forth." [5] By virtue of its very structure, the act is necessarily related to the source of its origin. The "pure ego," however, is not attached to any particular act, for not only this act but also others, even all acts, rise from it; all of them emerge from the same "pure ego." Hence the "pure ego," which obviously is not to be found on the noematic side, can no longer be defined as a real part, element, or moment of any noesis, since it is the same with respect to all noeses belonging to one stream of experience. What remains then, after the phenomenological reduction has been effectuated, is not only the field of noeses with their noematic correlates but also, over and above this, a special entity not to be bracketed, entirely situated within the domain of transcendentally purified consciousness and yet transcending every particular act belonging to this consciousness. So Husserl may characterize the "pure ego" as "a non-constituted transcendence—*a transcendence in immanence.*" In this conception consciousness is held to be polarized; in the *Cartesian Meditations* Husserl indeed speaks of a double polarization of the conscious acts: towards the object on the one hand and towards the identical and permanent ego on the other hand.[6]

Sartre again takes up the discussion of the question, and the outcome of his inquiry is a full vindication of Husserl's doctrine as maintained in the first edition of the *Logische Untersuchungen,* the ego-theory as laid down in the *Ideen* being incompatible, according to Sartre, with the very phenomenological conception of consciousness.[7]

A pure or transcendental ego may not be found as a datum when acts are considered as they are or have been experienced and unless one adopts the attitude of reflection with regard to them. I have just read a story, for example, and I recall my reading in seeking to account for my experience. There was a being conscious of the book, of the hero, of the narrated events, of the whole story in its progressive display; furthermore, there was an inner awareness of my being conscious of all this. Neither this being conscious of, however, nor the inner

4. *Ibid.,* p. 270.
5. *Ibid.,* p. 243.
6. Husserl, *Cartesian Meditations,* trans. D. Cairns (The Hague, 1960), § 31.
7. Jean-Paul Sartre, "La transcendance de l'ego," *Recherches Philosophiques,* VI (1936–37), pp. 85–123. (English translation by Forrest Williams and Robert Kirkpatrick, New York, 1957.)

awareness of it was in any way experienced as related to my ego. The latter did not appear at all. As long as an act is experienced or we follow the experienced act in its course, giving attention to the objects offering themselves through the act, rather than to the fact that the act in question is experienced (i.e., we do not objectivate the act, do not grasp it as a psychical event in our conscious life and as pertaining to the stream of consciousness), to that extent no ego will present itself in any mode of givenness whatever. No act, whether theoretical or practical, which confronts the experiencing consciousness with an object different from another act belonging to the same stream of consciousness as the act under discussion, bears any reference to the experiencing subject's ego. All these acts are impersonal in the sense that the subject in his dealing with the object, aware as he is of this dealing, is nevertheless in no way aware of his ego, much less of his ego's intervening in his dealing. Even so-called merely emotional reactions may be impersonal in the sense just defined. I see my friend in adversity, and I help him. What is given to me is "my-friend-in-need-of-aid." This "being-in-need-of-aid" is a feature belonging to the appearance of my friend, or, more correctly, belonging, so to speak, to my friend as he stands before my mind in this concrete situation. The world in which we live and act is peopled with items endowed not only with colors, warmths, smells, shapes, etc., but also with qualities like attractive, repulsive, agreeable, disagreeable, beautiful, fit for some purpose or other, and so forth. In this world there are actions done or to be done, and these actions deposit themselves like qualities upon the things with which they are connected. All qualities of the kind mentioned pertain to the things on which they appear; they contribute to shape the aspect under which the things with which we are concerned in our daily life are given to us and exist for us. These qualities are parts of the things, and in this sense they are objective.[8] Perceiving and reacting to such a quality is then, in principle, not different from the act of perceiving a red or a green. When I help my friend in need of aid, I make allowance in my behavior for certain objective features which act like forces upon my mind. Since my behavior is exclusively conducted by, and bearing upon, objective

8. These qualities dealt with under the headings of "demand characters," "physiognomic characters," and "functional characters" are held by Gestalt psychologists to belong to things and to be properties of certain objects. Although when these characters are to be explained in psychophysiological terms, it can be done only by the dynamic interplay between ego forces and environment forces, they do not belong to the ego but are found in the things themselves (cf. K. Koffka, *Principles of Gestalt Psychology* [New York, 1935], pp. 356–61, 391–93). In the present discussion we are not concerned with an explanatory theory, only with a descriptive statement; in this respect, there is complete agreement between Sartre and Gestalt psychology.

facts, the attitude I adopt is non-reflective. In fact, what I am conscious of is my friend in need of aid, the particular circumstances which bother him, the means I can render available to help him. But I am not concerned with my own ego and the disagreeable state provoked in my ego by seeing my friend's adversity, as though I helped him only to get rid of this disagreeable state by removing the cause which produces it. As far as emotional acts are experienced in the non-reflective attitude, i.e., do not bear on the experiencing subject's own mental states, they should then be accounted for without any reference to the experiencing subject's ego.

There is no place in the body of phenomenological doctrines for the pure or transcendental ego, since there is no function left which it might assume. In the ordinary way of thinking the function imputed to the ego is to institute unity among scattered mental facts. Phenomenology admits two kinds of unity in conscious life. There is, first, a unity among all those mental states, temporally separated as they may be from one another, through which the same object presents itself—for example, among all operations of adding two and two to make four. This unity exists in regard to the identical object upon which every one of the acts in question bears, so that all of them must be characterized as *consciousness of this object;* but this unity exists only in this respect, since in every other respect the acts may be separated in any way whatever. Hence it is no real unity. It depends upon the intentionality of consciousness. Since consciousness is defined by intentionality, no ego is required to institute the unity of this kind.[9] The unity of the other kind is a real one: it is the unity of the acts in their duration, the unification of act-moments into enduring acts, and the unification of acts present and past, so that conscious life becomes endowed with a streamlike character. It is highly significant, Sartre points out, that in accounting for this unity, in *Vorlesungen zur Phänomenologie des inneren Zeitbewusstseins,* Husserl never resorts to the unifying and synthesizing power of the ego. The unity of consciousness in no way depends upon the ego; conversely, the latter is rendered possible by the former. The hypothesis of the transcendental ego thus turns out to be quite useless. It is even prejudicial. Husserl insists upon the difference between the empirical and the transcendental ego. The latter should by no means be confused with the personality but must be considered as a bare formal principle. However formalized it may be and conceived as

9. W. James, *Principles of Psychology* (London, 1908), I, p. 459, also holds that the "sense of identity of the known object" does not rely on the "sense of identity of the knowing subject," i.e., on the "consciousness of personal identity." See also I, pp. 277–78.

empty of all content, nevertheless, Sartre thinks, it takes the shape of what is called a personality, although in an infinitely contracted form. Since in the egological conception of consciousness acts are held to issue or to emanate from the ego, consciousness itself gets substantialized and becomes something like a monad. Consequently the egological conception of consciousness is open to the same criticism which Husserl expressed against Descartes' views.

Both theoretical considerations and descriptive analysis lead to the following result: as long as we do not adopt the attitude of reflection, the ego does not appear. On the level of non-reflection there is no ego at all. A conscious act, inasmuch as it is free from reflection, does not deal with the ego and is not related to it in any way whatever. This holds good from the psychological standpoint as well as from that of transcendental phenomenology.

By reflection is meant the grasping of an act A by an act B, in order to make the former the object of the latter. The act B, however, in its turn is not grasped by a third act and made its object. The grasping act itself is experienced with a non-reflective attitude, exactly as in the case of an act bearing on some object other than a mental fact belonging to the same stream of consciousness. Although through the grasping act reflection is performed and is applied to the grasped act, this attitude is not adopted with respect to the act B. This act is not reflected upon, unless an act C is experienced which in its turn grasps the act B. (In this case all that has been stated about B would apply to C.) Inasmuch as the grasping act B is considered as an experienced mental state regardless of its object, all that has been said about acts experienced on the non-reflective level applies to it. If, then, the grasping act B deals with the ego, it does so not because of its being a conscious act but because of the particular object upon which it bears. Hence the relation of an act to the ego is not necessary, or, rather, it is no more necessary than the relation of an act to some other object.[10] As far as reflective acts are acts like those bearing on objects different from mental states of the experiencing subject, both the former and the latter are on the same footing in not being necessarily connected with the ego. Consciousness has no egological structure; it is not owned by the ego; its acts do not spring from a source or center called the ego.[11] Consciousness is defined by intention-

10. Cf. *ibid.*, I, pp. 274–75.
11. In dealing with the problems of attention, the present writer was also led to a non-egological conception of consciousness. (Cf. Aron Gurwitsch, "Phänomenologie der Thematik und des reinen Ich," *Psychologische Forschung*, XII [1929]. See above, "Phenomenology of Thematics and the Pure Ego: Studies of the Relation between Gestalt Theory and Phenomenology," chap. II, 7, chap. III, 19, chap. IV, 4.)

ality. It is consciousness of an object on the one hand and an inner awareness of itself on the other hand. Being confronted with an object, I am at once conscious of this object and aware of my being conscious of it. This awareness in no way means reflection: to know that I am dealing with the object which, for instance, I am just perceiving, I need not experience a second act bearing upon the perception and making it its object. In simply dealing with the object, I am aware of this very dealing. Therein consists the proper mode of existence pertaining to consciousness for which appearing is altogether the same as being, and on this account consciousness is endowed with absoluteness. What we are left with by the phenomenological reduction is transcendental consciousness as an a-personal and pre-personal field. The ego, like all other objects, falls under the phenomenological reduction, so that to speak correctly we ought to say, Sartre maintains, "There is a consciousness of this chair," instead of saying, "I am conscious of this chair."

In this conception of consciousness there is no place for an ego different from the psychical or the psychophysical one—that is to say, there is no ego except the empirical ego.[12] Now the latter may be conceived only as an object and as a transcendent existent. This is Sartre's view indeed. Hence the question arises as to the acts through which we become conscious of this object and as to its constitution for consciousness.

From what has been exhibited thus far, we may assume the self-presentation of the ego to be in some way connected with reflection. Let us consider what happens in reflection. I remember an excursion I recently made, and in doing so I again see the landscape which I went across. What, in a case like this, is the object of my thought? It is the landscape represented and, of course, no longer present, although it is represented as having been present. Since this act is experienced in the non-reflective attitude, it is free from all relatedness to the ego. Now let us reflect upon this act. When we do so, the landscape does not vanish from sight. The object of our thought is no longer simply the recalled landscape, however; rather, we become aware of the fact that certain acts bearing on the landscape were experienced and that

12. Thus we get rid of that paradoxical and contradictory entity which is the "pure ego," neither noetic nor noematic, neither an object nor a conscious fact. And along with this we also get rid of the troublesome and, I think, factitious problem of the "identity of the three egos": the empirical and worldly ego; the transcendental ego within the conscious life of which the whole world, the former ego included, is constituted; the ego-spectator who performs the phenomenological reduction and contemplates the constitution. Cf. E. Fink, "Die phänomenologische Philosophie Edmund Husserls in der gegenwärtigen Kritik," *Kantstudien,* XXXVIII (1933), pp. 355–57, 383.

they were so at a certain moment of conscious time, having a certain place within the stream of consciousness. That is what is expressed by saying "I saw the landscape," whereas the adequate expression of the former thought would be a description of the landscape itself, a statement about it. By the mere fact of being grasped by an act of reflection, the grasped act then acquires a personal structure and the relation to the ego which it did not have before it was grasped. *Reflection gives rise to a new object—the ego—*which appears only if this attitude is adopted. Since the grasping act is not itself grasped, the act continues having no egological structure. It deals with *the ego* as *an object* only; and it finds this object connected with its proper object, viz., the grasped act upon which it bears. Hence the ego in question is that of the grasped, not of the grasping act.

This statement leaves us with some questions. Reflection entails a modification of the acts concerned by it.[13] Because of its being grasped, the act is deprived to some extent of its spontaneity. Having simply been experienced, the act when grasped is objectivated; it becomes the terminus of another act bearing upon it. Along with the grasped act in its entirety, all its elements, components, and structures—the noetic as well as the noematic ones—undergo similar modifications.[14] Components and structures which contribute substantially toward shaping the act and its noematic correlate (that is, to make them what they are to the experiencing subject's mind) but which, as long as the act has simply been experienced, have not been given in an explicit manner are now given in this manner. Herein consists that which reflection brings about. It enables the experiencing subject to observe his experiences, to disclose and to disentangle what is involved in these experiences, and thus affords him explicit knowledge concerning his awareness and what he is aware of. Therefore reflection is the indispensable methodological condition for every analytic study of consciousness. On the other hand, what has been said about the alteration which reflection conveys to the acts concerned by it already contains an indication of the boundaries to which this alteration is confined. The alteration arises from the function of reflection which consists in observing the grasped act and in rendering its content explicit.[15] Consequently reflection does not at all mean a thorough modification of the acts concerned.[16] When an act is grasped, it is not as though it were just coming into existence owing to its being grasped; instead, the act stands forth as having existed, i.e., as having

13. Cf. Husserl, *Ideen*, I, § 78.
14. *Ibid.*, pp. 286–87.
15. Cf. Husserl, *Cartesian Meditations*, pp. 33f.
16. Husserl, *Ideen*, I, § 79.

been experienced, before it was grasped.[17] This holds good for all noetic and noematic components and structures of the act. If before it was grasped, the act was a certain consciousness of a certain object, it continues being so after it has been grasped. All of the act's components and structures are only disentangled and rendered explicit; none of them is given rise to by reflection.[18] Reflection is disclosing, not producing: the alteration it conveys to the act concerns the mode in which this act is experienced; it concerns the mode rather than the what of the awareness. Now in Sartre's theory, which, it seems to me, we must endorse, an act acquires relatedness to the ego through being grasped. In the very face of Sartre's non-egological conception of consciousness, this does not mean disclosing a structure which already existed before the act was grasped. On the contrary, it amounts to the assertion that the act is brought into relation to an object which did not appear before the act was grasped. In other words: reflection is held by Sartre to superinduce a new object and to be over and above the necessary condition of the constitution and existence of this object, viz., the ego. How then may reflection, as characterized above, give rise to a new object? What is the nature of the object thus given rise to? Under what aspect does this object present itself under the conditions in question? I must confine myself here to raising these questions, pointing out what I believe to be a gap in Sartre's argumentation.

When a grasped act appears as connected with the ego, the latter presents itself as exceeding this act. In fact the ego is connected not only with the act experienced and grasped at the time being but also with other acts, even with an indefinite number of them, and it is in this way that the ego appears. It offers itself as a permanent entity, as continuing to exist, beyond the grasped act which, like all mental states, is substantially perishing. The ego thus appears *through* rather than *in* the grasped act. All this is in conformity with the ego's being a transcendent existent. We must then inquire into its constitution. It is not, however, constituted in a direct way. The first constituted synthetic unities are dispositions (*états*), actions, and qualities. We must survey the constitution of these transcendent psychical objects before considering that of the ego.

Feeling repulsion against a man, I say, "I hate this man." The repulsion is an actual feeling which I grasp by an act of reflection, and there may be no doubt about the actuality of this feeling. What is meant by saying "I hate this man" is, however, more than a statement about this actual feeling. I mean that I have a permanent disposition

17. *Ibid.*, § 77.
18. Cf. *ibid.*, §§ 106, 108.

of hatred toward this man, that this disposition does not rise at the very moment at which my feeling of repulsion rises and that it will not vanish along with the actual feeling. On the contrary, I have long since hated this man, and I shall hate him forever. In fact, the same hatred which is manifested in my actual feeling was yesterday manifested in the repugnance I felt when I saw this man, and it may be expected to manifest itself in consonant feelings in the future whenever I shall have the occasion to meet that man, and so forth. This disposition is supposed to persist even without manifesting itself at all—when, for instance, I do not see that man and when I am too absorbed by some occupation to think of him. For this disposition, since it is permanent, the distinction between being and appearing is admitted. From this we may infer that it is not a conscious fact but is a transcendent psychic object constituted from conscious facts given in the mode of reflection. The hatred, identically the same as a constituted synthetic unity, is opposed to the multiple feelings of repulsion, aversion, disgust, etc., through which it appears. Through every one of these feelings the hatred appears in its entirety, not otherwise than as a material thing presents itself in its entirety through every one of its perspective variations. And as the material thing has to be distinguished from every one of its perspective variations or modes of appearance, so the hatred is not the same thing as a particular feeling through which it announces itself. By referring and being related to one another, the multiple feelings are united and polarized with respect to a transcendent unity, the permanent disposition; as a consequence, other similar feelings may be foreseen to happen in the future which will be related to the past and present feelings, and will be polarized with respect to that same unity pertaining to these feelings. To the naïve observer's mind, however, the hatred appears as a source from which the feeling of repulsion emanates; the disposition as a source and origin seems to exist before that which emanates from it—a proceeding characterized by Sartre as "magic" and about which we shall have more to say later.

This conception of psychic dispositions as transcendent objects and constituted synthetic unities entails two important consequences.

Like all entities of this kind, psychic dispositions are open to uncertainty and doubt. Every judgment concerning such a disposition which is founded upon an actual experience may be contradicted by further experiences. Believing that I hate a man, I can be mistaken not only in the sense that my disposition towards him may change, but even at the very moment at which I do feel repulsion against him and interpret this feeling as an expression of hatred, I may possibly be induced into error as to my true disposition. This is obvious in cases when, in a fit of anger, I say to a man, "I detest you," and a moment later withdraw it, saying, "No, it is not true, I said this in anger." What reflection ascertains and what is not open to doubt is my feeling of repulsion as an actually experienced mental state. But reflection does not reach further. The absolute certainty of its statement does not surpass the actual feeling as a fact of consciousness and does not extend to the objective and objectivated unity constituted by this conscious fact and of which the latter seems to testify. Reflection is not open to doubt as to facts of consciousness, but reflection is open to doubt as to transcendent unities constituted from out of these facts. The case is obviously not different from that of the perception of material things. Thus we may account for the possibility of error in our feelings in the sense of permanent dispositions without resorting to the hypothesis of unconsciousness.

The other consequence concerns the comprehension of other persons' minds. When I talk with my friend about his love, both of us have identically the same object in view—namely, a constituted psychic unity as distinct from the multiple conscious acts through which it appears. This object, his love, is for him no less open to uncertainty and doubt than it is for me. It is, of course, true that my friend becomes conscious of his love by means of acts quite different from those by means of which I become conscious of his love. Yet the sense of objectivity consists specifically in that the object, as identically the same, may and does present itself through acts different from one another not only numerically but also typically. My ego and my psychic facts, in contradistinction to the conscious acts, are then no longer my exclusive property, for they are accessible to other people, whereas my consciousness is not so; it is and remains closed and impenetrable for everyone except myself. The problem of the comprehension of other persons' minds is thus simplified and must be raised in quite new terms. The condition, however, of this simplification is the non-egological conception of consciousness. The psychical dispositions like love, hatred, etc., are substantially connected with the ego in a manner we shall survey. Were the ego an essential structure of consciousness, the impenetrability and inaccessibility of the latter would extend to psychic facts and to the ego as constituted out of these facts. Then indeed I could not understand my friend except by means of analogy. And this would be no understanding at all. All analogous representations, as far as I may go, would never confront me with the same object as that which is given to my friend and about which he is talking.

Besides dispositions there are two further kinds of constituted psychic objects. First, we discern *actions,* not only those bearing on external objects such as writing, driving a car, etc., but also merely psychic actions such as reasoning, meditating, doubting, investigating, furthering science and knowledge, and so on. All these actions may be projected, executed, discussed, remembered, and so forth. Their execution takes time, passes through phases, is articulated, has different moments, so that these actions turn out to be noematic unities in opposition to multiple acts and act-systems bearing upon them and contributing to their constitution. We have, secondly, such *qualities* as being irascible, hateful, rancorous, etc., conceived as potentialities and virtualities in regard to actions to be undertaken and dispositions to be adopted. All virtues, faults, tastes, talents, tendencies, etc., belong to this class of psychic objects.

The ego is then a synthetic unity of these psychic objects, chiefly of the dispositions and the actions—that is to say, it turns out to be a transcendent unity of transcendent unities. All these objects have their support in the ego, and the latter performs their permanent synthesis. It is not, however, a support distinct from that which is supported, such as a mere common center with respect to which materials are organized, so that it only institutes unity among these materials without belonging to them itself. Such a support would be more or less indifferent to what it supports. If the ego were a support of this kind, it could never be committed by its actions and dispositions. In truth, however, it is committed. What I do—in the broadest sense of the word—affects me and produces effects upon me. A support which is concerned by what happens in the materials supported by it may conceivably be the concrete organized totality of these materials only. This is the case of the ego: it is nothing other than the concrete totality of the dispositions and actions it supports, and it may be found nowhere outside these psychic unities. The ego is to psychic objects as the universe is to material things: the former and the latter have to be taken as infinite synthetic totalities. By the mere fact of their co-existence the psychic objects group into an organized unity; this is the ego. Hence it may never be apprehended in a direct way. It may be apprehended only in a reflection grasping a conscious act as related to a disposition; then *the ego appears* behind the disposition, *at the horizon.* This is in conformity with the fact that the ego is the all-embracing totality of the dispositions. Consequently with respect to a particular disposition, it is the horizon or a frame into which this disposition is inserted.

To naïve, i.e., non-analytical, observers' minds—and all of us are to some extent such observers—things appear in quite a different light. They think of the ego as much more than the all-embracing totality of dispositions, and they are not content to have a new disposition which has just risen join the older ones and thus enter into the ego. To them the ego seems to produce its dispositions from which the conscious acts, e.g., feelings, are held to emanate as mentioned above. Phenomenology teaches us to take the dispositions as objectivated unities constituted by means of conscious facts and to hold the ego to be the organized totality of the dispositions—that is to say, to be constituted out of these dispositions. To the common observer, however, the order is inverted. The ego becomes a source and an origin; and what in truth are first data, viz., the acts of consciousness, seem to be last products. If we allow for this naïve view, we come to a "real production" in an order contrary to that of the constitution. Thus the ego is bestowed with characteristics which belong exclusively to consciousness, as, for example, spontaneity. Hence the set of paradoxes which the ego involves. The procession of the dispositions from the ego becomes irrational, unintelligible, and in the end it may not be accounted for, Sartre thinks, except in "magic terms."

It seems to me that Sartre has gone much too far in allowing for the non-analytical, naïve view. The case is by no means as unique as it seems to be. For many centuries material things were believed to contain an innermost kernel or nucleus. This substance or essence was supposed not only to support the qualities of the thing but also to produce them, to be a kind of source from which issue the effects one thing exerts upon others; finally, it was above all not supposed to be altered when the thing underwent changes. From critical and analytical reflection it was progressively learned that there is no such kernel, much less an unchangeable substance as opposed to the modifications of the thing.[19] Material things, and perceptual things as given in everyday experience, are but organized unities of their qualities and attributes, although perhaps the structure of these unities and their organization has not yet been cleared up completely. The case of the ego will, it is assumed, be no different. As in regard to material things, thinking in terms of substantiality gave way to thinking in terms of functions and relations, so, I submit, it will have to do in all fields of experience.

The general result of Sartre's investigation may be formulated as follows: The ego exists neither *in* the acts of consciousness nor *behind* these acts. It stands *to* consciousness and *before* consciousness. It exists in the world as a worldly transcendent existent. This is true of my ego as well as that of other persons. Now a transcendent existent

19. Cf. the discussion of the question by G. F. Stout, "The Common-Sense Conception of a Material Thing," *Proceedings of the Aristotelian Society,* I (1901), New Series.

may be conceived only as an ideal noematic unity. Such is in fact the case of the ego; it turns out to be the noematic correlate of reflective acts. Through every act of this kind the ego appears in its entirety, but it presents itself under a special aspect—namely, so far as that disposition is incorporated in the ego to which the grasped act is related. As the totality of the dispositions and actions the ego may not appear except as seen from this or that disposition or action; its self-presentation is necessarily one-sided. Every apprehension of the ego involves empty meanings and intentions bearing on dispositions and actions which, for the time being, are not given, i.e., do not appear through a correspondent conscious fact grasped by reflection; these empty meanings and significations may of course be filled out in further apprehensions. Hence it follows that no evidence concerning the ego is apodictic, since in every apprehension of the ego we have in view more than is truly given. And any such evidence that may be acquired will be no more adequate, since what we have in view about the ego may, owing to the empty meanings and significations involved in the present apprehension, be contradicted by further apprehensions. Thus the ego is open to doubt. This does not mean that we may be in doubt whether we have an ego, or that the ego may possibly turn out to be a mere hypothesis. It simply means that whatever we know or believe we know about the ego—our own or that of other persons—and be this knowledge grounded upon a single apprehension or upon a certain number of apprehensions, however great, this knowledge is permanently in need of being confirmed by further apprehensions and is only valid under the condition that further apprehensions do confirm it. In this sense the ego's being carries with it a certain character of provisionalness. It partakes of this dubitability or, better, relativity, which is the essential and existential condition of all transcendent existents.

# 12 / William James's Theory

## of the "Transitive Parts"

## of the Stream of Consciousness [1]

WILLIAM JAMES'S THEORY of the "transitive parts" of the stream of consciousness will not be considered here from a historical point of view but will be gauged as a contribution to those problems which are of actual concern to present philosophical thought, especially those questions with which phenomenology deals. This orientation will also prevail in some historical considerations.

Since James intended his theory to provide a satisfactory solution for the problems of the immediately experienced continuity of consciousness, we shall begin by exhibiting this fundamental feature of conscious life as it has been brought out by James as well as by Husserl. In this respect there is a far-reaching agreement between the two thinkers. Continuity is here not understood in the mathematical sense but is meant to designate that unbroken chain and connection which is to be expounded presently. It will be shown that continuity of consciousness is identical with phenomenal time. From a discussion of the pertinent views of Hume it will appear that the classical British empiricism was unable to account adequately for the phenomenon in question. In discussing the general aspects of James's theory, the place which it holds in his thought, and its connection with some other theories of his, we shall endeavor to stress those aspects of the theory in question which make new problems arise and thus call for further investigations. The main purpose of the present analysis is to prepare those further investigations.

1. This study was written with the support of a grant from the American Philosophical Society (Penrose Fund). The writer wishes to express his gratitude both to the American Philosophical Society and to the Library of Harvard University for the hospitality extended to him and the kind permission to consult unpublished material. The article originally appeared in *Philosophy and Phenomenological Research*, III (1943).

[301]

Referring to James's works we shall use the abbreviations suggested by Professor Perry in his book, *The Thought and Character of William James.*

## [I] CONTINUITY AND TEMPORALITY OF THE STREAM OF CONSCIOUSNESS

ONE OF THE PRINCIPAL FACTS of conscious life is the continuity and coherence of this very life. Consciousness appears unbroken as it is immediately experienced and as the experiencing subject is aware of it in a "naïve" way, i.e., without or before resorting to reflection and introspective observation. Its "parts," phases, tracts hang together and are connected somehow. This connection need not be established. *The phases occur in some connection* which pertains to their experienced succeeding of each other, and connection is an immediately given feature of this very succession. The transition from one phase of conscious life to another never has the character of a sudden break; as though on the one side there were a brusque end, on the other side a no less sudden beginning, and between these two brusque events a breach which had to be bridged. Heterogeneous and indifferent to each other as the contents might be which fill two consecutive phases of conscious life, there is, at least at the beginning of the second phase, a certain awareness, though vague, dim, and indistinct, of what has just gone.

Every conscious act involves a certain reference to, or at least a certain reverberation of, what has preceded it. Thunder may be heard as breaking upon silence or else as continuing a series of thunderclaps.[2] In either case the actual datum is co-determined by those which have just been given, and the former varies according to the latter. This co-determination is sometimes a thoroughgoing qualification. In a sequence of musical notes, for example, each note, as it appears to the listener's mind, is affected by those which came before. If a sentence appears as a *conclusion,* it is because other sentences, the arguments, premises, reasons have been read or heard before; the sentence in question would not possibly have the character of a conclusion if, instead of these, other sentences or quite different experiences—for instance, visions of colors, auditions of musical notes, etc.—had occurred. Similarly, trying to clarify an idea we may come to a distinct thought and, at this very moment, have the experience, "*This* is what I

2. Cf. W. James, *Principles of Psychology* (New York, 1890), I, pp. 240f.

meant," [3] an experience which again refers back to the preceding confused meaning and to the attempt to clarify it.

Some kind of immediately experienced connection between the present act and those which have preceded it is also obtained, although less strikingly, if the contents of the consecutive acts are not so intimately related as they are in the foregoing examples. Thinking about a scientific problem, we may suddenly be induced to pay attention to what happens in the garden. Even in a case like this, there is no sudden break between the two succeeding phases of conscious life. In the initial phase of observing what happens in the garden we retain a certain reminiscence, perhaps fading very rapidly, of the scientific topic with which we have been dealing, a certain awareness of having dealt with it.

In the examples mentioned thus far, the continuity of the stream of thought, the unbroken transition from one phase to another, is felt and experienced, in that an echo of the past act enters into the present one.[4] This is not an objective after-effect which the past act has upon the present one, i.e., an after-effect ascertainable only from without by an observer. *The present act appears in its inner constitution tinged by the reference which it contains to the past act.* On the other hand, every act experienced in the present also contains a certain foretaste, a certain anticipation, however vague and indeterminate, of what is going to occur. Listening to a speaker we expect him to continue speaking in the same language and about the same topic; an expectancy which need not be explicit, much less formulated.[5] We furthermore expect the speaker to follow the same line of argument as he has done thus far, without rendering this expectancy any more explicit than the more "general" one. We may even more or less distinctly anticipate the conclusion of his argument. Doing something in order to obtain a result which we desire, we are, in our very action, looking forward, and we are experiencing our coming nearer to the goal of our activity and to the gratification of our desire.

As a last example we mention the *intrinsic temporality of an enduring act* in contradistinction to the transition from one act to another. When a note resounds for a certain time, the listener is aware of its duration; he is aware that he is listening to the same note now to which he was listening a moment ago, has been listening all the while, and which he expects to continue resounding for some time longer. The "present phase" of conscious life is pervaded by reminiscences

3. Cf. James, *Collected Essays and Reviews* (New York, 1907), pp. 380f.
4. Cf. James, *Principles*, I, p. 635.
5. Cf. *ibid.*, I, p. 262.

and expectancies: reminiscences of phases which have been present, i.e., which had the temporal character of an "actual now" but no longer have it, being only retained (*retentions*) as "having just been an actual now," and this in greater or lesser remoteness from what at the time being has the distinguished character of the "actual now." [6] The same holds true for the expectancies (*protentions*). All these retentions and protentions are interconnected and interrelated so as to make every retention appear as a retention of a less remote one. Such a series of concatenated retentions and protentions terminating in, and converging towards, the "actual now" constitutes the present phase of an enduring act.[7] To put it in the words of James, who took over S. H. Hodgson's notion of the "minimum of consciousness" and that of E. R. Clay of the "specious present": ". . . The practically cognized present is no knife-edge, but a saddle-back, with a certain breadth of its own on which we sit perched, and from which we look in two directions into time. The unit of composition of our perception of time is a *duration*, with a bow and a stern, as it were—a rearward and a forward-looking end." [8] What, properly and strictly speaking, should be called the present is an ideal limit-phase of conterminousness of the set of retentions and that of protentions, either set not only converging to that limit-phase, but each member of either set also intrinsically referring to it.[9] In fact, the "having just been an actual

6. As to "retention" ("primary memory") in contradistinction to "reproduction" ("secondary memory"), cf. James, *Principles*, I, pp. 630, 638, 646f.; and E. Husserl, *Vorlesungen zur Phänomenologie des inneren Zeitbewusstseins* (Halle, 1928), §§ 14, 19. The views of the two thinkers are in complete agreement in this respect.

7. Cf. Husserl, *Ideen zu einer reinen Phänomenologie und phänomenologischen Philosophie* (Halle, 1913), I, § 81. (Hereafter cited as *Ideen*. Page numbers are those of the first edition, corresponding to page numbers in the margins of the Louvain edition, ed. W. Biemel [*Husserliana*, Vol. III, The Hague, 1950].) See also *Vorlesungen zur Phänomenologie des inneren Zeitbewusstseins*, § 8; *Erfahrung und Urteil* (Hamburg, 1954), § 23a. The time-diagram which Husserl gives in *Vorlesungen zur Phänomenologie des inneren Zeitbewusstseins*, § 10, agrees perfectly with that proposed by James in *Principles*, I, p. 629. The parallelism and agreement between James's theory of the "specious present" and Husserl's analysis of duration have been shown by A. Schutz, "William James' Concept of the Stream of Thought, Phenomenologically Interpreted," *Philosophy and Phenomenological Research*, I (1941), p. 450. The latter study appears also in Schutz, *Collected Papers* (The Hague, 1966), Vol. III.

8. James, *Principles*, I, pp. 606ff. "The specious present has, in addition, a vaguely vanishing backward and forward fringe" (*ibid.*, p. 613). This leads to the connection as brought out before, between the presently enduring act and those acts which have been experienced and, respectively, are expected to occur.

9. Cf. Husserl, *Vorlesungen zur Phänomenologie des inneren Zeitbewusstseins*, p. 399. James (*Principles*, I, p. 608) thinks that "the strict present . . . is an altogether ideal abstraction. . . . Reflection leads us to the conclusion that it

now" derives its sense from the "being an actual now" which was distinguished, and it is in itself characterized as proceeding from the latter by modifications and iterations of modifications. The content of the complex "specious present" is incessantly subjected to continuous variations: at every moment what is an "actual now" becomes a "having just been an actual now"; a retention is transformed into a retention of a retention, a retention of any degree into a retention of a higher degree. It is, however, only the content filling these temporal forms, the matter bearing what James calls "time-coefficients," that undergoes these incessant changes and variations, whereas the temporal forms or "time-coefficients" themselves, the "actual now," the "not yet," the "just gone," etc., persist unaltered and unchanged.[10] The source and origin of these modifications is the "strict present"; the modifications arise from the "actual now" and are conveyed to the retentional phases and also, correspondingly, to the protentions. In the case of an enduring act,

---

*must* exist, but that it *does exist* can never be a fact of our immediate experience." It seems to us that the "strict present" can be called an abstraction only in that sense that it cannot be experienced without something else; in other words, it cannot be experienced except as the "nucleus in relation to a comet-tail of retentions." But it cannot be considered as an abstraction in that sense that it has to be assumed or inferred on the strength of "reasons." As an ideal limit-phase the "strict present" is in fact immediately given and experienced. Its absence or presence in, e.g., perceptual experience, makes the difference between a note which, having resounded for a while, still resounds and is, therefore, *perceived* and a note whose duration has elapsed, so that it no longer pertains to the present, even the "specious present" and, consequently, *is no longer perceived*. In fact, in the former case the note appearing in the temporal orientations of a retention, retention of a retention, and so on *also* appears in the distinguished orientation of the "actual now"; whereas in the latter case the note takes only the temporal orientations of retentions, in various degrees of iteration, but not the distinguished orientation, the "actual now." It is true, primarily we do not become aware of the "strict present" through a grasping and objectivating act. This, however, holds for any retentional phase as well. In either case what is grasped undergoes a temporal variation in the very moment of being grasped, the "actual now" becoming a "having just been an actual now," a retentional phase, a still more remote retentional phase (Husserl, *loc. cit.*, pp. 391, 400, 472f.). There is another modification emphasized by James himself which takes place when the stream of consciousness is grasped and objectivated instead of being simply experienced. Whereas the stream itself is continuous and is experienced as such, the acts of reflection by which certain moments or phases are grasped are discrete. Behind these discrete markings, however, the stream of experience goes on continuously. (*Principles,* I, p. 622; cf. also James's letter to Renouvier of September 30, 1884, in R. B. Perry, *The Thought and Character of William James* [Boston, 1935], I, p. 698 [hereafter cited as *Thought*].) Here we cannot go further into the details of the inner awareness of phenomenal time, or, equivalently, stated, the inner awareness which, at every moment, consciousness has of itself.

10. Cf. James, *Principles,* I, pp. 630, 636n.; Husserl, *loc. cit.*, p. 390 and Supplement I; *Ideen,* I, p. 237.

then, there is again continuous change and modification: a continuity of interrelated phases involved in continuous transformation.

Therefore no mental state, however elementary, is entirely confined to the "present"; none is without some elements pointing to both the past and the future. Whatever objects might appear through a *mental state*, the latter *besides being a consciousness of these objects is necessarily an awareness of time passing.*[11]

From what has been exhibited thus far one may see that the permanently experienced continuity of consciousness must be conceived in terms of temporality. In fact, this continuity is but the immediately experienced connection among different phases of conscious life. This connection necessarily takes the temporal forms of coexistence and succession, better transition. It is given in the very experiencing of these temporal forms. The fact that every conscious act refers in itself to the past and points to the future makes this act a segment conterminous with, and continuously leading into, another segment, so that in the transition from segment to segment consciousness is carried along unbroken. Thus, that continuity is bestowed upon consciousness, and therefore consciousness appears as a flow or a stream. *Continuity and temporality are then two names for the same fundamental structure of conscious life.* No theory of consciousness therefore may stand unless it adequately accounts for this fundamental fact as given in immediate experience at every moment of conscious life.

## [II]  HUME'S ACCOUNT OF TEMPORALITY

TEMPORALITY AS THE SUBSTANCE of consciousness is emphasized by Hume. He speaks of the mind as "a bundle or collection of different perceptions, which succeed each other with an inconceivable rapidity, and are in perpetual flux and movement. Our eyes cannot turn in their sockets without varying our perceptions. Our thought is still more variable than our sight; and all our other senses and faculties contribute to this change. . . . *The mind is a kind of a theatre, where several perceptions successively make their appearance; pass, re-pass, glide away, and mingle in an infinite variety of postures and situations.*"[12]

Such a succession of different data and items gives rise both to the

---

11. *C.E.R.*, pp. 380ff.; *E.R.E.*, p. 95; *P.U.*, pp. 282f. Cf. also A. N. Whitehead, *Adventures of Ideas* (New York, 1933), pp. 232ff., 246ff.

12. Hume, *A Treatise of Human Nature*, ed. L. A. Selby-Bigge (Oxford), pp. 252f. (italics added).

"impression" and "idea" of time. Time cannot "make its appearance to the mind" unless "some *perceivable* succession of changeable objects" is given.[13] To have the "idea" of time, it is necessary to conceive objects succeeding each other. *The experience of a succession of changeable objects is a necessary condition of the experience of time.*[14] Consequently, when something "steadfast and unchangeable" is given with no succession of different "perceptions"—in the broad sense in which Hume uses the term "perception" so as to include both "impressions" and "ideas"—neither the "impression" nor the "idea" of time may arise. Properly and exactly speaking, an unchangeable object cannot "be said to have duration"; it is only by "fiction" that the idea of time and duration may be applied to such an object. On the other hand, when time is experienced through a succession of "perceptions," no new "impression" or "idea" is aroused in addition to those which succeed each other.[15] In other words, the "impression" and "idea" of time stands for the very succession of contents, not for a particular and specific content which might be distinguished and separated from the former. The same is correspondingly true for space, the "impression" or "idea" of which is but the manner in which colored and tangible points are disposed and not that of a new sensational element in addition to the chromatic and tactile qualities. The ideas of both time and space are incomparable to those of colors, sounds, tastes, etc., in that the former are not ideas of objects, "no separate or distinct ideas, but merely those of the manner or order in which objects exist." [16] Since we continually experience different "perceptions" succeeding each other, "the idea of time" is "for ever present with us." [17]

Here we do not have to deal with Hume's principal thesis concerning space and time, viz., his contention of infinite divisibility and his assertion that both space and time have an atomistic

13. Unless otherwise indicated, all quotations from Hume in this section refer to *ibid.*, Book I, Part II, Section III.

14. It follows that there is no "empty time" ever given in either "impression" or "idea." This is in fact the thesis which Hume tries to prove (*ibid.*, pp. 36, 40, 65). In this respect James agrees with Hume. James maintains that "awareness of *change* is . . . the condition on which our perception of time's flow depends" and that this change "must be of some concrete sort," i.e., must occur in what fills the time (*Principles*, I, pp. 619f.). We shall see presently that the experience of a succession is more, in Hume's opinion, than a necessary condition of the experience of time.

15. Hume, *Treatise*, p. 36. "The idea of time is not derived from a particular impression mixed up with others, and plainly distinguishable from them; but arises altogether from the manner in which impressions appear to the mind, without making one of the number. Five notes played on a flute give us the impression and idea of time; tho' time be not a sixth impression, which presents itself to the hearing or any other of the senses."

16. *Ibid.*, pp. 39f.

17. *Ibid.*, p. 65.

structure.[18] We are concerned rather with the *experience of time* based on Hume's theory.

The "perceptions" which fill the "indivisible moments of time" and "whose succession forms the duration and makes it conceivable by the mind" are held by Hume to be of a perfectly definite nature. Both their qualitative and quantitative attributes have precisely determinate degrees in every respect. The "perceptions" are, futhermore, conceived as discrete as to each other. Hume repeatedly emphasizes the principle that "whatever objects are different are distinguishable, and whatever objects are distinguishable are separable by the thought and imagination." This principle applies to all "perceptions." [19] If a substance is defined as *"something which may exist by itself,"* perceptions "are . . . substances, as far as this definition explains a substance." [20] This discreteness, distinction, and separability of the "perceptions" with respect to each other implies that no "real bound" or "real connection" exists between them.[21] Every "perception" is a self-sufficient entity, entirely independent of, and unrelated to, any other "perception."

Keeping this in mind, let us examine the sequence of two impressions, i.e., the experience of time passing in its most simple form. What is given at the second phase of such a sequence is an impression B plus an idea *a,* the copy of that impression A which occupied the first phase of the sequence. Impression B and idea *a* are different, consequently separable. Their being together is extrinsic to either of them and is a mere accidental coincidence. There is no feature, no tinge in the impression which would result from its being accompanied by this idea rather than by that; the impression would remain in every respect what it is, even if the actually concomitant idea were replaced by some other one. The fact that it appears in a certain context has no bearing whatever upon the nature of any

18. *Ibid.*, Book I, Part II, §§ I–II. Leaving these problems out of consideration, we also abstain from discussing the theory, maintained among others by A. Lovejoy, "The Problem of Time in Recent French Philosophy," *Philosophical Review,* XXI (1912), pp. 336, 532ff., that phenomenal time has a discrete or discontinuous structure and is made up of indivisible elementary units, none of which has inner duration.

19. *Ibid.*, pp. 18ff., 634. "All perceptions are distinct; they are, therefore, distinguishable, and separable, and may be conceived as separately existent, and may exist separately, without any contradiction or absurdity." Cf. also Berkeley, *A Treatise Concerning the Principles of Human Knowledge,* Introduction, § 10.

20. Hume, *Treatise,* p. 233. ". . . Since all our perceptions are different from each other, and from every thing else in the universe, they are also distinct and separable, and may be conceiv'd as separately existent, and may exist separately, and have no need of any thing else to support their existence."

21. Cf. *ibid.*, pp. 259f., 636.

"perception." The sequence in question consists then in that impression A is superseded by a complex state composed of impression B and idea *a*, both contemporary but with no intrinsic connection with each other. On these grounds, time passing is a sequence of perfectly definite, self-sufficient and intrinsically unrelated "perceptions."

We have already mentioned that, according to Hume, when different "perceptions" succeed each other and thus time is experienced, no new impression of the senses is aroused in addition to those which form the sequence. Nor does any impression of reflection arise. Hume explicitly stresses that by the observation and contemplation of a succession of "perceptions" "no emotion in the mind," "no affection of any kind" is produced. The succession of "perceptions" is not accompanied by a "new original impression" of any kind whatever from which a "new original idea" (namely, that of time) might be derived. In other words: *the succession of "perceptions" is more than a necessary condition of the experience of time; it is this very experience itself.*[22] Hence Hume has difficulty in applying the idea of time and duration to an unchangeable object, i.e., to account for what has been described above under the heading of the intrinsic temporality of an enduring act. Besides those "perceptions" which succeed each other, there is no "primary and distinct impression," no specific fact standing for what is called awareness of time passing.

To this one might reply, following James, that "a succession of feelings, in and of itself, is not a feeling of a succession."[23] In fact, for a succession to be experienced as such, it is not sufficient for it only to take place effectively. If, when a later phase of a succession is present, there were no simultaneous knowledge, in some form or other, of the previous phases, consciousness would be confined to the actually present phase alone, and there would be no experience of the succession, although succession did effectively take place.

Hume's theory, however, does not seem to be open to this criticism.

22. *Ibid.*, p. 37. Time "can plainly be nothing but different ideas, or impressions, or objects dispos'd in a certain manner, that is succeeding each other."

23. James, *Principles*, I, pp. 628ff. (italics deleted). This critical remark is a special application of a general principle which James repeatedly stresses against Berkeley, Hume, and the classical British empiricism, namely, that what an idea *is* must not be confused with what that very idea *knows*. Thus according to these thinkers, "Two ideas, one of 'A', succeeded by another of 'B', were transmuted into a third idea of 'B *after* A.' An idea from last year, returning now, was taken to be an idea *of last year*; two similar ideas stood for an *idea of similarity* . . ." (p. 353). Or an "idea of pleasure" is held to be a "pleasant idea," an "idea of pain," a "painful one" (p. 497). Brentano's views on this matter are reported by Husserl, *Vorlesungen zur Phänomenologie des inneren Zeitbewusstseins*, § 3. Cf. also the discussion of the problem by Lovejoy, "The Problem of Time in Recent French Philosophy," *loc. cit.*, pp. 30, 331ff.

Hume himself emphasizes that to experience time it is necessary that the succession of "changeable objects" be "perceivable." [24] Moreover, his theory does provide for the knowledge of the previous phase at the moment of the later one. Again to take up the example given before, at the second phase not only B (present impression) is given, but $a$ ("idea" and copy of the foregoing impression) is also given. Indifferent to each other as B and $a$ might be, and although the only relation existing between them is their being together, they are together in consciousness. Consequently, at the present phase there is knowledge of the preceding one.

It appears questionable whether or not the actual knowledge of impression A as past is satisfactorily accounted for by the presence of idea $a$, which corresponds to the impression. With Hume impression and corresponding idea have the same content and only differ in the degree of "force," "vivacity," and "liveliness." [25] An "idea of the memory" differs from a corresponding "idea of the imagination" in that the former is more "lively and strong" than the latter and, therefore, "is somewhat intermediate betwixt an impression and an idea." The presence of an "idea of the memory" then means the appearance of a certain content with a certain intensity. This characterization of the "idea of the memory" is open to criticism, considering that what is given at the present moment is but the "idea" and that it is through it, and only through it, that we have any knowledge of the past. To maintain that impression and corresponding idea have the same content and differ in intensity, it is necessary to revive the past impression in order to compare it with the present idea. This is impossible, however, since at the moment nothing is given which refers to the past impression, except the present idea. Therefore, no means is provided for ascertaining sameness of content and difference in intensity.[26] It is hard to see how the appearance of a certain content with a certain intensity might be interpreted as recollection of the same content having appeared with greater intensity. The present idea, a content with a certain intensity, is a self-sufficient datum of a perfectly definite nature. How does such a datum come to represent, indicate, refer, or

24. Hume, *Treatise*, p. 35. "Wherever we have no successive perceptions we have no notion of time, even tho' there be a real succession in the objects."

25. *Ibid.*, Book I, Part I, §§ I, III; Hume, *An Enquiry Concerning Human Understanding*, § II.

26. It is this argument to which Hume resorts to invalidate the second criterion of the difference between memory and imagination, namely, that the former, in contradistinction to the latter, preserves "the original order and position of its ideas" (*Treatise*, p. 85). It is impossible "to recall the past impressions in order to compare them with our present ideas, and see whether their arrangement be exactly similar." *This argument then destroys Hume's entire theory of ideas as copies of antecedent impressions.*

point to another datum of the same content but of a higher degree of intensity? The datum is only what it is and nothing else; its intensity is one of its features. How can one degree of intensity be made to stand for another degree? According to Hume, the comparatively lower degree of intensity is experienced as pastness. This again is not understandable. The degree of intensity designates the strikingness and impressiveness of a datum, the force with which the datum imposes itself upon the experiencing subject's mind, draws attention, etc. This feature has nothing to do with a temporal character. In fact, how does a lower degree of impressiveness come to be consciousness of pastness? It may be true that, as Hume states, the more remote a remembered object is from the present moment, the more decayed and obliterated the idea through which it is remembered becomes.[27] We might even admit for the sake of discussion (and without making a point of it) that contents characterized as past are more faint, more feeble, less impressive, etc., than those which are characterized as present. Thus a correlation would be maintained to exist between two sets of characters of data. Even tentatively, in order to correlate the two sets of characters, regardless of the validity of the advanced correlation, both sets must be known. The temporal characters must then be given through facts other than degrees of intensity. Temporal characters cannot be conveyed by, and defined in terms of, degrees of intensity.

These difficulties concern Hume's general theory of ideas rather than the point at issue. We shall, therefore, not stress them, and, for the sake of the discussion, we shall grant that Hume's theory of ideas satisfactorily accounts for the fact of memory. The crucial question may then be formulated as follows. Of what nature does experience of time turn out to be on the assumption that time cannot be experienced unless through a succession of "perceptions," in Hume's sense, and that, when such a succession occurs, there is no specific fact in addition to the data which succeed each other?

As already mentioned, there is no intrinsic connection between impression B and idea *a* which at the second phase of a sequence are given together. Consequently, the second phase is not experienced as intrinsically connected with the first phase. Since at the second phase there is no other consciousness of the first phase except that which is conveyed by idea *a*, an intrinsic relationship between the two phases cannot be experienced unless through an intrinsic connection between B and *a*. According to Hume, such an intrinsic connection does not exist; impression B and idea *a* are independent of, indifferent to, and separable from each other. Since impression B is in no way tinged by

27. *Ibid.*, pp. 85f.

the merely concomitant idea *a*, the former cannot be said to point backwards, to be experienced as continuing or terminating that which was present at the preceding phase. The second phase of the sequence, then, cannot be characterized other than by saying: there is a present impression plus an additional knowledge that something different was given before. Thus from the fact that what is present now differs from that which was present a moment previously, the latter being given now in the form of an idea of memory, the mind becomes aware of the fact that change has occurred. According to Hume, this awareness of change and succession not only gives rise to, but actually is, the experience of time passing.

On the grounds of Hume's theory there is no other way of becoming aware of change, succession, and time. An awareness like that which has just been described is an awareness of "flux and movement," in terms, so to speak, not of movement itself but rather of the stages through which movement passes. *In Hume's account, the mind ascertains "flux and movement" which constitute its very life, as though mind were an external observer of itself*—namely, from the fact that different cuts made in the observed conscious life yield several different results. What Hume accounts for is the fact that one mental state *has succeeded* another rather than *the very succeeding* itself. Succession and transition can then not be immediately experienced but are merely inferred and constructed after the event.[28] Bergson's criticism endorsed by James of the mathematical treatment of physical movement may well be applied to this view of conscious life, a criticism which seems to us not to attain its proper goal, because it misconceives the substance of mathematical calculus.[29] As to Hume's view of conscious life, however, it is true that only positions, stages, extremities are taken into consideration, whereas the intervals among them and what flows throughout the intervals are overlooked. When consciousness is considered as composed of self-sufficient perceptions, unrelated to, distinct and separable from, each other, the

28. This view is consistent with, and even follows from, the thesis that time has a discrete structure. Lovejoy, who maintains the latter thesis (cf. above, n. 18), explicitly denies that there is an immediate experience or perception of succession (cf. his article, pp. 338f., 532ff.). According to Lovejoy (pp. 536ff.), this contention is necessary in order to avoid "the paradox of the simultaneity of the successive." In the account of phenomenal time which has been expounded in the preceding section, the paradox in question does not seem to arise, although immediate experience or direct perception of succession is admitted. Since the present phase of an act is constituted by a series of retentions and protentions, all interrelated with each other and convergent towards an ideal limit-phase, the first moment of an experienced succession, to put it in Lovejoy's words (p. 537), may be said to be "existentially present" in the second moment, although not "in exactly the same sense as the second moment."

29. James, *P.U.*, pp. 233ff.

"flux and movement" which characterize conscious life appear as a sequence of beaded entities.

Hume's views are at variance with what we tried to set forth in the first section of this analysis—namely the continuity of conscious life as experienced in experiencing time passing. "Consciousness . . . does not appear to itself chopped up in bits. Such words as 'train' or 'chain' do not describe it fitly as it presents itself in the first instance. It is nothing jointed; it flows. A 'river' or a 'stream' are the metaphors by which it is most naturally described." [30] The experiencing subject does not look at his own conscious life from the standpoint of an external observer, ascertaining what is going on in his mind in much the same way in which he records physical facts and events. He is aware of his conscious life not from without but from within, in a most immediate and intimate way; he is aware not only of the stages through which "flux and movement" pass but also and mainly of the very passing movement itself and of its continuity. This can be the case only owing to certain specific facts existing in and pervading conscious life, facts for which Hume fails to account.

## [III] Survey of the "Transitive Parts"

Besides Bergson and Husserl, it is James to whom we are indebted for the insights into the continuity and temporality of conscious life and the streamlike character of the latter. To James this continuity and coherence of experience was a topic of utmost concern, and his interest may be said to have revolved around this topic throughout all periods of his development.

Since the permanently experienced continuity of conscious life cannot be accounted for in terms of Hume's psychology, James is led beyond these terms in order to overcome the sensationalistic atomism instituted by Hume and accepted as well as developed in the school of classical British empiricism.[31] There is more in consciousness than those "definite images of traditional psychology" which in truth "form but the very smallest part of our minds as they actually live." [32] Searching further for this more, James is far from denying the existence of what he calls "'substantive parts' of the stream of thought," which may stand for Hume's "perceptions" although they do

30. James, *Principles*, I, p. 239.

31. As to James's indebtedness to J. Ward and S. H. Hodgson for overcoming the psychological atomism, cf. Perry, *Thought*, I, pp. 56ff.; II, pp. 611ff., 626. These obligations notwithstanding, "James' doctrine of the stream of thought was essentially his own" (II, p. 78).

32. James, *Principles*, I, pp. 243, 255.

not correspond exactly to the latter, since, as we shall see later, the "substantive parts" are not unaffected by other things existing in consciousness.[33]

Aiming at an introspective account more complete and more comprehensive than that of the traditional empiricists, James is, if not the first, at least among the first to call attention to the phenomena of *imageless thought*.[34] We may have in our mind the "shadowy scheme of the 'form' of an opera, play or book," of a scientific or philosophical system, without having sensorial imagery of any kind whatever. The case is the same in that "first instantaneous glimpse of some one's meaning which we have, when in vulgar phrase we say we 'twig it' " or in our intention of uttering a thought, before we have done it. In these cases we again experience specific mental states from which all imagery either of words or things is absent and for which it is impossible to account as long as consciousness is assumed to be composed, on the one hand, of sensations and, on the other hand, of ideas, representations, and images of a perfectly definite nature. Allowing for imageless thought, without trying to explain it away—for instance, by reducing it to images passing by too rapidly to be noticed —James went beyond not only any traditional theory but also the very terms in which these theories were conceived. The faint and dim bodily feelings, hardly heeded at all but nevertheless always present and permanently accompanying conscious dealing with any objects, may also be mentioned. They come to the foreground more in the experience of so-called "empty-time"; there are bodily feelings of a sort of which the innermost center of the self, the "Self of selves," is composed and upon which rests the feeling of personal identity.[35]

Another class of "transitive facts" are the *feelings of relation,* as various in kind and as numerous as the objective relations which exist in *rerum natura*.[36] Every conjunction, preposition, adverbial phrase, syntactic form, inflection of voice, and so on expresses some feeling of relation, and yet these feelings in their variety and manifoldness may not be exhausted by the means available to language. These feelings have a cognitive function: the objective relations are revealed to them, or, to put it subjectively, the stream of thought matches the objective relations "by an inward coloring of its own," which is but the feelings under discussion.

A special case of feelings of relation is the "sensation of difference." When two data *m* and *n* follow each other and are perceived to

33. Section VI, below.
34. James, *Principles*, I, pp. 253ff.
35. *Ibid.*, I, pp. 241f., 297ff., 341f., 619f.
36. *Ibid.*, I, p. 245.

be different, the latter, $n$, is not given as it would be if it appeared in a different context. In other words, it is not "bald $n$" that is experienced, but it is "$n$-different-from-$m$." The reason hereof is that the experience of the second term incorporates that of the "difference," a "transitive feeling," a "feeling of relation," a "shock of transition" with a quality of its own, independent of the nature of the terms. Thus the whole experience consists, according to James, of three phases: (1) "$m$"; (2) "difference"; (3) "$n$-different-from-$m$." Correspondingly, when the second datum is perceived to be similar to the first, a "shock of likeness" is experienced.[37]

Among the relations felt must be counted all kinds of logical relations.[38] Thus, James thinks, "we ought to say a feeling of *and*, a feeling of *if*, a feeling of *but*, and a feeling of *by*." Mere skeletons of logical relations like "naught but," "either one or the other," etc., and negatives such as "no" and "never" are understood when they are read or heard. That they are understood means that there is more in consciousness than a mere noise or a mere agglomeration of visible things called letters. It means that a certain affection of consciousness, a certain feeling is aroused by these words. That feeling is one of psychic movement, of transition from one phase of thought to another, from one item to that which is conjoined with the former by the "and," the "with," and so on. When these feelings are considered in passing and not in retrospection, i.e., as they are experienced before the term to which they lead is attained, they appear as states of expectancy of something to come, as states of directedness towards a more, as "sticking out" from the term from which the thought starts and as pointing in a certain direction.

On this account, the feelings of relation, taken in their living moments, appear akin to the *feelings of tendency*. Both the former and the latter are liable to fulfillment and to disappointment. An example of feeling of tendency is the aforementioned intention to say something, before it has been said. This intention is a specific state of mind with a nature of its own. Its peculiarity consists in pointing forward towards the actual utterance. When the utterance is made, it is experienced either as fulfilling or as disappointing the former tendency, depending upon whether or not it is felt to be a fit or unfit expression of what we wanted to say before we said it. The case is similar to the attempt to recall a forgotten name. The word being altogether absent, we nevertheless know what we mean and have in view. Here again we experience a specific and distinct state of mind which, moreover, varies along with the several different names we

37. *Ibid.*, I, pp. 495, 498, 529.
38. *Ibid.*, I, pp. 245f., 250ff.; James, *E.R.E.*, pp. 237ff.

have in view but are unable to utter. Such a state of mind may be characterized as a gap; but then it is an intensely active gap. Its activity becomes manifest in its selective power. It is by such a gap that we are guided in our reactions to words which are proposed to us, rejecting those which do not fit into the gap, accepting that which does. Feelings of tendency enable us, in reading a new text, to give a correct emphasis to every word actually before the eyes, i.e., to read this word with a prospect of that part of the sentence which is still to come, at least with a prospect of its mere grammatical structure. A good deal of psychic life consists of thoughts not only imageless but also inarticulate in the sense that they are experienced only as *feelings of direction,* as perspectives shooting out from the image actually in mind and pointing far beyond that image. In such a case a "substantive part" (word or image) forms the nucleus of the phenomenon. This nucleus is so fused with the sense of direction as to be taken and understood in the light of the latter, i.e., under the premonitory perspective of that which is to come, but is given at present only in the vague and indefinite shape of a direction felt. A mere sense of direction is aroused by words like *Wait!* and *Hark!* and *Look!;* an attitude of expectancy bears in a certain direction in which something is to appear, without any image, representation, often enough even without an imageless idea of what that something might be.

Finally, we must mention those mental states which James treats under the heading of "psychic overtones," "suffusions," "fringes": awarenesses in a "penumbral nascent way" of objects and relations— whole schemes of relations—"but dimly perceived." [39] Since we intend to discuss more thoroughly in a different context James's theory of "fringes," we do not dwell here upon it.

## [IV] THE STATUS OF THE "TRANSITIVE PARTS"

IT IS TRANSITIVENESS that characterizes these and related facts in contradistinction to the "substantive parts." Whereas the latter are places of comparative rest, the former are places of flight. "Their function is to lead from one set of images to another." [40] Experiencing one of these facts, the subject lives in a state of transition, either actual or virtual. The subject is either actually passing from one phase of thought to another (more correctly from one "substantive part" to

39. James, *Principles,* I, pp. 258ff.
40. *Ibid.,* I, p. 253. Cf. also p. 243: ". . . The main end of our thinking is at all times the attainment of some other substantive part than the one from which we have just been dislodged . . . ; the main use of the transitive parts is to lead us from one substantive conclusion to another."

the next), or, owing to the halos, fringes, feelings of relation, of tendency, of direction, etc., which surround, escort, and pervade any "substantive part," the subject retains, on the one hand, a certain awareness of that past transition which has led to the actual "substantive part" and, on the other hand, has a premonitory anticipation of other transitions as imminent which will lead away from the actual "substantive part." The latter is the case when for a certain time the subject abides by the "substantive part" which is present. When the pre-announced transitions are actualized, they are experienced as bringing fulfillment to the previously experienced tendencies and expectancies. On account of this transitiveness, we call the facts under discussion *transitive parts or states.*[41] These facts pervade all mental states and enter into them as ingredients. *Mental facts* are then *not self-sufficient, distinct, atomistic entities,* discrete and isolated from each other, as Hume holds them to be.[42] On the contrary, every mental state contains a pointing beyond itself to the past, the future, to other mental states so as to be experienced as linked to its neighbors.

The experiences of the "transitive parts" are experiences of these linkages. *Such are then,* according to James, *those specific facts owing to which the experiencing subject is at every moment aware from within of the temporality and streamlike continuity of his conscious life.*[43]

The intrinsic relationship between the experience of time and the "transitive parts" appears most clearly in the hypothesis which James advances as to the physiological processes underlying both phenomena.[44] At every moment brain-processes of different degrees of excitement occur together. While one of these processes is in the phase of maximal excitement, others have just been in this phase and are now waning, still others are waxing. All these processes overlap each other and thus form the *total* condition of the brain which corresponds to the *total* mental state experienced at that moment. The submaximally

41. The terminology used here differs from that of James in that by the term of "transitive states" he designates a sub-class only of the facts in question, distinguishing this sub-class from, e.g., "the feelings of tendency" (*ibid.*, I, pp. 249ff.), whereas here the term is applied to all the facts. We so use it because we find no better term for a general heading; James employs none.

42. "Traditional psychology talks like one who should say a river consists of nothing but pailsful, spoonsful, quarterpotsful, barrelsful, and other moulded forms of water. Even were the pails and the pots all actually standing in the stream, still between them the free water would continue to flow. It is just this free water of consciousness that psychologists resolutely overlook. Every definite image in the mind is steeped and dyed in the free water that flows round it. With it goes the sense of its relations near and remote, the dying echo of whence it came to us, the dawning sense of whither it is to lead" (*ibid.*, I, p. 255).

43. Cf. Perry, *Thought*, II, pp. 76f.

44. Cf. *Principles*, I, pp. 176, 235, 242f., 257f., 279ff., 634ff., 638n.

excited processes underlie, according to James, both the "specious present" and the "transitive states" and form their cerebral substratum. This applies also to the intrinsic temporality of an act, to a monotonously enduring sensation: processes which are fading co-exist with those which are dawning and those which are just maximally excited. Since all these processes correspond to the same sensation, the only difference among them must lie in their degrees of excitement.

This relationship as it appears in James's physiological hypothesis has been remarked upon and criticized by A. Marty in his review of the *Principles*. According to Marty, James is inconsistent with himself in this hypothesis, because he does not hold the experience of time to belong descriptively with the fringes.[45] As may be seen from this, Marty overlooks that aspect of the theory of "transitive states" which we are stressing here. He does not sufficiently allow for what seems to us the main purpose of the theory—namely, satisfactorily to account for the experienced continuity and temporality of conscious life.

Specific as the "transitive facts" are, they are vague, indefinite, and have no precise contours. In bringing out and stressing their existence, James tries to reinstate "the vague to its proper place in our mental life" over and against the view held by Berkeley and Hume that every mental state is of a perfectly definite nature.[46]

The "transitive parts" are devoid of definiteness; they are penumbral, dumb, and anonymous. In our naïve, conscious life we not only experience these facts but are also most often guided by them and by their several different shades. Indistinct and inarticulate as they are, every one among them has yet a specific nature of its own so as to be distinguishable not only from the "substantive parts" but also from "transitive parts" of another shade.[47] But it is hard to tell, in a particular case, what the differences between their shades and nuances are, hard also to assign names to them. Most often the "transitive parts" are named after the terms to which they lead; but then they are as if overshadowed by these terms because of the latter's stability and strikingness, so that the specific shades of the several "transitive parts" are suppressed.

Because of their vagueness as well as their transitiveness, the "transitive parts" confront introspective analysis with a peculiar difficulty which, James thinks, is partly responsible for their having

45. *Zeitschrift für Psychologie und Physiologie der Sinnesorgane*, III (1892), p. 316n. In the copy of Marty's review which was in his possession, James commented upon this criticism with the marginal note, "good!"
46. James, *Principles*, I, p. 254.
47. *Ibid.*, I, pp. 251f.

been overlooked.[48] The " 'substantive states' can be held before the mind for an indefinite time, and contemplated without change." To apply this procedure to the "transitive states" would be the same as trying to fix attention upon and to render clear and distinct what in itself is penumbral, vague, inarticulate. It would mean stabilizing what in itself is unstable and evanescent, stopping what in itself is motion and transition, bestowing duration upon what only exists in flight and on the wing. This procedure when applied to the "transitive states" must prove a failure, because it is contrary to their specific nature; the vague and penumbral escapes our attention; and, instead of what we are looking for (fringe, relation, tendency, and so on), we are left with some "substantive part" surrounded by the former or that to which it leads, "usually the last word we were pronouncing, statically taken, and with its function, tendency, and particular meaning in the sentence quite evaporated." From this we may see that, in James's opinion, the "transitive parts" not only make up a considerable part of conscious life but also possess more importance, significance, and value than the "substantive parts" to which they are attached.[49]

According to Marty, the only mental facts, if any, to which James's descriptions of the fringes might apply are the *"uneigentlichen Vorstellungen."* [50] By the latter are meant cognitive mental states which refer only indirectly to the intended object O. They do not represent O itself but designate another object O′ which stands in a certain relation to O. It follows that relational and conceptual thoughts, in contradistinction to James's opinion as interpreted by Marty, cannot be taken as *uneigentliche Vorstellungen*. Relational and conceptual thoughts are required by *uneigentliche Vorstellungen* as the very elements of which the latter are composed. It is true that the content of the *uneigentliche Vorstellung* of O is not similar to O. But it is similar to O′. With respect to O′ the *uneigentliche Vorstellung* is a direct and *eigentliche* representation. Would such not be the case, a *regressus ad infinitum* would be unavoidable. Therefore, the *uneigentlichen Vorstellungen* can by no means be characterized as devoid of any describable content. Thus, Marty states, James is mistaken as to the true nature of the only phenomenon which, if any, might eventually fall under the concept of fringes. To this James replies in a marginal note on page 327 of his copy of Marty's review, "But have I ever denied

48. *Ibid.*, I, pp. 243f., 246; cf. also pp. 643f.
49. *Ibid.*, I, p. 255. "The significance, the value of the image is all in this halo and penumbra that surrounds and escorts it." Meaningfulness is then, according to James, a matter of "transitive facts."
50. Marty, *loc. cit.*, pp. 326f.

that the conceptual and transitive states and fringes *had* an *eigentlicher Inhalt?*" On page 329, Marty comes back to the point again. There are undoubtedly some difficulties in describing *uneigentliche Vorstellungen.* This, however, does not entitle us to conclude that the facts in question are vague in themselves and have no describable content. There are no representations or acts of consciousness the content of which is vague or indeterminable in itself. Deficiencies of imperfect observation must not be attributed to the phenomenon observed. To this James remarks in a marginal note, "This is a *quotable* passage—it says briefly all that I have meant to say." We are inclined to interpret both marginal notes as reassertions of the specific nature of what James means by "transitive states," notwithstanding their descriptive vagueness. The connection which Marty tries to establish between fringes and *uneigentliche Vorstellungen* appears to us quite arbitrary. However, this discussion discloses a real problem which here can be stated only. It concerns James's assertion that facts of the distinction of logical relations are experienced through mental states of which descriptive vagueness and functional transitiveness appear as the essential characteristics.

## [V] THE EMPIRICIST TREND IN THE THEORY OF THE "TRANSITIVE PARTS"

JAMES'S ASSERTION of his view of consciousness as continuously streaming and his establishment of the theory of the "transitive parts" in which this streamlike continuity appears and upon which it rests brought him in opposition to the classical British empiricism. To lay down his theory of the "transitive states" James had to criticize explicitly views held by that school. But when he turned against the empiricist tradition, his aim was by no means to confute *empiricism as such.* Perry has most convincingly shown that James does belong to the British empiricistic school.[51] James's criticism is that of a reformer, not an adversary; the target of his criticism is a certain narrowness which had developed in the empiricistic tradition, not the basic principles from which this train of thought had sprung. Fully aware of the insufficiencies of certain doctrines which had grown in that tradition of empiricism and laying these insufficiencies bare himself, James, however, thinks that the remedy must be found within and not outside empiricism. It is only by a deeper understanding, a

51. Perry, *Thought,* chaps. XXVI, XXXIII, XXXV. As to James's affiliation with French temporalism, cf. Lovejoy, "The Problem of Time in Recent French Philosophy," *loc. cit.,* pp. 16ff.

more radical appeal, and a more consistent and a more deliberate application of the very principles of empiricism that those insufficiencies which had affected what, in his day, was empiricistic tradition and doctrine might be overcome. James's ultimate end is to rehabilitate empiricism, not to depart from it; thus an empiricistic trend is manifest in all his thinking.[52]

As far as the present topic is concerned, this trend appears in that feelings of relations, conjunctions, transitions, etc., according to James, not only exist and are as real as other feelings of "substantive parts" or terms but also and mainly have the same kind of psychic reality and existence as the latter feelings have.[53] The facts under discussion "involve no new psychic dimension," no "*actus purus* of Thought, Intellect, or Reason"; they are not due to a mental function superior in any sense whatever to that of sensible experience.[54] Terms as well as conjunctive and disjunctive relations are consubstantial; all of them are "affairs of experience" and are equally "integral members of the sensational flux." Both "substantive" and "transitive" parts belong to the same psychic level. This is so because there is but one psychic level—namely, the sensational temporal stream of experience.[55] It is then not the function of the "transitive parts" to overcome any separation existing between the terms. Insofar as separation is actually experienced, it is not overcome at all, but remains. Otherwise,

52. A particularly significant expression of this trend is to be found in the letter to Dickinson S. Miller of December 6, 1905: ". . . The concept of 'being' or 'fact' is not wider than or prior to the concept 'content of experience'; and you can't talk of *experiences being* this or that, but only of *things experienced as being* this or that." *The Letters of William James*, ed. Henry James (Boston, 1920), II, p. 236.

53. James, *Principles*, I, p. 245: "If there be such things as feelings at all, *then so surely as relations between objects exist in rerum natura, so surely, and more surely, do feelings exist to which these relations are known.*" Cf. also James, *E.R.E.*, pp. 25, 42f., 51, 62, 95; James, *Pragmatism* (New York, 1907), pp. 147f.; James, *P.U.*, p. 279.

54. James, "On Some Omissions of Introspective Psychology," *Mind*, IX, pp. 4, 8, 10; James, *Principles*, I, p. 245.

55. James, *E.R.E.*, p. 95: "Prepositions, copulas, and conjunctions: 'is,' 'isn't,' 'then,' 'before,' 'in,' 'on,' 'beside,' 'between,' 'next,' 'like,' 'unlike,' 'as,' 'but,' flower out of the stream of pure experience, the stream of concretes or the sensational stream, as naturally as nouns and adjectives do, and they melt into it again as fluidly when we apply them to a new portion of the stream." Cf. also p. 59, and James, *P.U.*, pp. 279f. As a consequence of this view, James asserts the consubstantiality of thought, universal and conceptual, and feeling or image. The difference between thought and feeling is that between the presence and absence of a fringe surrounding a nucleus, word or image. Fringes are as real and integral parts of experience as the nuclei which they escort. Therefore, thoughts and feelings turn out to be consubstantial under the "structural aspect" (insofar as both are subjective facts) as well as under the "functional aspect" (both are cognitions and have cognitive quality). Cf. James, *Principles*, I, pp. 477ff.n.; Perry, *Thought*, II, p. 39.

however, the terms do not come disjointed and isolated. James explicitly rejects a misinterpretation of the fringes as "some sort of psychic material by which sensations, in themselves separate, are made to cohere together." [56] In truth, fringes are as much consubstantial parts of the "object cognized" as substantive qualities are. What is *given* in experience is *not a simple quality to be related,* nor a feeling of such a quality to which a second feeling or thought of relations is added or superinduced, but a *quality fringed, swimming in a halo of relations,* a "quality in relation with something else," as, for example, "green-as-sequent-upon-the-red-and-contrasted-with-it." [57] Experience then turns out to be a *connective tissue.* In this sense, the "transitive parts" might also be called conjunctive parts.

The assertion of the felt immediacy of relations and conjunctions gives rise to the question as to whether it is as universally valid as stated by James. Are all relations and conjunctions, without any exception, integral parts of the sensational stream so that experience of them is fully consubstantial with that of the terms? The question is whether experience actually has but one level or whether the discrimination between sensational (or, better, perceptual) experience and categorical thinking must be admitted. Even if there are relations to which James's view applies, does this purport that it applies to all relations? The examination of this question leads to Husserl's distinction between perceptual and categorical unities.[58] This problem is mentioned, although it cannot be discussed here.

## [VI]  THE THEORY OF THE "TRANSITIVE PARTS" AND THE CRITICISM OF THE "MIND-STUFF" THEORY

THAT THE SUBSTANTIVE NUCLEI by themselves are given as fringed and related, and are not made to cohere subsequently by an additional suprasensational act, means that they are not only surrounded and escorted but also and chiefly *qualified* by the "transitive parts." The latter bestow a certain tinge or aspect upon their nucleus so as to make it *appear and,* as is also the case in the realm of consciousness, *be different* from what it would be if it were suffused

56. James, *Principles,* I, p. 258n.; cf. also James, *E.R.E.,* pp. 86f.
57. James, *Mind,* IX, pp. 9ff.; cf. also Perry, *Thought,* I, pp. 570f.
58. Husserl, *Philosophie der Arithmetik* (Halle, 1891), pp. 217ff.; Husserl, *Logische Untersuchungen* (Halle, 1913), II, iii, §§ 22–23, II, vi, §§ 43, 51, 61. Following this theory of Husserl, the writer has maintained that all categorical terms have a double meaning, the one categorical proper, the other designating a phenomenon of felt immediacy. See above, "Some Aspects and Developments of Gestalt Psychology," pp. 8, 29ff., 49ff.

with fringes, halos, etc., different from the actual ones.[59] A most striking example of the qualification of a nucleus by surrounding fringes is the phenomenal modification, as described by James, which a word undergoes when from being perceived in the normal way—i.e., as a word understood and having a meaning—it is taken as a mere noise or a mere aggregation of black strokes on white paper.[60] The meaningfulness of a word, according to James, is brought about by fringes.[61]

Consequently, when the same external stimulus repeatedly exerts the same action upon the same region of the same sense organ, one is in no way entitled to speak of the recurrence of the same state of mind. Even if the nucleus were the "same" in all these cases, it would nevertheless not be the same because of the several different fringes, halos, relations, etc., which surround and qualify it. One has then to admit as many different mental states, each one unique, as there are

59. This assertion is at variance with the thesis of "radical empiricism": that a piece of "pure experience" preserves its identity in different systems, i.e., that it is not qualified by the context into which it enters. Cf. James, *C.E.R.*, pp. 377ff., and "Does 'Consciousness' Exist?" in James, *E.R.E.* "Radical empiricism," on the other hand, rests on the admission of all kinds of relations and conjunctions as integral members of the experiential stream, on the "notion . . . of the through-and-through union of adjacent minima of experience, of the confluence of every passing moment of concretely felt experience with its immediately next neighbors." Cf. James, *P.U.*, p. 326. In fact, "to be radical, an empiricism must neither admit into its constructions any element that is not directly experienced, nor exclude from them any element that is directly experienced" (*E.R.E.*, p. 42). Cf. James's notes of 1897–98, published by Perry, *Thought*, II, pp. 368ff.; see also Perry, *Thought*, I, pp. 460f., 564, and *Present Philosophical Tendencies* (New York, 1929), pp. 365f. According to A. Lovejoy, "William James as Philosopher," *International Journal of Ethics*, XXI (1911), p. 148, and Perry, *Thought*, II, pp. 586, 590, the later philosophy of James grew, to a considerable part, from the development and the transposition into metaphysics of the views first laid down in the *Mind* article and in the chapter on the "stream of thought" in the *Principles*. It is the contradiction between that which "radical empiricism" presupposes and that which it asserts which finally brought James to embrace Bergson's anti-intellectualism. Cf. James, *P.U.*, chaps. VI–VII.

60. James, *Principles*, II, pp. 80f. Compare James's description of the phenomenon with that given by Husserl, *Logische Untersuchungen*, II, 1, pp. 66, 407ff. According to Husserl, "Der *sinnliche* Habitus eines Objektes ändert sich nicht, wenn es für uns die Geltung eines Symbols annimmt; oder umgekehrt, wenn wir bei dem normalerweise als Symbol fungierenden von seiner Bedeutsamkeit absehen. . . . Wohl aber hat der *eine und selbe* Inhalt seinen *psychischen* Habitus geändert" (italics added). With James, on the contrary: "Their sensible quality changes under our very eye . . . ; the sound itself appears to change . . . ; one may often surprise a change in the very *feel* of the word. . . . We felt it quite otherwise than as we feel it now divested and alone."

61. James, *Principles*, I, pp. 265, 472. James distinguishes the "dynamic meaning" which "is usually reduced to the bare fringe . . . of felt suitability or unfitness to the context and conclusion" from the "static meaning" consisting either of "sensory images awakened" or of "other words aroused."

stimulations. To be sure, all these different mental states not only are produced by the same object but also bear cognitive reference to it. Through all of them cognizance is taken of that object as identically the same. This, however, is far from making the different mental states recurrences of the same experience. It is the "ultimate law of our intellectual constitution," the "keel and backbone of our thinking," that an object may be thought of as identically the same through an indefinite number of mental states highly different from each other. Looking at a thing now one may be aware of it as the same which was looked at on a previous occasion. It is this very consciousness of the thing's sameness, no matter whether this consciousness belongs to the nucleus or to the fringes of the present thought, which constitutes an additional ingredient of the latter and makes it differ from the thought experienced on the previous occasion. Were the actual thought but the previous thought returning, the subject would simply revert to this previous thought. In this case there could not possibly be consciousness of the identity of the object appearing now and that which had appeared on the previous occasion.[62] Not only, then, is the "thought of the object's recurrent identity" not the same thing as the "identity of its recurrent thought," [63] but the former would even be rendered impossible by the latter. Because of the fringes, relations, etc., the object which is given as the same in a plurality of mental states appears now in this context, now in that, now in these relations, now in different ones; in every later mental state the object surely appears as the same but is taken in a new manner, freshly understood, seen from a different angle, and so on. The penumbral, dim context with which the nucleus is suffused somehow modifies the identity of the "thought's object," though sometimes only superficially.[64] No mental state can ever recur.[65] And no part of a mental state can recur, either

62. *Ibid.*, I, pp. 172ff., 354, 459f., 480f.; II, p. 290. The possible and actual cognitive reference of different mental states to the same object must be taken as an ultimate fact admitting of no reduction and even of no further explanation and account. In his personal copy of the *Principles*, James made the following entry on the interleaf, I, p. 553: "Perhaps I ought to say in a note that no explanation is intended either of *thought* or of any of its forms (such as that of seeing that two things are similar, or that the same thing is meant once again). We assume thought and the sorts of relations it can cognize, and simply seek to show, by cerebral conditions, what *things* at any moment come to be known in any of these relations."
63. Cf. James, *Principles*, I, p. 196. This confusion results from that between what James respectively calls the "object of thought" and "the psychologist's reality" (cf. *ibid.*, I, p. 184).
64. James, "On Some Omissions of Introspective Psychology," *Mind*, IX, p. 9; James, *Principles*, I, pp. 233, 255. Cf. also Perry, *Thought*, II, p. 77.
65. The fringes and kindred facts being related, as we have seen, to faint brain-processes and the latter depending upon the condition of the whole brain, the supposition that the same set of fringes might recur unchanged leads to the

in isolation or in a different context. Being qualified by what surrounds it, such a part would in one context be in fact different from what it is in another context.

Hence it follows that, to speak properly, the "thought's object" has no parts in the sense of components. Nuclei and fringes enter into the constitution of the "thought's object," and they do so on the same footing. Being ingredients, however, they are not elements out of which the "thought's object" were built up. The latter is a unitary whole, uncomposed of, and not decomposable into, elementary units.[66] It is thought of in a single pulse of consciousness. Consequently, when it is of some complexity it cannot be said to be the result of more elementary units compounding themselves. Thus, we are led to a theory held by James which occupies a central position in his *Principles*—namely, his assertion, over and against what he calls the "mind-stuff theory," that there is no self-compounding, blending, integration, synthesis, or whatever it may be called, among mental states.

## [VII] FORMULATION OF NEW PROBLEMS

JAMES'S THEORY of the "transitive parts" has been expounded here with reference to the continuity and temporality of

---

assumption that, at the second appearance, the total brain-state could be exactly what it was at the first appearance. This assumption is obviously absurd. Not only does what happens between the two appearances leave traces in the brain, so that the total condition of the latter is modified, but the brain is also after the first appearance no longer in the same state in which it was before this appearance; it has been modified by the very fact that this neurosis took place (*Principles*, I, p. 234). For his assertion that no mental state recurs, James refers not only to fringes and relations but also to facts discussed under the heading of constancy problems—constancy of color, shape, and size (*Principles*, I, pp. 231ff.). It is worth noting that James's assertion applies to what he calls the "thought's object," which, according to him, never can "have the same content," whereas in phenomenology, the identity of the "thought's object" is assumed and only the recurrence of what James would call the "thought," the act of experience is denied, since every conscious act is individualized by its position in phenomenal time. (Concerning the phenomenological theory, see above, "On the Intentionality of Consciousness.") E. G. Boring, *A History of Experimental Psychology* (1929), p. 499, also states that in his assertion James did not mean what Boring calls the "logical point," viz., the difference in time. According to Boring, with the assertion in question James anticipated the Gestalt theory, especially the repudiation of the "constancy hypothesis."

66. James, *Principles*, I, pp. 277ff. In "The Knowing of Things Together" James withdraws from the radical formulation as maintained in the *Principles* and allows "mental states" to be called complex and to have "parts." But the "parts" he admits now are not the elementary units of traditional psychology, which by aggregating themselves compound the mental state in which they are contained (see James, *C.E.R.*, pp. 396ff.).

consciousness. The theory must be seen under this perspective, and it is for the purpose of accounting for the continuity of consciousness that it was conceived by James himself. "Transitive parts" are experiences of continuity; it is through them that the mental state, into which they enter as ingredients, appears connected with, and linked to, both what came before and what is to come after. Since in the realm of consciousness *every thing is* what it *appears as* and *is experienced to be*, the "transitive parts" *by virtue of being experiences of continuity and temporality* may be said to *constitute this very continuity and temporality*. The "transitive parts" are not, on the other hand, scattered facts appearing now and then. On the contrary, there is no nucleus, no "substantive part" which is not pervaded by, and suffused with, fringes and "transitive states" of some description or other. Consequently, every mental state consisting, although not compounded, of "substantive" and "transitive" parts appears, because of the latter, in continuity with other mental states and is experienced as pertaining to the conscious stream and as forming a phase of this stream. The "transitive parts" thus bestow a temporal aspect upon every mental state. In fact, every mental state has duration, on the one hand, and is, on the other hand, integrated into a temporal order which is the continuously flowing stream of conscious life. *Temporality turns out to be the very substance of consciousness.* When consciousness appears at every moment as a temporal flux, it is because of the omnipresence, so to speak, of specific facts through which at every moment time is experienced.

Establishing the theory in question James has done more than advance a solution of a special problem. *What underlies the doctrine of the "transitive states" is a new conception of consciousness, the definition of consciousness in terms of temporality.* Herein lies the historical significance of the theory under discussion with which James may be said to have discovered temporality as the fundamental structure of conscious life.[67] James is not content with generally and abstractly stating temporality as an all-important and characteristic fact of consciousness. He tries to account for what he conceives to be the substantially fundamental feature of consciousness by pointing out specific facts through which time and continuity are experienced and by assigning to these facts a central position in his psychology, i.e., a position corresponding to the importance of what is experienced through these facts. Accordingly, brain-processes are so conceived that

67. Cf. Lovejoy, "William James as Philosopher," *loc. cit.*, pp. 146ff., and his discussion of Perry, *Present Philosophical Tendencies*, in *Journal of Philosophy*, IX (1912), pp. 631f.

what underlies the specific psychic facts in question appears as a cause present at every moment.[68]

Whatever exists in consciousness necessarily exhibits temporal aspects and structures and forms part of a temporal order. To set forth the continuity and temporality of consciousness, we referred at the outset to some examples; for instance, the experience of a proposition as a conclusion which could not possibly occur had consciousness not a temporal structure. In fact, a proposition derives its aspect as a conclusion from its relations to other propositions which occupied previous phases of thought. That a proposition be experienced as a conclusion, these previous phases must be retained at the very moment when the former is actually dealt with. Consequently, to a consciousness for which there was no time—i.e., which was confined to the present moment and from which all reminiscence of any previous phase had completely vanished—no proposition could possibly appear as a conclusion. We have tried to show elsewhere that for a consciousness of an atemporal nature there could exist no identity, no identical object.[69] In this sense *time* is a *necessary condition of consciousness*. Is time also a *sufficient condition*? May the specific characters of phenomena like the experience of a proposition as a conclusion, that of the fulfillment of an obscure and confused meaning by a clear and distinct thought, and so on, be satisfactorily disposed of merely in terms of temporality? When a proposition appears as a conclusion, previous phases of thought are retained. When we interrupt our dealing with a scientific topic to pay attention to something which happens in our environment, we also retain a certain awareness of our previous activity, at least at the beginning of the present one. There is, however, a sensible difference between the two cases. In the former case, what is retained is experienced to be *relevant* to what we are dealing with presently; whereas from the latter case any such experience of relevancy is altogether absent. Is it possible to account for the presence and absence of *relevancy* in terms of conscious time, or is another factor involved here? Speaking of an eventual other factor, we do not mean an individual element characteristic of a particular experience and varying from one experience to another. What we have in mind is a structural factor of much the same generality and general significance for consciousness as that which time has.

The same problem may be approached from a different point. Among the facts which James cites as examples of "transitive parts,"

68. Cf. James, *Principles*, I, pp. 632ff.
69. Above, "On the Intentionality of Consciousness," III.

there are genuine experiences of linkages among mental states and of transitions either actual or virtual: the "whence" and the "whither," the echo of what has just passed, the pointing towards what is to come. There are, however, other facts listed by James as "transitive" which at first sight do not seem to belong under this heading. We have already mentioned imageless thoughts of different descriptions, all kinds of relations, including logical relations and those which are expressed by the formal parts of speech, meaningfulness of words in general and what James calls the "dynamic" meaning in particular, universal and conceptual thought.[70] It may be added that even a non-perceptual presentation of objects otherwise perceivable is also accounted for by James in terms of transitional experiences and tendencies towards such experiences.[71]

From this provisional survey of the facts considered by James as "transitive" and from the manifold applications which he makes of the *concept of "transitive parts"* we may see that with him this notion has a *double meaning* and accomplishes a *double function. First, "transitive states" are experiences of connection, continuity, and temporality; and they constitute this very temporal continuity.* It is this aspect which we have tried to bring into the foreground. *Second, "transitive states" stand for imageless thought in the broadest sense.* By this we mean mental states from which, under the actual conditions, images happen to be absent, although they may, under different circumstances, contain images; we also include those which prove not to be reducible to images and imagelike entities, either not completely or not at all.[72]

70. Above, pp. 314ff., 321f.n. 55.
71. Cf. James, C.E.R., pp. 375ff.; E.R.E., pp. 54ff.
72. It is with respect to the latter function and only with this respect that the fringes have been considered by G. F. Stout who treats them under the general heading of "implicit apprehension" (*Analytic Psychology* [1896], Bk. I, chap. IV). By the latter Stout means apprehension of an item as part of a whole which, however, is not given in full sensible detail and in the form of an image. Stout objects to James's allowing for fringes in the higher mental states only and not in the lower ones as well—e.g., sense perception (*Analytic Psychology*, I, p. 93). A fringe is involved in the simple recognition of a sensory quality, inasmuch as for this recognition no actual recall of other instances is required, with which the sensory quality is compared and classified (pp. 182f.). In the perception of a thing more facts play a part and are given than merely those which appear in the form of sensations and images. Other examples of fringes on the lower level of mental life are, according to Stout (pp. 93f.), the perception of a melody, of the metrical form of a sonnet, of a series of changes, the visual perception of the movement of a body, etc. From this it appears that, to Stout, fringes are but one class of examples of imageless apprehension and that he completely disregards the other function which they have according to James—namely, as experiences of the continuity and temporality of the conscious stream. This is most conspicuous in Stout's discussion of the experience which we have when our

It is no ambiguity in the usual sense which appears in the double meaning of James's term. Imagelessness and transitiveness belong together, according to James, and are but two aspects of the same phenomenon.[73] Every mental fact which bears one of these features also exhibits the other. The genuine experiences of continuity, transition, etc., are in fact devoid of images and fall under the concept of imageless thought. Correspondingly, James holds that every mental state characterized by the fact that images are either absent from it or, if present, are irrelevant to its specific nature is an experience of continuity and transition. It is in accordance with the standards set by one special group of imageless thought that the whole class is interpreted. The originality of James's theory consists in his taking non-perceptual presentation of perceivable objects, meaningfulness of words, experiences of relations, and so on, as specific experiences of time, i.e., experiences through which the subject becomes aware of his passing from phase to phase. With respect to those "skeletons of logical relation" as expressed by "either one or the other," "although it is, nevertheless," etc., James speaks of *"signs of direction . . . of which direction we nevertheless have an acutely discriminative sense, though no definite sensorial image plays any part in it whatsoever. . . . These bare images of logical movement . . . are psychic transitions, always on the wing, so to speak. . . . Their function is to lead*

---

attention suddenly shifts from one topic to another of heterogeneous nature (pp. 218f.). "The subject which previously engrossed our attention may continue for a time to retain a considerable hold on our minds." For this awareness of the previous topic in, at least, the initial phase of our dealing with the present one, Stout refers to James's "transitive states." But Stout emphasizes exclusively the imagelessness of this awareness and does not even mention its other aspect, viz., as an experience of the continuity of the conscious stream. In point of fact, it is in and through phenomena like this that the temporal continuity of consciousness manifests itself the most strikingly. (In another context we shall discuss the controlling influence upon the train of thought which Stout, pp. 94f. and 182ff., attributes to the fringes.) From the standpoint of the "School of Würzburg," J. Orth (*Gefühl und Bewusstseinslage*, 1903, section III) has brought James's fringes in connection with K. Marbe's "Bewusstseinslagen"; see also K. Stumpf, "Erscheinungen und psychische Funktionen," *Abhandlungen der Preussischen Akademie der Wissenschaften* (Berlin, 1906), pp. 38f.

73. Marty, *loc. cit.*, pp. 316ff., notes the manifold applications which James makes of his concept. Marty is right in that James does group very heterogeneous facts under the heading of "fringes" or "transitive states." But when Marty objects to the lack of a principle with respect to which the heterogeneous phenomena belong to one and the same class, he fails to recognize the fact that there are two principles of classification which, according to James, are complementary to each other, so that whatever phenomenon falls under the one *eo ipso* falls under the other. This view, of course, is open to criticism, but not until it has been disclosed and rendered explicit so as to permit the discussion of the reasons which led James to consider each and every imageless thought as a "transitive fact."

from one set of images to another." [74] In experiencing a relation between terms, the subject experiences his transition, his being brought from term to term, a jump, as it were, from the one to the other, a flight from "resting-place" to "resting-place." This transitional experience which in itself is an awareness of time passing, is, in the temporal succession of the segments of the stream of consciousness, intercalated between those of the respective terms. This appears most clearly in James's account of the "sensation of difference" which has been mentioned above. [75] Here again the experience of the relation of difference is interpreted as awareness of time, of passing from one comparatively stable phase which has just gone to another as stable which is to come.

In a *temporalistic conception* of consciousness, i.e., a conception in which *temporality* is considered to be the *only general structural factor*, [76] the main difference among conscious states can be found only in their pace. There are phases of comparative rest and phases of flight. That mental state which cannot be considered, for some reason or other, as a phase of rest must then be classed as a state of flight and transition, the function of which consists in leading from next to next. With respect to mental states, such as conceptual thought, experiences of relation, non-perceptual presentation of perceivable objects, comprehension of meanings, etc., the question arises as to why James holds them to be descriptively vague and functionally transitive and as to whether or not they correspond to this characterization. If a closer examination shows that such is not the case and that the states under consideration cannot be accounted for in terms of temporal structures, it does not mean that they have no temporal aspect. When time is the necessary condition of whatever exists in consciousness, as it surely is, the mental facts in question must exhibit intrinsic temporal structures and be inserted into the temporal order of consciousness. That their specific nature cannot be accounted for in temporal terms leads again to the eventuality of another general structural factor besides time and to the problem of the relation between this factor and that of temporality. It is not the temporality of any conscious fact that is questioned, but merely a conception of consciousness which exclusively emphasizes temporality.

The question as to whether time is a condition necessary and

74. James, *Principles*, I, pp. 252f. Cf. Marty's pertinent critical remarks, *loc. cit.*, p. 318 (n.1).

75. Above, p. 314f.

76. A pregnant formulation of the temporalistic conception may be seen in the following passage: "In such a world (scl. of pure experience) transitions and arrivals (or terminations) are the only events that happen . . ." (James, *E.R.E.*, p. 63).

sufficient or only necessary also arises from a closer study of the "transitive states" insofar as they are genuine experiences of continuity and context. Are all conjunctions of the same type, only differing from each other gradually, according to intensity, intimacy, and so on, or have we to admit typical, even dimensional, differences among the experienced conjunctions? Were conjunctions merely temporal phenomena, they would all be of the same type, and there could exist among them but gradual differences. May the conjunction which exists between a conclusion and its premises be said to be of the same type as that between an actual thought and a previous one, the latter being retained at the moment of the former but quite irrelevant to it? The problem as to whether there is but one or several types of conjunctions leads to a *field theory* of consciousness. By the latter is meant an investigation into the form or forms of organization prevailing among those facts which at any given moment appear to consciousness. This study of the forms of organization in consciousness permits an approach to the problem of the qualification of one item by its context. Those types of contexts in which the item preserves its identity must be differentiated from those in which the item is so modified by what surrounds it as to be in one context different from what it would be in another.

# 13 / Contribution to the Phenomeno-
## logical Theory of Perception *

THE CONCEPT OF *perceptual adumbration* (*Wahrneh-mungsabschattung*) is so central to the phenomenological theory of perception that the discussion of all problems concerning the phenomenology of perception must take its departure from that concept.

The doctrine of perceptual adumbration is based on the obvious fact that every particular perception of a thing is relative to a determinate standpoint and occurs under certain circumstances and conditions. The perceived thing is seen from this or that side, appears under the aspect corresponding to the standpoint at which the perceiving subject happens to be placed. Furthermore, the thing presents itself in a certain orientation relative to the observer and his standpoint as near or far, as at the center of the visual field or more toward the periphery, etc. Finally, the manner of appearance of the perceived thing varies according to whether it is seen in bright daylight or at dusk, in a fog, and so forth. What has been said is by no means limited to visual perceptions alone. The note which a singer holds or which comes from a radio sounds different depending on whether we are in the same room as the source of the sound, hear it from the next room through a closed door, and so on. We make the assumption—essential for our purpose and possible in principle—that during the entire time no objective change of the note occurs: it is the same note which sounds the whole time, only appearing differently according to the varying circumstances.

With the foregoing we refer to the one-sidedness of every particular perception, which consists in the perceived thing presenting itself under *one among many possible* adumbrations, manners of appearance and exhibition. Although we speak at the beginning of this one-

* This article originally appeared in *Zeitschrift für philosophische Forschung,* XIII (1959).

sidedness as a fact, it is not to be understood as "mere fact" in the sense of a contingency which, perchance, originates in the imperfection of human mental and sensuous organization, as though things could be different in the case of a better or higher organization.[1] According to Husserl, this one-sidedness belongs essentially and necessarily to each particular perception of a spatial thing and event taking place in space (e.g., to the sounding note).[2] The notion that a perception would not be related to any standpoint, that the perceived thing would not be exhibited in it in any perspectival adumbration, or that the thing would appear in all possible adumbrations at once (or even simultaneously in a plurality of possible adumbrations) cannot be framed by any manner or means and thus proves utterly absurd. Whenever this one-sidedness is ascertained in a particular perception chosen at random, this observed fact is to be understood as an example or special case of a universal law, as a manifestation of an eidetic necessity. Furthermore, we must emphasize that the one-sidedness of which we speak, even when its eidetic necessity is taken into account, is not established from a standpoint outside or above the particular perception in question. It is not as though an observer, standing outside the perception and making it a topic for study, would discover the one-sidedness as eidetically necessary. Such an observer could be the perceiving subject himself, provided that he placed himself outside his own perceptions, reflectively looked at them, compared them with each other, etc.—in a word, studied them in an attitude comparable to that in which we can ascertain the deformation of our own memories in the course of time (possibly with the aid of documents in which the remembered event is recorded as it actually occurred). The one-sidedness of a particular perception is thus not established from without; rather, it belongs to the perception's phenomenal features.[3] *That perception is experienced in itself as one-sided* purports, and must purport, that *the perceived thing appears under a certain aspect but presents itself as susceptible of being perceived under different aspects.* This signifies, in turn, that *among the phenomenal features of the perception under consideration, references to further perceptions are included* through which the perceived

1. Husserl, *Ideen zur einer reinen Phänomenologie und phänomenologischen Philosophie*, ed. W. Biemel (*Husserliana*, Vol. III [The Hague, 1950]), I, p. 77. Hereafter cited as *Ideen*. The page numbers refer to the original edition, found in the margin of the *Husserliana* edition.

2. *Ibid.*, pp. 10, 315.

3. Let us note in passing that the disclosure of one-sidedness from "without," i.e., by a subsequent reflection directed to the perception, is possible only because the perception has already been previously experienced as one-sided before and independent of all reflection. For the performance and problematic of reflection, into which we cannot enter further here, see *ibid.*, §§ 77ff.

thing can appear under the several aspects possible for it.[4] This corresponds in fact to the phenomenal findings: what we perceive, to name one instance, is a house which we see from the front and which, through this very particular perception, presents itself as perceivable from other sides. We do not, however, simply perceive the front as though all relations to further possibilities of perception were cut off, as, for example, when we see a photograph of the front. Just as the one-sidedness of every particular perception is an eidetic necessity, so also is the phenomenon of reference in which that one-sidedness finds its phenomenal manifestation.[5]

The one-sidedness of every particular perception determines the sense of its *inadequacy*. Inadequacy concerns perception in the latter's presentative function, i.e., as apprehension of its object.[6] This, however, still does not do full justice to inadequacy. If each perception contains references to further perceptions through which the perceived thing presents itself under varying aspects, then this is not to be understood in the sense of full determinateness of these aspects. Even when it is a matter of a wholly familiar thing, one will hardly ever succeed in rousing fully and totally determinate images of the other aspects under which the thing can appear.[7] That the references under discussion are affected by indeterminedness in the case of only relatively familiar things is self-evident, not to speak of a completely new and unknown object when the perception in question is the first acquaintance with this object. It might seem that in the latter case the actual perception contains no references at all and that the unfamiliarity and novelty of the object manifest themselves phenomenally just in the absence of such references. This would be tantamount to asserting that the new and unknown object is completely exhausted for perceiving consciousness in one of its manners of appearance and exhibition, that the perceptual experience of it simply coincides with one of its adumbrational presentations, so that the question does not

---

4. *Ibid.*, pp. 77f.: ". . . Räumliches Sein . . . kann nur 'erscheinen' in einer gewissen 'Orientierung', mit welcher notwendig vorgezeichnet sind systematische Möglichkeiten für immer neue Orientierungen, deren jeder wiederum entspricht eine gewisse 'Erscheinungsweise', die wir etwa ausdrücken als Gegebenheit von der und der 'Seite' usw." Cf. also Husserl, *Cartesian Meditations*, trans. D. Cairns (The Hague, 1960), p. 44; Husserl, *Die Krisis der Europäischen Wissenschaften und die transzendentale Phänomenologie*, ed. W. Biemel (*Husserliana*, Vol. VI [The Hague, 1954]), § 45. (The latter is hereafter cited as *Krisis*.)

5. For this, see also A. Gurwitsch, *The Field of Consciousness* (Pittsburgh, 1964), Pt. IV, chap. I, 2.

6. For inadequacy in this sense, cf. Husserl, *Ideen*, I, pp. 10, 78, 297f., 310.

7. As we shall remark later (below, p. 343f.), the occurrence of such images is not essential for the reference-phenomenon as such, of which we speak here; but they play a role for explicating and rendering perception distinct, especially with respect to the perceptual noema.

arise at all as to how the object would look were it seen from another standpoint. In other words, there would be given a visual phantom but not the perceptual appearance of a spatial thing which, in the course of a perceptual *process,* presents itself from different sides.

The example of a completely unknown object—pre-eminently suited for bringing out the eidetic necessity of the reference-phenomenon—immediately shows that the indeterminacy, no matter how far it may reach, is never total. It is not as though no anticipations whatever were possible with respect to that which further perception yields, so that one would have to prepare oneself for anything and everything. The thing shows a certain shape, coloring, smoothness or roughness, and the like, at the side from which it appears at present. It is uncertain which form, which chromatic and tactile qualities the thing exhibits at sides from which it is not—not yet—perceived. But it is determined throughout that the thing has at those sides *some* form or other, *some* coloration or other, some tactile quality or other.[8] Thus, a definite range is circumscribed, the detailed filling in of which remains, however, undetermined. Certain possibilities exist for this filling in; but on the basis of the present perception, not only can no choice between these possibilities be made, but also no one of them appears as favored in some sense or other over against the others.[9]

The range which, in a certain sense, is determined, still can be more or less narrow or broad depending on relative acquaintedness or unacquaintedness with the perceived thing in question. Its indeterminateness concerning only the manner in which it is filled in hangs together with the fact that each object is perceived in the light of a certain typicality and is, by this means, essentially qualified as that as which it appears.[10] No perception is exhausted by what, in the rigorous and proper sense, is seen, heard, touched, etc. That which is given in genuine sense experience lies, as Husserl expresses it, in an "inner horizon," which functions for the perception in question as sense-determining or co-determining.[11] Every perception contains more than what merely falls into direct sense experience proper, or, in Husserl's formulation: "at any moment, this something meant" (*dieses Vermeinte*) in this perception "is more—something meant with something more—than what is meant at that moment 'explicitly' "—an

8. Husserl, *Cartesian Meditations,* p. 45.

9. In his *Erfahrung und Urteil* (Hamburg, 1954), § 21c, Husserl calls possibilities of this kind "open possibilities."

10. On the perceptual appearance of an object in the light of typicality, see *ibid.,* § 8.

11. The term "inner horizon" does not seem to us to be fortunately chosen, since, as will be shown later on, it really concerns only the noetic, not noematic, side of the phenomenon.

"intending-beyond-itself" (*Über-sich-hinaus-meinen*) which essentially belongs to perception.[12] The appearance of the object in the light of a certain typicality, the intervention of the "more" in the present perception, is exemplified by the perception of the object as a spatial thing *simpliciter* whose properties still remain largely undetermined, or, more specifically, by its perception as a machine whose purpose and functioning remain, however, completely unknown. A further example is the perception of a residential building whose architectural form is prominent only in gross and whose internal organization remains almost completely in the dark; yet it is determined that the building has *some* inner organization and that the latter must be in agreement with its total architectural form, and so forth.

Corresponding to the relative familiarity of the perceived object is the greater or lesser specification of the type in question. Unfamiliarity with the object thus does not purport lack of references; it purports their vagueness and emptiness, their want of specification. Obviously the typicality depends on the past of the perceiving subject—with which, however, we only indicate a problem.[13]

Finally, we must mention that the specification of the typicality is motivated by what is given in genuine sense experience in the present perception.[14] Let us suppose that we see a house for the first time and that we see it from the front. Since what we perceive is a building, the present perception contains references to the total architectural form of the house, to aspects under which it presents itself when it is seen from other sides, etc. No matter to what extent all these references may be undetermined, they are also specified in the sense that the total architectural form must be such that it can comprise the now-seen front as a part of itself, that the aspects under which the house appears when seen from other standpoints must harmoniously fit together with each other as well as with that aspect under which the house now presents itself. The *indeterminacy of references* can be described in full universality as follows: it *involves the way of detailed concretization of a type which, to be sure, can still be undetermined to a greater or lesser extent but is never totally undetermined. The concretization must satisfy a further restrictive condition—namely, that of agreement and harmony with both the present perception and*

12. Husserl, *Cartesian Meditations*, p. 46.
13. The problem does not concern the undeniable fact that past experience influences present perception, but instead it involves the way in which this influence is to be understood. We cannot enter further into the problem here, which, however, must be pointed out as such.
14. For the specific phenomenological sense of the concept of "motivation," see Husserl, *Ideen*, I, pp. 84f., 89f., 292.

*what is known about the perceived object from earlier experience.*[15]
Such knowledge about the object in question stemming from earlier
experience can and does figure in the present perception in the form of
references it includes to relatively determined aspects when the object
is experienced as known in many respects but is still unknown in
others.

The inadequacy of every particular perception thus consists not
only in its one-sidedness but also in that in every *"manner of
appearance . . . a core of 'what is actually exhibited'* (is) apprehended as surrounded by a *horizon of inauthentic 'co-givenness'* and
more or less vague *indeterminacy,"* the latter to be understood as
*"determinability of a fixed, prescribed style."* [16] Indeed, if every
perception refers to further perceptions, then a perception is related
not only to those through which the object appears again from sides
already known but also to such perceptions through which the object
will be determined above and beyond what is yielded by the present
perception. Accordingly, the phenomenology of perception finds itself
referred from single acts to perceptual concatenations.[17] Corresponding to every perceptual thing as well as to each of its properties
and determinations (e.g., its color, form, tactile qualities, etc.), there
is a multiplicity, or, more correctly stated, "a multiform system of
continuous multiplicities of appearances and adumbrations in which
all . . . objective moments are exhibited or adumbrated in definite
continua." [18] That these multiplicities form a system purports that
their members do not just co-exist with one another accidentally,
arbitrarily, or in any other merely external way. Instead, these
multiplicities are organized in a definite way so that the single
perceptions entering into them become *phases of a unitary process*
which, for its part, functions as a "continuously unitary, self-confirm-
ing experiential consciousness of the identical thing." [19] A "synthesis
of identification" is established between the perceptual phases—i.e., a

15. For the detailed presentation of this state of affairs we refer to our
*The Field of Consciousness,* Pt. IV, chap. II, 3.
16. Husserl, *Ideen,* I, p. 80.
17. .*Ibid.,* p. 205: ". . . Wahrnehmung (ist) nicht ein leeres Gegenwärtigha-
ben des Gegenstandes . . . es (gehört) . . . zum eigenen Wesen der Wahrnehmung . . . , 'ihren' Gegenstand . . . als Einheit eines *gewissen* noematischen
Bestandes zu haben, der für andere Wahrnehmungen vom 'selben' Gegenstande
immer wieder ein anderer, aber immer ein wesensmässig vorgezeichneter
ist . . . es (gehört) zum Wesen des jeweiligen, objektiv so und so bestimmten
Gegenstandes . . . , gerade in Wahrnehmungen solcher deskriptiven Artung
noematischer zu sein und nur in ihnen es sein zu können."
18. Husserl, *Ideen,* I, § 41; *Cartesian Meditations,* § 17; *Krisis,* § 45.
19. Husserl, *Ideen,* I, pp. 74f.

*"connectedness that makes the unity of one consciousness,* in which
the unity of an intentional objectivity, as the 'same' objectivity
belonging to multiple modes of appearance, becomes 'constituted.' " [20]
From the standpoint of Husserlian constitutive phenomenology, any
object whatever, any entity, not merely the perceptual thing, is
universally treated as a "clue" or "index" for a systematically organized multiplicity of manners of appearance and presentation.[21] To
express it differently, this multiplicity is the "equivalent of consciousness of the respective kind of 'reality,' " the "equivalent correlate" corresponding to the object in question.[22] ". . . According to
absolutely fixed essential laws the existing object ⟨is⟩ the correlate . . . for concatenations of consciousness of an entirely definite
essential content, just as, conversely, the being of concatenations of
the structure mentioned is equivalent with the existing object." [23] That
correlation emerges as one of the central problems and themes of
constitutive phenomenology.[24] The task is to understand how the
multiplicities in question, owing to their inner organization, function
as consciousness of *one* object presenting itself from different sides
yet appearing as identical in and through these diverse manners of
presentation.[25]

For the sake of completeness, we indicate, though only in passing,
a third sense of inadequacy of perceptual experience. This results
from the presumptive character of perceptual evidence not only in
relation to single perceptions but also in relation to every finite
perceptual process.[26]

On the basis of the foregoing presentation of Husserl's adumbrational theory of perception we can now introduce his concept of
*perceptual noema.* Obviously, the perceptual noema makes up a
special case of the general concept of *noema at large.* With the
doctrine of the noema we find ourselves in the midst of Husserl's
theory of *intentionality.*

That an act of consciousness is intentional, is directed to an object,

20. Husserl, *Cartesian Meditations,* § 18. In *Krisis,* p. 161, Husserl prefers to
speak of a "synthesis of unification" instead of "identification." Cf. also his
comment in *Ideen,* I, p. 78: "Im Wesensbau dieser Mannigfaltigkeiten liegt
es . . . , dass sie Einheit eines *einstimmig gebenden* Bewusstseins herstellen, und
zwar von dem *einen,* immer vollkommener, von immer neuen Seiten, nach immer
reicheren *Bestimmungen* erscheinenden Wahrnehmungsdinge."
21. Husserl, *Cartesian Meditations,* § 21; *Krisis,* §§ 38, 41, 48, 50.
22. Husserl, *Ideen,* I, p. 319 and § 142. See also § 135.
23. *Ibid.,* p. 177.
24. Cf. G. Funke, *Zur Transzendentalen Phänomenologie* (Bonn, 1957), pp.
42ff.
25. Husserl, *Ideen,* I, §§ 86, 150.
26. *Ibid.,* §§ 46, 138, 143, 149; Husserl, *Cartesian Meditations,* § 28.

is experienced as consciousness "of" an object, signifies not only that an object is presented through that act of consciousness but also that the object is presented in a certain manner or fashion. Not only is the object intended (*gemeint*) in the act, but it is also meant (*vermeint*) as this or that. Acts directed to the same object can, with respect to the manner in which it is meant, still differ one from the other. If at one time we conceive 3 < 4 and, at another time, 4 > 3, then both times we deal with the same relational state of affairs (object), apprehended the one time from the standpoint of one of its members, the other time from the standpoint of its other member. Similarly, the representations "Victor at Austerlitz" and "Vanquished at Waterloo" are related to the same person, although he is represented in different roles, under different aspects, in a different light.[27] By *noema* Husserl understands not the *object simpliciter,* as it is in itself, per se, but *the object as it is meant,* the object just—precisely just, but also only just —as it appears through the act of consciousness in question, as it is apprehended and intended through this act, the object in the perspective, orientation, illumination, and role in which it presents itself.[28] Other and briefer designations for this are expressions such as "the meant as such" (*das Vermeinte als solches*), "that of which there is consciousness as such" (*das Bewusste als solches*), or, in Husserl's later manner of speaking, the *"cogitatum qua cogitatum."* [29] The concept of noema has universal significance so far as it is operative in acts of all kinds, in all acts of perception, remembering, representing, willing, judging, etc.[30]

27. In the sphere of linguistic expression the difference which we have in mind here corresponds to that between the object named by the expression and the meaning of the expression; cf. Husserl, *Logische Untersuchungen* (Halle, 1913), II, i, § 12.

28. For Husserl's concept of noema in general and perceptual noema in particular see *Ideen,* I, §§ 87ff.

29. Husserl, *Cartesian Meditations,* §§ 14ff.

30. It is of historical, although not only historical, interest to mention the fact that the concept of judicative noema had already been anticipated in a certain way by W. James. In *The Principles of Psychology* (New York, 1890), I, p. 275, James introduces the concept of the "object of thought" and defines it as follows: "The object of every thought . . . is neither more nor less than all that the thought thinks, exactly as the thought thinks it, however complicated the matter, and however symbolic the manner of thinking may be." Using the example of the sentence, "Columbus discovered America in 1492," James argues that the entire sentence must be considered as "object," while Columbus, America, the discovery of America form the "topic" or "subject of discourse." We can compare this to Husserl's description of the judicative noema, especially his distinction between what is judged (*Geurteilte*) and what is judged about (*Beurteilte*). *Ideen,* I, p. 194: ". . . *Das gesamte geurteilte Was* und zudem genau so genommen, mit der *Charakterisierung,* in der *Gegebenheitsweise,* in der es im Erlebnis 'Bewusstes' ist, bildet das *volle noematische Korrelat,* den . . . 'Sinn' des Urteilserlebnisses. Prägnanter gesprochen, ist es der 'Sinn im Wie seiner Gegebenheitsweise,' soweit

In the *Logische Untersuchungen,* in which the term "noema" does not yet appear, Husserl speaks of the "matter of the act" as the "sense of the apprehension of the object" or the "apprehensional sense." [31] Not only does it depend upon the "matter" that "the act apprehends the object in question, but *what* the act apprehends the object *as* also depends on the matter—which features, relations, categorial forms it imputes by itself to it." In the *Ideen,* in which Husserl has overcome the noetic orientation, i.e., the orientation towards the acts (which had prevailed in the *Logische Untersuchungen*), the concept of "matter" is transformed into the concept of noema: more precisely, the concept of the "noematic sense," where "noematic sense" designates a core in the full, concrete noema. [32]

In the present context this "core" holds a special interest. Expressing it again in the language of the *Logische Untersuchungen,* the difference between noema and object can be formulated as that between the "object as it is intended" (*so wie er intendiert ist*) and the "object *simpliciter,* which is intended" (*schlechthin der Gegenstand, welcher intendiert ist*). [33] This terminology offers the advantage of making it clear that for an object to be *meant and intended simpliciter,* it must be intended in a certain way, must be apprehended and *meant as this or that.* In other words, the directedness of the act to the object depends entirely upon the noema to which the act in question corresponds. [34] However, it would be a misunderstanding to construe the noema as an "immanent" or "mental object," as a kind of intermediary entity mediating the act and object. [35] Starting from the distinction between the object as intended and the object *simpliciter,* we are led to contrast *one* "apprehensional sense" in which the object is meant to the totality or the system of "apprehensional senses" in

---

diese an ihm als Charakter vorfindlich ist." What James calls "topic" corresponds precisely to what Husserl calls the judged-about or the "object-about-which" (*Gegenstand worüber*), one judges.

31. Husserl, *Logische Untersuchungen,* 2d ed., II, pp. 415f.

32. Husserl, *Ideen,* I, §§ 129f.

33. Husserl, *Logische Untersuchungen,* II, pp. 400f.

34. In *Ideen,* I, §§ 87ff., Husserl explicitly emphasized that the noema is no real part, element, or component of the act, of the noesis. Consequently, the noema's "being contained" in the noesis is to be understood not in the sense of the relation of part to whole but in the sense of a correlation, to which the frequently used expression, "intentional correlate," also points. In our article, "On the Intentionality of Consciousness" (see above, pp. 124ff.), we have tried to show that the central phenomenon of the intentionality of consciousness is this correlation, in which, fundamentally, a single identical noema corresponds to an indefinite multiplicity of acts distinguishable from one another.

35. In this connection, see Husserl, *Logische Untersuchungen,* II, v, § 11; *Ideen,* I, § 90.

which the object can be meant. Accordingly, the relation between noema and object comes to be defined precisely as that between a member of a system and the system as a whole.[36] Because the noema is defined as the object as it presents itself, in contrast to the object as it is in itself, a rigorous descriptive orientation must be followed in the description and analysis of the noema. The object as it presents itself must be taken *precisely* just, but also *only* just, as it appears through the act of consciousness in question, as it is meant and intended by that act. Any moment which figures in a noema must be allowed for, and it must be taken into account in the role which it plays for the concrete noema in question and at the place which it occupies in its total structure. On the other hand, nothing must be imputed to a noema unless it can be found in its structure.

The concept of the perceptual noema results from the general concept of noema at large by suitable specialization. The noema at large being defined as that which is meant as such, the perceptual noema must, accordingly, be determined as the "perceived as such." [37] It turns out to be the perceived thing, just as it presents itself through a concrete act of perception—namely, as appearing from a certain side, in a certain perspective, orientation, etc. In this sense all *manners of appearance and presentation* which we mentioned above in connection with the adumbrational theory of perception are to be considered as *perceptual noemata*. As to the multiplicities, to which the phenomenology of perception finds itself referred with regard to any single thing, they obviously are multiplicities of both noemata and noeses: the thing itself appears as a unity over against the noetic and noematic multiplicities related to it.[38] Furthermore, we note in passing that the noetic multiplicity turns out to be multi-dimensional in comparison with the noematic multiplicity so far as every noema— i.e., every single member of the noematic multiplicity—is itself coordinate to an indefinite multiplicity of noeses.

At the beginning we mentioned the essential one-sidedness of every particular perception of a thing and emphasized that, just by virtue of the references to other perceptions of the same thing contained in it, the perception in question is experienced as one-sided. Since, as mentioned, noematic observation must adopt a strictly descriptive orientation, it is incumbent upon it to account and allow for the phenomenon of references in the description and analysis of

36. For the special case of the relation between the perceptual noema and the perceived thing, see Gurwitsch, *The Field of Consciousness*, pp. 218f., 221ff.
37. The expression stems from Husserl, *Ideen*, I, pp. 182ff.
38. Cf. *ibid.*, pp. 207f.

the perceptual noema. References relate to aspects under which the thing can appear but under which it does not presently appear. In other words, the references are to noemata to which perceptions other than the present one correspond. This purports that *in the concrete perceptual noema under consideration, further noemata are contained or present in a certain way*, the sense of being contained and being present deriving from the fact that what is in question are *references* to these other noemata. Hence the following question arises: how are we to understand a thus determined containedness of other noemata in the total structure of a randomly chosen noema?

Husserl has dealt with the phenomenon pre-eminently, if not exclusively, from a noetic point of view.[39] He, for example, characterizes the sides of the perceptual thing which are "also meant" (*mitgemeint*) and to which the "genuinely perceived sides" refer as "not yet perceived but only anticipated and, at first, with a non-intuitional emptiness (as the sides that are 'coming' now perceptually)." Quite generally, Husserl speaks of "potentialities" belonging to consciousness which are "implied" in every actual mental state. By these potentialities he means possible perceptions—namely, such as I can experience or expect to experience when I move my eyes or head in another way, when I orient myself in another way with respect to the thing than I do now, when I observe it from a standpoint different from my present one, and so forth. Likewise, when we remember a thing which we earlier perceived from a certain side, there comes into play an awareness of aspects under which we could have perceived the thing if we, at that time, had comported ourselves in our perceptual activity in the appropriate manner with regard to the thing. What determines the sense for all these potentialities is, according to Husserl, consciousness of "I do," "I can," "I can do otherwise than I do": in other words, consciousness that their actualization is at least dependent in principle on the experiencing and perceiving subject.

To speak of a horizon, an "inner horizon," seems thoroughly apt with respect to the noetic side of the phenomenon. It expresses the fact that the present perception does not stand alone but is surrounded and accompanied by retentions and protentions—in short, by potentialities of consciousness. Accompaniment must not be understood in the external sense of mere simultaneous occurrence. Instead, potentialities are intertwined and interwoven with consciousness in the mode of actuality in such an intimate way as to become co-determining of the sense of what is yielded by actual consciousness. Actual consciousness is inserted into and imbedded in potentialities such that only in this

39. For what follows, see Husserl, *Cartesian Meditations*, § 19.

horizon does it fully become what it is experienced as being.[40] It would be, it seems, completely within the sense of Husserl's intent to say that, taken in full concreteness, the act of perception comprises both perception in the genuine sense and potentialities; moreover, the distinction between actual and potential consciousness can be made only within this concrete whole.

The question previously raised by us concerns the noematic parallel to what is described noetically as the "inner horizon." Considering Husserl's insistence, since the *Ideen,* on noetico-noematic parallelism, this question not only appears justified on the basis of his conception but seems pre-emptory. Husserl's noetic analyses suggest seeing the noematic correlate of the potentialities of consciousness in representations and images accompanying that noema—again, obviously, not in the external sense of a mere juxtaposition but in the sense of a concrete relatedness. Thus, one could speak of a noematic inner horizon so far as what is given in actual and genuine perception, the perceptual noema in the pregnant sense, finds its expansion and continuation in the components of the noematic inner horizon and in this manner is co-determined by horizonal components. To speak of references would, indeed, have here a prevalently noetic sense, indicating the possible actualization of the potentialities of consciousness as left to the freedom of the perceiving subject.

This conception of the noematic inner horizon may account for the perceptual noema *if and to the extent that it is explicated.* Of "phenomenological explication" of the perceived as such, Husserl says that it "makes clear what is included and only non-intuitively co-intended in the sense of the cogitatum (for example, the 'other side'), by making present in phantasy the potential perceptions that would make the invisible visible." [41] In the course of this explication, there

40. Husserl, *Krisis,* p. 152: ". . . Das jeweils aktive Bewusste und korrelativ das aktive Bewussthaben, Darauf-gerichtet-, Damit-beschäftigt-sein (ist) immerfort umspielt von einer Atmosphäre stummer, verborgener, aber mitfungierender Geltungen, von einem *lebendigen Horizont.* . . ." It is noteworthy that this description characterizes horizonal consciousness as such and, therefore, applies to both the "inner" and "outer" horizon. Husserl, to be sure, has established the distinction between the two kinds of horizon both terminologically and conceptually (cf. *Krisis,* p. 165, and Husserl, *Erfahrung und Urteil,* pp. 26ff.) without, however, pursuing the matter sufficiently. In our *The Field of Consciousness,* Pt. V, 9, we have tried to analyze this difference in greater detail.

41. Husserl, *Cartesian Meditations,* p. 48. The whole of § 20, which describes the "peculiar nature of intentional analysis" as opening up the "horizon structure belonging to every intentionality," is, similarly, primarily noetically oriented. The opening up is presented as the disclosure of "noetic multiplicities of consciousness and their synthetic unity," as "penetrating the anonymous 'cogitative' life," as uncovering the "*definite* synthetic courses of the manifold modes of consciousness and . . . modes of Ego comportment," and the like.

may appear more or less intuitive images of what will be yielded in the mode of originary experience through further perceptions of the thing in question. However, the phenomenon under discussion is by no means a product of the explication. If we perceive a house, it is, to be sure, seen only from a certain side; but it presents itself through this very perception as perceivable from other sides unseen at the moment. Let us recall that the perceivableness of the house under further aspects belongs to the noematic sense of the particular perception, essentially one-sided and experienced as one-sided. In a strict descriptive orientation the perceived as such is to be described here as a house presenting itself perceptually from a certain side among other possible sides. But that holds prior to all explication and independently of whether the perception in question and its noema are explicated at all. On the other hand, the occurrence of images of just those unseen sides of the house is, certainly, not essential for the perception and its noema. Even the complete absence of such images in no way impairs the perception and its perceptual noema, as can be seen in any example whatever of perceptual experience.[42] Our problem concerns the structural moment of the perceptual noema by virtue of which other noemata are contained in the former, and it also concerns the sense of this containedness.

To advance this problem it appears opportune to resort to lines of thought and concepts borrowed from Gestalt theory, or at least which can be developed in affiliation with it.[43] According to Gestalt theory a percept must not be considered as consisting in and being composed of parts or elements, nor must it be conceived as divisible into such elements. Elements have traditionally been characterized by their isolation and independence from one another. This purports that each element has properties and determinations belonging to it in itself and which it possesses in its own right, totally irrespective of other elements with which it might happen to be conjoined. Such conjoining can mean no more than the occurring together of the elements in question. The properties peculiar to, and characteristic of, any of the several elements are in no way affected by such occurring together. Each one of them preserves its phenomenal identity when it is transplanted from one set of elements into another, and it would even retain its phenomenal identity in the case of complete isolation—if such could ever be realized at all.

42. Probably one of the first to point out the irrelevance of such images was G. F. Stout, *Analytic Psychology* (1896), II, pp. 5, 21ff., and *A Manual of Psychology*, 4th ed. (London, 1929), pp. 205ff.

43. Because of the lack of space we refer here for what follows to the presentation we have given in our *The Field of Consciousness*, Pt. II, esp. 6, 8, 10–11, of Gestalt theory in view of its application to phenomenological problems.

In opposition to the traditional view, which rests on the self-sufficiency of elements, or, more correctly stated, takes this self-sufficiency for granted, Gestalt theory sees in the parts of percepts whole-parts (*Ganzteile*) or, to follow Wertheimer, " 'parts' in whole-processes" (*Ganzvorgänge*).[44] Each such part is related essentially to the whole to which it belongs so far as it plays a definite, specific role in and for it—a role assigned to it by the structure of the percept as a whole, and which only has sense within this whole. In figuring in a definite place within the whole in the role characteristic for it, the part in its turn contributes to the percept as a whole according to the measure of importance of its role. Any elementary musical context, melodic as well as rhythmic, may serve to illustrate this state of affairs. Any part which occurs within such a context fulfills a certain specific function: e.g., the function of the initial phase of an ascending tonal movement. The note exists with and in a functional significance characteristic for it and defined in terms of the context in question. On the other hand, by its occurrence at a certain place in the context and by virtue of the functional significance characterizing it, the note makes its specific contribution to the structure of the context as a whole—that contribution which is possible and requisite at that definite place.

Quite in general: *every part actualizes the whole, whose part it is, at its place and in the manner which corresponds to its functional significance.* To emphasize the point, this must be understood in a twofold way. By virtue of its own peculiar structure the whole imposes conditions on its parts and requires at the places in question parts of a certain entirely definite functional significance rather than some other; it prescribes to the parts the roles they have to play. But for a part to be given in its own peculiar role and functional significance, it requires a whole structured in a definite way and thus, in turn, prescribes conditions for the whole into which the part, characterized by its functional significance, can be integrated. Both formulations express the same state of affairs seen from different sides.

The foregoing sketchy presentation of the Gestalt theoretical conception requires two important supplements.

I. At the outset, we must avoid misunderstanding by stating that the characteristics which accrue to the parts from the whole—we comprise them here under the heading of functional significance for the whole—are not properties, so to speak, of a higher order—i.e., such as are added to certain fundamental qualities, presupposing the

44. M. Wertheimer, "Untersuchungen zur Lehre von der Gestalt," *Psychologische Forschung*, I (1922), p. 52.

latter and superimposing themselves upon them. One is tempted to consider as fundamental qualities those which the part possesses in and for itself, independently of any context, thus those which the part exhibits when it is isolated as far as possible. The achievement of Gestalt theory does not consist in having discovered properties bestowed on parts by wholes, as though they were additional properties among others. Gestalt theory maintains, instead, that parts not only have their functional significance but are qualified by it, existing only in and with it. *Each part possesses its phenomenal qualification exclusively as the bearer of its role and function; by functional significance and only by it does a part become determined as to what it is in concreto within an organized totality.* A part's phenomenal being is defined by and coincides with its functional significance. There can be no question of a part preserving its phenomenal identity when it is removed and isolated from its context or when it is transferred from one context to another—even though in all these cases the objective stimuli may be the same. If a note which, objectively speaking, is the same, occurs in two different musical contexts, it is often phenomenally changed to the point where it is unrecognizable.

2. According to Gestalt theory, the whole cannot be separated from its parts; it is not something "over and above" them, nor is it added to them "from without." The whole is nothing else but the totality of the parts, taken in their full determinedness and qualification by their respective functional significances—to the extent that each part is what, and only what, its functional significance makes it to be. To express it more pregnantly: *the whole is the system of functional significances mutually dependent upon and attuned to one another.* Such a system needs no special unifying factors since it has its unity from within and in itself by virtue of its own peculiar organizational form. In a system organized along such lines, "all parts mutually support each other;" in so doing, each one of them possesses "its place and property as part of a whole." [45] Earlier we said that each part has its functional significance for the whole in terms of which the functional significance is defined. We can now make this more precise: the functional significance of any part is essentially related to that of other parts and determined by such relatedness. By virtue of this form of organization operative between them, the other parts set conditions for each *locus* in the system which they fashion, and they set these conditions for the sake of the inner coherence of the system. Conversely, the functional significance of any part motivates requirements concerning the system as a whole, i.e., all the other parts in

45. K. Koffka, "Psychologie," in *Lehrbuch der Philosophie*, ed. Max Dessoir (Berlin, 1925), II, p. 551.

their respective functional significances. In thoroughgoing reciprocity, all parts determine and condition one another.

Let us apply this conception of Gestalt theory to the analysis of the perceptual noema.[46] The latter is defined as the perceived as such, as the thing appearing from a certain side, taken just and precisely just as it offers itself through the perception in question. Stated noematically, the one-sidedness of every perception, phenomenally manifested in references to further perceptions, purports that the corresponding noema contains "more" than merely what is given in genuine sense experience, i.e., what is directly given.

It is now the task to interpret this "more" of which Husserl speaks from the standpoint of Gestalt theory, or to so reinterpret it that it loses its quantitative sense.[47] When we perceive a house from a certain standpoint, part of an architectural form is given to us in genuine sense experience, and *what is thus given appears as a part.* According to the Gestalt theoretical view concerning the relation of part and whole, the seen part has its functional significance with regard to the total architectural form, hence also with respect to the parts of this form, unseen at the present moment; and this functional significance determines and qualifies the seen part, making it into what it phenomenally is. If aspects under which the perceived thing can, but does not at the present moment, appear, are contained, present, represented, and the like in the actual aspect, that is to be understood neither in the sense of the supervention of accompanying images nor as though other noemata were somehow enclosed or encased in the noema in question. *Containedness purports nothing else than that the present perceptual noema is phenomenally constituted by its relatedness to those other noemata, or at least co-constituted, that it exhibits this relatedness as one of the determinations and qualities peculiar to it, as one of the moments which belong to its phenomenal qualification.*

The corresponding noetic correlate is the Husserlian inner horizon or what he calls potentialities of consciousness—namely, references to further perceptions by which the noemata in question can be actualized. Whether one also speaks of a *noematic inner horizon* is a mere terminological question. At any event, this manner of speaking must not be permitted to convey the idea that what is given in genuine sense experience is only imbedded in a horizon and appears in its

46. In our essay "Phenomenology of Thematics and of the Pure Ego" (section I, Appendix), we have attempted to present the justification for utilizing descriptive results of Gestalt theory for phenomenological problems and to point out the noematic relevance of these results.

47. See above, pp. 335f.

perspective while yet retaining a certain independence and separableness with regard to the horizon. Precisely the opposite is the case here. The noematic inner horizon, if we use this term, does not *surround* what appears in genuine sense experience but rather *pervades* and *permeates it*. What is given in genuine sense experience presents itself as a member of a system, becoming what it phenomenally is by its relatedness to the system, by the role which it plays in it, by its significance for it. From the noematic point of view, reference does not have the sense of a supervenient component, but that of an inherent and immanent moment belonging to phenomenal qualification.

From the noematic point of view, Gestalt theoretical interpretation also allows us to account for that indeterminacy by which every perception is affected.[48] We have seen that this indeterminacy obtains within the more or less precisely delineated boundaries of a certain range. Of primary importance here is the repeatedly emphasized strict reciprocity in the parts or members of the system determining one another. Since a perceived object always appears in the light of a certain typicality, this determinedness as to type (besides all undeterminedness, however extensive, with respect to details) also belongs among the phenomenological and descriptive features of the perceptual noema in question. Consequently, definite conditions are imposed upon the total noematic system in order that the perceptual noema in question may be integrated into and find its place within the system. The aforementioned harmony with the perception experienced at present, understood in formal generality, is the supreme condition. The particular conditions which come into play in the diverse concrete cases, changing from case to case according to their material particularization, are to be considered as various specifications of the supreme formal condition. With regard to the Gestalt theoretical interpretation of the structure of the perceptual noema, the supreme formal condition can be formulated as follows from the noematic point of view: *the total noematic system must be of such a kind as to be capable of receiving the present perceptual noema as a part or member of itself*. We propose to designate this supreme formal noematic condition as the *principle of conformity to sense (Sinneskonformität)*, of which Wertheimer's law of *"good continuation" (kurvengerechte Fortsetzung)* seems to us to be a special case.[49]

Let us now turn our attention from the results attained to the process of perception in whose course the thing in question presents itself from different sides and under changing perspectives. In view of

48. Above, p. 334.
49. Wertheimer, "Untersuchungen zur Lehre von der Gestalt," II, *Psychologische Forschung*, IV (1923), pp. 322ff.

the fact that, noematically speaking, the total system of noemata is to be considered as the "equivalent of consciousness" or the "equivalent correlate" of the perceptual thing,[50] the perceptual process can be characterized as the progressive actualization of one member of the system after the other. However, it must be added that members which were actual in earlier phases lose their actuality in later ones.[51] More correctly perhaps, we may say that in the course of the perceptual process the total noematic system itself and as a whole is actualized, but in the diverse phases of the process from the standpoint of always different members of the system. Since, as established, the relatedness and orientation to the total system, the functional significance for it, make up an essential moment of phenomenal qualification concerning every particular perceptual noema belonging to the system, the perceptual process proves to be a progressive actualizing and unfolding of that very particular perceptual noema. That holds, obviously, for any perceptual noema whatever belonging to the system. Conversely, we can speak from the standpoint of the latter, even in a noematic sense, with Merleau-Ponty of a "contraction of a whole possible process into a single perceptual act." [52] For the sake of simplicity, let us suppose that the perceptual process related to a certain thing takes place smoothly and uninterruptedly, without any revisions or re-determinations. In that case, all phases of the process continue one another and mutually confirm each other. The dynamic development of the process reflects the structure of the perceptual noema as this structure is disclosed in static analysis. Conversely, the static structure of the perceptual noema can be considered as the germinal cell from out of which the process develops in its dynamism.

TRANSLATED BY FREDERICK KERSTEN

50. See above, p. 338.

51. See Husserl, *Ideen,* I, p. 80.

52. M. Merleau-Ponty, *Phénoménologie de la Perception* (Paris, 1945), p. 306. Merleau-Ponty's theory of perception coincides, though broadly, with the present one; this agreement consists more in the descriptive formulation of the phenomenal state of affairs than in the theoretical interpretation. We cannot attempt here a critical discussion of Merleau-Ponty's theory because it would have to be very wide-ranging. It would have to enter into the basis for the divergency which lies in Merleau-Ponty's very differently oriented line of inquiry. He has not undertaken an investigation of perception with respect to its noetico-noematic structure, but instead he has related perception to the organism (*corps phénomenal*), which is considered by him as *"sujet de la perception"* (pp. 235ff.). Accordingly, he refers the structure of perception to corporeal organization (cf. pp. 174ff., 266ff., 366ff.; see also the especially pregnant formulation on p. 216: "L'identité de la chose à travers l'expérience perceptive n'est qu'un autre aspect de l'identité du corps propre au cours des mouvements d'exploration, elle est donc de même sorte qu'elle . . .*"*). We have dealt with a few relevant points in our *The Field of Consciousness,* Pt. IV, chap. III, 5.

# 14 / Philosophical Presuppositions of Logic[1]

LIKE MATHEMATICS, logic may be constructed and developed in the spirit of pure positivity, that is, with inner consistency as the sole concern. Let us take the widest view of logic and define it as the science of possible forms: forms of propositions as well as forms of objects. Among the latter such forms as multiplicities, sets, combinations, permutations, coordinations, relations of every kind, etc., have to be included. In elaborating logic as a positive science, one begins by defining the most elementary forms and the fundamental operations. By applying one of these operations to a given form, a new form is obtained. There is the possibility of indefinite reiteration for every logical operation.[2] When a higher-order form is constituted through the application of a certain operation to a primitive form, that higher-order form can in turn be subjected to the same or a different operation.[3]

Instead of performing permitted operations on elementary forms so as to construct progressively complex ones, one may move in the opposite direction and, starting from a form of some complexity, go back to the more elementary forms from which the given form derives

1. This essay was originally published in *Revue de Métaphysique et de Morale*, LVI (1951). It was reprinted in the collection of essays *Phénoménologie—Existence* (Paris, 1953).

2. On the *law of reiteration*, see Husserl, *Formale und transzendentale Logik* (Halle, 1929), pp. 46, 167. Cited hereafter as *Logik*. In the following analyses we will comment upon and develop some ideas advanced by Husserl in the *Logik* expounded in a masterly fashion by Jean Cavaillès in his *Sur la Logique et la Théorie de la Science*, III, published posthumously by Canguilhem and Ehresmann (Paris, 1947).

3. Cf. Husserl, *Logische Untersuchungen* (Halle, 1913), II, iv, § 13; *Logik*, § 13. In writing the *Logische Untersuchungen*, especially the first volume, Husserl has done more than any other writer to found and justify the autonomy of logic as a positive science.

by construction. In such a procedure one retraces the *history* of the form which was chosen as a point of departure for the regressive movement. So as not to mistake what is meant by history in this sense, let it be emphasized that here it is not a question of history in the empirical or psychological sense. It is not a matter of explaining the mechanism of the process in the course of which the given complex form has actually arisen, a process taking place in a real consciousness under certain conditions and under the influence of diverse factors. Since the validity—that is to say, the mathematical existence of the complex form—depends upon that of the more elementary forms and upon the legitimacy of the operations involved, it follows that every complex form refers, in its very sense, to the more elementary forms and to the operations by means of which it proceeds from these elementary forms. The latter are contained within the complex form. They do not, however, make up a part of its explicit content; rather, they are contained within it as *implications* and *sediments*. It is as referred to, and pointed to, that forms pertaining to a more elementary level are concealed within the unity of meaning which is the complex form. Components of sense and meaning figure within the complex form in a hidden and implicit way but contribute in their silent effectiveness no less essentially to constituting the complex form in question.

When we speak here of analysis, the term must not be taken in its usual sense of a decomposition of a real whole into its real parts. Let us recall that the unities of sense and meaning dealt with by logic and mathematics are not real but ideal entities. The analysis of meanings which Husserl calls *intentional analysis* consists in uncovering the silently effective components of meaning, in rendering implications explicit, in disengaging the sediments, and, finally, in going back to the source in which the sediments take their origin, re-inserting them in the very processes of their formation. Consequently, the history of logical forms, retraced by the regressive method of intentional analysis, reveals itself as a "history of sense," just as the genesis of forms in the course of the process of construction must be understood as a "genesis of sense." It is the specific nature of intentional analysis, as well as that of the structures made discoverable by it, which, it seems to us, led Husserl to his general conception of history, to which Ricoeur has devoted an excellent study.[4]

Pursuing regressive analysis to its limit, with respect to the forms of objects, one arrives at last at individual objects which have not yet undergone any logical or, more precisely, any categorial formation,

4. P. Ricoeur, "Husserl et le sens de l'histoire," *Revue de Métaphysique et de Morale*, LIV (1949).

such as, for example, articulation into parts (but without real division, of course), explication in terms of attributes, putting in relation to other objects, combination with other objects into a multiplicity, and the like. As to the forms of propositions, regressive analysis terminates in simple categorical propositions of the form "S is P." In a proposition of this form, an "ultimate" predicate—that is, one no longer reducible —is attributed to an "ultimate" subject, also irreducible, as, for example, in the proposition "This table is brown." [5] Individual objects, divested of all categorial form, the "ultimate substrates," as Husserl says, are precisely the objects as they present themselves in perceptual experience, prior to all categorial operations, but lending themselves to these operations and serving as their material or basis so that every categorial operation is founded on the perceptual appearance of objects.[6] Furthermore, an "ultimate proposition," in the sense defined, refers to an individual object as it appears in pure perceptual experience; it renders explicit this perceptual appearance and must be taken as the most elementary logical or categorial operation that may be applied to objects given in perceptual experience. In the final reckoning, *regressive analysis leads to perceptual experience prior to all categorial operation,* or, as Husserl calls it, to "pre-predicative experience." [7] Let us add that the objects appearing in pre-predicative experience must, of course, be considered as they present themselves to perceptual consciousness, apart from all *mathematical idealization.* The spatial forms of perceived objects must be taken as they present themselves in their perceptual physiognomy and as determined only in terms of certain morphological types.[8] Perceived spatial forms must not be referred to geometrical ideals, e.g., the "circle," the "straight line," the "sphere," etc., as such notions are conceived in mathematics even at the level of the geometry of Euclid, i.e., in a geometry which is still "intuitive" because it has not yet undergone arithmetization.[9] Although mathematization and geometrical idealization hardly play a role in the analyses which follow, we mention the point because of its importance for the philosophical problems which Husserl raises with regard to geometry and the modern physical sciences.[10]

It is to pre-predicative perceptual experience then that one must

5. Husserl, *Logik,* §§ 82–84.
6. On this subject, see Husserl, *Logische Untersuchungen,* II, vi, chap. VI.
7. Husserl, *Erfahrung und Urteil* (Hamburg, 1954), §§ 4–6.
8. Husserl, *Ideen zu einer reinen Phänomenologie und phänomenologischen Philosophie* (Halle, 1913), I, § 74. Hereafter cited as *Ideen.* See also M. Merleau-Ponty, *Phénoménologie de la Perception* (Paris, 1945), pp. 316–17.
9. Cf. Husserl, *Erfahrung und Urteil,* § 10.
10. Husserl, *Die Krisis der Europäischen Wissenschaften und die transzendentale Phänomenologie* (The Hague, 1954), §§ 8–12.

return for a radical clarification and for the definitive justification of logic. The first task which confronts the philosophical theory of logic consists in accounting for the origin of the "ultimate" categorical propositions in the very pre-predicative experience.[11]

In speaking of the philosophy of logic, we are contrasting it to logic as a technique or as a positive science. Let us define that contrast in a preliminary way. While the technical logician is engaged in constructive work, establishing the techniques of calculation, the philosopher of logic raises questions as to the very sense of the constructive and calculative procedure. *The perceptual world as it presents itself in pre-predicative experience appears* in our analyses *as one of the fundamental presuppositions of logic.*

At the center of the formal sciences, logical as well as mathematical, are such notions as "object," "property," "relation," "plurality," "number," "quantity," "whole," "part," etc. These notions are considered by Husserl as pure forms derived from the concept of "something at large" (*Ableitungsgestalten des Etwas überhaupt*).[12] It must be emphasized that although they refer to objects whose specific and qualitative nature is left indeterminate, the terms which figure in the forms of propositions as well as numbers have reference to objects nonetheless.

As we have sought to bring out, at every level of formalization the very meanings of the terms contain references either to individual objects or to notions which, from the viewpoint of degree of formalization, have to be considered as subordinate. Given the gradation of levels of formalization it becomes apparent that in the final analysis every formal term has reference, either directly or through intermediary referrals, to individual objects which pertain to the world of experience. We are merely expressing the matter differently when we say that mathematics has possible application.

This applicability is not to be thought of as accidental or extrinsic to mathematics. On the contrary, applicability to objects, be it only so far as they are exclusively determined by the formal properties of the relations between them, belongs to mathematics intrinsically, even to purely formal and purely analytic mathematics. This is so because of the very nature of the meanings of the symbols and hence because of the nature of the theorems.[13] To be sure, from the positive viewpoint— that is to say, from the point of view of the constructive elaboration of mathematics—its actual or possible application is without interest.

11. This is precisely one of the main problems to which Husserl devotes a major part of his *Erfahrung und Urteil.*

12. Husserl, *Logische Untersuchungen*, II, p. 252; *Logik*, p. 68.

13. Husserl, *Logik*, § 40.

The effective development of mathematics can indeed be carried out and has in fact been carried out without any question being raised regarding the existence of objects to which mathematics can be applied, a question which is irrelevant indeed from the positive or merely technical point of view. From the viewpoint of philosophical interpretation, however, the relation between purely formal and analytic mathematics and possible objects proves to be highly important, because the *applicability of mathematics betrays its origin in the experience of a world of objects*. Yet this origin must not be considered as a pure empirical fact noted by the historian who, so to speak, follows from without the development of mathematics under the influence of the experience of the world and under the pressure of practical problems imposed by the exigencies of life in the world. On the contrary, it is by way of disclosure and explication of components of meaning contained in the mathematical notions as sediments and in a "concealed" or "silent" form that the reference, imbedded in these notions, to objects of the world comes to be uncovered. When we speak here of historicity, we therefore have in mind *intentional historicity* or *historicity of sense* as the term has been defined. If mathematics has its roots in the experience of the world, it is not solely and above all not chiefly because of the actual course of its development, but by virtue and on account of its very sense. Since the origin of the mathematical disciplines in the experience of the world determines the very sense of their notions, these disciplines have to be defined as sciences concerned with the formal structure of a world—not only and not necessarily of the real world as it is in fact and as we know it, but of a possible world as such. By virtue of its "genesis of sense" analytical mathematics is constituted as the most general science of the form of any possible world *qua* world.

The notion of proposition with which purely analytical logic is mainly concerned is that of a proposition given in the "evidence of distinctness" (*Evidenz der Deutlichkeit*).[14] A proposition is given in the "evidence of distinctness" if it arises or may arise out of a spontaneous synthetic activity of thought, by which the component partial meanings are combined into an articulated unity of meaning which is the meaning of the proposition itself as a whole. To express it in a less atomistic way, one may say that by the spontaneous activity of thought, the partial meanings are grasped, each in its place and contributing function within the articulated unity which is the total meaning. The evidence of distinctness is the originary and primordial consciousness of the proposition (*Selbstgegebenheit*); which means

14. *Ibid.* §§ 16–17.

the consciousness through which the proposition presents itself directly and immediately. Consciousness of that kind is to propositions as perception is to material things. It must be added that what is given and presents itself directly and immediately in the evidence of distinctness is the *proposition as such* and not the state of affairs to which it refers or the accord or conformity between the proposition and the state of affairs in question. The latter evidence is designated by Husserl as the "evidence of clarity" (*Evidenz der Klarheit*).[15]

One is referred to the experience of a coherent world within which objects of every kind have something to do with one another and are interconnected in the most diverse relations, of both compatibility and incompatibility.[16] *The limitation imposed on the free and arbitrary choice of terms which may be substituted for the formalized symbols reveals the intentional origin of the proposition in the experience of the world.* Its intentional genesis or history thus defines the condition on which the very existence of the proposition depends as it is considered in the logic of mere consistency—that is to say, the possibility of being brought to the evidence of distinctness.

In the perceptual experience of a coherent world are also grounded the limitations which the laws of "purely logical grammar" impose on the free variation of the terms which may figure in a proposition. The philosophy of logic must begin with accounting for the structure of the categorical proposition by relating this structure to those of pre-predicative perceptual experience and deriving it from those structures.

At every level of logic—"purely logical grammar," logic of mere consistency, logic of truth—there is a reference to the perceptual experience of a coherent world which, therefore, appears as a presupposition at each of these levels.

If, at every level of logic, perceptual experience and the existence of a coherent world are encountered as a "presupposition," this is not a "presupposition" in the sense of a premise which one had simply forgotten to state and which might be formulated after the event; nor is it "presupposed" in the sense of an axiom which has a well-defined place within a deductive system and entails certain consequences, such that the change of the axiom in question would invalidate the consequences and entail different ones. Rather, logic and mathematics presuppose the world as the spring from which they flow or as a

15. *Ibid.*, §§ 16b, 75. Let us stress, following Husserl, that the notion of validity which pertains to the logic of mere consistency must not be confounded with that of truth, which denotes the relation of conformity between a proposition and the corresponding state of affairs.

16. *Ibid.*, § 89b.

nutritive soil in which they have their roots, since the entities and forms constructed and studied by these sciences depend, as to the very possibility of their existence, upon the reference to the presupposed world. The presupposition of the world appears nowhere in the patent theoretical content of logic, although it shores up the whole edifice. *It is in the nature of such presuppositions—which are not presuppositions in the usual technical sense but are conditions of possibility and hence presuppositions in the philosophical sense—to be effective everywhere and, at the same time and perhaps for that very reason, to be able to pass unnoticed.* Precisely because the presupposition of the world is effective everywhere and because logic, as to its existence and its very possibility, is founded upon it, the presupposition in question does not figure as one premise among others, and no determinate place within the system of logic can be assigned to it.

The presupposition of the world is not the sole or even the most fundamental among those which we try to set forth here. According to Husserl's analyses, the world proves to be the intentional correlate of acts of consciousness, especially acts of perception, organized into groups and systems which have well-determined structures.[17] In this sense the world presupposes consciousness and appears as relative to conscious life, above all to perceptual consciousness. If then logic presupposes the world, it further presupposes—in an equally implicit form—the constitutive consciousness of which the world is the intentional correlate.

With respect to any proposition, we have the certainty of being able to return to it as identically the same as often as we wish. When a mathematical demonstration terminates in the formulation of a certain theorem, we are conscious of being able to take up this theorem again, either to repeat or re-examine the demonstration or to continue the mathematical reasoning, so that the theorem, which has just appeared as a result, will now serve as a point of departure for further deductions. The proposition which is simply posited can be doubted, it can be submitted to further examination and be reaffirmed with the consciousness that it is identically the same which was first posited, then underwent doubt, etc. As we have seen, the application of logical operations to given propositions generates new propositions whose structures develop with increasing complexity. It is the same proposition $p$ which can be posited as an independent proposition and which, when a certain operation is applied to it, enters as a component into a more complex proposition, within which it has a definite function. It is the same $p$ and the same $q$ which figure, as antecedent and consequent respectively, in the hypothetical proposition $p \supset q$ or which appear in the disjunctive one $p \lor q$. There is always the *ideal identity* of propositions—that is to say, there is the possibility of re-verting to them, whenever one wishes to, as identically the same—and also the ideal possibility of reiterating logical operations.[18] The ideal identity of the propositions plays a role of first importance, not only for the thought of the solitary logician, but also for inter-subjective com-munication. When we submit our results to other thinkers and examine theirs in turn, in every discussion and collaboration, whether in the sciences or in daily life, it is tacitly presupposed and taken for granted that the propositions and systems of propositions in question are the same for everyone.

The ideal identity of propositions is nowhere mentioned among the axioms or among the premises which figure explicitly in logical construction. Nevertheless, it is continuously used; indeed, it is impossible to abstain from such usage.

In speaking of the ideal identity of propositions, we contrast the *one* and identical proposition with the *multiplicity* of acts, real or possible, through which the proposition is grasped or may be grasped. These acts can differ from one another in several ways. In the case of the repeated positing of the same proposition by the same subject, the acts of positing differ from one another at the least by their places within phenomenal time and by whatever follows from the difference in temporal placement.[19] Furthermore, the same proposition may be posited by diverse subjects, in which case the acts of positing belong to different streams of consciousness. Besides the differences in temporal placement there may be differences in what Husserl calls the "quality of the act," when, for example, the same proposition is at one time simply posited, at another time doubted, questioned, subsequently reaffirmed, negated, etc., whether by the same person or by a plurality of subjects.[20] Finally, let us mention differences such as those between an act by which a certain proposition is posited as independent and another act by which the same proposition is posited as the component part of a more complex proposition. All the entities of logic and mathematics reveal themselves in philosophical reflection as inten-tional correlates or even as products of acts of consciousness and of groups of acts systematically concatenated with one another. Philo-sophical reflections on logic such as those which we have developed can, therefore, lead and have in fact led Husserl to establish the

18. Husserl, *Logik,* §§ 73–74.
19. See Husserl, *Logische Untersuchungen,* II, i, §§ 11, 30–31.
20. *Ibid.,* II, v, § 20.

principle of *phenomenological idealism* according to which whatever exists and has validity derives the sense of its existence and its validity from conscious life and can find its ultimate clarification and final justification only by means of analyses of acts and of groups of acts in which it presents itself as existing and as valid.[21]

Phenomenological idealism must be understood, above all, as the formulation of a vast program of concrete research. The first task to be tackled is, in terms of constitutive consciousness, to account for the perceptual world—familiar to us in everyday existence—in which we find ourselves and within which our whole life and all our activities take place. To this end, one must analyze particular perceptual acts as well as the groups and systems into which the particular acts are inter-concatenated. Correspondingly, the same questions can be raised concerning the constitution of "higher" universes, such as those of science, logic, mathematics, etc. Again one has to go back to the acts, the groups of acts, the specific operations and procedures of consciousness, in and through which the universes in question present and constitute themselves (here one can even speak of construction) as those for which we take them in our conscious life. If we say of these universes that they are a "higher" order, it is because, as Husserl has shown with respect to the physical sciences [22] and as, following Husserl, we have tried to bring out in the example of logic, the universes in question presuppose the perceptual world and imply it by their very sense.

TRANSLATED BY ABIGAIL L. ROSENTHAL

21. Husserl, *Logik*, § 94.
22. Husserl, *Krisis*, § 9; *Erfahrung und Urteil*, § 10.

# 15 / Gelb-Goldstein's Concept of "Concrete" and "Categorial" Attitude and the Phenomenology of Ideation[1]

*Written in Honor of Kurt Goldstein, Teacher and Friend, on the Occasion of His 70th Birthday, November 6, 1948*

HUSSERL'S THEORY of universals as general objects and specific ideal entities very soon acquired widespread notoriety, although often in a grossly misinterpreted and misrepresented form, partly as a result of the not very fortunately chosen term of "intuition of essences" (*Wesenserschauung*). When Husserl established his theory of ideation for the first time in the *Logische Untersuchungen,* he hardly went beyond asserting the specific nature and irreducibility of those acts through which universals in contradistinction to particular things are meant and apprehended and, correspondingly, asserting the specific nature and irreducibility of the objects apprehended through the acts in question. For this purpose, Husserl had to engage himself in a thoroughgoing analysis and discussion of the theories of abstraction prevailing in the tradition of classical British empiricism.

Most of the essential ideas which Husserl developed in the course of his critical discussion and refutation of the empiricist theories of abstraction have been fully confirmed by the results to which Gelb and Goldstein have been led in their studies of brain injuries. Considering that Gelb and Goldstein carried out their investigations within a mere neurological and psychopathological setting and in complete independence of phenomenological and, quite in general, philosophical points of view and theories, their corroboration of the pertinent views of Husserl appears the more significant and conclusive. After having set forth the convergence between Husserl's and Gelb-Goldstein's theories, we shall embark upon formulating further phenomenological problems of ideation which arise on the basis of this convergence, also

1. This study was originally published in *Philosophy and Phenomenological Research,* X (1949).

taking into account Husserl's later contributions toward the problem under discussion.

## [I] CATEGORIAL EQUALITY AND QUALITATIVE HOMOGENEITY

EMPIRICIST THEORIES deny universals as ideal entities and objects *sui generis*. Ideation is reduced to, or, at least, explained by, apprehension of similarity or likeness between particular things. General terms are, accordingly, held to denote classes of similar particular things. When a general term is predicated of a particular thing, the meaning of such predication can be but the assertion that the given thing belongs to a certain class, i.e., bears similarity or likeness to other particular things.

In his refutation of the empiricist theories, Husserl points out that every relation of similarity or likeness between particular things presupposes a point of view from, and a respect in, which the particular things are similar or alike.[2] If two things are alike as to their color or their form, the point of view with reference to which the relation of likeness obtains is, in the former case, the *eidos* of color, in the latter case, that of form; both *eide* have to be considered as identical ideal entities. Every object bears similarity to a great many objects; to some in one respect, to others in a different respect. To put it otherwise, every object belongs to a great many classes comprised of objects which are similar to each other. Emphasizing the classes founded on similarity or likeness, but denying the identical ideal *eidos* with reference to which the relations of similarity or likeness obtain, one is confronted, as Husserl shows, with the insuperable difficulty of accounting for the constitution and unification of the very classes and also for that which separates the classes from each other and keeps them apart. A red sphere is similar to both a green sphere and a red cube; the similarities involved in either case are of a different kind. Hence similarities prove to admit of differences in kind. As with the objects themselves, so similarities between objects may be compared with each other and thus turn out to be similar or alike or else to differ from each other. Similarities too may, therefore, be grouped and classified according to species. Again the problem arises as to the point of view with reference to which similarities are similar to, or different from, each other. In other words, the very problem of the *eide* from

2. Husserl, *Logische Untersuchungen* (Halle, 1913), II, ii, chap. I. Cf. the condensed but faithful rendering by M. Farber, *The Foundation of Phenomenology* (Cambridge, Mass., 1943), chap. IXA.

which we started is transferred from the objects between which similarities obtain to the similarities themselves. On the grounds of the empiricist denial of the *eide* as identical ideal units and entities, there remains but the resorting to similarities between similarities, and this shows that a *regressus in infinitum* is unavoidable.

Equality or likeness with reference to an *eidos* as point of view, or, as we shall likewise say, categorial equality or likeness, is defined by Husserl as that relationship which obtains between objects that fall under one and the same species.[3] Since every *eidos* necessarily constitutes and defines a class—namely, the class of objects which fall under it [4]—the relation of categorial equality may be said to obtain between objects by virtue of the latter's belonging to one and the same class. To state for any objects that they belong to the same class or that they stand in the relation of categorial equality are but two expressions of the same state of affairs. Objects between which the relation of categorial equality is ascertained to obtain are not taken in themselves in all their individualities and particularities but are considered with reference to a certain species as particularizations of the latter or as representatives of the class to which they belong by virtue of their actualizing the *eidos* in question.

From equality in the categorial sense there is to be distinguished the sensuous factor of equality (*das sinnliche Gleichheitsmoment*), the latter being to the former what *figurale Momente* by means of which pluralities are perceptually recognized are to pluralities as apprehended through genuine representation.[5] For the apprehension of a plurality in the latter mode, as many acts are required as the plurality contains elements, each element being apprehended through one of these acts; in addition to these acts of individual apprehension, there is an act of synthesis through which the individually apprehended elements are colligated and united.[6] Such genuine apprehension of a plurality by means of explicit colligation cannot be assumed to occur when, for example, looking at the sky we instantaneously see "many" stars or entering a hall perceive at a glance "a lot" of people.[7] To account for the apprehension of pluralities under circumstances which preclude explicit colligation, Husserl refers to *quasi-qualitative*

3. Husserl, *Logische Untersuchungen*, II, 1, p. 113: "Gleichheit ist das Verhältnis der Gegenstände, welche einer und derselben Species unterstehen." Cf. Husserl, *Erfahrung und Urteil* (Hamburg, 1954), p. 393: ". . . *Gleichheit nur ein Korrelat der Identität eines Allgemeinen.* . . ."
4. Husserl, *Erfahrung und Urteil*, p. 423.
5. Husserl, *Logische Untersuchungen*, II, 1, p. 282n.
6. Husserl, *Philosophie der Arithmetik* (Halle, 1891), pp. 79f.
7. *Ibid.*, pp. 219ff.

*Momente* or *figurale Momente* as perceptual features exhibited by certain groups.[8] In speaking of the perception of a "row of trees," a "column of soldiers," a "swarm of birds," etc., we render by the terms "row," "column," and "swarm" a certain aspect, a certain characteristic property or organizational form with which the group in question presents itself in our very sense experience. Geometrical configurations, all kinds of arrangements of points and lines belong here, as well as the characteristic aspect of the chessboard pattern, the specific nature of a rhythm, a melody, etc. *"Figurale Momente" denote characters, properties, aspects of groups, and are no more and no less a matter of mere sense experience than the groups themselves and the "elements" of which the groups consist.* Among such group aspects there must also be reckoned—deserving special attention in the present context—the perceptual feature of qualitative homogeneity. We see at a glance "a heap of apples" or "a heap of nuts," without resorting to, and, in most cases, without even being able to resort to, $\frac{n(n-1)}{2}$ comparisons, $n$ being the number of elements involved.[9] The group in question displays the perceptual feature of qualitative homogeneity of a specific kind, by virtue of which the "heap of apples" presents a group aspect different from that of a "heap of nuts." Qualitative homogeneity is involved, but differently specified, in both cases.

There is then a mere perceptual apprehension of equality in the sense of qualitative homogeneity which neither requires nor implies any reference to an *eidos*. Sensuous equality between the members of a perceived group is exhibited by the group as a specific perceptual character of its own, as a *figurales Momente* of a special kind. By the same token, the group character in question, like every *figurales Momente*, is confined and restricted to the very group as experienced in actual perception. Let us take the perception of a certain number of red objects, all of identical chromatic properties (as to hue, brightness, etc.). For the perception of such a group, the perceptual apprehension of qualitative homogeneity specified in a certain determinate manner is characteristic. Still, the *perception of the group* in question *with its*

8. *Ibid.*, pp. 228ff. Cf. Farber, *The Foundation of Phenomenology*, pp. 46ff. In the present context we cannot dwell at length on Husserl's concept of *figurale Momente;* we wish, however, to point out that the phenomena referred to by Husserl are the same which C. von Ehrenfels studied in his important article, "Über Gestaltqualitäten," *Vierteljahrsschrift für wissenschaftliche Philosophie,* XIV (1890). Concerning the complete agreement between Husserl and von Ehrenfels as to the theoretical interpretation of the phenomena in question, see above, "Some Aspects and Developments of Gestalt Psychology."

9. Husserl, *Philosophie der Arithmetik*, p. 233.

*characteristic group aspect is not only entirely different from, but does not even convey or found the idea of, the class of red objects,* no more than that of the class of red objects whose chromatic determination is completely particularized. Such a class, understood as the extension of a concept or *eidos*, which is a necessary correlate of the *eidos*, is essentially an infinitely open class, comprising whatever objects have the properties in question, whether or not they happen to be given in actual experience.[10] Considered as that perceptual phenomenon which it presents itself as being in experience, qualitative homogeneity, on account of its sensuous nature and the ensuing restriction to actual sense experience, contains no motivation leading beyond actual perception, in particular toward the idea of a class in the conceptual sense. On the other hand, a genuinely conceptual class, e.g., that of red objects, which, as shown before, cannot be constituted and unified except with reference to an *eidos*, obviously does not present itself as an experiential or perceptual whole.[11] Its unity is not of a sensuous nature but is derived from the unity of a categorial intention, the class itself being the correlate of that intention. It follows that in contradistinction to sensuous equality or qualitative homogeneity, categorial equality, defined as the relationship between objects which belong to a certain class, or, equivalently stated, which fall under the corresponding *eidos*, proves a mere conceptual relationship established by categorial thought and not a relationship of sensuous or perceptual nature.

As a result of Husserl's discussions and distinctions, we may state the unaccountability of ideation in terms of equality, so far as categorial equality presupposes, and is rendered possible by, the apprehension of an *eidos*, whereas qualitative homogeneity does not found the presentation of a class in the conceptual sense, at least not without the intervention of specific mental activities and operations.

## [II]   GELB-GOLDSTEIN'S ANALYSIS OF A CASE OF AMNESIA OF COLOR NAMES

HUSSERL'S VIEWS have found hitherto unnoticed corroboration in Gelb's and Goldstein's concepts of "categorial" and "concrete" attitude, concepts which those authors have laid down on the basis of their studies of numerous psychopathological cases presenting

10. Husserl, *Erfahrung und Urteil*, § 82 and pp. 422f.
11. Husserl, *Logische Untersuchungen*, II, 1, pp. 282f.

a great variety of symptoms. For the sake of conciseness and brevity, we shall essentially limit ourselves to their analysis of a case of amnesia of color names,[12] the symptoms involved being closely related to the phenomena dealt with by Husserl.

## 1. The Symptoms and the Perceptual Experience of the Patient

GELB'S AND GOLDSTEIN'S PATIENT, T., manifested the familiar difficulty in naming a color shown to him; even the suggestion of the correct name was of little, if any, avail. Presented with color samples and requested to choose a sample fitting to a color name, T. repeatedly uttered the name, but it seemed that the word had no meaning for him. He could no more indicate the name of the color of an object which was mentioned to him than he was able to point out a color corresponding to a color name. If, however, instead of being asked to *name* the color of an object, the patient was requested to choose a sample fitting to the object in question, he succeeded very well due to his excellent visualization, provided that a fitting specimen was there. He never chose a wrong color. If the specimen did not match perfectly the color of the mentioned object, T. was not satisfied and continued looking for better fitting ones.

Particularly interesting and revealing was the behavior of the patient when he was given a color specimen (e.g., a red one) and was requested to sort out all those specimens that agreed with the former in hue, though they might differ as to brightness, warmth, etc.[13] T. proceeded with much uneasiness and hesitation. Sometimes he tried to assort specimens of equal or very similar hue, sometimes specimens which, though of different hue, agreed as to brightness. It happened not infrequently that, having already chosen a correct specimen (a red one), he laid it aside or that he paid no attention at all to the red specimens. Some of his choices appeared quite incomprehensible. There arose the impression, rejected, as we shall see, by Gelb and Goldstein, that the patient was unable to abide by his principle of coordination and shifted from one principle to any other; assorting sometimes according to hue, sometimes according to brightness. The patient himself was far from satisfied by his own procedure. Having made a first selection of specimens, he again and again compared each one of the selected specimens with the sample of reference until he finally accepted a few, but very few only, as fitting, not without

12. A. Gelb and K. Goldstein, "Über Farbennamenamnesie. . . . ," *Psychologische Forschung*, VI (1924).
13. *Ibid.*, I, § 3.

expressing doubts as to whether he might not find still better fitting ones. The meticulousness with which the patient proceeded in choosing a color specimen corresponding to the color of an object, either presented or merely mentioned, reappeared in his sorting. For T. to be satisfied with his choice, the color specimens had to agree in both color and brightness, i.e., to be identical. In fact, when his task was to match identical nuances, the patient succeeded perfectly.

Starting from the procedure of their patient in sorting color specimens, Gelb and Goldstein explain all the symptoms presented by T., as well as by other patients who had been studied by various authors, as effects of a general reduction from the level of "categorial" behavior and attitude to that of "concrete" attitude. Confronted with a color specimen, the patient has of the latter a characteristic perceptual experience in which, according to the objective qualities of the specimen, the factor of hue, that of brightness, or some other factor may prevail.[14] *It is by that characteristic experience with its individuality and particularity that the patient abides and cannot help abiding.* When, for example, in the experience of the specimen of reference the factor of hue is predominant, whereas in that of another sample which T. compares with the former the factor of brightness prevails, the patient cannot persuade himself to group the two: "they do not fit" on account of the difference in brightness, though both are of the same hue, say red. Conversely when the factor of brightness prevails in the experience of either specimen and when the latter are of the same, or nearly the same, brightness, the patient considers them as fitting together, the eventual difference in hue notwithstanding. It goes without saying that T. sometimes grouped specimens agreeing in hue. Whether or not two color specimens appear to him as fitting together depends entirely and exclusively upon whether or not he has the experience of *concrete agreement, accordance,* and *coherence (konkretes Kohärenzerlebnis)* on account of the particular, characteristic individual aspects which the specimens present to him. In the case of identical specimens, the patient obviously experiences concrete agreement to the highest possible degree; hence he is prompt and unhesitating in sorting such specimens. On the other hand, when the samples selected by the patient are not identical but merely very close to each other, he still sorts them by virtue of his experience of concrete accordance. The latter, however, appears to him as not quite perfect and somehow increasable; therefore he does not feel completely satisfied with his choice. If in the case of T., the experience of concrete accordance depended upon factors like hue or brightness, it could be,

14. *Ibid.*, pp. 148f.

and was in other cases, attached to aesthetic effects, suitability for practical purposes, etc.[15]

Confronted with the same task as the patient, *viz.*, the task of grouping color specimens according to hue, the normal person unhesitatingly sorts two, say red, specimens, though the one may be very dark, the other rather bright. In so doing, the normal person is not unaware of the difference between the specimens. Carrying out the assignment given to him, however, the normal person does not take the specimens in their particularity and individuality; rather, he sees in both a special case of redness. To express it in Husserl's terminology, the normal person does not depend for his sorting upon sensuous equality or likeness but may, and does, group specimens according to the relation of equality in the categorial sense, which obtains between the specimens in question insofar and *only* insofar as the latter are considered as particularizations and actualizations of the *eidos* of redness. In his grouping, the normal person is not confined to abiding by the immediately given experiential features of perception, including among the latter the experience of concrete agreement and accordance. He may impose a principle of classification upon the data of perception; he may consider these data from a certain point of view, in the case under discussion from the point of view of hue.

It is just this attitude, the "categorial" attitude, that brain-injured patients are utterly unable to adopt, an inability which, according to Gelb and Goldstein, defines the essential difference between normal persons and patients. Confined to the content of perception as actually experienced, the patients abide by that content in all its singularity and particularity; they are unable to see in it the representative of a color species or of a category or class of colors.[16] To the patient's mind, the given color specimen stands out as that as which, and exactly as it, presents itself in perceptual experience without any reference whatever to any thing beyond itself. In particular, the patients cannot regard their perceptual experience in the light or under the perspective of a principle extraneous to that perceptual experience in the sense that is not imbedded in, but is somehow imposed upon, the latter. Hence the patients prove unable to refer their actual experience to any ideal or conceptual order; they cannot take a stand or a view with regard to their perceptual experience, not to speak of varying views so that, according to the view taken, sometimes these, sometimes other

15. Cf. K. Goldstein, "L'analyse de l'aphasie et l'étude de l'essence du langage," *Psychologie du Langage* (Paris, 1933), pp. 480f.

16. Gelb and Goldstein, "Über Farbennamenamnesie," *loc. cit.*, pp. 152f.; Goldstein, "L'analyse de l'aphasie," *loc. cit.*, pp. 453ff., 473ff. Cf. E. Cassirer, *Philosophie der symbolischen Formen* (Berlin, 1929), III, pp. 258ff.

features of the perceptual content appear as particularly relevant or essential.[17]

Every brain injury entails, according to Goldstein, a regression to the level of merely concrete behavior and attitude.[18] Only that exists for the patient which offers itself in perceptual experience. Within the content of actual experience, there is no differentiation between the experiential features as to their relevancy and significance. All features of the perceptual content are of equal importance for the patient; each of these features is of paramount importance for the mere reason that it is encountered in actual perception. The patients are somehow overwhelmed and overpowered by actual experience imposing itself upon them by a force of constraint from which they cannot emancipate themselves. Thus the patients are unable to conceive of eventual changes or modifications in the experiential content, i.e., to conceive of the latter as possibly being different from what it actually is. This goes so far that brain-injured patients cannot make or even repeat statements which are at variance with actual experience as, for example, repeating the sentence, "Today the weather is bad, and it is raining," when in fact the sun is shining.[19] All that these patients can do is act (in the broadest sense of the word) under the suggestions and imperatives arising from the given concrete situation. To the extent to which problems can be solved in this direct and immediate way, the patients succeed, for their actions, oriented with regard to, and dictated by, the experienced concrete situation, prove adequate to the latter. When, however, the patients are confronted with problems that cannot be solved by actions directly and immediately induced by the very experiential situation, they always fail. One might say, the patients are at the mercy of actualities so as not to be able to conceive of possibilities or to look at the given situation from a distance.[20] The latter attitude requires and implies a certain detachment from the experienced concrete situation, which, without losing its character of actuality and reality, yet loosens its grasp upon the experiencing subject's mind so as to permit him to consider the given situation under varying angles, from different points of view, and to display some initiative in its respect. Since it has

17. Cassirer, *Philosophie der symbolischen Formen,* III, pp. 261ff.

18. Goldstein, "L'analyse de l'asphasie," *loc. cit.,* pp. 453f., 470; K. Goldstein, *Der Aufbau des Organismus* (The Hague, 1934), pp. 18ff.

19. Cassirer, *Philosophie der symbolischen Formen,* III, pp. 295f., 314. Cf. W. Hochheimer, "Analyse eines Seelenblinden von der Sprache aus," *Psychologische Forschung,* XVI (1932), pp. 30f.

20. Goldstein, *Der Aufbau des Organismus,* p. 19; A. Gelb, "Remarques générales sur l'utilisation des données pathologiques pour la psychologie et la philosophie du langage," *Psychologie du Langage* (Paris, 1933), pp. 415f.

become impossible for the patients to detach themselves from the given situation and to look at the latter from a distance, they prove deprived of any initiative whatever.

## 2. Theoretical Interpretations

CONSIDERED IN THE LIGHT of Gelb's and Goldstein's general characterization of the "concrete" and "categorial" attitudes, the behavior of their patient T. in sorting color samples becomes understandable. Already holding in his hand a sample agreeing with the specimen of reference as to hue, the patient, as mentioned above, not infrequently put the "correct" sample aside to choose another one of different hue but of equal or nearly equal brightness as the specimen of reference. It must not be concluded from this that the patient inconsistently shifted from one principle of classification to another. To sort color specimens with reference to a principle of classification requires adoption of the "categorial" attitude, whether the principle of classification is adhered to consistently or is adopted for a brief moment only. Maintaining that their patient is utterly unable to adopt the "categorial" attitude, Gelb and Goldstein conclude that he has no principle of classification at all.[21] Hence T.'s behavior has to be explained by an alternation and succession upon each other of different experiences of concrete agreement. Suppose the specimen of reference is experienced in concrete agreement as to hue with specimen a, and suppose further that the patient at this moment notices another sample, b, which, though of different hue, is highly similar to the specimen of reference as to brightness, even more similar in the respect mentioned than a is as to hue. While the factor of hue had thus far prevailed in the experience of the specimen of reference, that of brightness now becomes predominant. An experience of concrete coherence based on brightness supersedes the previous experience of concrete coherence based on hue. Guided exclusively by that experience of concrete accordance which proves stronger and more imperative, the patient is thus led to prefer b to a.

This interpretation is borne out by Gelb's and Goldstein's observations of their patient H.[22] Requested to sort out those color samples which seemed to him to fit with a given specimen of reference, H., differently from T., selected a rather great number. A closer examination of H.'s choices revealed that any two specimens selected in immediate succession were highly similar to each other as to certain

21. Gelb and Goldstein, "Über Farbennamenamnesie," *loc. cit.*, pp. 149ff.; Gelb, "Remarques pour la psychologie," *loc. cit.*, pp. 409f.
22. Gelb and Goldstein, "Über Farbennamenamnesie," *loc. cit.*, pp. 171f.

optical qualities (e.g., hue, brightness, warmth, and other properties hard to describe and to formulate), so that they may well have been experienced to be in concrete accordance. Such, however, was not the case when all the selected specimens were compared with the given specimen of reference. In the course of sorting samples, H., in contradistinction to T., did not abide by the given specimen of reference. His specimen of reference varied from moment to moment in that at any moment the sample which he had last chosen became the specimen of reference for the subsequent selection. T. performed *one single process of selection* in that he persistently referred his choices to the given specimen of reference and thus, after many vacillations and hesitations, he came to assemble only very few samples, since only these few were experienced in concrete accordance with the specimen of reference. When H. selected a great many specimens and established a series in which two neighbors, but only neighbors, stood to each other in the relation of concrete accordance, it was because, instead of one single process of selection, he performed a *set of partial choices* with varying specimens of reference, looking out at each choice for a sample agreeing with that which he had selected just before. Whatever the difference in the procedure of the two patients, both of them were guided in their choosing exclusively by the experience of concrete agreement and coherence.

To gain more insight into the procedure of sorting color samples on the basis of the experience of concrete accordance, let us describe the phenomenal aspect of that experience. Gelb and Goldstein point out that the experience of concrete coherence must not be misconstrued as a secondary experience supervenient to those of the specimens themselves and their chromatic qualities.[23] In other words, it is not that the specimens in question are first experienced independently of each other, each one determined by definite chromatic properties of its own and are then, subsequently, related by concrete accordance. Rather, the specimens in question are experienced only *within the relation of concrete coherence*. This is to say, the specimens—for the sake of simplicity let us assume there are but two—present themselves as members or "parts" of a *contexture of which, on account of its uniformity, the phenomenon of concrete agreement is the specific and distinctive feature*. With regard to the specimens, the uniformity of the contexture of which they are "parts" appears as qualitative homogeneity. The two specimens present themselves as platforms on the same plane, with no rise or fall from the one to the other, with no tension between them. Obviously this characterization holds for the

23. *Ibid.*, p. 153 (n. 2).

specimens as members of the contexture in question, which offers the typical aspect of a level-phenomenon.[24] Within this contexture, each specimen occupies a definite place and plays a specific role which, in a contexture of the kind considered here, is the same for both. It is from the contexture with the properties which it has of its own and with reference to all the other members of the contexture that each one of the members derives its functional significance and that qualification which defines its phenomenal status in a given concrete case. All the examples to which Husserl refers for *figurale Momente* and von Ehrenfels for *Gestaltqualitäten* are contextures with characters and properties of their own, though, of course, not all of them are of the type of the "level-phenomenon," as is easily seen in the case of a melody, a rhythm, an ascending scale, etc. Accordingly, the component members of a contexture do not always have the same functional significance. However, what holds for the members of any contexture, of whatever type and kind, is that each member is experienced with, and as defined by, a specific functional significance which, in turn, is determined by the role which the member plays within the contexture in question. The structure of such contextures has to be accounted for in Gestalt theoretical terms of the kind which we have used. A further clarification of these terms is not within the scope of the present discussion.

Sorting color specimens on the basis of concrete agreement, the subject looks for samples best lending themselves to forming a contexture together with the specimen of reference. All he has to do is to select specimens which are experienced as belonging together with the specimen of reference in the sense of concrete agreement to the highest possible degree. For that purpose, the subject does not need to go beyond the very experience of concrete agreement. In particular, it is not necessary for him to analyze the latter experience and to recognize the agreement as agreement by equality of, say, brightness.[25] It may well happen that the agreement is in fact based upon the factor of brightness, which thus actually determines the perceptual experience. Still, the factor of brightness is, so to speak, silently effective. The subject acts under the imperatives of its silent effectiveness, without disengaging and apprehending the factor of the brightness as to the role which it actually plays for the experience of concrete coherence. When, on the other hand, specimens *are* sorted

24. As to level-phenomenon in contradistinction to step-phenomenon cf. K. Koffka, "Perception: An Introduction to the Gestalt-Theorie," *Psychological Bulletin,* XIX (1922), pp. 540ff. Koffka has introduced these concepts in discussing quite different problems.

25. Cf. Gelb, "Remarques générales," *loc. cit.,* p. 411.

with reference to brightness as the point of view and principle of classification, there may again occur, at the outset, an experience of concrete agreement. Here, however, the subject does not merely experience concrete coherence but proceeds from that experience toward disengaging the factor which is constitutive for that very experience. Apprehending the concrete agreement as founded upon equality of brightness, the subject discloses the factor of brightness in its effectiveness and may then choose the factor thus thematized as principle of classification. The difference is between, on the one hand, concrete coherence founded in fact on brightness and, on the other hand, concrete coherence explicitly recognized and apprehended as thus founded: between the factor of brightness actually effective and the thematization of that factor in its determinant role. Previously we mentioned a certain detachment from experienced situations as prerequisite to the adoption of the "categorial" attitude. Such detachment permits the normal person not only to experience the actual situation and to undergo the effectiveness of operating factors but also to explicate the given situation, to apprehend and thematize effective factors, and, eventually, to orient his actions with respect to factors thus rendered explicit. Reduced as the patients are to passively accepting experiential situations in their actuality and to acting only under their direct inducements, explication and thematization have become operations impossible for them to perform.

If Gelb's and Goldstein's patient T., who had an excellent capacity of visualization, found no difficulty at all in choosing a specimen whose color matched that of an object pointed out or mentioned to him, it is because the "categorial" attitude is not required for that purpose. Evoking a mental image of the object in question, all the patient had to do and did in fact was to select a specimen whose color was experienced by him to be in concrete accordance with that of the object.[26] Normal persons do not act differently when they are confronted with the same task.

Required to sort out specimens of the same color as that of a certain object, we select, like the patient, very few shades only, *viz.*, those which exactly fit and concretely cohere with the color of the object. Asked, e.g., to point out the color of blood, we do not accept a pink specimen any more than we do a green one. Actual mental visualization of the object in question is not even indispensable for the accomplishment of the task under discussion.[27] The selection may and, more often than not, does take place on the basis of mere recognition of a specimen as fitting with the color of the object, no mental image

26. Cf. Gelb and Goldstein, "Über Farbennamenamnesie," *loc. cit.*, I, § 2.
27. *Ibid.*, pp. 135f.

of the latter being evoked. What is important, and is alone important, is the occurrence of the immediately "intuitive experience of fitting-ness" (*das anschauliche Erlebnis des Passens*), whether on the basis of visualization or mere recognition. It is obviously with respect to only very few specimens that the experience in question takes place, whereas other specimens of the same hue, but of a brightness, saturation, and other chromatic properties different from those of the object in question appear inappropriate and incongruous. Under certain circumstances, in the face of certain tasks, normal persons also adopt the "concrete" attitude. When, however, we are given the assignment to sort samples of the same hue as a certain specimen of reference, we select all specimens that fall under the class represented by the specimen of reference. Prevented from adopting the "categorial" attitude, T. resorts to the same procedure with respect to either task. Reappearing here is the difference between the behavior of the patient and that of normal persons.[28]

Finally we have to mention the interpretation which Gelb and Goldstein give to certain speech affections. Since these patent affections of speech are the most conspicuous and most striking symptoms in amnesic aphasia, older theoreticians have explained the latter by a deficiency of words, at least by a considerable difficulty on the part of the patients to find certain words. Against this explanation, Goldstein points out that the very same words which the patients are unable to find under *certain circumstances* are spontaneously and easily uttered under *different circumstances*.[29] Whether or not a certain word is found by a patient does not depend upon the word itself but depends upon the meaning with which the word is to be used in a concrete situation of speech.[30] Color names like "red," "blue," etc., do not designate individual and particular chromatic phenomena in all their singularity; rather, they denote classes or categories of colors. It is with this categorial meaning that the subject has to use the terms in question when he is asked to name a color shown to him or to point out a color to which a given name applies. Since patients suffering from amnesia of color names are not able to consider a given color as representative of a class of colors, words whose significations are of as predominantly a conceptual nature as they are in the case of color names have lost all meaning for those patients.[31] The inability of the

28. *Ibid.*, p. 150.
29. Goldstein, "L'analyse de l'aphasie," *loc. cit.*, pp. 471ff.; also pp. 449f.
30. As to this view, first advocated by H. Jackson, cf. Cassirer, *Philosophie der symbolischen Formen*, III, pp. 245ff.
31. Gelb and Goldstein, "Über Farbennamenamnesie," *loc. cit.*, I, § 5; Gelb, "Remarques générales," *loc. cit.*, pp. 411f.; Goldstein, "L'analyse de l'aphasie," pp. 475ff. The pre-eminently eidetic signification of color names also appears in

patients to use words which have an essentially eidetic signification and the patients' characteristic behavior in sorting color specimens thus appear, according to Gelb and Goldstein, as two manifestations of the same fundamental modification, *viz.*, regression from the "categorial" to the "concrete" level. Neither manifestation, however, must be considered as the cause of, or in any sense primary with respect to, the other. Each must be regarded as coordinate to the other and must equally directly be referred to the fundamental modification of attitude.

When T. speaks of colors, he often uses expressions such as "grassy," "like a cherry," "like a violet," etc.[32] Of another patient Goldstein reports that she consistently used color names like "red," "green," etc., with reference to only a few determinate shades, mostly highly saturated ones. As to other shades, those terms did not apply; in their stead, the patient had expressions like "dark yellow," "bright blue," "leaf green," or "fashion color," "spring color," etc.[33] If inferences from the verbal formulations of the patients to their chromatic experiences are warranted, one might presume that colors appear to the patients not as "pure qualities" but as attributes and properties of objects, in attachment to, and adherence in, objects. Tendencies to designate colors after objects have also been observed among primitive peoples.[34] We may also refer to the thesis of Pradines, who asserts the priority, from the genetic, especially the phylogenetic, point of view, of colors as well as sounds as essentially related to agents and objects over colors and sounds divested of objective significance and thus given the status of "pure qualities." [35] According to Pradines, "pure qualities" are not primary data, not even data at all, but are products of mental opera-

---

that mentioning the correct color name, even its utterance by the patient himself, hardly produces any effect in contradistinction to cases of amnesia of names of objects (Gelb and Goldstein, *loc. cit.*, pp. 184ff.; Goldstein, *loc. cit.*, pp. 487ff.). This not only leads to the question, discussed by Gelb and Goldstein, as to whether all terms which are of general applicability have by this very token a genuine eidetic signification; it also gives rise to the problem as to whether there are εἴδη with reference to all objects, of whatever kind and description, and to all properties, attributes, characters, etc., of any objects. In the present context, we must confine ourselves to noting that a problem debated in Platonism as well as in platonizing philosophies (e.g., that of Malebranche) also arises out of a mere discussion in psychopathology.

32. Gelb and Goldstein, *ibid.*, pp. 133f.; Goldstein, *ibid.*, p. 476.

33. Goldstein, *ibid.*, pp. 480f., 483f. As to both denominating and sorting colors, the patient exhibited the symptoms of amnestic aphasia.

34. Cf. D. Katz, *Der Aufbau der Farbwelt* (Leipzig, 1930), pp. 4f.; Cassirer, *Philosophie der symbolischen Formen*, III, pp. 265ff.; and the remarks by Gelb and Goldstein, *ibid.*, p. 134.

35. M. Pradines, *Philosophie de la Sensation*, Vol. I (Paris, 1928), Bk. I, chap. IV; cf. M. Merleau-Ponty, *Phénoménologie de la Perception* (Paris, 1945), p. 352, who distinguishes between *couleur-fonction* and *couleur-qualité*.

tions by means of which the realm of sensibility is surpassed. It thus seems that their reduction to the "concrete" level of behavior and attitude purports for the patients the inability not only to consider a given color as member of a class—i.e., to perceive the color with reference to a species—but also to sever the relatedness of the color to some object whose property and attribute it is. Such severance is necessary for the conception of a purely qualitative order, i.e., an order in which colors figure as mere chromatic phenomena, as "pure qualities," detached from objects to which they adhere. We thus venture the hypothesis that if patients reduced to the "concrete" attitude speak of colors in terms implying essential reference to objects, it is because their confinement to accepting actual experience in all its concreteness prevents them from performing mental operations upon the data of experience—in the case under discussion, divorcing colors from the objects whose attributes they are and thus experiencing the colors as pure chromatic phenomena, with the exception, perhaps, of the limiting case of identity of shades or similarity to such high degree as borders upon identity. The propounded conception of colors as originally and primarily attributes of objects also makes understandable the fact previously pointed out that even normal persons do not adopt the "categorial" attitude when they are required to sort specimens whose color matches that of some object mentioned to them. Under the conditions of the assignment, the color reassumes its primary function; it is perceived with reference to some object; it is experienced, so to speak, as an envelope of the latter which in a certain specific manner announces itself in the very chromatic experience. A closer examination of the phenomenal impliedness and involvement of objects in colors or, for that matter, in sounds, cannot be attempted here. It has its place within the broader frame of the phenomenology of perception.

## [III]   PHENOMENOLOGICAL PROBLEMS OF IDEATION

### 1. Convergence of Husserl's Views with the Gelb-Goldstein Theory

HUSSERL'S DISTINCTION BETWEEN EQUALITY in the categorial sense and sensuous equality appears, in the light of the Gelb-Goldstein theory, as a special case of the distinction between acts which are performed in the "categorial" attitude and those which belong to the "concrete" attitude. We cannot discuss here the question as to whether, and, if so, in which sense, the same holds for Husserl's distinction between multiplicities apprehended through acts of genuine explicit colligation and multiplicities which in sense experience are perceived as such by means of *figurale Momente*. Sensuous equality, as previously mentioned, is counted by Husserl among *figurale Momente*.[36] When we speak of the distinction between sensuous and categorial equality as a *special* case of that between "concrete" and "categorial" acts, it is because the latter two concepts comprise much more than the phenomena which, for the sake of the discussion, had to be emphasized in the present context.

Guided in his sorting of color specimens by the experience of concrete agreement, coherence, and accordance—i.e., in Husserl's terminology, by the experience of sensuous equality to the highest possible degree—Gelb's and Goldstein's patients prove utterly unable to conceive of the relationship of equality in the categorial sense. This observation of Gelb and Goldstein bears out our previous conclusion as to the impossibility of accounting for ideation by apprehension of equality.[37] *Husserl's theory and that of Gelb and Goldstein converge toward recognizing ideation as an act* sui generis *with a specific nature of its own.* Patients of the kind considered here have become unable to perform acts of ideation, an inability which also appears in that color names, when used in an eidetic sense, no longer have any meaning for them. It is the specific act of ideation that renders possible the apprehension of a particular thing or of a plurality of particular things with reference to, or under the perspective of, an *eidos*.[38] Among the latter acts, there are to be included those through which a particular thing is conceived of as belonging to a class which, in turn, is constituted with respect to an *eidos*. Husserl's distinctions and theoretical ideas further clarify and complement the Gelb-Goldstein concepts.

Expounding T.'s procedure in sorting color specimens and emphasizing the difference between the patient's procedure and that of a normal person, Gelb writes: "To take together . . . skeins of equal brightness because they agree in fact—and because at the present moment this grouping imposes itself rather than a different one—is quite different from knowing those skeins *as similar* by brightness and then choosing that property as a principle of classification." [39] This argument of Gelb is reminiscent of Husserl's discussion of the logical presentation "*all* A." For the latter presentation to be conceived, it is not sufficient to survey in fact all A, even if the number of the

36. Cf. above, pp. 361ff.
37. Cf. above, pp. 362ff.
38. Cf. Husserl, *Logische Untersuchungen*, II, ii, § 1; Farber, *The Foundation of Phenomenology*, pp. 246f.
39. Gelb, "Remarques générales," *loc. cit.*, p. 411.

individuals in question is finite. "No matter how many particulars we . . . might go over and how eagerly we may colligate them, at best, all A would be presented if the extension of the concept were really exhausted, and yet '*all* A' would not be presented, the logical presentation would not be effectuated." [40] In both Gelb's and Husserl's arguments, reference is made to an operation of consciousness which we propose to term *thematization,* which is to signify disengagement and disclosure of factors which previously to the operation in question are present to consciousness in a rather implicit form. In Gelb's example, the nature of thematization is quite obvious. It denotes the aforementioned transition of the factor of equality by brightness from the state of silent effectiveness in determining the phenomenal aspect of perception to the state of explicit apprehension. [41] It is just this transition which cannot be performed in the case of amnesia of color names. As to the example referred to by Husserl, it is conceivable that in proceeding from one A to another and thus actually exhausting the extension of the concept, the experiencing subject is not aware at all of his covering all A. Under these conditions, there is no thematization, any more than there is a motivation to form the logical presentation "*all* A." We therefore consider the case in which at the end of his survey the subject is aware of all A having been covered. Still the logical presentation "*all* A" cannot be conceived, the totality of the A cannot be explicitly apprehended and stated, unless the awareness mentioned is rendered explicit and thematized, rather than accompanying, in an implied and involved form, the act of consciousness experienced in the final phase of the survey. To both the apprehension of logical forms and the process of ideation, the operation of thematization proves essential. [42] Concerned with ideation, we have to assign to the operation of thematization its systematic place within the whole process of ideation.

## 2. The Problem of the Perceptual Basis of Ideation

To OBTAIN AN IDEA of the phenomenal aspect which the heap of color specimens presents to their patient, Gelb and Goldstein had a few normal persons move the specimen of reference back and

40. Husserl, *Logische Untersuchungen,* II, 1, p. 173. Cf. Farber, *The Foundation of Phenomenology,* p. 268.

41. Cf. above, pp. 370ff.

42. As to the apprehension of logical forms, cf. Husserl, *Formale und Transzendentale Logik* (Halle, 1929), pp. 69f. Husserl's operation of "nominalization" (*Logische Untersuchungen,* II, v, §§ 35f.; *Ideen zu einer reinen Phänomenologie und phänomenologischen Philosophie,* ed. W. Biemel [*Husserliana,* Vol. III (The Hague, 1950)], §§ 119ff., 134, 148) seems to us a special case of thematization.

forth over the heap.[43] These observers were instructed to look at the heap as passively as possible and especially to refrain from placing themselves at a point of view or adopting a principle of classification. Specimens identical with, or extremely similar to, the specimen of reference appear in concrete accordance and coherence with the latter. When there are no identical or highly similar specimens, the heap sometimes presents an aspect of instability, fluctuation, unrest, and agitation. Incipient contextures between color samples are formed and dissolved almost at once. Different groupings of color specimens conflict with each other. Experiences of concrete agreement and accordance of various descriptions compete with and supersede each other. It is more or less under this phenomenal aspect that Gelb and Goldstein presume the heap of color specimens appears to their patient. When, however, under the influence of a given assignment, e.g., that of sorting all red specimens, the normal person abandons his heretofore passive attitude, the instability and agitation of the heap, the vacillation of conflicting contextures, the alternation between and fluctuation of inchoate groupings, dissolved almost as soon as formed, etc.—all at once give way to a reorganized perceptual field. All red specimens acquire predominance and emerge from the rest, which in turn form a more or less irrelevant background. Since the organization and grouping of colors is not immaterial to the phenomenal appearance of the latter, Gelb and Goldstein conclude that their patient's experience of colors differs from the chromatic experience which the normal person has, when he adopts the "categorial" attitude.[44] In the Gelb and Goldstein theory, the behavior of the patient is not interpreted as a mere intellectual deficiency, *viz.*, the loss of the ability to subsume perceived colors under categories, while the very perceptual experience of colors remains unaltered, i.e., is with the patient the same as with normal persons. Merleau-Ponty sees here the "existentialist" rather than "intellectualist" character of their theory: ". . . Before being thought or knowledge, categorial activity is a certain manner of relating oneself to the world and, correlatively, a style or a configuration of experience." Accordingly, ". . . The disturbance of thinking which is discovered at the basis of amnesia . . . does not so much concern the judgment but rather the experiential milieu in which the judgment arises; it concerns less the spontaneity than the grasp of that spontaneity on the sensible world and our power of projecting any intention onto it." [45]

Emphasizing the difference between the chromatic experience of

43. Gelb and Goldstein, "Über Farbennamenamnesie," *loc. cit.*, pp. 151ff.
44. *Ibid.*, p. 162.
45. Merleau-Ponty, *Phénoménologie de la Perception*, pp. 222ff.

their patient and that of a normal person adopting the "categorial" attitude, Gelb and Goldstein still seem to admit, at least in their article on "Farbennamenamnesie," that there is hardly any difference between the chromatic experience of the patient and that of a normal person, provided the latter adopts the "concrete" attitude. This is borne out by their explanation of the failure to detect anomalies in the chromatic perception of their patient by means of certain ophthalmological methods.[46] What is examined by the methods in question is but the experience of homogeneity and inhomogeneity between colors. For that experience, the adoption of the "categorial" attitude is not required. To the extent to which the normal person perceives colors in a mere intuitive, i.e., "concrete," attitude, his chromatic experience is not assumed by Gelb and Goldstein to differ substantially from that of their patient. Yet in an article written after the one on "Farbennamenamnesie," Gelb cautions against assimilating the perception of the patient to that which the normal person has when he adopts the "concrete" attitude.[47] From the fact that the normal person may and, with respect to certain tasks, does adopt the "concrete" attitude, the conclusion must not be drawn that the patient experiences and acts as the normal person does in the "concrete" attitude. Whereas the patient is reduced and confined to the "concrete" attitude, the latter is with the normal person but *one phase* of a more comprehensive process; it is integrated into a total process of experience which also includes phases of "categorial" attitude, of detachment and contemplation from a distance. In the life of the normal person, the "categorial" and "concrete" attitudes—the latter more immediate and direct, more "manual"—fecundate each other, and it is from this integration into the total process of experience that either derives its full meaning and significance.

Gelb's remarks, it seems to us, must not be construed to mean that the integration in question is a fact ascertainable by an onlooking observer but not by the experiencing subject himself. On the contrary, we submit that a perception experienced in the "concrete" attitude appears in itself as integrable into a wider context, is descriptively characterized as a phase of a more comprehensive process. For a perception thus to present itself, it must include a specific phenomenal tinge or feature by means of which a more encompassing context is referred to, through which the possibility of the "categorial" attitude is somehow pre-announced and anticipated in the very perception experienced in the "concrete" attitude.

To formulate more precisely what we mean by the inclusion in an act pertaining to the "concrete" attitude of a possible "categorial"

46. Gelb and Goldstein, "Über Farbennamenamnesie," *loc. cit.*, pp. 161f.
47. Gelb, "Remarques générales," *loc. cit.*, pp. 413ff.

attitude, let us proceed by way of contrast. Confined to abiding by perceptual data as they actually present themselves, the patient cannot experience such data except in that organizational form in which they impose themselves upon him. If, as in the case of a heap of color samples which contains no identical or highly similar shades, the perceptual field exhibits no unambiguously determined organization, the field appears unstable and fluctuating with conflicting groupings superseding each other. The normal person, on the contrary, may adopt the "categorial" attitude and impose upon the perceptual field an organizational form which that field does not possess in its own right. He may even impose upon the field varying forms of organization according to different points of view. As we have seen, the perceptual field accepts organizational forms determined by the point of view at which the subject chooses to place himself.[48]

In the perception of the normal person, there is then a certain readiness to receive forms of organization imposed from without, a certain *ambiguity* and *plasticity* which are in marked contrast to the rigidity characteristic of the perception of the patient. To the normal person's mind, the things perceived do not appear as *mere* actual data and facts, as they do to the patient, but appear, without in the least being divested of their character of real things given in actual experience, as *eventual examples,* as *potential varieties of an invariant.* Even when the normal person does not adopt the "categorial" attitude, his perception is not mere perception in a "pure" state but, we tentatively submit, is pervaded and permeated by some consciousness or awareness of possibilities, of possible reference to a non-perceptual order. Such consciousness of possibilities does not necessarily exist in an entirely explicit and distinct state; more often than not it assumes the form of greater or lesser inarticulation, latency, and implicitness. The reference is, especially in the latter case, to the realm of possibilities as such rather than to any specified possibility. To a greater or lesser degree of implicitness, the perceptual experience of the normal person is oriented with respect to non-perceptual orders and possibilities so that, even when a thing is perceived in itself and for its own sake, without actual reference to a conceptual order, it still is experienced as *referable* to such an order; even when it is not perceived as an example, it still appears as thus *perceivable.* All perceptual experience is encompassed by the horizon of at least a potential consciousness of possible non-perceptual perspectives. In every perception experienced in the "concrete" attitude, there is implied a more or less vague, indistinct, and inarticulate con-

48. Cf. above, p. 376f.

sciousness of, and reference to, a possible transition to the "categorial" attitude. It is by the plasticity just sketched that experiences which the normal person has, when he happens to adopt the "concrete" attitude, seem to us to differ substantially from those of the patient who by virtue of the profound modification which he has undergone is confined to the "concrete" attitude.

## 3. The Operation of "Free Variation"

ALREADY IN *Logische Untersuchungen* Husserl mentions the operation of "free variation." To be sure, there the operation in question is not introduced to account for the apprehension and phenomenological constitution of *eide* but is used as a method for establishing *a priori* laws between *eide*, as, for example, between the *eidos* of color and that of extension.[49] In the very performance of "free variation," certain limitations become apparent which the operation in question is bound to respect. Eidetic laws *a priori* are formulations of such limitations. Starting, for example, from a colored surface, we may imagine the surface to vary arbitrarily as to size and shape, and still the color remains unaltered. When, however, we go as far as imagining the size of the surface to decrease until the extension vanishes altogether, we see that the color vanishes as well.[50] Color and extension do not co-exist merely accidentally. It appears from the mental experiment by way of "free variation" that no instance of color can exist except in connection with an instance of extension. By virtue of an eidetic law *a priori* there is an essential and necessary relationship between color and extension. Because this relationship is founded on the very *eide* of extension and color, it extends to every instance of either *eidos*.

Even when it starts from some actual experience, the operation of "free variation" leads—of necessity, as we shall presently see—to forms which are not and have not been given in actual experience, which for empirical reasons will, perhaps, never be actually experienced. Since eidetic science is interested not in matters of fact but in possibilities, the eventual existence or non-existence of forms arrived at in the process of "free variation" is of no relevancy whatever.[51]

49. Husserl, *Logische Untersuchungen*, II, iii, chap. I. Cf. Farber, *The Foundation of Phenomenology*, chap. XA.

50. This argument has been advanced by C. Stumpf, *Über den psychologischen Ursprung der Raumvorstellung* (Leipzig, 1873), pp. 112ff. Taking over the argument, Husserl (*Logische Untersuchungen*, II, iii, §§ 4ff.) presents it in an ontological rather than psychological setting.

51. Cf. Husserl, *Ideen*, I, §§ 4, 7, 70; Husserl, *Cartesian Meditations*, trans. Dorion Cairns (The Hague, 1960), § 34.

Geometry, which is an eidetic science itself, sets the example. Arbitrarily modifying his figures, passing from form to form by way of continuous transformations, the mathematician is not in the least concerned with the question as to whether or not the products of his geometrical imagination correspond to something in empirical reality. To assure the geometrical validity of these forms, it is both necessary and sufficient that they may be contrived in the process of "free variation" oriented in a certain direction. In other eidetic fields, the situation is not different. Setting out to disclose the *eidos* "material thing," we may be led to consider golden mountains and winged horses. As far as their function as exemplifications of the *eidos* in question is concerned, the products of the fancy are no more and no less valid possibilities than are stones and trees given in actual experience.[52] Since *eide* are exemplified in facts of actual experience as well as in creations of the imagination, the operation of "free variation" is not bound to start from real existents. Products of the imagination may serve as starting points as well.[53] In any event, whatever its starting point, the operation of "free variation" must lead to and pass through merely fictive forms. Otherwise the process would be confined to actualities which form but a subclass of possibilities, whereas it is the very purpose of the process of "free variation" to yield a survey of what is possible in a certain domain, regardless of its actualization in empirical reality. Imagination thus proves the "organ" of eidetic knowledge.[54] The process of "free variation" by means of which not only eidetic laws and relations between *eide* are established but *eide* themselves are apprehended and constituted is carried out in imagination.

If the process of "free variation" leads to the constitution of *eide*, it is because certain features and structures prove to remain unaltered throughout the process in question. Starting from a musical sound, whether actually experienced or merely imagined, we engender a series of auditory phenomena which originate from each other by way of variation and transformation. All members of the series prove congruent in a certain respect, the members of the mentioned series differing from those of that series which would have been engendered if we had started from a color and applied to it the process of variation and transformation. Throughout all varieties which are encountered in the

52. *Ideen*, I, § 149.
53. *Ibid.*, p. 12, "[Wir] können . . . , ein Wesen selbst und *originär* zu erfassen, von entsprechenden erfahrenden Anschauungen ausgehen, *ebensowohl aber auch von nicht-erfahrenden, nicht-daseinserfassenden, vielmehr 'bloss einbildenden' Anschauungen.*"
54. Cf. F. Kaufmann, "On Imagination," *Philosophy and Phenomenological Research*, VII (1947), pp. 372f.

very process of "free variation," there appears an *invariant general form, an invariant structure* exhibited by every member of the series. Different as the members in question are from each other and must be on account of their origination, they all exhibit congruity as to an *invariant identical content.*[55] Congruity with other members of the series as to the invariant is the condition for any member to belong to the series in question, the latter being conceived as generated by "free variation" and transformation of a certain exemplar, e.g., a musical sound. *Ideation reaches final completion with the disengagement, disclosure, explicit apprehension—briefly, thematization—of the invariant in question.* This invariant is the *eidos* in the Platonic sense, to be conceived without any metaphysical connotation.

Constituted as an invariant which manifests itself in the very process of "free variation," the *eidos* presents itself in genuine apprehension as ἐν ἐπὶ πολλῶν: i.e., in opposition and therefore in *necessary* relatedness to a multiplicity of varieties which, however differing from each other, are all actualizations of the same invariant form.[56] The *eidos* is apprehended as an identical ideal entity in contradistinction to, and with reference to, an infinite multiplicity of possible varieties. Since the significance of the *eidos* lies in its being invariant with regard to all possible varieties of a certain domain— e.g., that of musical sound—the reference obviously cannot apply only to those varieties which have actually been considered in a given process of "free variation" which, like any process actually performed, is by necessity finite. Though the process is in fact broken up after a certain number of steps, it is carried out with the consciousness that it can be continued *ad libitum.*[57] It is this consciousness of a possible continuation that renders possible the reference of the *eidos* not only to the varieties which have actually been taken into account but also to more varieties to be contrived *ad libitum.* The very phenomenological constitution of the *eidos*, which we can but roughly sketch here, accounts for the above-mentioned essential correlation between the *eidos* and its extension as an infinitely open class.[58] It also appears that the extension in question does not comprise real objects and their

55. Husserl, *Erfahrung und Urteil,* § 87a, e.
56. *Ibid.,* § 87c; *Logische Untersuchungen,* II, 2, p. 162, ". . . Gegenüber der Mannigfaltigkeit von einzelnen Momenten einer und derselben Art, diese Art *selbst,* und *zwar als eine und dieselbe vor Augen* stehen kann . . . wir werden uns . . . auf Grund mehrerer individueller Anschauungen der Identität des Allgemeinen bewusst. . . ."
57. Husserl, *Erfahrung und Urteil,* § 87b: "Es kommt . . . darauf an, dass die Variation als Prozess der Variantenbildung selbst eine *Beliebigkeitsgestalt* habe, dass der Prozess im Bewusstsein beliebiger Fortbildung von Varianten vollzogen sei."
58. Cf. above, p. 363.

real properties; rather, it embraces pure possibilities, i.e., possible varieties.[59] If it is justifiable to speak of an empirical extension of an *eidos,* and if eidetic relationships hold, and hold even necessarily and *a priori,* for matters of fact, it is because every real occurrence may and must be considered as a possible variety which happens to be actualized. By the same token, the distinction, upon which we previously insisted, between a class in the conceptual sense and a perceptual grouping which exhibits the *figurales Moment* of, for example, qualitative homogeneity, finds here its ultimate validation.

As already mentioned, the process of "free variation" is carried out in imagination. All the forms which originate from each other by way of transformation and variation play their roles as, and *only* as, possible varieties, i.e., as possibly contrivable in imagination. This holds without exception for every member of the series generated in the process under discussion. It also holds for the member from which the process starts, even when the member in question happens to be a real occurrence. For the process of ideation to apply to an object given in actual experience, the latter object must be subjected to what Husserl occasionally calls "eidetic reduction." [60] By eidetic reduction, the real existent is divested of its actuality, of its existential character, its spatio-temporal determinations from which it derives its individualization, and of all those characters that accrue to it on account of its integration into the real world.[61] Every real existent can be regarded as an actualized possibility. Under the eidetic reduction, the fact of its actualization is considered as immaterial and, hence, is disregarded. What is encountered as a matter of fact, is "irrealized"; i.e., considered as to its imaginableness and not as to its actuality, it is transformed into a "pure possibility" among other possibilities.[62] From the status of a real existent, it is transferred to that of an example or exemplar lending itself to "free variations" and thus becoming apt to function as starting point for an infinitely open series of possible (i.e., imaginable) varieties.[63] Eidetic reduction is obviously a necessary condition for a real existent to play a role in ideation. Only possibilities can find insertion into a process whose very purpose is to yield a survey of what is possible in a certain domain.

Recalling Goldstein's characterization of the modification under-gone by brain-injured persons, we can, in the light of the results which we have now attained, understand the incapacity of the patients

59. Husserl, *Erfahrung und Urteil,* §§ 90f.

60. Husserl, *Ideen,* I, p. 4. Emphatically, "eidetic reduction" ought not to be confounded with phenomenological or transcendental reduction.

61. Cf. *ibid.,* § 2; *Erfahrung und Urteil,* § 89.

62. Husserl, *Cartesian Meditations,* pp. 70f.

63. Husserl, *Erfahrung und Urteil,* pp. 410f.

mentioned to perform any operation which involves ideation.[64] Overwhelmed by the actuality of factual experience, the patients in question are unable to conceive of possibilities; they cannot imagine any actual experience to be possibly different from what it actually is.[65] In the case of the patients, the very pre-condition of ideation, which we found to be conception of facts as actualized possibilities and free variability of the latter in and by imagination, is not realized. Expressing it in Kantian terms, Merleau-Ponty speaks of an affection of productive imagination rather than understanding (*entendement*).[66] By its very structure, the perceptual experience of the patients resists being subjected to imaginational operations, processes, and transformations. Thus we are brought back before the rigidity in the perception of the patients in contrast with what we tentatively described as plasticity in the perceptual experience of normal persons.[67] When we refer to psychopathological findings, it is because, by way of contrast, these findings permit us to disclose conditions which, just on account of their realization in the case of normal persons, are likely to be taken for granted and hence to be overlooked. The structure of perceptual experience proves, we submit, a necessary condition of ideation and, therefore, an important problem for the phenomenology of ideation. It is to this problem that we wish to call attention.

64. Cf. above, pp. 366ff.
65. We wish to stress that the modification in question is not peculiar to amnesia of color names alone. Impairment of imagination in the sense mentioned has been observed by Gelb and Goldstein in numerous patients exhibiting the most diversified symptoms.
66. Merleau-Ponty, *Phénoménologie de la perception*, p. 224.
67. Cf. above, p. 379

# 16 / On a Perceptual Root of Abstraction[1]

ACCORDING TO HUSSERL, a distinction has to be made between generalizing and formalizing abstraction.[2] By means of generalizing abstraction one arrives at notions such as "red," "color," "sensuous quality," or "triangle," "planimetric figure," "spatial form," etc. Each of these notions refers to what Husserl calls a "material region"—that is to say, a region circumscribed and defined by a certain qualitative content of whatever pertains to it. If, therefore, an object, a fact, a phenomenon, can be considered as an instance of one of these notions, it is because of its material and qualitative nature. Each of the notions in question expresses an *invariant* with regard to variations and varieties. Starting from a certain red, for example, one can vary, if only in imagination, its brightness; one can even vary its shade or hue while taking care that all the resulting variations remain red. Since the variations concern a certain qualitative and material content some traits of which remain constant, the corresponding invariant—the notion "red" in the example considered—is also material and qualitative in nature.

The case is quite different with regard to the notions obtained by formalizing abstraction. Such purely formal notions as "object," "property," "relation," "symmetrical relation," "transitive relation," "multiplicity," "class," "member of a class," "number," "whole," "part," etc. have no reference to any specific material region. All these notions which have a preponderant importance in the purely formal sciences —that is, in logic and in strictly analytical mathematics, or which,

1. This essay was originally published in *Actes du XI*ᵉ *Congrès International de Philosophie* (Amsterdam, 1953).

2. Husserl, *Logische Untersuchugen* (Halle, 1913), II, iii, §§ 11f. *Ideen zu einer reinen Phänomenologie und phänomenologischen Philosophie* (Halle, 1913), I, §§ 13, 16; *Erfahrung und Urteil* (Hamburg, 1954), §§ 62, 85.

more correctly, are the only ones to play a role in these sciences—are considered by Husserl as derivative forms of the concept of "something at large." Since they refer to no material region in particular, notions of this kind refer or can refer to every one of these regions— that is to say, to any object, content, or phenomenon, whatever its qualitative and material nature. Hence the universal and unrestricted validity and applicability of mathematical and logical notions. For the same reason, formal notions in no way may be obtained by means of variation of material and qualitative contents. None of these notions can be considered as an invariant with regard to such variations. In contrast to the transition to the general, the formal is reached by substituting, for qualitative and material contents, terms which are quite indeterminate as to their material signification and which are defined solely by their mutual relations. At a higher level of formalization, even the specific nature of the relations themselves is left indeterminate, and they are defined by their formal properties alone.

These views established by Husserl are in almost complete agreement with those of Piaget. According to Piaget, "abstraction on the basis of the object" (*abstraction à partir de l'objet*) must be distinguished from "abstraction on the basis of action" (*abstraction à partir de l'action*).[3] The formal notions which figure in logic and mathematics—arithmetic as well as geometry—arise, according to Piaget, by way of "abstraction on the basis of action." In the final analysis, these notions are derived from the simplest actions or, more precisely, from the coordinations between such actions. By simplest actions are meant classing or grouping of objects, serial arrangement, joining, disjoining, displacement, etc. Studying, from the genetic point of view, the gradual elaboration of operative deductive systems—such as arithmetic and geometry in their fully developed form—Piaget goes back to the simplest actions as they are performed at the beginning of life and emphasizes their stabilization and progressive coordination in the course of development. The most important aspect of this stabilization is the development of the actions toward reversibility. Since the actions in question are independent of the specific nature of the objects to which they apply, they may be applied to objects of any sort —the objects being, so to speak, but aliments for the function or activity. The universal validity, or, to express it in Husserl's terms, the entirely formal character, of mathematical notions is easily explained by their being derived from "abstraction on the basis of action" and not from "abstraction on the basis of the object."

A discussion, from the phenomenological point of view, of Piaget's

3. J. Piaget, *Introduction à l'epistémologie génétique* (Paris, 1950), I, chap. I, §§ 1–2, 12.

theory both in general terms as to the very idea of a genetic epistemology and with reference to the particular problem here in question, would be very interesting and highly instructive. Here we cannot enter into such a discussion. In making use of some views of Piaget and of some results obtained in Gestalt theory, we are seeking to delineate with some precision certain perceptual structures from which, it seems to us, the abstractive processes, generalizing as well as formalizing, take their departure. Our analyses will be guided by Husserl's principle that logical forms have their origin in structures of perceptual consciousness.[4] We are far from overlooking the difference between generalization and formalization. Still, this distinction plays a lesser role in a study of the perceptual basis of the abstractive processes than it would in an analysis of the processes of abstraction themselves.

The perceptual structure which seems to deserve most attention in the present context is what, following Husserl, we will call the inner horizon.[5] A thing perceived is not merely a sum of sensuous qualities given to the senses at the moment of perception, such as, for example, a certain color, form, size, some auditory datum, tactile or thermal properties, etc. Nor is the perceived thing a sum of such actually given qualities to which are added remembered qualities of a similar kind. Through particular perception, the perceived thing presents itself in a merely unilateral way; it appears under a certain aspect, to the exclusion of every other, from one determinate side, in this orientation rather than in another. Every unilateral presentation of a thing contains references to aspects under which the thing does not appear at the moment but under which it would present itself under certain conditions—for example, if the perceiving subject assumed a different determinate point of observation. These references must not be considered as memories or images simply superadded to what is given in sensory experience. On the contrary, they are part and parcel of the actual appearance of the thing and contribute in an essential way to determining the sense of what is perceived, so much so that the latter would not be what it is for perceptual consciousness were it not for the references in question.

To illustrate, consider the perception of a house. What we perceive is not the façade of a house but is the house itself presenting itself from a certain side. By the very sense of what presents itself in the

4. Husserl has formulated and, to a very large measure, realized this principle in two of his works which must be counted as pertaining to the "later period" of his thought: *Formale und transzendentale Logik* (Halle, 1929) and *Erfahrung und Urteil* (previously cited).

5. For the relevant theories of the phenomenology of perception, see A. Gurwitsch, *The Field of Consciousness* (Pittsburgh, 1964), Pt. IV, chaps. I–II.

present perception, the latter refers to further perceptions through which the house will appear under different aspects. Such references may be determined to a higher or lesser degree. That is to say, the sides which are not seen at the moment but to which the present perception contains references can be given with greater or lesser determinateness as to their details. If we perceive the house for the first time, not being familiar with the façades other than that we see, the references in question will be entirely indeterminate. Nevertheless, for what we perceive to be a house presenting itself from a certain side, the present perception must contain references to other sides, whatever the condition of their details and the indeterminateness of the latter.

The phenomenon of the inner horizon manifests the dependence of present perception upon previous experience. If, however, the past has efficacy for the present, it is not because residues of previous experiences—images or memories—are superadded to present sensory data. To learn from experience means, according to Gestalt theory, acquiring modes of seeing, hearing, perceiving, also of acting.[6] The efficacy of the past results from the permanence of certain structures and forms of organization developed through the appropriate experiences in the past. In Piaget's terminology, in the course of the evolution of the individual, "schemes" are formed, established, and come to be consolidated.[7] By virtue of its assimilating power, each of these "schemes" applies or at least tends to apply to whatever object is encountered. For that reason, Piaget considers these "schemes" as functional sensory-motor equivalents of concepts.[8] However—and here we are following ideas which derive from Gestalt theory rather than from those of Piaget—reorganization and restructuring concern not only the psychic function (that function which is crystallized in "schemes") but also and above all the objective correlates of this function: namely, the objects, whether assimilated or still to be assimilated to "schemes."[9] The objects become what the assimilating "schemes" make them to be—for example, "something for writing," "something to be handled in a certain way." Objects appear in the light of "schemes"; they are perceived under the perspective of the latter. Its assimilation—whether actual or possible—to a certain "scheme" determines and defines the object as it figures in conscious life—that is, as it presents itself and therefore as that which it is from the phenomenal point of view. For this reason, the inner horizon has

6. W. Köhler, *Gestalt Psychology* (New York, 1929), chaps. VI, X; K. Koffka, *Principles of Gestalt Psychology* (1935), chaps. III, XII–XIII.
7. J. Piaget, *La naissance de l'intelligence chez l'enfant* (Paris, 1936).
8. *Ibid.*, pp. 92, 241ff.
9. Cf. Gurwitsch, *The Field of Consciousness*, Pt. I, chap. II, 3 d.

to be considered as an intrinsic, essential, and constitutive component of every perceptual presentation of an object. The same also holds for the simple actions from which, according to Piaget, logical and mathematical operations finally emerge. Once these actions are established and coordinated with one another, any object appears or may appear as assimilable to them, as lending itself to a certain manipulation corresponding to a certain action, or at least as a possible aliment of the function in question, the reason being the elementary or fundamental character, hence the universality of the actions under discussion. Let us stress again the assimilating of the "schemes."

Since the reference to a certain "scheme of assimilation" is among the constitutive characters of the sense of the perceived as such, the objects which we perceive always appear in a certain generic typicality. What we perceive are not simply singular and individual things; they belong instead to a certain class or a certain type: they exhibit a certain style. Type and style may be given with greater or lesser determinateness. However, even in the extreme case—that is, when we perceive an object for the first time so that all its details not seen at present are unknown to us and therefore totally indeterminate—the object in question still presents itself as pertaining to a certain type of which, at least, some characteristic outlines are relatively determined. Hence total unfamiliarity proves to be a privative mode of familiarity.[10]

Such is the perceptual structure from which, we submit, one has to start in accounting for the process of abstraction. Within the limits of the present discussion we cannot embark upon the analysis of that process itself. Let us restrict ourselves to two final remarks. In the process of abstraction, the operation of thematization must come into play. Thematization consists in disengaging and rendering explicit a number of factors which, previous to that operation, were already efficacious but were so only implicitly and, so to speak, tacitly. What is disengaged may be the actions themselves and their mutual inter-coordinations, or else it may be that which, when thematization is accomplished, will appear as principle or point of view with respect to which certain objects have been or may be handled or subjected to a determinate operation. This operation may, moreover, be completely interiorized. According to the direction taken by thematization, one arrives in the first case at formalizing abstraction and in the second case at generalizing abstraction.

TRANSLATED BY ABIGAIL L. ROSENTHAL

10. Husserl, *Erfahrung und Urteil*, p. 34: ". . . *Unbekanntheit* ist jederzeit zugleich ein *Modus der Bekanntheit*." Cf. above, "Contribution to the Phenomenological Theory of Perception."

# 17 / On the Conceptual Consciousness[1]

MANY CONTEMPORARY LOGICIANS seek to account for the notion of class in terms of propositional function. Let $f$ signify, for example, "is red" or "is a dog." Then one has the propositional function $f(x)$ which, $x$ being a variable, has the meaning "$x$ is red" or "$x$ is a dog." By substituting individual terms for the variable, the propositional function gives rise to propositions which, according to the substitutions which are made, are true or false. One then defines the class as the set of individual terms which, substituted for the variable, confer a value of truth upon the propositions derived from the original propositional function by means of these substitutions.[2]

By proceeding in this way, one not only defines the concept in extension, because it has been defined in terms of class (which appears opportune from the operational point of view), but it also seems possible to avoid all "Platonism" and to exempt oneself from having recourse to "metaphysical" entities such as the Idea or the concept taken in intension. In fact, the procedure just sketched does not seem to rely on any presupposition. All that is required is the verification of propositions such as "This book is red." The very notion of concept being thus avoided, no ontological problem can consequently be raised with regard to it.

It is certainly legitimate to make a propositional function correspond to every class and to define the latter as the set of individual terms satisfying the condition mentioned. From the formal point of view, this presentation certainly offers advantages. However, it re-

1. This essay was originally published in *Edmund Husserl 1859–1959* (*Phaenomenologica*, Vol. IV [The Hague, 1959]). An English translation has appeared in K. Sayre and F. Crosson (eds.), *The Modeling of Mind* (Notre Dame, 1963).

2. Cf. C. Serrus, *Traité de logique* (Paris, 1949), pp. 176–77; J. Piaget, *Traité de logique*, p. 53.

mains to be seen whether, by proceeding in this fashion, one can succeed in accounting for the notion of class and of conceptual thought in general. In particular it must be asked whether the process itself by which propositions of the type in question are verified does not contain hidden presuppositions.

In this regard the pathology of language has some significant findings. Gelb and Goldstein have drawn attention to patients suffering from amnesic aphasia who, when presented with very familiar objects—for example a pencil, an umbrella, a knife, etc.—are not capable of saying what these objects are called.[3] It is not that the patients no longer recognize them: on the contrary, by using circumlocutions, the patients describe adequately the use for which these objects are intended. Nor is it that they have forgotten the words. When they are presented with a series of words, they almost never make an incorrect choice, indeed they seize upon the proper word for the object presented.[4] Moreover, the patients readily use words such as "handkerchief," "penholder," etc., but they do so only when these words have a function other than that of serving as *names designating a certain class or category of objects.* It is only when the words assume this function of designation that the patients are no longer capable of finding them.

Gelb and Goldstein explain these phenomena as the result of a weakening or even a total loss of the "categorial attitude." According to these authors, the patients are reduced to the "concrete attitude." Of these rather complex notions, let us retain only the following characteristics.[5] To be reduced to the "concrete attitude" means to be captivated by the present concrete situation in which one finds oneself, to be dominated by the imposed reality in all its massiveness, to the point where it becomes impossible to establish any distance between

3. For what follows, we refer to the articles of A. Gelb, "Remarques générales sur l'utilisation des données pathologiques pour la psychologie et la philosophie du langage," and of K. Goldstein, "L'analyse de l'aphasie et l'étude de l'essence du langage," pp. 471–91. The two articles appeared in the *Journal de Psychologie Normale et Pathologique* (1933) and have been reprinted in the collection of articles, *Psychologie du langage* (Paris, 1933). We refer also to the book of Goldstein, *Language and Language Disturbances* (New York, 1948), chaps. IVA, VB, VIII.

4. We leave aside the case of amnesia of the names of colors, where the difficulties which the patients experience increase further because of the very nature of color names. Cf. Goldstein, "L'analyse de l'aphasie," pp. 487–89.

5. For a general characterization of "concrete" and "categorial" attitudes, cf. Gelb, "Remarques générales," *loc. cit.*, pp. 415–17; Goldstein, "L'analyse de l'aphasie," pp. 454–56; *Language and Language Disturbances*, pp. 6–8; Goldstein, *The Organism* (New York, 1939), p. 30. See above, "Gelb-Goldstein's Concept of 'Concrete' and 'Categorial' Attitude and the Phenomenology of Ideation."

oneself and the present situation of the moment. It means, further-more, to know how to act and manipulate things, but without being able to render an account of what one does. The objects with which the patient has to do present themselves to him as linked and bound to a situation of practical action. The objects appear to him in the light of the role which they play within a concrete situation, and they appear to him only under that light. As they exist for the patients, the objects are completely determined by the function which they fulfill within a concrete situation. On the basis of the particular periphrases employed by the patients,[6] it may even be said that in their eyes the objects are defined by the usage to which they lend themselves, that they are as it were impregnated by the sense which they derive from their practical role, and that their sense is exhausted by that role. Thus, the patients are not capable of detaching an object presented to them from the situation of action in which that object is meant to function, so as to relate it to a context other than that of concrete action. In particular, the patients are no longer capable of regarding an object under the aspect of its similitude with other objects, of taking a given object as representative of similar objects which, by reason of their similarity, can be considered as belonging to the same class. The patients can no longer apperceive the object presented to them as an example or a particular case of a type or of a concept. To envisage an object in that manner, it is in fact necessary to extract it from the context of concrete action and to refer it to a conceptual order. This is precisely what the patients can no longer do. Consequently, words, to the extent to which they express a conceptual classifying of things and hence require for their understanding the adoption of the "categorial" attitude, have lost all meaning for the patients.

The theory just summarized, perhaps too succinctly, allows us to bring out a presupposition which, without being formulated or made explicit, lies at the base of the explanation mentioned above of the notion of class in terms of propositional function and verified proposition. In fact, in order for a proposition such as "This book is red" or "This is a pencil" to be verified, it is not enough that a red book or a pencil be present or perceived. The book must be perceived *as red*, the pencil *as pencil*.[7] These objects thus do not appear so much in the

6. Cf. Goldstein, "L'analyse de l'aphasie," *loc. cit.*, pp. 472, 490, and *Language and Language Disturbances*, pp. 248–50, 254, 287–88, for some representative examples of these periphrases.

7. With respect to a patient who was suffering from amnesia of color names and who was no longer able to arrange skeins of wool according to a principle of classification such as fundamental hue, brightness, etc., Gelb, "Remarques géné-rales," *loc. cit.*, p. 411, writes: "Rapprocher . . . les teintes egalement claires, parce qu'elles s'accordent en fait . . . est tout autre chose que de connaître ces

light of a context of concrete action as in the role which they play with respect to the propositional function and the proposition to be verified. More precisely, the object in question must be envisaged in reference to the propositional function within which it is substituted for the variable, in reference also to the proposition which, resulting from that substitution, acquires a value of truth from the fact of referring to that object. It is not enough for the object to possess in fact the attributes and the qualities which make a pencil or a red book; it must be regarded as presenting these qualities which, in their turn, must be apprehended as corresponding to the meanings which figure in the proposition in question. Nor must the verification of the latter be taken for an event which simply occurs. At the very least, it is an *event ascertained:* that is, the object must be conceived of as conferring a value of truth on the proposition which refers to it. Furthermore, by the very fact that the object in question is substituted for a variable, it refers to other objects which could equally be substituted and which would also confer a value of truth on the resulting proposition, thereby entering into the same class with it.

Obviously all this is possible only in the "categorial" attitude which proves to be the indispensable condition of conceptual thought. The Platonic problem thus persists, transferred, it is true, from the ontological plane to that of consciousness. What is in question, at least at first, is not the existence of universals nor their mode of being but the conceptual consciousness itself, whose specific and irreducible nature must be recognized.

We have referred to the pathology of language because the study of patients who have lost the faculty of adopting the "categorial" attitude makes clear a pre-condition of conceptual thought which, just because it is always fulfilled in normal persons, can easily be taken for granted and thus escape attention. It should be noted that the observations of Gelb and Goldstein fully confirm the views and the distinctions on which Husserl insisted in the *Logische Untersuchungen*.[8] Moreover, the full philosophical significance of the theory of Gelb and Goldstein is best brought out when their work is placed in the perspective of Husserlian phenomenology.

While insisting on the specific character of conceptual consciousness, we are far from contesting its link with perceptual consciousness. Following the general direction in which Husserl was

---

teintes *en tant qu'analogues* par la clarté, puis de choisir cette propriéte comme principe de classement." This remark expresses clearly the presupposition we have in mind.

8. In this regard, cf. above, "Gelb-Goldstein's Concept of 'Concrete' and 'Categorial' Attitude and the Phenomenology of Ideation."

oriented, especially in the last period of his life, we maintain that in order to account for conceptual thought it is necessary to go back to pre-predicative experience. Let us indicate the terms in which this problem is to be raised.

In pre-predicative experience, we do not find ourselves, as a rule, before beings and objects wholly unique and particularized down to the last details. Except for a few beings and things which have for us the significance of unexchangeable individuals, in the vast majority of cases we perceive *objects and beings of a certain kind.* We perceive trees, automobiles, dogs, human beings, etc. In our practical life, we handle the objects which we encounter in the way in which objects of such and such a kind are treated. Perceived objects appear to us with generic determinations and in a certain typicality.[9] But—and this is the decisive point—*to perceive an object of a certain kind is not at all the same thing as apperceiving that object as representative or as a particular case of a type.*[10] In other words, pre-predicative perceptual consciousness is indeed pervaded by the generic and typical; but the latter is enveloped in the perceived objects, inherent in them, incorporated in them. The words which we use in ordinary language seem to us to express that typicality in which things present themselves. In fact, as some logicians have long since noted, if one speaks of a blue fabric, this does not mean placing that fabric in the same class as the sky, the Mediterranean, some inks, certain persons' eyes, etc.[11] We would rather say that the word "blue" here renders a typical chromatic quality, that manner of being blue which fabrics have in distinction, for example, to inks.[12] Moreover, it seems to us that if patients suffering from amnesic aphasia sometimes use words which they cannot find when these words have a categorial meaning, i.e., when they designate objects as belonging to a certain class, this is because

9. This characteristic, very essential to perceptual experience, had been brought out by Husserl in *Erfahrung und Urteil* (Hamburg, 1954), § 8. It was explored and developed by A. Schutz in several of his works, of which in particular we mention the articles, "Language, Language Disturbances and the Texture of Consciousness," *Social Research,* XVII (1950) (written *a propos* of Goldstein's book), and "Common-sense and Scientific Interpretation of Human Action," *Philosophy and Phenomenological Research,* XIV (1953). (Both of these articles have been reprinted in A. Schutz, *Collected Papers,* Vol. I [The Hague, 1962].) We have spoken of the characteristic in question in connection with the phenomenological theory of perception, which we have developed in our book, *The Field of Consciousness* (Pittsburgh, 1964), Pt. IV, chap. II, 3.

10. Gelb, "Remarques générales," *loc. cit.,* p. 411.

11. Cf. Serrus, *loc. cit.,* p. 213.

12. See also M. Merleau-Ponty, *Phénoménologie de la perception* (Paris, 1945), p. 361: "Une couleur n'est jamais simplement couleur, mais couleur d'un certain objet, et le bleu d'un tapis ne serait pas le même bleu s'il n'était un bleu laineux."

those words, in the eyes of the patients, express generic traits linked to the objects and imbedded in them. Goldstein characterizes these words as "proper names" or as sonorous complexes which, properly speaking, convey no meanings at all but belong to the object as qualities among others.[13] However, we believe that the expression "proper name" must not be taken too strictly. In fact, if in the eyes of the patients a word is appropriate to a certain object, for example to a knife, it is not that the word is appropriate only to this individual knife to the exclusion of every other. We would say that the word is appropriate to the use which can be made of the knife, hence to its generic typicality, which—let it be emphasized—remains inherent in it.[14] The same explanation can be given of the fact already mentioned that patients confronted with an object whose name they cannot find almost always choose the correct word among those proposed to them.

The first step in the constitution of conceptual consciousness consists in effecting a dissociation within the object perceived in its typicality. The generic traits which until then were immanent and imbedded in the perceived thing are detached and disengaged from it. Made explicit, these traits can be apprehended in themselves and crystallized into a new and specific object of consciousness. This object is the concept taken in intension. By virtue of this dissociation, *the generic becomes the general.* As such it is opposed to the thing perceived from which it has just been disengaged. Now the thing is transformed into an example, a particular instance, and, in this sense, into a representative of the concept. By the same token, one can conceive the idea of a set of particular instances of the concept in question, instances which can all represent, i.e., stand for, one another in the sense that, with respect to the concept, they are all equivalent.[15] This is the notion of the concept in extension, or, as modern logicians say, the notion of class. The disengagement of the generic and its transformation into the general can found a second operation by which ideal concepts are constituted, normative in some way: that is, Ideas in the Platonic sense. They must be understood, at least in the initial phases of the analysis, purely as objects of consciousness so far as they are meant and intended by conceptual consciousness and without any ontological preoccupation.

The dissociation or disengagement just referred to seems to us to be a particular form of a very general operation for which we propose the name *thematization.* It consists in unfolding and articulating a

13. Goldstein, "L'analyse de l'aphasie," *loc. cit.,* p. 476; *Language and Language Disturbances,* pp. 61–63, 257–58, 269.
14. For a confirmation of this interpretation, see *ibid.,* pp. 471–73, 488–89.
15. Cf. Piaget, *loc. cit.,* p. 213.

noesis or a noema into its constituents. The latter, which before thematization were imbedded in the initial noesis or noema and had an implicit efficacy—but nonetheless an efficacy—are now unraveled and displayed. Consequently, they can be apprehended and become themes themselves, whereas previously they only contributed to the constitution of another theme within which they played merely a silent role. The result to which thematization leads obviously depends on the nature of the constituents in question. Since, in the case which interests us here, thematization is effected on generic traits and characters, it yields the general and the conceptual. It is to the operation of thematization that we wish to call attention; because of its universal scope, this operation of consciousness seems to us to merit more intensive study.

TRANSLATED BY F. J. CROSSON

# 18 / The Last Work
## of Edmund Husserl[1]

IN 1936 HUSSERL PUBLISHED the first of an intended series of articles which were to deal with the general intellectual crisis of our time, especially the crisis of the sciences, and with transcendental phenomenology as a way, the *only* way, to overcome that crisis.[2] The series would have become the principal document of the last phase of Husserl's phenomenology and would have provided the center of reference of his other writings pertaining to that phase: *viz.*, *Formale und transzendentale Logik* (1929) and *Erfahrung und Urteil* (edited by L. Landgrebe and published in 1939, after Husserl's death; reissued in 1954). Because of his final illness, Husserl had to discontinue all work after August, 1937, so that the planned series was never completed, the article of 1936 having thus far been the only one to appear in print.

In collaboration with the Archives-Husserl at the University of Louvain—founded and directed by H. L. van Breda—Walter Biemel of the Husserl-Archiv at the University of Köln has edited the article of 1936 and its continuation by Husserl, as far as Husserl was able to proceed with it.[3] The present volume furthermore contains the enlarged text of a lecture which Husserl delivered in Vienna in May, 1935, "Die Krisis des europäischen Menschentums und die Philo-

1. This discussion was originally published in *Philosophy and Phenomenological Research*, XVI (1956), XVII (1957).
2. E. Husserl, "Die Krisis der europäischen Wissenschaften und die transzendentale Phänomenologie: Eine Einleitung in die phänomenologische Philosophie," *Philosophia*, I (Belgrade, 1936). A French translation of this article by Edmond Gerrer appeared in *Les Études Philosophiques*, N.S. IV (1949).
3. Husserl, *Die Krisis der europäischen Wissenschaften und die transzendentale Phänomenologie*, ed. W. Biemel (*Husserliana*, Vol. VI [The Hague, 1954]).

sophie"[4] as well as two elaborated and comparatively self-contained essays, "Realitätswissenschaft und Idealisierung: Die Mathematisierung der Natur" and "Naturwissenschaftliche und geisteswissenschaftliche Einstellung: Naturalismus, Dualismus, und psychophysiche Psychologie." As a novelty in the *Husserliana* series Biemel has included a certain number of research manuscripts which enlarge and complement the main text.[5] These manuscripts shed light on the genesis of Husserl's last great work. Since Husserl did not live to see the completion of his last work, a further research manuscript has been selected by Biemel to serve as a conclusion.

All students of phenomenology are highly indebted to Biemel for the masterly fashion in which he has rendered accessible *Die Krisis*, this most important work of Husserl. The edition of the present volume again shows the skillful, reliable, and devoted craftsmanship to which the editors of *Husserliana* have accustomed their readers.

The volume under discussion bears the subtitle "An Introduction into Phenomenological Philosophy." However, it is not an introduction like *Cartesianische Meditationen*, for example, in which the main problems and central theories of phenomenology are gradually developed. The reader is to be led towards phenomenological philosophy as a line of thinking which alone offers a way out of the crisis that has befallen Western man.[6] Unlike Husserl's other writings, the present volume opens up vistas and offers general indications of direction rather than results of analytical work on particular phenomena. Therefore we shall confine ourselves to retracing, in some detail, the general lines of Husserl's exposition without embarking upon special problems. Such discussions and critical examinations are best left to future studies which this great work will certainly inspire. It appears opportune to divide this report into two parts, the first dealing with Husserl's historical reflections and reflections on history, while the other part pertains to the new approach to phenomenology which Husserl opens up in the volume under consideration.

4. The original title of the Viennese lecture was "Die Philosophie in der Krisis der europäischen Menschheit." A different version of the enlarged text of this lecture has been translated into French by P. Ricoeur in *Revue de Métaphysique et de Morale*, LV (1950). In November, 1935, Husserl lectured in Prague, in both the German and the Czech universities. "Die Krisis der europäischen Wissenschaften und die transzendentale Phänomenologie" grew out of the Prague lectures.

5. Two of the research manuscripts are by E. Fink. One of Husserl's research manuscripts had already been edited by Fink under the title "Die Frage nach dem Ursprung der Geometrie als intentional-historisches Problem" and published in *Revue Internationale de Philosophie*, I (1939); cf. its careful and detailed analysis by D. Cairns in *Philosophy and Phenomenological Research*, I (1940), pp. 98ff.

6. Husserl speaks of "Europe" and "European man" but notes explicitly that these terms are not meant to be understood in a geographical sense. We may therefore safely replace his terms by the wider ones of "West" and "Western man."

## [I] WESTERN PHILOSOPHY AND SCIENCE

### 1. The Meaning of the Present Crisis and the Historicity of Philosophy

WHAT IS THE NATURE of the present crisis to which phenomenological philosophy is asserted by Husserl to offer a solution? If the existence of Western man appears critical and problematical, it is because he has allowed himself to become unfaithful to his idea, the very idea that defines and constitutes him as Western man. That idea is no other than the idea of philosophy itself: the idea of a universal knowledge concerning the totality of being, a knowledge which contains within itself whatever special sciences may grow out of it as its ramifications, which rests upon ultimate foundations and proceeds throughout in a completely evident and self-justifying fashion and in full awareness of itself. Closely connected with this idea, whose inception in ancient Greece in the 7th and 6th centuries B.C. marks the historical beginning of Western man, is the idea of a truly human, i.e., philosophical, existence, an existence oriented towards the ideas, ideals, and norms of autonomous reason, which alone permits Western man to live in conformity and at peace with himself.

Paradoxically enough, it is owing to the one-sided and, therefore, distorting as well as distorted realization of the idea of philosophy since the Renaissance—*viz.*, its realization through the positive sciences—that Western man has lost sight of the idea which makes him what he is and has thus become alienated from himself. In the course of their development, expansion, and growth (which Husserl is ready to admire), the sciences have undergone a process of specialization and technization. Perhaps this was unavoidable; but it has led to forsaking those very philosophical aspirations out of which Western science was born and by which it had been sustained in the 17th and 18th centuries. Who indeed can today look at science as the thinkers of those centuries did? Who can still maintain that science has the function of enabling Western man to renew himself under the idea of his rationality, to lead an authentic existence as a rational being, to order freely and reasonably his relations to his environment, his fellow-men, and himself? In the prevailing positivistic interpretation, the sciences appear as expedients to predict facts and events and to manipulate them. All questions concerning human reason, which is but a title for "eternal" or atemporal ideas and norms—among them true knowledge, authentic value, genuinely good action, etc.—are eliminated from the sciences, not only from the natural sciences which anyhow confine themselves to the corporeal aspect of reality, but from the humane sciences as well. In the latter, too, man is regarded merely as to his factuality, as an object like any other one in whose study the objectivistic methods of the natural sciences must be emulated.[7] However, if the human mind and human rationality are either overlooked or explained away in a naturalistic fashion, the sciences themselves become unintelligible. Since they are products and creations of the human mind, the foundations upon which they rest, the sense of their procedures and accomplishments, and the limitations of their legitimacy cannot be brought to light except by referring the very products to the generating and producing (*leistende*) mental activities. If this most essential context is overlooked— in recent times it has increasingly become the tendency to disregard it —the sciences appear as most ingenious technical devices which one may learn to use and which, if properly handled, will yield most remarkable, even marvelous, results but whose interior mechanism and functioning remain utterly obscure.

The crisis of the Western sciences does not concern their technical validity. What is in question is the meaning of the sciences in a philosophical sense and, no less important, their human significance. They familiarize us with facts and their concatenations, with the conditions under which certain facts occur. In a world in which there are merely facts and in which man himself appears as nothing but a most complex fact, there is no room for the norms and ideas of reason. They become unintelligible. Science, it seems, has nothing to say regarding things that matter most for human existence.[8] Hence the growing skepticism, if not hostility, with regard to the sciences extends to reason itself, whose paramount manifestations and creations the sciences are. Losing faith in reason, Western man loses faith in himself. All the irrationalistic and anti-intellectualistic tendencies which have of late made their appearance on the Western scene are symptoms of the disease which has befallen Western man, of his estrangement from himself, of his betrayal of himself, that paradoxical betrayal through partial realization. For his salvation, Western man must not try to escape from himself; on the contrary, he must endeavor to find himself again. At this point phenomenological

7. We have set forth the naturalistic conception of man as it prevails especially in the contemporary psychological and social sciences in our article "On Contemporary Nihilism," *Review of Politics*, VII (1945).

8. Husserl argues exclusively on the theoretical level, since he had not yet the opportunity to appreciate the crisis of Western science under the politico-practical aspect with which we have become acquainted during the last decade. This aspect has been brought to the fore by E. Voegelin in his most illuminating article "On the Origins of Scientism," *Social Research*, XV (1948).

philosophy appears in its historical significance and mission. It purports the return to the *idea of philosophy*, though certainly not to any philosophical system of the past. Resuscitating the idea of philosophy in the classical sense in which it was conceived in Greece, re-orienting Western man towards this idea as the τέλος of his historical existence, phenomenology permits him to become again true to himself.[9]

It is not by an accident or through a blind fate that Western man has fallen into his present existential crisis. To show how that crisis grew organically in the history of Western thinking and to convince his readers that at the present historical stage phenomenology is necessitated by the meaning of Western history, or, more correctly, by the sense of the historicity of Western man, if the very foundations of his historical existence are to be retrieved, Husserl engages himself in historical considerations of a particular kind.[10] In view of the vital role which, according to him, philosophy has played for Western culture, his historical studies bear upon the history of philosophy. The purpose of his historical considerations is not to satisfy an interest in the past for its own sake. The contemporary philosopher has to be made aware of his position within a historical context and of the task which he has to assume if he is to be faithful to his vocation as a philosopher. It is the essential *inner historicity* of the philosopher and of the realization of the idea of philosophy that has to be disclosed. Husserl's history of philosophy is at the same time, and even primarily, a philosophy of history.

What Husserl sets out to study is not a plurality of philosophical systems, considered as historico-cultural phenomena and the logical or other concatenations that might obtain between them; nor does he emphasize their dependency and influence upon the products of other historico-cultural activities. Rather, he embarks upon the *history of the very idea of philosophy*, its inauguration in Greek antiquity, its renewal in the Renaissance, its subsequent transformations. Such an idea can be apprehended and have efficacy in different modes, that of explicitness to a greater or lesser degree as well as those of compara-

9. Husserl's description of the crisis of Western science is reminiscent of that which Max Weber had given about 20 years before. Cf. "Wissenschaft als Beruf," in *Gesammelte Aufsätze zur Wissenschaftslehre* (1922), pp. 537ff. There is, however, a significant difference. Whereas Weber is prepared to resign himself to the given state of affairs, Husserl holds out the prospect of a regeneration of Western man under the very idea of philosophy, into the unity of which the sciences have to be reintegrated.

10. Husserl's late orientation towards, and his conception of, history and historicity have been analyzed in an excellent and highly instructive article by P. Ricoeur, "Husserl et le sens de l'histoire," *Revue de Métaphysique et de Morale,* LIV (1949).

tive obscurity, sedimentation, and mere traditionality. Its historical
effectiveness consists in orienting and polarizing the intentions of the
philosophers, thus unifying from within the historical process whose
τέλος the idea in question is. If the history of philosophy is more than a
mere sequence of conflicting and contradictory systems, if it has
context and coherence, this is by virtue of a "concealed unity of
intentional interiority" (*verborgene Einheit intentionaler Innerlich-
keit*). To disclose and to render explicit that "concealed unity" is the
purpose of Husserl's historico-teleological reflections. Such reflections
differ from historical studies in the usual sense insofar as they cannot
be carried out in an "inductive" manner by the analysis and comparison of texts and other documents, including the self-interpretations of
the historical philosophers. Behind and beneath all documentary
evidence, there is the orientation of the philosopher towards the
teleological idea of philosophy, that very idea which gives unity and
meaning to the historical process as a whole. A teleological idea which,
because it displays itself in the medium of history, by necessity
undergoes transformations and yet preserves its identity defines an
*infinite task*. All philosophical theories as formulated in documents
must be seen under the perspective of that infinite task. They must be
considered as to the fulfillment which they bring to that task at the
respective phases within the encompassing historical context. The
historical significance of a philosophical theory consists precisely in its
contribution towards the infinite task.

Made aware of the essential reference of every philosophical
endeavor to a teleological idea and of the place of that endeavor within
a teleologically organized and unified context, we at once become
aware of the inner historicity of philosophy. We, the philosophers of
the present age, are by no means free arbitrarily to choose our
directions, our problems, our points of departure. Assuming the
vocation and the responsibility of philosophers, we find ourselves
within a certain historical situation, and we have to accept that
situation. History does not denote a past behind us and extraneous to
us. On the contrary, the past is contained and implied within our
present. Our intentions as philosophers of the present age continue,
and are in continuity with, the intentions of our intellectual ancestors,
because we not only possess a historical heritage but are historical
beings throughout (*durch und durch . . . historisch-geistig Gewor-
dene*).

Such efficacy of the past within the present can assume two forms.
Either the past is but a sediment, merely a tradition, a transmitted
acquisition which we silently accept as a matter of course (*Selbstverständlichkeit*) without being aware of its historical nature. Or else

the acquisitions of the past may be revitalized and re-instated, resuscitated from their sedimentary condition and this by referring them to the very motives which instituted them originally and determined their formation. Far from satisfying a mere curiosity in the past, Husserl's historico-teleological reflections are meant to enable us, the contemporary philosophers, to see and to understand ourselves —that is, to find our specific task within the infinite task. Through such reflections, the historical context of philosophy is to be revivified so that we may become aware of our place within that context and of the specific task assigned to us at that place. As matters stand, our specific task is no other than a renewal and a new transformation of the very idea of philosophy. If, as Husserl contends, transcendental phenomenology proves to be the specific task which we have to assume at the present historical period, phenomenological philosophy is not a private concern of an individual philosopher or of a particular school, nor is it one possible philosophy among others equally possible. Rather, it appears as a historical "necessity"—that is, as demanded at the present phase of the history of philosophy by that history in its totality, by the very idea of philosophy itself.

## 2. The Rise of Philosophy in Ancient Greece

IN THE VIENNESE LECTURE Husserl concerns himself mainly with the institutive inception of philosophy in Greek antiquity. This inception purports a radical modification of, or departure from, the pre-philosophical and pre-theoretical attitude. To understand this departure, we have to describe briefly the pre-theoretical attitude.

Normally and originally man lives naïvely in a specific "world" (*Umwelt*) which he takes for granted and unquestionably accepts as reality. Prior to a philosophical and theoretical culture of Greco-Western style, the *Umwelt* is essentially and even necessarily of a mythico-magical nature. Deities, demons, mythical powers of every description are to be counted among the realities of the *Umwelt;* their influence extends to things and happenings of all kinds. The *Umwelt* is thus thoroughly imbued with meaning and signification; it is constituted by the sense which is bestowed upon it by the members of a certain community. To them their *Umwelt* is their reality: the world as it appears to them, as they take it to be, conceive of it, interpret it.[11]

11. If in the historical and other humane sciences (*Geisteswissenschaften*) reference is made to the world or even to the physical world, the reference is to the *Umwelt* and not to an "objective" universe "as it really is," a notion of objectivity which is of central importance for the mathematico-physical sciences of Galilean style but has no place whatever within the historico-humane sciences.

Conceptions and interpretations may and do change in the course of the history of a given community, and this purports a corresponding transformation of its *Umwelt*. For the same reason, the *Umwelt* of one community may be highly different from that of another one. *Umwelt* has an essentially mental denotation. As the product of the collective mentality of a community, *Umwelt* proves relative to that community at a certain period of its history.

As long as the pre-theoretical attitude prevails, all activities not only take place within the *Umwelt* and are oriented by the accepted traditional conceptions, but they are also pursued for the sake of living and finding one's way within the *Umwelt*. All activities, including those of cognitive or speculative nature, are motivated by, and essentially related to, practical human interests. Practicality must not be construed in a crude utilitarian sense; it purports reference to human purposes and to the general welfare of individuals as well as the community. Notions like knowledge, error, truth, falsity, reality, appearance, etc. are here relative not only to the nature and structure of the *Umwelt* in question but also to a given specific situation, to needs and desires to be satisfied at the moment, to courses of action to be taken, to plans and designs to be carried out, etc. Cognitive and speculative activities remain confined within a finite horizon, the sense of finitude being defined by the relativities mentioned. At the level in question, neither the relativity nor the finitude can obviously be disclosed and apprehended as such.

According to Plato and Aristotle, "wondering" ( θαυμάζειν ) marks the beginning of philosophy. "Wondering" is interpreted by Husserl as suspension (*epoché*) of all practical interests and adoption of the attitude of the detached onlooking observer (*unbeteiligter Zuschauer*). In this new attitude, as contrasted with the practico-mythical one, there arises the conception of "being as it really is in itself" (ὄντως ὄν) in contradistinction to the many *Umwelten*, that of the philosopher's own community as well as those of other communities.[12] Every such *Umwelt* is now relegated to the status of an appearance or, as Husserl puts it, representation of the world (*Weltvorstellung*). Along with the notion of "being as it really is in itself" there is conceived the idea of knowledge in the sense of ἐπιστήμη: i.e., knowledge of "being as it really is in itself" in contradistinction to "opinion" ( δόξα ) which is related to *Umwelt* and to situations within the *Umwelt*. The goal of the philosopher who has devoted himself to the theoretical life is to attain ἐπιστήμη—that is, absolute truths valid

12. In Husserl's presentation, the relationship between the attitude of "wondering" and the conception of "being as it really is in itself" is hardly made a topic of explicit discussion. The relationship calls for further analysis and clarification.

always and for everybody, regardless of the situation in which one might find oneself, independently of any practical purposes and needs, irrespective of the community to which one belongs. Such truths can only be about entities which are not subject to change or variation but remain forever identical with themselves. In other words, they can only be about ideal entities like the Platonic archetypes in which the particular things partake and which these things approximate to a higher or lesser degree or like the ideal geometrical elements (point, straight line, plane) and whatever ideal geometrical figures can be constructed by means of these elements, in contradistinction to the empirical spatial configurations which are given in a more or less vague typicality and are, therefore, affected by a comparative indeterminateness or unpreciseness. *Philosophy and* θεωρία *in general originate in the disclosure of infinite horizons and the apprehension of ideal entities.* Empirical things are referred to ideal norms or, which is the same, limit-poles, i.e., ideal poles located at infinity. As contrasted with the man of the pre-theoretical attitude, who concerns himself only with what pertains to his *Umwelt* and in the pursuit of all his activities remains within a finite horizon, the philosopher, who conceives of ideal entities as "being as it really is in itself," orients himself towards infinity and finds himself confronted with infinite tasks.[13] An infinite task is denoted by the very idea of ἐπιστήμη itself, an idea which proves an ideal norm and an ideal limit-pole with respect to every cognitive endeavor. Not only is every truth concerning matters of fact referred to the idea of absolute truth in the sense of ἐπιστήμη, of which the former is a relative approximation, but every single theoretical result, every single truth within the meaning of ἐπιστήμη acquires the sense of a transitional phase within an infinite process oriented towards an ideal pole: *viz.,* the idea of ἐπιστήμη as totally and definitively accomplished.

Conceived with regard to the theoretical domain, which in the strict sense is constituted by this very conception, the notion of ideal norms and ideal limit-poles to which empirical occurrences are to be referred is in no way confined to that domain. On the contrary, the conception in question becomes relevant for every domain of culture;

13. In the main text (§ 8), Husserl confines Greek geometry and mathematics in general to finite tasks, though mathematics deals with ideal entities and limit-poles conceived of under Platonic inspiration. To remove this discrepancy, pointed out by Ricoeur ("Husserl et le sens de l'histoire," *loc. cit.,* p. 300), we suggest that in the Viennese lecture Husserl does not so much concern himself with the factual condition of Greek mathematics and philosophy from a strictly historical point of view but focuses on potentialities of the notion of ἐπιστήμη, potentialities which did not come to full development before the renewal of Platonism during the Renaissance.

it revolutionizes all traditional norms such as justice, beauty, morality, and the like. In a sense in which this holds for no other culture, Western culture, even beyond the theoretical domain, proves essentially *Ideenkultur*, oriented towards ideal norms, assuming infinite tasks, and growing within infinite horizons. This distinctive feature results from the central and vital role which the idea of philosophy, as the idea of an infinite task, not a particular philosophical system as a historical fact, played at the institutive beginning and therefore also during the historical growth of Western culture. On account of the historical inception of Western culture, the idea in question proves to be its immanent τέλος. The rise of the idea of philosophy in Greek antiquity marks the appearance on the historical scene of a new type of man who in all his finitude assumes infinite tasks (*in der Endlichkeit lebend, auf Pole der Unendlichkeit hinlebt*) and whose historicity has the sense of *Entwerden des endlichen Menschentums im Werden zum Menschentum unendlicher Aufgaben*. This new type of man must not be considered as just one anthropological type beside others. The appearance of Western man purports the incipient actualization of a potentiality proper to man as such. As Ricoeur has expressed it: ". . . *Être européen est moins une gloire qui particularise qu'une responsabilité qui relie à tous.*" [14] For his well-being, his wholesomeness, his very existence, Western man must remain faithful to his idea and immanent τέλος which make him to be what he is.

## 3. Galileo's Inauguration of Modern Science

DURING THE RENAISSANCE the closely related ideas of "being as it really is in itself" and knowledge in the sense of ἐπιστήμη are at once revived and transformed. This transformation finds its expression in the work of Galileo. Reality comes to be conceived of as a thoroughly rational universe accessible to a totally rational (i.e., mathematical) science. The mathematization of nature is Galileo's consequential accomplishment by which all future development of the modern period has been decisively determined.

Galileo inherited the traditional Euclidean geometry, which he accepted as a self-contained and autochthonous science, i.e., a science having no roots or foundations outside of itself. However, perceptual experience of common everyday occurrences within the world in which we live and within which we pursue all our activities, the *Umwelt* or *Lebenswelt*, is prior to and underlies geometry as a "foundation of sense" (*Sinnesfundament*). In the *Lebenswelt* we

---

14. Ricoeur, "Husserl et le sens de l'histoire," *loc. cit.*, p. 291.

encounter bodies whose spatial forms are only typically determined, i.e., determined within a more or less vaguely circumscribed range of variability. Spatial forms, magnitudes, etc. present themselves more or less in fluctuation, when observed under varying conditions. Practical necessities lead to the development of the art of measurement by which the vagueness, the lack of precision, and the relativity of the perceptual experience of spatial configurations are overcome to the extent to which this is required by the demands of the given situation and the conditions of social life. Not only does the accuracy of measurement depend upon the available techniques, but the practice of measuring, determining, obtaining more precise results, etc. is throughout oriented towards practical goals. Techniques may be perfected: if they are actually perfected, they are so with a view to practical purposes and tasks. Whatever measurement meets the demands of a given practical situation is accepted as sufficiently accurate and satisfactory.

On this basis, geometry arises by the process of *idealization,* a specific mental operation *sui generis* through which there is constituted a universe of ideal entities, ideal limit-forms (*Limesgestalten*), the geometrical figures in the proper sense. Such figures can be determined with absolute accuracy, i.e., exactness; they are absolutely identical with themselves and free from every vacillation; their properties can be ascertained in a totally unambiguous manner. Spatial configurations and forms as given in perceptual experience may now be referred to the geometrical figures as ideal poles which the former approximate to a greater or lesser degree. Moreover, geometry develops methods of constructing more and more complex geometrical figures out of a very few elementary ones, like straight lines, triangles, circles, etc. In the final analysis, all possible geometrical figures may be generated by means of constructive operations upon the elementary ideal entities. Geometry provides a method of definitively overcoming the relativism of perceptual experience and the limitations of the practical art of measurement. Geometrical methods yield a body of results valid in all situations and under all conditions. Because of their cogent conclusiveness these results must be accepted by everyone who applies those methods. In other words, the methods of geometry lead to the discovery of absolute truths, i.e., truths holding for everybody, and to the disclosure of "being as it really is in itself." Here the idea of ἐπιστήμη seems finally attained.

Established, developed, and practiced in the course of centuries, the method of geometry grows into a technique which may be acquired and become habitual, which one may learn to master and to use. This process is at the same time one of consolidation and obfuscation,

obfuscation, namely, of the historico-intentional "origin" of geometry, its rootedness in the pre-geometrical experience of the *Lebenswelt*. The latter remains what it is, and we continue living and pursuing all our activities within it whether or not we are in the possession of the geometrical method or, for that matter, any scientific method. It is but the last phase of the process of origination of geometry, the accomplished result to which this process leads, that is retained, while the process itself is lost sight of. When geometry is thus taken as constituted and established, in severance from the very process of its origination, it undergoes a certain transformation of sense. It is not understood as a *mental accomplishment of a higher order,* involving the process of idealization and, therefore, founded upon and presupposing pre-geometrical experience of the *Lebenswelt* upon which idealization is performed. Having become a tradition, an established and consolidated acquisition at the disposal of whomever learns to master its methods, geometry appears to rest on its own grounds. The validity of its results seems self-evident, the function of its method to yield ἐπιστήμη seems to involve no problem whatever and is taken for a matter of course.

For Galileo, geometry exists already in the historical form of traditionality, i.e., it has undergone the mentioned transformation of sense. He inherits geometry as an established science which, on account of its absolute and universal validity, he considers as the prototype, model, and standard of knowledge. Consequently geometry must be applied to experience in order to discover reality as it is in itself in contradistinction to the varying appearances and phenomena. The geometrical method, and this method alone, allows for disclosure within experienced things of that content which belongs to those things as they really are and which is not affected by changes in their manner of appearance. Again the notions of "being as it really is in itself" and genuine knowledge prove correlative of one another.

Galileo's first step consists in an *abstraction.* Only the corporeal aspect of things and of the world at large is taken into consideration. The only subjects of study are spatial configurations and spatio-temporal events. Spatiality and temporality play a privileged role also in the pre-theoretical experience of the *Lebenswelt;* no matter what the nature of the things encountered in the *Lebenswelt* might be, they exhibit spatial and temporal characteristics. Space and time provide the framework within which things are experienced in the *Lebenswelt*. The mathematization of the spatial and temporal features and characteristics purports their quantification. The art of measurement which, historically speaking, underlies geometry in the sense that, as mentioned, geometry arises out of it by means of the operation of idealization, acquires, in turn, a new meaning in the light of geometry and mathematics at large, once they are established. To be sure, the accuracy of every actual measurement is still relative to the available technique and will remain so forever. Yet, the perfection of techniques of measurement is now emancipated from the concern with practical goals and needs arising in concrete situations. Because of the reference to ideal limit-poles, actual perfections of techniques come now to be conceived of under the perspective of the idea of infinite perfectibility (infinite in principle, of course, not in fact). A series of measurements performed by means of progressively perfected techniques not only yields results of increasing accuracy, but these results can now be interpreted as closer and closer approximations to a numerical value which, though it might not be obtainable by any actual measurement, determines the quantity in question as that quantity really is. Spatial configurations, temporal intervals, etc. are in themselves numerically determined, in the sense of geometrico-mathematical exactness, though our knowledge of them takes by necessity the form of an asymptotic process. In the things as they are in themselves, there are realized, as their determinations, those very ideal limit-poles towards which the actual empirical measurements converge.

Far from being confined to static phenomena, the mathematization of nature extends to change and variation as well. As given in common everyday experience, the *Lebenswelt* not only extends into an indefinitely open spatio-temporal horizon, but it also exhibits causality of a certain style. Changes do not occur at random but with typical uniformity. Variations in some respect are regularly accompanied or followed by variations in another respect. In all variation and change the world presents an invariant general style of variation and change. On this account things are connected and hang together; the world as a whole appears as a unified totality (*Alleinheit*). Regularity, uniformity, the invariant style of the world, make possible inductions and predictions, though on a rather limited scale and of relative accuracy. To obtain genuinely philosophical knowledge of the world, one has to go beyond the empty generality that all happenings are causally determined. A method must be found which permits specification of the general causality of the world and construction of infinities of causal connections on the basis of what is accessible to actual experience, finite and fragmentary. Such a method is mathematization, more specifically, algebraization. Phenomena which change along with one another are symbolized by variables between which laws of functional dependency are established as hypotheses. These hypotheses lend themselves to verification; the phenomena in question are subjected to measurement under the perspective, of course, of ideal limit-poles to be approximated. Still this method is of limited application as long as merely spatial configurations and temporal intervals but not the specific qualities—color, sound, thermal and tactile phenomena—are accessible to quantification, i.e., measurement of increasing accuracy and oriented towards ideal limit-poles. The general causality which prevails in the *Lebenswelt* involves spatio-temporal configurations and specific qualities alike. Every change, whether in the former or the latter, occurs in typical and uniformly regular connection with some other change. In physics of the Galilean style, all happenings and changes which concern the specific qualities are referred to spatio-temporal events in such a manner that all qualitative aspects of the world are conceived of as causally dependent upon spatio-temporal events. Qualitative phenomena indicate spatio-temporal events, i.e., events completely describable in terms of spatiality and temporality and, hence, accessible to mathematization. These events have come to be considered as the objective content of the specific qualities—i.e., the real condition of things, a condition which at once reveals and conceals itself in their qualitative aspects. It must be stressed that the occurrences experienced in the *Lebenswelt* in no way motivate the interpretation of the specific qualities as causally dependent, and unilaterally so dependent, upon spatio-temporal events. This interpretation which is the distinctive mark of modern physics is regarded by Husserl as a *hypothesis* which, all verification notwithstanding, forever remains a hypothesis. "Verification" here means a sequence of particular verifications: a sequence of correct theories, special hypotheses, and their verifications —briefly, nothing less than the historical process of the development of science. By its very nature, science of the style inaugurated by Galileo is a *progressive historical process* which passes from phase to phase, each phase being the "science of a certain time." This historical process is progressive so far as it approximates an ideal goal, *viz.*, "nature as it really is in itself." Nature as modern science conceives it really to be in itself proves to be an ideal infinite pole towards which an infinity of theories and verifications converge.

By means of referring the specific qualities to underlying spatio-temporal processes, an indirect mathematization of the former is accomplished such that laws of functional dependency may now encompass all features and aspects of experience. Formulated as mathematical equations, these laws permit predictions and inductions surpassing by far, both in scope and accuracy, those of pre-theoretical common experience. The causality of the *Lebenswelt*, which merely purports typical regularity and uniformity, is also idealized and mathematized: all events in "nature as it really is in itself" are strictly determined by exact laws. Laws of nature are the formulae of functional dependency by which the mathematized phenomena are correlated with one another. These laws of functional dependency, the laws of nature stated in mathematical form which is their proper and genuine form, are considered to express the true condition of nature.

Thus the mathematization of nature is completed. A universe of ideal mathematical entities related to one another by exact laws is substituted for the *Lebenswelt,* which is relegated with all its features to the status of a mere subjective phenomenon or appearance. In whatever disguise nature may present itself in experience, especially perceptual experience, taken as it is in itself, it must be considered as a "mathematical manifold." Subjective phenomena have significance only so far as they may serve as indications of the true—i.e., mathematical—condition of things, indications which are vague and, moreover, are merely by way of concealment. A specifically modern concept arises which we may term *nature of the physicist* in contradistinction to nature as experienced. Experienced nature is the fundamental stratum of the *Lebenswelt,* our reality and our only one, which alone is and may ever be given in experience. Nature of the physicist proves to be a tissue of ideas and ideal constructions (*Ideenkleid*). Under the import of the growing prestige of the developing physics, a prestige stemming from its success, both theoretical and practical, that tissue of ideas which a closer philosophico-historical analysis reveals as result and product of a special method and, hence, as correlate of specific mental operations, has come to be considered, by scientists and educated laymen alike, as reality, as "nature as it truly and objectively is" to the total disregard of the *Lebenswelt.* So completely has the latter been eclipsed that up to the present time even philosophical reflections on science, its meaning and bearing, not to speak of scientific discussions in the technical sense, start from, and abide by, idealized and mathematized nature, no question ever being raised as to the genealogy of nature of the physicist.[15] Considered from a philosophical point of view, the abandonment of the principle of determinism in contemporary microphysics and the other departures from classical physics prove to be, according to Husserl, of less radical significance than they are often

15. As far as the social sciences are concerned, the problem of the origin of scientific concepts in the pre-theoretical experience of the *Lebenswelt* has been formulated in a masterly fashion by A. Schutz, "Common-sense and Scientific Interpretation of Human Action," *Philosophy and Phenomenological Research,* XIV (1953). (Reprinted in A. Schutz, *Collected Papers,* Vol. I [The Hague, 1962].)

presented to be. All the innovations in question concern only mathematized nature—i.e., nature as interpreted in terms of mathematical entities and formulae. The very existence of the *Lebenswelt* is lost sight of, and, hence, its relation to nature of the physicist is not seen as a problem at all.

By way of abstraction and idealization, Galileo arrives at the conception of nature as a closed and self-contained corporeal world within which all events are determined in advance. With this the path is opened up for the later Cartesian dualism. The very idea of the world undergoes a radical transformation so far as the world is divided into mind and matter. Notwithstanding the utter heterogeneity of the extended and the thinking substances, the latter is conceived after the model of the former. Mental states, "modifications of consciousness," are supposed to occur according to causal laws of a style analogous to those which prevail in physical nature. This naturalistic conception of the mind as well as the idea of a "mechanistic" biology—i.e., a biology reducible in the final analysis to the general laws of physics—are expressions of the physicalistic objectivism or rationalism which is established and gradually consolidated in consequence of Galileo's inauguration of the "new science." Reality is seen throughout as a systematic context in which all occurrences are rationally determined; the new idea of reality is an extension and generalization of the idea of nature of the physicist. The cognitive style of Galilean physics defines the ideal of scientific knowledge in general. Philosophy as the universal science of the totality of being must assume the form of a universal mathematics as in Spinoza's *Ethica,* the first universal ontology *more geometrico.*

## 4. The Dawn of Transcendental Subjectivism

RATIONALITY NECESSARILY REFERS to a mind, whether human or divine, as its principle or source. It is in conformity with the logic of the historical situation as it developed under the impact of Galileo's institution of the "new science" that, along with the conception of the world as a rational system and universe of ideal entities accessible to mathematical knowledge, those mental functions and operations come to the fore whose products and creations are the mathematical theories. The objectivistic trend seems to motivate a complementary trend in the opposite direction, *viz.,* towards the subjective realm, the realm of consciousness. In no thinker does the duality and polarity of these trends, which soon prove antagonistic to one another, appear more clearly than in Descartes.

Descartes conceives the idea of a new philosophy as a universal mathematics, and he gives to this idea a partial realization in his analytical geometry. By the arithmetization of geometry he anticipates Leibniz' idea of a *mathesis inversalis* and prepares the way for the complete formalization of mathematics which has been brought to culmination in our day. For us, mathematics has become a technique or an art of combining and manipulating symbols which are devoid of any meaning and are merely defined in terms of the operations which may be performed upon them, operations, which, in turn, are also defined only by certain exclusively formal properties, as, for example, commutativity. To avoid misunderstandings, let us stress that Husserl insists upon the legitimacy and even necessity of the formalization and technization of mathematics and mathematical physics, provided only that we do not lose sight of the source from which the formalizing methods derive their sense and their cognitive significance. On the other hand, intending to lay down ultimate foundations for physicalistic objectivism and rationalism, Descartes was led to the discovery of the realm of consciousness. He thus inaugurated a development in the course of which the very idea of that rationalism came to be uprooted altogether. Two philosophical trends whose antagonism marks the history of modern philosophy take their departure from Descartes: on one side, the rationalistic trend as represented by Malebranche, Spinoza, Leibniz, and, in Husserl's interpretation, Kant; on the other, the empiricistic trend as developed by Locke, Berkeley, and Hume.

Husserl interprets Descartes' discovery of the *ego cogito* in the light of the development which the Cartesian doubt is given in phenomenology under the heading of the "phenomenological reduction." By this interpretation Husserl claims to disengage hidden implications of Descartes' universal doubt, or, as Husserl also says, the "Cartesian *epoché*," implications of which Descartes was perhaps not fully aware himself, which at any event he failed to render completely explicit, but in which Husserl sees the driving force and the τέλος of modern philosophy. Descartes' universal doubt discloses the absolute and apodictic certainty of the existence of the ego as the doubter and performer of the *epoché* as well as of the totality of his acts of consciousness (*cogitationes*). To every *cogitatio* there belongs inseparably its *cogitatum*, i.e., that which presents itself to the mind through the *cogitatio* in question. The universal *epoché* engulfs all certainties, convictions, and beliefs, those of our scientific as well as prescientific life. It also engulfs the belief in the existence of the *Lebenswelt* as given in perceptual experience, that world in which we live, which we take for granted as the basis for all our endeavors. Certainties do not discontinue being experienced. However, they may now be taken only as *experienced convictions;* we forsake making use of them as valid convictions on the basis of which to proceed. The *Lebenswelt* continues to appear, to be perceived; but it is now regarded merely as an experienced world, as a world presenting itself, a *cogitatum* of *cogitationes,* an "idea," or, as Husserl likewise says, a phenomenon. It remains a real world, but its reality is no longer simply accepted as a matter of course, as a certainty upon which further certainties may be built. In Husserl's interpretation, Descartes' *epoché* yields more than merely the axiomatic proposition *ego cogito* or *sum cogitans.* In other words, the *epoché* discloses the realm of *cogitationes* and corresponding *cogitata* as an apodictic sphere of absolute being which has priority and precedence with regard to every domain of being and existence so far as it proves its absolute apodictic presupposition.

Descartes identifies the ego (i.e., the realm of consciousness) with the human soul, while the human body falls under the *epoché.* The notion of a pure soul as different from the body is, however, the result of an abstraction, that very abstraction which leads to the concept of a pure corporeal nature. The soul proves to be what remains of the world after corporeity has been abstracted. However, the abstraction in question is not performed within the *epoché.* Rather, it is taken over from considerations previous to the *epoché*—specifically, considerations based upon the unquestioned belief in the existence of the world. In other words, Descartes relies upon the Galilean certainty that there exists a corporeal nature whose true being, as it really is in itself, is accessible to mathematical knowledge. His goal is to provide an ultimate foundation and justification for Galilean science and physicalistic objectivism as yielding metaphysically valid knowledge. Having discovered the *cogito* and identifying it with the soul, Descartes finds himself confronted with the task of transcending the ego, of arriving, by way of inferences, at existents "exterior" to the ego. In his interpretation of the ego, this must mean exterior to the psychological domain. By his insistence on subjectivity, Descartes has opened up an entirely new direction and orientation for modern philosophy. However, his conception of subjectivity proves affected by an ambiguity. On the one hand, it is to the realm of consciousness that he refers all validities and resorts for the validation of objective science and also of the existence of the world. Herein appears the motive of transcendental subjectivism in its earliest form. On the other hand, the ego is identified with the soul, and the realm of consciousness with the psychological domain. Hence the ego is conceived of as a mundane existent to be dealt with in the objective science of psychology, objective so far as it is patterned after the model of physics. Considering that the world and all mundane existents, including the ego or the "I" in the psychological sense, are constituted through, and derive the sense of their existence (*Seinssinn*) from, *cogitationes* and functions of the ego as disclosed by the *epoché*, it is obviously absurd to conceive of the latter ego as a mundane existent. These ambiguities, incompatibilities, and inconsistencies have impelled Husserl to reinterpret and to radicalize the Cartesian *epoché* or, as he puts it, to disengage its full meaning and true import far beyond what Descartes had seen himself. The ego which is disclosed by the *epoché* proves to be, when rightly understood, the transcendental ego with reference to which one can no longer meaningfully speak of "exteriority."

In a certain sense Locke seems to take over from Descartes the problem of accounting for the objectivity of knowledge and science. However, in Locke's treatment the problem is transformed into that of the natural history of human cognitive functions and their accomplishments. The mind is conceived of as a kind of closed and self-contained "space" in which data appear, disappear, and are combined with one another in a variety of forms. Setting out to trace the psychological genesis of the combinations and complications of data, Locke describes the history of a mundane existent (the mind), and he takes it for granted that this mundane existent has its history among, and under the influence of, other mundane existents: *viz.*, external bodies and events which act upon sense organs and thus give rise to "ideas of sensation." Descartes' problem as to how *cogitationes* as occurrences in the closed interiority of the soul can acquire cognitive significance with regard to existents exterior to the soul is supplanted in Locke by an inquiry into the psychological and even psycho-physiological genesis of acquisitions whose objective validity is not seen as a problem at all.

The motive of transcendental subjectivism, which seems altogether absent from Locke's philosophy, reappears in its full force in Berkeley and, still more, in Hume. Inheriting from Locke the sensualistic conception of the mind and developing it to its utmost consequences, Hume arrives at a complete skepticism. All objective categories prove to be fictions; those of scientific thinking like number, quantity, continuity, geometrical figure, etc. no less than those of common experience of the perceptual world as the identity of persisting thing, the identity of the self, the causal connection. What the psychological analysis discovers are nothing but appearing and vanishing data, "impressions" and "ideas" (in the specific Humean sense), and regularities, as a result of the various forms of association, in the appearance and grouping of "ideas." It is possible to give a psychological explanation of the origin of those fictions; to do that is Hume's endeavor. But the fictions have to be seen and recognized as fictions.

A highly paradoxical situation arises in which Husserl sees the germ or even the incipient phase of the present crisis of the sciences. They are in a flourishing growth, they proceed from one theoretical conquest to the other, not to speak of their practical success. They seem to bear the stamp of exemplariness and finality. The ways of reasoning and the methods of the sciences, especially the mathematical and physical sciences, cannot but appear conclusive and absolutely evident to whomever follows those lines of thought. Yet, when the attempt is made to account for this conclusiveness and for the accomplishments of science in terms of the functions and operations of the mind whose products and creations the sciences are, it appears in the light of Hume's analysis that the sciences and the evident conclusiveness of their methods are utterly unintelligible.

Still more important than Hume's theoretical failure which finds its expression in his skepticism—a failure resulting from his sensualistic conception of consciousness—is, according to Husserl, his formulation of the problem in question. Hume's formulation, Husserl maintains, surpasses in radicalness even that of Descartes. It is not sufficient to establish, as Descartes did, the indubitability and priority of consciousness. Both the constructed universe of science in its specific objectivity and the perceptual world of common experience (the *Lebenswelt*) have to be referred to consciousness; they must be seen as *cogitata* of *cogitationes,* as deriving their existence from functions and operations (*Leistungen*) of consciousness. To Hume the naïveté of our common experience becomes a problem, our very naïveté in taking for granted as an unquestioned certainty and a matter of course (*Selbstverständlichkeit*) the existence of the world in which we find ourselves. Behind Hume's skepticism Husserl discerns the discovery of a world-riddle (*Welträtsel*) of an entirely new type: "das Rätsel einer Welt, deren Sein *Sein aus subjektiver Leistung* ist." Solving this riddle purports nothing less than accounting for the world, its objectivity, and the unquestioned certainty of its existence in subjective terms, or, to put it differently, revealing the world as a correlate and product of subjective functions, activities, and operations. By raising this problem, Hume challenges the objectivism not only of the mathematical and mathematizing sciences but also of common experience and all traditional thinking. Thereby the very idea of philosophy is transformed in a most radical way. Its task is no longer to construct or to discover true and objective reality, reality as it is in itself behind and beneath the appearances. Rather, philosophy is concerned with the world and the universes of a higher order, like that of science, as originating in consciousness. Philosophy passes from objectivism to transcendental subjectivism.

Kant, as Husserl sees him, does not pursue what Husserl considers as the true Humean problem. Kant's interpretation of, and reaction to, Hume's sensualism and skepticism is determined by his affiliation with the rationalistic tradition as represented by Leibniz and Wolff. When Kant speaks of dogmatism, he has in view not the certainties of common experience in pre-theoretical everyday life but the rationalistic philosophy whose metaphysical claims he endeavors to invalidate. Human knowledge, resulting from the interplay of "sensibility" and "understanding," has to confine itself to the realm of experience and cannot penetrate into any "reality" behind experience. On the other hand, since Kant stresses subjectivity over and against objectivism, his philosophy has to be regarded as genuine transcendental philosophy, though not yet in a definitive form, because it is not resting upon ultimately clarified foundations. More or less the same is to be said about Kant's successors, the thinkers who belonged to the school of German idealism.

Since the time of Galileo up to the present day, modern philosophy, Husserl maintains, is torn between the opposite tendencies of objectivism and transcendentalism. Objectivism has found its realization in the establishment and growth of the positive sciences, which, in the course of time, have undergone increasing specialization and technization. Technization of the sciences means their transformation into arts by means of which one may accomplish many admirable things but which rest on unclarified foundations and on unquestioned presuppositions. Art in this sense is certainly not ἐπιστήμη. By its very nature, ἐπιστήμη demands going back to the ultimate sources of sense, radical disclosure of presuppositions and examination of foundations. The technization of the sciences implies their severance from philosophy. Thus the idea of a universal objectivistic philosophy, which had been the driving force behind Galileo's inauguration of physics and the great aspiration and inspiration of the beginning of the modern era, has degenerated from within, a process which has entailed the loss of faith in reason itself. As to the subjectivistic trend, there have been most impressive attempts at establishing a transcendental philosophy. But, Husserl points out, none of the thinkers who embarked upon such an attempt has thus far attained a full awareness of the very task and program of a transcendental philosophy; none, moreover, has succeeded in elaborating a clear and workable conceptual apparatus. With regard to Kant and German idealism, Husserl speaks of constructive mythical concepts beset by obscurities. In these attempts one has to see prefigurings that have the greatest value and importance, to be sure, and yet are no more than preliminaries.

At the root of the present crisis of philosophy, Husserl discerns the breakdown of objectivism, on the one hand, and, on the other hand, the failure of transcendental subjectivism to consolidate itself. In this situation two problems have to be faced. The one concerns the *Lebenswelt,* for which, as we have seen, modern science has substituted a tissue of ideal constructions which passes for reality. The other problem is that of an adequate conception of the mind; this leads to a discussion of modern psychology and of the very idea of psychology itself. In what follows we shall survey Husserl's reasoning along the lines mentioned, which will be seen to converge towards transcendental phenomenology.

## [II] THE LEBENSWELT

### 1. General Characteristics of the *Lebenswelt*

UNDER THE IMPACT of modern science as inaugurated by Galileo, the *Lebenswelt*—i.e., the world of common experience—has been superseded by the objectively true and valid universe of science which, in the thinking of modern Western man, passes for reality. Whereas no "objective" entity—objective in the sense of science—is, in principle, accessible to direct and immediate experience in the proper sense of the term, the Lebenswelt does present itself, actually or virtually, in such experience, perceptual experience as well as its derivative forms like memory, representation, imagination, etc. Since the universe of science proves to be a tissue of ideal constructs, or, as Husserl puts it, a theoretico-logical superstructure, its conception and apprehension is of the same nature as that of any infinite ideas, e.g., geometrical ones. The construction of the universe of science involves, as a mental accomplishment, certain specific operations, especially that of idealization. Obviously, idealization presupposes materials to be idealized. By virtue of its intrinsic sense as a superstructure, the universe of science requires a foundation upon which it rests and upon which it is constructed. This foundation is no other than the Lebenswelt and the evidence of common experience—the term "evidence" denoting, as always with Husserl, bodily presence or self-presentation of the object in question. All theoretical truth—logical, mathematical, scientific—finds its ultimate validation and justification in evidences which concern occurrences in the Lebenswelt. If Husserl assigns to the evidences of the *Lebenswelt* a privileged status with respect to those of objective and scientific theory, it is in the sense of the latter being founded upon the former. That is to say, the mental operations, whose products and constituted correlates objective theory and the objective universe of science are, presuppose those acts of consciousness through which the *Lebenswelt* appears as ever-present and pre-given, i.e., as existing independently of, and prior to, all scientific activity. For an ultimate clarification of the universe of science, one has, therefore, to turn to the *Lebenswelt* and to bring out the role which it plays, in several respects, in the construction and constitution of science.

Radical philosophical reflection must begin by rendering explicit the universal "presupposition" which underlies all our life and all our activities. This "presupposition" is the unquestioned and even unformulated acceptance of the world in which we find ourselves and with which we always have a certain familiarity. At every moment of our life, we concern ourselves in some mode or other, with things, animals, fellow-men, etc., which present themselves as mundane existents, and we conceive of ourselves as also belonging to the world. None of those existents is ever given in isolation. Every one of them refers to a context into which it is inserted; it appears within an all-encompassing and indefinitely extended horizon: the *world-horizon*. Unlike particular mundane existents which may occasionally appear and disappear, the world is continually present to our mind as the universal field of all our actual and possible activities of any nature whatever. If the world is always there as pre-given, if living means living in the world, it is because the world announces itself along with the appearance of every particular mundane existent with which we might be dealing. The inexplicit and inarticulate awareness of the world pervades all our activities and enters into them as their most general, though unformulated, "premise" or "presupposition." Correspondingly, the world, silently accepted as a matter of course, proves to be the ground upon which we pursue all our activities, whatever their orientation.

To be sure, the world includes nature. The nature here in question is obviously nature as given in direct and immediate experience and not the idealized nature of physics. However, the world comprises more than mere nature. Among the existents by which we find ourselves surrounded, there are not only natural things—i.e., objects which may exhaustively be described by indicating their color, shape, size, weight, etc.—but also instruments, books, objects of art, and so on: in short, objects which have human significance, serve human ends and purposes, satisfy human desires and needs. Because the world contains objects of this kind and, therefore, proves to be the frame within which we lead our human existence, we speak of it as our *Lebenswelt*.

Within the *Lebenswelt*, we encounter our fellow-men and take it for granted that they not only exist in the world but are also aware of it, that they are confronted with the same things and objects as we are, though to each one of us, depending upon his point of view, the objects and the world at large may and do appear under varying aspects and perspectives. It is one of the unquestioned and even unformulated certainties of common experience that the world is one and the same for all of us, a common intersubjective world.

Encountering our fellow-men in the common world, we may adopt with regard to them, and they with regard to us, the attitude of detached and disinterested observers, or else we may become involved with one another and enter into the manifold relationships of cooperation and collaboration. We then not only live in the same world but live, function, and operate in it together and corporately; we interlock and interlink our intentions, designs, and activities with theirs in thoroughgoing mutuality and interplay. If on account of its reference to human life and existence the world assumes the character of a *Lebenswelt*, the reference is not only to individuals but also, and even primarily, to a historical community whose societal life consists in the interrelatedness and interplay of thought and action in various forms. *The term* Lebenswelt *has essentially a historico-social connotation:* a *Lebenswelt* is relative to a certain society at a given moment of its history; it must be taken as it is conceived by the historical community whose world it is—e.g., in mythico-magical interpretation, as in the case of societies and civilizations which had not yet been influenced by the Greek idea of philosophy and θεωρία. Whether we happen to act alone or, cooperating with others, engage in common pursuits, the things and objects with which we are confronted as well as our own plans and designs, finally the world as a whole, appear to us in the light of beliefs, opinions, conceptions, certainties, etc. that prevail in the community to which we belong. Community may here be understood in the largest and most encompassing sense so as to denote the whole historical civilization to which we belong or in the more restricted sense of a special group within a given society, e.g., the group of contemporary scientists, doctors, scholars, artists, philosophers, etc. The *Lebenswelt* proves to be the ground of our existence, a ground which is accepted as a matter of course, as pre-given and existing independently of, and previous to, all our activities, individual as well as collective, and which these activities presuppose for their pursuit. Upon this ground, common to all of us, we meet one another as mundane existents among mundane existents. Besides being *objects in the Lebenswelt*, we are at the same time *subjects with respect to the Lebenswelt*, so far as it derives its meaning and the sense of its existence from our collective mental life, from our acts (concatenated and interlocked with those of our fellow-men) of perceiving, experiencing, reasoning, purposefully acting, etc. Collective accomplishments become part and parcel of the *Lebenswelt* which not only is as it is conceived of by the respective community but also comprises all communal creations, both material and mental. In and through the life of a community, the interplay of the activities of its members, its *Lebenswelt* undergoes transformation, change, reinterpretation, etc. Reflecting upon this, we become aware of the *Lebenswelt* as a mental acquisition (*geistiger Erwerb*), as having grown and continuing to grow: i.e., we come to disclose its historical character and its relativity to a living community.

## 2. Science as a Cultural Accomplishment in the *Lebenswelt*

SCIENTIFIC PURSUITS must be reckoned among the collective activities of the kind under consideration. Einstein, Husserl points out, relies upon Michelson's experiments. When physicist A refers to the work and results of physicist B, the reference is obviously not to a psychological or psychophysical construction of B which would reveal him as "he really and objectively is in himself," although both A and B as well as the laboratory, the apparatus used, the books, papers, etc. may be subjected to an investigation in the sense of objective positive science. To the working physicist A, B appears rather as a collaborator who lives in the same world, shares with him certain interests, and is engaged in pursuits of the same kind. Meeting B in the same *Lebenswelt* and finding himself in communion with him, on account of their common purpose and general orientation of thinking, A tries to grasp and to comprehend B's ideas; he appropriates or, if he sees fit to do so, modifies them; he uses B's results as premises for further conclusions or avails himself of them in some other form for his own work, which he then submits to his fellow scientists for further criticism and discussion, etc. Science results from, and grows in, such interplay of the mental activities of the members of the scientific community which, of course, is comprised not only of contemporary scientists but also of their predecessors upon whose accomplishments the former are building; it is, moreover, an open community in the sense that the work accomplished thus far will be continued by future generations. The interplay in question consists in a general debate, in mutual criticism, confirmation, and, eventually, correction; all this in view of reaching justifiable agreement. Science thus appears as a collective cultural accomplishment, not too different, in principle, from the productions of other cultural activities. With respect to scientific pursuits, Husserl significantly speaks of a practice of a special kind—*viz.,* the practice of theorizing (*theoretische Praxis*).

For a clarification and account of science, one has to proceed to an examination and analysis of the mental functions and operations involved in the elaboration of science and to investigate the various forms in which mental activities come to be intersubjectively concatenated and interlinked. Inasmuch as humane science (*Geisteswissenschaft*) deals with the mental life of man and with the creations originating in that life, natural science of the Galilean style, since it is a product of the human mind, falls under the purview of *Geisteswissenschaft*.[16] "Objective nature," "nature as it really is in itself," must not be construed to refer to a reality behind or beneath the appearances in the *Lebenswelt,* a hidden reality which may be revealed by means of appropriate methods and techniques. Rather, it denotes the idea of an infinite intersubjective accomplishment, an idea with respect to which the members of the scientific community orient their work and which is approximated by the products of their interlocking activities. Those products are the scientific theories which mark the successive phases of the historical development of science.

Like every other cultural activity, the pursuit of scientific knowledge is carried on in the *Lebenswelt.* Scientific problems arise within the *Lebenswelt* and concern special aspects of it singled out by abstraction, as, for example, the spatio-temporal or corporeal aspect. Continuously the scientist avails himself of occurrences in the *Lebenswelt* in which he performs his experiments, finds his apparatus, reads his pointers, etc. To avail oneself of such occurrences for and in the construction of scientific theories is, however, not the same as to conceive and to interpret those occurrences in scientific terms. To the scientist, the laboratory in which he works is a place of study and research, it appears to him with reference to the specific human activities it serves; he does not consider it as to what, in the light of a completed universal scientific explanation of all phenomena, it would prove "really and objectively to be in itself," not any more than, as mentioned, he conceives of his collaborators as physico-chemical systems. The purpose to be attained by scientific endeavors also relates to human existence in the *Lebenswelt;* it is one among the several

16. In opposition to the traditional naturalistic tendencies to base the humane sciences upon the natural sciences and to look for physico-chemical explanations as, in the final analysis, ultimate and definitive, Husserl insists upon *Geisteswissenschaft* as the more encompassing and more fundamental discipline. An account of the various creations of the mind—among them science, as we know it since Galileo—can be given only by an autonomous universal science of the mind itself, a science which is certainly not of the Galilean style.

purposes which we pursue in our collective practice and through our intersubjectively concatenated activities. If this purpose is of a specific nature, so is every other purpose which orients our cultural life. The specific purpose in question is to enlarge, both as to scope and accuracy, the possibilities of prediction and induction infinitely beyond those proper to pre-scientific common experience. As Husserl puts it, in this way we come to replace "knowledge" in the sense of the familiarity which we have with the *Lebenswelt* in our everyday life, and which suffices for our practical needs and our orientation in the *Lebenswelt*, by knowledge in the strict sense, conceived of with reference to the ideas of "objective truth" and "being as it really is in itself." Again, as in the case of all cultural activities, the results and products of scientific endeavors are superadded to the *Lebenswelt*. It hardly needs mentioning that the existence of science and scientific theories form an integral part of the historico-cultural reality of modern Western man, i.e., of his *Lebenswelt*. This does not mean, as it has traditionally been understood, that the universe constructed by science is true reality which is to supplant the *Lebenswelt*. It does, however, purport among other things that to Western man nature as given in common experience appears as lending itself to, and, therefore, under the perspective of, possible scientific interpretation and explanation.

The *Lebenswelt* proves the foundation upon which the universe of science is built as a superstructure; the specific logico-mathematical evidence refers, by its very nature, to evidence pertaining to common experience. It does not follow from this that the *Lebenswelt* is to be considered as a mere point of departure for making the transition to another sphere of being. It might seem as though there were two sorts of truth: subjective and relative truth concerning practical situations in the *Lebenswelt,* and objective and scientific truth which, notwithstanding its reference to the former, is intrinsically not affected by this reference. However, as Husserl insists, the *Lebenswelt* does intervene in the elaboration of science; the *Lebenswelt* is given to us, and we experience ourselves as existing within it, whether or not we happen to be engaged in scientific pursuits. Mankind has existed and has lived in respective *Lebenswelten* prior to the rise of science in the modern sense. Finally, science is comprised in the specific *Lebenswelt* of Western man. The ideas of "objective truth" and "being as it really is in itself," by means of which the subjectivity and relativity of common experience are to be overcome, insofar as these ideas guide and direct the specific human activity which Husserl calls *theoretische Praxis*, pertain themselves to the domain of the mental, the subjective, hence the relative.

At the outset, it might have seemed that the problem of the *Lebenswelt* was raised for the sake of the philosophical clarification of science. Now it is seen that the philosophy of science, whatever its importance, deals merely with a special or partial theme. The *Lebenswelt* appears not only as a theme in its own right but also as the more universal and, therefore, the foremost theme.

## 3. Invariant Structures of the *Lebenswelt*

A SCIENCE OF THE *Lebenswelt* which respects its specific character and takes it as it presents itself in direct experience (the notion of experience understood in the sense of pre-scientific life, and not to be interpreted in terms of sense data) can obviously not be a science of Galilean style in which a theoretical logico-mathematical superstructure supersedes the *Lebenswelt*. First of all, according to Husserl, we have to perform an *epoché concerning "objective science."* [17] This does not mean ignoring the existence of "objective science" or pretending to live in a world from which "objective science" is absent. It does not mean denying nor even doubting its validity. "Objective science" and its results and accomplishments remain what they always have been, *viz.*, cultural facts pertaining to our *Lebenswelt*. We are far from abandoning our interests in "objective science." However, under the *epoché*, we abstain from pursuing those interests; we suspend them, put them out of play. We refrain from being involved in the pursuit of "objective science"; we adopt the attitude of disinterested neutrality with regard to those pursuits. Such an attitude consists not only in withholding assent to theories of "objective science" but also in abstaining from taking *any* critical position with respect to the truth or falsity of such theories; this precludes denial and doubt as specific critical positions. Valid theories of "objective science" remain valid for us. However, under the *epoché* we consider them merely as accepted as valid, without ourselves proceeding upon their accepted validity which we are equally far from making use of as from challenging. No theory, no result, no assertion of "objective science" will be permitted to intervene in our reasoning as an established truth, point of departure, premise, or argument of any kind. Of course, the *epoché* concerns not only specific theories and results but also the very idea of "objective science" itself. Without losing sight of this idea as a driving force in our cultural life, we shall yet refrain from being motivated and determined by it.

This *epoché* enables us to take the *Lebenswelt* at face value as we

17. To avoid misunderstandings, we shall use the expression "objective science" (in quotation marks) to denote science of the Galilean style.

experience it as our historico-cultural reality, without referring it to, or having it superseded by, "being as it really is in itself." Yet the idea of a general science of the *Lebenswelt* seems beset by an insuperable difficulty. Such a science, though not of Galilean style, must admit of a certain objectivity and validity of its own; it must develop methods by means of which true and warranted assertions can be established—i.e., assertions which appear as conclusive and cogent to whomever uses those methods. This, however, seems incompatible with the essential relativity of the *Lebenswelt* to a given community and even to a certain phase in the history of that community. Would not each one of these indefinitely many *Lebenswelten* require a science of its own? Is there room for a general science of the *Lebenswelt* as such?

Notwithstanding its *relativity*, the *Lebenswelt* exhibits an invariant structure: more precisely, an invariant structural framework within which the relative and changeable finds its place. Prior to, and independently of, "objective science," the *Lebenswelt* appears extended in space and time. The space in question is, of course, that which we experience and in which we live and not a mathematical space; it does not contain any ideal geometrical entities (points, planes, etc.); it is not infinitely divisible; it does not form an infinitesimal continuum, etc. The same holds with respect to time. In the *Lebenswelt* we encounter corporeal things, but they are not bodies in the sense of geometry or physics. Finally, the *Lebenswelt* displays causality, not in the sense of laws of nature formulated in equations of functional dependency, but rather regularity, typical uniformity, typicality of behavior. As Husserl puts it, things have their "habits" (*Gewohnheiten*) of behaving in similar ways under typically similar conditions.

Let us note that the categories pertaining to the *Lebenswelt* and expressing its invariant structures are denoted by the same terms as the objective categories which are unfolded in *a priori* sciences such as logic and the different branches of mathematics. The identity of denotation must not be allowed to conceal the distinction between the *a priori* pertaining to the *Lebenswelt* and the objective *a priori*. What the identical denotation does indicate is the essential reference of the objective *a priori* to the *a priori* of the *Lebenswelt* as its foundation. On the basis of the *a priori* of the *Lebenswelt*, the objective *a priori* is generated by the operation of idealization. Raising the problem of the origin of geometry, Husserl accordingly insists upon the historico-intentional investigations taking their departure from the invariant content of spatial configurations or, more generally, the invariant structure of perceptual and experienced space and spatiality, as known in pre-geometrical experience and not from the transient apperceptions of a special historical period (e.g., the mythico-magical conceptions) which, as a matter of historical record, were involved in and to some extent certainly influenced the rise of early geometry.

The general science of the *Lebenswelt*, as conceived by Husserl, concerns itself with the invariant general style or the invariant formal structure of the *Lebenswelt*, the essential typicality (*wesensgesetzliche Typik*) which prevails in it.[18] This science need not confine itself to our *Lebenswelt*—i.e., the specific *Lebenswelt* of Western man—nor even to actual *Lebenswelten* of communities which exist or existed in historical reality. Passing from one actual *Lebenswelt* to another and ascertaining the differences between them, we may emancipate ourselves from all considerations of actuality. Starting from any actual *Lebenswelt*, we may freely vary it in imagination and thus contrive varieties of possible *Lebenswelten* merely as possible, with regard to which the question of their historical actuality is immaterial. The objective of this procedure is to disclose what essentially and necessarily pertains to a *Lebenswelt* as such, considered merely as to its possibility. Husserl thus arrives at the idea of an *ontology* of the *Lebenswelt* as such understood as a possible world of intersubjective experience. Structures disclosed by this ontology are exhibited by every factual *Lebenswelt*, whatever its historically varying and, in this sense, accidental content. It must be noted that an ontology of the *Lebenswelt* differs fundamentally from the ontologies of the modern tradition which have been dominated by the constructive notion of "being as it really is in itself" conceived of as a mathematical manifold. Traditional ontologies have been resting upon the objective *a priori*, whereas the ontology which Husserl has in view is concerned with the *a priori* of the *Lebenswelt*. In bringing out the idea of an ontology of the *Lebenswelt*, Husserl hardly goes beyond formulating it. His main interest lies in a different direction.

## [III] THE GENERAL PROGRAM OF PHENOMENOLOGY

### 1. The Natural and the Phenomenological Attitude

THROUGHOUT OUR CONSCIOUS LIFE we concern ourselves with objects which, however diversified, all belong to the world. Living in the world means taking it for granted as the universal all-encompassing horizon which comprises all that passes for reality,

18. It would be of considerable historical interest to examine the science of Aristotle, which Husserl does not mention at all, under the perspective of the idea of a general science of the *Lebenswelt*.

within which we pursue all our activities, into which fall the objectives of all our interests, the goals of all our actions, etc. Taking the world for granted does not, however, purport explicit disclosure of its character as universal horizon. To be sure, every object and existent appears as mundane, i.e., presents itself within the universal horizon in such a manner that its appearance conveys the horizonal awareness of the world. In this sense, the world is always there for us (*vorgegeben*). Its being there is tacitly accepted as a matter of course; as a rule it is not disengaged, thematized, rendered explicit.

Instead of abiding by this attitude, which is that of our naïve and natural life, we may direct our attention to the subjective modes in which the world and mundane existents of every description present themselves to us. Such appearance of objects in subjective modes, and even of the same object in a variety of modes, occurs, of course, throughout all our conscious life. In the naïve attitude which we naturally and normally adopt, we are too much concerned with the objects themselves, their properties and attributes; we are too much interested in what the objects are, whether as objects of the *Lebenswelt* or considered in the specific scientific orientation under the idea of "being as it really is in itself"; we are too much engrossed by our mundane pursuits, both practical and theoretical; we are too much absorbed by our goals, purposes, and designs, whether transient or comparatively permanent—to pay attention to the modes and forms in which mundane existents and the world at large present themselves to our minds. The acts of consciousness through which the world and whatever it contains become accessible to us are lived, but they remain undisclosed, unthematized, and, in this sense, concealed. Their disclosure is a matter of the decision of our will. Breaking with the naïve and natural attitude, we establish a new theoretical interest in things, not as they are, but as they offer themselves; more precisely, we take an interest in their appearances and presentations and also, and even especially, in the systematic connections and concatenations of the appearances and presentations. Generally speaking, our topic is no longer the world but is the texture of conscious life, the syntheses of acts of consciousness owing to which we have the permanent awareness of the world as always being there (*vorgegeben*). Consistently proceeding in this direction, we approach the threshold of phenomenology, whose general program may be formulated as the attempt to *account for the world at large as well as mundane existents in particular and, for that matter, for all objective entities whatever, in terms of experiences, acts, operations, and productions (Leistungen) of consciousness.* Such an account amounts to revealing the world and the mentioned objective entities as products and correlates of systematically concatenated and synthetized multiplicities of conscious acts from which the former derive the sense of their validity (*Geltung*) and existence.

To carry out that program, we have to perform a second *epoché*, this time with respect to the *Lebenswelt* itself. Again *epoché* purports suspension, putting out of action, withholding, and not denial, elimination, or withdrawal. The whole texture of conscious life, in and through which appear existents of every description and the *Lebenswelt* at large, remains unaffected by the *phenomenological reduction* which is the second *epoché*. While living all these acts in their intertexture and interwovenness, we refrain, however, under the phenomenological reduction, from living *in* those acts. In other words, we no longer allow ourselves to be involved and engaged in them. Our attitude is that of a detached and disinterested observer who, rather than *partaking in, looks at* the stream of conscious life, which flows on independently of the attitude adopted, as a field of descriptive and analytical investigations. Acts which, in the natural attitude, are simply lived are now thematized and made topics of reflective analysis. In this sense Husserl speaks of an *attitude above the life of consciousness*, both subjective and intersubjective, through which, in the natural attitude, the world is simply there, unquestioned. Correspondingly, none of the mundane existents nor the *Lebenswelt* at large undergoes any modification. Mundane existents are, however, no longer simply accepted as they are in the natural attitude. Rather, they are regarded as experienced entities, to be taken exactly as they appear; they are considered as entities presenting themselves as real, etc. All mundane existents and the *Lebenswelt* as a whole are transformed into *phenomena* in the specific sense of being referred to the acts of consciousness through which they are given, and of being taken exactly as they stand before the mind of the subject experiencing those acts. The existential character or claim of mundane objects is neither accepted nor rejected; it is neither doubted nor even examined as to its legitimacy. It is merely regarded as an experienced claim—i.e., as one among the characteristics and features which the object in question exhibits in its presentation.

## 2. Outline of the Phenomenology of the Perceptual World

BY VIRTUE of the phenomenological reduction, objective entities are disclosed as correlates of acts of consciousness. With this disclosure the field of phenomenological research is laid open. Phenomenology is nothing but the systematic and comprehensive study of the correlation between the world and the consciousness of the world —more generally, between being of every kind and description and acts of consciousness through which being appears and in which it originates.

To illustrate the problems which arise in the field opened up by the phenomenological reduction and the nature of phenomenological analytical work, Husserl refers in the main to the phenomenology of perception as established in his earlier writings, especially *Ideen zu einer reinen Phänomenologie und phänomenologischen Philosophie* and *Cartesianische Meditationen.*[19] Keeping in line with the general orientation of the *Krisis*, Husserl does not develop the theory of perception in a systematic fashion. Rather, he brings out some of the pertinent topics as representative examples of phenomenological problems.

A thing may be seen, touched, smelled, etc. These perceptions differ from one another; still, they are all experienced as perceptions of the same thing. Abiding by visual perceptions, we again find that the same thing may be seen from different sides, under varying aspects and perspectives. To acquire perceptual acquaintance with the thing, it is necessary to pass from perception to perception, so that the thing may show itself from many sides and progressively reveal its attributes and properties. What presents itself through each particular perception is the thing itself appearing, to be sure, in a one-sided manner, and yet experienced as perceivable from different points of view, as capable of appearing in further modes of presentation. Each particular perception thus contains more than it offers in direct and actual sense experience. This "more" consists in references to, or anticipations of, further perceptual appearances of the same thing. Every actual perception implies an horizon—the *inner horizon*—of possible perceptions which are expected to occur when the thing is seen from the appropriate point of observation. Here we encounter the role which inactualities of consciousness play in actual experience. Among such inactualities are the acquisitions of the past—i.e., acquisitions which once had the mode of actuality but no longer have it, though they may be reactivated. Even when they are not reawakened, they contribute towards determining the present actual experience which proves to be encompassed by a horizon or immersed in an atmosphere of inactualities which function only implicitly but function nevertheless.

In addition to the perception of a thing being pervaded and permeated by references, anticipations, and other inactualities, the thing perceived appears amidst other things simultaneously perceived,

19. Both published in the *Husserliana* series, respectively, as Vol. III and Vol. I (The Hague, 1950). The *Cartesian Meditations* have been translated by D. Cairns (The Hague, 1960).

within a perceptual field or *outer horizon*. To be sure, the perceptual field is not the world; yet it is experienced as a segment of the world. The outer horizon points and refers beyond itself; these pointing references convey our permanent awareness of the world as the universe of possible objects of perception.[20]

If, in the course of the perceptual process, the anticipations implied in previous perceptions are fulfilled by subsequent ones, a synthesis of identification, or, as Husserl here prefers to say, of unification (*Einigung*), takes place between these perceptions. By virtue of this synthesis of unification, the particular perceptions, rather than merely succeeding upon one another in time, organize themselves into phases of one coherent, sustained process. Yieldings of previous phases are not only retained at later phases but are also continued and complemented by those of later phases. The thing perceived which, in several respects, was indeterminate to some degree gradually unfolds itself in increasing determinateness. The perceptual process derives its intrinsic coherence from its various phases mutually confirming each other by virtue of the fulfillment of expectancies and anticipations, as well as from their enlarging and continuing one another (*Sinnbereicherung und Sinnfortbildung*). The varying modes of perceptual presentation in which the thing perceived appears in the course of the perceptual process depend upon movements of the experiencing subject's body. For the thing to appear under a certain aspect, the observer has to come nearer to it or to recede from it, to walk around it, to move his head or his eyes in an appropriate manner, to stretch out his hand so as to touch it, or to turn it around in his hand, etc. Our own body with its sense organs plays a role in all perceptual experience, a role which becomes manifest in the correlation between the kinaesthesias and the perceptual presentations of the thing perceived. (Let us mention in passing the problem of the appearance of our own body itself through a multiplicity of experiences which are organized with one another in a specific manner.) It may well happen that anticipations implied in previous phases are not fulfilled in the further course of the perceptual process. The thing perceived proves to be different from what at first it appeared to be. Subsequent phases correct rather than confirm preceding phases. By this token there arises the phenomenon of modalization: what we see in the show window at first unquestionably

20. For a comparatively detailed study of Husserl's notion of horizonal consciousness, cf. H. Kuhn, "The Phenomenological Concept of 'Horizon,'" in *Philosophical Essays in Memory of Edmund Husserl*, ed. M. Farber (Cambridge, Mass., 1941). The connection between horizonal consciousness and the awareness of the world has been brought out by L. Landgrebe, "The World as a Phenomenological Problem," *Philosophy and Phenomenological Research*, I (1940).

appeared to be a human being; now this becomes doubtful; it is possible, presumable, probable, etc. that it is a dummy.

No perceiving subject is ever alone. Throughout our life, even during periods of solitude, we are aware of our existing among our fellow-men with whom we communicate either actually or virtually, and we are also aware of their communicating with one another. As in my own conscious life, perceptions and series of perceptions confirm, continue, enlarge, and, eventually, correct one another, so, by means of communicating with my fellow-men, my own perceptual systems and syntheses enter into the same relationships with theirs. Disagreements and discrepancies may well occur. These are removed, at least they are considered as removable, by discussion and mutual criticism. Through intercommunication, i.e., interlinking my perceptual life with those of my fellow-men, there arises, for each one of us, the consciousness of *the one and the same perceptual world,* as the universal horizon within which all real things exist, the one world in which all of us live and which all of us experience, though each one does so from his particular point of view. I may and do perceive the same thing as my fellow-man, but the same thing presents itself to each of us from a different side, under a different aspect and perspective. Every such perceptual presentation implies in its inner horizon references to further perceptual presentations, all belonging to one total system. For the consciousness of each one of us, there arises the distinction between the actual perceptual presentation of a thing and the thing itself. Especially in view of possible discrepancies between my perceptual experience and those of my fellow-men, that distinction assumes the sense of that between "mere" appearance, "mere" representation of a thing, and the thing as it objectively is. Note that the thing as it is objectively is given to nobody in actual perception, since it is, for the consciousness of everybody, nothing other than the systematic unity of an indefinitely open multiplicity of perceptual experiences, his own as well as those of his fellow-men.

From the preceding outline, however superficial, of the phenomenological theory of perception, a principle emerges whose generalization permits us to formulate the ultimate aim of phenomenological philosophy. Every objective entity, of any description whatever—every object, as we shall say for the sake of brevity—is correlated to, and is an *index* of, multiplicities of modes of appearance and presentation (*Gegebenheitsweisen*). If these presentations are related to the object in question and "contain" it as their "object-pole" (*Gegenstandspol*), this is by virtue of their being oriented with regard to one another and their being systematically organized into a synthesis of unification which, since it extends from subject to subject, proves to be an *intersubjective synthesis* in the full sense of the term. The forms of

organization and systematization which prevail among the multiplicities in question must not be regarded as a matter of mere
factuality, not to speak of contingency. On the contrary, *the correlation between an object and the multiplicity of its modes of presentation is dominated by* a priori *laws; it is throughout a matter of
essential necessity.* Unless certain appearances and presentations are
intersubjectively organized in a determinate specific form, the object
in question either does not exist at all or not as an object of a certain
particular kind. In this sense the object may be said to derive its
existence and the meaning of its existence from intersubjectively
concatenated and interlocking experiences, and we may speak of the
"intersubjective constitution" of the world: that is, of the world as
originating in intersubjectively interlinked experiences.

Phenomenological analysis refers what in the naïve and natural
attitude is simply taken for an "accomplished entity" (*Fertig-Seien-
des*) to the multiplicities of experiences through which it presents
itself. Retracing the "finished" and accomplished product to the
sources of its formation and production in no way means stripping the
object of its existence, reality, or objectivity. It is not the task to found
objectivity, or to guarantee it, or to argue about it, any more than to
demonstrate the actual existence of the world. It is not in the least
doubtful that the world exists and that all of us exist within it as
human beings. The task is rather to *render intelligible* this conviction
which underlies all our life as a matter of course and remains so under
the phenomenological reduction. Final intelligibility cannot be
achieved except by analysis of intersubjective consciousness in and
through which the world arises as it presents itself to us, as being
there and as always having been there (*Vorgegebenheit*). Quite in
general, ultimately to understand objectivity, we have to study objects
of a given type in their gradual display and unfolding through
multiplicities of experiences, modes of appearance and presentation,
systematically interconcatenated with one another. In and through
such systematically organized multiplicities of experiences there
accrues to the objects in question the specific sense of their objectivity.

### 3. The Transcendental Ego and the Problem of Intersubjectivity

HUSSERL ADVOCATES an egological conception of consciousness. Every act of consciousness emanates or issues from the
ego who lives in that act which by this very token is experienced as
*his.* The whole of conscious life, all syntheses, all modalizations, etc.

are centralized in the ego, or, as Husserl prefers to say, ego-pole, as the identical performer of all operations and productions (*identischer Vollzieher aller Geltungen*). It is the identical ego-pole who passes from one phase to the next of his conscious life, retains past experiences, and connects them with the present ones, anticipates such further experiences as will fit into a progressively growing coherent system. Through a multiplicity of presentations the ego directs himself towards the object-pole (that which appears in varying modes or that towards which the varying modes are polarized) as the goal of his intention, an intention which, in the course of the process of experience, is eventually fulfilled. By means of his activities, which may assume different forms, the ego explicates the objects as to their attributes and properties; his activity may be solicited by affections, etc. Correspondingly, intersubjectivity is interpreted as interlinkage between a plurality of egos, as I-Thou synthesis or We synthesis. The intersubjectively identical *Lebenswelt* is, as we have seen, an *index* of multiplicities of modes of appearance and presentation, systematically organized. Through these multiplicities, the several egos—and each one not merely through his own—direct themselves towards, intend, and experience the world as the common field of all *their* activities.

In the light of Husserl's egological conception of consciousness and mental life, the correlation between mundane objects and the world at large, on the one hand, and, on the other hand, multiplicities of systematically organized experiences purports that the former originate in, and derive their existence from, egological operations, performances, and activities (*ichliche Leistungen*). That the world is intersubjectively constituted comes to mean that it is the communal product of an indefinite plurality of egos communicating and cooperating with one another, thereby interrelating, coordinating, and interlinking their egological mental lives. Such a plurality of egos is mankind: in the wider sense, the human race in its totality; in the narrower sense, a more or less confined socio-historical group (e.g., a certain civilization). Hence the correlation under discussion seems to obtain between world and mankind "*als die in Vergemeinschaftung intentional die Leistung der Weltgeltung zustandebringende Subjektivität.*" If—as it seems we must—we mean by egos human beings, an apparently insuperable paradox is bound to arise. Human beings are themselves mundane existents among other such existents; they belong to, and are part of, the world. How then is it possible for a part to constitute and to produce the very whole of which it is a part? If the general program of phenomenology is to account for the world in terms of human subjectivity or intersubjectivity, this program proves to be beset by an utter absurdity, because it amounts to accounting for the world in terms which by their very nature imply and presuppose that which is to be accounted for. Obviously, the paradox hinges on the dual role of man, who is at the same time both a mundane existent among others, an object within the world, and a subject with respect to the world, i.e., a subject from whose experiences and mental operations the world derives the sense of its existence.

To surmount that paradox and to achieve some clarity concerning the ambiguous position of man, it is, according to Husserl, both necessary and sufficient to perform the phenomenological reduction with utmost consistency. Undoubtedly, we encounter our fellow-men, of whom we conceive as human beings and persons like ourselves, in the world and as mundane existents. This, however, means that, under the phenomenological reduction, they have to be treated as phenomena, not differently from any other mundane existents. Under the phenomenological reduction, we may not speak of mankind except in the sense of the "phenomenon of mankind"; we are not entitled simply to refer to, and to make use of, the conscious lives and mental activities of our fellow-men. Because of its universality, the program of phenomenology extends to me as a mundane human being and to my fellow-men as well. Performing the phenomenological reduction, I am no longer a human being among other human beings, all living in, and pertaining to, the world. The performance of the phenomenological reduction puts the performer into an "incomparable philosophical solitude" (einzigartige philosophische Einsamkeit) in which the world and whatever it comprises, including himself as a human being and his fellow-men as beings like himself, become phenomena, i.e., themes and topics of transcendental phenomenological investigation. Two problems of phenomenological constitution arise in this connection. The first is that of my auto-constitution. It concerns those acts through which I experience myself, in a variety of modes of appearance, as a person, as I-the-man, as a mundane human being. Hence the ego-pole from which, according to Husserl, all my conscious acts issue and in which all activities, operations, performances, etc. of my consciousness are centralized (Funktionszentrum aller Konstitution) must not be mistaken for the soul, the person, the "I" in the sense of I-the-human-being—in brief, for a mundane ego, be it even a merely psychological ego. For this reason, Husserl speaks of an ego-pole rather than an ego; in other passages he insists upon distinguishing the transcendental ego or, especially in earlier writings, the pure ego from the mundane ego, in any sense of mundaneity whatever. The second problem concerns the constitution and apperception, in and through acts of *my* experience, of others, *alter egos,* the likes of me and yet different from me, and of a community of the likes of me into which I insert myself. To ascribe a transcendental function to my fellow-men was, therefore, not incorrect, but premature, because it lacked a justification. What is required is a phenomenological theory of the constitution of intersubjectivity within my own experience, for me, in this sense "within" me.[21] On the basis of such a theory, it becomes legitimate to assert that every human being "contains" a transcendental ego so far as, constituted as the likes of me, the fellow-man is conceived of as capable of performing the phenomenological reduction, as I am capable of doing, and of disclosing his ego-pole in its transcendental function. Thus Husserl arrives at the notion of *transcendental intersubjectivity,* a community of ego-poles to which my own ego-pole also belongs, though it enjoys a privileged position, since it remains forever the ego-pole with respect to which every other ego-pole appears as an *alter ego-pole.* If the world is experienced as common to, and the same for, all of us, this is because it proves to be the correlate of transcendental intersubjectivity, the communal product of an indefinitely open community of ego-poles communicating with one another and thereby interlinking their constitutive functions.

By the consistent and radical performance of the phenomenological reduction, Descartes' identification of the ego of the *ego cogito* with the soul—i.e., a mundane existent—is definitively dissolved, this identification which has given rise to so many perplexities. Transcendental subjectivity can now be recognized in its uniqueness: as a privileged realm by virtue of, and owing to, which alone there is a world and which as a necessary condition and presupposition of every mundane domain can therefore not be such a domain itself.

On the other hand, the mere formulation of the problems of the auto-constitution and the constitution of other human beings sheds light on the position of man. Mundane subjectivity and intersubjectivity—i.e., mankind—prove self-objectivations of transcendental subjectivity. For this reason, transcendental phenomenology stands in a close relation to psychology as the systematic study of the mundane ego or the soul: that is, among other things, of the mental life of human beings who find themselves in the world, perceive things, entertain representations and conceptions about the world, pursue purposeful activities in it, etc. In fact, all the acts, performances, and operations of consciousness which under the perspective of transcendental phenomenology are considered as to their presentational

21. This theory, to which the present work contains but scant references, is developed at length in Husserl, *Cartesianische Meditationen,* V.

and constitutive function—*viz.*, as experiences through which the world and whatever it contains appears and reveals itself to us—are also encountered within the psychological setting, where they have the sense of mundane occurrences pertaining to mundane psychosomatic unities (human beings). Results of transcendental phenomenology may thus be translated into psychological terms. Conversely, psychological analyses of human mental life, especially of the forms and modes in which we experience the world, of human conceptions, representations, and images of the world, acquire phenomenological significance, provided allowance is made for those specific acts of apperception and objectivation from which mental life derives its mundaneity—i.e., owing to which experiences and representations of the world come to be conceived of as mundane events occurring in mundane existents. From transcendental phenomenology to psychology, a transition in both directions is always possible. Accordingly, Husserl embarks upon opening up a second avenue of approach to phenomenology by taking his departure from psychology. Along this way, an important gap will be filled: a conception of the mind is still missing. To provide such a conception is the essential task of psychology. But, as it has historically developed, psychology has utterly failed to fulfill this task. In order to formulate the problems which arise for a genuine psychology, we have first to bring out the reasons of the failure of traditional psychology.

## [IV] PROBLEMS OF PSYCHOLOGY

### 1. Presuppositions of Traditional Psychology

MODERN PSYCHOLOGY HAS DEVELOPED under the impact and influence of Galilean physics whose methods and procedures have come to be regarded as standards and models of all scientific knowledge. Physics being concerned with the corporeal aspect of reality, psychology was from the outset conceived of as a complementary science, parallel to physics. Its subject matter is the aspect or part of reality which does not fall under the purview of physics—*viz.*, souls, their mental life, occurrences in them, etc. Modern psychology rests on the Cartesian dualism of *corpus* and *mens* which in some form or other has prevailed in the whole modern tradition. The world consists of two "substances" or, at least, orders of reality, of which only one, the "extended substance," proves a self-contained independent context, whereas souls, because they are attached to bodies, remain separated from, and external to, one another and do not form a coherent universe. Man and, at least in the later post-Cartesian tradition, animals as well are conceived of as composed of two utterly heterogeneous strata between which certain regular connections obtain. Psychology and physics divide among themselves the two strata. The dualism of the two substances or strata of reality reappears in the distinction between "internal" and "external" experience, the former being of psychological phenomena, souls, and occurrences in souls, the latter yielding physical phenomena in which there manifests itself nature "as it really is in itself"—in the sense with which this term is understood in the mathematico-physical sciences. As physics relies on external experience, so does psychology rely on internal experience.

Notwithstanding the utter heterogeneity of the two substances or strata of reality, the cognitive style of psychology must be modeled after that of physics. The ideal under whose predominance modern psychology has developed is that of a universal objectivistic science *more geometrico*. It is taken for granted that souls have the same mode of existence and reality as material bodies, different though they are from one another as to their structure. Hence between psychological occurrences there obtain causal relations of the same sort as between physical events. Quite in general, the psychological domain can and must be explained by means of theories of the same nature as the theories of physics. Accordingly, the soul is regarded as a self-contained sphere (analogous to a closed space) comprising psychological data, especially sense data which, in turn, are taken for some kind of atoms or complexes of atoms; psychological dispositions are interpreted by analogy with physical forces as indicating causal properties of the soul, etc. Throughout its history, modern psychology has striven for exactness in the sense of physics. Yet, not only has it not attained, not even approximated, its ideal, but its history has been a sequence of crises. The reason for this failure is the absurdity of the ideal itself. By its very nature, the psychological domain does not lend itself to idealization and mathematization. Hence it is not only hopeless but even meaningless to search for exact psychological laws and theories and to aim at exact theoretization of the psychological domain—exactness after the model of the theories of physics.

All suppositions of traditional modern psychology hinge upon, and even follow from, the *fundamental presupposition* which is none other than *the very existence of Galilean science*.[22] Modern psychology did

22. Cf. above, "The Phenomenological and the Psychological Approach to Consciousness," in which we have tried to bring out, from a slightly different point of view, the historico-logical continuity between modern psychology and Galilean physics.

not derive its concept of the soul and of the psychological from direct experience but took over the Cartesian dualistic concept which, in turn, had been determined by the constructive ideas of a mere corporeal nature and a mathematical science of that nature.

## 2. The Mind–Body Problem

PSYCHOLOGY, like every other science, has to take its departure from findings in the *Lebenswelt* and must respect these findings. It is in the *Lebenswelt* that we encounter souls, in the first place human souls, and they are encountered as embodied. Questions arise as to how each one of us experiences his own body as an articulate system of organs at his disposal, how he experiences his inhabiting and functioning in (*Walten*) his body—experiences which in primordial and originary form every one can have only with respect to his own body. Examples of such functioning in bodily organs are pushing, pulling, lifting, etc.—in brief, kinaesthesias by means of which alone we are able to act upon external things and whose role in perceptual experience has already been mentioned previously.

To be sure, the motions of my body and its organs, e.g., my hand, take place in space. However, my hands' being at my command and disposal, the acting and functioning of the kinaesthesias is not itself a motion in space. It is only indirectly localized, so far as my hand in which the kinaesthesias are incorporated occupies a position in space. Quite in general, Husserl maintains, if souls are localized in space-time as the universal form of the *Lebenswelt*, they are so only indirectly. They merely *partake* of spatio-temporal localization by virtue of their being embodied. Embodiment is originarily experienced by every one of us in and through his inhabiting his body and, within certain limits, having it at his free disposal.

Accordingly, if souls exist "in" the world, as they do, their existence has not the same sense as that of material bodies, nor is it possible to ascribe to animated beings as psychosomatic unities the same sort of reality as to inanimate things. As to the later, their *principium individuationis* is spatio-temporal localization. A soul, on the contrary, has its individuality and uniqueness in its own right and does not derive it from the localization of its body in space and time. Similarly, connections between psychological occurrences or between psychological and somatic occurrences are not of the same nature as causal relations, i.e., relations of functional dependency between physical events.

## 3. Intentionality

TAKING INTO CONSIDERATION that every science starts from the *Lebenswelt* and that the domain of physics is defined by an abstraction—*viz.*, a deliberate exclusive concentration upon the corporeal aspect of objects encountered in the *Lebenswelt* (this abstraction serves as presupposition and basis for the ensuing idealization and mathematization)—one may raise the question as to whether psychology must not follow a similar procedure, that of a complementary abstraction or counter-abstraction. Along this line of reasoning, the dualism of traditional psychology, especially its theoretical practice, would appear legitimate and justified if we disregard the just-mentioned difficulties related to the mind-body problem which have beset the traditional dualism. Apart from such a counter-abstraction, there seems to be no way to disclose the psychological domain in the proper sense—i.e., consciousness and mental life. Everything will now depend upon the nature and meaning of the counter-abstraction.

Even superficially surveying conscious life, our own or that of other persons, but taking it as it is actually lived and not permitting any preconceived theories to intervene in its description, we do not find the sense data of traditional psychology. What we do find are acts which are most adequately described by saying "I perceive a tree," "I remember my childhood," "I am sorry that my friend is sick," etc. Every such act must be characterized as an *act of consciousness of something;* that is what is meant by *intentionality of consciousness.* We have to take our departure from human beings consciously dealing in various modes with objects, events, things, etc. in the *Lebenswelt.*

Already at this point, the traditional distinction between external and internal experience (the latter alone being considered as psychological experience) proves to be unfounded. Undoubtedly, there are significant differences between experiences of stones or rivers and those of feelings of joy or anger or of inhabiting one's body. Still, both the former and the latter are acts of consciousness, subjective experiences. Hence both of them come under the purview of psychology as the universal science of consciousness and mental life: in short, subjectivity.

The intentionality of consciousness must not be misconstrued into an additional character or tinge of data, nor should it be conceived as a property of man among his other properties, as though some mundane existents were endowed with the faculty of experiencing the other existents and acquiring knowledge about them. Through an act of consciousness, an object appears and stands before the experiencing subject's mind in a certain manner of presentation. That object has to be taken such, exactly and only such, as it actually presents itself through the act under discussion. In the case of the perception of a tree, for example, we have the perceived tree appearing under a certain aspect and perspective, in a certain orientation, as near or far, etc.: in other words, the tree as perceived presents itself in a certain perceptual appearance (*wahrgenommener Baum als solcher*). Whereas the tree as a real thing may be consumed by fire, obviously no such event can happen to the perceptual appearance of the tree, i.e., the tree as appearing in a certain perceptual presentation. Quite in general, to every act of consciousness belongs the "object" of which the act conveys consciousness, such as the "object" appears, presents itself, is meant and intended through that act. This is the *cogitatum qua cogitatum*, the "intentional object" of the act, or, as Husserl said in previous writings, its noema. The "intentional object" belongs to the act as its correlate, its sense or meaning.[23] Taken in its full and concrete sense, the term "intentionality of consciousness" *expresses just this correlation or correspondence* between acts and their "intentional objects." [24] As the correlate of the act, the "intentional object" is inseparable from it, so that no description of an act of consciousness is adequate unless allowance is made for its intentional correlate.

Human beings concern themselves, through their conscious acts, with mundane realities like animals, houses, fields, etc. Intentionality thus seems to denote a real relation between a person and some mundane reality. Every descriptive statement about a person and his acts of consciousness necessarily oversteps the psychological domain, i.e., the domain of what properly belongs to the subjective life of the person, inasmuch as the statement must contain reference to the mundane reality with which the person deals through the act under discussion. To disclose and delimit the psychological or subjective domain, the psychologist must perform what Husserl calls the "phenomenologico-psychological reduction." The person studied by the psychologist is confronted with mundane realities presenting themselves as simply existing or else as doubtful, presumable, likely, etc.; they

23. In phenomenology, the term "meaning" is used in a sense wider than the usual one in which the term is confined to meanings of verbal symbols. Taken in this wider sense, "meaning" denotes the same as "intentional object," *viz.*, that which through a given act of consciousness appears to the subject's mind, such as it actually presents itself. Meanings of verbal symbols are a special class of meanings in the wider sense.

24. For the theory of the intentionality of consciousness, see above, "On the Intentionality of Consciousness," and "On the Object of Thought." Recently Q. Lauer, *Phénoménologie de Husserl* (Paris, 1955), has presented a detailed study of Husserl's theory of intentionality and has pursued its development through Husserl's major writings.

may appear as endowed with values, as having practical utility; finally, in the eyes of the person in question they may be charged emotionally or affectively. Concerning all this, the psychologist has, or may have, convictions of his own which may, or may not, coincide with those of the person he studies. The phenomenologico-psychological reduction consists in the psychologist neither endorsing nor opposing nor in any way challenging the existential beliefs and convictions—in the broadest sense—of his subjects. In these matters, the psychologist must refrain from taking a stand. He has to adopt the attitude of a detached and disinterested observer of the mental life of his subjects—disinterested in the sense of abstention from involvements. To be sure, the psychologist takes notice of and tries to understand the interests of the persons he studies, but he does not share those interests in any of the possible forms of sharing. If his subject finds himself confronted with some mundane reality, the psychologist must take it as it presents itself to his subject and for what it is in his subject's eyes, without referring that reality, such as it appears and is experienced, to the true and objective state of affairs. Studying an act of perception, for example, the psychologist must consistently abide by the thing perceived as it is actually perceived. No question as to whether that thing exists in reality and is truly such as it is perceived must be permitted to intervene in psychological descriptions and analyses. In other words, *the psychologist deals with "intentional objects,"* only and exclusively. They, and they alone, are his themes and constitute his field of research. Disclosing mental life, the psychologist finds, at least to begin with, acts of consciousness and "intentional objects" which, as correlates of the acts, are inseparable from them. Nothing else must play a role for the psychologist, since as soon as he allows for some reality other than an experienced and meant reality (taken exactly as it is meant and intended), he goes beyond the psychological domain.

## 4. From the Psychology of Intentionality to Transcendental Phenomenology

THE PHENOMENOLOGICO-PSYCHOLOGICAL REDUCTION takes the place of, or rather is, the counter-abstraction whose possibility we considered at the beginning of the preceding section. But may one properly speak here of an abstraction, comparable to that by which physics starts? In the case of physics, the fundamental abstraction consists in concentrating exclusively upon the corporeal aspect of the *Lebenswelt* to the disregard of the rest. Under the phenomenologico-psychological reduction, no mundane object and no aspect of any mundane object, actually given in experience (in whichever form and mode), is disregarded, not to speak of discarding. To be sure, no such object is simply accepted as a reality upon which to proceed in psychological reasoning or as a standard to which "intentional objects" might be referred and by which they might be measured. However, as experienced and taken such as it actually presents itself, in other words considered as an "intentional object," every mundane reality reappears by necessity within the scope of psychology. The claim to universality which Husserl lays for the psychology of intentionality is announced here.

To justify this claim, we have to examine the manner in which the phenomenologico-psychological reduction must be performed. It has to be applied to every conscious act of every person the psychologist considers or might consider. A possible way of performing the reduction—a way which suggests itself at first—would be to proceed from one conscious act of a given person to the next and also to pass from one person to the other. Such a procedure would yield a series of consecutive reductions. Its universality would be distributive in character and would result from the fact that, in principle, no act of any person is to be left out. Consequently, if one might speak here of *one* universal reduction, then only in the sense of the sum total of the several reductions.

To this way of performing the phenomenologico-psychological reduction, Husserl objects that it would be misleading, would rest on a misunderstanding. He insists upon the *reduction being performed all at once and at a single stroke* with regard to all possible persons, including the psychologist himself, and this means, correspondingly, with respect to all mundane existents or, to be more precise, the *Lebenswelt* as a whole. To satisfy ourselves of the necessity of proceeding in the manner which Husserl prescribes, let us recall that, although at every moment and through every particular act the experiencing subject deals with particular mundane existents, each of these presents itself within a certain perceptual environment or horizon which, however large or narrow, appears as a segment of the world. Owing to its reference to the world at large, every mundane existent is experienced as mundane. Performing the reduction with respect to a particular thing, withholding assent to, but also dissent from, an existential belief or conviction about it, therefore requires the generalization of this modification of attitude so as to extend it to the *Lebenswelt* as a whole. This purports transforming the *Lebenswelt* with whatever it contains into a phenomenon in the specific sense in which this term is used by Husserl. Obviously, the transformation in question also concerns the psychologist himself—the performer of the phenomenologico-psychological reduction—as well as all the persons whose conscious lives he may make topics of investigation: that is to say, it concerns all of his fellow-men. All persons, including the psychologist himself, inasmuch as they perceive and experience themselves as human beings, hence as mundane existents, are transformed into phenomena and, by the same token, disclosed as subjects of intentional conscious life.

Performing the reduction upon himself, the psychologist, in analyzing his own conscious life, becomes aware of its relationship to, and connectedness with, the conscious lives of other persons. Under the reduction, his own existence as a human being has acquired the sense of an experienced phenomenon. However, he cannot experience himself as human being unless he experiences himself as living in a certain historical present which, in turn, refers to both a historical past and future. In his very experience of himself as a human being are implied references to other human beings, to an open horizon of humanity (*menschheitlich offener Horizont*) and co-subjectivity (*Mit-subjektivität*). Experience of oneself proves to be inseparable from that of others. Under the phenomenologico-psychological reduction, all human beings are reduced to subjects of conscious life, so that any historico-social group now appears as a community of transcendental subjects to which the performer of the reduction also belongs, himself a pure subject of intentional life.

The reference to such a community proves an essential and constitutive component of the experience of the *Lebenswelt*. Though the world has been reduced to the status of a phenomenon, it still retains the sense of one identical world, the same for all of us. Every one perceives this common world from his point of view and in a certain orientation; this implies its being perceived or, at least, perceivable by other subjects from different points of view and in different orientations. Experiencing the world as a common world, one must and does allow for one's experiences being confirmed, corrected, enlarged, and enriched by those of other subjects. Such mutual confirmation and correction takes place in actual intercourse between conscious subjects. Even if one happens to be alone, one's experience of the world, inasmuch as it presents itself as a common world, is essentially determined by allowance for possible experiences of others with which one's own experiences must be harmonized.

Developing the psychology of intentionality far enough, we come to discover the phenomenon of intersubjectivity in its full concreteness. Souls must not be considered as closed and self-contained spheres forever separated from one another because the bodies to which they are attached are, in fact, external to each other. On the contrary, it appears from the psychology of intentionality, especially the analysis of the experience of the world as common *Lebenswelt*, that in every Ego and his conscious life there are implied other Egos and their conscious lives, even an open and indefinite plurality of such Egos. All souls interpenetrate, are interlinked and interlocked—terms which are to be understood in the light of the mentioned orientation of everyone's experience with respect to that of other subjects. Under the perspective of the psychology of intentionality, souls prove to form one universal context, unified from within—*viz.*, by virtue of the interconcatenation and interwovenness of their respective intentional acts, operations, activities, and performances.

The preceding discussion leads us back to a problem and phenomenon which we already encountered when we presented the general program of phenomenology: the world as an intentional correlate of, and as constituted in, intersubjective syntheses. Developed with utmost consistency, *the psychology of intentionality turns into transcendental phenomenology*. Likewise, if *the phenomenologico-psychological reduction* is performed in the universal manner upon which Husserl insists, it *proves to be nothing other than the transcendental reduction*. The two lines along which Husserl has pursued his analyses are now seen to converge. Starting from the *Lebenswelt* and its essential structure, Husserl sets himself the task to account for it and whatever mundane existents it comprises as well as for objects and objectivities of a higher order (like those which pertain to the sciences) in terms of their multiple and diversified modes of appearance and presentation, i.e., in terms of acts of consciousness and mental life. Obviously, the systematic study both of particular conscious acts and of the various forms of synthesis and synthetic unity into which they may enter leads to the disclosure of intentionality as the essential feature of mental life. On the other hand, after the psychology of intentionality has brought us before the problem of the world as intersubjective communal product of an indefinitely open community of subjects whose conscious lives are interlocked and interlinked, the very logic of this development impels us to take a last step. It consists in bringing out the problem concerning the acts, complexes and systems of acts through which the "absolutely solitary pure psychologist" (*der sich absolut vereinsamende reine Psychologe*) —i.e., the psychologist who, by means of the radical performance of the phenomenological reduction, has disclosed himself as a pure transcendental Ego or Ego-pole—apprehends and experiences alter Egos with whom he enters into intercourse and communication, so as to constitute, by such intersubjective cooperation in its multiple forms, the one and identical world, common to all.

Psychology as a positive science, patterned after the model of the other positive sciences, has never existed and cannot exist. All endeavors to attain in psychology the exactness of physics are doomed to failure because of their intrinsic absurdity. It is just the pursuit of this chimerical aim that has prevented the development of a genuine and pure psychology, genuine and pure in the sense of concerning itself with what properly belongs to the essential nature of the soul and the mind. *Pure psychology* in this sense is not only inseparable from but is *identical with transcendental phenomenology.* This is not to preclude the legitimacy of psychology as a science in the natural, as opposed to the phenomenological, attitude: i.e., a science which establishes itself on the grounds of the *Lebenswelt* and deals with the souls and the mental life of human beings—and, perhaps, of animals —considered as mundane existents. Having performed the phenomenological reduction, we are free to relinquish it and to return to the natural attitude, though not to the former naïveté in which we lived previously to performing the reduction. We can understand but not reassume that naïveté. After the transcendental dimensions have been disclosed, no return to the natural attitude is ever able to undo that disclosure, though it might lose its actuality at times. When, returning to the natural attitude, we take mundane existents as such, they will now appear in a light in which they had not appeared prior to the performance of the phenomenological reduction—*viz.,* in the light of the disclosed transcendental dimensions to which they will continue referring. If, for the legitimacy of psychology as a science in the natural attitude, Husserl insists upon a *return,* it is because transcendental phenomenology proves to be the fundamental *a priori* science with regard to empirical psychology which has to respect, and to avail itself of, phenomenological insights and results.

## [V]  Concluding Remarks

In our day and age it has become fashionable to denounce rationalism as a source of evil and to hold it responsible for the present crisis, both intellectual and moral. This view is the more dangerous because it contains a half-truth. According to Husserl, the present crisis is the crisis of naturalistic objectivism or objectivistic rationalism, the crisis of Western science in the phase of extreme technization in which it has forsaken those philosophical aspirations from which it historically arose. In other words, it is the crisis of a specific historical form of rationalism, the form which rationalism has assumed since the Renaissance. *Historical forms of rationalism,* however, must be distinguished from the *idea of rationalism* or rationality, a Platonic idea which is specified and approximated in those historical forms. Surmounting a certain historical form of rationalism is one thing; abandoning the very idea of rationalism is quite another.

Since philosophy aims at knowledge, universal, ultimately founded, and totally justified, *philosophy and the idea of rationalism are one and the same.* Abandoning rationalism is forsaking philosophy altogether. More is at stake than a technical discipline or a special cultural activity. Western man in his specific historicity, we remember, makes his first appearance along with, and owing to, the rise of the idea of philosophy or rationalism in Greek antiquity. This idea defines essentially the sense of his existence and determines his history. The appearance of Western man means more than the appearance of one possible human type besides others. It marks the first disclosure of a possibility pertaining to man as such. Surrender to the anti-rationalistic and anti-intellectualistic tendencies, a surrender urged upon us from many quarters, is nothing short of self-betrayal of Western man and betrayal of the teleological destiny and idea of man at large. This destiny is none other than the autonomy of reason which actualizes itself in a historical process, *viz.*, through the historical transformations of the idea of rationalism.

Just the faithful adherence to the idea of rationalism may become a compelling motive to surmount a historical form of rationalism whose limitations have become apparent. As to the specific modern form of rationalism, its limitations spring from its constructive character. In the elaboration and development of mathematical and other rational systems (the sciences and scientific theories), the producing activity of reason which is involved in these elaborations, and whose accomplished products those systems are, is overlooked, and, moreover, the *Lebenswelt,* the necessary base of departure for all theoretical constructions, is eclipsed. Engrossed in, and preoccupied with, his products, the scientist and theoretician effaces himself; he loses sight of the processes of production and of whatever these processes presuppose. Along the same line of argument, Husserl points out the failure of Hume and also of the psychologists of the late 19th century to see that the activity of reason which gives rise to their psychological theories, and whose products these theories are, must itself be accounted for in terms of sensations, laws of association, and whatever other data of consciousness and laws of psychological causality are assumed as elementary: i.e., in the very terms in which the theories in question conceive of consciousness and mental life. Traditional modern rationalism proves to be affected by a naïveté which, according to Husserl, has led to the present crisis. Overcoming the crisis requires surmounting that naïveté by making the mind increasingly aware of itself or, to use an expression of Hegelian provenience, by making the mind return to itself.

Phenomenology, Husserl claims, opens up a new chapter in the history of rationalism by establishing a new form of rationalism which, on account of its radicalism, is to supersede the historically transmitted forms—radicality understood in the etymological sense of going to the roots. It is the very idea of rationalism that motivates and necessitates this transition at the present phase of the historical development of both philosophy and the sciences. Far from abandoning the idea of rationalism, phenomenology brings it to higher fulfillment.

In concluding, let us contrast the general orientation of phenomenology with that of traditional rationalism, not only modern but also ancient which culminated in the philosophy of Plato. Throughout history, ἐπιστήμη was opposed to δόξα; for δόξα was conceived as related to the world of common experience, ἐπιστήμη to the realm of "being as it really is in itself," a realm with regard to which the world of common experience has been relegated to a position of inferiority in some sense or other. Under the heading of the *Lebenswelt,* the world of common experience is rehabilitated by phenomenology as *the reality* from which all conceptions and constructions of other domains of existence start and to which these domains essentially refer. Accordingly, the δόξα is reinstated in its rightful place. Moreover, defined in a broad and all-inclusive sense, the *Lebenswelt* comprises the products and accomplishments of all cultural activities, hence also the sciences, their results and theories. This means that ἐπιστήμη in the traditional sense, e.g., specific scientific ἐπιστήμη, also falls under the concept of δόξα, differences of level and scope notwithstanding. Yet phenomenology does not relinquish the search for ἐπιστήμη. However, ἐπιστήμη in the specific phenomenological sense is not ἐπιστήμη as opposed to δόξα. Rather it is the ἐπιστήμη of the very δόξα, of all possible δόξα. It is ἐπιστήμη concerning the mind and its life in which originate the *Lebenswelt* as well as whatever other domains of being and existence there are, along with all their specific objectivities and validities.

# Index